LET'S GO

■ THE RESOURCE FOR THE INDEPENDENT TRAVELER

"The guides are aimed not only at young budget travelers but at the independent traveler; a sort of streetwise cookbook for traveling alone."

—*The New York Times*

"Unbeatable; good sight-seeing advice; up-to-date info on restaurants, hotels, and inns; a commitment to money-saving travel; and a wry style that brightens nearly every page."

—*The Washington Post*

"Lighthearted and sophisticated, informative and fun to read. [Let's Go] helps the novice traveler navigate like a knowledgeable old hand."

—*Atlanta Journal-Constitution*

"A world-wise traveling companion—always ready with friendly advice and helpful hints, all sprinkled with a bit of wit."

—*The Philadelphia Inquirer*

■ THE BEST TRAVEL BARGAINS IN YOUR PRICE RANGE

"All the dirt, dirt cheap."

—*People*

"Anything you need to know about budget traveling is detailed in this book."

—*The Chicago Sun-Times*

"Let's Go follows the creed that you don't have to toss your life's savings to the wind to travel—unless you want to."

—*The Salt Lake Tribune*

■ REAL ADVICE FOR REAL EXPERIENCES

"The writers seem to have experienced every rooster-packed bus and lunar-surfaced mattress about which they write."

—*The New York Times*

"Value-packed, unbeatable, accurate, and comprehensive."

—*The Los Angeles Times*

"[Let's Go's] devoted updaters really walk the walk (and thumb the ride, and trek the trail). Learn how to fish, haggle, find work—anywhere."

—*Food & Wine*

P9-DEV-378

LET'S GO PUBLICATIONS

TRAVEL GUIDES
Australia 8th edition
Austria & Switzerland 2005
Brazil 1st edition
Britain & Ireland 2005
California 2005
Central America 9th edition
Chile 2nd edition
China 5th edition
Costa Rica 2nd edition
Eastern Europe 2005
Ecuador 1st edition **NEW TITLE**
Egypt 2nd edition
Europe 2005
France 2005
Germany 12th edition
Greece 2005
Hawaii 2005
India & Nepal 8th edition
Ireland 2005
Israel 4th edition
Italy 2005
Japan 1st edition
Mexico 20th edition
Middle East 4th edition
Peru 1st edition **NEW TITLE**
Puerto Rico 1st edition
South Africa 5th edition
Southeast Asia 9th edition
Spain & Portugal 2005
Thailand 2nd edition
Turkey 5th edition
USA 2005
Vietnam 1st edition **NEW TITLE**
Western Europe 2005

ROADTRIP GUIDE
Roadtripping USA **NEW TITLE**

ADVENTURE GUIDES
Alaska 1st edition
New Zealand **NEW TITLE**
Pacific Northwest **NEW TITLE**
Southwest USA 3rd edition

CITY GUIDES
Amsterdam 3rd edition
Barcelona 3rd edition
Boston 4th edition
London 2005
New York City 15th edition
Paris 13th edition
Rome 12th edition
San Francisco 4th edition
Washington, D.C. 13th edition

POCKET CITY GUIDES
Amsterdam
Berlin
Boston
Chicago
London
New York City
Paris
San Francisco
Washington, D.C.

LET'S GO

THAILAND

SARAH SELIM EDITOR
ANNE PATRONE ASSOCIATE EDITOR

RESEARCHER-WRITERS
ANNA BYRNE
STEPHEN FAN
DAN RAMSEY
NITIN SHAH

CLIFFORD EMMANUEL MAP EDITOR
BRIANA CUMMINGS MANAGING EDITOR

ST. MARTIN'S PRESS ✠ NEW YORK

HELPING LET'S GO. If you want to share your discoveries, suggestions, or corrections, please drop us a line. We read every piece of correspondence, whether a postcard, a 10-page email, or a coconut. **Address mail to:**

> Let's Go: Thailand
> 67 Mount Auburn Street
> Cambridge, MA 02138
> USA

Visit Let's Go at **http://www.letsgo.com**, or send email to:

> feedback@letsgo.com
> Subject: "Let's Go: Thailand"

In addition to the invaluable travel advice our readers share with us, many are kind enough to offer their services as researchers or editors. Unfortunately, our charter enables us to employ only currently enrolled Harvard students.

Maps by David Lindroth copyright © 2005 by St. Martin's Press.

Let's Go: Thailand Copyright © 2005 by Let's Go, Inc. All rights reserved. Printed in the United States of America. No part of this book may be used or reproduced in any manner whatsoever without written permission except in the case of brief quotations embodied in critical articles or reviews. Let's Go is available for purchase in bulk by institutions and authorized resellers. For information, address St. Martin's Press, 175 Fifth Avenue, New York, NY 10010, USA. www.stmartins.com.

Distributed outside the USA and Canada by Macmillan, an imprint of Pan Macmillan Ltd.
20 New Wharf Road, London N1 9RR
Basingstoke and Oxford
Associated companies throughout the world
www.panmacmillan.com

ISBN: 0-312-33568-7
EAN: 978-0-312-33568-7
First edition
10 9 8 7 6 5 4 3 2 1

Let's Go: Thailand is written by Let's Go Publications, 67 Mount Auburn Street, Cambridge, MA 02138, USA.

ADVERTISING DISCLAIMER. All advertisements appearing in Let's Go publications are sold by an independent agency not affiliated with the editorial production of the guides. Advertisers are never given preferential treatment, and the guides are researched, written, and published independent of advertising. Advertisements do not imply endorsement of products or services by Let's Go, and Let's Go does not vouch for the accuracy of information provided in advertisements.

If you are interested in purchasing advertising space in a Let's Go publication, contact: Let's Go Advertising Sales, 67 Mount Auburn St., Cambridge, MA 02138, USA.

CONTENTS

v

PRICE RANGES >> THAILAND

Our researchers list establishments in order of value from best to worst; their favorites are denoted by the Let's Go thumbs-up (☝). Since the best value is not always the cheapest price, however, we have also incorporated a system of price ranges, based on a rough expectation of what you will spend. For **accommodations,** we base our range on the cheapest price for which a single traveler can stay for one night. For **restaurants** and other dining establishments, we estimate the average amount a traveler will spend. The table below tells you what you will *typically* find in Thailand at the corresponding price range; keep in mind that no system can allow for every individual establishment's quirks.

ACCOMMODATIONS	RANGE	WHAT YOU'RE *LIKELY* TO FIND
1	Under $2 Under 80฿	Dorm rooms or dorm-style rooms. Expect bunk beds and a communal bath; you may have to provide or rent towels and sheets.
2	$2-7 80-280฿	Upper-end hostels or guesthouses. You may have a private bathroom, or there may be a sink in your room and communal shower in the hall.
3	$7-12 280-480฿	A small room with a private bath. Should have decent amenities, such as phone and A/C. Breakfast may be included in the price of the room.
4	$12-18 480-720฿	Similar to 3, but may have more amenities or be in a more touristed area.
5	Over $18 Over 720฿	Large hotels or upscale chains. If it's a 5 and it doesn't have the perks you want, you've paid too much.

FOOD	RANGE	WHAT YOU'RE *LIKELY* TO FIND
1	under $0.75 under 30฿	Perhaps the best way to eat in Thailand, street stalls and vendors.
2	$0.75-2 30-80฿	Small Thai restaurants and as much fruit as you can eat!
3	$2-4 80-160฿	Already approaching the more expensive side, in this range you should be able to afford a sit-down meal at a restaurant.
4	$4-6 160-240฿	And now you're having several courses at that restaurant or eating at a more touristy, foreign-themed restaurant.
5	Over $6 Over 240฿	In this range you should not only be getting delicious food but impeccable service and atmosphere, regardless of what type of food you're eating.

HOW TO USE THIS BOOK

Thailand is an aesthetic heaven; from golden Buddhas to turquoise waters, the visual landscape will thrill you. *Let's Go* lists 1000-year-old temples and immaculate white-sand beaches, but the adventure is yours to find. Relish the uncertainty of life on the road. Let our "Sights" section guide you as you cruise from *wat* to *wat*. Swat mosquitos with this book on the beach. Let these pages and your instinct be your guides. Trust no other.

INTRODUCTORY MATERIAL. The first chapter, **Discover Thailand,** provides an overview of travel in the region. The **suggested itineraries** give an idea of the places you shouldn't miss and how long it takes to see them. **Essentials** outlines practical travel information that you'll need before you leave and once you're there. **Life and Times** offers a piece of Thai history, culture, politics, and customs. The **Appendix** has useful **conversions,** a handy **phrasebook,** and a **climate** chart.

COVERAGE. The chapters each cover a region and are listed alphabetically. The **black tabs** in the margins—and knowing that "S" comes after "N"—will help you to navigate the chapters quickly and easily. First stop is **Bangkok** (p. 93), the flashy, dynamic jumping-off point for travelers heading all over Southeast Asia. Next come the historical sights of **Central Thailand,** like the ancient capital of Ayutthaya (p. 160) and the real bridge on the River Kwai (p. 175). Sleepy **Northeast** cities like Ubon Ratchathani (p. 218) are a relaxing retreat from the tourist-heavy areas of the rest of the country. Next are the **Northern** mountains and the cultural center of Chiang Mai (p. 265). Our coverage ends in sunny **Southern Thailand,** exemplified by the beaches of Phuket (p. 362) and gorgeous dive sites off Ko Tao (p. 415).

FEATURES. For your reading enjoyment, we have included sidebars of information ranging from how to purchase your very own *tuk-tuk* (p. 236) to how not to pick up a prostitute (p. 398). Savor one of Thailand's greatest assets—the food!—with our features describing uniquely Thai brands (p. 165), and market offerings (p. 112).

PRICE DIVERSITY. The small numbered icons next to our food and accommodations choices denote the price range (p. VI) of that particular establishment. Everything is ranked in order of quality—from the best value to the least—and our researchers give the coveted ▨thumbpick to their favorites.

LANGUAGE AND OTHER QUIRKS. There is no standard system of transliteration between Thai and English. Therefore, you may come across the Thai words we include in various forms during your travels. Fear not, however—the spellings will usually be similar enough to be recognizable.

ALTERNATIVES TO TOURISM. Interested in doing more? Try volunteering at an orphanage (p. 85), working with endangered animals (p. 82), or teaching English (p. 85). Or take "study abroad" to a whole new level at a Thai university (p. 86).

A NOTE TO OUR READERS. The information for this book was gathered by *Let's Go* researchers from February through August of 2004. Each listing is based on one researcher's opinion, formed during his or her visit at a particular time. Those traveling at other times may have different experiences since prices, dates, hours, and conditions are always subject to change. You are urged to check the facts presented in this book beforehand to avoid inconvenience and surprises.

RESEARCHER-WRITERS

Anna Byrne   *Bangkok, Central Thailand*

Despite her irrational fear of collapsing malls, Anna got to participate in some of her favorite pastimes: shopping, getting massages,
sunbathing, and consuming large tropical drinks, while merrily
distributing Let's Go picks all over the place. Along the way, Anna
did an amazing job, seeking out hidden gems in the frenetic labyrinth that is Bangkok. We have no doubt Thailand will miss her as
she tackles her next challenge. We will too.

Stephen Fan   *Northeast Thailand*

Making new friends at every turn, Steve wandered through the rustic villages of Thailand's northeastern plateau. We wish we could
say that he enjoyed himself, but his mouth was always too full of
food for us to understand what he was saying on the phone. Having
gotten a taste of life on the road, next year will see Steve appren-
ticed to a violin-maker in Germany and traveling to Hong Kong.
Ever the doting son, he would like to thank his mom and dad.

Dan Ramsey   *Northern Thailand*

Hailing from the American South, Dan chose to switch it up on his
second researching stint for *Let's Go*, trekking through the mountains of northern Thailand. Despite his Indiana Jones-style antics,
including riding a motorbike and jumping onto moving trains, Dan
completed his copy in top form. After whetting his appetite for
adventure, Dan is back in the US, busy pursuing a career in Washington, D.C.

Nitin Shah   *Northern Thailand, Southern Thailand*

After narrowly escaping death by coconut, Nitin did an amazing job
finishing up his route (the doctors say there won't be any permanent damage). Although he had the cushiest route (where else
would sitting on the beach be called "work"?), Nitin managed to
keep his editors laughing all summer with his clever research and
his witty accounts of his misadventures. Nitin's future plans are
rather nebulous, but no matter where he ends up, he's sure to shine.

CONTRIBUTING WRITERS

Ted Osius edited and contributed to various *Let's Go* Guides from 1980 to 1984. Since
1989, he served for the US Department of State in Manila, Philippines; as a political and
administrative officer at the US Embassy to the Vatican; and as an assistant to the Permanent Representative to the UN. In 1997, he opened the US Consulate General in Ho
Chi Minh City. From 1998 to 2001, he served as Senior Advisor on International Affairs
to former Vice President Al Gore. He is now a Regional Environmental Affairs Officer in
Southeast Asia, for the US Embassy. Ted is also the author of *The U.S.-Japan Security
Alliance: Why It Matters and How To Strengthen It* (CSIS/Praeger, 2002.)

Brett Renfrew is currently working and living in Bangkok as a teacher and a corporate
writer. He also runs a project to import used computers for use in rural schools.

Sarah Selim is the editor of this book and spent six months living in Thailand volunteering at the Pattaya Orphanage. She loves Thailand so much she jumped at the chance to
share her experiences there.

ACKNOWLEDGMENTS

TEAM THAILAND THANKS: Brie for being the best ME a bookteam could ever wish for (with impeccable taste in chocolate); Anna, Nitin, and Steve for their tireless work and constant good humor, and for never giving us cause to worry; Cliff for his amazing proficiency with both map software and people; Charlotte, Jesse, Scottie, and Stef for keeping life interesting and making the pod the best place to work, *ever;* J Zac for his sharp eyes and way with the ladies; Vicky and Adam for their technological genius; Shelley and Richard for midnight chats; and 7-Eleven for graciously satisfying our late-night caffeine needs.

SARAH THANKS: Anne, who managed to get all her work done, even if she doesn't know where the capital of Thailand is, Rabia for getting it, my roomates and friends who made sure I had fun, my family and the Cranberry crew, ice cream (and everyone who helped me eat it), chocolate in all its forms, and CAKE! SiSi, I love you.

ANNE THANKS: Sarah for being wonderful, even if she *is* a dirty, dirty, wench; Shelley for Roswell lunches, Chinese pastries, and for listening to me babble; Barb for making me laugh and putting up with me when I'm stressed; LT for her key-tar and the Phelpedo; Kathy for general fabulousness; my family for dealing with my deadlines; and Trader Joe's for all the comfort food I could ever want.

CLIFF THANKS: Sarah and Anne for their hardwork, delightful mapland visits, and equally delightful culinary treats, Andrea for experimental cookery, and RWs for making it all possible.

Editor
Sarah Selim
Associate Editor
Anne Patrone
Managing Editor
Briana Cummings
Map Editor
Clifford Shawn Emmanuel
Typesetter
Dustin Lewis

LET'S GO

Publishing Director
Emma Nothmann
Editor-in-Chief
Teresa Elsey
Production Manager
Adam R. Perlman
Cartography Manager
Elizabeth Halbert Peterson
Design Manager
Amelia Aos Showalter
Editorial Managers
Briana Cummings, Charlotte Douglas, Ella M. Steim, Joel August Steinhaus, Lauren Truesdell, Christina Zaroulis
Financial Manager
R. Kirkie Maswoswe
Marketing and Publicity Managers
Stef Levner, Leigh Pascavage
Personnel Manager
Jeremy Todd
Production Associate
Victoria Esquivel-Korsiak
IT Director
Matthew DePetro
Web Manager
Rob Dubbin
Associate Web Manager
Patrick Swieskowski
Research and Development Consultant
Jennifer O'Brien
Office Coordinators
Stephanie Brown, Elizabeth Peterson

Director of Advertising Sales
Elizabeth S. Sabin
Senior Advertising Associates
Jesse R. Loffler, Francisco A. Robles, Zoe M. Savitsky
Advertising Graphic Designer
Christa Lee-Chuvala

President
Ryan M. Geraghty
General Manager
Robert B. Rombauer
Assistant General Manager
Anne E. Chisholm

DISCOVER THAILAND

Requiring almost no introduction, Thailand is a sensuous paradise full of all kinds of adventure. Regardless of the pictures you see, books you read, and movies you watch before your trip, you will inevitably be astounded by Thailand's natural beauty and compelling culture. Perhaps the most accessible destination in Southeast Asia, Thailand is filled with aesthetic charms from celestial beaches to glittering golden *chedis* to savory culinary delights. Explore the ancient cities of central Thailand, where the ruins of once-great kingdoms now lie in silent majesty, testament to a glorious past. Swim in the world's bluest waters and search for a different kind of wildlife than the backpackers you encounter on shore. Meditate amid saffron-cloaked Buddhist monks in temples adorned with mother-of-pearl inlay and frescoes older than the Magna Carta. Throughout Thailand, mouth-watering cuisine will be your sustenance, delightfully warm people will be your companions, and a smile will be your currency. Get ready to dive right in.

FACTS AND FIGURES

Official Name: Kingdom of Thailand
Government: Constitutional monarchy
Capital: Bangkok
Land Area: 514,000 km²
Geography: Borders Malaysia, Myanmar, Laos, and Cambodia. Northern Thailand and the Burmese border to the west are mountainous.

Climate: Dry (high) season Nov.-Mar., rainy (low) season Apr.-Oct.
Major Cities: Bangkok, Chiang Mai
Population: 60,200,000
Language: Thai
Religions: Theravada Buddhism (95%); Muslim, Christian, Hindu (5%)
Average Income Per Capita: US$2000

WHEN TO GO

Thailand has rainy and dry seasons, which roughly correspond to low and high tourism seasons. During the low season, sights are less crowded and prices are reduced, but fewer services are offered. In the north, fewer trekking opportunities are available and in the south some beaches and islands completely close down. The rainy season spans May to September in the north and runs later in the year the farther south you travel. The dry season is split into hot and dry (Mar.-May) and cool and dry (Oct.-Feb.), although the actual temperature difference is very small. Essentially, Thailand is hot and humid; temperatures fluctuate around 27°C (80°F) year-round everywhere except the extreme uplands of the mainland, where night-time temperatures can drop dramatically (see **Average Temperatures,** p. 422). For a rough conversion from °C to °F see p. 422.

WHAT TO DO

Thailand has enough *wats*, beaches, jungles, museums, and markets to keep you busy for the rest of your life. But if you don't plan to stay in Thailand forever, where are you supposed to start? When there are sharks to swim with, handicrafts to shop for, religions to learn about, cultures to understand, species to save, and nirvanas to reach, what do you do first? The editors of *Let's Go Thailand* challenge you to do it all. Because in Thailand, you can.

BACKPACKER CENTRAL

If you're looking for a backpacker scene, Thailand is the undisputed mecca. With the proliferation of charming guesthouse communities and the Southeast Asian gateway city of Bangkok, it's no surprise that tourists under thirty permeate Thailand. You may run into your best friend from primary school buying spring rolls in **Bangkok** (p. 93) or that crazy guy you met two weeks ago in Vietnam getting a sun tan on **Ko Chang** (p. 153). You'll definitely meet people who have crazy stories about near-death experiences with dysentery, malaria, wild tigers, Burmese border guards, or the hyped-up narcotic of the week. Most of these stories are true. **Khaosan Road** (p. 93) is the best place for these story-telling sessions. **Ko Samet** (p. 143), on the east coast, is the spot for low-key chilling, swimming, and snorkeling. **Chiang Mai** (p. 265), the largest city in Northern Thailand, has cultural and commercial attractions that also suit the *farang* crowd. In the northeast, **Chiang Khan** (p. 248) is a hidden gem—essentially a backpacking destination without the tourists. The scene in the southern *kos* is even more relaxed and is a break from green curry three times a day. **Ko Samui** (p. 420) has been a backpacker haven since its discovery in the 1970s. And what backpacker trip would be complete without a **Full Moon party** on **Ko Phangan** (p. 420)? Enjoy the spirit of the culture and bond over banana pancakes, but make sure you leave time to get stories of your own.

NOURISH YOUR SPIRIT

With over 300 *wats*, including its most famous, **Wat Phra That Doi Suthep** (p. 283), whose golden *chedi* glows for miles, **Chiang Mai** is known for its cultural heritage. For that matter, Bangkok is no lightweight when it comes to *wats*. **Wat Phra Kaew** (Temple of the Emerald Buddha, p. 115), is certainly **Bangkok's** most visited *wat* and perhaps the most impressive. **Ayutthaya's** (p. 160) collection of *wats* is among the oldest in Thailand, but many were ruined when the Burmese ransacked it in 1767. Brightly colored **Wat Thawet** (p. 311) in **Sukhothai** has a maze of Buddhist sculptures. Also in Sukhothai, **Wat Mahathat** (p. 311) has a lotus-shaped *chedi*, characteristic of the era when Sukhothai was the capital of the Thai empire. In **Khorat**, **Wat Sala Loi's** (p. 202) inner sanctuary is shaped like a ship, symbolizing the passage of its devoted students to nirvana. **Wat Khaek** (p. 243) in **Nong Khai** was designed according to Buddhist cosmology and has some bizarre sculptures, a few towering five stories. Hidden among the millions of guesthouses and drunken *farang* in southern Thailand is **Wat Borommthat Chaiya** (p. 400) in **Chaiya**. Besides being an anomaly in terms of location, it is also one of Thailand's rare Mahayana Buddhist (as opposed to Theravada Buddhist) *wats*. **Wat Suwannakuha** (p. 360) is composed of several attached caves near **Phang-Nga**. Nearby, **Wat Tham Sua** (p.360) has Buddha's footprints, a Tiger Cave, and an inhabited monastery.

TASTE THAILAND

Forget main courses, the fruit in Thailand is among the strangest and most delicious in the world. From the indigenous durian often banned from public places because of its pungent, pervasive odor, to the ridiculous-looking, yet incredibly refreshing, flame-red rambutan, to the much sought-after golden mango, the fruit in Thailand offers a feast fit for (and often indulged in by) a king. The best place to sample such delicacies is at the day markets such as those in **Nan** (p. 340) and **Chanthaburi** (p. 148) or find a restaurant that serves a set Thai menu, since most Thai meals end with a platter of mouth-watering fruit. Seafood lovers should sample the local specialities in **Si Racha** (p. 130) on Thailand's East Coast with their spicy red fish sauce. **Sukhothai** (p. 311) markets have yummy *nam rik noom*, a chili-paste dip. Fried scorpions and ants are protein-packed snacks; buy them from vendors in **Bangkok** (p. 93) or **Pattaya** (p. 135). **Udon Thani** (p. 234) has Isaan specialties like sausages, insects, and sticky rice. Savor *kung den*, live shrimp, as they pop around your plate and in your mouth in **Chiang Khan** (p. 248). Way down south on the Malaysian border, **Sungai Kolok** (p. 389) stirs up the local specialty of *gaeng tai plaa*—spicy curry with fermented fish kidney. Southern Thailand has sweet delicacies too, like crepes with shredded coconut in **Hat Yai** (p. 385). **Phuket** (p. 362) is famous for Chinese crepes and *kanom jin Phuket* (breakfast noodles in spicy curry). It's never too early for curry in Thailand.

MEDICATE, EDUCATE, OR MEDITATE

There are countless opportunities to medicate and educate yourself and others, and countless monasteries with teachers to guide you to spiritual healing. **Lampang Medical Plants Conservation Center** (p. 317) does botanical research and also has a spa for all your physical healing needs. **Wat Pa Nanachat,** a forest monastery outside **Ubon Ratchathani,** invites serious students of Buddhism to stay there (p. 218). Meditation retreats at **Wat Suan Mokkha Phalaram** in **Chaiya** (p. 400) are terrific for the travel-weary. The **Population and Community Development Association (PDA)** in **Chiang Rai** (p. 334) is a major organization that accepts volunteers who are willing to help with rural development and AIDS education/outreach. PDA is one of many, many organizations in need of volunteers. Opportunities abound for travelers interested in teaching English or almost any special skill. For more specific information about volunteering at community development organizations, NGOs, clinics, animal refuges and preserves, see **Alternatives to Tourism** (p. 81).

TRIBAL TRIBULATIONS

Northern Thailand is full of a variety of hill-tribe groups who migrated to Thailand from various parts of Southeast Asia (including China and Myanmar) seeking security. Over 99.5% of all refugees in Thailand are Burmese. In **Sangkhlaburi** (p. 181), a **Mon** village of ethnic Burmese refugees is connected to a Thai village by a wooden bridge, with the halfway point distinguishing the territories. **Pha Maw Yaw** (p. 181) is home to an affluent White Karen community. The **Red Karen** state is just across the border from **Mae Hong Son** (p. 291), and the much publicized **Long-Necked Karen** village with "giraffe women" is nearby. Mae Hong Son also accommodates the **KMT** camps and **Shan, Lisu, Hmong,** and **Lahu** hill tribes. The **Hmong villages** in **Chiang Khong** (p. 331) are accessible only by bike during the dry season. **Nan National Museum** in **Nan** (p. 340) displays a thorough history of Thai hill tribes. **Village Weaver Handicrafts** in **Nong Khai** (p. 239) has silk products made by Isaan women. The night market in **Chiang Rai** (p. 334) has hill-tribe handicrafts. For those interested in the hill-tribe lifestyle, check out the **Living Museum** near **Mae Salong** (p. 327).

SNORKELERS' DELIGHT

And scuba divers' too! As the largest diving-training center in Southeast Asia, **Ko Tao,** with over 20 dive schools, is the first stop on a scuba tour. Leopard sharks and rock "swim-throughs" are just the beginning. Snorkelers will love the island's **Ao Leuk** and **Ao Thian** (p. 415) or the off-beach snorkeling in **Ao Ta-Note.** A daytrip from Ko Tao to **Ko Nang Yuan** (p. 420) also has great snorkeling. Gurus hail **Hat Karon** and **Hat Kata** beaches on **Phuket** (p. 362) as homes to some of the world's best marine life, particularly around the Similan Islands. Near Trang, **Ko Tarutao National Marine Park** (p. 388) is an archipelago of 51 islands that is nothing short of an aquatic enthusiast's visual paradise. Off **Ko Samui,** the **Ang Thong Marine National Park** (p. 409) is made up of 40 limestone islands that offer phenomenal snorkeling and diving, particularly at **Ko Sam Sao** (Tripod Island) and **Hat Chan Charat** (Moonlight Beach). The **Outer Islands of Ko Chang** on the east coast, **Ko Rang** and **Ko Wai** (p. 158), are almost completely coral and spotted with sharks.

ISLAND	DESCRIPTION	BEACHES	HIGHLIGHTS
Ko Samet Central	Best beaches on the east coast.	Ao Cho, Ao Kiu, Ao Kiu Na Nai, Ao Nuan, Ao Phai, Ao Phrao, Ao Thian, Ao Tup Tim, Ao Wai, Ao Wong Duan, Hat Lung Dum, Hat Sai Kaew	Snorkeling in Ao Kiu's coral reefs, hanging out at Ao Phai, and camping under the stars on Ao Thian.
Ko Chang Central	An increasingly commercialized hotspot.	Hat Kai Bae, Hat Khlong Phrao, Hat Sai Khao	Exploring Ko Chang National Marine Park.
Ko Phi Phi South	Natural paradises fighting encroaching tourism.	Ao Lo Dalam, Ao Maya, Ao Thon Sai, Hat Hin Kohn, Hat Yao (Long Beach), Laem Him, Ma Prao	Plenty of dive sites, tours of stunning Ao Maya, and longtail boat trips.
Ko Tao South	Southeast Asia's biggest dive-training site.	Hat Sai Ree, Ao Chalok Ban Kao, Ao Leuk, Ao Tanote, Ao Thian, Laem Taa Toh, Mae Hat	Fantastic snorkeling and scuba diving just about anywhere on the island.
Ko Phangan South	Sun-soaked beaches by day, drunken tourists by night.	Hat Khuat (Bottle Beach), Hat Rin Nai, Hat Rin Nok, Thong Sala, Thong Nai Paan Yai, Thong Nai Paan Noi	Wild full moon parties, soothing Bottle Beach, and refreshing waterfalls.
Ko Samui South	An island of extremes, from McDonald's to the jungle.	◼Hat Chaweng, Ao Thongsai, Ao Yai Noi, Hat Bangrak (Big Buddha Beach), Hat Choeng Mon, Hat Lamai, Hat Mae Nam, Laem Thongson, Na Thon	The Big Buddha, Hat Chaweng's nightlife, Ang Thong Marine National Park, and beautiful inland waterfalls.
Phuket South	Thailand's biggest and most touristy island.	Hat Ao Bang Tao, Hat Chalong, Hat Kamala, Hat Karon, Hat Kata, Hat Nai Yang, Hat Patong, Hat Rawai, Hat Surin, Sing Cape, Hat Mai Khao, Friendship Beach	Great snorkeling and diving around Hat Karon and Hat Kata, gorgeous Hat Surin, first-class resorts, and nightlife hub Hat Patong.

ANCIENT ELEPHANTS

The most revered animal in Thailand, elephants hold a special place in the heart of every Thai citizen. They are considered very lucky: people will even pay money to walk under an elephant and absorb some of its luck. White elephants have especially great significance, symbolizing royalty, prosperity, fertility, and knowledge, stemming from the story of the Buddha. Celebrate these majestic beasts during the **Elephant Roundup,** a two-day festival in **Surin** (p. 213) in mid-November. **Ruammit,** the Karen Elephant Camp, near **Tha Ton** (p. 322) rescues the jungle creatures and rehabilitates them. To help out with the bathing and feeding, see **Alternatives to Tourism** (p. 81). Just outside **Lampang** (p. 317), the **Thai Elephant Conservation Center** trains elephants to do manual labor, under the belief that they can make them useful once again, despite the technology that forced them into unemployment. Currently, elephants are often seen wandering the streets of Bangkok with their riders, since development of rural areas has reduced the need for their services.

VENERATED BUDDHAS

Bangkok's **Wat Phra Kaew** (p. 115) houses the famous **Emerald Buddha** and nearby **Wat Pho** (p. 116) has the largest reclining Buddha in Thailand. Glass paintings and wooden Burmese dolls adorn the inside of **Wat Chong Klang** in Mae Hong Son (p. 291). **Wat Tha Ton** (p. 322) has life-size Chinese, Hindu, and Buddhist figures. Also in Tha Ton is the **golden, dragon-headed Buddha** not to be missed. A trip to **Sukhothai** (p. 316) will bring you to **Wat Sri Chum** and King Ramkhamhaeng's famous talking Buddha. In Thai history, it is not uncommon for a bolt of lightning, a *wat*-sacking, or an accident to destroy a Buddha, only to reveal a more valuable Buddha underneath—as happened with the Emerald Buddha. Most recently, in 1955, an 800-year-old stucco Buddha was dropped, breaking the stucco shell around a stunning, 5½-ton gold Buddha in **Wat Traimit** in Bangkok (p. 93). Remember, it is illegal to remove Buddha images from the country without the permission of the Fine Arts Department. Luckily, souvenir Buddhas are not subject to these regulations.

EXOTIC WATERFALLS

It may take three days, but the trek to **Pa La-u Falls** (p. 195), with its 11 tiers of cascades, is worth it. Its rival might be **Nam Tok Krathing** in **Khao Khitchakut National Park** (p. 150) near Chanthaburi, where you can swim in six of the 13 tiers of falls. After coming up from a shallow dive into the thirteenth, you emerge from the water into a swarm of hundreds of golden butterflies. And, of course, the trail up is marked by a sitting Buddha. The jungle pool at **Than Mayom Falls** (p. 158) was the royals' pick at the turn of the 20th century. Deserted and soothing, the **Pha Peung** upper waterfalls in **Tak** (p. 306) are stunning. Head to **Khao Yai National Park** (p. 200) to see **Haew Narok** where even elephants have been known to fall to their death. Swim in the second tier of the **Than Thip Falls** in **Sangkhom** (p. 246) and hike to **Na Muang Waterfall** in **Ko Samui** (p. 401). Famous for waterfalls, the **Than Sadet Historical Park** on **Ko Phangan** (p. 409) has giant cascades with tiny pools.

▓ LET'S GO PICKS: THAILAND

BEST PLACE FOR A SWIM: Larn Sak Waterfall in **Tak** (p. 306) with its multiple tiers, or one of Thailand's many other multi-tiered natural marvels.

BEST PLACE TO FEEL LIKE A MAN: The nightly transvestite shows at **Alcazar** in **Pattaya** (p. 135) are billed as family entertainment and draw thousands of visitors each year.

BEST PLACE TO CATCH AN ELEPHANT (PLAYING SOCCER!): The **Elephant Roundup** in **Surin** (p. 213) lasts for 2 days in November and features demonstrations of the revered beasts' strength.

BEST SPA: The natural hot springs off the Mae Yen River in **Pai** (p. 286) soothe you before your traditional Thai massage. ·

BEST KARMA: With a level for each enlightenment, **Wat Pu Thok** in **Nong Khai** (p. 239) is not to be missed.

BEST PLACE TO SNAG JEWELS: 50-60% of the world's sapphires and rubies travel down Si Chan Rd. in **Chanthaburi** (p. 148) on the way to counters near you.

BEST PUPPETEER: Visit Suchart Sabsin, the award-winning puppet-maker at the **Shadow Play House** in **Nakhon Si Thammarat** (p. 391) and watch him both build and perform with his puppets.

BEST WAY TO CHAT UP A MONK: Visit **Wat Chedi Luang** in **Chiang Mai** (p. 265), one of several *wats* that offers **Monk Chat,** an opportunity to learn about Buddhism and Thai life from monks.

BEST BUDDHAS: The "thousand Buddhas" tucked into caves in **Phetchaburi** (p. 183) almost beat the Emerald Buddha in **Bangkok** (p. 93).

BEST FOOD: Anywhere in Thailand!

DISCOVER

SUGGESTED ITINERARIES

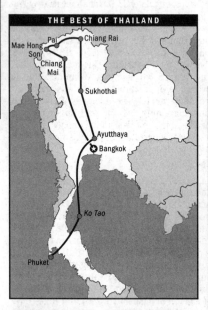

THE BEST OF THAILAND

THE CULTURAL CONNECTION

choice, but if you are seeking more than just relaxation, **Ko Tao** (p. 415) and **Phuket** (p. 362) are the best destinations for aquatic activities.

FROM PAGODAS TO PATPONG
THE BEST OF THAILAND
(6 WEEKS)

Begin where all good trips should, in bustling **Bangkok** (p. 93). Head north, reaching the hills of **Chiang Mai** (p. 265), where the best trekking and aesthetic treats of the region await you. To find it, look for the city's golden *chedi*—it will beckon from miles away. The infamous **Threesome** of Chiang Mai, **Mae Hong Son** (p. 291), and **Pai** (p. 286) brings together the best of indigenous Thai culture, amazing mountain views, and a respite from the sizzling Southeast Asian summer. Having conquered the three, move on to the gentler **Chiang Rai** (p. 334) for more insights into northern culture. Venture to the west for exposure to Burmese refugee camps and hill tribe villages along the **Myanmar border.** Shoot south via the ancient capitals of **Sukhothai** (p. 311), in whose ruins echoes the long history of Thailand, and **Ayutthaya** (p. 160), a UNESCO World Heritage Site with a concentrated collection of ancient *wats*. End your trip with a relaxing stroll on the beaches of the *ko* of your

THE CULTURAL CONNECTION
(4 WEEKS)

Fly into **Bangkok** (p. 93), and proceed with the requisite tour of museums and *wats*. Visit the ancient ruins at both **Ayutthaya** (p. 160) and **Sukhothai** (p. 311) and absorb the region's history at their museums. Travel on to **Chiang Mai** (p. 265) and spend your first days at the **Chiang Mai Cooking School** (p. 265) in their renowned cooking class. Take your pick of instruction in meditation, massage, and Muay Thai, and then go to **Mae Hong Son** (p. 291) for tribal villages and forest monasteries. Head to **Pai** (p. 286) and set up a trek through the north with one of the local outfits. If that isn't enough for you, come to **Nan** for a **home stay** (p. 340) to live and work with a local hill-tribe family. Visit the **Thai Payap Project,** which sells hill-tribe handicrafts to fund community development programs in the area. On your way east, stop at **Nong Khai** and **Phu Phra Bat** (p. 239) to see the prehistoric paintings. For

Southeast Asia's most significant archaeological site, travel to **Ban Chiang** in **Udon Thani** (p. 234), another World Heritage Site. Finish up your trip with Wat That Phanom in **That Phanom** (p. 229), for the most sacred structure in Isaan culture.

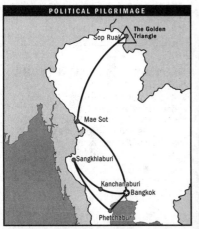

POLITICAL PILGRIMAGE (3 WEEKS)

After seeing the palaces and parliament buildings in **Bangkok** (p. 93), travel south to see **Phetchaburi's** (p. 183) historical park and national museum, which showcases the intermingling of Chinese and Western influences in Thailand. Continue on to **Sangkhlaburi** (p. 181), and visit Burmese Karen and Mon refugee camps. If you have more time, perfect the trip with a hands-on experience—teach English to refugees, or get involved with a local community development program (see **Alternatives to Tourism**, p. 81). Take Rte. 323 down to **Kanchanaburi** (p. 170), stopping at the historical sights and park along the way. The notorious River Kwai Bridge (Death Railway Bridge) was built in Kanchanaburi by local workers and Japan's Allied POWs. Swing back by Bangkok and then check out **Mae Sot** (p. 299), farther north, where you'll run into more armed border police than local refugees. Much farther north, finish the tour at the **Golden Triangle** (p. 330), whose drug trade is the source of major political controversy.

BEACH BABY: ISLAND-HOPPING (3 WEEKS)

Begin your trip on **Ko Chang** (p. 153), with your back to the jungle, your feet sinking into the sand, and your eyes focused on the vibrant sunset. Next, spend time on **Ko Samet** (p. 143) exploring the crystal-clear water or simply relaxing on the immaculate beaches. From there, head to the peninsula where **Ko Phangan** (p. 409) awaits you with its exhilarating full moon parties. A quick boat ride will bring you to **Ko Tao** (p. 415), one of the best diving and snorkeling sites in the world. Head farther south to **Trang** (p. 381) for wild orchid-covered coves and cave spelunking at **Hat Yong Ling**. Nearby **Ko Ngai** (p. 385) is a sweet dive spot with pristine beaches. The **Ko Tarutao National Marine Park** (p. 388) has 51 islands worth of scuba diving excellence. Then it's off to **Ko Phi Phi Ley** (p. 375) for the hot springs and endangered species in **Khao Nawe Choochee Lowland Forest.** Stop at **Phuket** (p. 362) for one last dose of beach and aquatic sports before going to **Ko Panyi** (p. 362) to see the three-centuries-old **Muslim fishing village.**

DISCOVER

SPIRITUAL PICK-ME-UPS (AS LONG AS YOUR HEART DESIRES)

Start the rejuvenation journey with a traditional Thai massage by Mr. Noi in **Bangkok** (p. 93). Then head far south to **Surat Thani** for a meditation retreat at **Wat Suan Mokkha Phalaram** (p. 395) to center your thoughts and focus your energy. After this spiritual renewal, hop on a boat for **Ko** Phangan (p. 409). Skip the full moon party in favor of a healthier option: **The Sanctuary.** Remarkably secluded for the crowded island, the spa specializes in yoga and ten-day fasts. Then treat yourself to one more of Thailand's best massages in **Trat** (p. 151) on the east coast. Complete your revitalization with a trip to the revolutionary **Udorn Sunshine Fragrant Orchid Farm** (p. 234), where the plants are bred to have healing powers of all kinds. And if nothing else, the orchids are just plain beautiful.

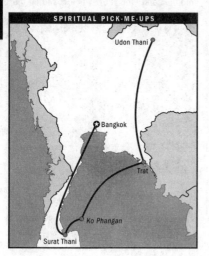

SPIRITUAL PICK-ME-UPS

Udon Thani

Bangkok

Trat

Ko Phangan

Surat Thani

THE WHOLE SHEBANG (YOUR NATURAL LIFE)

Seeing and doing everything in Thailand will undoubtedly take you the rest of your natural life, but it will be worth it. Explore all the *wats* and jungles and volunteer at every possible opportunity. Take this book with you.

LIFE AND TIMES

The only country in Southeast Asia never to have been colonized, Thailand has a proud and independent history that infuses the spirit of Thai society even today, in spite of the hordes of tourists who tramp through the country's beaches, temples, and jungles. A period of economic depression has made living very cheap for foreigners, even as the Thai economy slowly begins the road to recovery. While 15 years ago, a million people descended on the "Land of Smiles" yearly, today that number has risen to an estimated 10 million, and catering to tourists has become the country's lifeblood. There are sights to suit every taste: beachgoers head to the picturesque islands off the eastern and southern coasts, while more adventurous travelers trek through hill tribe homelands in the mountainous north. Others explore the ancient cities of Central Thailand, where the ruins of once-great kingdoms now lie in silent majesty, a testament to a glorious past. For travelers new to Southeast Asia, there's no better place to start than "Amazing Thailand."

◪ HIGHLIGHTS OF THAILAND

BEACHES. Idyllic **Ko Samet** (p. 143) and **Ko Chang** (p. 153) off the east coast are cheap and mellow. Down south, **Ko Samui** (p. 401), **Ko Phangan** (p. 409), and **Ko Tao** (p. 415) offer a more raucous brand of sun and fun with a broader slate of aquatic activities. **Krabi's** (p. 375) seaside cliffs offer world-class climbing.

HIKING AND TREKKING. Northern Thailand (p. 265) offers the greatest range of affordable treks. Less-touristed **Mae Hong Son** (p. 291) and **Sangkhlaburi** (p. 181) have activities ranging from elephant excursions to river rafting.

HANGING OUT. Towns along the Mekong, including **Chiang Khan** (p. 248) and **Nakhon Phanom** (p. 230), are unparalleled spots to unwind and take in stunning natural settings. Nothing tops **Kanchanaburi** (p. 170) for top-notch accommodations and tasty victuals. Tiny **Pai** (p. 286), nestled in the northern highlands, has much to explore.

CULTURAL HERITAGE. The temples and palaces of **Bangkok** (p. 93), the ancient capitals of **Sukhothai** (p. 181) and **Ayutthaya** (p. 160), and the Khmer ruins of **Phimai** (p. 208) are engrossing and accessible. **Chiang Mai** (p. 265) is not to be missed for its stunning architectural legacy and religious significance.

NIGHTLIFE. Bangkok (p. 93), **Chiang Mai** (p. 265), **Ko Phangan** (p. 409), **Ko Samui** (p. 401), and **Khon Kaen** (p. 255) rock on when the rest of the kingdom goes to bed.

LAND

With nearly every topological feature short of a frozen steppe, Thailand is a geography teacher's dream and a cartographer's nightmare. *Kos* (islands) off the coast of the "elephant trunk" peninsula have attracted tourists with claims of paradise. Best known for their white beaches, coral reefs, gushing waterfalls, and shimmering turquoise waters, the *kos* uphold their promise. The range of terrain extends from seashore to mountain peak: Doi Inthanon in the pine-forested north is Thailand's highest point at 2576m. The semi-arid Khorat plateau of the northeast is a far cry from the mangrove forests scattered around the Gulf of Thailand. Farther east, several rivers converge at the lush "Emerald Triangle" where Laos, Cambodia, and Thailand meet, leaving the rice paddies of central Thailand behind. The climate is largely tropical, with extreme temperatures in the drier northern regions. Despite seasonal monsoons, Thailand often has regional droughts.

PEOPLE

DEMOGRAPHICS

Use of the word "Thai" began in the 20th century as a political and geographical designation referring to all citizens of Thailand. "Tai," however, refers to the ethnic Tai-Kadai people, who speak Tai-based languages, live mostly in China, Laos, and Myanmar (where they are known as the Shan), and who account for 75% of the population of Thailand. At about 12% of the population, the **Chinese** are Thailand's largest minority. Homeland starvation and poverty are the leading causes behind the high Chinese immigration rate over the past decades. Hill-tribe groups, including the **Karen, Hmong, Yao, Lahu, Akha,** and **Lisu,** are concentrated in the north, while the country's six million Muslims are concentrated mainly in the south. Ever tolerant, Thais have interwoven elements of all ethnicities into the national culture, in part due to the proliferation of intermarriage.

LANGUAGE

Like the people themselves, the Thai language has evolved with influences and adaptations from English, Chinese, and Sanskrit (to name only a few), while still retaining the characteristic five tones, monosyllabic words, and ancient alphabet. King Ramkhamhaeng of Sukhothai created the first **Thai aphabet** in 1283 as a combination of Sanskrit syntax and Khmer characters, and this alphabet has survived almost entirely intact to this day. This standardized language has lent the Thais a sense of cultural identity and national unity. **Grammar** is delightfully simple: there are no suffixes, genders, articles, declensions, or plurals in spoken Thai. Like English, it is written from left to right, but it lacks capital letters and punctuation. The national language has four major **dialects** that have developed geographically: Central, Northern (Tak), Northeastern, and Southern. See the Appendix (p. 421) for specific phrases. Aside from regional dialects, Thai also employs different vocabulary and syntax depending on the social status of the speaker relative to his audience. The most distinctive of these is the royal language, **rachasap,** used mainly for state or official occasions. Below *rachasap* are the **ecclesiastical language,** the **polite vernacular** used most commonly on a daily basis, and, finally, the spicy **slang** used only between close friends. The Thai vocabulary readily lends itself to adaptation. Somewhat like German, Thai combines existing words to create new meanings. For example, the word "ice" in Thai, *nam khaeng*, literally translates to "solid water." Western concepts and scientific and technological terms are somewhat more difficult to create by combining existing Thai words, however. To remedy the situation, the **Royal Institute** convenes a committee of linguists to concoct new vocabulary words by delving into Pali and Sanskrit.

RELIGION

Although the Thai Constitution requires the reigning monarch to be Buddhist, it does not name Theravada Buddhism as the state religion and guarantees complete freedom of religion for its citizens, a right that Thailand has upheld for centuries. Speech that insults Buddhism is strictly prohibited, however. Foreign missionaries—those formally registered with the government and otherwise—can work in the country free of harassment, but since 1984, the government has not recognized any new faiths, including the Church of Jesus Christ of Latter Day Saints. Since 1999, government-issued National Identity Cards include a religious designation, in the interest of those who wanted an easier means of identifying individuals requiring a Muslim burial. However, this designation is optional; card-holders can choose whether or not they would like to declare their faith.

THERAVADA BUDDHISM. The religion of more than 90% of the Thai people, Theravada Buddhism informs both their faith and their lifestyle. The Thai outlook is better understood in light of the **Four Noble Truths of Buddhism:** there is suffering; the source of suffering is desire; there is a cessation to suffering; and that cessation is achieved through an adherence to the **Eightfold Path,** which is a path of virtue, mental cultivation, and wisdom. Anti-materialism, forgiveness, and a vigorous spirit that has mastered tranquility are all characteristics of this highly scriptural religion and of the Thais themselves. The **Spirit of Free Enquiry** is central to Buddhism: the Buddha encouraged his followers to investigate His Teaching for themselves instead of adhering to it blindly. This teaching inspires a high degree of tolerance for difference—racial, religious, or ethnic—and teaches kindness and compassion in the hope that individuals can live in harmony with the people, creatures, and natural environment around them. Monks are a common sight in Thailand. Their saffron robes, shaved heads, and gentle manner serve as a reminder of the search for inner peace that is the mainstay of Theravada Buddhism. It is an accepted **male rite of passage** to serve temporarily (usually about three months) in the monkhood. The goal of this religious service is increased maturity and spirituality in everyday life. Only below the monarchy in the social hierarchy, monks are discussed and addressed with language that denotes great respect.

MAHAYANA BUDDHISM. Buddhism evolved over time into two schools, Theravada ("tradition of the elderly") and Mahayana ("the great vessel"). The latter teaches that it is impossible for individuals to achieve their own **nirvana**—rather, they can only approach it. According to Mahayana Buddhism, nirvana will only come when all of humankind is ready for salvation. This belief leads Mahayana Buddhists to work to relieve universal suffering. Although it is more popular today in other parts of Southeast Asia, Mahayana Buddhism is still practiced in Thailand, mainly by ethnic Chinese and Vietnamese immigrants. There is a particularly large ethnic Chinese community in Phuket that practices a combination of Mahayana Buddhism and Taoism.

ISLAM. Thailand's largest religious minority, Muslims account for approximately 4% of the population. Thailand's Muslim inhabitants are overwhelmingly Sunni, with a Shi'a distribution of only 1 or 2%. They live mostly in southern Thailand, close to the Malaysian border, and many are originally of **Malay** descent. In fact, in the south there are more mosques than *wats*. Although Islamic law necessitates a lifestyle significantly different from that of Theravada Buddhists or nihilist backpackers, Muslims are well assimilated into Thai culture. In the south, employers observe Muslim holidays and holy days, and all employees are given four months paid leave to travel to Mecca. But in the wake of violent attacks in southern Thailand, the government has become more wary of possible separatist movements in that region (see **Southern Discomfort,** p. 14).

CHRISTIANITY. Christianity first appeared in Thailand in the 16th and 17th centuries, brought by missionaries of varying Christian sects. Thailand's Christian population however remains proportionally the smallest of any Asian nation (at 0.5%), with almost half residing in Chiang Mai and the surrounding area. The religion suffered a setback when foreigners were expelled from Siam (p. 15). When they were eventually allowed back, King Rama IV is reported to have remarked to a missionary friend, "What you teach us to do is admirable, but what you teach us to believe is foolish." A few hill tribes converted to Catholicism, but efforts by the government to bring them into the Buddhist fold have eroded Christianity's popularity.

LIFE AND TIMES

HINDUISM. Although it has been diluted over the centuries, Thai culture is infused with Hinduism from early contact between the Thai and Khmer. This influence is particularly apparent in early art and architecture (p. 26). Only a small percentage of modern Thai are Hindu—mostly immigrants from India—and the majority of them live in Bangkok, where there are four main Hindu temples. Since mandatory religious instruction in schools is solely concentrated in Buddhism and Islam, the Hindu community keeps traditional subjects like Hindi and Sanskrit alive by running its own school in Bangkok

ANIMISM. Predating both Hinduism and Theravada Buddhism, Animism formed the first layer of Thai religion, later incorporating Theravada Buddhism. Followers of Animism believe that everything has a spirit. The ubiquitous Thai spirit houses, provided to shelter the spirits, reflect these deep-seated beliefs (p. 24). Today, most Animists are found among the northern hill tribes or the Chao Lay of the Andaman Sea (p. 388).

FLORA AND FAUNA

Thailand's diverse topology and unique geographical location yield a wealth of plant and animal species. This great variety means that the country makes it onto every international "best" list: best scuba diving, best bird-watching, best trekking. Even the world's best veterinarians travel to Thailand to care for the country's endangered wildlife in the many sanctuaries and nature preserves.

PLANTS

FLOWER POWER. The white or pink **lotus,** seen floating on a pond or depicted in Buddhist art, is a sacred symbol of fertility, purity, peace, and compassion. It gained religious significance when one blossom grew from each of the young Buddha's first seven footsteps. A hot commodity in the Western hemisphere and the national flower of Thailand, **orchids**—over 1000 species—grow everywhere in Thailand. Though the flowers are still on the endangered species list, the orchid industry is a major source of income for Thais. Typically a flower associated with Christian winters in the West, the scarlet **poinsettia** is quite popular in Thailand, especially in Chiang Mai province. Interestingly, it is more common during the winter months because its bright, cheerful poisonous blooms help to compensate for the fewer hours of daylight. Traditional Thai remedies employ many common roots and berries, used for medicinal purposes and to inspire creativity.

RICE AND EVERYTHING NICE. Thailand's most important crop is not significant simply because it is a staple of local cuisine but also because of its religious symbolism. Rice is celebrated as an example of nature providing sustenance. Early every morning (mostly in smaller villages), people leave offerings of rice for the Buddhist monks who collect donations of food and basic daily necessities, collectively known as *binderbaht.* These offerings are particularly significant during harvest festivals (timing varies by region), when it is customary to celebrate all of earth's living things as well as man's labor, which brings these fruits into the home.

RELIGIOSI-TREE. It is believed that Buddha attained enlightenment in the shade of the **Bodhi tree.** Those grown from a cutting of the original tree in India are the most precious, but all Bodhi trees command respect. Long-reaching branches, an irregularly shaped trunk, and heart-shaped leaves are its most noticeable traits. Buddha also sat in the shade of the **Rose Apple** tree, meditating on man's sufferings. Its enormous branches (13m) protected Buddha thousands of years ago; they now do the same for Thais. The **Chomphu Phukha** tree in Nan's Doi Phuka National Park (p. 344), is extremely rare, though it isn't the only one in the world, as locals claim. When it blooms in February, it becomes a regional attraction.

WILDLIFE

MAKING HEADLINES. Unlike many other peoples, the Thai take their animals very seriously—to the point of personification. Thanks to the Buddhist influence, Thais tend to regard animals in the same way they would regard other human beings. Almost daily, special interest articles appear in the well-respected *Bangkok Post* about various animals whose names, personalities, and salient characteristics are well known. Rare animal sightings, the transfer of an animal from one zoo to another, or even an ordinary event at a zoo makes national headlines. One recent saga involved a celebrity orangutan named **Mike,** who was the star of the Lopburi Zoo. Having contracted herpes from a contaminated piece of food fed to him by a visitor at the zoo, Mike was admitted to Chulalongkorn Animal Hospital and fed intravenously for two weeks. He died of pneumonia soon afterward, at age 17. Fans had been following Mike even before he married his first mate, **Zuzu** from Taiwan, in 1996. The wedding was celebrated by a festival in Lopburi complete with a parade, ceremony, and international media coverage. He was laid to rest with a hero's funeral attended by 500 people who threw roses on his coffin as Buddhist monks chanted in the background. His body will be kept in storage until a decision is reached about whether to bury him or preserve his body for public viewing in a mausoleum, and a statue will be erected in his memory.

ELEPHANTS. Culturally and historically, elephants are the good luck charms of Thailand. They are on the national currency, the national flag, and are the symbol of the monarchy. Thailand is even geographically shaped like an elephant's head and trunk. Used for centuries as the main means of transportation in Thailand and as battle animals, today they are drugged to be docile as they pose for cheesy photographs with tourists, or are overworked and underfed by illegal loggers. **White elephants** are considered particularly lucky, as they once only belonged to kings. Today, when a white elephant is found, it immediately becomes the property of the reigning monarch. Despite the efforts to save these precious beasts, their numbers have diminished by almost 40% in the past ten years.

ENDANGERED ANIMALS. The **Asiatic Black Bear** and the **Malaysian Sun Bear,** the world's smallest bear, are two species native to Thailand, but poaching has put both on the endangered species list. A popular pet in Southeast Asia, the Sun Bear's skin is so loose that when it's grabbed by an attacker, it is able to turn around completely and counter-attack. Though it is illegal, both species are poached for their skins, and older bears are killed for medicinal purposes. The recipes for many traditional remedies for inflammation, fevers, and liver disease include the gallbladder and bile of these bears. Herbal alternatives to these recipes exist, but the products containing actual animal parts are far more popular. Tourists, mostly from Korea, visit Thailand in order to eat bear-paw soup, which appears on Thai menus for over US$1000 per bowl. Discovered in 1974, **Kitti's Hog-Nosed Bat** is also on the endangered species list. Found thus far only in Thailand, it may be the world's smallest mammal, not much larger than a bumblebee. At the other end of the scale, the **Giant Mekong Catfish,** weighing in at up to 300kg, is also endangered (p. 331).

In an attempt to protect wildlife, Thailand has set aside 13% of its land for natural preserves. Deforestation threatens the Kitti's Bat population in Sai Yok, the national park created specifically for it, but the preserves' effects—negative or otherwise—have yet to be seen on the Black Bear and Sun Bear populations.

HISTORY

PREHISTORY

IMPORTANT DATES		
4000 BC Farmers settle in Khorat Plateau.	**AD 651** First kingdom of Thai tribes form.	**7-12th Centuries** Tai-Kadai tribes found kingdoms.

Scholars disagree about the origins of the Thai people. Some argue that their ancestors came from Mongolia or northern China and were driven south to Yunnan, where the tribes coalesced and established the kingdom of Nanchao in AD 651. Others trace the sources to northeast Thailand. Human remains discovered at Ban Chiang (p. 239) in the Khorat Plateau suggest that farmers settled there around 4000 BC, before leaving for Nanchao two centuries later. In the next four centuries, various tribes of the Tai-Kadai moved south into northern Myanmar, Thailand, and Laos, establishing minor kingdoms and city states.

THE SUKHOTHAI PERIOD (1238-1350)

IMPORTANT DATES		
1238 Kingdom of Sukhothai founded by King Si Inthrathit.	**1275** King Ramkhamhaeng ascends the throne.	**1283** Thai alphabet established by King Ramkhamhaeng.

Taking advantage of the weakening Khmer and Srivijaya, two Thai chieftans, **Khun Bang Klang Thao** and **Khun Pha Muang,** rebelled and moved north. In 1238, **King Si Inthrathit** (formerly Khun Bang Klang Thao) founded the kingdom of **Sukhothai,** considered by most to be the first true Thai polity. Sukhothai, meaning "Dawn of Happiness," reached its zenith in power and size (incorporating present-day Laos, Thailand, Singapore, Malaysia, and much of Myanmar) in 1275, when **King Ramkhamhaeng the Great** ascended the throne. Modern Thai ideals of the benevolent monarch and his place in society originate in the Sukhothai period. Ramkhamhaeng's rule marked the first unification of Thais under a single monarch, and he worked tirelessly to better the condition of his people, abolishing slavery and codifying laws. He also invited Ceylonese monks to come to Sukhothai to purify the kingdom's Buddhism. As a result, the Ceylonese school of Theravada Buddhism was established as the national religion. Sukhothai is commonly celebrated as a utopian golden age in Thai history, which, to a certain degree, it was. It has often been conveniently overlooked, however, that Thai states such as **Lanna** (established by King Mengrai in Chiang Mai) and **Phayao,** in the northern part of modern Thailand, also flourished contemporaneously. A famous inscription from this period reads, "In the water there are fish, in the fields there is rice. Whoever wants to trade in elephants, so trades…Whoever wants to trade in silver and gold, so trades. The faces of the citizens are happy." It's no wonder everyone was smiling: King Ramkhamhaeng levied no taxes and made himself available to his citizens, building a bell in front of his palace so that his subjects could ring it at any time, confident that he would arbitrate justly. In 1283, the king introduced the Thai **alphabet** as a symbol of the nation's cultural and political independence. Except for a few later changes, mostly in the late 17th century under **King Narai,** King Ramkhamhaeng's script remains intact today.

LIFE AND TIMES

THE AYUTTHAYA KINGDOM (1351-1767)

IMPORTANT DATES

1350 Kingdom of Ayutthaya founded.	**13-16th Centuries** Ayutthaya grows in stature and number of temples.	**1511** Portuguese establish contact with Ayutthaya.	**1605-1662** Spanish, Dutch, English, Danish, and French arrive.	**1688** French expelled from the kingdom.

In 1350, **King U Thong** (later called King Ramathibodi I) established the magnificent island-city of **Ayutthaya,** which served as the capital of Siam for the next four centuries. Ayutthaya incorporated many Khmer court customs, such as the idea of an absolute monarch, into its traditions. By this time, Thai cultural and national identity had established itself, and the kingdom of Ayutthaya merely consolidated and expanded the existing kingdom of Sukhothai. With its capital in modern Thailand's central plains region, Ayutthaya was safe from external invasions during the rainy season, which was marked by massive flooding. Relatively impregnable, Ayutthaya turned inward and developed a complex system of administration, the forerunner of the modern Thai bureaucracy. To compliment this administrative structure, Thai society began to develop internal hierarchies that persist to this day. The lowest rung on the social ladder was **phrai,** commoners and slaves; above them were **khunnang,** or nobles. At the top were **chao,** the princes. Ever classless, the **monks** remained the one social group that could bridge these divisions.

The rise of Ayutthaya also coincided with the inevitable arrival of the first Europeans. A dispute over the Melaka territory brought the **Portuguese** into the picture in 1511. The Portuguese were followed by a veritable stampede of curious foreign visitors, beginning with the **Spanish,** followed by the **Dutch, English** and **Danish,** and concluding with the **French** in 1662. Under **King Narai,** Ayutthaya reached its peak of power and influence, boasting a population nearly double that of contemporaneous London. But in 1688, while the king was seriously ill, his chief minister, a Greek named **Constantine Phaulkon,** was accused of conspiring to replace the king with a puppet-king loyal to France. He had successfully kept the Dutch and English at bay but permitted the French to station over 500 troops throughout Ayutthaya. That year, King Narai cut off relations with the French and executed Phaulkon for his French connections. The degree to which this incident has become a part of the Thai national psyche is clear from the modern word for "foreigner," *farang,* a derivative of the word for "French." Although Ayutthaya had limited contact with foreigners after the debacle with France, they still maintained trade relations with a number of countries.

THE FALL OF AYUTTHAYA (1767-82)

IMPORTANT DATES

1767 Burmese annex, sack, and burn Ayutthaya.	**1767-83** General Taksin reclaims Thai kingdom.	**1782** King Rama I comes to power.

After a year-long siege, Burmese forces stormed Ayutthaya in 1767. They burned it to the ground, destroying culturally and religiously significant manuscripts, paintings, and sculptures. Only a few thousand out of over one million original inhabitants escaped the slaughter, including **General Phraya Taksin** and a few hundred of his followers. The Thai have never forgiven the Burmese or forgotten what they did to the kingdom of Ayutthaya, and much of the modern conflict between the two countries is a result of this historical grudge. Regrouping on the east coast, Taksin led an army of several thousand men to expel the Burmese and gain revenge. Within 15 years, the Thais had successfully recaptured Chiang Mai, Cambodia and parts of Laos. Taksin ruled from his new capital at **Thonburi,** just across the river from Bangkok. Soon after he won the war, however, King Taksin began to suffer from the unfortunate misconception that he was a reincarnation of the Buddha, most likely due to some form of mental illness. He also made the ill-advised decision to proclaim this publicly. Needless to say, his declaration was poorly received in court. He was executed in royal fashion: thrown into a velvet sack (so as not to spill any royal blood) and then beaten to death with a sandalwood club. Commander-in-chief **Thong Duang** was recalled from his campaign in Cambodia and crowned **King Rama I** in 1782, founding the **Chakri** dynasty.

THE EARLY BANGKOK PERIOD (1782-1868)

IMPORTANT DATES		
1785 Bangkok becomes capital; King Rama I builds Grand Palace.	**1851** King Rama IV ascends the throne.	**1855** King signs treaty with British, imports Western technology.

When Thonburi became too vulnerable to the Burmese and unable to accommodate major expansion, Rama I moved the capital across the Chao Phraya River to **Bangkok.** There he built his most lasting legacy, the Grand Palace and Royal Chapel (Temple of the Emerald Buddha), and unified the kingdom's many fiefdoms. Due to its many errors, he ordered an editorial overhaul of the **Tripitaka,** the Buddhist scriptures, by a learned council. He also codified and edited Thai law into the *Kotmai Tra Samdung* (Three Seals Code), which set economic, political, and military rules and was the major achievement of his reign. It was also during this period that Chiang Mai was added to the Thai kingdom.

The reign of King Mongkut, or **King Rama IV,** was one of the most significant transitional periods of modern Thailand. Unfairly portrayed as a flippant and frivolous monarch in Margaret Landon's *Anna and the King of Siam*, Mongkut was actually a serious man, having spent the reign of his half-brother, **King Rama III,** in the monkhood, traveling extensively throughout the kingdom and accumulating experience that would later prove invaluable. Seeking to strengthen Siam and silence his Western critics, Rama IV negotiated a foreign trade treaty with the British in 1885, reversing 150 years of virtual isolation. Intellectually stimulated by the cultures and ideas brought to Siam by Western missionaries, he studied English and French and imported Western technologies and organizational techniques.

COLONIALISM AVERTED (1868-1932)

IMPORTANT DATES				
1868-1910 King Rama V attains god-like status.	**1893** Frano-Siamese Crisis: French ships enter Bangkok.	**1897** Rama V is the first Thai monarch to travel to Europe.	**1908** First statue of a Thai king (Rama V) erected.	**1909** Siam gives up claims to peninsular Malaysia.

Malaria cut short Mongkut's rule, however, and the government fell into the able hands of his teenage son, **Prince Chulalongkorn,** who was crowned **King Rama V.** His 42 years of rule were marked by the abolition of slavery, reforms in the Thai justice, education, and public welfare systems and a courageous foreign policy in an era of aggressive European colonialism. In 1893, after prolonged tension between **France** and Siam in the northeast, two French gunboats shelled Siamese defenses at the mouth of the Chao Phraya River and sailed into Bangkok. Thanks to the swift diplomatic action of Foreign Minister **Prince Devawongse,** war between the two countries was narrowly averted. A subsequent 1896 treaty with the French established Siam as a regional **buffer state,** guaranteeing its independence. In return, Siam ceded much of the territory that is modern Laos and Cambodia to the French and what is now peninsular Malaysia to the British.

By his death in 1910, Rama V had become one of the most revered Thai monarchs in modern history. **King Vajiravudh** was the next in line for the throne in 1910. The pride and popularity the Thais accorded royalty during Rama V's reign were all but destroyed during **Rama VI's** 15-year term. A graduate of Oxford, King Vajiravudh wrote *The Jews of the Orient*, a work about the overseas Chinese in Thailand. This intense focus on nationalism was only heightened through Vajiravudh's adoption of the concept of surnames (which had not previously existed in Thailand), coining hundreds of them himself. Under this system, Siam's ethnic Chinese were forced either to assimilate or brand themselves as foreigners. Vajiravudh's financial finesse was equally dubious. His massive expenditures incurred a tremendous debt that damaged the Thai economy long after his reign. Against the better judgement of the king's advisors, Thailand joined **WWI,** declaring war against Germany in 1917 and sending a small number of troops to fight with the Allies. After the war's end, Thailand became one of the original members of the **League of Nations** in 1920.

THE RISE OF THE MILITARY (1932-1942)

IMPORTANT DATES

1932 Absolute monarchy abolished; People's Party comes to power in a bloodless coup.	**1933** Dr. Pridi Banomyong advocates socialist economic plan.	**1935** King Rama VII goes into voluntary exile in England.	**1941** Tokyo Convention: France returns Indochinese territory to Thailand.	**1941** War of Greater East Asia breaks out.

During the Great Depression, the Thai treasury nearly went bankrupt from the millions of *baht* poured into public works projects. Prominent academics and intellectuals, blaming the royal government, demanded a civil constitution. In June 1932, government workers and the military launched a bloodless coup. Proclaiming themselves the **People's Party,** the revolutionaries, led by **Major Luang Phibun Songkhram** (commonly known as **Phibun**) and Dr. Pridi Phanomyong, moved quickly to occupy high government posts. Phanomyong agitated for a socialist economic plan that would nationalize land and labor. More conservative leaders in the Thai government were horrified by his proposal and forced him into exile. During this period, the Thai **military,** the pet project of King Rama VI, became increasingly influential. Unable to satisfy the demands of his people, **King Rama VII** abdicated in 1935 and went into a voluntary exile in England, where he died six years later. He was replaced by his nephew, 10-year-old **Ananda Mahidol** (later **King Rama VIII**), who was studying abroad in Switzerland at the time. As the country experimented with **constitutions** granting varying degrees of democracy, the pendulum of Thai political power swung back and forth between the military and the civilian bureaucratic elite. Thailand received its modern name in 1939, when Phibunsongkhram officially renamed the country *Muang Thai*, or "Land of the Free." In 1940, Phibun requested that France return the territories that it had taken just a few decades earlier. The French were reluctant, to say the least. The resulting military skirmishes only ended with the arbitration by the occupying **Japanese.** The 1941 **Tokyo Convention** returned much of French Indochina to Thai control. Unfortunately, later that year, the **War of Greater East Asia** merged with World War II, and Thailand joined up with the Japanese forces against the Allies.

THE WORLD WAR II ERA (1942-1971)

IMPORTANT DATES

1942 Thai Field Marshal declares war on Allies; ambassador refuses to honor declaration.	**1946** Thailand joins the United Nations.	**1957** Military *coup d'état* during general elections; Field Marshal Sarit Thanarat takes over.	**1964** First US military personnel stationed in Thailand.	**1967** Association of Southeast Asian Nations (ASEAN) founded.

Field Marshal **Phibun Songkhram**, having aligned himself with Japan, declared war on the Allies in 1942. Thai Ambassador to the US, **Seni Pramoj,** reluctantly went to to American Secretary of State Hull, saying he was obligated to deliver a declaration that he didn't want to deliver. Hull's innovative suggestion was that he not deliver it. Seni Pramoj concurred, and many now understand the events to mean that Thailand remained neutral during WWII. After this brush with disastrous foreign policy, the Thai Ambassador organized the people against Field Marshal Phibun Songkhram, who ultimately resigned, only to come to power again after the death of King Rama VIII. In 1946, after his brother was found shot dead under suspicious circumstances, **King Rama IX** began his reign. Thailand continued to develop economically through the late 1940s and early 50s and attempted to adopt increasingly democratic practices, although corruption persisted in the government. The country also became more actively involved in international affairs, joining the **United Nations** in 1946 and even sending troops on a UN mission to Korea in 1950. In 1957, the military staged a *coup d'état* during the general elections, and Field Marshal **Sarit Thanarat** took over. The new government abolished the Consititution and re-established full military control while cracking down on the drug trade and suppressing Communist propaganda. By the time Thanarat died in 1963, Thailand had become a staunch US ally in Southeast Asia. Under his successor, **Thanom Kittikachorn,** US forces were permitted to build air bases in Thailand to support the war in Vietnam.

MILITARY REPRESSION (1971-1976)

IMPORTANT DATES

1973 Students and workers hold pro-democracy demonstrations.	**1974** Interim government establishes new constitution.	**1976** Government quells demonstrations, resulting in the October Massacre.

By late 1971, Thailand had reverted to full military rule. However, the nation's patience with new constitutions, coups, and regime changes was wearing thin. In June 1973 students and workers held demonstrations in the streets, calling for a democratic government. Radicals left the cities to join Communist guerrilla forces, leftist activists were emboldened, and by October 13, 250,000 people had gathered in front of the **Democracy Monument** in Bangkok (built to commemorate the end of absolute monarchial rule) in the largest protest in Thai history. The military attacked the crowd the very next day, killing 75. In response, King Bhumibol called for the resignation of Field Marshal Thanom (who fled the country), and appointed **Professor Sanya Dharmasakti** as interim prime minister. Many Thais celebrate October 14 as "Thai People's Rights and Freedom Day." A new constitution sparked a short-lived era of democratic rule, cut short by Thanom's return to Thailand. Responding to a sit-in at **Thammasat University** in October of 1976, military troops, accompanied by violent rightist gangs, were sent in to quell demonstrations. More than 300 protestors were shot, clubbed to death, and hanged, and more than 1700 were arrested, in what was called the **October Massacre.** The military seized power of the government that night. Even today, the events of 1971-1976 are taboo and rarely taught in Thai schools.

TOWARD DEMOCRACY (1976-1992)

IMPORTANT DATES

1988 First elected, non-military Prime Minister since 1977.	**1991** Army launches bloodless coup, dissolves legislature, abolishes Constitution.	**1992** Troops kill hundreds of protestors on Suchinda's orders.

An 11-year stretch of rotating prime ministers, failed constitutions, economic decline and constant coups left the Thai people desirous of a new form of government. In 1988, after 16 coups in 40 years, public dissatisfaction and shrinking support for the military culminated in general elections and the end of military rule. Early in 1991, the army launched a successful bloodless coup under **General Suchinda Kraprayoon,** who abolished the constitution, dissolved the legislature, and curtailed general freedoms. Accusations that the army influenced the framing of the new constitution to institutionalize its rule spurred hundreds of thousands of pro-democracy protesters to hold a demonstration in May 1992. The military killed or injured hundreds of people, many of whom were strategically located in front of the Democracy Monument and Western TV cameras. Horrified, King Bhumibol forced Suchinda out of office and appointed **Anand Panyarachun** as transitional prime minister.

END OF MILITARY RULE (1992-1998)

IMPORTANT DATES

1992-96 Economic prosperity slows down.   **1996** Stock market crashes.   **1997** Asian Financial Crisis.

Panyarachun fired the top four military officers in August 1992, kicking off a new era in Thai politics that was marked by an effort to separate the government and the military. The following regimes, however, faced charges of corruption and mismanagement, and the resulting political instability damaged Thailand's previously spectacular 8-10% annual growth rates. In 1996, Thailand had a 5.9% inflation rate—the highest in five years—0% export growth, and a drop of 30% in stock market prices. Then **Prime Minister Banharn Silpa-archa** was harshly criticized for meddling in economic affairs and was held responsible for the nation's dire economic situation. Tougher times were still to come. In July 1997, heavy external debts, financial deregulation, and an unsustainable fixed exchange rate culminated in the collapse of the Thai *baht* in what became known as the **Asian Financial Crisis.** From 1985 to 1995, Thailand had maintained the highest growth rate in the world—a whopping 9% annually. But in January of 1998, the *baht* hit the lowest point in history: 56 *baht* to the US dollar. Economists discovered the hard way that the national economic infrastructure, riddled with corruption and hidden debt, was too weak to absorb the shock and rebound. Waves of **currency devaluations,** accompanied by economic and political havoc, spread across Southeast Asia. The **International Monetary Fund (IMF)** initiated a US$17.2 billion emergency international rescue package for Thailand in August 1997. In spite of (or perhaps as a result of?) IMF intervention, the *baht*'s value fell 40%, over 350 factories shut down, and Thailand's stock market hit a nine-year low.

THAILAND TODAY

LIFE AND TIMES

IMPORTANT DATES		
2000 "Amazing Thailand" launched by TAT.	**2001** PM Thaksin Shinawatra elected in landslide victory.	**2004** Violence erupts in the south of Thailand.

With positive growth rates since 1999, Thailand seems to be well on its way to economic recovery. The Tourism Authority of Thailand (TAT) inaugurated the ambitious **Amazing Thailand** campaign to boost the economy, and by February 2000, officials declared the worst of the economic crisis to be over. Today, Thailand leads Southeast Asia in economic growth, largely due to the efforts of charismatic Prime Minister Thaksin Shinawatra. However, violence broke out in the predominantly Muslim south (p. 13) starting in January 2004, when there was a series of bombings and attacks on the government. It remains unknown how this situation will affect the Prime Minister's popularity, especially when added to accusations that he covered up the severity of bird flu in Thailand.

KING BHUMIBOL ADULYADEJ (RAMA IX)

King Rama IX was born in December 1927 in Cambridge, Massachusetts while his parents were studying medical-related fields at Harvard University and Simmons College. After his father's death, the King's family moved to Switzerland. Ascending the throne when he was only 18, the young king's actual coronation was postponed by four years so he could finish his education. As the longest-reigning monarch in the world, he's revered for his dedication to the underprivileged, his role in resolving government conflicts, and his commitment to the peace and unity of his country. As a constitutional monarch, he may have no direct legal power, but his word commands tremendous loyalty and respect. His official titles are Head of State, Upholder of Religions, and Head of the Armed Forces. The three "rights" that go along with these positions are outlined as follows: to encourage, to warn, and to be consulted. Since 1974, he has become particularly active in **reforestation projects** in order to preserve Thailand's flora and fauna. Heavily influenced by his parents' medical careers, King Bhumibol also places a great deal of emphasis on **health care.** While he's not busy governing the kingdom, the King devotes himself to a variety of hobbies. He is a world-class **yachtsman** as well as a famous **composer** with 43 jazz and blues compositions to his name.

HOOKED ON THAILAND

According to the United States Central Intelligence Agency, Thailand is considered a **drug money-laundering center.** Despite the low percentage of Thailand's narcotics production in comparison to its Southeast Asian neighbors, the backpacker mythology about drug abuse in Thailand, particularly in the south and the northeast, has resulted in a nation-wide crackdown. Some backpackers in Thailand, however, don't seem to understand the new "zero tolerance" policy.

The erroneous mythology has its origins in the northeastern treks of the 1970s. Guides, who had little or no knowledge of the hill tribes' customs, told foreigners that **opium** was an integral part of hill-tribe culture, used to welcome guests and to ease the aches of manual labor. Later anthropological study revealed that most hill tribes viewed opium as a privilege reserved for elderly men. Gradually, however, the villagers realized the financial advantages of selling opium and **heroin** to foreign tourists. Unfortunately, the new local dealers began experimenting with the drugs themselves, and soon most of the money they made selling the drugs to foreigners was spent on their own addictions. In many northeastern villages today, as much as 80% of the population is addicted to either opium or heroin. With the rapid spread of **AIDS/HIV** through intravenous drug use, these poppy derivatives are creating a difficult problem in Bangkok. Now, however, much of the energy formerly devoted to poppy cultivation has turned to the production and consumption of **methamphetamines** (locally known as *ya ba*, see **Crazy Medicine,** p. 414), which are much less easily detected by authorities. Backpacker tales of full moon acid parties on Ko Phangan have become the stuff of legends, inspiring many travelers to venture south in search of the perfect tropical high. Full moon parties don't just draw tourists, however; the police are also out in full force (see **Sex, Drugs, and Lunar Cycles,** p. 412).

Thailand declared itself "drug-free" on the king's birthday in 2003, after a year-long effort to rid the country of its drug problem—an effort that resulted in more than 2,700 deaths and tens of thousands of arrests. While this campaign has helped to crack down on the drug trade, some fear that its violence may only make it harder to identify and treat intravenous drug users with HIV/AIDS.

AIDS

A thriving sex and intravenous drug industry drove the **Acquired Immune Deficiency Syndrome (AIDS)** to epidemic status in parts of Thailand during the late 1990s. By the end of 1999, 66,000 people had died of HIV/AIDS in Thailand, the first country in Southeast Asia to experience the epidemic. Medical researchers warned that the country's AIDS-related deaths would total approximately 286,000 by the beginning of the new millennium, and many feared that the disease was spreading to new sectors of Thai society. Today, these trends are slowly reversing. The effects of **safe-sex practices** such as condom use, first advocated in the early 1990s by **Senator Mechai Viravaidya** (justly dubbed "Mr. Condom") and his "100 Percent Condom" plan, are now becoming apparent in HIV/AIDS statistics. The use of condoms in commercial sex is up from 14% to over 90%, and protective measures have resulted in a 90% decrease in the rate of sexually transmitted diseases (STDs). Traditionally, AIDS prevention efforts have focused on **prostitutes** and those intimately involved in the skin trade. A large percentage of workers in the sex industry are illegal immigrants, who have little to no access to federally funded HIV/AIDS prevention and treatment programs. Now, however, **drug users** are seen as the main obstacle in Thailand's path to victory over HIV because the proportion of new infections in this category has grown steadily. Recent budget cuts have also severely hampered the efforts of **AIDS awareness programs.** Thailand introduced an inexpensive **AIDS cocktail** during the summer of 2002 designed to consolidate patients' medications. The generic Thai form of the drug created by three Western pharmaceutical companies will cut patients' medical bills in half, making the retroviral medicine accessible to more people. As of now, however, only about 10% of Thailand's estimated 200,000 HIV-positive patients receive the drug cocktail from the government. Despite budget constraints, the government hopes to raise that percentage to 20% in the near future.

SOUTHERN DISCOMFORT

Although the Thais pride themselves on their religious tolerance, some conflicts cannot be avoided. In January 2004, armed men in the southern provinces of Narathiwat, Pattani, Songkhla, and Yala burned schools, looted weapons, and killed four Thai soldiers. In response, Thailand declared martial law, deploying troops to the region. Scattered bombings and shootings plagued the area until the conflict came to a head in April of 2004, when militants raided police stations and government buildings. The police fought back, killing an estimated 112 fighters.

The southernmost provinces, once the independent Sultanate of Pattani, only came under Thai rule in 1902 and have complained of religious, cultural and economic isolation. The population is largely Muslim, many of them ethnic Malays. The government fought to dispel separatist groups in the 1980s, but separatist elements have allied with those organizing crime in the underdeveloped region. Some speculate that the problem lies in the encouragement of clerics and other religious officials. Thailand's government, however, links the uprisings with crime and poverty in the area. In a recent statement, Prime Minister Thaksin Shinawatra declared his intentions to bring "peace and prosperity" back to the region through education reform and public works projects that would create jobs.

While the militants first only attacked government buildings and officials, they soon attacked Buddhist citizens as well, in what seems like an attempt to spread conflict between Muslims and Buddhists, in addition to the Muslim/government dispute. By August of 2004, more than 300 casualties had been reported.

SURVIVING "SURVIVOR"

For centuries, Ko Tarutao and the surrounding islands of the Andaman Sea near the Thai-Malaysian border have been home to the Chao Lay, or Sea Gypsies, who maintain their own distinct language, nomadic lifestyle, and animist religion. Recovering from the lawless days of World War II, when it was a famed pirate hide-out, Tarutao and the 51 surrounding islands became Thailand's first national marine park in 1974, The park is home to approximately 25% of the world's species of fish, and three endangered species of migratory sea turtles.

In the local language, Tarutao means "old," "mysterious," or "primitive." Perhaps it was this mystique that drew executives at the American CBS television network to the island when they were searching for a site for the fifth season of the reality TV show "Survivor," shot during the summer of 2002. However, controversies arose during filming over the Thai government's preferential treatment of the Americans over the Thai fishermen who use the abundant marine life in the area as the source of their livelihood. The provincial governor requested that the "Survivor" production team allow local fishermen seeking shelter from torrential monsoon rains, which drench the area from May to October, to dock their boats on the island. However, fishermen still reported being chased away from the sheltered bays during the monsoon rains by the production company's patrol boats. They were also forbidden from fishing within 2km of Tarutao for fear they would disrupt filming. Suthichai Viriyakosol, chief of the marine park, agreed that locals had to be kept away, but the Law Society of Thailand insisted that CBS was guilty of human rights violations. The National Film Board denied that fishermen were prevented from landing on the island.

A similar uproar arose after Danny Boyle's 2000 film *The Beach* was shot on location on Ko Phi Phi Don, a small island accessible from Phuket (see p. 364). The island, once largely unnoticed, filled up with garbage, guesthouses and tourists so quickly that the government considered closing it down for a year. So far development has reigned unchecked on the island, part of a national park system. A slew of backpacker-friendly businesses and services have cropped up all over the island, irreversibly transforming its once-unspoiled landscape.

BORDER RELATIONS

Thailand is bordered by Cambodia, Laos, Malaysia, and Myanmar and has had a tempestuous relationship with all of its neighbors. From historical battles to present-day policy fights, a variety of events have contributed to the tension often felt around Thailand's 8000km perimeter. Present-day cooperation, however, such as major transportation projects currently underway, seems to suggest that this corner of Asia is settling down.

THAI-BURMESE RELATIONS. Since the Burmese sacked the Thai capital of Ayutthaya in 1767 (p. 15), Thai-Burmese relations have been off-and-on at best. Thai and Burmese officials both claim that relations are complicated by a lack of "mutual understanding." The issue of illicit drugs adds to the Thai-Burmese bout, as Burmese drug lords have long been producing methamphetamine and smuggling it into Thailand, China, and India. The most recent controversy between the two neighbors erupted in May 2002 when officials in Yangon, Myanmar accused the Thai military of firing shells over the border in support of ethnic Shan rebels. Thailand denied the charges and Myanmar closed all border checkpoints with Thailand indefinitely. After a five-month closure of the border, however, the two countries managed to reestablish relations and have turned their attention to other issues, such as the flourishing drug trade. Currently, the two governments are discussing possible ways to curb drug-trafficking.

THAI-CAMBODIAN RELATIONS. Although relations between the two neighbors have always been tense, tempers flared at the beginning of 2003 as a result of vicious rumors. In January 2003, the *Rasmei Angkor* (a Cambodian newspaper), published an article based on rumors that Thai soap opera star Suvanant Kongying (known popularly as Phkay Proek) had claimed that Angkor Wat was rightfully Thailand's. This article incensed the Cambodian people, who began to riot at the Thai embassy in Phnom Penh. After a series of continued misunderstandings, the Thai embassy was ransacked, along with several Thai businesses. Thailand responded by closing the borders and evacuating all Thai personnel. By mid-February, however, the two sides were talking again and the borders had been reopened. Currently, the two countries appear to be united against a common enemy as they work together to combat human trafficking across the border.

CULTURE

CUSTOMS AND ETIQUETTE

FARANG, FARANG. As a traveler in Thailand, the single word you're most likely to hear is *farang*, meaning "foreigner". Derived from the word meaning "French", this term is now universally applied to all non-Asian visitors.

THE THREE SPIRITS

The Thai attitude toward life rests on three major concepts. The first, *jai yen*, or "cool heart," explains the Thai aversion to any sort of confrontation, especially in public. Most Thais avoid raising their voices or displaying any visible irritation, instead embracing the idea of *mai pen rai*, literally translated as "it can't be helped, so why bother?" This verbal equivalent of a shrug is ideally complemented by the last of the three Thai spirits, *sanuk*, which literally means "fun." Thais believe that everything in life should have a little bit of *sanuk*, or else everything degenerates into mere drudgery. Join in the national water fight during Songkran in April (see **Festivals,** p. 24) for a healthy helping of *sanuk*.

HEADS UP

According to an ancient Hindu belief (now incorporated into Buddhism), the head is the most sacred part of the body, and by extension, the feet are the most unclean. A pat on the head in Thailand is neither playful nor cute—it's simply disrespectful. Similarly, don't point your feet toward an image of the Buddha in a temple or toward another person, especially if he or she is older. Shoes, even more unclean than feet, are unwelcome in temples and most private homes.

WAI NOT?

To show respect, put palms together at chest level, pointing your fingers away from you, and gently bow your head. This is a traditional greeting, called a *wai*. The degree to which you should bend your waist while performing a *wai* is determined by your social status relative to the other person. Older people receive lower, more respectful *wais*. Younger people or those of inferior social standing *wai* first. You should never perform a *wai* to a child; you will only embarrass yourself and make everyone around you uncomfortable. Inanimate objects that should receive a *wai* include **spirit houses,** miniature temples blessed by Brahman priests that house the spiritual guardians of the land on which the house resides.

TABLE MANNERS

When dining out with a group in Thailand, many dishes are ordered and food is served family-style, as opposed to the practice of one dish per person. The oldest or most successful person at the table pays for the meal. Taking a large portion from a communal dish is frowned upon; small portions are most polite. Most Thai meals are eaten with a spoon in the right hand and a fork in the left, to help guide the food onto the spoon. Eating off the fork itself is as rude as eating off the knife in Western countries. Chopsticks are only used with noodle dishes. And remember — while eating with your hands is not the social faux pas it is in many Western countries, never use your left hand!

TABOOS

The tourism industry has so successfully marketed Thailand for its tolerance that many travelers mistakenly think that the Thai take a generally laissez-faire attitude. This is simply not the case. Don't ever speak disparagingly of the Monarchy, and avoid dropping, defacing, or stepping on currency or stamps, which carry the king's portrait. When near a portrait of King Bhumibol or any past Thai king, never raise your head above the head in the portrait. Be especially careful in restaurants and public buses, often plastered with royal portraits. In short, don't mess with the man whose name means "Strength of the Land, Incomparable Power." The Thai speak in a special language of higher respect when referring to the Monarchy.

Always remove your **shoes** when entering a home or temple, even though your Thai hosts may assure you it's okay to keep them on. Thais appreciate foreigners who make an effort to follow customs. Clothing should be modest: both men and women should wear long sleeves and long pants or skirts, especially when visiting a *wat*. Women should never touch a monk or give him anything directly, as this will violate an important part of his vows. Similarly, **public displays of affection** between lovers are frowned upon. Affectionate same-sex caresses or hugs are commonplace and rarely have sexual overtones. Despite its tolerance of different cultures, Thailand does imprison foreigners for actions considered sacrilegious.

STAND AND DELIVER

Remember your national anthem? The Thais certainly remember theirs. Visitors to Thailand are struck by how citizens respond so patriotically to their national anthem and the national flag. Whether they're in the bus station, on the street, or in the market, all Thai people stop what they're doing when they hear the anthem (and they do, indeed, hear it often). In some smaller cities, traffic comes to a screeching halt. Thailand's flag is raised each morning at 8am and lowered each evening at 6pm to the accompaniment of the national anthem. If you don't stand still, old ladies will stare with disapproval, children will laugh and point, and you will never feel more like a *farang*. Respect Thailand's national custom—be still and stand up when the anthem is played before movies and public events.

THE FLAG

Historians believe that the first appearance of a Thai national flag was in 1680 when a French diplomatic ship visited Thailand. The ship wished to fire a gun salute, but needed a raised national flag to do so, prompting the Thai fort to create a makeshift flag out of a red piece of cloth. In 1816 Singapore declared that Siamese ships needed a more distinctive flag for trading purposes. King Rama II added a white elephant, the sacred Thai symbol of royalty, with its trunk facing the flag post. Nearly a hundred years later, however, King Rama IV saw the flag being flown upside down in a rural village. He promptly set to work on redesigning the flag, choosing five horizontal stripes in white and red. Being both horizontally and vertically symmetrical, the flag could never be flown upside down. Blue replaced red for the center stripe in honor of the king's birthday (blue was the king's color). The colors of the *Trairong* (tricolor) are said to represent different aspects of Thailand: red for the nation, white for Buddhism, and blue for the monarchy. The modern flag, which is raised and lowered in daily ceremonies, was officially declared as such on September 28, 1917.

FOOD

FRUIT

As if to top the wildlife and scenery, Thailand's fruit is colorful, exotic, and occasionally dangerous. The **custard apple**'s *(noina)* bumpy light-green skin looks like a crocodile-skin hand grenade, and the grainy and creamy pulp's aroma is similar to the guava. The **durian** *(thurian)* has such a potent smell that the green spiky fruit has been banned from public places. A large fruit from an enormous tree, they are custard-like and high in protein, minerals, and fats, making excellent milk shakes and ice cream. **Guavas** *(farang)* have a grainy white or pink flesh; they're often eaten unripe with sugar and salt. The **jackfruit** originated in India but frequents the Thai marketplace. Its bumpy green shell protects the largest edible tree-grown fruit, growing up to 80 lbs. and three ft. in length. A close relative of the jackfruit is the **breadfruit,** which has an identity complex. A fruit when ripe, vegetable when mature, it usually just tastes like a potato. It's thin, bumpy rind ranges in color from green to yellow-brown. The most popular fruit in China, the **lychee** *(lin jii)* has been cultivated for over a millennium. Until 1950, it was only available as a nut, with dried fruit inside the shell; now the juicy, delicate fruit can be eaten by biting through the squash-ball-sized shell. Don't eat the seed, though: it's toxic. The **longan** *(lamyai)*, a close relative of the lychee, is Thailand's greatest fruit export. This small fruit resembles the lychee, but has a brownish, pebbled rind. Lamphun holds a yearly longan festival (p. 31), complete with a parade consisting of floats decorated with longan. Another close relative is the **Rambutan** *(ngo)*, with fiery red sea-urchin skin. **Mangosteens'** *(mang khut)* dark red (purple if past ripe) rinds protect sweet pearl-white segments inside. The skin of the **sapodilla** *(lamut)* resembles a bald kiwifruit; inside, its brownish flesh is as sweet as molasses.

COCONUTS

Close on the heels of the tomato fruit-or-vegetable debate is the coconut fruit-or-nut dispute. Actually, the coconut is all three: fruit, vegetable, and nut—and tech-

LIFE AND TIMES

nically classified as a drupe! The hard, green, oval fruit is 300-450mm long and has a thick husk around its *copra* (nut), and the young coconut palm is a vegetable. According to an Indonesian proverb, the coconut has more uses than there are days in a year. Vegetable oil, milk, alcohol, sugar, rope, and porcupine wood are among its products. First documented in Sanskrit and then introduced to Europe in the 6th century, the coconut was finally named by the Portuguese in the 15th century. A combination of the proximity of palm trees to the ocean and the buoyancy of the fruit facilitated the coconut's quick spread throughout the tropics.

HERBS

One of the most familiar Thai ingredients, **chili,** was actually not incorporated into the cuisine until Portuguese missionaries brought it over from South America in the 17th century. The Thais have been using it since—and in massive quantities. This can cause stomach discomfort or other unsavory digestive problems for the unaccustomed traveler. The phrase *mai pet* is a useful one to learn for those who don't like their food overly spicy. **Lemon grass,** the integral ingredient in most curries, is native to Thailand and actually looks like long grass. Thais also use relatives galanga and ginger for flavoring, as well as basil, shallots, cilantro, dill, mint, cardamon, cumin, and tumeric. In addition to their culinary uses, all these herbs have several **therapeutic properties,** including gastronomic, respiratory, cardiac, antimicrobial and diuretic benefits.

TRADITIONAL DISHES

Though internationally considered distinct, Thai food today is actually a collection of influences and spices from Asia, India, South America, and Europe. The Chinese brought the technique of frying to Southeast Asia, and, while taking ideas from India, Thais replace their ingredients with native essentials.

Traditional Thai food varies from region to region. Although it is a sea-based cuisine, with most of its ingredients (fish, vegetables, and herbs) taken directly from the rivers and oceans, Thailand's staple food, just like its Asian neighbors, is rice. However, even this staple has variations; in Central Thailand plain rice is usually eaten, whereas the Northern Thai specialty is **sticky rice,** or *khao niaw*, a glutinous breed of the grain, is everywhere and eaten with everything, even desserts. A **traditional Thai meal** is composed of a harmony of spices, tastes, and textures. It always includes a fish plate, a vegetable dish, a curry with condiments, and soup. By the time they leave the country, backpackers will inevitably have eaten their weight in **pad thai,** claimed to be Thailand's national dish. Pan-fried noodles, garlic, bean sprouts, ground peanuts, eggs, dried red chili, and shallots are the defining ingredients in this common dish. Fried and veggie-stuffed **spring rolls,** or *po pia thot*, are similarly ubiquitous. **Green curry,** made of lemon grass, coriander root, garlic, green chilis, and galanga, is mixed with meat or fish for another common meal.

THE ARTS

HISTORY

ARCHITECTURE. Thai architecture, while encompassing a broad range of influences (Myanmar, China, India, Sri Lanka, and the Khmer count among its major sources), and forms (including royal palaces and wooden houses), is best illustrated through its most common manifestations, **religious structures.** Buddhist **wats** continue to be the finest examples of traditional Thai architecture. A compound with separate buildings, each with its own distinct purpose, the *wat* has a variety of social functions, including a monastery, a school, and a gathering place for the community. The **bot,** or main chapel, which often faces east, is a tall, oblong build-ing with a three-level, steeply sloped roof that houses the principal Buddha image and serves as the site of most ceremonies. Similar to the *bot* but often larger, the **wihaan** holds fewer Buddha images and functions primarily as a worship hall, uti-lized for meetings, meditation, and sermons. The **sala** is an open, gazebo-like struc-ture for meditation and preaching. Above some monastic compounds looms a tapering, spire-like tower, called a **chedi.** Derived from the Indian **stupa,** the *chedi* is the reliquary for the possessions and cremated remains of high priests, mem-bers of royalty, and the Buddha. Another tower found in Thai architecture is the **prang,** which is more cob-shaped than the rounder bell-like *chedi.*

Most *wats* are constructed of carved sandstone (later brick), their various pieces held together by vegetable glue. In the heavily-forested north, wood was often the major building material. While the most spectacular example of classical Thai religious architecture is Bangkok's intricate and detailed **Wat Phra Kaew** (p. 115), **Wat Benchamabophit** (p. 118), built in 1899 in Bangkok's Dusit district, is widely considered the most impressive example of modern Thai Buddhist architecture.

By the 20th century, increased contact with Europeans led to the steady decline of traditional Thai architecture. Western styles and materials (often concrete) were adopted, making Thailand's modern architecture remarkably similar to that in cities elsewhere. However, some intrepid Thai architects still study historical styles, utilizing modern materials for the construction of traditional forms.

DANCE AND DRAMA. The earliest Thai dramatic forms are believed to be **nang yai** (shadow plays) and **hun puppets,** both performed at Ayutthaya. *Nang yai* and its smaller and more elaborate counterpart, *nang talung,* depict scenes from other popular dramas but use puppets made from the hides of water buffalo that are then held against back-lit screens. The story line is chanted. The larger *hun* mari-onettes were themselves believed to be the continuation of an oral tradition.

The three main types of dramatic media in Thai culture are **khon, lakhon,** and **likay,** utilizing both dance and drama. The first two forms are generally patronized by the elite, but *likay* is favored in the countryside among poorer Thais, making it the most popular of the three. *Khon,* or masked dance drama, is based on Indian temple dances and rituals; its various stories come exclusively from the Indian epic, the *Ramayana,* known in Thai as the **Ramakien,** which recounts the triumph of good over evil. The plot follows the adventures of the hero, **Phra Ram,** on his quest to recover his consort, **Nang Sida,** who was abducted by wicked **King Thotsa-kand of Longa.** Over the centuries, this Indian tale has been adapted to Thai culture, with certain portions expanded and others reduced or dropped completely.

During the Ayutthaya period, only men performed *khon* drama. Women didn't appear on stage until the mid-19th century because the movements were consid-ered too strenuous for the female frame. With the exception of the leading male and female characters, all actors wear elaborate masks. As in Greek drama, verses are recited by a chorus that sits next to a small band known as a **piphat.** *Khon* is performed with a great deal of stylized action; the movements are suggested by motifs in the music. The *lakhon* form of drama is less structured and stylized than *khon.* Masks are not used except in the case of animals and demons. Like *khon, lakhon* is derived from the *Ramakien* but also adds stories from Thai folk tales and Buddhist *Jatakas.* **Lakhon chatri** is a simple play performed at shrines for the benefit of gods. **Lakhon nai,** traditionally with an all-female cast, dramatizes roman-tic stories and focuses on graceful movements. **Lakhon nok,** once performed only by men, is characterized by a bawdy sense of humor, fast-paced music, and move-ments to match. In contrast to *khon* and *lakhon,* the *likay* style is bawdy and humorous with loud, sharp music, improvisation, pantomime, lyrics sprinkled with sexual innuendos, and social satire. It's often performed at festivals, its plot combining local references and court stories.

LITERATURE. The most enduring work of Thai literature is the *Ramakien*, the Thai version of the Indian epic, the *Ramayana*. Early versions of this lengthy document were lost when Ayutthaya was sacked in 1767. By far the most famous of the three surviving versions was written in 1798 by **King Rama I.** This version, written in conjunction with several courtiers who were close to the king, incorporates uniquely Thai and Buddhist attributes and portrays the rites, traditions, and customs of the Ayutthaya state. Given early Thai literature's focus on religion, poet **Sunthon Phu** (1786-1855) revolutionized the tradition with his portrayal of the emotions and adventures of common people in a common language that all classes could understand. His 30,000-line **Phra Aphaimani** is arguably Thailand's most famous literary work. It details the physical and emotional journey that an exiled prince must complete before he can return victorious to his kingdom. Modern Thai literature, shaped both by foreign influences and by changing perceptions of the individual's place in society, has picked up on this trend of addressing personal and social problems.

MUSIC. Assimilating elements of the Indian, Mom and Khmer traditions, Thailand boasts over 50 kinds of musical instruments. Uniquely Thai instruments have onomatopoetic names such as **krong, chap, ching, krap,** and **pia.** The oldest surviving Thai songs are from the Sukhothai period. In the Ayutthaya period, music was an official part of court life as territorial expansion brought musical instruments and styles from neighboring regions such as Myanmar, Malaysia, and Java. During this period, rules defining musical forms were introduced. Songs were composed in a form called **phleng ruang,** a suite of melodies. Three orchestral types of music, appropriate to different occasions, order Thai musical form: **piphat** is used at ceremonies and in the theater; **kruang sai** is used in performance at village festivals; and **mahori** often accompanies solo vocalists. Thai music emphasizes variation in pitch and rhythm, with individual changes in tempo creating a dense layering effect.

Instead of a five-note scale like that used in many other Asian countries, Thai music works on a **seven-note scale.** The music composed in this unique system has been passed down orally, but many today fear that the institutional memory of traditional Thai music may soon run out. Many modern Thai musicians are therefore working to invent a system by which traditional Thai music can be translated into Western musical notation and thus recorded for future generations.

PAINTING. Like classical architecture and literature, most traditional Thai painting was restricted to religious subjects or was designed for temples, palace interiors, or manuscript illustrations. Rather than stand-alone artistic statements, classical Thai **mural paintings** were meant to complement and enhance the beauty of their surroundings as well as to inspire faith and meditation in their beholders. Subjects were often taken from the *Jataka* stories or scenes from the Buddha's life. Landscapes were usually flat backgrounds for detailed action, and the size and position of various figures was based on their social importance, not a Western idea of artistic perspective. The original palette of five colors—red, yellow, blue, white, and black—was first supplemented by Chinese pigments during the Bangkok period and then by chemical pigments from the West in the 1800s. Most of the traditional Thai mural paintings that are still in good condition today are from the Ayutthaya, Thonburi, and Bangkok periods. The murals at Bangkok's **Wat Suthat** (p. 117) and Chiang Mai's **Wat Phra Singh** (p. 277) are widely considered the finest extant examples of this traditional style of Thai painting. Recently, a greater number of Thai artists are being trained in the Western style, and their works have blended the two traditions.

SCULPTURE. Ancient Thai sculpture focused strongly on the production of Buddha images, emphasizing the spirituality of the image rather than anatomical details. Rigid artistic rules ensured that a relatively uniform tradition passed from generation to generation. The giant seated Buddha at Sukhothai's **Wat Sri Chum** (p. 316) is a prominent example of the artistic achievement of the Sukhothai period.

Lying closer to maritime trading routes, **southern** Thailand developed unique styles of sculpture influenced by Indian and Khmer culture. Images of Hindu gods add a layer of complexity to the Thai religious landscape. Khmer artistic traditions have exerted the greatest influence over the sculpture of the **northeast.** In Thailand, Khmer art is referred to as the **Lop Buri style,** which consists of stone and bronze sculptures mainly of Hindu gods, Bodhisattvas, or Tantric Buddhist deities. Images of the Buddha often portrayed him seated on a coil of the famous seven-headed *naga*, Muchalinda. Also significant are the distinctive Khmer **lintels** of northeastern temples featuring detailed carvings of Hindu stories.

WEAVING. Even before it became a cottage industry, weaving was an important part of rural life-cycle rituals. A woman spent much time and energy handweaving the material for her wedding dress. Similarly, for the most important day in a man's life, when he entered the monkhood, his mother prepared his saffron robes. The female head of the household also handwove all the shrouds to be used at the funerals of each family member. For centuries, village women in the northeast bred silkworms and worked at hand looms to produce bolts and bolts of traditional Thai silk. However, cheaper fabrics imported from China and Japan devastated the industry in the second half of the 19th century. Revived by famous American expatriate **Jim Thompson** (see **The Mystery of Jim Thompson,** p. 120) after World War II, the silk industry soon became symbolic of Thailand on the international market. Today, the company founded by Thompson at **Pak Thong Chai** (p. 208) is still the largest hand-weaving facility in the world. Each region has its own special style and technique, though the most famous Thai silk is still woven in the northeast. The **mud-mee** style of silk weaving, characterized by geometrical and zoomorphic designs, is particularly popular.

CURRENT SCENE

DRAMA. The Hun Lakhon Lek Joe Louis Troupe (☎ 252 9683; joelouistheater@hotmail.com), under the guidance of founder and "National Artist" Sakorn Yangkhiawsod ("Joe Louis" himself), daily performs their own updated version of traditional Thai puppetry. Their repertory mostly consists of tales from the *Ramayana*. The staff also offers tours of the theater and puppet- and mask-making demonstrations. The troupe has toured internationally, but their new permanent home is the Joe Louis Theater in Bangkok (p. 119).

LITERATURE. Former Prime Minister **M.R. Kukrit Pramoj** wrote prolifically. Among his most notable works are **Si Phandin,** describing court life between the reigns of King Rama V and Rama VII, and **Phai Daeng,** about the conflict between Communism and Buddhism. **Seni Saowaphong,** or Sakdichai Bamrungphong, often writes about class exploitation and the widening gulf between the rural and the urban. Similarly, the protagonist of the late **Suwanee Sukhontha**'s most famous novel, **Khao Chu Kan,** is a young doctor with a promising career lined up in a big city who leaves to work in a rural area where the peasants have little access to modern medicine. **Krisna Asokesin** also reveals a more personal side, writing almost exclusively about issues such as love and family life. All the authors mentioned above have been awarded National Artist status in Thailand or Southeast Asian literary awards, indicating both the accessibility of their styles and the popularity of their subjects.

FILM. While cinemas are common in large cities, about 2000 mobile film units travel from village to village in rural areas of Thailand, offering open-air screenings for large numbers of people. Most of the movies shown are either of the Chinese *kung-fu* or Hollywood variety. Thai films are less popular. Traditionally low-budget productions packing a sensationalist punch, 2001 seems to have been a turning point for the industry, and Thai movies are beginning to gain recognition on the international film circuit. *Tropical Malady*, by director Apichatpong Weerasethakul, won the 2004 Jury Prize at Cannes, after being the first Thai film to be shown in competition there. Co-directed by the Pang brothers from Hong Kong, *Bangkok Dangerous* is a dramatic thriller to a frenetic techno beat—a change for Thai audiences, who usually favor upbeat comedies. Many film critics have enthusiastically noted the release of director Nonzee Nimibutr's third film, *Jan Dara* (2001, Buddy Films), as possibly indicating a new stage of maturity for the Thai film industry. Based on a novel by journalist Pramoon Un-hathoop (who writes under the pen name of Utsana Pkleungtham), the movie only passed Thailand's film censorship board after repeated screenings. *Jan Dara* ran into trouble with this official body because of the prevalence of sexual themes throughout: the protagonist is caught in a web of Oedipal lusts and primal urges. Prince Chatreechalerm Yukol's much anticipated film, *Suriyothai*, details the life of a young princess as a 16th-century battle for the throne of Thailand rages above her head. Yuthlert Sippapak's debut film, *Killer Tattoo*, takes place in an ambiguous post-IMF future and thinly conceals an anticolonialist ideology—rare for Thai cinema given that Thailand has no colonial experience—underneath a slapstick surface. Foreign films are increasingly being shot in Thailand, from Oliver Stone's Alexander the Great epic to the *Bridget Jones' Diary* sequel to the latest *Star Wars*. The Thai government actively promotes the shooting of foreign films in Thailand because it boosts state revenue, but all scripts have to be approved. Over 15 Western productions are expected to film in Thailand yearly, and the potential environmental damage from the shooting of large commercial films and Western television shows (p. 22) is becoming a very real concern both to the government and to local NGOs.

MUSIC. Contemporary Thai music takes many forms. Regional folk music, studied less frequently than classical music, is still common. One of the most popular styles is **luk thung** (country music), which, much like American country music, tells tales of woe in daily rural life. *Luk thung* has recently developed upbeat electronic versions. In the 1960s, Thai pop met folk to create the genre of **protest songs,** called *plaeng peua chiwit* or "songs for life," which focused primarily on criticizing the US military presence in Thailand. The Thai student band **Caravan** filled the musical vacuum of the '70s with pro-democracy songs that fused Western and Thai styles. Caravan inspired other bands to take up causes. The most famous rock band in modern Thailand, **Carabao,** also sings about social issues, such as the AIDS crisis. In the late 1980s, there was a movement to promote ethnic Thai pop music, led by Grammy Entertainment Company. Currently, Thai music centers around bubblegum pop and rock, often by attractively packaged bands.

SPORTS AND RECREATION

MUAY THAI (THAI BOXING)

Muay Thai is a martial art that has been around since the early days of Thailand, but was especially encouraged to keep Thai soldiers battle-ready during the 15th and 16th centuries. The first boxer to win historic recognition was **Nai Khanom Tom.** Captured by the Burmese, he won his freedom after dispatching 10 Burmese soldiers one by one in a boxing challenge. Muay Thai reached the peak of its popularity in the first decade of the 18th century during the reign of Phra Chau Sua, when he promoted it as a national sport. Due to an alarming number of injuries and even deaths, Muay Thai was banned in the 1920s. It was reinstated in 1937, however, when it underwent a series of regulations that shaped the sport to its present form. Today these fights, full of ritual, music, and blood, are put on display throughout Thailand. Every blow imaginable is legal, with the exception of head-butting. Fighters exchange blows for five three-minute rounds; the winner either knocks out his victim or takes the bout by points (most bouts are decided in the latter manner). Fights are packed with screaming fans, most of whom have money riding on the outcome. While many provinces have venues, most of the best fighting occurs in **Bangkok's Ratchadamnoen** and **Lumphini Boxing Stadiums**.

TRADITIONAL PASTIMES

Every year during the hot season, a strong wind lifts handmade **kites** high over Bangkok. **Kite-fighting,** which has been popular for over 700 years, is enjoyed by kings as well as commoners. In a more gruesome fight, crowds watch and bet on **Siamese fighting fish.** When let loose in a tank, these fish battle to the death in a flurry of fins and scales. The fish are so aggressive that they will often kill themselves trying to attack fish in nearby tanks. Raised in Thailand since the Sukhothai period, breeders are constantly developing new varieties. Their international popularity is a great source of pride. In the countryside, **cockfighting** is also popular.

HOLIDAYS AND FESTIVALS (2005)

The Thai, Buddhist, and international holidays listed below are current as of the book's publishing date. Many of the religious days, whose dates are not determined by a lunar cycle, will be given a date by the Royal Family or religious VIPs at the beginning of 2005. The listed dates are subject to change. Make sure to check with the Tourism Authority of Thailand before attending one of the festivals or holiday celebrations. Note that on national holidays, all banks and most establishments are closed.

DATE	NAME AND LOCATION	DESCRIPTION
Jan. 1	New Year's Day	International celebration of the passing year.
Jan. 14-16	Bosang Umbrella Festival, Chiang Mai	Vivacious celebration of Bosang's famous umbrellas with fairs, crafts, and contests.
Feb. 4-6	Flower Festival, Chiang Mai	Thailand's tropical answer to the Rose Parade.
Early Feb.	Phra Nakhon Khiri Fair, Phetchaburi	Local cultural performances, art shows, and contests.
Feb. 9-10	Chinese New Year	Celebrated by nearly all of Thailand, as most Thais have Chinese blood. Most businesses close for at least 3 days.
Feb.	Dragon & Lion Parade, Nakhon Sawan	Golden Dragon, lion, and ancient deity parade with bands and the Chinese community.
Feb. 23	Makha Bucha	Full moon of third lunar month. Commemoration of the 1250 disciples of Buddha coming to hear him preach. Public holiday.
Mar.-Apr.	Poi Sang Long, Mae Hong Son	Stunning Shan tribal celebration of the ordainment of boys as novice monks.
Apr. 6	Chakri Day	National holiday to commemorate the first king of the present dynasty to ascend to the throne.
Apr. 13-15	Songkran, Thai New Year	Best in Chiang Mai, the holiday is known for water: washing with scented water and throwing water at everyone.
Apr.	Pattaya Festival, Phuket	Delicious food, floral floats, and fireworks.
May 1	Labour Day	Banks, factories, and offices closed.

DATE	NAME AND LOCATION	DESCRIPTION
May 5	Coronation Day	National holiday.
May	Royal Ploughing Ceremony, Bangkok	Official beginning of rice-planting outside the Royal Palace, with re-enactments of ancient Brahman rituals. Government holiday.
May	Boon Bang Fai Rocket Festival, Yasothon	Celebration for a plentiful upcoming rain season for rice-planting. Homemade rockets launched.
May 22-23	Visakha Bucha	Full moon of sixth lunar month. Birth, enlightenment, and death of Buddha. Holiest holiday, celebrated at every temple with candlelight processions.
May-June	Wai Kru Day	Usually a Thursday, specific date varies from school to school. A day for students to honor their teachers for their important role in children's lives.
June	Phi Ta Khon, Dan Sai, Loei	People dress as spirits and carry Buddha images while monks read the story of the visit of his incarnation.
July 21	Khao Pansa Day: Buddhist Lent begins. Candle Festival, Ubon Ratchathani	Townspeople celebrate the monks' Buddhist Rains Retreat by walking up to the temple with ornate, huge candles. A time of giving up indulgences, the first day is commemorated with particular attention by students.
Aug.	Rambutan Fair, Surat Thani	Anniversary of the first rambutan tree planted in Surat Thani is commemorated with fruit floats and performing monkeys.
Aug.	Cake Festival	Chamber of Commerce holiday for Southern Thailand's yummy pastries.
Aug. 12	The Queen's Birthday, Mother's Day	Best celebration is in Bangkok, as the city is draped in lights. Thais celebrate their queen's birthday by honoring their own mothers.
Sept. 4-5	Boat Races, Phichit	Annual regatta down the Nan River.
Sept.	Barbecue Festival	Chamber of Commerce holiday for Thai food.
Oct. 3-11	Vegetarian Festival, Phuket	Chinese festival enjoyed since the 1800s with parades, rituals, and of course only vegetarian food to honor two emperor gods.
Mid Oct.	Wax Castle & Boat Racing Festival, Sakhon Nakhon	Procession of beeswax carvings of Buddhist temples to mark the end of the Buddhist Rains Retreat, followed by regatta.
Oct.	Buffalo Races, Chonburi	Water buffaloes stop work and race each other and farmers.
Oct.	Nakhon Phanom Boat Procession	Evening ritual in which thousands of exquisitely carved boats with lights atop them are launched on the Mekong.
Oct. 23	Chulalongkorn Day	King Rama V died on this day. National holiday.
Nov. 19-20	Elephant Roundup, Surin	Celebration of the revered animal, with performances by over 100 elephants, some even in costume.
Nov.	Hill Tribe Festival, Chiang Rai	Cultural performances and handicrafts.
Early Dec.	River Kwai Bridge Week, Kanchanaburi	Remembrance of the site, with historical and archaeological exhibitions; rides on vintage trains available.
Nov. 15	Loi Krathong & Candle Festival	Best in Sukhothai, where it originated, with fireworks and folk dancing. Also good in Ayutthaya and Chiang Mai.
Dec.	Trooping of the Colors, Bangkok	In the Royal Plaza, the elite Royal Guards, dressed in bright colors, renew their allegiance to the Royal Family.
Dec. 5	His Majesty's birthday, Father's Day	Thais celebrate the king's birthday by honoring their own fathers.
Dec. 10	Constitution Day	Thai military pays homage to the constitutional statue in Bangkok, but no festivities ensue. National holiday.
Mid Dec.	World Heritage Site Celebration, Ayutthaya	Celebration of the past with exhibitions and traditional performances.
Dec. 25	Christmas	Not a public holiday, but celebrated by schoolchildren.

ADDITIONAL RESOURCES

GENERAL HISTORY

The Chastening: Inside the Financial Crisis that Rocked the Global Financial System and Humbled the IMF, by Paul Blustein (2002). A cogent study of the Asian Financial Crisis.

Southeast Asia: An Introductory History, by Milton Osborne (1995). A basic survey of Southeast Asian history, revised and updated many times.

Thailand's Durable Premier: Phibun through Three Decades 1932-1957, by Kobkua Suwannathat-Pian (1996). A biography of Thailand's most controversial and influential political leader, Field Marshal Phibunsongkhram.

The Lands of Charm and Cruelty: Travels in Southeast Asia, by Stan Sesser (1994). A collection of compelling essays originally published in the New Yorker.

Modern Thailand: A Volume in the Comparative Societies Series, by Robert Slagter and Harold Kerbo (1999). A review of contemporary Thai institutions and social change.

Thailand: A Short History, by David Wyatt (1982). Excellent history of Thailand.

CULTURE

Night Market: Sexual Cultures and the Thai Economic Miracle, by Ryan Bishop and Lillian Robinson (1998). Explores the trade-off between the lives of young Thai women who are lured into the prostitution industry and the country's economic recovery.

When Elephants Paint: The Quest of Two Russian Artists to Save the Elephants of Thailand, by Dave Eggers, Vitaly Komar, and Alexander Melamid (2000). This book tells the artists' story of their struggle to support Thai elephant sanctuaries with profits made by the elephants themselves—through the sale of their jumbo-sized artistic masterpieces.

Genders and Sexualities in Modern Thailand, ed. by Peter Jackson and Nerida Cook (2000). Essays interpreting roles and patterns of gender in Thailand since the 1800s.

Peoples of the Golden Triangle: Six Tribes in Thailand, by Paul and Elaine Lewis (1998). A historiography of local hill tribes in northern Thailand, with personal vignettes.

Endangered Relations: Negotiating Sex and AIDS in Thailand, by Chris Lyttleton (2000). Describes the intersection of Thai conceptions of sexuality and public health measures to reverse the nation's infamous AIDS/HIV trend.

The Buddhist World of Southeast Asia, by Donald Swearer (1995). A comprehensive academic text covering Buddhist scripture and tenets, the relationship between Buddhism and the government, and the changes in Buddhism in the past 30 years.

FICTION AND NON-FICTION

Singing to the Dead: A Missioner's Life Among Refugees from Burma, by Victoria Armour-Hilleman (2002). Journal of a missionary working with Mon refugees in an illegal camp.

4,000 Days: My Life and Survival in a Bangkok Prison, by Warren Fellows (1998). True story of an Australian who was caught trafficking heroin and spent 12 years in jail.

The Beach, by Alex Garland (1997). A page-turner narcotics adventure about backpackers in search of paradise. A perfect beach read.

Ban Vinai, by Lynellyn Long (1992). Narrative based on the author's ethnographic research in Ban Vinai, a Thai camp sheltering Lao and Cambodian refugees.

Silk Umbrellas, by Carolyn Marsden (2004). Children's book about a young girl's attempt to help contribute to her struggling family. Contains a small glossary of Thai terms.

Jasmine Nights, by S.P. Somtow (1995). A brilliant and hilarious coming-of-age story that paints a colorful and rich picture of Thai culture, contrasting it with its Western counterpart. Thailand's most widely-published author.

Monsoon Country, by Pira Sudham (1988). Personal account of the period of tumult and revolution experienced by Thai culture and politics during 1954-1980. Sudham was nominated for the Nobel Prize for this work. His *People of Esarn* (1987) is highly informative background reading for those traveling to northeast Thailand.

The Force of Karma, by Pira Sudham (2001). The sequel to *Monsoon Country,* depicting the Thai massacres of 1973, 1976 and 1992.

A Fortune-Teller Told Me: Earthbound Travels in the Far East, by Tiziano Terzani (2001). A journalist's trek through Southeast Asia, focusing on myths, religions, and mysticism.

Siam: Or the Woman Who Shot a Man, by Lily Tuck (2000). A novel highlighting cultural misunderstandings and an obsession with a lost American entrepreneur.

FILM

The Bridge On the River Kwai, directed by David Lean, starring Sir Alec Guinness and William Holden (1957). A WWII epic based on a true story about Allied POWs forced to build a bridge connecting Thailand to Burma. The film won 7 Academy Awards, including Best Picture, and causes hundreds of tourists flock to Kanchanaburi each year.

The Iron Ladies, directed by Youngyooth Thongkonthun (2000). A comedy about an underdog volleyball team, composed mostly of gays, transvestites and transsexuals.

Mysterious Object at Noon, conceived and directed by Weerasethakul (2001). Fiction tale crafted by the many people the director encountered as he traveled through the Thai countryside. Documentary film provides a glimpse into Thai traditions and culture.

Ong Bak: Thai Warrior, directed by Prachya Pinkaew (2003). Action film follows a Muay Thai boxer as he tracks down his village's stolen Buddha statue.

Suriyothai, directed by Chatrichalerm Yukol (2001). Historical epic set in the Ayutthaya period that follows events in the life of Queen Suriyothai.

Tropical Malady, directed by Apichatpong Weerasethakul (2004). This surrealistic film won the Jury Prize at Cannes in 2004.

TRAVEL BOOKS

Dream of a Thousand Lives: A Sojourn in Thailand, by Karen Connelly (2001). A young Western woman's experience working and studying on a small Thai farm.

Travelers' Tales: Thailand, ed. by James O'Reilly and Larry Habegger (1993). Collection of stories about Thailand, Thai culture, and traveling.

Travels in the Skin Trade: Tourism and the Sex Industry, by Jeremy Seabrook (2001). In-depth look at the relationship between tourism, Western media, and the sex industry.

Thailand: The Golden Kingdom, by William Warren and Luca Tettoni (1999). Photograph-filled travel companion book that details Thai art, history, and culture.

ON THE WEB

Tourism Authority of Thailand (www.tourismthailand.org). Official website of TAT is possibly the best launching pad for information on visiting Thailand, containing travel tips, a constantly-updated events list, and a general overview of the country.

Thailand Youth Hostel Association (www.tyha.org). The name says it all: solid budget accommodations. Individual hostel information and Internet booking available.

Thailand.com (www.thailand.com/travel). Info on nightlife, accommodations, and more.

Learning Thai the Easy Way (www.learningthai.com). A comprehensive website from Sriwittayapaknam School, offering basic Thai phrases and online resources.

ESSENTIALS

PLANNING YOUR TRIP

> **ENTRANCE REQUIREMENTS**
> **Passport** (p. 36). Required of all travelers. Must be valid for at least 6 months after intended period of stay.
> **Visa** (p. 37). Visas are required of all travelers staying more than 30 days.
> **Inoculations** (p. 48). Visitors who have been in Africa or South America must have a certificate of vaccination against yellow fever. *Let's Go* lists other specifically recommended inoculations, including Japanese encephalitis.
> **Work Permit** (p. 37). Required for all foreigners planning to work in Thailand.

EMBASSIES AND CONSULATES

THAILAND CONSULAR SERVICES ABROAD

Australia: Embassy: 111 Empire CTT, Yarralumla 2600, Canberra, ACT (☎06 273 1149; http://members.tripod.com/posit/index2.html). **Consulates:** 2nd fl., 75-77 Pitt St., Sydney NSW 2000 (☎02 9241 2542); 5th fl., Silverton Place, 101 Wickham Terrace, Brisbane QLD 4000 (☎07 3832 1999); 6th fl., 277 Flinders Ln., Melbourne VIC 3000 (☎03 9650 1714); 1st fl., 72 Flinders St., Adelaide SA 5000 (☎08 232 7474); 135 Victoria Ave., Dalkeith WA 6009 (☎09 386 8092).

Canada: Embassy: 180 Island Park Dr., Ottawa ON K1Y OA2 (☎613-722-4444; www.magma.ca/~thaiott/mainpage.htm). **Consulate:** 1040 Burrard St., Vancouver BC V6Z 2R9 (☎604-687-1143; www.thaicongenvancouver.org).

New Zealand: Embassy: 2 Cook St., P.O. Box 17-226, Karori, Wellington 6005 (☎04 476 8617; www.thaiembassynz.org.nz).

UK: Embassy: 29-30 Queen's Gate, London SW7 5JB (☎020 7589 2944; www.thaiembassyuk.org.uk).

US: Embassy: 1024 Wisconsin Ave. NW, Suite 401, Washington, D.C. 20007 (☎202-944-3600; www.thaiembdc.org). **Consulates:** 351 E. 52nd St., New York, NY 10022 (☎212-754-1770); 700 N. Rush St., Chicago, IL 60611 (☎312-664-3129); 611 N. Larchmont Blvd., 2nd fl., Los Angeles, CA 90004 (☎323-962-9574; www.thai-la.net).

CONSULAR SERVICES IN THAILAND

Australian Embassy: 37 South Sathorn Rd., Bangkok 10120 (☎02 287 2680). Open M-Th 8:30am-12:30pm and 1:30-4:30pm.

Canadian Embassy: Abdulrahim Bldg., 15th fl., 990 Rama IV Rd., Bangkok 10500 (☎02 636 0540). Open M-Th 7:30am-4pm, F 7:30am-1pm. **Consulate:** 151 Moo 3 Superhighway, Tambon Tahsala, Chiang Mai 50000 (☎053 242 292).

New Zealand Embassy: M Thai Tower, 14th fl., All Seasons Place, 87 Wireless Rd., Lumphini, Bangkok 10330 (☎02 254 3856). Open M-F 7:30am-noon and 1-4pm.

UK Embassy: 103 Wireless Rd., Bangkok 10330 (☎02 305 8333). Open M-F 7:30am-noon and 1-3:30pm. **Consulate:** 198 Bumrung Rat Rd., Muang, Chiang Mai 50000 (☎053 263 015). Open M-F 9-11:30am.

US Embassy: 120-122 Wireless Rd., Bangkok 10300 (☎02 205 40 00). Consular services M-F 8-11am and 1-2pm. **Consulate:** 387 Witchayanond Rd., Chiang Mai 50300 (☎053 252 629). American citizen services open M and W 1-3:30pm.

TOURIST OFFICES

Tourism Authority of Thailand (TAT): www.tat.or.th or www.tourismthailand.org. 75 Pitt St., 2nd fl., Sydney 2000 (☎61 2 9247 7549); Brook House 98-99 Jermyn St., 3rd fl., London SW1Y 6EE (☎44 207 925 2511); 61 Broadway, Suite 2810, New York, NY 1006 (☎212-432-0433); 611 North Larchmont Blvd., 1st fl., Los Angeles, CA 90004 (☎323-461-9814). Webpage regularly updated for dates of festivals and recent news.

Ministry of Foreign Affairs: www.mfa.go.th Sri Ayudhaya Rd., Bangkok 10400 (☎66 2 643 5000). Provides info about traveling in Thailand as well as foreign policy updates.

DOCUMENTS AND FORMALITIES

PASSPORTS

REQUIREMENTS

You need a valid passport to enter Thailand and to return to your home country. Federal Aviation Administration (FAA) regulations require that your passport be valid for six months beyond your anticipated departure date. If you are not entering Thailand by plane you may be able to use a passport that will expire sooner than six months from your departure date, although this is not recommended.

NEW PASSPORTS

Citizens of Australia, Canada, Ireland, New Zealand, the UK, and the US can apply for passports at certain post offices, passport offices, or courts of law. Any new passport or renewal applications must be filed well in advance of the departure date to ensure procurement, although many passport offices offer rush services for a very steep fee.

PASSPORT MAINTENANCE

Photocopy the page of your passport with your photo, as well as your visas, traveler's check serial numbers, and any other important documents. Carry one set of copies in a safe place, apart from the originals, and leave another set at home. Consulates also recommend that you carry an expired passport or an official copy of your birth certificate in a part of your baggage separate from other documents.

If you lose your passport, immediately notify the local police and the nearest embassy or consulate of your home government. To expedite its replacement, you will need to know all info previously recorded and show ID and proof of citizenship. In some cases, a replacement may take weeks to process, and it may be valid only for a limited time. Any visas stamped in your old passport will be irretrievably lost. In an emergency, ask for immediate temporary traveling papers that will permit you to re-enter your home country. American citizens may want to notify someone at home who can contact Overseas Citizen Services (☎202-647-5225).

VISAS, INVITATIONS, AND WORK PERMITS

VISAS

American, Australian, British, Canadian, European, New Zealand, and South African citizens can stay for 30 days without a visa. For longer stays, travelers can buy a 10-day extension (500฿) at an immigration office in Thailand or apply for a 60-day tourist visa (US$25 per entry) from any Thai consulate prior to arriving in

Thailand. Visas must be used within three months of issue. If you wish to sojourn in nearby countries, obtain a re-entry permit at an immigration office before departure. Double-check entrance requirements at the nearest embassy or consulate of Thailand (see **Embassies and Consulates Abroad,** p. 35) for up-to-date info before departure. US citizens can consult http://travel.state.gov/foreignentryreqs.html. US citizens can also take advantage of the **Center for International Business and Travel** (☎ 800-925-2428), which secures visas for travel to almost all countries for a service charge. Any traveler remaining in Thailand beyond their visa expiration date will be charged a fine upon departure payable immediately.

If your reason for entering Thailand is not tourism you may need to purchase a non-immigrant or transit visa prior to your arrival. In addition to the visa application form, two passport-size pictures, and a valid passport, travelers applying for other visas may need to submit a letter from a Thai contact detailing the purpose of their visit. For more info on specific requirements please contact any Thai embassy or consulate (p. 35) or check out the visa info at www.mfa.go.th.

If you have a 60-day visa and you go to Myanmar, Cambodia, Malaysia, or Laos for a daytrip, you will lose your visa and will need to reapply. To avoid having to get a new visa when you hop across the border for a day, make photocopies of your passport (usually 5฿). Then proceed directly to Thai border control, at whichever border point you are hoping to cross, with your two photocopies of your passport. Surrender your passport to the Thai authorities, who will stamp the photocopies. Take your newly stamped photocopies and the border crossing fee to the border control authorities of the country you are entering. They will stamp your photocopies and keep one of them. All stamps are on the copies, so when you return to Thailand, you get your unmarked passport back. Foreign authorities will keep one photocopy, Thai authorities the other. Either way, when you surrender your passport photocopies, you will receive a very thin piece of paper—that piece of paper is your passport. Hold on to it if you ever want to see home again.

WORK PERMITS
Admission as a visitor does not include the right to work, which is authorized only by a work permit. Entering Thailand to study or teach requires that you apply for a non-immigrant visa and submit a letter from the educational institution with which you will be working. For more info, see **Alternatives to Tourism** (p. 81).

IDENTIFICATION
When you travel, always carry at least two forms of identification on your person, including at least one photo ID. A passport and a driver's license or birth certificate is usually adequate. Never carry all of your IDs together. Split them up in case of theft or loss, and keep photocopies of all of them in your luggage and at home.

STUDENT, TEACHER, AND YOUTH IDENTIFICATION
The **International Student Identity Card (ISIC),** the most widely accepted form of student ID, is accepted in Thailand for discounts on some sights and services such as cinemas and upscale restaurants. Check out the ISIC discount database (www.istcnet.org/DiscountDatabase) for more info. Cardholders also have access to a **24hr. emergency** helpline. US cardholders have basic insurance benefits (see **Insurance,** p. 48). Applicants must be full-time secondary or post-secondary school students at least 12 years of age. Because of a rise in fake cards, some services (particularly airlines) require additional proof of student identity.

The **International Teacher Identity Card (ITIC)** offers teachers the same insurance coverage as the ISIC and similar but limited discounts. For travelers who are up to 25 years old but are not students, the **International Youth Travel Card (IYTC)** also offers many of the same benefits as the ISIC.

Each of these identity cards costs US$22 or £7. ISIC and ITIC cards are valid for roughly one academic year (depending on when you purchase the card); IYTC cards are valid for one year from the date of issue. Many student travel agencies (see p. 55) issue the cards. For a list of issuing agencies or more info, see the **International Student Travel Confederation (ISTC)** website (www.istc.org).

The **International Student Exchange Card (ISE)** is a similar identification card available to students, faculty, and youth aged 12 to 26. The card provides discounts, medical benefits, a **24hr. emergency** helpline, and access to student airfares. The card costs US$25. Call US ☎ 800-255-8000 for more info, or visit www.isecard.com.

CUSTOMS

Upon entering Thailand you must declare certain items from abroad and pay a duty on the value of those articles if they exceed the allowance established by that country's customs service. Note that goods and gifts purchased at **duty-free** shops abroad are not exempt from duty or sales tax at your point of return and thus must be declared as well. In order to expedite your return, make a list of any valuables brought from home and register them with customs before traveling abroad, and be sure to keep receipts for all goods acquired abroad. Travelers may bring one still camera with five rolls of film or one video camera with three tapes, 200 cigarettes, and one liter of alcohol. These restrictions are meant to ensure the film/equipment is for personal use only and are flexible. The total amount of currency taken out should not exceed the amount taken in (max. US$10,000). No authentic Buddha or Bodhisattva images, or fragments thereof, may be exported without permission from the Bangkok National Museum (☎ 02 224 1333) and the Department of Fine Arts; you must prove you are a practicing Buddhist or are using them for cultural or academic purposes. Such certification often takes three to five days to process; so make sure you leave enough time. These rules do not apply to souvenirs. For art purchased in the country, keep receipts for customs. For more detailed info on exportation of Buddha images or antiquities see www.mfa.go.th/web/808.php.

Additionally, the Thai government has harsh penalties for **drug possession and trafficking,** which are often considered synonymous. The import of **firearms, weapons,** and **pornography** is prohibited. Travelers should note that though Thailand's regulations are among the most stable, customs requirements do vary.

MONEY

CURRENCY AND EXCHANGE

The Thai **baht (฿)** comes in denominations of 10 (rare), 20, 50, 100, 500, and 1000฿ notes. Coins come in 1, 5, 10฿, and 25 and 50 satang (100 satang equals 1฿), although you will rarely pay less than 1฿ for anything. The currency chart below is based on August 2004 exchange rates between local currency and Australian dollars (AUS$), Canadian dollars (CDN$), European Union euros (EUR€), New Zealand dollars (NZ$), British pounds (UK£), and US dollars (US$). Check the currency converter on websites like www.xe.com or www.bloomberg.com or a large newspaper for the latest exchange rates.

As a general rule, it's cheaper to convert money in Thailand than at home. While currency exchange will probably be available in your arrival airport, it's wise to bring enough foreign currency to last for the first 24 to 72 hours of your trip. Travelers can get foreign currency from the comfort of home through **International Currency Express** (US only ☎ 888-278-6628) or Online FX (UK ☎ 020 7224 5799), which deliver currency or traveler's checks within two business days.

THAI BAHT (฿)	AUS$ 1 = 30.02฿	10฿ = AUS$ 0.33
	CDN$ 1 = 31.98฿	10฿ = CDN$ 0.31
	EUR€ 1 = 51.04฿	10฿ = EUR€ 0.20
	NZ$ 1 = 27.91฿	10฿ = NZ$ 0.36
	UK£ 1 = 75.45฿	10฿ = UK£ 0.13
	US$ 1 = 41.46฿	10฿ = US$ 0.24

When changing money abroad, try to go only to banks or change bureaus that have at most a 5% margin between their buy and sell prices. Since you lose money with every transaction, **convert large sums** (unless the currency is depreciating rapidly), **but no more than you'll need.**

If you use traveler's checks or bills, carry some in small denominations (the equivalent of US$50 or less) for times when you are forced to exchange money at disadvantageous rates, but bring a range of denominations since charges may be levied per check cashed. Store your money in a variety of forms. Ideally, at any given time you will be carrying some cash, some traveler's checks, and an ATM and/or credit card. Travelers should consider carrying **US dollars,** as many establishments in Thailand prefer them.

TRAVELER'S CHECKS

Traveler's checks are one of the safest and least troublesome means of carrying funds. American Express and Visa are the most recognized brands. Many banks and agencies sell them for a small commission. Check issuers provide refunds if the checks are lost or stolen, and many provide additional services, such as toll-free refund hotlines abroad, emergency message services, and stolen credit card assistance. The preferred currency of traveler's checks in Thailand is US dollars, although sterling and Australian dollars will be accepted as well. Checks are readily accepted in most cities in Thailand, although travelers to more rural areas should carry sufficient *baht* to last the duration of their trip. Also, due to high incidences of fraud, Thai bank clerks tend to be suspicious of signatures so be confident with yours. Ask about toll-free refund hotlines and the location of refund centers when purchasing checks, and always carry emergency cash.

American Express: Checks available with commission at select banks, at all AmEx offices, and online (www.americanexpress.com; US residents only). American Express cardholders can also purchase checks by phone (☎800-721-9768). Checks available in Australian, Canadian, European, Japanese, British, and US currencies. For purchase locations or more info contact AmEx's service centers: in Australia ☎800 68 80 22; in New Zealand 0508 555 358; in the UK 0800 587 6023; in the US and Canada 800-221-7282; in Thailand 02 504 3435; elsewhere, call the US collect at 801-964-6665.

Visa: Checks available (generally with commission) at banks worldwide. For the location of the nearest office, call Visa's service centers: in the UK ☎0800 89 5078; in the US 800-227-6811; elsewhere, call the UK collect at 44 173 331 8949. AAA (see p. 62) offers commission-free checks to its members. Checks available in Canadian, Japanese, European, British, and US currencies.

Travelex/Thomas Cook: Issues Visa traveler's checks. Members of AAA and affiliated automobile associations receive a 25% commission discount on check purchases. In the US and Canada call ☎800-287-7362; in the UK call 0800 62 21 01; elsewhere call the UK collect at 44 1733 31 89 50.

CREDIT, DEBIT, AND ATM CARDS

Where they are accepted, credit cards often offer superior exchange rates, up to 5% better than the retail rate used by banks and other currency exchange establishments. Credit cards may also offer services such as insurance or emergency help, and are sometimes required to reserve hotel rooms or rental cars. **Mastercard** and **Visa** are the most welcomed; **American Express** cards are also commonly accepted.

ATMs are widespread in Thailand. Depending on your home bank's system, you can most likely access your bank account from abroad. However, many foreign ATMs will automatically withdraw money from your checking account without asking if you would prefer to take money from a savings account. There are ATMs in Thailand that will let you withdraw money from either account, but you may need to try several different ones. ATMs get the same wholesale exchange rate as credit cards, but there is often a limit on the amount of money you can withdraw per day (usually around US$500). There is typically also a surcharge of US$1-5 per withdrawal. The two major international money networks are Cirrus (US ☎ 800-424-7787; www.mastercard.com) and Visa/PLUS (US ☎ 800-843-7587; www.visa.com).

American Express cards can be used at Bangkok Bank ATMs throughout Thailand. Cardholders (enrolled in the Express Cash program) can withdraw cash from their checking accounts at any of AmEx's major offices and many representative offices. For more info, call ☎ 800-227-4669 in the US. The AmEx international assistance number is ☎ 800-732-1991. For more info see www.americanexpress.com.

GETTING MONEY FROM HOME

If you run out of money while traveling, the easiest and cheapest solution is to have someone back home make a deposit to the account linked to your credit card or ATM card. Failing that, consider one of the following options. The online **International Money Transfer Consumer Guide** (http://international-money-transfer-consumer-guide.info) may also be of help.

WIRING MONEY

It is possible to arrange a **bank money transfer,** which means asking a bank back home to wire money to a bank in Thailand. This is the cheapest way to transfer cash, but it's also the slowest, usually taking several days or more. Note that some banks may only release your funds in local currency, potentially sticking you with a poor exchange rate. Inquire about this in advance. At Bangkok Bank you do not need to have an account in order to receive money transfers; however, you will need to present photo ID in order to claim your transfer (there is a 0.25% fee levied on every transaction; min. 200฿, max. 500฿). Money transfer services like **Western Union** are faster and more convenient than bank transfers, but also much pricier. Western Union has many locations worldwide. To find one, visit www.westernunion.com, or call in Australia ☎ 800 501 500, in Canada 800-235-0000, in the UK 0800 83 38 33, or in the US 800-325-6000. Several banks in Thailand, including Bank of Asia and Bank of Ayudhya, are authorized Western Union agents.

US STATE DEPARTMENT (US CITIZENS ONLY)

In serious emergencies only, the US State Department will forward money within hours to the nearest consular office, which will then disburse it according to instructions for a US$30 fee. If you wish to use this service, you must contact the Overseas Citizens Service division of the US State Department (☎ 317-472-2328; nights, Sundays, and holidays 202-647-4000). Other nationals should contact their embassies for info on emergency loans.

COSTS

The cost of your trip will vary considerably, depending on where you go, how you travel, and where you stay. The most significant expense will probably be your round-trip **airfare** to Thailand (p. 54). Traveling in Thailand can be done on a rather small budget, although it is possible to spend quite a lot of money in Thailand as well. Before you go, spend some time calculating a reasonable daily **budget** that will meet your needs. Always keep emergency reserve funds (at least US$200) when planning how much money you'll need.

STAYING ON A BUDGET

The cost of living in Thailand is very low compared to most Western countries, especially because the price difference between the cheapest options and the mid-range options is often very small, giving the budget traveler the option of an occasional relative night of luxury. Travelers looking to spend more than a single night in comfort also have that option, especially in the more populated areas and at beach resorts. At the moment, package tours are on the rise. Often, they offer efficient travel while still being affordable, but for many travelers, packaged deals can feel limiting. In any case, travel in Thailand need not drain your savings.

To give you a general idea, a bare-bones day in Thailand (camping or sleeping in hostels/guesthouses, buying food at supermarkets) would cost about US$5 (200฿). A slightly more comfortable day (sleeping in hostels/guesthouses and the occasional budget hotel, eating one meal per day at a restaurant, going out at night) would cost US$10 (400฿). And for a luxurious day, the sky's the limit. Don't forget to factor in your emergency reserve funds when planning how much money you'll need.

TIPS FOR SAVING MONEY

Some ways to save money include searching out free entertainment and splitting accommodation and food costs with trustworthy fellow travelers. Although budget travelers are often accustomed to seeking out supermarkets for food, in Thailand it is often cheaper to buy meals from street stalls or small restaurants than to buy and cook it yourself. Do your **laundry** in the sink (unless you're asked not to). That said, don't go overboard. Though staying within your budget is important, don't do so at the expense of your health or a wonderful travel experience.

TIPPING AND BARGAINING

Tipping and especially bargaining in the developing world is a quite different and much more commonplace practice than you may be accustomed to. There are many unspoken rules to which tourists must adhere. Tipping in Thailand is not customary but much appreciated. A general rule is that the more Western the establishment, the more likely a tip is expected. If an establishment includes a service charge in the bill, tipping is not necessary. In restaurants that don't levy service charges, a 15% gratuity is appropriate. Most people will welcome the extra *baht*, as the average yearly income for some regions of Thailand is as low as US$150. Foreigners should expect to pay higher entrance fees than native Thais at some places, including beaches, museums, and monuments.

Most officials are unwilling to accept bribes from foreigners, and it is unwise to initiate an under-the-table transaction. If an official demands a fee or fine that you feel may be illegal, proceed with caution. Paying the bribe might be preferable to the alternative, but keep in mind that it is also illegal. If you politely ask for a receipt, or to speak with the official's superior, you might be able to defuse the situation. As a last resort, threatening to contact your embassy may also be effective.

THE ART OF THE DEAL. In Southeast Asia, bargaining is more than a pricing system. It is an art form, a crucial part of everyday social interactions, and, if your attitude is right, a great deal of fun. Bargaining in Thailand is a given: vendors will automatically quote you a price that is several times too high; it's up to you to get them down to a reasonable rate. But put your cut-throat attitude aside; this game of skill is built on a foundation of mutual respect and cheeky smiles of understanding. With the following tips and some finesse, you might be able to impress even the most hardened hawkers:

1. **Bargaining needn't be a fierce struggle laced with barbs.** Quite the opposite: good-natured wrangling with a cheerful face may prove your best weapon.

2. **Use your poker face.** The less your face betrays your interest in the item the better. If you touch an item to inspect it, the vendor will be sure to "encourage" you to name a price or make a purchase. Coming back again and again to admire a trinket is a good way of ensuring that you pay a ridiculously high price. Never get too enthusiastic about the object in question; point out flaws in workmanship and design. Be cool.

3. **Know when to bargain.** In most cases, it's clear when it's appropriate. Most private transportation fares, like those for *tuk-tuks* and motorcycle taxis, are all fair game. Don't bargain on metered taxis or buses. Bargaining for lodging is possible, but success varies dramatically. Your chances will increase if you can state a specific reason for a better rate, like low-season discounts. It is acceptable to bargain for souvenirs at a market, but it is not customary in stores. Never bargain for produce or prepared foods on the street or in restaurants. In some stores, signs will indicate "fixed prices". When in doubt, ask tactfully, "Is that your lowest price?" or whether discounts are given.

4. **Never underestimate the power of peer pressure.** Bargaining with more than one person at a time always leads to higher prices. Alternately, try having a friend discourage you from your purchase—if you seem to be reluctant, the merchant will want to drop the price to interest you again.

5. **Know when to turn away.** Feel free to refuse any vendor or driver who bargains rudely, and don't hesitate to move on to another vendor if one will not be reasonable about the final price he offers. However, to start bargaining without an intention to buy is a major *faux pas.* Agreeing on a price and declining it is also poor form. Turn away slowly with a smile and "thank you" upon hearing a ridiculous price—the price may plummet.

6. **Start low.** Never feel guilty offering a ridiculously low price. If it's too low the vendor simply won't sell it to you! Your starting price should be no more than one-third to one-half the asking price.

TAXES

There is a 7% VAT (value-added tax) in Thailand levied on most items, including hotel rooms and food; it's usually already included in stated prices. Menus, tariff sheets, etc., specify if VAT is not included in the listed price. There is also a departure tax which you must pay in the airport before leaving. The value of this tax varies depending on which airport you leave from and your flight destination.

PACKING

Pack lightly: Lay out only what you absolutely need, then take half the clothes and twice the money. The Travelite FAQ (www.travelite.org) is a good resource for tips on traveling light. The online **Universal Packing List** (http://upl.codeq.info) will generate a customized list of suggested items based on your trip length, the expected climate, your planned activities, and other factors. If you plan to do a lot of hiking, also consult **Camping and the Outdoors**, p. 68. Don't forget that you can purchase all necessary items in Thailand for a fraction of the cost.

Luggage: If you plan to cover most of your itinerary by foot, a sturdy **frame backpack** is unbeatable. (For the basics on buying a pack, see p. 70.) Toting a **suitcase** or **trunk** is fine if you plan to live in one or two cities and explore from there, but not a great idea if you plan to move around frequently. In addition to your main piece of luggage, a **daypack** (a small backpack or courier bag) is useful. Plastic bags will keep things dry and sorted.

Clothing: No matter where you're traveling, it's a good idea to bring a warm jacket, a rain jacket (Gore-Tex® is both waterproof and breathable), sturdy shoes or hiking boots, and thick socks. However, in general, the clothes you bring to Thailand should be light, comfortable, and quick-drying. Flip-flops or waterproof sandals are must-haves for grubby showers. You may also want one outfit for going out, and a nice pair of shoes. Remember that dress in Thailand is considered very important and Thais dress well. If you plan to visit religious or cultural sites you will need modest and respectful dress. In order to enter many temples in Thailand, dress that covers both the arms and the legs is required, as well as shoes that (at a minimum) have a strap around the heel.

Sleepsack: Some hostels require that you either provide your own linen or rent sheets from them. Save cash by making your own sleepsack: fold a full-size sheet in half the long way, then sew it closed along the long side and one of the short sides. If you plan to camp, a sleeping bag is a good idea. Either way, you'll want something between you and the bed in most hostels in Thailand.

Converters and adapters: In Thailand, electricity is 220V AC, enough to fry any 120V North American appliance. Americans, Brits, and Canadians should buy an adapter (US$5) which changes the shape of the plug, and a converter (US$20) which changes the voltage. Don't make the mistake of using only an adapter, unless appliance instructions explicitly state otherwise. New Zealanders and Australians (who use 230V at home) won't need a converter, but will need a set of adapters to use anything electrical. For more on all things adaptable, check out http://kropla.com/electric.htm.

Toiletries: Toothbrushes, towels, cold-water soap, talcum powder (to keep feet dry), deodorant, razors, tampons, and condoms are often available, but may be difficult to find, especially in the more rural areas of Thailand. Bring extras. **Contact lenses** are likely to be expensive and difficult to find, so bring enough extra pairs and solution for your entire trip. Also bring your glasses and a copy of your prescription in case you need emergency replacements. If you use heat disinfection, either switch temporarily to a chemical disinfection system (check first to make sure it's safe with your brand of lenses), or buy a converter to 220/240V.

First-aid kit: For a basic first-aid kit, pack bandages, a pain reliever, antibiotic cream, a thermometer, a Swiss Army knife, tweezers, moleskin, decongestant, motion-sickness remedy, diarrhea or upset-stomach medication (Pepto Bismol or Imodium), an antihistamine, sunscreen, insect repellent, burn ointment, and a syringe for emergencies (get an explanatory letter from your doctor). If you are traveling in a malarial area of Thailand (p. 47), also bring your malaria medication.

Film: Less serious photographers may want to bring a disposable camera or two rather than an expensive non-disposable one. Despite disclaimers, airport security X-rays can fog film, so buy a lead-lined pouch at a camera store or ask security to hand-inspect it. Always pack film in your carry-on luggage in an easily accessible place, since higher-intensity X-rays are used on checked luggage.

Other useful items: For safety purposes, you should bring a **money belt** and small **padlock.** Basic **outdoors equipment** (plastic water bottle, compass, waterproof matches,

ESSENTIALS

pocketknife, sunglasses, sunscreen, hat) may also prove useful. **Quick repairs** of torn garments can be done on the road with a needle and thread; also consider bringing electrical tape for patching tears. If you want to do laundry by hand, bring detergent, a rubber ball to stop up the sink, and string for a makeshift clothesline. Other things you're liable to forget are an **umbrella;** sealable **plastic bags** (for damp clothes, soap, food, shampoo, and other spillables); an **alarm clock;** safety pins; rubber bands; a flashlight; earplugs; garbage bags; and a small calculator. A **cell phone** can be a life-saver on the road. See p. 65 for info on acquiring one that will work in Thailand.

Important documents: Don't forget your passport, traveler's checks, ATM and/or credit cards, adequate ID, and photocopies of all of the aforementioned in case these documents are lost or stolen (p. 37). Also check that you have any of the following that might apply to you: a hosteling membership card (p. 66); international driver's license (see p. 62); travel insurance forms; and/or an ISIC card (p. 37).

SAFETY AND HEALTH

GENERAL ADVICE

In any type of crisis situation, the most important thing to do is **stay calm.** Your country's embassy abroad (p. 35) is usually your best resource when things go wrong: registering with that embassy upon arrival in the country is often a good idea. The government offices listed in the **travel advisories** box (p. 45) can provide info on the services they offer their citizens in case of emergencies abroad.

LOCAL LAWS AND POLICE

Thai police enforce strict drug policies and will arrest and heavily fine foreigners (and Thais) for possession and trafficking of illicit drugs. Beware of anyone offering a "free trip to Thailand" in exchange for help transporting "luggage" or "gifts" into the country, as this method of drug trafficking has been employed in Thailand.

The monarchy of Thailand is a respected institution and it is a criminal offense to make any derisive comments about the monarchy or its members. Called "lese majeste," offenses against the King or his family can result in imprisonment. These include stepping on or destroying any image of the King, such as Thai bank notes.

The **tourist police** in Bangkok can be reached by calling ☎ **1155** and are generally a useful resource either in emergency situations or simple complications. Any issues related to tourist scams should be related to them or the local tourist police. The countrywide **emergency** number is ☎ **191**. It is probably preferable to contact the tourist police before using this number.

DRUGS AND ALCOHOL

Drugs are easily accessible in Thailand and, especially in some rural communities, drug use may seem to be common and public. Despite the glamour surrounding the Thai drug scene, which is often connected to the skin trade or the backpacker community, narcotics are illegal and travelers do get caught. Buying or selling *any* type of drug may lead to a stiff prison sentence. For serious drug offenses, Thailand has imposed the death penalty. If you break the law, your home embassies will visit you in jail, but they cannot do anything else to help you. Often they do not even learn of arrests until a few days after they occur.

Thailand has no established minimum drinking age; however, some clubs do have a minimum age requirement (although they often do not ask for IDs from foreigners). Whenever you drink, *Let's Go* recommends that you use alcohol responsibly. Also, take extra safety precautions, as there have been cases of travelers being robbed after accepting drugged food or drink from casual acquaintances.

SPECIFIC CONCERNS

Periodically, Thailand suffers from severe flooding during the rainy season (June to November). Also, strong currents off Thailand's southern beaches occasionally result in fatalities. Travelers should educate themselves about natural dangers specific to the regions in which they are about to travel.

Similarly, travelers should always check travel advisories and world news before departure. The box on **travel advisories** lists offices to contact and webpages to visit to get the most updated travel warnings and info. It is always helpful—and sometimes essential—to be aware of the political situation in the region. Using current, proper titles for government officials and organizations is a must.

Recently, northern Thailand and its border with Myanmar have been prone to violence due to the a **ethnic conflict.** Check the news and your embassy for the latest before going to these areas (p. 22). Even more recently, tensions in the south have swelled into violent conflict between Muslim separatists and the current Thai government (p. 21). During the spring of 2004 government troops were sent in to reduce the bloodshed. Although violence has not been directed at tourists, travelers are advised to closely monitor the situation before making travel plans, particularly in the provinces of Naratiwat, Pattani, Yala, Satun, and Songkhla.

In general, Thailand has a good safety record. Nevertheless, scams abound: taxi and *tuk-tuk* drivers, guesthouse operators, and fellow travelers have all been known to attempt various con-games. On buses and trains and in the airport, be careful when accepting food or drink from strangers: travelers have been drugged and robbed. Most likely friendliness is genuine, but exercise common sense. Crime committed against foreigners is usually petty thievery; violence is rare. **All narcotic drugs in Thailand are illegal,** despite what anyone may tell you. Penalties for drug-related crimes can be very stiff. Thailand has even begun imposing the death penalty for severe violations.

TRAVEL ADVISORIES.

Australian Department of Foreign Affairs and Trade: ☎ 13 00 555135; faxback service 02 6261 1299; www.dfat.gov.au.

Canadian Department of Foreign Affairs and International Trade (DFAIT): In Canada and the US ☎800-267-8376, elsewhere 613-944-4000; www.dfait-maeci.gc.ca. Call for their free booklet, *Bon Voyage...But.*

New Zealand Ministry of Foreign Affairs: ☎04 439 8000; fax 494 8506; www.mft.govt.nz/travel/index.html.

United Kingdom Foreign and Commonwealth Office: ☎020 7008 0232; fax 7008 0155; www.fco.gov.uk.

US Department of State: ☎202-647-5225, faxback service 647-3000; http://travel.state.gov. For *A Safe Trip Abroad*, call ☎202-512-1800.

PERSONAL SAFETY

EXPLORING AND TRAVELING

Be careful about leaving yourself vulnerable to thieves. As pickpockets know, tourists carry a lot of cash and are not as street-savvy as locals. You can reduce your risk of getting robbed or hurt by **keeping a low profile.** Try to blend in as

ESSENTIALS

much as possible. Respecting local customs (in many cases, dressing more conservatively than you would at home) may placate would-be hecklers. Be openminded and courteous: a smile goes a long way. If you show genuine interest in the local language and practices, the locals are more likely to make sure you are not harassed. This is particularly true in Thailand, where not many travelers can be bothered to learn the language. Even a few phrases of conversational Thai will immediately elevate your status in the eyes of the people you meet.

Familiarize yourself with your surroundings before setting out, and carry yourself with confidence. Check maps in shops and restaurants rather than on the street. If you are traveling alone, be sure someone at home knows your itinerary, and never admit that you're alone. When walking at night, stick to busy, well-lit streets. If you ever feel uncomfortable, leave the area as quickly as you can.

There is no sure-fire way to avoid all the threatening situations you might encounter while traveling, but a good **self-defense course** will give you concrete ways to react to unwanted advances. **Impact, Prepare, and Model Mugging** can refer you to local self-defense courses in the US (☎800-345-5425;www.impact-safety.org). Workshops (1½-3hr.) start at US$75; full courses (20-25hr.) run US$350-400. However, don't let fear pervade your trip: careful exploration will build confidence and make your stay more rewarding.

Renting a **motorbike** is one of the cheapest and most convenient ways to explore Thailand, but you should understand the risks involved before you hop on. Motor-vehicle crashes are a leading cause of injury among travelers. Wear a helmet and drive with care to reduce the chance of serious injury. Remember, you don't necessarily need to do anything wrong to be in an accident; watch out for other drivers. If you are using a **car,** learn local driving signals and wear a seatbelt. Officially, Thais drive on the left side of the road, but most drive on the right side with equal frequency. Children under 40 lbs. should ride only in specially-designed carseats, available for a small fee from most car rental agencies. Study route maps before you hit the road, and if you plan on spending a lot of time driving, consider bringing spare parts. If your car breaks down, wait for the police to assist you. For long drives in desolate areas, invest in a cellular phone and a roadside assistance program (p. 62). Thailand has well-maintained roads, but is notorious for heavy traffic. Park your vehicle in a garage or well-traveled area, and use a steering wheel locking device in larger cities. **Sleeping in your car** is one of the most dangerous (and often illegal) ways to rest. Not for the weak-hearted, the roads of Thailand are an adventure in themselves. For info on the perils of **hitchhiking,** see p. 62.

POSSESSIONS AND VALUABLES

Never leave your belongings unattended; crime occurs in even the most demure-looking hostel or hotel. Bring your own **padlock** for hostel lockers, and don't ever store valuables in any locker. Be particularly careful on **buses** and **trains:** horror stories abound about thieves who wait for travelers to fall asleep. Carry your backpack in front of you where you can see it. When traveling with others, sleep in alternate shifts. When alone, use good judgment in selecting a train compartment: never stay in an empty one, and use a lock to secure your pack to the luggage rack. Try to sleep on top bunks with your luggage stored above you (if not in bed with you), and keep important documents and other valuables on your person.

There are a few steps you can take to minimize the financial risk associated with traveling. First, **bring as little with you as possible** and **never carry your wallet in your back pocket.** Second, buy a few combination **padlocks** to secure your belongings either in your pack or in a hostel or train station locker. Third, **carry as little cash as possible.** Keep your traveler's checks and ATM/credit cards in a **money belt**—not a "fanny pack"—along with your passport and ID cards. Fourth, **keep a small cash** reserve separate from your primary stash. This should be about US$50 (US$ are best) sewn into or stored in the depths of your pack, along with your traveler's check numbers and important photocopies.

In large cities **con artists** often work in groups and may involve children. Beware of certain classics: sob stories that include a request for money, rolls of bills "found" on the street, mustard spilled (or saliva spit) onto your shoulder to distract you while they snatch your bag. **Never let your passport and your bags out of your sight.** Beware of **pickpockets** in city crowds, especially on public transportation. Also, be alert in public telephone booths: if you must say your calling card number, do so very quietly; if you punch it in, make sure no one can look over your shoulder. Be aware of your surroundings and look sure of yourself. Confidence is the greatest anti-theft device you can have.

If you will be traveling with electronic devices, such as a laptop computer or a PDA, check whether your homeowner's insurance covers loss, theft, or damage when you travel. If not, you might consider purchasing a separate insurance policy. **Safeware** (US ☎ 800-800-1492; www.safeware.com) specializes in covering computers and charges $90 for 90-day international travel coverage up to $4000.

PRE-DEPARTURE HEALTH

In your **passport,** write the names of any people you wish to be contacted in case of a medical emergency and list any allergies or medical conditions. Matching a prescription to a foreign equivalent is not always easy, safe, or possible, so if you take prescription drugs, consider carrying up-to-date, legible prescriptions or a letter from your doctor stating the medication's trade name, manufacturer, chemical name, and dosage. Bangkok will have most over-the-counter medications that you will need; stock up here before you travel out. While traveling, be sure to keep all medication with you in your carry-on luggage. For tips on packing a basic **first-aid kit** and other health essentials, see p. 43.

Common drugs are essentially known by the same generic names in Thailand as they are elsewhere. However, some specific brands are Duran or Nurofen (ibuprofen), Decolfed (decongestant and antihistamine), and Biscadyl (laxative).

IMMUNIZATIONS AND PRECAUTIONS

Travelers over two years old should make sure that the following vaccines are up to date: MMR (for measles, mumps, and rubella); DTaP or Td (for diphtheria, tetanus, and pertussis); OPV (for polio); HbCV (for haemophilus influenza B); and HBV (for hepatitis B). See **Inoculation Requirements & Recommendations** (p. 48) for a list of inoculations you might need. For recommendations on immunizations and prophylaxis, consult the CDC (p. 49) and check with a doctor for guidance.

Malaria is prevalent in most of Thailand. The CDC also provides info about malaria risk by region. Strains resistant to certain prophylactics are common, so ask your doctor to recommend the best preventative drug for your region of travel. There are many schools of thought about malarial medication. In general, malarial medication is not recommended for travelers staying in major cities such as Bangkok, Chiang Mai, Pattaya, and Phuket. However, anyone traveling in rural areas along Thailand's borders should talk to a doctor about buying medication. Be aware that not all drugs are available everywhere in Thailand, so stock up before you go. For more info see p. 50.

Adults traveling to Thailand on trips longer than four weeks should consider the following additional immunizations: Hepatitis A vaccine and/or immune globulin (IG), an additional dose of polio vaccine, typhoid and cholera vaccines, particularly if traveling off the beaten path, and a meningitis vaccine. The Japanese encephalitis vaccine is recommended for anyone traveling in rural regions for longer than one month, particularly in the Northeastern parts of Thailand. The vaccine consists of a series of three shots, which can occasionally have severe side-effects. Japanese encephalitis is one of many diseases found in Asia that is transmitted by mosquito. Additionally, the rabies vaccine and yearly influenza vaccines are recommended. While **yellow fever** is only endemic to parts of South America and sub-Saharan Africa, Thailand may deny entrance to travelers arriving from these zones without a certificate of vaccination.

> ### ! INOCULATION REQUIREMENTS & RECOMMENDATIONS
> The inoculations needed for travel in Thailand vary with the length of your trip and the activities you plan to pursue. Visit your doctor at least 4-6 weeks prior to your departure to allow time for the shots to take effect. Be sure to keep your inoculation records with you as you travel: you may be required to show them to border officials.
>
> **Diphtheria and tetanus, measles, and polio:** regular boosters recommended.
> **Typhoid:** strongly recommended.
> **Hepatitis A** or **Immune Globulin (IG)**: recommended.
> **Hepatitis B:** if traveling for 6 months or more, or if exposure to blood, needle-sharing, or sexual contact is likely. Important for health care workers and those who might seek medical treatment abroad.
> **Japanese encephalitis:** only if you will be in rural areas for 4 weeks or more, or if there are known outbreaks in the regions you plan to visit. Elevated risk usually from May to October.
> **Rabies:** if you might be exposed to animals while you travel.
> **Yellow Fever:** if you are traveling from South America or sub-Saharan Africa or other infected areas, a certificate of vaccination may be required for entry into Thailand. There is no risk in Thailand.

INSURANCE

Travel insurance covers four basic areas: medical/health problems, property loss, trip cancellation/interruption, and emergency evacuation. Though regular insurance policies may well extend to travel-related accidents, consider purchasing separate travel insurance if the cost of potential trip cancellation, interruption, or emergency medical evacuation is greater than you can absorb. Prices for travel insurance purchased separately generally run about US$50 per week for full coverage, while trip cancellation/interruption may be purchased separately at a rate of US$3-5 per day, depending on length of stay.

Medical insurance (especially university policies) often covers costs incurred abroad; check with your provider. **US Medicare** does not cover foreign travel. **Canadian** provincial health insurance plans increasingly do not cover foreign travel. Check with the provincial Ministry of Health or Health Plan Headquarters for details. **Homeowners' insurance** often covers theft during travel and loss of travel documents (passport, plane ticket, railpass, etc.) up to US$500.

ISIC and **ITIC** (p. 37) provide basic insurance benefits to US cardholders, including US$100 per day of in-hospital sickness for up to 60 days and US$5000 of accident-related medical reimbursement (see www.isicus.com for details). Cardholders have access to a toll-free **24hr.** helpline for medical, legal, and financial emergencies overseas. **American Express** (US ☎ 800-528-4800) grants most cardholders automatic collision and theft car rental insurance and ground travel accident coverage of US$100,000 on flight purchases made with the card.

ESSENTIALS

INSURANCE PROVIDERS

STA (p. 55) offers a range of plans that can supplement your basic coverage. Other private insurance providers in the US and Canada include: Access America (☎800-284-8300; www.accessamerica.com); Berkely Group (☎800-797-4514; www.berkely.com); Globalcare Travel Insurance (☎800-821-2488; www.globalcare-cocco.com); Travel Assistance International (☎800-821-2828; www.europ-assistance.com); and Travel Guard (☎800-826-4919; www.travelguard.com). Columbus Direct (☎020 7375 0011; www.columbusdirect.co.uk) operates in the UK and AFTA (☎02 9264 3299; www.afta.com.au) in Australia.

USEFUL ORGANIZATIONS AND PUBLICATIONS

The US **Center for Disease Control and Prevention** (**CDC;** ☎877-FYI-TRIP; fax 888-232-3299; www.cdc.gov/travel) maintains an international travelers' hotline and an informative website. The CDC's comprehensive booklet *Health Information for International Travel* (The Yellow Book), an annual rundown of disease, immunization, and general health advice, is free online or US$29-40 via the Public Health Foundation (☎877-252-1200; http://bookstore.phf.org). The **United States State Department** (http://travel.state.gov) compiles consular info sheets on health, entry requirements, and other issues for most countries of the world. Government agencies of other countries offer similar services: consult the appropriate government agency of your home country for consular info sheets on health, entry requirements, and other issues for various countries (see the listings in the box on **Travel Advisories,** p. 45). For quick info on health and other travel warnings, call the **Overseas Citizens Services** (M-F 8am-8pm ☎888-407-4747; after-hours 202-647-4000; from overseas 317-472-2328) or contact a passport agency, embassy, or consulate abroad. For info on medical evacuation and travel insurance firms, see the US government's website at http://travel.state.gov/medical.html or the **British Foreign and Commonwealth Office** (www.fco.gov.uk). For detailed info on travel health, try the **International Travel Health Guide,** by Stuart Rose, MD (purchase for US$19.95 or download for free at www.travmed.com). For general health info, contact the **American Red Cross** (☎800-564-1234; www.redcross.org). For a Thailand-specific overview of diseases check out MDtravelhealth.com (www.mdtravelhealth.com).

STAYING HEALTHY

Common sense is the simplest prescription for good health while you travel. Drink lots of fluids to prevent dehydration and constipation, and wear sturdy, broken-in shoes and clean socks. Sunscreen and heavy-duty bug spray are absolute essentials; make sure you apply them regularly to stay burn- and bite-free.

ONCE IN THAILAND

ENVIRONMENTAL HAZARDS

Heat exhaustion and dehydration: Heat exhaustion leads to nausea, excessive thirst, headaches, and dizziness. Avoid it by drinking fluids, eating salty foods, abstaining from dehydrating beverages (e.g. alcohol and caffeinated beverages), and wearing sunscreen. Adding salt or lemon juice to water can help. Continuous heat stress can lead to heatstroke, characterized by a temperature, severe headache, delirium, and cessation of sweating. Victims should be cooled off with wet towels and taken to a doctor.

Sunburn: Always wear sunscreen (SPF 30 is good) when spending excessive amounts of time outdoors. If you are planning on spending time on the beaches of Thailand, you are

ESSENTIALS

at a higher risk of getting burned, even through clouds. In the case of sunburn, drink more fluids than usual and apply an aloe-based lotion. Severe sunburns can lead to sun poisoning, a condition that affects the entire body, causing fever, chills, nausea, and vomiting. Sun poisoning should always be treated by a doctor.

High altitude: Trekking in northern Thailand can take you to areas of high altitude. Allow your body a couple of days to adjust to taking in less oxygen before exerting yourself. Note that alcohol is more potent and UV rays are stronger at high elevations.

INSECT-BORNE DISEASES

Many diseases are transmitted by insects, mainly **mosquitoes.** Be careful in wet or forested areas, especially while hiking and camping. Wear long pants and long sleeves, tuck your pants into your socks, and sleep under a mosquito net. While traveling in the *kos* and rural areas, you should be particularly careful. Use insect repellents containing DEET. Consider soaking or spraying your gear with permethrin (licensed in the US for use on clothing), but be aware that permethrin can cause an allergic reaction. Natural repellents include vitamin B-12 and garlic pills. Sleeping with a mosquito net is a good way to prevent being bitten at night. Mosquitoes—responsible for malaria, dengue fever, yellow fever, and Japanese encephalitis, among others—are particularly prevalent around the borders of Thailand. To stop the itch after being bitten, try Calamine lotion or topical cortisones like Cortaid, or take a bath with a half-cup of baking soda or oatmeal.

Malaria: Transmitted by *Anopheles* mosquitoes that bite at night. The incubation period varies anywhere between 10 days and 4 weeks. Early symptoms include fever, chills, aches, and fatigue, followed by high fever and sweating, sometimes with vomiting and diarrhea. See a doctor for any flu-like sickness that occurs after travel in a risk area. To reduce the risk of contracting malaria, use mosquito repellent, particularly in the evenings and when visiting forested areas. Make sure you see a doctor at least 4-6 weeks before a trip to a high-risk area to get up-to-date malaria prescriptions and recommendations. A doctor may prescribe oral prophylactics, like **mefloquine** (sold under the name Lariam) or **doxycycline** (ask your doctor for a prescription). Be aware that mefloquine can have very serious side effects, including paranoia, psychotic behavior, and nightmares, and doxycycline can result in severe sunburns.

Dengue fever: An "urban viral infection" transmitted by *Aedes* mosquitoes, which bite during the day rather than at night. The mosquitoes are distinguishable by their stripped legs. The incubation period is 3-14 days although the onset usually occurs between 4-7 days. Early symptoms include a high fever, severe headaches, swollen lymph nodes, and muscle aches. Many patients also suffer from nausea, vomiting, and a pink rash. If you experience these symptoms, see a doctor immediately, drink plenty of liquids, and take fever-reducing medication such as acetaminophen (Tylenol). *Never take aspirin to treat dengue fever.* There is no vaccine available for dengue fever.

Japanese encephalitis: Another mosquito-borne disease, most common during the rainy season in agricultural areas near rice fields and livestock. Aside from delirium, most symptoms are flu-like: chills, headache, fever, vomiting, muscle fatigue. Since the disease carries a high mortality rate, it's vital to go to a hospital as soon as symptoms appear. While the JE-VAX vaccine, usually given in 3 shots over a 30-day period, is effective for a year, it has caused serious side effects in some people. According to the CDC, there is little chance of being infected if you take proper precautions, such as using repellents containing DEET and sleeping under mosquito nets. The vaccine is recommended if you are planning on spending more than one month in rural Thailand.

Yellow fever: A viral disease transmitted by mosquitoes. Derives its name from one of its most common symptoms, the jaundice caused by liver damage. While most cases are mild, the severe ones begin with fever, headache, muscle pain, nausea, and abdominal pain before progressing to jaundice, vomiting of blood, and bloody stools. While there is no specific treatment, there is an effective vaccine that offers 10 years of protection. Thailand does not require that travelers have this vaccine unless they have traveled to an infected area (see www.thaiembdc.org for more info).

Other insect-borne diseases: Lymphatic filariasis is a roundworm infestation transmitted by mosquitoes. Infection causes enlargement of extremities and has no vaccine. The **plague** is still a risk as well. Early symptoms include fever, nausea, sore throat, and swollen lymph nodes. A vaccine is available for the plague; both diseases can be treated. In northern Thailand, travelers who eat raw or undercooked fish are at risk of picking up **liver flukes,** parasites found in the water, especially in the waters of Nong Han, the largest fresh-water lake in northeast Thailand.

FOOD- AND WATER-BORNE DISEASES

Thailand's **tap water** is not potable. It is not even safe for brushing teeth. Prevention is the best cure: be sure that your food is properly cooked and the water you drink is clean. Peel fruits and vegetables and avoid ice cubes and anything washed in tap water, like salad. Watch out for food from markets or street vendors that may have been cooked in unhygienic conditions.

Other potential culprits are raw shellfish, unpasteurized milk, and sauces containing raw eggs. Buy bottled water, or purify your own water by bringing it to a rolling boil or treating it with **iodine tablets.** Note, however, that some parasites such as *giardia* have exteriors resistant to iodine treatment, so boiling is more reliable. Most Western establishments, or Thai establishments that cater to tourists, serve water and ice that have been purified. The menu will usually say, but it never hurts to ask. Always wash your hands before eating or bring a purifying liquid hand cleaner. It may seem like a hassle, but your bowels will thank you.

Traveler's diarrhea: Results from drinking fecally contaminated water or eating uncooked and contaminated foods. Symptoms include nausea, bloating, and urgency. Try quick-energy, non-sugary foods with protein and carbohydrates to keep your strength up. Over-the-counter anti-diarrheals (e.g. Imodium) may counteract the problems. The most dangerous side effect is dehydration: drink 8 oz. of water with ½ tsp. of sugar or honey and a pinch of salt, try uncaffeinated soft drinks, or eat salted crackers. If you develop a fever or your symptoms don't go away after 4-5 days, consult a doctor. Consult a doctor immediately for treatment of diarrhea in children.

Cholera: An intestinal disease caused by a bacteria found in contaminated food. Symptoms include severe diarrhea, dehydration, vomiting, and muscle cramps. See a doctor immediately: if left untreated, it may be deadly, even within a few hours. Antibiotics are available, but the crucial treatment is rehydration. There is no vaccine in the US.

Dysentery: Results from a serious intestinal infection caused by certain bacteria in contaminated food or water. The most common type is bacillary dysentery. Symptoms include bloody diarrhea (sometimes mixed with mucus), fever, and abdominal pain and tenderness. Bacillary dysentery generally only lasts a week, but it is highly contagious. Amoebic dysentery, which develops more slowly, is a more serious disease and may cause long-term damage if left untreated. A stool test can determine which kind you have: seek medical help immediately. Dysentery can be treated with the drugs norfloxacin or ciprofloxacin (commonly known as Cipro). If you are traveling in high-risk (especially rural) regions, consider obtaining a prescription before you leave home. Dehydration can be a problem: be sure to drink plenty of water or eat salted crackers.

Hepatitis A: A viral infection of the liver acquired primarily through contaminated water, including through shellfish from contaminated water. Symptoms include fatigue, fever, loss of appetite, nausea, dark urine, jaundice, vomiting, aches and pains, and light stools. The risk is highest in rural areas and the countryside, but it is also present in

ESSENTIALS

urban areas. Ask your doctor about the Hepatitis A vaccine (Havrix or Vaqta) or an injection of immune globulin (IG; formerly called gamma globulin).

Giardiasis: Transmitted through parasites (microbes, tapeworms, etc.) and acquired by drinking untreated water from streams or lakes. Symptoms include diarrhea, abdominal cramps, bloating, fatigue, weight loss, and nausea. If untreated it can lead to severe dehydration.

Schistosomiasis: A parasitic disease caused when the larvae of a certain freshwater snail species penetrate unbroken skin. Symptoms include an itchy localized rash, followed in 4-6 weeks by fever, fatigue, headaches, muscle and joint aches, painful urination, diarrhea, nausea, loss of appetite, and night sweats. To avoid it, try not to swim in fresh water in areas with poor sanitation. If exposed to untreated water, rub the area vigorously with a towel and apply rubbing alcohol.

Typhoid fever: Caused by the salmonella bacteria. **Common in villages and rural areas in Thailand.** While mostly transmitted through contaminated food and water, it may also be acquired by direct contact. Early symptoms include a persistent, fever, headaches, fatigue, loss of appetite, constipation, and sometimes a rash on the abdomen or chest. Antibiotics can treat it, but the vaccination (70-90% effective) is recommended.

Leptospirosis: A bacterial disease caused by exposure to fresh water or soil contaminated by the urine of infected animals. Able to enter the human body through cut skin, mucus membranes, and through ingestion, it is most common in tropical climates. Symptoms include a high fever, chills, nausea, and vomiting. If not treated it can lead to liver failure and meningitis. There is no vaccine. Consult a doctor for treatment.

OTHER INFECTIOUS DISEASES

Rabies: Transmitted through the saliva of infected animals. Fatal if untreated. By the time symptoms (thirst and muscle spasms) appear, the disease is in its terminal stage. If you are bitten, wash the wound thoroughly, seek immediate medical care, and try to have the animal located. A rabies vaccine, which consists of 3 shots given over a 21-day period, is available and recommended for developing world travel, but is only semi-effective. Rabies is found all over the world and is often transmitted through dogs.

Hepatitis B: A viral infection of the liver transmitted via blood or other bodily fluids. Symptoms, which may not surface until years after infection, include jaundice, loss of appetite, fever, and joint pain. It is transmitted through activities like unprotected sex, injections of illegal drugs, and unprotected health work. A 3-shot vaccination sequence is recommended for health-care workers, sexually-active travelers, and anyone planning to seek medical treatment abroad. It must begin 6 mo. before traveling.

Hepatitis C: Like Hepatitis B, but the mode of transmission differs. IV drug users, those with occupational exposure to blood, hemodialysis patients, and recipients of blood transfusions are at the highest risk, but the disease can also be spread through sexual contact or sharing items like razors and toothbrushes that may have traces of blood on them. Usually, no symptoms, but if there are any, they can include loss of appetite, abdominal pain, fatigue, nausea, and jaundice. If untreated, it can lead to liver failure.

Severe Acute Respiratory Syndrome (SARS): A viral respiratory illness transmitted through droplets. Early symptoms include fever, chills, headache, and muscle ache. Steroids and antiviral agents such as oseltamivir and ribavirin have been used as therapy; in many cases, however, SARS is fatal.

AIDS, HIV, and STDs: Travelers seeking pleasure in the quasi-legal bars, massage parlors, and brothels of Patpong and similar red light districts stand a good chance of bringing back unwanted viral souvenirs of their trip. The best advice is to follow all precautions that apply to any sexual encounter: use a condom with spermicide, and avoid sex with strangers or with people who engage in high-risk behavior (such as IV drug use, promiscuity or unprotected sex). Many prostitutes do not know that they are infected, and even if they do, they probably won't tell their clients. Though protected commercial sex has risen to over 90%, there's still roughly 10% who aren't careful (p. 21). Condoms aren't always easy to find when traveling; and even if you do find them, Western brands tend to be more reliable, so bring a supply with you. *Never* share intravenous drug, tattooing, or other needles. For detailed info on Acquired Immune Deficiency Syndrome (AIDS) in Thailand, contact the Thai Red Cross Anonymous Clinic 104 Thanon Ratchadamri, Pathumwan, Bangkok, 10330 (☎02 252-2568), the US Centers for Disease Control's **24hr.** hotline (☎800-342-2437), or the Joint United Nations Programme on HIV/AIDS (UNAIDS), 20, ave. Appia, CH-1211 Geneva 27, Switzerland (☎41 22 791 3666; fax 22 791 4187). Gonorrhea, chlamydia, genital warts, syphilis, herpes, and other STDs are more common than HIV and certainly something to avoid. **Hepatitis** B and C can also be transmitted sexually. **Syphilis** and Hepatitis C can be deadly. Though condoms may protect you from some STDs, oral or even tactile contact can lead to transmission. If you think you may have contracted an STD, see a doctor immediately.

OTHER HEALTH CONCERNS

MEDICAL CARE ON THE ROAD
Hospitals in Thailand vary from region to region, but, generally, larger, centralized cities like Bangkok and Chiang Mai have high-quality facilities. Thailand's health-care system is balanced between public and private institutions. The public system often has limited technical support and is overcrowded and bureaucratic. Private hospitals are more likely to have English-speaking doctors, language interpreters, foreign insurance claim assistance, international emergency medical evacuation access, and embassy liaison services. Private healthcare is so good that an epidemic of medical tourism (both cosmetic and essential) has broken out. Not only is healthcare in Thailand much cheaper in most private hospitals than in the Western world, but foreigners are very well-taken care of.

General practitioners and dentists are readily available. Most medical staff at large medical institutions speak very good English. Thai medical services are always available: walk-in services are common during the daytime and many hospitals offer **24hr. emergency** room service. Unfortunately, emergency hotlines are only useful if you speak Thai. Watch closely to make sure that any instruments used during your treatment are thoroughly sanitized, and if you ever need an injection make sure the medical practitioner unwraps a new syringe.

If you are concerned about obtaining medical assistance while traveling, you may wish to employ special support services. The *MedPass* from **GlobalCare, Inc.,** 6875 Shiloh Rd. East, Alpharetta, GA 30005, USA (☎800-860-1111; fax 678-341-1800; www.globalcare.net), provides **24hr.** international medical assistance, support, and medical evacuation resources. The **International Association for Medical Assistance to Travelers** (IAMAT; US ☎716-754-4883, Canada 519-836-0102; www.cybermall.co.nz/NZ/IAMAT) has free membership, lists English-speaking doctors worldwide, and offers detailed info on immunization requirements and sanitation. **International Security Overseas (ISOS);** 331 N. Bridge Rd., #17-00 Odeon Towers, Singapore 188720 (www.internationalsos.com) provides medical services, travel insurance, and around-the-clock emergency assistance services. ISOS offers medical insurance for both short-term and long-term travel. Couples and families can purchase cheaper packages. Call ☎800-523-8930 for more info or to enroll in a plan. If your regular **insurance** policy does not cover travel abroad, you may wish to purchase additional coverage (p. 48).

Those with medical conditions (such as diabetes, or heart conditions) may want to obtain a **Medic Alert** membership (first year US$35, annually thereafter US$20), which includes a stainless steel ID tag and a **24hr.** collect-call number, among other benefits. Contact the Medic Alert Foundation, 2323 Colorado Ave., Turlock, CA 95382, USA (☎888-633-4298, outside US 209-668-3333; www.medicalert.org).

WOMEN'S HEALTH

Women traveling in unsanitary conditions are vulnerable to **urinary tract** and **bladder infections,** common and severely uncomfortable bacterial conditions that cause a burning sensation and painful, frequent urination. Over-the-counter medications can sometimes alleviate symptoms, but if they persist, do not hesitate to see a doctor. Thailand's hot and humid climate also makes women especially susceptible to **vaginal yeast infections.** Wearing loose trousers or a skirt and cotton underwear will help, as will over-the-counter remedies like Monistat or Gynelotrimin. Bring supplies from home if you are prone to infection. In a pinch, some travelers use natural alternatives such as a plain yogurt and lemon juice douche.

Since **tampons, pads,** and reliable **contraceptive devices** are sometimes hard to find, bring supplies from home. Most toiletries can be found in Western establishments like UK's Boots on Khaosan Rd. and malls on Silom Rd. in Bangkok. Women using birth control pills should bring enough to allow for possible loss or extended stays. Also bring a prescription, since forms of the pill vary considerably. However, if you need contraceptive services, contact the Planned Parenthood Association of Thailand in Bangkok, 8 Soi Vibhavadi-Rangsit 44, Superhighway, Ladyao, Chatuchak, Bangkok 10900 (☎02 941 2320; ppat@samart.co.th; www.ipp.org). English is the primary language spoken at the branch. **Abortion** is legal in Thailand, but only in cases where the woman's health is in danger or she has been raped.

TOILETS

If you've never been to the developing world before (and even if you have), you may never have seen toilets quite like those you'll find in Thailand. While many tourist-oriented establishments have Western toilets, some don't, especially the farther away you get from big cities. If you do encounter a squat toilet, don't panic; using one may take some practice, but it is very manageable. Most squat toilets are porcelain bowls set in the ground with raised foot grooves on either side. You are expected to put a foot on either side of the bowl and then squat down. Remember to take your time—you don't want to lose your balance. Next to the toilet there will be a container of water and a small bucket, which is used both to wash yourself and flush the toilet (scoop water in the bucket, pour the water in the toilet, and the water will disappear). Many foreigners choose to carry toilet paper with them in case they need to use a squat toilet, but putting this in the toilet is not a good idea. Instead, many establishments put a wastepaper basket next to the toilet for their disposal. Also, a bottle of hand sanitizer comes in handy after using a squat toilet—just remember, there's a reason people don't eat with their left hands!

GETTING TO THAILAND

BY PLANE

When it comes to airfare, a little effort can save you a bundle. If your plans are flexible enough to deal with the restrictions, courier fares are the cheapest. Tickets bought from consolidators and standby seating are also good deals, but last-minute specials, airfare wars, and charter flights often beat these fares. The key is to hunt around, to be flexible, and to ask persistently about discounts. Students, seniors, and those under 26 should never pay full price for a ticket

Thailand has four major **international airports:** Bangkok (p. 93), Chiang Mai (p. 265), Phuket (p. 362), and Hat Yai (p. 385). Many international airlines fly to these destinations, including **Thai Airways** (US ☎800-426-5204 or Thailand 02 1566; www.thaiairways.com) and **Bangkok Airways** (US ☎866-226-4565 or Thailand 02 265 5555; www.bangkokair.com).

AIRFARES

Airfares to Thailand peak between July and August. Holidays are also expensive. During the rest of the year, the fares should be about the same. Midweek (M-Th morning) round-trip flights run US$40-50 cheaper than weekend flights, but they are generally more crowded and less likely to permit frequent-flier upgrades. Not fixing a return date ("open return") or arriving in and departing from different cities ("open-jaw") can be pricier than round-trip flights. For example, a New York-Chiang Mai and Bangkok-New York trip tends to be pricier than a round-trip to Bangkok and a one-way flight to Chiang Mai would be. Patching one-way flights together is the least economical way to travel. Flights between Thailand's capitals or regional hubs, such as Chiang Mai and Ko Samui, will tend to be cheaper, and domestic flights can usually be purchased just hours in advance.

If Thailand is one stop on a more extensive globe-hop, consider a round-the-world ticket. Tickets usually include at least five stops and are valid for about a year. Prices range US$3400-5000. Try **Northwest Airlines/KLM** (US ☎800-447-4747; www.nwa.com) or **Star Alliance,** a consortium of 22 airlines, including United Airlines (US ☎800-241-6522; www.staralliance.com). For a more localized trip, look into Southeast Asia regional package tickets offered by **Cathay Pacific Airlines** (www.cathaypacific.com).

Fares for round-trip flights to Bangkok from the US or Canadian east coast cost US$800-4000; from the US or Canadian west coast US$700-2500; from the UK, UK£450-1500; from Australia AUS$1400-3000; from New Zealand NZ$1400-3000.

BUDGET AND STUDENT TRAVEL AGENCIES

While knowledgeable agents specializing in flights to Thailand can make your life easy and help you save, they may not spend the time to find you the lowest possible fare because they get paid on commission. Travelers holding **ISIC** and **IYTC cards** (p. 37) qualify for big discounts from student travel agencies. Most flights from budget agencies are on major airlines, but in peak season some may sell seats on less reliable chartered aircraft.

CTS Travel, 30 Rathbone Pl., London W1T 1GQ, UK (☎0207 290 0630; www.ctstravel.co.uk). A British student travel agent with offices in 39 countries including the US (Empire State Building, 350 Fifth Ave., Suite 7813, New York, NY 10118; ☎877-287-6665; www.ctstravelusa.com).

STA Travel, 5900 Wilshire Blvd., Suite 900, Los Angeles, CA 90036, USA (24hr. reservations and info ☎800-781-4040; www.sta-travel.com). A student and youth travel organization with over 150 offices worldwide (check their website for a listing of all their offices), including US offices in Boston, Chicago, L.A., New York, San Francisco, Seattle, and Washington, D.C. Ticket booking, travel insurance, railpasses, and more. Walk-in offices are located throughout Australia (☎03 9349 4344), New Zealand (☎09 309 9723), and the UK (☎0870 1 600 599).

Travel CUTS (Canadian Universities Travel Services Limited), 187 College St., Toronto, ON M5T 1P7 (☎416-979-2406; www.travelcuts.com). Offices across Canada and the US, including Los Angeles, Montreal, New York, San Francisco, and Vancouver.

USIT, 19-21 Aston Quay, Dublin 2 (☎01 602 1777; www.usitworld.com). Ireland's leading student/budget travel agency has 22 offices throughout Northern Ireland and the Republic of Ireland. Offers programs to work in North America.

COMMERCIAL AIRLINES

The commercial airlines' lowest regular offer is the **APEX** (Advance Purchase Excursion) fare, which provides confirmed reservations and allows "open-jaw" tickets. Generally, reservations must be made seven to 21 days ahead of departure, with seven- to 14-day minimum-stay and up to 90-day maximum-stay. These fares carry hefty cancellation and change penalties (fees rise in summer). Book peak-season APEX fares early. Use **Airtreks** (www.airtreks.com), **Expedia** (www.expedia.com), or **Travelocity** (www.travelocity.com) to get an idea of the lowest published fares, then use the resources outlined here to try and beat those fares.

AIR COURIER FLIGHTS

Those who travel light should consider being an air courier. Couriers transport cargo on international flights by using their checked luggage space for freight. Generally, couriers must travel with carry-ons only and deal with complex flight restrictions. Most flights are round-trip only, with short fixed-length stays (usually one week) and a limit of one ticket per issue. Most of these flights also operate only out of major gateway cities, mostly in North America. Round-trip courier fares from the US to Thailand run about US$600. Most flights leave from Los Angeles, Miami, New York, or San Francisco in the US, and from Montreal, Toronto, or Vancouver in Canada. Generally, you must be over 21 (in some cases 18). In summer, the most popular destinations usually require an advance reservation of about two weeks (you can usually book up to two months ahead). Super-discounted fares are common for "last-minute" flights (three to 14 days ahead). For more info about courier flights check out www.aircourier.org or www.courier.org.

TICKET CONSOLIDATORS

Ticket consolidators, or **"bucket shops,"** buy unsold tickets in bulk from commercial airlines and sell them at discounted rates. The best place to look is in the Sunday travel section of any major newspaper (such as the *New York Times*), where many bucket shops place tiny ads. Call quickly, as availability is typically extremely limited. Not all bucket shops are reliable, so insist on a receipt that gives full details of restrictions, refunds, and tickets, and pay by credit card (in spite of the 2-5% fee) so you can stop payment if you never receive your tickets. For more info, see www.travel-library.com/air-travel/consolidators.html.

TRAVELING FROM THE US AND CANADA

Travel Avenue (☎800-333-3335; www.travelavenue.com) searches for the best published fare and then uses several consolidators to attempt to beat it. **NOW Voyager,** 315 W. 49th St. Plaza Arcade, New York, NY 10019 (☎212-459-1616; www.nowvoyagertravel.com) arranges discounted flights, mostly from New York to Bangkok. Other consolidators worth trying are **Rebel** (☎800-732-3588; www.rebeltours.com), **Flights.com** (www.flights.com), **Cheap Tickets** (☎800-652-4327; www.cheaptickets.com), and **TravelHUB** (www.travelhub.com). Remember these are just suggestions to get you started: *Let's Go* does not endorse any of these agencies—be cautious, and research companies before you hand over your credit card number.

TRAVELING FROM THE UK AND IRELAND
In **London,** the Air Travel Advisory Bureau (☎ 087 0737 0023; www.atab.co.uk) can provide names of reliable consolidators and discount flight specialists.

TRAVELING FROM AUSTRALIA AND NEW ZEALAND
In **Australia** and **New Zealand,** look for consolidator ads in the travel section of the *Sydney Morning Herald,* the *New Zealand Herald,* and other papers

CHARTER FLIGHTS

Charters are flights a tour operator contracts with an airline to fly extra loads of passengers during peak season. Charter flights fly less frequently than major airlines, make refunds particularly difficult, and are almost always fully booked. Schedules and itineraries may also change or be cancelled at the last moment without a full refund, and check-in, boarding, and baggage claim are often much slower. However, they can also be cheaper. Discount clubs and fare brokers offer members savings on last-minute charter deals. Study contracts closely; you don't want to end up with an unwanted overnight layover.

AROUND SOUTHEAST ASIA

Flights between countries in Southeast Asia are inexpensive. Find the best deals on tickets in capital cities. Popular airlines include Air Asia (southeast Asia's first budget carrier; flights within Thailand can be as little as US$10), Malaysia Airlines, Singapore Airlines, Thai International, Cathay Pacific, and KLM Airlines. Booking tickets should be relatively worry-free, but travel agents can scam you. Be sure to make sure your deal is legitimate before you buy. *Let's Go* lists reliable tourist offices and travel offices in the **Practical Information** section of large cities. In general, use common sense—don't trust agents vending tickets in coffee bars. Always reconfirm with the airlines after receiving your ticket.

BY BUS

Thailand can be reached by bus from Cambodia, Laos, Malaysia, and Myanmar. A/C buses are usually very comfortable and reliable, but others offer sparse leg room and bumpy rides. Inquire about purchasing tickets, as some buses require reservations in advance, whereas others sell tickets upon departure and don't leave the station until completely full. Check visa availability before taking a bus ride; visas may not always be available at the border and must be acquired in advance in other towns. Most tourist cafes can help you with info and reservations.

BY BOAT

Boat trips from Malaysia to Thailand are possible, particularly from one point on the Malay peninsula to another. There's a ferry from Pulau Langkawi in Malaysia to Satun (180), though boats are not the best way to travel in Southeast Asia. They're generally slow and unreliable.

BY LAND

Overland border crossing points represent legal points of transit between Southeast Asian countries. Check local news agencies and embassies to confirm which border crossing points are open. Though Thailand's border crossing regulations remain stable, those of its neighboring countries do not. The result is unpredictable closings of crossing points, particularly with Malaysia and Myanmar.

ESSENTIALS

BORDER CROSSINGS

CAMBODIA. Border crossings include: **Aranyaprathet** to **Poipet** (p. 160), from **Chong Jiam** (p. 216), or via a **Trat-Sihanoukville** boat (p. 153).

LAOS. Border crossings include: **Chiang Khong** to **Houie Xay** (p. 334), **Nong Khai** to **Vientiane** (p. 245), **Nakhon Phanom** to **Tha Kaek** (p. 231), **Mukdahan** to **Savannakhet** (p. 228), **Chong Mek** to **Vang Tao** (p. 224).

MALAYSIA. Border crossings include: **Satun** to **Kuala Perlis**, **Padang Besar** to **Kangar**, **Betong** to **Keroh**, or **Sungai Kolok** to **Kota Bharu** (p. 389).

MYANMAR. Border crossings include: **Mae Sai** (p. 327), **Mae Sot** (p. 302), or the **Three Pagoda Pass** (p. 184). These border crossing points close the most frequently and unexpectedly, so check at the local embassy first.

GETTING AROUND THAILAND

Thailand has every type of vehicle imaginable. From buses to *tuk-tuks*, you'll find detailed info on transportation options in the **Local Transportation** section of each city. Here's a glimpse of Thailand's most common mechanical marvels:

LOCAL TRANSPORTATION	
Motorcycle taxi	A death-defying ride on the back of a speeding motorcycle. One passenger only.
Samlor	A three-wheeled vehicle, more primitive than the tuk-tuk. Can be man-powered (pedaled) or motorized.
Songthaew	Four-wheeled pickup with two rows of seats added to the bed. More room but less spunk than a tuk-tuk.
Tuk-tuk	An opinionated and noisy three-wheeled truck that spitters and sputters on every road in Thailand.

BY PLANE

It is possible to travel by plane within Thailand, but be aware of possible safety risks. Thai Airways (p. 55) has a near-monopoly within the country, with extensive domestic connections. Bangkok Airways' (p. 55) most popular destinations include Ko Samui and Phuket. Other airlines include Air Andaman (www.airandaman.com), Air Asia (www.airasia.com), and PBAir (www.pbair.com); all offer flights to Thailand's major cities.

AIRCRAFT SAFETY. The airlines of developing world nations do not always meet safety standards. The *Official Airline Guide* (www.oag.com) and many travel agencies can tell you the type and age of aircraft on a particular route. This can be especially useful in Southeast Asia, where less reliable equipment is often used for internal or short flights. The **International Airline Passengers Association** (US ☎800-821-4272, UK 020 8681 6555) provides region-specific safety info. The **Federal Aviation Administration** (www.faa.gov) reviews the airline authorities for countries whose airlines enter the US. **US State Department** travel advisories (☎202-647-5225; http://travel.state.gov/travel_warnings.html) sometimes involve foreign carriers, especially when terrorist bombings or hijackings may be a threat.

BY TRAIN AND BUS

The **State Railway of Thailand** (☎02 220 4334; www.thailandrailway.com) operates an efficient, cheap rail system with three main train routes starting in Bangkok: north to Chiang Mai, south to Malaysia and Singapore, and northeast to Nong Khai and Ubon Ratchathani. Minor routes connect Bangkok to Kanchanaburi and cities north of the eastern seaboard. For long rides (over 3hr.), **third-class** travel can be uncomfortable. Unless otherwise specified, train fares given in this book are for third class travel on regular trains. Depending on the type of train and class of travel, your fare may vary. **Second-class** sleeping berths carry an additional charge of 100-320฿ (depending on the type of train, fan or A/C, and upper or lower bunk) and often sell out. **Rapid** (40฿ extra), **Express** (60฿ extra), and **Special Express** (80฿) trains come next in price and are speedier than ordinary trains.

Public buses are the cheapest and easiest way to travel short distances but blue A/C buses are recommended for longer transits. These buses generally cost twice as much, make fewer stops, and are mostly used by tourists.

BY CAR

Travel by car is largely unnecessary because of the wide range of public transportation options available to travelers. Other rental options, such as bicycles and motorbikes, are also plentiful. A good resource for info on international automobile travel is the **Association for Safe International Road Travel** (www.asirt.org).

RENTING

Car rental is not only rare but unreliable. If you do choose to rent a car, make reservations before you leave by calling major international offices in your home country. However, occasionally the price and availability info they give won't jive with what the local offices will tell you. Try checking with both offices to make sure you get the best price and most accurate info. Local desk numbers are included in town listings. For home-country numbers, call your toll-free directory. Rental agencies, particularly Western ones like AVIS and Budget, are fairly safe, although a safe car won't protect you from bad road conditions and other drivers. AVIS and Budget both rent cars all over Thailand. Below is a listing of their primary locations. Other locations can be found on their respective websites.

Generally, the minimum age to rent a car is 21 in Thailand. Some agencies require renters to be 25, and most charge those aged 21-24 an additional surcharge. Policies and prices vary from agency to agency. Small local operations occasionally rent to people under 21, but be sure to ask about the insurance coverage and deductible, and always check the fine print. Higher-end hotels will arrange a **"self-service"** (rental) car for you.

AVIS, (www.avis.com), has a location at the **Bangkok International Airport** on the first floor of Meeting Hall. Open daily 7am-midnight. Other locations in **Bangkok:** 2/12 Wireless Rd., Bangkok 10330 (☎02 255 5300), open daily 8am-6pm; Le Meridien President Hotel, 971 Ploenchit Rd., Bangkok 10330 (☎02 253 0444), open daily 8am-6pm. In **Chiang Mai:** Royal Princess Chiang Mai Hotel, 122 Changklan Rd., Chiang Mai (☎053 281 0336), open daily 8am-8pm; 60/27 **Chiang Mai Airport,** Chiang Mai 50200, open daily 8am-9pm.

Budget Rental, (US and Canada international reservations ☎800-467-9337; www.budget.com) has three main locations in **Bangkok:** Tesco Lotus Rama 4, 3300 Rama 4, Kwang Klongton, Bangkok 10230; 19/23 Royal City Avenue, New Phetchburi Rd., Bangkok 10320; 335/16 Don Muang Railway Station, Viphavadee Rungsit Rd.,

Do you travel ?
get online !

A website made for travel enthusiasts.

www.GLOBOsapiens.com®

Get the hottest

insider travel tips

**Pictures - Travel Reports - Slide Shows
Chat - Forum - Friendships
Hostels - Member Pages - E-Cards**

it's free!
LG078
Registration code

If you are into travel, you are going to love **GLOBOsapiens**®!

Bangkok 10320. In **Chiang Mai:** Tambon Haiya 201/2 Mahidol Rd., Tumbon Suthep Muang, Chiang Mai 50100.

COSTS AND INSURANCE

Rental car prices start at around 1500฿ a day for a compact car. Expect to pay more for larger cars and 4WD. Cars with **automatic transmission** can cost more than standard manuals (stick shift), and in some places can be hard to find. It is virtually impossible, no matter where you are, to find an automatic 4WD.

Many rental packages offer unlimited kilometers, while others offer a certain number of kilometers per day with a surcharge for every kilometer after that. Return the car with a full tank of petrol to avoid high fuel charges at the end. Be sure to ask whether the price includes **insurance** against theft and collision. Remember that if you are driving a conventional vehicle on an **unpaved road** in a rental car, you are almost never covered by insurance. Ask about this before leaving the rental agency. Beware that cars rented on an **American Express** or **Visa/Mastercard Gold or Platinum** credit cards in Thailand might *not* carry the automatic insurance that they would in some other countries: check with your credit card company. Insurance plans almost always come with an **excess** (deductible) for conventional vehicles which is higher for younger drivers and 4WD. This means you pay for all damages up to that sum, unless they are the fault of another driver. The excess you will be quoted applies to collisions with other vehicles; collisions with non-vehicles, such as trees ("single-vehicle collisions") will cost even more. The excess can often be reduced or waived if you pay an additional daily charge.

National chains often allow pickup in one city and drop-off in another. There is usually a minimum hire period and sometimes an extra drop-off charge.

ON THE ROAD

> **! DRIVING PRECAUTIONS.** Bring substantial amounts of water (a suggested 5 liters per person per day) for drinking and the radiator. For long drives to unpopulated areas, register with police before beginning the trek, and again upon arrival at the destination. Check with the local automobile club for details. When traveling for long distances, make sure tires are in good repair and have enough air, and get good maps. A **compass** and a **car manual** can also be very useful. You should always carry a **spare tire** and **jack, jumper cables, extra oil, flares, a flashlight,** and **heavy blankets** (in case your car breaks down at night or in the winter). If you don't know how to **change a tire,** learn before heading out, especially if you are planning on traveling in deserted areas. Blowouts on dirt roads are exceedingly common. If you do have a breakdown, **stay with your car:** if you wander off, there's less likelihood trackers will find you.

Driving in Thailand can be confusing at best, and downright dangerous at worst. Avoid driving in Bangkok at any cost. In the rest of Thailand, drivers tend to ignore international driving rules, and cars travel on both sides of the road without discrimination. While road signs are constantly being updated, many are still only in Thai script. Asking for directions can be difficult if locals do not speak English. If you decide to drive, get a good road map, like the **Thailand Atlas,** by Lotus Image, or the **Road Atlas of Thailand,** by Asia Books. Local tourist offices or guesthouses may also have maps. **Gasoline** prices vary, but average about 18 *baht* per liter.

A better option may be **chauffeured vans,** which can be rented out to small groups. The driver, who often serves as an impromptu tour guide, can take you wherever you wish. The vans are comparably priced to rental cars, and arrangements can be made by most upscale hotels.

CAR ASSISTANCE. International SOS, 331 North Bridge Road, #17-00 Odeon Towers, Singapore, 188720 (☎ 65 6338 2311; www.internationalsos.com) provides roadside assistance to members, along with other emergency services.

DRIVING PERMITS AND CAR INSURANCE

INTERNATIONAL DRIVING PERMIT (IDP)

If you plan to drive a car while in Thailand, you must be over 18 and have an International Driving Permit (IDP). An application for an IDP usually requires one or two photos, a current license, an additional form of ID, and a fee. To apply, contact a branch of your home country's automobile association. Thailand can also grant IDPs if you take the road test, but unless you speak fluent Thai, get it at home. Be careful when purchasing an IDP online or anywhere other than your automobile association. Many vendors sell fake permits for higher prices.

CAR INSURANCE

Most credit cards cover standard insurance. If you rent, lease, or borrow a car, you will need a **green card,** or **International Insurance Certificate,** to certify that you have liability insurance and that it applies abroad. Green cards can be obtained at car rental agencies, car dealers (for those leasing cars), some travel agents, and some border crossings. Rental agencies may require you to purchase theft insurance in countries that they consider to have a high risk of auto theft.

BY MOTORBIKE AND BICYCLE

Almost every kind of personal vehicle short of a pogo stick can be rented in Thailand. Motorbikes and bicycles are the most common and often quite convenient. Always rent a helmet. If possible, ask other travelers in the area what their experience has been with local rental agencies before renting.

BY FOOT

Walking around in Thai cities can be a bit confusing. The street numbering system (see below) and street signs are indecipherable to the uninitiated. As there is no official transliteration system, Thai street names are often spelled in multiple ways, even in the same city. Minor roads that split off a main thoroughfare are called *sois* (alleys), although they can often be sizable roads.

> **TIP** **1, 2, 3, 5...4?** You're not on the wrong block. Street numbers, called Laek Ti, often consist of two pairs of numbers, divided by a slash. The numbers before the slash refer to the lots numbers, which are assigned according to the order in which they were drawn on to the city plan, and not to their relative locations. Numbers after the slash refer to the buildings within the lots; thankfully, most of these numbers are ordered numerically to their relative locations.

BY THUMB

> **!** *Let's Go* never recommends hitchhiking as a safe means of transportation, and none of the info presented here is intended to do so.

Let's Go strongly urges you to consider the risks before you choose to hitchhike. Though the Thai people are kind and generous, hitchhiking is never a safe option. Pay the extra *baht,* and take something official.

ESSENTIALS

KEEPING IN TOUCH

BY MAIL

SENDING MAIL HOME FROM THAILAND

Airmail is the best way to send mail home from Thailand. **Aerogrammes,** printed sheets that fold into envelopes and travel via airmail, are available at post offices. Write "airmail," *"par avion,"* or "airmail" in your language on the front. Most post offices will charge exorbitant fees or simply refuse to send aerogrammes with enclosures. **Surface mail** is by far the cheapest and slowest way to send mail. It takes one to two months to cross the Atlantic and one to three to cross the Pacific—good for heavy items you won't need for a while, such as souvenirs, or other articles you've acquired along the way that are weighing down your pack.

SENDING MAIL TO THAILAND

Mail in Thailand is quite reliable. To ensure timely delivery, mark envelopes "airmail," or "par avion." Expect standard mail to take 2-3 weeks to reach major cities and longer to get to rural areas. In addition to the standard postage system whose rates are listed below, **Federal Express** (Australia ☎ 13 26 10, Canada and US 800-463-3339, Ireland 1800 535 800, New Zealand 0800 733 339, UK 0800 123 800; www.fedex.com) handles express mail services from most countries to Thailand. For example, they can get a letter from New York to Thailand in 1-3 days for US$37, and from London to Thailand in 2-3 days for UK£33.

RECEIVING MAIL IN THAILAND

There are several ways to arrange pick-up of letters sent to you by friends and relatives while you are abroad. Mail can be sent via **Poste Restante** (the international phrase for General Delivery) to almost any city or town in Thailand with a post office, usually for no surcharge. Address *Poste Restante* letters to the recipient, with the last name underlined and in capital letters: "Stephen FAN, Poste Restante, Bangkok, Thailand." The mail will go to a special desk in the central post office, unless you specify a post office by street address or postal code. It's best to use the largest post office, since mail may be sent there regardless. It is usually safer and quicker, though more expensive, to send mail express or registered. Bring your passport (or other photo ID) for pick-up. If the clerks insist that there is nothing for you, have them check under your first name as well. *Let's Go* lists post offices in the **Practical Information** section for each city and most towns.

    American Express's travel offices throughout the world offer a free **Client Letter Service** (mail held up to 30 days and forwarded upon request) for cardholders who contact them in advance. Address letters as shown above. Some offices offer these services to non-cardholders (especially AmEx Travelers Cheque holders), but call ahead to make sure. *Let's Go* lists AmEx office locations for most large cities in **Practical Information** sections. For a complete free list, call US ☎ 800-528-4800.

BY TELEPHONE

CALLING HOME FROM THAILAND

A **calling card** is probably your cheapest bet. Calls are billed collect or to your account. You can frequently call collect without even possessing a company's calling card just by calling their access number and following the instructions. **To**

obtain a calling card from your national telecommunications service before leaving home, contact the appropriate company listed below (using the numbers in the middle column). To **call home with a calling card,** contact the operator for your service provider in Thailand by dialing the appropriate toll-free access number (listed below in the right-most column). International calling booths abound. For a small fee, some may let you receive a call as well if you ask nicely. Many hostels also have International Direct Dial (IDD) facilities.

COMPANY	TO OBTAIN A CARD, DIAL:	TO CALL ABROAD, DIAL:
AT&T (US)	800-364-9292	001 999 11111
British Telecom Direct	800 34 51 44	001 999 44 1066
Canada Direct	800-561-8868	001 999 15 1000
MCI (US)	800-777-5000	001 999 12001
Telecom New Zealand	3 374 0253	001 999 64 1066
Telstra Australia	13 22 00	001 800 611 9999

You can usually also make **direct international calls** from pay phones, but if you aren't using a calling card, you may need to drop your coins as quickly as your words. Prepaid phone cards and occasionally major credit cards can be used for direct international calls, but they are generally less cost-efficient. Placing a **collect call** through an international operator is even more expensive, but may be necessary in case of emergency. You can place collect calls through the service providers listed above even if you don't have one of their phone cards. Alternatively, **the Communications Authority of Thailand** (CAT) has many offices throughout Thailand offering various telecommunications resources, including international phones.

PLACING INTERNATIONAL CALLS. To call Thailand from home or to call home from Thailand, dial:

1. The **international dialing prefix.** To call from **Australia,** dial 0011; **Canada** or the **US,** 011; **Ireland, New Zealand,** or the **UK,** 00; **Thailand,** 001.
2. The **country code** of the country you want to call. For **Australia,** dial 61; **Canada** or the **US,** 1; **Ireland,** 353; **New Zealand,** 64; the **UK,** 44; **Thailand,** 66.
3. The **city/area code.** Let's Go lists the city/area codes for cities and towns in Thailand opposite the city or town name, next to a ☎. If the first digit is a zero (e.g., 020 for London), omit the zero when calling from abroad (e.g., dial 20 from Canada to reach London).
4. The **local number.**

CALLING WITHIN THAILAND

The simplest way to call within the country is to use a coin-operated phone. **Prepaid phone cards** (available at many guesthouses, shops, and restaurants), which carry a certain amount of phone time depending on the card's denomination, usually save time and money in the long run. Just insert them into the phone and proceed with your call. Other prepaid phone cards come with a Personal Identification Number (PIN) and a toll-free access number. Call the access number and follow the directions on the phone to make both international and domestic calls. Purchase them in advance from major telephone companies in your country, and make sure that company services the region where you'll be traveling. Phone rates typically tend to be highest in the morning, lower in the evening, and lowest on Sunday and late at night. When a telephone number listed has six digits it should be preceded by the full dialing prefix for the city being called (including the 0) when being called from out of town. Conversely, numbers beginning with 01, 06, or 09 are cell phones and should be dialed as listed.

CELLULAR PHONES

Cell phones are extremely popular in Thailand, from the normal garden-variety flip phone to the more exotic (and entertaining, one can guess) karaoke phone. All varieties can be found in cell phone or electronic stores in most large towns and cities. Cell phones in Thailand operate on **GSM**, a system that began in Europe and has spread to much of the rest of the world. To make and receive calls in Thailand you will need a **GSM-compatible phone** within the 900-MHz range and a **SIM (subscriber identity module) card,** a country-specific, thumbnail-sized chip that gives you a local phone number and plugs you into the local network. SIM cards are sold virtually everywhere; most convenience stores carry them. Many SIM cards are **prepaid,** meaning that they come with calling time included and you don't need to sign up for a monthly service plan. Incoming calls are frequently free. When you use up the prepaid time, you can buy additional cards or vouchers to get more. For more info on GSM phones, check out www.telestial.com, www.orange.co.uk, or www.roadpost.com. 1-2-Call Co. has the best overall coverage throughout Thailand. Companies like **Cellular Abroad** (www.cellular-abroad.com), **Planet Omni** (www.planetomni.com), and **Travel Cell** (www.travel-cell.com) rent cell phones that work in a variety of destinations around the world, providing a simpler option than picking up a phone in-country.

> **TIP** **GSM PHONES.** Just having a GSM phone doesn't mean you're necessarily good to go when you travel abroad. The majority of GSM phones sold in the United States operate on a different **frequency** (1900) than international phones (900/1800) and will not work abroad. Tri-band phones work on all three frequencies (900/1800/1900) and will operate through most of the world. As well, some GSM phones are **SIM-locked** and will only accept SIM cards from a single carrier. You'll need a **SIM-unlocked** phone to use a SIM card from a local carrier when you travel.

Before settling on a calling card plan, be sure to research your options in order to pick the one that best fits both your needs and your destination.

TIME DIFFERENCES

Thailand is seven hours ahead of **Greenwich Mean Time (GMT)**. It is 14 hours ahead of Vancouver and San Francisco, 11 hours ahead of New York, six hours ahead of London, three hours behind Sydney, and five hours behind Auckland, although the actual time differences depend on **Daylight Saving Time (DST),** which Thailand does not observe (see inside back cover). A useful resource is the World Time Server (www.worldtimeserver.com), which lists the current time in numerous locations worldwide, as well as whether the location is operating on Standard Time or DST.

BY EMAIL AND INTERNET

Internet cafes are everywhere in Thailand. Many guesthouses have Internet access, and you can often log on for free at a public library. *Let's Go* lists Internet access locations in the **Practical Information** sections of most cities and towns. Often Internet access is listed as **CATNET,** an access network.

Though in some places it's possible to forge a remote link with your home server, in most cases this is much slower (and more expensive) than taking advantage of free **web-based email accounts** (e.g., www.hotmail.com or www.yahoo.com).

ACCOMMODATIONS

Choosing accommodations in Thailand can sometimes be a gamble, as electricity, running water, and air-conditioning have not yet reached many rural areas. Finding inexpensive accommodations, however, never proves to be a problem. For a few dollars, facilities can vary from a shared room with several beds to a single room with a private bath and fan. Modern and more expensive hotels can be found in highly touristed areas, allowing for a cooler, more comfortable stay.

While you should make reservations at the more expensive lodgings, finding a hotel on a day's notice is not difficult. It is not uncommon, and often you are expected, to ask to see rooms before committing to a hotel. This also makes it easier to bargain. Some hotels and guesthouses require that you leave your passport with them during your stay. If you feel uncomfortable about doing this, some places will allow you to leave your customs slip from immigration.

HOSTELS

Many hostels are laid out dorm-style, often with large single-sex rooms and bunk beds, although private rooms that sleep two to four are becoming more common. They sometimes have kitchens and utensils for your use, bike or moped rentals, storage areas, transportation to airports, breakfast and other meals, laundry facilities, and Internet access. There can be drawbacks: some hostels close during certain daytime "lockout" hours, have a curfew, don't accept reservations, impose a maximum stay, or, less frequently, require that you do chores. In Thailand, a dorm bed in a hostel will average around 60-120฿ and a private room around 100-300฿. All dorm prices throughout the book are listed per person.

> **A HOSTELER'S BILL OF RIGHTS.** There are certain standard features that we do not include in our hostel listings. Unless we state otherwise, you can expect that every hostel has no lockout, no curfew, a kitchen, free hot showers, some system of secure luggage storage, and no key deposit.

HOSTELLING INTERNATIONAL

Joining the youth hostel association in your own country automatically grants you membership privileges in Hostelling International (HI), a federation of national hosteling associations. Non-HI members may be allowed to stay in some hostels, but will have to pay extra. HI hostels are generally concentrated in central and northern Thailand. The Thai Youth Hostels Association's web page (www.tyha.org), which lists the web addresses and phone numbers of all hostels, can be a great place to begin researching hosteling in a specific region. Other comprehensive hosteling websites include www.hostels.com and www.hostelplanet.com.

Most HI hostels also honor **guest memberships**—you'll get a blank card with space for six validation stamps. Each night you'll pay a non-member supplement (one-sixth the membership fee) and earn one guest stamp. Get six stamps, and you're a member. Most student travel agencies (p. 55) sell HI cards, as do all of the national hosteling organizations listed below. All prices listed below are valid for **one-year memberships** unless otherwise noted.

Australia: Australian Youth Hostels Association (AYHA), 422 Kent St., Sydney, NSW 200 (☎02 9261 1111; www.yha.com.au). AUS$52, under 18 AUS$19.

Canada: Hostelling International-Canada (HI-C), 205 Catherine St. #400, Ottawa, ON K2P 1C3 (☎613-237-7884; www.hihostels.ca). CDN$35, under 18 free.

the new way to go on holiday

Book Hostels all over the World!

Hostelsclub provides budget travellers and backpackers with an online booking engine for destinations all over the world:

Europe, North America, South America, Asia, Oceania, and Africa

You can make secure, guaranteed bookings for hostels, hotels and camping grounds for thousands of locations in just minutes.

www.hostelsclub.com

ESSENTIALS

Ireland: An Óige (Irish Youth Hostel Association), 61 Mountjoy St., Dublin 7 (☎01 830 4555; www.anoige.ie). €20, under 18 €10.

New Zealand: Youth Hostels Association of New Zealand (YHANZ), Level 1, Moorhouse City, 166 Moorhouse Ave., P.O. Box 436, Christchurch (☎0800 278 299 (NZ only) or 03 379 9970; www.yha.org.nz). NZ$40, under 18 free.

Scotland: Scottish Youth Hostels Association (SYHA), 7 Glebe Crescent, Stirling FK8 2JA (☎01786 89 14 00; www.syha.org.uk). UK£6, under 18 £2.50.

UK: Youth Hostels Association, Trevelyan House, Dimple Rd., Matlock, Derbyshire DE4 3YH, UK (☎0870 770 8868; www.yha.org.uk). UK£14, under 18 UK£7.

USA: Hostelling International-USA, 8401 Colesville Rd., Suite 600, Silver Spring, MD 20910 (☎301-495-1240; www.hiayh.org). US$28, under 18 free.

BOOKING HOSTELS ONLINE. One of the easiest ways to ensure you've got a bed for the night is by reserving online. Click to the **Hostelworld** booking engine through **www.letsgo.com,** and you'll have access to bargain accommodations from Argentina to Zimbabwe with no added commission.

HOTELS AND GUESTHOUSES

Hotel singles in Thailand cost about US$7-15 (280-600฿) per night; doubles US$10-20 (400-800฿). Rooms typically share a hall bathroom. A private bathroom may cost extra, as may hot water. Smaller (and more common) **guesthouses** tend to be less expensive. If you make **reservations** in writing, indicate your night of arrival and the number of nights you plan to stay. The guesthouse will send you a confirmation and may request payment for the first night. Often it is easiest to make reservations over the phone with a credit card.

 At most budget and mid-range hotels, rooms are priced as singles or doubles according to the number of beds, not the number of guests. To save a few *baht*, check into a single with a partner—if you don't mind sharing the covers. Keep in mind that this does not apply if the second "guest" appears late at night.

OTHER TYPES OF ACCOMMODATIONS

UNIVERSITY DORMS

Many **colleges and universities** open their residence halls to travelers when school is not in session. Some do so even during term-time. Getting a room may take a couple of phone calls and require advanced planning, but rates tend to be low, and many offer free local calls and Internet access.

HOME EXCHANGES AND HOSPITALITY CLUBS

Home exchange offers various types of homes (houses, apartments, and condominiums), plus the opportunity to live like a local and cut down on accommodation fees. For more info, contact HomeExchange.Com, P.O. Box 787, Hermosa Beach, CA 90254 USA (☎800-877-8723; fax 310-798-3865; www.homeexchange.com).

Hospitality clubs link their members with individuals or families abroad who are willing to host travelers for free or a small fee to promote cultural exchange and general good karma. In exchange, members usually must be willing to host travelers in their own homes. A small membership fee may also be required. **GlobalFreeloaders.com** (www.globalfreeloaders.com) and **The Hospitality Club** (www.hospitalityclub.org) are good places to start. **Servas** (www.servas.org) is an established, more formal, peace-based organization, and requires a fee and interview. An Internet search will find many similar organizations, some of which cater to special interests (e.g., women or gay and lesbian travelers) As always, use common sense when planning to stay with or host someone you do not know.

LONG-TERM ACCOMMODATIONS

Travelers planning to stay in Thailand for extended periods of time may find it most cost-effective to rent an **apartment**. A basic one-bedroom (or studio) apartment in Bangkok will range 15,000฿ and up per month. Serviced apartments seem to be easier to procure but are also more expensive: 18,000฿ and up per month. Besides the rent itself, prospective tenants usually are also required to front a security deposit (frequently one month's rent) and the last month's rent.

CAMPING AND THE OUTDOORS

Camping in Thailand is a viable option for budget travelers. Many national parks provide campsites, tent rentals, bungalows, or some combination of the three. The **Great Outdoor Recreation Pages** (www.gorp.com) provides excellent general info for travelers planning on camping or spending time in the outdoors.

USEFUL PUBLICATIONS AND RESOURCES

A variety of publishing companies offer hiking guidebooks to meet the educational needs of novice or expert. For info about camping, hiking, and biking, write or call the publishers listed below to receive a free catalog.

Sierra Club Books, 85 Second St., 2nd fl., San Francisco, CA 94105, USA (☎ 415-977-5500; www.sierraclub.org). Publishes general resource books on hiking and camping.

The Mountaineers Books, 1001 SW Klickitat Way, Suite 201, Seattle, WA 98134, USA (☎ 206-223-6303; www.mountaineersbooks.org). Boasts over 600 titles on hiking, biking, mountaineering, natural history, and conservation.

NATIONAL PARKS

Thailand's national parks are among its secret treasures. From the deep jungle to the sparkling beaches, thousands of acres of land in over 100 parks are preserved as refuges for endangered species of wildlife and for *farang* who need a break from each other. Tourists may be uncommon in these parts, but they may also be endangered if they're are not cautious. The beautiful habitats have precious sights to uncover, but travelers should be sure to be careful while enjoying them.

WILDERNESS SAFETY

THE GREAT OUTDOORS

Staying **warm, dry,** and **well-hydrated** is key to a happy and safe wilderness experience. For any hike, prepare yourself for an emergency by packing a first-aid kit, a reflector, a whistle, high-energy food, extra water, raingear, a hat, and mittens. For warmth, wear wool or insulating synthetic materials designed for the outdoors. Cotton is a bad choice since it dries painfully slowly.

Check **weather forecasts** often and pay attention to the skies when hiking, as weather patterns can change suddenly. Always let someone—either a friend, your hostel, a park ranger, or a local hiking organization—know when and where you are going hiking. Know your physical limits and do not attempt a hike beyond your ability. See **Safety and Health** (p. 44), for info on medical concerns.

WILDLIFE

If you are hiking in an area that might be frequented by **bears**, which is most of northern and northeastern Thailand, ask local rangers for info on bear behavior before entering any park or wilderness area and obey posted warnings. If you're close enough for a bear to see you, you're too close. If you see a bear at a distance, calmly walk (don't run) in the other direction. If it seems interested, back away slowly while speaking to the bear in firm, low tones, and head in the opposite direction or toward a settled area. If you are attacked by a bear, get in a fetal position to protect yourself, put your arms over the back of your neck, and play dead. In all situations, remain calm, as loud noises and sudden movements can trigger an attack. Don't leave food or other scented items (trash, toiletries, the clothes that you cooked in) near your tent. **Bear-bagging,** hanging edibles and other good-smelling objects from a tree out of reach of hungry paws, is the best way to keep your toothpaste from becoming a condiment. Bears are also attracted to **perfume,** as are bugs, so cologne, scented soap, deodorant, and hairspray should stay at home.

Look out for unwanted critters at all times. Shake out your shoes before putting them on, sleep with a mosquito net, and always wear repellent with DEET. Leeches are quiet predators: buy leech guards and cover every inch of flesh. If you are bitten by any creature of the wild, get help immediately. For more info, consult *How to Stay Alive in the Woods*, by Bradford Angier (Macmillan Press, US$8).

CAMPING AND HIKING EQUIPMENT

WHAT TO BUY

Good camping equipment is both sturdy and light. North American suppliers tend to offer the most competitive prices. While weather in Thailand is generally quite hot, temperatures can drop significantly at night, particularly in the north. See the **Appendix** (p. 421) for more info on climate and average temperatures.

Sleeping bags: Most sleeping bags are rated by season: "summer" means 30-40°F (around 0°C) at night; "four-season" or "winter" often means below 0°F (-17°C). Bags are made of **down** (warm and light, but expensive, and miserable when wet) or of **synthetic** material (heavy, durable, and warm when wet). Prices range US$50-250 for a summer synthetic to US$200-300 for a good down winter bag. **Sleeping bag pads** include foam pads (US$10-30), air mattresses (US$15-50), and self-inflating mats (US$30-120). Bring a **stuff sack** to store your bag and keep it dry.

Tents: The best tents are free-standing (with their own frames and suspension systems), set up quickly, and only require staking in high winds. Low-profile dome tents are the best all around. Worthy 2-person tents start at US$100, 4-person at US$160. Make sure your tent has a rain fly and seal its seams with waterproofer. Other useful accessories include a **battery-operated lantern**, a plastic **groundcloth**, and a nylon **tarp.**

Backpacks: Internal-frame packs mold well to your back, keep a lower center of gravity, and flex adequately to allow you to hike difficult trails, while **external-frame packs** are more comfortable for long hikes over even terrain, as they carry weight higher and distribute it more evenly. Make sure your pack has a strong, padded hip-belt to transfer weight to your legs. There are models designed specifically for women. Any serious backpacking requires a pack of at least 4000 in^3 (16,000cc), plus 500 in^3 for sleeping bags in internal-frame packs. Sturdy backpacks cost anywhere from US$125 to 420—your pack is an area where it doesn't pay to economize. On your hunt for the perfect pack, fill up prospective models with something heavy, strap it on correctly, and walk around the store to get a sense of how the model distributes weight. Either buy a **rain cover** (US$10-20) or store all of your belongings in plastic bags inside your pack.

Boots: Be sure to wear hiking boots with good **ankle support.** They should fit snugly and comfortably over 1-2 pairs of **wool socks** and a pair of thin **liner socks.** Break in boots over several weeks before you go to spare yourself blisters.

Other necessities: Synthetic layers, like those made of polypropylene or polyester, and a pile jacket will keep you warm even when wet. A **space blanket** (US$5-15) will help you to retain body heat and doubles as a groundcloth. Plastic **water bottles** are vital. Look for shatter- and leak-resistant models. Carry **water-purification tablets** for when you can't boil water (you should already have these for backpacking in Thailand). Although most campgrounds provide campfire sites, you may want to bring a small **metal grate** or **grill.** For those places that forbid fires or the gathering of firewood, you'll need a **camp stove** (the classic Coleman starts at US$50) and a propane-filled **fuel bottle** to operate it. Also bring a **first-aid kit, pocketknife, insect repellent,** and **waterproof matches** or a **lighter.**

WHERE TO BUY IT

The mail-order/online companies listed below offer lower prices than many retail stores. A visit to a local camping or outdoors store will give you a good sense of the look and weight of certain items.

Campmor, 28 Parkway, P.O. Box 700, Upper Saddle River, NJ 07458, USA (US ☎888-226-7667; www.campmor.com).

ESSENTIALS

MADE TO MEASURE

Ladies & Gents Custom Tailoring / BESPOKE SUITS & SHIRTS

To make an appointment with the Most Awarded Tailor
visit at: **www.smartfashion.com/form.htm**

On our next visit to Europe / UK we will introduce the latest and finest fabric collection from Super 120's wool and cashmere.

SPECIAL OFFER

2 Suits
2 Extra Pants
2 Shirts
2 Ties

from US$ 159

Fax & Voicemail
UK No: 020 7681 1794
E-mail: somsak11@inet.co.th
Website: www.smartfashion.com

For free pick up in Bangkok
Call: 02 253 2993

Hong Kong Tailors

Address: 28-28/1 Sukhumvit Soi 19 (Soi wattana) Bangkok 10110, Thailand
Tel: 00 662 253 2993   Fax: 00 662 255 4518

SAM'S LODGE

BANGKOK

Special Opening Rates @US$15 and up

GUESTHOUSE WITH COMMON CLEAN HYGIENIC BATHROOM. ACCESS TO EVERY FLOOR WITH ELEVATOR AND A NICE GARDEN ROOF TOP WITH AN EXCELLENT VIEW.

E-mail: stay@samslodge.com
For more information please visit:
www.samslodge.com

CENTRALLY LOCATED IN SUKHUMVIT AREA (SOI 19)
EASY 1 MINUTE REACH BY SKY TRAIN (ASOKE STATION)

FOR FURTHER INFORMATION, PLEASE CALL **02 253 6069**

28-28/1 Sukhumvit Soi 19 (Soi Wattana) Wattana, Bangkok, Thailand.
Booking: 02 253 2993 or 02 255 4516   Fax: +66 2 255 4518

Discount Camping, 880 Main North Rd., Pooraka, South Australia 5095, Australia (☎08 8262 3399; fax 8260 6240; www.discountcamping.com.au).

Eastern Mountain Sports (EMS), 1 Vose Farm Rd., Peterborough, NH 03458, USA (☎888-463-6367; www.ems.com).

L.L. Bean, Freeport, ME 04033 (US and Canada ☎800-441-5713, UK 0800 891 297; www.llbean.com).

Mountain Designs, 51 Bishop St., Kelvin Grove, Queensland 4059, Australia (☎07 3856 2344; www.mountaindesigns.com).

Recreational Equipment, Inc. (REI), Sumner, WA 98352, USA (US and Canada ☎800-426-4840, elsewhere 253-891-2500; www.rei.com).

ORGANIZED ADVENTURE TRIPS

Organized adventure tours offer another way of exploring the wild. Activities include hiking, biking, skiing, canoeing, kayaking, rafting, climbing, photo safaris, and archaeological digs. Tourism bureaus often can suggest parks, trails, and outfitters. Organizations that specialize in camping and outdoor equipment like REI and EMS (see **Where to Buy It,** p. 70) also are good sources for info.

Specialty Travel Index, 305 San Anselmo Ave., Suite 309, San Anselmo, CA 94960 (US ☎888-624-4030, elsewhere 415-455-1643; www.specialtytravel.com). Offers a variety of tours worldwide.

HILL TRIBES AND TREKKING

The safest bet when searching for tour guides is to use companies that meet **TAT** and **Northern Thailand Jungle Club** regulations (p. 279). Ask around when picking a company and talk to fellow travelers. Reputable operations make reports from former customers available. Treks affiliated with guesthouses are generally safer than the packages arranged by independent organizations. TAT publishes a list of trekking agencies, indicating those that use licensed guides (who have studied at the Tribal Research Institute in Chiang Mai). Trekking companies, guides, and customers are required by TAT regulations to be registered with the tourist police. Most companies provide insurance, food, accommodations, transportation, and extra supplies like small backpacks. Bring water with you. Go in a group of eight or fewer people, as smaller groups are less disruptive. The best way to learn about hill-tribe culture is to hire a personal guide (500฿ per day). Make sure your guide speaks both English and the languages of the villages on your itinerary.

HEALTH AND SECURITY

Bring a first-aid kit, sunscreen, a hat, mosquito repellent, a water bottle, and long pants. Baby wipes and anti-bacterial cream are also a good idea. Some regions contain malarial mosquitoes; be sure to get the proper medications before you go (see **Insect-Borne Diseases,** p. 50). Before embarking on a trek, try to find a safe place to leave valuables in your absence. TAT recommends that trekkers utilize a bank safety deposit box: there have been numerous reports of credit cards being lifted from guesthouse "security" boxes. Bandits have been known to raid trekking groups. Should this occur, hand over your belongings to the bandits to avoid physical harm. TAT discourages independent trekking.

TREKKING ETIQUETTE

Hill-tribe societies are being rapidly integrated into Thai society. Their unique, centuries-old cultures are ever-changing, and there's no question that tourism speeds up the process. **Always ask permission from the specific people you want to pho-**

ESSENTIALS

tograph before doing so. Some individuals or even whole villages may object even if your guide says it's okay. Respect people, space, and things, particularly hill-tribe beliefs, and be careful about what you touch. For example, the gate at the entrance to Akha villages marks the point past which spirits may not enter: don't touch this. Use the old hiking maxim: see as it is, leave as it was.

WHEN TO GO

Of northern Thailand's three distinct seasons, the cool season (Oct.-Feb.) is the best time for trekking. The vegetation is most lush, and temperatures are usually in the mid-20s (°C) by day, falling to near freezing at night. In the rainy season (July-Sept.), paths are muddy, and raging rivers make rafting fun but dangerous. In the hot season (Mar.-May), the land is parched and the air is dry.

WATER SPORTS

Most scuba agencies require that you have a **Professional Association of Diving Instructors (PADI)** certification in order to dive with them. The **Open Water Diving** course is the beginner course. The "performance-based" progress means that it will last as long as it takes for you to be good enough. Most courses consist of a knowledge section, a skill training section, and four training dives. There is a 183m nonstop swimming requirement or 300m nonstop snorkel and a 10min. treading water or floating session. **Ko Tao** is the largest diving training center in Southeast Asia. In addition to having some of the best snorkeling and diving in the world, it also has a plethora of scuba agencies, which are the island's primary source of income. (For specific listings, see **Ko Tao,** p. 420.) All of Ko Tao's scuba agencies are PADI certified which means that there can be no more than eight students with an instructor at any time. To get certification before your trip, see the listings of PADI certification sites in Australia, Canada, the United States, and Europe at the PADI web site: www.padi.com. The site also has listings of dive sites worldwide.

SNORKELING

Unlike scuba diving, snorkeling requires no training—anyone can grab a mask and start snorkeling. Since most snorkeling takes place in water that is only 1m deep, popping your head above water is always an option. The breathing technique is an adjustment, however, so practice by the shore before heading for deeper waters. Travelers can also take classes at scuba centers: nearly all cater to both activities.

HEALTH RESTRICTIONS

While PADI only mandates average health for certification, a prudent traveler will check with his or her doctor before signing up for a scuba course. Travelers with respiratory and heart ailments should be particularly careful with both diving and snorkeling. Contact lens wearers should not have a problem using them with a scuba or snorkeling mask, but prescription masks are also available.

SAFETY

Before you go out, check with local agencies and fellow backpackers about water conditions, currents, geological features of the area, and weather conditions. A strong current or an unexpected boulder can be extremely dangerous. Always check your equipment in shallow water before using it, and swim with a buddy.

When buying gear, make sure that the retailer is both reliable and reputable. There are many discount stores offering top quality merchandise, but keep in mind that the oxygen meter needs to be precise when you're 20m under the sea.

CORAL PRESERVATION

Learn about the marine life in the waters you hope to explore. This will not only improve the quality and enjoyment of the excursion, but it will give you an idea of which species are particularly delicate and prone to destruction. Never stand or kneel near coral. Simply touching it can kill it. Try not to disturb the environment: passive observation will provide better sights anyway.

SPECIFIC CONCERNS

SUSTAINABLE TRAVEL

As the number of travelers on the road continues to rise, the detrimental effect they can have on natural environments becomes an increasing concern. With this in mind, *Let's Go* promotes the philosophy of **sustainable travel.** Through a sensitivity to issues of ecology and sustainability, today's travelers can be a powerful force in preserving and restoring the places they visit.

Ecotourism, a rising trend in sustainable travel, focuses on the conservation of natural habitats and using them to build up the economy without exploitation or overdevelopment. Travelers can make a difference by doing advance research and by supporting organizations and establishments that pay attention to their impact on their natural surroundings and strive to be environmentally-friendly.

Traveling through Thailand takes visitors into ecologically sensitive areas. Avoid buying natural souvenirs such as teeth, hides, coral, butterflies, or turtle shells. Products made of animals often come at the expense of endangered species. Women should consider buying hygiene products with minimal packaging. Choose glass bottles over marginally recyclable plastic equivalents and reuse plastic bags. Bucket showers and squat toilets are more water-efficient than their Western counterparts. Carry a water bottle or canteen; where tap water is unsafe, purifying tablets or iodine drops save buying countless plastic water bottles.

> **TIP**
>
> **ENVIRONMENTALLY RESPONSIBLE TOURISM.** The idea behind responsible tourism is to leave no trace of human presence behind. A campstove is a safer (and more efficient) way to cook than using vegetation, but if you must make a fire, keep it small and use only dead branches or brush rather than cutting vegetation. Make sure your campsite is at least 150 ft. (50m) from water supplies or bodies of water. If there are no bathrooms, bury human waste (but not paper) at least four inches (10cm) deep and above the high-water line, and 150 ft. or more from any water supplies and campsites. Always pack your trash in a plastic bag and carry it until you reach the next trash receptacle. For more info on these issues, contact one of the organizations listed below.
>
> **Leave No Trace Center for Outdoor Ethics,** P.O. Box 997, Boulder, CO 80306, USA (☎800-332-4100 or 303-442-8222; www.lnt.org).
>
> **Earthwatch,** 3 Clock Tower Place #100, Box 75, Maynard, MA 01754, USA (☎800-776-0188 or 978-461-0081; www.earthwatch.org).
>
> **National Audubon Society,** Nature Odysseys, 700 Broadway, New York, NY 10003, USA (☎212-979-3000; fax 212-979-3188; www.audubon.org).
>
> **The Centre for Environmentally Responsible Tourism,** (www.c-e-r-t.org).
>
> **International Ecotourism Society,** 733 15th St. NW, Washington, D.C. 20005, USA (☎202-347-9203; www.ecotourism.org).

ESSENTIALS

RESPONSIBLE TRAVEL

The impact of tourist revenue on the destinations you visit should not be underestimated. The choices you make during your trip can have potent effects on local communities, for better or for worse. Travelers who care about the destinations and environments they explore should become aware of the social and cultural implications of the choices they make when they travel.

Community-based tourism aims to channel tourist revenue into the local economy by emphasizing tours and cultural programs run by members of the host community and that often benefit disadvantaged groups. An excellent resource for general info on community-based travel is *The Good Alternative Travel Guide* (UK£10), a project of **Tourism Concern** (☎020 7133 3330; www.tourismconcern.org.uk). **Earthfoot** (www.earthfoot.org) also provides info on community-based tourism, as well as other environmentally-conscious forms of tourism.

People for the Ethical Treatment of Animals (PETA) has called attention to the alleged mistreatment of elephants in Thailand's elephant camps. Some of these camps may employ inhumane training techniques. Keep this in mind when planning itineraries including elephant treks or elephant camps.

TRAVELING ALONE

There are many benefits to traveling alone, including independence and greater interaction with locals. On the other hand, a solo traveler is a more vulnerable target of harassment and street theft. Try not to stand out as a tourist, look confident, and be especially careful in deserted or very crowded areas. Never admit that you are traveling alone. Maintain regular contact with someone at home who knows your itinerary. For more tips, pick up *Traveling Solo* by Eleanor Berman (Globe Pequot Press, US$18), visit www.travelaloneandloveit.com, or subscribe to **Connecting: Solo Travel Network,** 689 Park Rd., Unit 6, Gibsons, BC V0N 1V7, Canada (☎604-886-9099; www.cstn.org; membership US$28-45).

WOMEN TRAVELERS

Women exploring on their own inevitably face some additional safety concerns, but it's easy to be adventurous without taking undue risks. If you are concerned, consider staying in hostels which offer single rooms that lock from the inside or in religious organizations with rooms for women only. Stick to centrally located accommodations and avoid solitary late-night treks or metro rides.

Always carry extra money for a phone call, bus, or taxi. **Hitchhiking** is never safe, even for two women traveling together. Look as if you know where you're going and approach older women or couples if you're lost or uncomfortable.

Generally, the less you look like a tourist, the better off you'll be. Dress conservatively, especially in rural areas. Wear shirts with sleeves and pants/skirt that fall below the knee. The more coverage the better. Wearing a conspicuous **wedding band** sometimes helps to prevent unwanted overtures.

Your best answer to verbal harassment is no answer at all: feigning deafness, sitting motionless, and staring straight ahead at nothing in particular can be very effective strategies. The extremely persistent can sometimes be dissuaded by a firm, loud, and very public "Go away!" Don't hesitate to seek out a police officer or a passerby if you are being harassed. Memorize each city's emergency numbers (☎191 is the standardized number for regular emergencies; all others are listed in the **Practical Information** sections). For tourist police in Bangkok, the number is always ☎1155. Consider carrying a **whistle** or an airhorn on your keychain. A self-defense course will both prepare you for a potential attack and raise your level of awareness (p. 46). Learn how to say "help" in Thai (see **Useful Phrases,** p. 423). If you feel threatened, **shout** your heart out. Also be sure you are aware of the health concerns that women face when traveling (p. 54). For general info, contact the **National Organization for Women (NOW),** 733 15th St. NW, 2nd fl., Washington, D.C. 20005, USA (☎ 202-628-8669; www.now.org).

GAY, LESBIAN, BISEXUAL, AND TRANSGENDERED (GLBT) TRAVELERS

The spirit of Buddhist tolerance and non-confrontation make Thailand largely accepting, if not actively supportive, of same-sex relationships. Most Thais are horrified at the idea of discriminating against someone because of his sexual orientation and would regard it as unthinkable to spurn a child because he is gay. There are no legal restrictions against homosexuality between consenting adults, and little social stigma is attached to it. Yet, due largely to familial structures that stress carrying on the family lineage, most lesbians and gays feel pressured to stay closeted.

The absence of blatant discrimination based on sexual orientation in Thai society takes away any impetus for the gay community to mobilize itself. It comes as no surprise, then, that informal social networks predominate over political organizations. That said, there is an interesting social dynamic associated with homosexuality. On the one hand, many educated, upper-class Thais have absorbed homophobic prejudices from Westerners. On the other hand, Thai homosexuals who have had contact with Western gay movements have returned to Thailand to spearhead domestic awareness campaigns. Thai health officials are beginning to connect homosexuality with the skin industry in their crusade against HIV/AIDS, so more attention is likely to be focused on the gay community in the future.

The boundary between homosexual and heterosexual, which is so concrete in the West, is much more fluid in Thailand. Homosociality (camaraderie between members of the same sex, particularly between men) is much more common than travelers may be used to. Hand-holding between men cannot be interpreted according to typical Western norms. Many even describe the country as a "gay paradise." However, most Thais believe that sexuality is a private matter and should be treated with discretion, regardless of one's sexual orientation. **Public displays of affection are not acceptable under any circumstance.**

Regardless, a booming gay nightlife—much of it divorced from the sex industry—remains quite accessible to foreigners. Thai tourism officials have seen the financial benefits of tolerating gay bars and establishments. Conversely, lesbian communities, often inaccessible to outsiders, remain largely underground, their nightlife comparatively subdued.

To avoid hassles at airports and border crossings, transgendered travelers should make sure that all of their travel documents consistently report the same gender. Many countries (including the US, the UK, Canada, Ireland, Australia, and New Zealand) will amend the passports of post-operative transsexuals to reflect their physical gender, although governments are generally less willing to amend documents for pre-operative transsexuals and other transgendered individuals.

Listed below are contact organizations, mail-order bookstores, and publishers that offer materials addressing some specific concerns. **Out and About** (www.planetout.com) offers a bi-weekly newsletter addressing travel concerns and a comprehensive site addressing gay travel concerns. The online newspaper **365gay.com** also has a travel section (www.365gay.com/travel/travelchannel.htm).

Utopia, 116/1 Soi 23, Sukhumvit Rd. (☎ 02 259 9619; www.utopia-asia.com). Bangkok's best resource for gay and lesbian listings and support groups.

Dreaded Ned's, (www.dreadedned.com). Detailed info on gay venues in Thailand.

Gay's the Word, 66 Marchmont St., London WC1N 1AB, UK (☎20 7278 7654; www.gaystheword.co.uk). Largest gay and lesbian bookshop in the UK. Mail-order service.

Giovanni's Room, 1145 Pine St., Philadelphia, PA 19107, USA (☎215-923-2960; www.queerbooks.com). International lesbian and gay bookstore. Mail-order service.

International Gay and Lesbian Travel Association, 4331 N Federal Hwy. #304, Fort Lauderdale, FL 33308, USA (☎954-776-2626 or 800-448-8550; www.iglta.com). An organization of over 1350 companies serving gay and lesbian travelers worldwide.

International Lesbian and Gay Association (ILGA), 81 rue Marché-au-Charbon, B-1000 Brussels, Belgium (☎2 502 2471; www.ilga.org). Provides political info, such as homosexuality laws of individual countries.

> **FURTHER READING: GLBT.**
> *Spartacus 2003-2004: International Gay Guide.* Bruno Gmunder Verlag (US$33).
> *Damron Men's Travel Guide, Damron Accommodations Guide, Damron City Guide,* and *Damron Women's Traveller.* Damron Travel Guides (US$11-19). For info, call ☎800-462-6654 or visit www.damron.com.
> *Ferrari Guides' Gay Travel A to Z, Ferrari Guides' Men's Travel in Your Pocket, Ferrari Guides' Women's Travel in Your Pocket,* and *Ferrari Guides' Inn Places.* Ferrari Publications (US$16-20).
> *The Gay Vacation Guide: The Best Trips and How to Plan Them,* Mark Chesnut. Kensington Books (US$15).

TRAVELERS WITH DISABILITIES

Thailand is ill-equipped to accommodate disabled travelers and has a history of not accepting people with disabilities. Often people with physical disabilities have been thought to have been immoral in past lives and to be bearers of bad luck. Further, it is also a cultural belief that a person's physical disabilities are emblematic of other mental and emotional disabilities. While these attitudes still persist in Thailand, they are slowly changing. The 1997 Constitution and 1998 Declaration on the Rights of Thai People with Disabilities have reflected the government's attempts to give the issue national attention as well as to facilitate the participation of people with disabilities in society. In 2001, Thailand received the Franklin D. Roosevelt International Disability Award for its progress toward fulfilling the goals set out by the United Nations World Programme of Action Concerning Disabled Persons. Thai people with disabilities rarely come out in public. Despite this, bold travelers will find many people eager to aid them.

Those with disabilities should inform airlines and hotels of their disabilities when making arrangements for travel: some time may be needed to prepare special accommodations. Call ahead to restaurants, museums, and other facilities to find out if they are handicapped-accessible. Hospitals cannot be relied upon to replace broken braces or prostheses. Orthopedic materials, even in Bangkok, are often faulty at best. All public transportation is completely inaccessible. Rural areas have no sidewalks, and larger cities are packed with curbs and steps. **Guide dog owners** should inquire as to the quarantine policies of their destination. Some useful organizations include:

Access Abroad, www.umabroad.umn.edu/access. A website devoted to making study abroad available to students with disabilities. The site is maintained by Disability Services Research and Training, University of Minnesota, University Gateway, Suite 180, 200 Oak St. SE, Minneapolis, MN 55455, USA (☎612-626-1333).

Accessible Journeys, 35 West Sellers Ave., Ridley Park, PA 19078, USA (☎800-846-4537; www.disabilitytravel.com). Designs tours for wheelchair users and slow walkers.

Directions Unlimited, 123 Green Ln. Bedford Hills, NY 10507, USA (800-533-5343). Books individual vacations for the physically disabled. No an information service.

Flying Wheels, 143 W. Bridge St., P.O. Box 382, Owatonna, MN 55060, USA (☎507-451-5005; www.flyingwheelstravel.com). Specializes in escorted trips for people with physical disabilities. Plans custom accessible trips worldwide.

Mobility International USA (MIUSA), P.O. Box 10767, Eugene, OR 97440, USA (☎541-343-1284; www.miusa.org). Provides publications containing info for disabled travelers.

Society for Accessible Travel & Hospitality (SATH), 347 Fifth Ave., #610, New York, NY 10016, USA (☎212-447-7284; www.sath.org). An advocacy group that publishes free online travel info and the travel magazine *OPEN WORLD*. (Annual subscription US$13, free for members. Magazine is currently not printing; check website for updates.) Annual membership US$45, students and seniors US$30.

Moss Rehab Hospital Travel Information Service (www.mossresourcenet.org). An information resource center on travel-related concerns for those with disabilities.

OLDER TRAVELERS

Travel in Thailand has the potential to be particularly taxing for senior citizens, despite being one of the most developed nations in Southeast Asia. There may be some extra benefits to age, however, including greater respect from the people you encounter. The books *No Problem! Worldwise Tips for Mature Adventurers* by Janice Kenyon (Orca Book Publishers, US$16) and *Unbelievably Good Deals and Great Adventures That You Absolutely Can't Get Unless You're Over 50* by Joan Rattner Heilman (McGraw-Hill, US$15) are both excellent resources. A few agencies for senior group travel are:

Elderhostel, 11 Ave. de Lafayette, Boston, MA 02111, USA (☎877-426-8056; www.elderhostel.org). Programs in Thailand and other countries in Southeast Asia. Programs last 1-4 weeks. Must be 55 or over (spouse can be of any age).

ElderTreks, 597 Markham St., Toronto, ON M6G 2L7, Canada (☎800-741-7956; www.eldertreks.com). In addition to Thailand, tours are also offered in Cambodia, Indonesia, Laos, Malaysian Borneo, Myanmar, and Vietnam.

MINORITY TRAVELERS

People in Thailand are largely accepting of minority travelers. However, travelers of African descent have reported stray incidents of harassment and discrimination. To be safe, these travelers are advised not to travel alone in rural areas.

DIETARY CONCERNS

Although Thai food often contains meat or uses meat bases, **vegetarian** dishes abound. The travel section of The Vegetarian Resource Group's website, at www.vrg.org/travel, has a comprehensive list of organizations and websites that are geared toward helping vegetarians and vegans traveling abroad. Vegetarians will also find numerous resources on the web: try www.vegdining.com and www.happycow.net for starters. For more info about vegetarian travel, see **Overcoming the Veggie Woes,** (p. 188), or contact the **North American Vegetarian Society,**

P.O. Box 72, Dolgeville, NY 13329, USA (☎518-568-7970; www.navs-online.org), which publishes *Vegetarian Asia* ($10).

While **kosher** meals are practically nonexistent, the 5% Muslim presence in Thailand makes **halal** food an integral part of the national cuisine (especially in the Malay-speaking regions). If you are strict in your observance, consider preparing your own food on the road. Contact synagogues in larger cities for info on kosher restaurants. Your own synagogue or college Hillel should have access to lists of Jewish institutions across the nation. A good resource is the *Jewish Travel Guide*, edited by Michael Zaidner (Vallentine Mitchell; US$18). For more info, visit your local bookstore, health food store, or library, and consult *The Vegetarian Traveler: Where to Stay If You're Vegetarian, Vegan, Environmentally Sensitive*, by Jed and Susan Civic (Larson Publications, US$16)

OTHER RESOURCES

Let's Go tries to cover all aspects of budget travel, but we can't put *everything* in our guides. Listed below are books and websites that can serve as jumping-off points for your own research.

TRAVEL PUBLISHERS & BOOKSTORES

Thailand Insight, Asia Books Co, Ltd. 5 Sukhumvit Rd., Soi 61 Wattana, Bangkok, 10110, Thailand (☎662 715 9000; fax 662-714-2799; www.thailandinsight.com). Website specializing on Thailand and Southeast Asia, from art to wildlife.

Hippocrene Books, Inc., 171 Madison Ave., New York, NY 10016, USA (☎212-685-4371, orders 718-454-2366; www.hippocrenebooks.com). Publishes foreign language dictionaries and language learning guides.

Travelers' Tales, 330 Townsend St., Suite 208, San Fransisco, CA 94107 (☎415-227-8600, orders 419-281-1802; www.travelerstales.com). Specializes in books containing personal accounts and advice from world travelers.

WORLD WIDE WEB

There is a wealth of info about Thailand available on the World Wide Web. Many regional newspapers, including the *Bangkok Post*, have online English-language editions. Listed here are some regional and travel-related sites to start you off. Other relevant websites are listed throughout the book. Because website turnover is high, use search engines (such as www.google.com) to strike out on your own.

 WWW.LETSGO.COM Our freshly redesigned website features extensive content from our guides; community forums where travelers can connect with each other and ask questions or advice—as well as share stories and tips; and expanded resources to help you plan your trip. Visit us soon to browse by destination, find information about ordering our titles, and sign up for our e-newsletter!

Atevo Travel: www.atevo.com/guides/destinations. Travel tips, and detailed info.

Australia National University: http://coombs.anu.edu.au/WWWVL-AsianStudies.html. Maintains a fantastic "virtual library" of Asia-related materials.

Bangkok Post: www.bangkokpost.com. Major daily newspaper printed in English.

BBC: www.bbc.co.uk. Current events info on Thailand in Asia-Pacific news section.

BootsnAll.com: www.bootsnall.com. Numerous resources for the independent traveler.

Business Day: www.bday.net. Thai newspaper looking at business and financial issues.

Chiang Mai News: www.chiangmainews.com. A northern newspaper with a unique view.

CIA World Factbook: www.odci.gov/cia/publications/factbook/index.html. Tons of vital statistics on Thailand's geography, government, economy, and people.

Cornell University Southeast Asia Program: www.einaudi.cornell.edu/southeastasia. Has links to hundreds of websites dealing with Thailand.

Geographia: www.geographia.com. Highlights, history, and people of Thailand.

How to See the World: www.artoftravel.com. A compendium of great travel tips.

MyTravelGuide: www.mytravelguide.com. Country overview and live web cam coverage.

Time-Asia: www.time.com/time/asia. An international edition of *Time Magazine*.

Travel Intelligence: www.travelintelligence.net. Travel writing by distinguished writers.

Travel Library: www.travel-library.com. Fantastic links for general info and travelogues.

TravelPage: www.travelpage.com. Links to official tourist office sites in Thailand.

World Travel Guide: www.columbusguides.com/country.asp. Helpful practical info.

World Hum: www.worldhum.com. "Travel dispatches from a shrinking planet."

TEACH. TRAVEL. GET PAID!

languagecorps

An Adventure in Teaching. An Experience in Learning.

Create your personal adventure teaching English abroad. Training, guaranteed placement into paid jobs, and close-at-hand local support.

www.LanguageCorps.com

ALTERNATIVES TO TOURISM

A PHILOSOPHY FOR TRAVELERS

Traveling in Thailand is likely to be one of the most beautiful and unique experiences of your life. However, it can also be one of the most eye-opening, especially if you manage to see beyond the banana pancakes to the person making them. *Let's Go* believes that the connection between travelers and their destinations is an important one. Over the years, we've watched the growth of the 'ignorant tourist' stereotype with dismay, knowing that many travelers care passionately about the communities and environments they explore—but also knowing that even conscientious tourists can inadvertently damage natural wonders and harm cultural environments. With this chapter, *Let's Go* hopes to promote a deeper understanding of Thailand and enhance your experience there.

In the developing world, there several options for those who seek alternatives to tourism. Opportunities for **volunteering** abound, both with local and international organizations, on a short-term basis or as the main component of your trip. As a volunteer in Thailand you can participate in projects from raising babies in Pattaya to raising baby gibbons in Phuket. You can learn why sea turtles no longer fill the Andaman Sea and how many Thai children are infected with HIV/AIDS. Later in this section, we recommend organizations that can help you find the opportunities that best suit your interests, whether you're looking to pitch in for a day or a year.

Studying is another rewarding option, and can be pursued either in the form of direct enrollment in a local university or as an independent research project. Often universities offer special programs for foreigners interested in learning more about Thailand and East Asia in general. Such programs usually include Thai language classes, although the primary classes are taught in English. For fluent Thai speakers, it is possible to enroll directly in many of the universities in Thailand. One reason people might choose to study in Thailand is that the cost of education, not to mention the cost of living, is much less than it is in the Western world.

In general, *Let's Go* discourages **working** in the developing world due to high unemployment rates and weak economies. However, there are situations in which your particular knowledge, whether it is a grasp of the English language or a comprehensive understanding of economics, can be used to aid development rather than hinder it. Additionally, cultural exchange in general, when pursued respectfully and tolerantly, offers innumerable benefits to our global society.

With all these options, we leave it up to you how to best spend your time exploring Thailand. The following are some exciting choices to get you started!

Start your search at ▓ www.beyondtourism.com, *Let's Go*'s brand-new searchable database of Alternatives to Tourism, where you can find exciting feature articles and helpful program listings by country, continent, and program type.

VOLUNTEERING

Thailand, while rich in culture and history, has significant concerns related to conservation, development, and health, especially with regards to HIV/AIDS. Volunteering can be one of the most fulfilling experiences you have in life, especially if you combine it with the thrill of traveling in a new place. Of course, many of the challenges specific to volunteering in the developing world are related to learning to live and function in a different culture, but such challenges generally help make any project more worthwhile. Do not underestimate these challenges, however, as trying to adapt to a new climate, society, and culture can be very difficult. Similarly, remember that your role as a volunteer is to provide any type of aid that you can, not to pass judgement on existing practices or beliefs. Perhaps the best way to approach any kind of volunteering is to keep an open mind and recognize your limitations; any contribution you are able to make will be greatly appreciated.

People who volunteer in Thailand often do so on a short-term basis, at organizations that make use of drop-in or once-a-week volunteers. The best way to find opportunities that match up with your interests and schedule may be to check the *Bangkok Post* or look for listings through universities or local organizations. Many people you talk to will be able, and eager, to suggest projects to you.

Many volunteer services charge you a fee to participate. These costs can be surprisingly hefty (although they frequently cover airfare and most, if not all, living expenses). Most people choose to go through a parent organization that takes care of logistical details and, frequently, provides a group environment and support system. There are two main types of organizations—religious and non-sectarian—although there are rarely restrictions on participation for either.

CONSERVATION

Thailand is known for the beauty of both its environment and its wildlife; unfortunately, these wonders are currently threatened by development and simple lack of understanding. The groups below offer volunteer activities related to conservation in Thailand, from preserving elephant habitats to monitoring turtle hatchings.

Earthwatch, 3 Clocktower Pl. Suite 100, Box 75, Maynard, MA 01754, USA (☎800-776-0188 or 978-461-0081; www.earthwatch.org). Arranges 1- to 3-week programs to promote conservation of natural resources. Sometimes offers volunteer programs in Thailand. Fees vary based on location and duration, costs average $1700 plus airfare.

Ecovolunteer, 1st fl. 577/579 Fishpends Rd., Bristol, BS16 3AF, UK (☎0117 965 8333; www.ecovolunteer.org). Volunteer opportunities with wildlife in Thailand. See website for more information.

International Conservation Holidays, BTCV Conservation Centre, 163 Balby Rd., Doncaster, South Yorkshire DN4 0RH, UK (☎01302 572 244; www.btcv.org/international). They offer conservation ecology trips throughout Thailand and Southeast Asia.

Wild Animal Rescue Foundation of Thailand, 65/1 3rd fl. Pridi Banomyong Building, Sukhumvit 55, Klongton, Wattana, Bangkok 10110 Thailand (☎66 22 619 670; www.warthai.org). Recruits paying volunteers to work with various animal conservation projects throughout Thailand, including gibbons and sea turtles.

DEVELOPMENT

It is one thing to travel to a foreign country and criticize their public transportation system; it is another to jump in and do something about it. Between government-instituted programs and the work of non-governmental organizations, Thailand is quickly developing in many sectors. Such development work is not easy; the following organizations are recruiting volunteers to work in Thailand.

PROFESSIONAL DEVELOPMENT

ACDI/VOCA, 50 F St. NW, Suite 1075, Washington, D.C. 20001, USA (☎800-929-8622 or 202-383-4961; fax 202-626-8726; www.acdivoca.org). Volunteer opportunities in Thailand for professionals with a minimum of 5 years experience, lasting from 2 weeks to 3 months. Volunteers provide short-term technical assistance in banking, business and cooperative planning, and agricultural production. All expenses paid.

Institute for Cultural Ecology Internships, P.O. Box 991, Hilo, HI 96721, USA (☎866-230-8508; http://www.cultural-ecology.com). Offers internships to American or Canadian citizens in a variety of fields ranging from publishing to ecology. Positions last anywhere from 4 weeks to 1 year.

International Executive Service Corps, 901 15th St. NW Suite 350, Washington D.C. 20005, USA (☎202-326-0280; www.iesc.org). Sends professionals to Indonesia, the Philippines, and Thailand. Volunteers serve as consultants to businesses, government organizations, and non-profits. Assignments last from 2 weeks to 3 months; IESC can also arrange longer-term work. Major expenses paid; spouse's expenses covered if project lasts for at least 1 month.

Peace Corps, Peace Corps Headquarters, 1111 20th St. NW, Washington, D.C. 20526, USA (☎800-424-8580; www.peacecorps.gov). Opportunities in 70 developing nations, including Thailand and the Philippines. Volunteers must be US citizens ages 18+ willing to make a 2-year, 3-month commitment. A bachelor's degree is usually required.

Voluntary Service Overseas, VSO Canada, 806-151 Slater St., Ottawa, Ontario KIP 5H3, Canada (☎613-234-1364; fax 613-234-1444; www.vsocan.org). Opportunities to work in Indonesia, Laos, the Philippines, Thailand, and Vietnam on a wide range of projects. Most volunteer positions require at least 2 years experience, though some shorter-term placements are available. VSO covers expenses; stipend provided.

URBAN AND RURAL DEVELOPMENT

CUSO, 500-2255 Carling Ave., Ottawa, Ontario, Canada, K2B 1A6 (☎613-829-7445 or 888-434-2876 in Canada); fax 613-829-7996; www.cuso.org). 2-year volunteer opportunities for Canadian citizens in Thailand. CUSO volunteers work in human rights, legal advocacy, and development. Airfare, housing, and a stipend provided.

GAP Activity Projects (GAP) Limited, GAP House, 44 Queen's Road, Reading, Berkshire RG1 4BB, UK (☎0118 959 4914; www.gap.org.uk). Organizes volunteer work placements for those between the ages of 17 and 20 in a "transition year" after secondary education. Programs are 5-6 months and costs vary from US$2600 to 4000. Financial aid is available. Programs are designed for British and Irish citizens, but applicants of other nationalities may be accepted.

Global Service Corps, 300 Broadway Suite 28, San Francisco, CA 94133, USA (☎415-788-3666, ext. 128; www.globalservicecorps.org). Programs and internships in education, health care, and environment (can be specialized) for 3-10 weeks ($2000+).

Greenway, P.O. Box 21, Hat Yai Airport, Hat Yai, Songkhla 90115, Thailand (☎074 473 506; fax 074 473 508; camps@greenwaythailand.org; www.greenwaythailand.org; www.greenwaybizland.com). Volunteer your help to indigenous communities throughout the country, including a hill tribe in northern Thailand. Applications must be completed in your home country.

Habitat for Humanity International, 121 Habitat St., Americus, GA 31709, USA (☎229-924-6935, ext. 2251 or 2252; www.habitat.org). In Thailand, SSP Tower 12A

Floor, 555 Sukhumvit 63, Klongton-Nua, Wattana, Bangkok 10110, Thailand (☎ 02 711 6934). Offers international opportunities in Indonesia, Malaysia, Singapore, Thailand, Vietnam, and the Philippines to live with and build houses in a host community. Costs range US$2000-3800.

Human Development Foundation (www.fatherjoe.org). Devoted to the grassroots development of Bangkok's poorest neighborhood, Khlong Toei. The founder, Father Maier, constantly needs donations and volunteers for his schools, HIV/AIDS and drug prevention programs, legal aid projects, and infirmaries.

Maryknoll Mission, P.O. Box 307, Maryknoll, NY 10545, USA (☎ 800-818-5276 or 914-762-6364; www.maryknoll.org). Become a Maryknoll Missioner and work to build Christian communities in Thailand.

United Nations Volunteers, UNDP Thailand 12th fl. UN Bldg., Radamnern Nok Avenue, Bankok 10200, Thailand (☎ 02-228-2148; www.unv.org). Assignments vary in length and are located throughout several Southeast Asian countries (sometimes Thailand). Inquire for information about specific projects' language and skill requirements. Minimum monthly stipend provided.

MEDICAL OUTREACH

Recent estimates suggest that 670,000 people are living in Thailand with HIV/AIDS, including 21,000 children, and this is merely one of the health-related concerns which plagues the country. Additionally, the costs of medical treatment for those not covered by insurance can be staggering. The following organizations all contribute in some manner to health-care in Thailand.

Doctors Without Borders, 333 7th Ave. 2nd fl., New York, NY 10001, USA (☎ 212-679-6800; www.doctorswithoutborders.org). Provides emergency aid to victims of armed conflict, epidemics, and natural and man-made disasters worldwide. Their focus in Thailand is primarily care and treatment of HIV/AIDS victims. Requirements for medical positions are at least 2 years professional experience.

Operation Smile, 6435 Tidewater Dr., Norfolk, VA 23509, USA (☎ 757-321-7645; www.operationsmile.org). Provides reconstructive surgery and related health care, as well as training and education to health care professionals in Cambodia, the Philippines, Thailand, and Vietnam.

Population and Community Development Association, 8 Sukhumvit, Soi 12, Bangkok 10110, Thailand (☎ 66 2 229 4611; www.sli.unimelb.edu.au/pda). Has programs specializing in everything from environmental research and rehabilitation to family planning and AIDS education. Volunteers are especially welcome on health-related projects in Chiang Rai (p. 339).

The Rejoice Urban Development 70/1 Amarin Court Klong Cholarpratan, Moo 6, T. Suthep A. Muan, Chiang Mai 50200, Thailand (☎ 053-806-227; www.rejoicecharity.com). This project brings badly needed medical welfare resources to those suffering directly and indirectly from AIDS. One of only a handful of NGOs working directly with the HIV-infected community, **Rejoice** has implemented both a formula milk program and educational scholarships for orphaned children, in addition to their medical services. Qualified nurses, doctors, social workers, and medical students, as well as those who can serve in administrative or technical positions, are welcome to volunteer for stints of 2 weeks to 2 months. Volunteers are expected to cover their own room and board. Donations are welcome, or visit their office to buy handicrafts made by people affected by AIDS. Contact the founder, Gareth, for more information.

YOUTH AND THE COMMUNITY

In general, children are particularly vulnerable since they cannot defend themselves from exploitation or harm, and Thailand is no exception. Statistics indicate that anywhere from 60,000 to 200,000 children are involved in prostitution, and 289,000 have been orphaned as a result of AIDS. Many organizations are involved in child welfare in Thailand; the following are just a few options.

Chaiyapruk Foundation, P.O. Box 5, Ongkharak-Nakhon Nayok 26120, Thailand (☎66 1 495 362). An orphanage that has taken in several abandoned children and provides them with a home as well as a good education. Accepts volunteers for 1-year periods.

Fountain of Life, 3/199 Moo 6, Soi Chalermphrakiet 3, Naklua, Banglamung, Chonburi 20150, Thailand (☎66 38 361 720). A daycare center that strives to provide the children of the slums of Pattaya with a nurturing environment in which to grow.

Pattaya Orphanage, P.O. Box 15, Pattaya City, Chonburi 20150, Thailand (☎66 38 716 628; www.pattayaorphanage.org.uk). One of the Redemptorist Social Projects in Pattaya, the orphanage takes in children of all ages. The orphanage needs long-term and short-term volunteers whose responsibilities range from taking care of babies to teaching English at the Vocational School for the Physically Handicapped.

Right to Play, 65 Queen Street West, Thomson Building, Suite 1900, Box 64 Toronto, Ontario, M5H 2M5 Canada (☎416-498-1922; www.rightoplay.com). A Canadian organization that uses sports to enhance child development in several countries around the world, including Thailand. Volunteers are accepted for 1-year positions.

Tree of Life, 166/23 Na Watpa Amphur Muang Changwat, Buriram 31000, Thailand (www.geocities.com/heartland/vista/8459). Takes care of several orphans in northeastern Thailand, some of whom may be HIV positive.

TEACHING ENGLISH

Teaching jobs abroad, with the exception of some elite American private schools, are rarely well-paid. Volunteering as a teacher is nevertheless a popular option. Volunteer teachers often get some sort of a daily stipend to help with living expenses. Although salaries at schools, even private schools, may seem low, Thailand's low cost of living makes it much more profitable. In almost all cases, you must have at least a bachelor's degree to be a full-time teacher, although undergraduates can often get summer positions teaching or tutoring.

Many schools require teachers to have a **Teaching English as a Foreign Language (TEFL)** certificate. Not having this certification does not necessarily exclude you from finding a teaching job, but certified teachers often find higher paying jobs. Native English speakers working in private schools are most often hired for English-immersion classrooms where no Thai is spoken. Those volunteering or teaching in public, poorer schools are more likely to be working in both English and Thai.

Placement agencies or university fellowship programs are the best resources for finding teaching jobs in Thailand. The alternative is to make contact directly with schools or just to try your luck once you get there. If you're going to try the latter, the best time of the year is several weeks before the start of the school year. The organizations listed below are extremely helpful in placing teachers in Thailand. However, do not stop here. There is tremendous demand for English teachers in Thailand and it's always possible to find work as an English teacher. Not all places will be able to provide work permits; the "visa run" (a brief departure from the country to renew one's visa) is a common phenomenon among permanent visitors. If you are trying to find work in Bangkok, the *Bangkok Post*'s Classified section is a good resource. The **Australia Center** (p. 271) in Chiang Mai is a good source of information and provides a leaflet on working in the area. If these resources are not right for your plans, keep looking or simply show up—many travelers have been hired on-site.

American University Alumni Language Center, Head office 179 Rajadamri Rd., Bangkok 10330, Thailand (☎2 528 170; www.auathailand.org). Hires foreign teachers at a rate of 250฿ per hr. for teachers-in-training and 300฿ for teachers under contract. Locations all over Thailand.

English and Computer College, 430/17-24 Chula 64, Siam Square, Patumwan, Bangkok 10330, Thailand (☎66 2 253 3312; fax in the US 425-930-5421, in the UK 0870 161 1256; www.eccthai.com). Constantly recruiting teachers for schools all over Thailand, from the most rural to the most urban. Also offers courses in teaching certification, with a guaranteed job placement after completion of the course.

Global Service Corps. See **Volunteering** (p. 83).

International Schools Services (ISS), 15 Roszel Rd., Box 5910, Princeton, NJ 08543-5910, USA (☎609-452-0990; fax 609-452-2690; www.iss.edu). Hires teachers for more than 200 overseas schools, including several in Thailand. Candidates should have experience with teaching or international affairs. 2-year commitment expected.

Involvement Volunteers Association Inc., P.O. Box 218, Port Melbourne, Victoria 3207, Australia (☎03 9646 9392; www.volunteering.org.au). The service offers a variety of placements in Thailand (and around the world) for a placement fee of AUS$250.

Kanchanaburi, Catholic School. Teachers receive room and board as well as a stipend. The school requests 1-month, 3-month, or 1-year commitments. Contact the school directly at ☎66 98 890 050 and ask for Orawan.

Office of Overseas Schools, US Department of State, Room H328, SA-1, Washington, D.C. 20522, USA (☎202-261-8200; www.state.gov/m/a/os/). Keeps a comprehensive list of schools abroad and agencies that arrange placement for Americans to teach abroad, including schools in Cambodia, Indonesia, Laos, Malaysia, Myanmar, the Philippines, Singapore, Thailand, and Vietnam.

Teach in Asia, www.teach-in-asia.net/jobs. This website posts teaching jobs of all types, giving information about salary and necessary experience for each opening.

STUDYING

Study abroad programs range from basic language and culture courses to college-level classes, often for credit. In order to choose a program that best fits your needs, research as much as you can before making your decision: determine costs and duration, as well as what kind of students participate in the program and what sort of accommodations are provided.

In programs that have large groups of students who speak the same language, there is a trade-off. You may feel more comfortable in the community, but you will not have the same opportunity to practice a foreign language or to befriend other international students. For accommodations, dorm life provides a better opportunity to mingle with fellow students, but there is less of a chance to experience the local scene. If you live with a family, there is a potential to build lifelong friendships with natives and to experience day-to-day life in more depth, but conditions can vary greatly from family to family.

VISA INFORMATION

To volunteer, study, or work for less than 30 days, American, Australian, Canadian, European, New Zealand and South African citizens do not need a visa. However, if you plan to stay past the 30-day free ride, you can buy a tourist visa for 60 days (US$25). If you've set up a job or volunteer placement before arriving in Thailand, you may be eligible for a 90-day non-immigrant visa (US$50), which covers work in medical and educational fields.

If you are among the truly devoted or hard-working and you wish to stay in Thailand for the long term, you must apply to a Thai embassy for an extension. Extensions are granted from within the country if you already have a 90-day visa; if you don't, you must leave Thailand and apply for an extension at a Thai embassy. In either circumstance, the Thai government will require a letter from your academic institution, volunteer project, hospital, NGO, or place of work indicating their need for your assistance. It generally does not take more than two weeks to process the extension, whose length is dependent on your request and the length of the program or project. Extensions are largely given on a case-by-case basis, so contact the Thai embassy before your visa runs out and before you leave the country to find out the most up-to-date procedures. When you leave Thailand to apply, keep in mind that if you go to another country in Southeast Asia that is politically hostile to Thailand (i.e. Myanmar) your application may take longer to process. Also, remember that if your remaining time in Thailand is less than 30 days you simply need to cross the border and re-enter the country, not apply for a visa.

UNIVERSITIES

Most university-level study abroad programs are conducted in Thai, although many programs offer classes in English as well as beginner- and lower-level language courses. Those relatively fluent in Thai may find it cheaper to enroll directly in a university abroad, although getting college credit may be more difficult. You can search **www.studyabroad.com** for various semester-abroad programs that meet your criteria, including your desired location and focus of study. The following is a list of organizations that can help place students in university programs abroad, or that have their own branch in Thailand.

DOMESTIC PROGRAMS

AFS, 17th fl. 71 West 23rd St., New York, NY 10010, USA (☎800-237-4636 or 212-807-8668; www.afs.org). Runs study abroad and community service programs for both students and educators. Volunteers live with host families in Indonesia, Malaysia, Thailand, and dozens of other countries around the globe. Programs last from several months to a year. Cost varies widely with program type and duration.

Council on International Educational Exchange (CIEE), 7 Custom House St. 3rd floor, Portland, ME 04101, USA (☎888-268-6245 or 800-407-8839; www.ciee.org/study). Sponsors study abroad programs and teaching programs in Thailand.

International Association for the Exchange of Students for Technical Experience (IAESTE), 10400 Little Patuxent Pkwy. Suite 250, Columbia, MD 21044-3519, USA (☎410-997-3519; www.aipt.org). 8- to 12-week programs in Thailand for college students who have completed 2 years of technical study. Application fee US$25.

Lexia International, 23 South Main St., Hanover, NH 03755, USA (☎800-775-3942 or 603-643-9898; www.lexiaintl.org). Students live at Payap University in Chiang Mai, study Thai, and choose a field research project in Thai culture.

Pacific Challenge, P.O. Box 3151, Eugene, OR 97401, USA (☎800-655-3513 or 541-343-4124; www.pacificchallenge.org). Experiential adventure travel program in Cambodia, Laos, Thailand, and Vietnam. US$5000 includes round-trip international flight, internal travel, program activities, accommodations, and visas.

School for International Training, College Semester Abroad, Admissions, Kipling Rd., P.O. Box 676, Brattleboro, VT 05302, USA (☎800-257-7751 or 802-257-7751; www.sit.edu). Runs the **Experiment in International Living** (☎800-345-2929; fax 802-258-3428; www.usexperiment.org), 3- to 5-week summer programs that offer high-school students cross-cultural homestays, opportunities for community service and ecological adventure, and language training in Thailand (US$1900-5000).

Teaching & Projects Abroad, Aldsworth Parade, Goring, Sussex, BN12 4TX, UK (☎44 0 1903 708 300; www.teaching-abroad.co.uk). Projects include care/community action and teaching English. Programs can be combined with projects in other countries (US$2000 for 3 months).

Where There Be Dragons, P.O. Box 4651, Boulder, CO 80306, USA (☎800-982-9203; info@wheretherebedragons.com). Runs youth summer programs and short adult trips to Cambodia, Laos, Thailand, and Vietnam. Youth programs range from US$6000-6500. Adult programs range from US$4000-5000. Fee includes food, accommodations, and internal travel.

Youth International, 92 Grenadier Rd., Toronto, Ontario M6R 1R3, Canada (☎416-538-0152; www.youthinternational.org). A community service and experiential learning program in Thailand and Vietnam. Each program's fees are US$7500 and cover all expenses, including airfare.

THAILAND'S PROGRAMS

It is quite easy to spend some time studying in Thailand: many universities like to attract international students in order to increase the diversity of their campuses. The most common places to find universities that will accept foreign students are Bangkok and Chiang Mai, although other universities occasionally offer international programs. The universities below offer programs that foreign students can apply to directly and have classes taught in English.

Assumption University, Ramkhamhaeng 24, Hua Mak, Bangkok 10240, Thailand (☎66 2 300 4543; www.au.edu). Students can apply directly to Assumption University.

Payap University, A. Muang, Chiang Mai 50000, Thailand (☎66 53 241 255; www.payap.ac.th/english). Foreign students can enroll either in the Thai and Southeast Asian Studies program or directly into the International College.

Rangsit University, 52/347 Muang-Ake, Paholyothin Rd. Lak-hok, Pathum Thani 12000 (☎66 2 997 2222; http://vishnu.rsu.ac.th/ic). The International College offers international students the opportunity to study alongside Thai nationals in subjects ranging from business to philosophy.

Thammasat University, 1st floor Dome Building, 2 Prachan Rd., Bangkok 10200 (☎66 26 132 009). Offers a Thai Studies Program open to international students. All classes are taught in English.

LANGUAGE SCHOOLS

Language schools can be independently run international or local organizations or divisions of foreign universities. They rarely offer college credit. They are a good alternative to university study if you desire a deeper focus on the language or a slightly less rigorous courseload. These programs are also good for younger high school students who might not feel comfortable with older students in a university program. Some good programs include:

BABY BLUES

gnoring him was hard. From the corner of my eye I could just see his legs thrashing around on the floor. I looked straight ahead. I had promised myself I would do this, no matter how hard it was. In my lap, Wenika squirmed and let out a whimper. I glanced down and realized she had finished her bottle and was straining to reach the ne Bua had dropped next to us. I laughed and ently moved her away.

SiSi was now pounding the floor with both his eet and his fists, his whole body shaking from is sobs. I felt a pang as I consciously avoided ooking at him. I knew he was angry with me, but s much as it hurt us both, he needed to learn that was not there for him alone.

On my other side, Kavin released the Fisher-rice car he was using to support himself, took ne terrifying step toward the gate of the eranda, and fell into a heap on the ground, tears f frustration appearing in his eyes before he ven hit the floor. I gathered him up with the arm ot tickling Wenika and stroked his back until his ears subsided into hiccups.

I risked a glance at SiSi and was distraught to ee him writhing about, his bawling unchecked. I canned the veranda to see if anyone one else as going to do what I longed to; Matilde and tine were involved in a fierce game of *mai, mai ai* (dog, no dog), Iben had her hands full of attha and a pile of cloth diapers, and the legion f nurses was fully engaged in its daily battle with ae baby room floor, mops and buckets in hand.

I was torn. In the four months I had been living the Pattaya Orphanage I had spent countless ours with these children, especially SiSi. Of the) babies (and 200 children) I interacted with aily, he was the one I had developed a special ond with—this not-quite-two-year-old Thai boy ith funny ears.

We even had a daily routine. When I entered the aby room in the morning, he would launch himself me, not satisfied until he had been flipped upside-own several times and twirled around. Then we ould cruise the baby room, stopping to examine e pictures on the wall. We took baths, ate cookies, d played games. Until, of course, I picked up other child. Then he practically turned green, fusing to look at me or striking both at me and the child I had chosen to look after.

Usually I could only stand his tantrums for so long before I would rush to placate him, often carrying him in one arm while tending to the other children. But I had begun to realize just how dangerous this was. I only had two months left in Thailand before I would be saying goodbye to the orphanage and SiSi. In four months, SiSi had come to trust me; if he was still dependent on me in two months, what would happen to him when I left?

As one of eleven volunteers living at the orphanage, I had come to Pattaya to help, but I had never imagined that the line between ser-vice and injury could be so thin. I recalled Kavin's behavior when I first arrived at the orphanage. He had been lethargic and despon-dent—the result, I had been told, of his favorite volunteer leaving. Each volunteer had a special child, an instinctive favoritism stemming, it seemed, as much from our need to give as their need to receive. What right did we have to enter their lives, love them, and then leave? If I loved SiSi as much as I thought I did, how could I hurt him?

Looking at him, my heart broke. He was so mis-erable, pouring his heart out on the cold tile. But even as I began to stand, SiSi raised his head. His clear eyes gazed at me expectantly. What I had imagined to be eyes red from crying were inquisi-tively sizing me up. When he realized I was look-ing he immediately dropped his head and began to wail again, but I was indignant.

This was the child I claimed to love? This sneaky little devil...Groaning over my susceptibil-ity and inflated sense of worth, I turned my atten-tion back to Wenika, who had somehow managed to wriggle completely out of her diaper and was in the process of putting it on her head. As she gurgled with pleasure, happily relinquishing the diaper to gnaw on my finger, I felt a nudge.

Looking over my shoulder I saw SiSi, his back pressed to mine, busily examining the latest addi-tion to the baby room toy collection: a yellow duck. As I stared in astonishment at the child who, thirty seconds ago, had been putting on the performance of his life, he glanced up at me and smiled. *Mai* (dog) he said, pointing to the duck as he crawled into my lap. *Mai mai* (no dog), I replied, hugging him.

Sarah Selim volunteered at the Pattaya Orphanage fox six months in 2003. For more information on the orphanage and the Redemptorist Social Projects in Pattaya, see Alternatives to Tourism (p. 81)

THE HIDDEN DEAL

ISAAN HOMESTAYS

Because most Isaan towns are market centers for farmers to deposit money at the bank, much of Isaan's allure lies in the opportunity to experience rural traditions and lifestyles. But if you don't speak Thai or the local dialect, this may prove difficult. Luckily, some guesthouses, like Pirom's in Surin (p. 193), can arrange tours that will get you in closer contact with the villagers. Homestays are another option, where you'll have the opportunity to immerse yourself in the local rituals and ways of life. Here is a list of organized homestays in the northeast:

Ban Prasat, in Nakhon Ratchasima province. This picturesque village of wooden homes raised on stilts is located on the Tam Prasat River. Here, you can observe the silk-making process, beginning with worms and ending with fabric, as well as watch weavers make floor mats. Nearby excavations have uncovered 3000-year-old burial sites, predating those of Ban Chiang in Udon Thani province. *To get to Ban Prasat, take any bus from Khorat bound for Phimai. Ban Prasat is located off Rte. 2, 46km from Khorat. (Ecotourism Society, 282 Moo 7, Tambon Tan Prasat, Amphoe Non Sung. Contact Teim Laongkarn ☎04 436 7075. It's recommended that you arrange your homestay through TAT in Khorat. Dinner and 2 breakfasts included. 400฿ per person for one overnight stay.)*

[Cont'd on next page...]

American University Alumni Language Center (AUA), 73 Rajadamnern Rd., Muang, Chiang Mai 50200, Thailand (☎66 53 278 407; www.auathailand.org). This respected language center offers different levels of Thai classes each with an average of 60 hours of instruction (10hr. per week for 6 weeks). AUA has locations throughout Thailand.

Berlitz Language Center, 25th Fl. Times Square Bldg., 246 Sukhumvit Rd. 12-14 Klongtoey, Bangkok 10110, Thailand (☎66 26 533 611; www.berlitz.com). This well-known language center offers Thai language classes at 5 locations in Bangkok.

Chulalongkorn University, Perspectives on Thailand Program, 7th Floor Sasin Graduate Institute of Business Administration, Chulalongkorn University Bangkok 10330, Thailand (☎66 2 218 4899; www.arts.chula.ac.th/miscell/int_thai.htm). The most prestigious university in Thailand, Chulalongkorn offers intense 5-week language classes for 25,000฿ (housing not included).

Union Language School, CCT Building, 109 Surawong Rd., Bangkok, Thailand (☎66 2 233 4482). This language center offers 4-week courses in Thai (80 hours of instruction).

OTHER STUDY ABROAD

COOKING SCHOOLS

As a general rule at most cooking schools in Chiang Mai, one day will teach you the basics of curry, while a two-day course is enough to cover basic Thai dishes. Depending on your interest, check whether a market tour is included, and whether you can choose the dishes you learn. A free recipe book should be standard. One-day courses cost 700-900฿.

A Lot of Thai, 165 Soi 9 Lampoon Rd., T. Nonghoy Muang, Chiang Mai 50000 (☎66 53 800 724; www.alotofthai.com). This family-run cooking school offers cooking classes in an intimate environment. 1-day 700฿, 2-day 1400฿, 3-day 2000฿, 4-day 2600฿. They also offer a short class in the evenings for 500฿. Check out their comprehensive website for more information.

BeBe's Wok-N-Roll. In Pai (see **Entertainment,** p. 290).

Benjarong Cooking Class, at the Dusit Thani Hotel, Rama IV Rd., Bangkok 10500 (☎66 22 366 400). Offers Thai cooking classes every Sat. 9:30am-12:30pm taught by the head chef of their exceptional restaurant. The full course consists of 12 classes and participants receive a certificate upon completion.

Chiang Mai Cooking Schools. In Chiang Mai (see **Courses and Forums,** p. 280).

Samui Institute of Culinary Arts, 46/6 Moo 3, Chaweng Beach, Ko Samui 84320 (☎66 77 413 172; www.sitca.net). Offers cooking classes, vegetable- and fruit-carving classes, and professional training classes. Prices range from 2000 to 100,000฿.

HOMESTAYS AND CULTURAL LEARNING

Center for Cultural Interchange, 17 North Second Ave., St. Charles, IL 60174, USA (☎866-684-9675; www.cci-exchange.org), offers 2-to 14-week family homestays for US$900, including room and board, for the purposes of cultural exchange.

Global Routes, One Short St., Northampton, MA 01060, USA (☎413-585-8895; www.globalroutes.org). Has high school programs focused on construction and college teaching internships throughout the world; both involve homestays. Programs cost around US$4000 plus airfare.

Lanna Boxing Camp (www.lannamuaythai.com), in Chiang Mai 50300. Learn to box like the pros. 1 day 250฿; for longer training periods, price varies.

Mama Nit, Baan Nit, 1 Chaiyaphum Rd. Soi 2, Chiang Mai 5000 (☎01 366 8289). Mama Nit learned her unique blend of deep tissue and nerve therapy massage from her Chinese grandfather when she was 13. Ever since, she has been able to help those with nagging back pain and piercing nerve twinges. Those taking the 10-day to 1-month massage courses follow Mama's technique with translation from aides. A 1hr. massage is 150฿, but if you want to have it with Mama Nit, it'll cost you 200฿. Courses run: 2-day 1000฿; 10-day 3800฿; 15-day 5800฿; 1-month 9500฿. Open M-Sa roughly 9:30am-5pm. (See also **Courses and Forums,** p. 280.)

The Old Medicine Hospital, 238/8 Wuolai Rd., Chiang Mai 50100 (☎275 085; http://www.thaimassageschool.ac.th), the *soi* is opposite and slightly south of the Chiang Mai Cultural Center. The hospital garners praise for its relaxing massages. 10-day course starting on the first and middle Monday of each month (4000฿). Students receive a certificate for Thai Massage, overseen by Thailand's Ministry of Education. Herbal sauna 60฿; 1½hr. massage 150฿, with A/C 200฿. Open daily 9am-4pm. (p. 280.)

Tribal Museum (☎210 872), in Chiang Mai can help interested visitors arrange homestays in hill-tribe villages in the area surrounding Chiang Mai.

Khampom Village, Khon Kaen province. Learn how farmers cultivate rice and how weavers create silk cloth and bamboo mats, visit a local school, and learn how to cook a traditional Isaan meal. The highlight will probably be talking with locals through your translator/guide. *(Isaan Discovery Travel Co., 100 Moo 1, Ban Khampon, Amphoe Phra Yuen. Contact Hank ☎01 872 5670 or 04 326 6179; www.thaitraveldreams.com. 3 dinners and 2 breakfasts included. 4 days, 3 nights 3500฿ per person; discounted rates available for larger groups. Price includes translator and transport to and from Khon Kaen.)*

Phuthai Khok Kong, Kalasin province. 3km off Hwy. 2042, about 87km northeast of Kalasin. Home to the Phu Thai ethnic group, this village is predominantly populated by rice farmers descended from southern China. Activities include participating in the Ban Sri tradition (rice offerings to spirits), sampling *Pa-lang* cuisine (such as mushroom wrapped in banana leaves and seasonal insects), watching music and dance performances, exploring local waterfalls, and observing the silk-weaving process. *Contact Mr. Seethued Traiyawong, the village headman at (☎04 385 2003 or 04 385 1225). It is recommended that you reserve a homestay through TAT in Khon Kaen, as very few villagers speak English. (☎244 498. 1- or 2-day stays; 2 days and 1 night 750฿.)*

SPAS AND HERBAL MEDICINE

Lampang Medical Plants Conservation Center (☎350 787), in Lampang. Offers herbal everything for self-healing. Massages, body scrubs, and vapor baths are available, too. They have remedies for every ailment and ache. (See also **Lampang: Sights,** p. 319.)

The Sanctuary, on Ko Phangan. Although a backpacker place, it is still quiet, secluded, and impeccably clean. Free evening meditations. Many are happy to pay 60฿ for a dorm bed and splurge on yoga classes (150฿) and oil massages (400฿). Singles and doubles with bath 200-1000฿. (See also **Ko Phangan: Sights,** p. 415.)

Tamarind Springs (☎77 424 436; www.tamarindretreat.com), on Ko Samui, offers alternative medicine and outstanding spa facilities, including a hot spring pool amid ancient boulders.

 ## FOR FURTHER READING ON ALTERNATIVES TO TOURISM

Alternatives to the Peace Corps: A Directory of Third World and U.S. Volunteer Opportunities, by Joan Powell. Food First Books, 2000 (US$10).

How to Get a Job in Europe, by Sanborn and Matherly. Surrey Books, 1999 (US$22).

How to Live Your Dream of Volunteering Overseas, by Collins, DeZerega, and Heckscher. Penguin Books, 2002 (US$17).

International Directory of Voluntary Work, by Whetter and Pybus. Peterson's Guides and Vacation Work, 2000 (US$16).

International Jobs, by Kocher and Segal. Perseus Books, 1999 (US$18).

Overseas Summer Jobs 2002, by Collier and Woodworth. Peterson's Guides and Vacation Work, 2002 (US$18).

Work Abroad: The Complete Guide to Finding a Job Overseas, by Hubbs, Griffith, and Nolting. Transitions Abroad Publishing, 2000 ($16).

Work Your Way Around the World, by Susan Griffith. Worldview Publishing Services, 2001 (US$18).

Invest Yourself: The Catalogue of Volunteer Opportunities, published by the Commission on Voluntary Service and Action (☎718-638-8487).

ESSAY CONTEST WINNER!

beyondtourism.com

Last year's winner, Eleanor Glass, spent a summer volunteering with children on an island off the Yucatan Peninsula. Read the rest of her story and find your own once-in-a-lifetime experience at **www.beyondtourism.com!**

"... I was discovering elements of life in Mexico that I had never even dreamt of. I regularly had meals at my students' houses, as their fisherman fathers would instruct them to invite the nice gringa to lunch after a lucky day's catch. Downtown, tourists wandered the streets and spent too much on cheap necklaces, while I played with a friend's baby niece, or took my new kitten to the local vet for her shots, or picked up tortillas at the tortilleria, or vegetables in the mercado. ... I was lucky that I found a great place to volunteer and a community to adopt me. ... Just being there, listening to stories, hearing the young men talk of cousins who had crossed the border, I know I went beyond tourism." - Eleanor Glass, 2004

LET'S GO

ALTERNATIVES TO TOURISM

BANGKOK

After a day or two in the city, most travelers are amazed that Bangkok still remains standing at each sunset. Armadas of BMWs and Mercedes meet at intersections littered with infuriating traffic as legions of people battle for territory on the city sidewalks and spill out of every bus. Bangkok wasn't fashioned by city planners; it was hewn from unsuspecting rice paddies by the double-edged sword of Thailand's growing economy. A consummate Western city, computer games take children permanently away from their mothers, 7-Elevens are on every corner, and modern medicine, education, and technology are taken for granted.

Bangkok is the tourism hub of Southeast Asia. The vast majority of tourists to the region pass through here, many several times, though some purists claim that visitors to Thailand should spend as little time here as possible. It's true that the traffic, noise, pollution, and crowds make the city unbearable for some. But this urban center of over 10 million people is the center of Thailand's government and culture, and has much to offer. The city is home to cultural, religious, and historical sights, the revered royal family, mind-boggling shopping markets and malls, an incredibly diverse nightlife, and great restaurants and entertainment.

Bangkok is perhaps the only city that sees history buffs drooling over the National Museum's treasures while steps away travel-weary backpackers reach their modern mecca on frenzied, narcotic Khaosan Road. Southeast Asia's best DJs blast the latest hits next to the pinnacles of royal Buddhism and ancient architecture in the Grand Palace. The Emerald Buddha poses contemplatively for praying worshipers as Muay Thai kickboxers battle it out in front of screaming fans. Chefs bargain for meat at the sunrise floating markets just hours after the "meat market" in the Patpong red light district closes down. A businessman cruises by on a cell phone and passes a parade of orange-robed, smiling Buddhist monks. It is a city of constant surprises—no two people know the same Bangkok.

✈ INTERCITY TRANSPORTATION

BY PLANE

Most flights to Thailand arrive at **Don Muang International Airport,** 171 Vibhavadi-Ransot Rd. (the main northern highway), 25km north of the city center. The airport includes **International Terminal 1** (departure info ☎535 1149, arrival 535 1310), **International Terminal 2** (departure info ☎535 1386, arrival 535 1301), and **Domestic Passenger Travel** (departure info ☎535 1192, arrival 535 1253). The **24hr. post office,** in the departure hall of International Terminal 1, has **international phones, EMS,** and **stamps.** Each terminal has **baggage storage** (70฿ per bag per day, over 3 mon. 140฿ per day). Departure tax is 500฿ for international flights, 60฿ for domestic. The prices below are based on a round-trip fare.

DESTINATION	PRICE	DESTINATION	PRICE
Chiang Mai	4500฿	Phuket	5500฿
Hanoi	12,500฿	Singapore	10,500฿
Kuala Lumpur	11,500฿	Udon Thani	4000฿
Phnom Penh	11,000฿	Vientiane	10,000฿

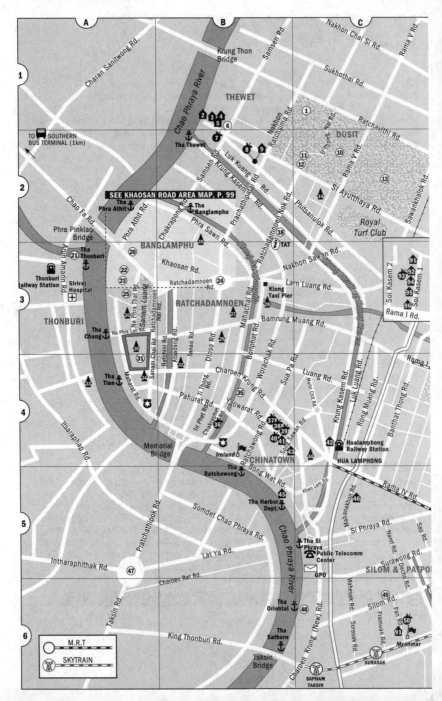

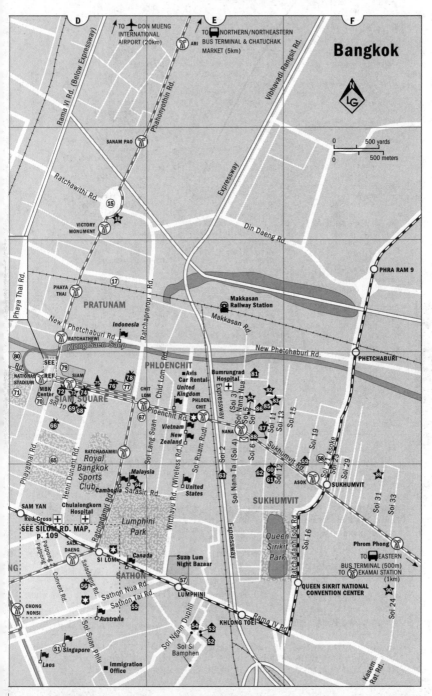

Bangkok

see map p. 94-95

🏠 ACCOMMODATIONS

🌙 NIGHTLIFE

🍎 FOOD

🛕 WATS

⭕ SIGHTS

As you exit customs, take one of the waiting taxis (250-400฿ depending on the traffic) or the useful, comfortable A/C airport buses, which run four routes into the city center. A1, A2, and A3 run every 30min. 5am-midnight. A4 runs every hour, or when eight people get on. All buses cost 100฿. To get to Khaosan Rd., take A2.

ROUTE #	STOPS
A1: DON MUANG-SILOM	Don Muang Tollway, Dindaeng Rd., Pratunam, Ratchadamri Rd., Lumphini Park, Silom Rd., Charoen Krung Rd., Silom Rd.
A2: DON MUANG-SANAM LUANG	Don Muang Tollway, Dindaeng Rd., Rachavithi Rd., Victory Monument, Phyathai Rd., Phetchaburi Rd., Larn Luang Rd., Tanao Rd., Phrasumen Rd., Chakrapong Rd., Banglamphu (Khaosan Rd.), Democracy Monument, Ratchadamnoen Klong Rd., Sanam Luang.
A3: DON MUANG-THONGLOR	Don Muang Tollway, Dindaeng Expressway, Sukhumvit Rd., Asok, Eastern Bus Terminal (Ekamai), New Phetchaburi Rd., Thonglor Rd.
A4: DON MUANG-HUALAMPHONG	Don Muang Tollway, Dindaeng Expressway, Ploenchit Rd., Siam Square, Phayathai Rd., Mahboonkrong, Rama IV Rd., Wongwien 2, Hualamphong.

A cheaper way to get from the airport to the city is to cross the bridge to the Don Muang Train Station and catch an inbound **train** to Hualamphong Railway Station (10-15฿), and then take a **city bus.** Night service is infrequent.

Suffocating **public buses** are available on the highway just outside the exit for 3.50-16฿ (regular #3, 24, 52; A/C #504, 510, 529), though other modes of transportation are more reliable. A list of fares and schedules can be found at the **Tourist Authority of Thailand (TAT)** in the arrivals area of Terminal 1. (Open **24hr.**)

BY TRAIN

Second only to elephant transport in style and peanut-holding capacity, train travel is cheap, efficient, and safe. Four train lines, traveling north, northeast, east, and south, start and end at **Hualamphong Railway Station** (☎220 4334, 24hr. info 1690), on Rama IV Rd. in the center of the metropolis. *Klongs* (canal) and river ferries, coupled with public buses (p. 100), provide the easiest transportation to the station from the city. Metered taxis or *tuk-tuks* at the side entrance of the station are the best ways into town from the station. The new **subway** line also terminates at Hualamphong. Bus #29 runs from the airport through Siam Square to the station. Otherwise, walk down Rama IV Rd. to a bus stop from which A/C bus #501 and regular buses #29 and 34 go to Siam Square. Walk down Sukhumvit Rd. for regular bus #53 to Banglamphu (Khaosan Rd. area), which continues to Thewet.

Daily ticket booking is left of the main entrance; advance booking is to the right. The lower information counter has train schedules. Upper-class seats have bathrooms and A/C; lower-class seats put you right in the middle of many friendly Thai people. Sleeper berths are popular, so buy tickets eight to ten days before departure. In order of increasing speed, price, and service, the trains are: ordinary *(rot thamada)*, rapid *(rot reaw)*, express *(rot duan)*, and special *(rot pheeset)*.

> **THE PRICE IS RIGHT!** Prices listed are ranges of fares. Add 40฿ for fast trains, 60฿ for express trains, and 80฿ for specials. Sleeper cars cost 100-500฿ extra, depending on class. Duration listed is for rapid trains; add 2-3hr. per 10 hr. for normal trains.

Platform 12 has a **luggage storage center.** (☎215 1920. 10-30฿ per day depending on bag size. 4-month max. Open 4am-11pm.) Other services include: an **information booth**; a **24hr. ATM** near the main entrance; a **police booth** (☎225 0300), left of the main entrance; and a **post office** outside. (Open M-F 7am-7pm, Sa 8am-4pm.)

DESTINATION	DURATION	FREQUENCY/TIME	PRICE
CHIANG MAI LINE (NORTHERN)			
Ayutthaya	2hr.	20 per day 6am-11:40pm	15-20฿
Chiang Mai	10-14hr.	7 per day 6am-10pm	181-1253฿
Don Muang Intl. Airport	1hr.	20 per day 6am-11:40pm	5-10฿
Lampang	13hr.	7 per day 6am-10pm	166-1172฿
Lopburi	3hr.	10 per day 6am-10pm	28-64฿
Phitsanulok	7hr.	11 per day 6am-10pm	129-974฿
UBON RATCHATHANI LINE (NORTHEASTERN)			
Surin	8hr.	8 per day 5:45am-11:40pm	173-946฿
Ubon Ratchathani	12hr.	5 per day 5:45am-11:25pm	175-1080฿
Nong Khai	13hr.	daily 8:45am, 10pm	183-1117฿
BUTTERWORTH LINE (SOUTHERN)			
Hat Yai	17hr.	5 per day 1-10:50pm	269-1394฿
Hua Hin	4hr.	12 per day 7:45am-10:50pm	164-842฿
Surat Thani	12hr.	11 per day 12:25-10:50pm	227-1179฿
EASTERN LINE			
Pattaya	3½hr.	daily 6:55am	31฿
Aranyaprathet	5½hr.	daily 5:55am, 1:05pm	48฿

BANGKOK

WHEELS ON THE BUS

Government buses depart from four terminals. The **Eastern Bus Terminal (E; ☎391 2504)** is on Sukhumvit Rd., and accessible via the Skytrain's Ekamai Station, local A/C bus #1, 8, 11, or 13, and regular bus #2, 23, 25, 38, 71, 72, or 98. The **Northern (N; ☎936 2852)**, **Central (C; ☎936 1972)**, and **Northeastern (NE; ☎936 3660) Bus Terminals** are in a new building west of Chatuchak Park. Take the Skytrain's Sukhumvit Line to Mo Chit and a motorcycle taxi (5min., 30฿) from there to the terminals. The **Southern Bus Terminal (S; ☎435 1199)** is on Boromat Chonnani (Pinklao-Nakhonchaisi) Rd. across the river in Thonburi. Tickets for government and **private buses** can be bought at the Southern Bus Terminal. To get there, take A/C bus #503 or 511 from the Democracy Monument, regular bus #19 from Phra Athit Rd., or regular bus #30 from Sanam Luang. Although private companies can be cheaper and more convenient, and sometimes offer more modern accommodations, they have higher scam and accident rates.

DESTINATION	DURATION	TERMINAL, FREQUENCY	PRICE
Ayutthaya	1½hr.	C, every 20min. 5:40am-7:20pm	41-52฿
Ban Phe (to Ko Samet)	3½hr.	E, every hr. 5am-8:30pm	124฿
Chanthaburi	4hr.	E, every 30min. 4am-midnight	115-148฿
Chiang Mai	9hr.	N, 74 per day 5:30am-10pm	314-625฿
Chiang Rai	11-13hr.	N, 32 per day 7am-9:30pm	264-700฿
Hat Yai	12hr.	S, 14 per day	535-830฿
Khon Kaen	7½hr.	NE, 27 per day	202-400฿
Krabi	12hr.	S, 1 per day	459-710฿
Mae Hong Son	14hr.	N, 1 per day 6pm	569฿
Nong Khai	7½-10hr.	NE, 19 per day 4:10am-9:45pm	195-545฿
Pattaya	2½hr.	E, every 20-30min. 4:40am-11pm	73-90฿
Phang-Nga	12hr.	S, 7 per day	441-685฿
Phrae	8hr.	N, 30 per day 6am-9:30pm	177-319฿,
Phuket	11½hr.	S, 8 per day	486-755฿
Rayong	3hr.	E, every 30min. 4am-10pm	101-117฿
Si Racha	2hr.	E, every 20-30min. 5am-9pm	55-70฿
Sukhothai	7hr.	N, 32 per day 7am-10:50pm	142-256฿
Surat Thani	9hr.	S, 7 per day	380-590฿
Surin	6-8hr.	NE, 30 per day 7am-11pm	146-385฿
Trat	5hr.	E, every hr. 4am-midnight	147-221฿
Ubon Ratchathani	5hr.	NE, 18 per day 7am-10:40pm	297-570฿

■ ORIENTATION

Beyond the backpacker-infested shelters of **Khaosan Road** lies a bastion of unclaimed sights and experiences. The north-south **Chao Phraya River** is a worthy landmark and launch site. To the river's east rests **Banglamphu**, the heart of the city. Home to Khaosan Rd., it's immediately north of **Ratchadamnoen/Ko Rattanakosin,** the location of Bangkok's major sights, including Wat Pho, Wat Phra Kaew, and the Royal Palace. Farther north is **Thewet/Dusit,** a backpacker area and the location of the Dusit Zoo and the former royal mansions. Heading southeast along the river leads to **Pahurat** the Indian district, **Chinatown,** and the **Hualamphong Railway Station.** Farther south is the wealthy **Silom** financial district and its less-upstanding bedfellow, the **Patpong** red light district. East of the Hualamphong Railway Station is **Siam Square,** the hub of the

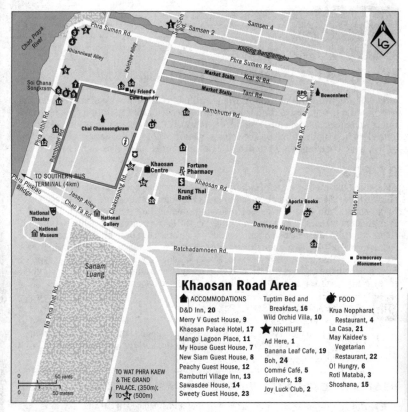

Khaosan Road Area

⌂ ACCOMMODATIONS
D&D Inn, **20**
Merry V Guest House, **9**
Khaosan Palace Hotel, **17**
Mango Lagoon Place, **11**
My House Guest House, **7**
New Siam Guest House, **8**
Peachy Guest House, **12**
Rambuttri Village Inn, **13**
Sawasdee House, **14**
Sweety Guest House, **23**

Tuptim Bed and
Breakfast, **16**
Wild Orchid Villa, **10**

★ NIGHTLIFE
Ad Here, **1**
Banana Leaf Cafe, **19**
Boh, **24**
Commé Café, **5**
Gulliver's, **18**
Joy Luck Club, **2**

🍎 FOOD
Krua Noppharat
Restaurant, **4**
La Casa, **21**
May Kaidee's
Vegetarian
Restaurant, **22**
O! Hungry, **6**
Roti Mataba, **3**
Shoshana, **15**

BANGKOK

BTS Skytrain and home to huge shopping malls and cinemas. **Rama I Road** slices through the city, connecting Wat Phra Kaew in the west with Bangkok's eastern edge and the **Sukhumvit Road** area, where Thais and *farang* party until the wee hours. The *Bangkok Tourist Map* (40฿) or Nancy Chandler's *Map of Bangkok* (200฿) will make all of this clearer than we ever could. Our own guide to the neighborhoods, however, might offer a different kind of help:

BANGLAMPU AND KO RATTANAKOSIN	This area offers the best sights in Bangkok within distance of the cheap accommodations of Khaosan Rd.
DUSIT AND THEWIT	Quiet and affordable, with less-visited sights and Thailand's largest zoo, this area is a nice break from the human zoo on Khaosan Rd.
CHINATOWN, PAHURAT, AND HUALAMPHONG	Home to the Chinese and Indian immigrant populations, this area is home to a lively street culture, especially at night.
PATPONG	Bangkok's red light district; no further explanation required.
SILOM ROAD	Grand hotels, neighborhood cafes, and the expansive Lumphini Park make this a great neighborhood for wandering.

SIAM SQUARE	Known for its shopping, this area offers giant malls for the avid consumer, as well as pleasant accommodations located conveniently close to the Skytrain.
SUKHUMVIT ROAD	Expensive restaurants and a thriving nightlife make this the place to splurge.

⊟ LOCAL TRANSPORTATION

Maneuvering through Bangkok traffic is enough to drive anyone crazy. Traffic has decreased recently, but getting from north to south is still frustrating. Taking canal boats and river taxis means less time sweating on buses and breathing exhaust. Travelers hoping to utilize public transportation will love the **Bangkok Tourist Map** (40฿), which has bus, water taxi, and Skytrain routes, as well as sight info.

BY BUS

The shiny, happy bus system, run by the Bangkok Metropolitan Transit Authority (BMTA), is extensive and cheap. Red-and-cream and white buses have no A/C (4-5฿); orange, blue-and-white, and yellow-and-white buses all have A/C (10-20฿). Pea-green **minibuses** (3.50฿) supposedly run the same routes as the buses but tend to stray easily. **Microbuses** cover long distances and stop only at designated places (5am-10pm, 30฿); the higher price guarantees a seat and fewer stops. A/C buses run 5am-midnight; regular buses run **24hr.** Make sure you get on the right type of bus, not just the right route number. Below is a sample listing; there are many, many buses, so for more options, pick up a free **bus map** at any TAT office.

> **TIP** **BACKPACKER'S BUS.** Regular bus #15 is especially important for those staying in Khaosan. It connects that area with Siam Square, where passengers can hop onto the Skytrain to access the eastern parts of the city, like Sukhumvit, Silom, Patpong, and Chatuchak Market. Alternatively, a taxi from Khaosan to Siam costs 60-90฿.

REGULAR BUSES WITH NO A/C (RED-AND-CREAM OR WHITE)

#1: Wat Pho—Yaowarat Rd. (Chinatown)—General Post Office (GPO)—Oriental Hotel

15: Banglamphu (Phra Athit Rd., Phrasumen Rd.)—Sanam Luang—Democracy Monument—Wat Saket—Siam Sq.—Ratchadamri Rd.—Lumphini Park—Silom Rd.

18 and **28:** Vimanmek Teak Museum—Dusit Zoo—Chitralada Palace—Victory Monument

25: Wat Phra Kaew—Wat Pho—Charoen Krung Rd.—Rama IV Rd. (near Hualamphong Railway Station)—Phayathai Rd.—Mahboonkrong Center—Siam Sq.—World Trade Center—Ploenchit Rd.—Sukhumvit Rd. to outer Bangkok

48: Sanam Chai Rd.—Bamrung Muang Rd.—Siam Sq.—along Sukhumvit Rd.

59: Don Muang International Airport—Victory Monument—Phahonyothin Rd.—Phetchaburi Rd.—Larnluang Rd.—Democracy Monument—Sanam Luang

70: Democracy Monument—TAT—Boxing Stadium—Dusit Zoo

72: Ratchaprarop Rd.—Si Ayutthaya Rd.—Marble Temple—Samsen Rd.—Thewet

74: Rama IV Rd. (outside Soi Ngam Duphli)—Lumphini Park—Ratchadamri Rd.—World Trade Center—Pratunam-Ratchaprarop Rd.—Victory Monument

115: Silom Rd.—Rama IV Rd.—along Rama IV Rd. until Sukhumvit Rd.

116: Sathorn Nua Rd.—along Rama IV Rd. (passes Soi Ngam Duphli)—Sathorn Tai Rd.

204: Victory Monument—Ratchaprarop Rd.—World Trade Center—Siam Sq.—Bamrung Muang Rd.

A/C BUSES (BLUE-AND-WHITE, YELLOW-AND-WHITE, OR ORANGE)

#501: Wat Pho–Charoen Krung Rd.–Rama IV Rd. (near Hualamphong Railway Station)–Phayathai Rd. (Mahboonkrong Center)–Siam Sq.–along Sukhumvit Rd.

508: Sanam Luang–Bamrung Muang Rd.–Rama I Rd.–Ploenchit Rd.–outer Bangkok

510: National Assembly (Ratchavithi Rd.)–Dusit Zoo–Chitralada Palace–Victory Monument–Phahonyothin Rd.–Don Muang International Airport

511: Khaosan Rd.–Phra Sumen Rd.–Democracy Monument (Ratchadamnoen Klong Rd.)–Phetchaburi Rd.–World Trade Center–Sukhumvit Rd.

BY BOAT

Chao Phraya River Express ferries (6am-6:40pm, 4-25฿) are the best way to travel along the river and provide easy access to the Skytrain. Buy tickets at the booth on the pier or from the ticket collector on board. Specify your stop, as boats will otherwise stop only if there are passengers waiting. Disembark quickly and carefully.

The main stops, from north to south, are **Thewet** (for the National Library and Dusit guesthouses), **Phra Athit** (for Khaosan Rd./Banglamphu), **Thonburi Railway Pier** (for Thonburi Railway Station and Royal Barges), **Chang** (for Wat Phra Kaew and the Royal Palace), **Tien** (for Wat Pho), **Ratchawong** (for Chinatown and Hualumphong Railway Station), **Si Phraya** (for GPO), **Oriental** (for the Oriental Hotel and Silom), and **Sathorn** (for the Skytrain to Silom). During peak transit times special rush-hour express ferries with orange (10฿) or yellow (15-25฿) flags stop at only some of the major piers (6:30am-9pm and 4-7pm). Small, brown, box-like ferries with bench seats, easily confused with river taxis, shuttle across the river to every major stop (2฿). A small sign identifies each *tha* (pier).

Klongs are small canals that zig-zag through the city's interior. Thonburi, west of Chao Praya, has an extensive network, and Bangkok proper has two useful lines. **Klong Saen Saep** links Democracy Monument near Banglamphu with the area around Siam Sq. and the World Trade Center (10min.). Another route links **Klong Banglamphu** and **Klong Phadung Krung Kasem**. From Tha Banglamphu, at the Chakraphong and Phrasumen Rd. intersection, you can reach Hualumphong Railway Station (15min.). Boats run every 30min. during peak hours and every 45min. 6am-6:40pm during off-peak hours and weekends. A single trip costs 7-20฿.

THE LOCAL STORY

RED LIGHT, GREEN LIGHT

Love it or loathe it, Bangkok's red light district cannot be denied. Three Bangkok locales—Patpong, Nana, and Soi Cowboy—host a concentration of "entertainment centers."

Most innocent are regular bars staffed by Thai women, who sit with male customers as they drink. Next are hostess bars, almost exclusively for Japanese tourists. Well-dressed Japanese women wait to accompany their clients into karaoke bars for food, drinks, and singing. Third are go-go bars, which feature topless and/or bottomless dancing, in addition to topless and bottomless girls for "company." Many of these have back rooms for live sex shows. Needless to say, additional "services" can be purchased at any of these locations.

At first sight, Patpong appears to be another of Bangkok's tourist attractions, with families and couples roaming the streets. But as the "show lists" indicate, the goings-on are not as innocent as the crowds. Go-gos host plenty of older white men and curious younger tourists. "Boy go-gos" provide the gay equivalent.

Longtail boat rentals are available at almost every pier for tourist destinations on the river and *klongs*. Agree on a price before setting off. Usual rates are 600฿ for the first hour, 400฿ each additional hour.

BY SKYTRAIN

The **Skytrain** (Bangkok Mass Transit System, **BTS**), a monorail train launched on December 5, 1999 to celebrate the King's 72nd birthday, is an A/C delight. Incredibly useful for navigating Siam Sq., Silom, and Sukhumvit, the train has two lines that meet at Siam Sq. The **Sukhumvit Line** runs from Mo Chit, next to Chatuchak Market, goes past the Victory Monument to Siam Sq., continues through Sukhumvit Rd., and terminates at On Nut, beyond the Eastern Bus Terminal. The **Silom Line** runs from the National Stadium past Siam Sq. and Lumphini Park, and along part of Silom Rd., before terminating at Taksin Bridge. All stations have useful **maps. Fares** are based on distance (10-40฿), and ticket purchase is automated. Trip passes (10-, 15-, and 30-ride) are the most cost-effective for students; flaunt your ISIC card (200-540฿, with ISIC card 160-360฿; passes must be used within 30 days of purchase). Unlimited one-day (100฿) and three-day (280฿) passes are also available. Insert the card at the turnstile to enter the station; **hold onto it and insert it at the turnstile at your destination to leave the station.** The Skytrain operates daily 6am-midnight. There is a BTS information office in the Siam Center stop. (☎617 7340. Open daily 8am-8pm.)

BY METRO

The newest addition to Bangkok's public transportation system is the clean, cool underground metro. Unfortunately, the metro was designed more to accommodate commuters and alleviate road traffic than to shuttle tourists, but the single line does connect a few attractions. The metro runs from Bang Sue in the north in a southeast semi-circle to Hualamphong in the south, passing through Chatuchak Market, Sukhumvit Rd., Lumphini Park, Suan Lum Night Bazaar, and Silom Rd. The Sukhumvit Rd. and Silom Rd. stations are close to BTS Skytrain Asok and Sala Daeng stations, respectively. Tickets are priced by distance (single ride 14-36฿) and can be purchased in the underground stations. (☎246 6733; www.mrta.co.th. Open 6am-midnight.)

BY TAXI

Your lungs will thank you for using Bangkok's extensive taxi system. Simple and cost-efficient, taxis are under-utilized by most travelers. The fare is 35฿ for the first 2km and 2฿ per additional 0.4km. Waiting time is also factored into the fare. Always insist on the driver using the meter—there is no such thing as a flat rate, unless you are coming from the airport. The only official extra fees are expressway tolls. Single women find taxis much safer than *tuk-tuks* or motorcycle taxis.

BY TUK-TUK

Tuk-tuks scour the city and squeeze through the traffic that brings taxis to a halt. Negotiation is key: drivers may charge you twice what they would a local. Skillful negotiators can get prices 30% cheaper than taxi fares. *Tuk-tuks* are best for short distances; if a *tuk-tuk* tries to charge you more than 50฿, save yourself from exhaust inhalation and the likelihood that you're getting ripped off, and take a taxi.

BY MOTORCYCLE TAXI

Motorcycle-taxi drivers loiter on street corners in brightly colored vests. Though faster in traffic and 10-25% cheaper than *tuk-tuks*, motorcycle taxis carry only a

TIP

TOURIST SCAMMING. *Tuk-tuk* drivers are often con artists and have been known to harass women travelers. Drivers have also been known to drive off with passenger luggage, push the skin industry, deliver passengers to expensive restaurants, or tell travelers that sights are closed and take them to jewelry and tailor shops instead. To entice *farang*, they offer tours of the city for low rates (10-20฿ per hr.), but all you'll get is a sales pitch and inflated prices. Beware of these words: *free, sexy, massage, jewelry, tailor shop,* and *go-go* (unless, of course, you really want to go to a masseur, jeweler, tailor, or prostitute). *Tuk-tuks* aren't all bad—just be firm and make it clear that you want to go to your intended destination and nowhere else.

single passenger, are dangerous, and require calm nerves. Travelers should insist on a helmet, as police will fine non-wearers.

BY CAR

Travelers should avoid cars, as driving in Bangkok can be dangerous. An **International Driver's Permit** (p. 62) and major credit card are required. Rental agencies include **Avis,** 2/12 Witthayu Rd. (☎255 5300). Renting a small sedan costs 1400-2000฿ per day, including collision insurance. Personal accident insurance costs an extra 160฿ per day. A passport, driver's license, and major credit card are needed to rent. (☎535 4052. Branch at airport. Open M-F 7am-7pm, Sa-Su 7am-6pm.)

⓵ PRACTICAL INFORMATION

PHONE CODE   The phone code for all of Bangkok is ☎02.

TOURIST AND FINANCIAL SERVICES

Tourist Office: TAT, 4 Ratchadamnoen Nok Rd. (☎282 1672; www.tourismthailand.org). Ratchadamnoen Nok is the broad boulevard that begins at the 8-way intersection east of the Democracy Monument; the office is 500m down on the right, just past the tourist police station. Very helpful staff doles out **free maps** and advice in English, French, Japanese, bad Italian, and worse German. Open daily 8:30am-4:30pm.

Tourist Information: (☎1672), receives calls 8am-8pm. Tourist information booths are scattered throughout the city: Chakrapong Rd., opposite Khaosan Rd. (☎281 5538; open M-Sa 8:30am-5pm); and Chakraphet Rd., near the Grand Palace (☎225 7612; open daily 9:30am-5pm).

Immigration Office: 507 Soi Suan Phlu (☎287 3101), off Sathorn Tai Rd. 30-day transit visas extended for 10 days; 60-day tourist visas extended for 30 days (1900฿). Bring 4x6cm passport photo. Open M-F 8:30am-4:30pm.

Embassies and Consulates: Cambodia, 185 Ratchadamri Rd. (☎254 6630). Consular services around the corner off Sarasin Rd. on the first *soi* on the left. 30-day visa; 2-day processing (1000฿). Open M-F 9-11am and 1:30-4pm. **China,** 57 Ratchadaphisek Rd. (☎245 7043). Open M-F 9-11:30am. **Indonesia,** 600 Phetchaburi Rd. (☎252 3135). Take regular bus #2 or 11; or A/C bus #505, 511, or 512. Open M-F 8am-noon and 1-4pm. **Laos,** 502/1-3 Soi Ramkhamhaeng 39 (☎539 6667). Visa 300฿; 2-day processing. Open M-F 8am-noon and 1-4pm. **Malaysia,** 33-35 Sathorn Tai Rd. (☎679 2190). Open M-F 8:30am-noon and 1-4pm. **Myanmar,** 132 Sathorn Nua Rd. (☎233 2237). Consular services on Pan Rd., off Sathorn Nua Rd., 1½ blocks from the Skytrain Surasak Station. 30-day visa 800฿ (inquire at embassy for up-to-date status of land crossings); 24hr. processing. Open M-F 8:30am-noon and 2-4:30pm. **Singapore,** 129

Sathorn Tai Rd. (☎286 2253). Open M-F 8:30am-noon and 1-4:30p. **Vietnam,** 82/1 Witthayu Rd. (☎251 5836). Visa 2050฿; 2- to 3-day processing. Open M-F 8:30-11:30am and 1:30-4:30pm. For other embassies see p. 35.

Currency Exchange: 24hr. ATMs abound. Those with "ATM" spelled in blue dots or with a purple hand holding an ATM card accept AmEx/Cirrus/MC/V. You can't throw a stone in Bangkok without hitting a bank, particularly in **Silom.**

American Express: Offices in Terminal 1 (☎504 3181) and Terminal 2 (☎504 3176) at Don Muang Airport. Open **24hr.** Also branches at **G.M. Tour and Travel,** 273 Khaosan Rd. (☎282 3979; fax 281 0642; open M-F 9am-7pm, Sa 9am-4pm) and Sukhumvit Soi 7 (☎655 7719; open daily 10am-9pm).

LOCAL SERVICES

Luggage Storage: The **airport** is the most reliable but a bit pricey (70฿ per day). Open **24hr.** Also available at **Hualamphong Railway Station** for 10-30฿ per day. Open daily 4am-11pm. Guesthouses may also offer this service, but it may not be as secure.

Books: Aporia Books, 131 Tanao Rd. (☎629 2552), opposite the end of Khaosan Rd. One of the best bookshops in Bangkok, with new and used books for sale, trade, or rent. Open daily 9am-8pm. **Used bookstores** are very common in the Khaosan area; Mango Lagoon Hotel runs a great one (open daily 9am-7pm). The omnipresent chain **Asia Books** has a selection of fiction, non-fiction, guidebooks, and lots of Stephen King, John Grisham, and Clive Cussler. **Branch:** Siam Discovery Center, 4th fl. (☎658 0418) Open daily 10am-9pm. Sukhumvit **branch** (☎252 7277).

Local Publications: *The Bangkok Post* is an English daily sold everywhere (20฿). *The Nation* is a more incisive, independent English daily (20฿). Monthly ■ *Metro* divulges the trendiest nightlife secrets (100฿). *BK Magazine* is a weekly publication with similar content (■ free). *Farang* monthly magazine reviews accommodations, restaurants, and the hottest nightlife in Bangkok; also includes entertaining travel articles about various Southeast Asian destinations.

Gay and Lesbian Resources: *Metro* (above) has extensive gay nightlife listings. *Thai Guys* is a gay newsletter and guide to gay life in Bangkok, published 10 times yearly and distributed free at most gay venues.

EMERGENCY AND COMMUNICATIONS

Tourist Police: Tourist-specific complaints handled. Most useful office located next to TAT, 4 Ratchadamnoen Nok Rd. (☎282 1144). All others will refer you here. **Branches** at 2911 Unico House Bldg., Soi Lang Suan (☎652 1721), off Ploenchit Rd. in Siam Sq., and at the corner of Khaosan and Chakraphonh Rd. English spoken. **24hr.** booths opposite Dusit Thani Hotel in Lumphini Park and at Don Muang International Airport.

Pharmacy: Fortune Pharmacy (Banglamphu), in front of Khaosan Palace Hotel on Khaosan Rd. Open daily 9am-2am. **Siam Drug** (Silom/Financial), at the cul-de-sac of Patpong 2 Rd. Open daily 11am-3:30pm. Many pharmacies cluster on **Sukhumvit Road** between Soi Nana and Soi II. Most open daily 8am-late.

Medical Services: Bumrungrad Hospital, 33/3 Sukhumvit Soi 3 (Soi Nana; operator ☎667 1000; emergency 667 2999). BTS: Nana. Thailand's only internationally accredited hospital. Open **24hr. Chulalongkorn Hospital,** 1873 Rama IV Rd. (☎252 8181). Ambulance service. The best public hospital is **Siriraj Hospital** (Thonburi), 2 Pran Nok Rd. (☎411 0241). Take regular bus #19 from Sanam Luang. **24hr.** ambulance. Cheapest vaccinations at **Red Cross Society's Queen Saovabha Institute** on Rama IV Rd.

Telephones: Make domestic calls at "cardphone" booths (5฿ per 3min.) and international calls at yellow "international cardphone" booths. Upper right metal button connects directly to an AT&T operator. Offices offering 10-15฿ international calls abound on Khaosan Rd. The **Public Telecommunication Service Center** (☎614 2261), next to GPO, offers fax and telex. Open **24hr.**

Internet Access: Try **Khaosan Road** and all other guesthouse areas listed. Khaosan rates 40฿ per hr. Elsewhere in Bangkok 60฿ per hr.

Post Offices: GPO (☎233 0700), in CAT building on Charoen Krung Rd. near Soi 32. *Poste Restante.* Mail held for 2 months. Pick-up fee 1฿ per letter, 2฿ for parcels. Open M-F 8am-8pm, Sa-Su 8am-1pm. **Banglamphu Office,** off Khaosan Rd.; turn left onto Tanao Rd. and walk to the corner of Kraisi Rd. *Poste Restante.* Open M-F 8:30am-5:30pm, Sa 9am-noon. **Patpong Office,** 113/6-7 Thanon Surawong Center. Head up Patpong 1 Rd. and turn left on Surawong Rd.; the post office is at the end of the next dead-end *soi* on the left. Open M-F 8:30am-4:30pm, Sa 9am-noon. **Sukhumvit Rd. Office,** 118-122 Sukhumvit Rd. (☎251 7972), between Soi 4 (Nana Tai) and Landmark Plaza. International calls 8am-10pm. Open M-F 8:30am-5:30pm, Sa 9am-noon. To track packages, go to www.thailandpost.com.

Postal Code: GPO 10210; Banglamphu 10203; Patpong 10500; Sukhumvit 10110; *Poste Restante* 10112.

ACCOMMODATIONS

Accommodations in Bangkok are as varied as the exotic fruits lining its streets. Options range from dirt-cheap flophouses to five-star hotels and every level of guesthouse in between. Always ask to see rooms to discern differences in quality.

ACCOMMODATIONS BY PRICE

UNDER 80฿ (❶)		280-480฿ (❸)	
Bangkok International Youth Hostel	Dusit	D & D Inn	Bang
80-280฿ (❷)		Pranee Building	Siam
Baan Sabai	Bang	Rambuttri Village Inn	Bang
Khaosan Palace Hotel	Bang	Sri Ayuttaya	Dusit
Lee Guest House 3	Silom	The Bed and Breakfast	Siam
Lee Mansion 4	Silom	The Atlanta	Sukh
Merry V. Guest House	Bang	Tuptim Bed and Breakfast	Bang
My House Guest House	Bang	White Lodge	Siam
New Siam Guest House	Bang	**480-720฿ (❹)**	
Original Sawutdee Guest House	Dusit	Mango Lagoon Place	Bang
Peachy Guest House	Bang	New Siam II	Bang
S.V. Guest House	Sukh	P.B. Hotel	Sukh
Sala Thai Daily Mansion	Silom	River House Guest House	China
Sawasdee House	Bang	Wendy House	Siam
▨ Shanti Lodge	Dusit	**Over 720฿ (❺)**	
Station Hotel	China	Bangkok Christian Guest House	Silom
▨ Suk 11	Sukh	Chinatown Hotel	China
Sweety Guest House	Bang	New Empire Hotel	China
Tavee Guest House	Dusit	Reno Hotel	Siam
T.T. Guest House	China	YWCA	Silom
Wild Orchid Villa	Bang		

BANGLAMPHU AND KO RATTANAKOSIN

Within walking distance of Wat Phra Kaew, Wat Pho, the Grand Palace, and the National Museum, this hub of Buddhism and architecture functions as a kind of decompression chamber for international travelers and budget backpackers as they enter Thailand. The heart of the fanfare is just to the north along **Khaosan Road,** a dubious backpacker mecca of cheap accommodations, free-flowing

Chang beer, and fake designer clothing. Rooms are often cramped, noisy, and full—reserve ahead by phone. The area just west between Chakrapong Rd. and Phra Athit Rd. is less noisy, just as popular with the *farang*, and can have more rooms available. Khaosan can be cheap, but rooms are often little more than beds with white sheets and walls. About as un-Thai an experience as Diesel shirts and Hollywood movies, Khaosan is laden with drunken *farang*, who haggle with Thais for overpriced goods and swap travel stories over banana pancakes.

GETTING TO BANGLAMPHU. Chao Phraya River Express stop: Banglamphu Pier. Buses: Airport Bus AB2, regular bus #15, A/C bus #511.

New Siam Guest House, 21 Soi Chana Songkram (☎ 282 4554). On the small *soi* that connects the *wat* to the river. Though a few banana pancakes pricier than the competition, this recently renovated guesthouse has a comfortable feel that's worth the extra *baht*. Very popular, and the sheets have maps of Thailand on them. 24hr. Internet 1฿ per min. Singles 200฿; doubles 245฿, with bath 395฿, with bath and A/C 500฿. ❷

New Siam II, New Siam Guest House's sister establishment a block away, is a more upscale version of Siam, with luxurious furniture and a small pool. Doubles with fan 620฿, with A/C 690฿. Low-season discounts. ❹

Wild Orchid Villa, 8 Soi Chana Songkram (☎ 629 4378), across from New Siam. The brightly colored rooms are a welcome change from many Khaosan guesthouses. Unfortunately, some of the fan rooms do not have windows facing the outside. Extremely popular **24hr.** restaurant and bar. Pizza (recommended) 100-175฿. Singles with fan 200฿; doubles with fan 290฿, with bath and A/C 550฿. ❷

Baan Sabai, 12 Soi Rongmai Thanon Chaofa (☎ 629 1599). Slightly outside the busiest tourist areas, Baan Sabai is quieter, less expensive, and better kept than the typical Khaosan guesthouse. The shared baths are clean and the lobby has a large plantation-style porch with a garden. Singles with fan 150฿; doubles with fan 230฿, with window 290฿, with bath and A/C 390฿. ❷

D & D Inn, 68-70 Khaosan Rd. (☎ 629 0526). This upmarket guesthouse offers a Khaosan address and a spic-and-span, impersonal room. Ask to stay in the new section. The rooftop pool is party central. Every room has A/C and private bath. Very popular: book ahead by phone. Singles 450฿; doubles 600฿. Low-season discounts. ❸

Sawasdee House, 147 Soi Rambhuttri (☎ 629 3457). From Khaosan Rd., cross Chakrapong Rd. and walk down the *soi* along the right side of the temple wall; it's halfway down on the right. A socialite's dream, it's practically a backpacker convention. Beautiful restaurant and loads of traditional decor. Rooms are well kept but often full—reserve ahead. Singles with fan 200฿, with A/C and bath 350฿; doubles with fan 380฿, with A/C 400฿, with A/C and bath 550฿. Low-season discounts. ❷

My House Guest House, 37 Soi Chana Songkram (☎ 282 9263). From Khaosan Rd., go toward the river and across the temple grounds; it's 50m to the right. Manages to be close to cafes and bars, but still maintain a quiet atmosphere. An excellent selection of newly released, Western movies keeps crowds transfixed all day. Singles 150฿, with bath 190฿; doubles 250฿, with bath 350฿, with bath and A/C 500฿. ❷

Mango Lagoon Place, 30 Soi Rambuttri Phra Athit Rd. (☎ 281 4783). A little slice of luxury in Khaosan. The cheery rooms are well furnished and all have A/C, hot water, and TV. Doubles 650฿, low-season 500฿; suites 800฿/600฿. ❹

Peachy Guest House, 10 Phra Athit Rd. (☎ 281 6471). High ceilings, spacious rooms, and highly polished dark-wood floors give this guesthouse a comfortable feel. No shoes upstairs. Serene garden, Internet cafe (1฿ per 2min.), and bar are bonuses. Singles with shared bath 120฿; doubles 160฿, with shower, toilet, and A/C 400฿. ❷

Rambuttri Village Inn, 95 Soi Rambuttri Chakrapong Rd. (☎282 9162). A large, new establishment with plain, clean rooms in a hotel-like atmosphere. Singles with fan 290฿, with A/C 400฿; doubles 350฿/450฿. Minibus to airport 70฿ per person. ❸

Merry V. Guest House, 33-35 Soi Chana Songkram (☎282 9267). Walk through the cafe of lazy-eyed backpackers to a guesthouse with cramped, cheap rooms typical of most accommodations in the area. That it's not on Khaosan Rd. makes it worthwhile. All rooms with fan and shared bath. Singles 120฿; doubles 180฿. ❷

Tuptim Bed and Breakfast, 82 Rambuttri Rd. (☎629 1535). From Khaosan Rd. walk to Chakrapong Rd., turn right, and right again onto Rambuttri Rd.; it's about halfway down on the right. Bright, clean rooms, and smiling staff. Filling breakfasts included. All rooms with A/C and shared bath. Singles 400฿; doubles 550฿. ❸

Sweety Guest House, 49 Ratchadamnoen Rd. (☎280 2191). Walk away from the river to the end of Khaosan Rd., cross Tanao Rd., and go 100m down the *soi* to the right. One of the cheapest places in town. Singles 100฿; doubles 150฿, with bath 250฿. ❷

Khaosan Palace Hotel, 139 Khaosan Rd. (☎282 0578), walk down the alley beneath the large green neon sign. For party animals willing to pay, the Palace is in the heart of the action, but the rooms show it. Rooms include private bath and towels. Singles with bath 280฿, with A/C, hot shower, and TV 400฿; doubles 350-580฿; triples 730฿. ❷

DUSIT AND THEWET

Just a quiet bus ride, boat trip, or walk from the sights of Ko Rattanakosin and Banglamphu, the guesthouses behind the National Library in Thewet are some of Bangkok's best-kept secrets. Catering to those who wish to escape Khaosan Rd.'s frenetic atmosphere while retaining its affordability and accessibility, the area is quiet, with little nightlife. Laid-back tropical ease pervades the guesthouses that line the end of Si Ayutthaya Rd. Some taxi and *tuk-tuk* drivers don't even know where this area is; be sure to tell them to go to Thewet, behind the National Library. Conversely, Dusit is dominated by heavily trafficked, wide avenues and large government buildings, and does not have many accommodation options.

> **GETTING TO DUSIT.** Chao Phraya River Express stop: Thewet. Regular buses #16, 23, 30, 32, 33, and 72. A/C bus #505. One bus from each *soi* stops near Thewet, check local listings for more complete schedules.

 Shanti Lodge, 37 Si Ayutthaya Soi 16 (☎281 2497). Billed as "The Oasis of Bangkok," Shanti is one of the best choices in the city. With smoking and shoes prohibited inside, the place feels like paradise. Impeccably clean rooms, sparkling shared baths, and a vegetarian restaurant open 7:30am-11pm. In high season reserve 1-2 weeks ahead. Dorms 100฿; doubles 300฿, with shower 400-500฿, with A/C and shower 600฿. ❷

Tavee Guest House, 83 Si Ayutthaya Soi 14 (☎280 1447). Cozy common spaces with natural wood furniture and a popular restaurant open **24hr.** Rooms are clean and tidily decorated. Dorms 90฿; singles 200฿; doubles 250฿, with bath 300฿, with A/C 350฿. ❷

Sri Ayuttaya, the Tavee Guest House's street-side, upscale sister establishment gleams with shiny, dark-wood-carved furniture. Singles 300฿; doubles with bath 450฿. ❸

Original Sawutdee Guest House, 71 Si Ayutthaya (☎281 0757). Similar to Shanti and Tavee but less character and cheaper. All rooms with fans and clean, shared baths. Singles 150฿; doubles 200฿. ❷

Bangkok International Youth Hostel (HI), 25/2 Phitsanulok Rd. (☎281 0361). Head south on Nakhon Ratchasima Rd. and turn right on Phitsanulok Rd.; it's 20m on the right. Spacious dorm rooms. Sex-segregated. No alcohol, and smoking in permitted areas only. HI members only; non-members can buy a year-long membership on the spot for 300฿ or 50฿ per night. Dorm-style rooms 70฿, with A/C 120฿; singles with A/C and private bath 280฿; doubles with fan 250฿, with A/C and private bath 350฿. ❶

CHINATOWN, PAHURAT, AND HUALAMPHONG

A notch below those in other neighborhoods, Chinatown accommodations line **Yaowarat Road, Pahurat Road, Chakraphet Road,** and **Rong Muang Road.** Travelers staying here are either evading *farang* hordes or jumping on and off early-morning trains. Chinatown offers few budget rooms that are clean and safe. Some are rip-offs, others welcome only Asians, and many are brothels.

> **GETTING TO CHINATOWN, PAHURAT, AND HUALAM-PHONG.** Chao Phraya River Express stop: Ratchawong. Regular buses #1, 4, 25, and 73. A/C bus #501. Boat taxi is easy and enjoyable.

T.T. Guest House, 516-518 Soi Sawang, Si Phraya Rd. (☎236 2946; ttguesthouse@hotmail.com). Exit Hualamphong, take a left on Rama IV Rd., turn right on Mahanakhon Rd., and take the 1st left; it's a 15min. walk or 30฿ *tuk-tuk* ride total. Popular in high season (reserve ahead) with clean rooms and a friendly atmosphere. English library. Midnight lockout. Dorms 100฿; singles 160฿, with window 200฿; doubles 250฿. ❷

Chinatown Hotel, 526 Yaowarat Rd. (☎225 0226; www.chinatownhotel.co.th). One of the few hotels in Chinatown catering to *farang*, the staff wears dandy Chinese clothing. All rooms have A/C and TV. Restaurant open 6:30am-10:30pm. Internet 60฿ per 30min. Doubles 800฿. ❺

New Empire Hotel, 572 Yaowarat Rd. (☎234 6990), opposite the Bank of Ayudhya near Wat Traimit. Functional rooms with some basic luxuries line the dim, cavernous halls at this impersonal hotel. Deluxe rooms are newer and better decorated. All rooms have A/C, TV, and private bath. Standard 750฿, low-season 580฿; deluxe 800฿/650฿. ❺

River House Guest House, 768 Soi Panurangsri (☎234 5429). From Tha Harbor Department, exit the pier, turn left on Soi Duang Tawan, and follow the noise. On the southeastern outskirts of Chinatown, a short walk away from Sampaeng Lane market. The neighborhood is every bit as colorful as Chinatown and even more confusing; women walking alone in the area at night may feel uncomfortable. Spacious rooms with A/C and TV. Doubles 690฿. ❹

Station Hotel (☎214 2794), opposite the Hualamphong Railway Station. Entrance is down the small *soi.* Good for those with a train to catch, but there's no other reason to stay here. All rooms have private bath. Singles 250฿; doubles 250฿, with A/C 400฿. ❷

SILOM ROAD

Although towering skyscrapers dominate **Silom Road,** the surrounding area is home to diverse neighborhoods. On **Pan Road,** a Burmese community lives between the Burmese Embassy and the Hindu temple. The world-famous **Patpong** red light district explores the raunchier side of Bangkok, while the wealthy saunter in and out of the Oriental Hotel. Some of the best budget establishments in Bangkok cluster 2km from Silom Rd. along **Soi Ngam Duphli** and **Soi Si Bamphen** off Rama IV Rd., a bus or *tuk-tuk* ride away. Silom is a nightlife center that attracts hip Thais, expats and tourists alike.

> **GETTING TO SILOM RD.** Chao Phraya River Express: Oriental or Sathorn/Central Pier to access the Skytrain. Skytrain: Saladaeng. Regular buses #15, 76, 77, 115. A/C buses #502, 504,50 5, 515.

Sala Thai Daily Mansion, 15 Soi Sapankoo (☎287 1436). From Rama IV Rd., walk up Soi Ngam Duphli and turn left onto Soi Si Bamphen; take the 1st *soi* to the left and then turn right. Quiet during the low season and happenin' during the high. Sala Thai features sizable rooms with shared bath, a sitting area with cable TV, and a rooftop garden. Singles 200-300฿; doubles 300-400฿. ❷

Lee Mansion 4, 9 Soi Sapankoo (☎286 7874). All rooms are clean and bright with small balconies and private baths. Small rooms 160฿; large 200฿. ❷

Lee Guest House 3, 13 Soi Sapankoo (☎679 7045), next to Sala Thai, offers clean, fan rooms at reasonable prices. Singles 120฿; doubles 150฿, with private bath 200฿. ❷

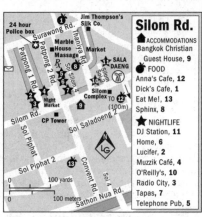

Silom Rd.

▲ ACCOMMODATIONS
Bangkok Christian
Guest House, 9
♦ FOOD
Anna's Cafe, 12
Dick's Cafe, 1
Eat Me!, 13
Sphinx, 8
★ NIGHTLIFE
DJ Station, 11
Home, 6
Lucifer, 2
Muzzik Café, 4
O'Reilly's, 10
Radio City, 3
Tapas, 7
Telephone Pub, 5

YWCA, 13 Sathorn Tai Rd. (☎679 1280), accessible through BMW dealership on Sathorn Rd. Small rooms located within walking distance of Lumphini Park, Suan Lum Night Bazaar, and the Silom/Patpong area. Women only. Bookstore, badminton courts, and restaurant. Singles 750฿; doubles 1000฿. Monthly rate: singles 8,000฿; doubles 9,500฿, plus service and utilities. 5% discount for members. 3% credit card charge. ❺

Bangkok Christian Guest House, 123 Soi Saladaeng 2 (☎233 6303; www.bcgh.org), 1 block from Silom Rd. and the Saladaeng Skytrain stop. Neat and simple rooms for the traveler who can't stay far from the Silom/Patpong nightlife, though the strict rules may make this self-defeating. No alcohol or smoking (or, it goes without saying, prostitution). Breakfast included. Singles 1000฿; doubles 1400฿. ❺

SIAM SQUARE

In the shadow of Bangkok's ritziest malls, **Soi Kasem San 1** lies off Rama I Rd., opposite the National Stadium. Quieter than Khaosan and almost tout-free, Siam Sq. claims a loyal following of travelers. Prices run high, but accommodations are a good deal for those willing to splurge a little. Proximity to the Skytrain makes much of Bangkok's nightlife and the Eastern Bus Terminal easily accessible. Guesthouses can be reached by taking Exit 3 at the National Stadium Skytrain stop, one stop away from Siam Square.

GETTING TO SIAM SQUARE Skytrain: Siam Sq. Regular buses #15, 25, and 204. A/C bus #501.

Wendy House, 36/2 Soi Kasem 1 (☎214 1149). This popular guesthouse is clean and simple. Convenience sets it apart from its neighbors. All rooms have A/C and private hot water bath. Laundry 50฿ per kg. Internet 65฿ per hr. Reserve ahead. Doubles 550฿, weekly 3465฿, with TV and fridge 650฿/4095฿; triples 750฿/4725฿. ❹

The Bed and Breakfast, 36/42-43 Soi Kasem 1 (☎215 3004). Fairly clean rooms and steel frame beds. A/C, phone, and hot shower. For the price, it's a respectable enough place to hang your hat. Breakfast included. Reserve ahead Nov.-Feb. Singles 380฿; doubles 480-550฿; triples 650฿. ❸

White Lodge, 36/8 Soi Kasem 1 (☎216 8867). Bright white halls and the odd nice piece of furniture give this place a cheery feel. All rooms with A/C, private bath, and telephone. Singles and doubles 400฿. ❸

B A N G K O K

Reno Hotel, 40 Soi Kasem 1 (☎215 0026). If the rooms were as nice as the lobby, this place would be a gold mine. Internet, pool, and cafe. Doubles 840฿, with TV 980฿. ❺

Pranee Building, 931/12 Soi Kasem 1 (☎216 3181). A/C doubles are like the Mercedes outside the guesthouse: old and worn, but retaining a hint of past glory. The fan-cooled rooms remind you that you're paying extra for location but not luxury. Doubles 400฿, with hot-water bath 450฿; triples 500฿. ❸

SUKHUMVIT ROAD

Beneath the Skytrain, Sukhumvit Rd.'s accommodations boast proximity to some of Bangkok's trendiest nightlife, great restaurants, and easy access to the Skytrain and Eastern Bus Terminal. The area also hosts a red light scene second only to Patpong. Accommodations range from sketchy places that rent rooms "part time" to some of Bangkok's most luxurious five-star hotels. In between are some good budget hotels and the delightful **Suk 11.** The area is popular with expats and is one of the best places to find long-term accommodation.

> **GETTING TO SUKHUMVIT RD.** Skytrain: Nana or Asok. Regular buses #2, 25, 38, 40, 48, 90. A/C buses #501, 508, 511, 513.

 Suk 11, 1/13 Sukhumvit Rd. Soi 11 (☎253 5927; www.suk11.com), 10m down the *soi* on the left. A truly beautiful enclave in the heart of Bangkok's nightlife. All rooms (even dorms) have A/C, and are worth every *baht*. 2 common rooms with cable TV and DVDs. All baths have hot water. **Internet** access and laundry service available. Dorms 250฿; singles 450฿, with bath 500฿; doubles 550฿/600฿. ❷

The Atlanta, 78 Soi 2 Sukhumvit Rd. (☎252 6069), at the very end of the road. This budget hotel has 60s character, style, and sass. Attracts artists, intellectuals, and those with a sense of humor about where they stay. Singles with fan, balcony, and cold-water bath 330฿, with A/C and hot-water 450฿; doubles 450฿/570฿; triples 570฿/690฿. Funky, spacious suites also available—singles 500฿; doubles 620฿; triples 740฿. ❸

S.V. Guest House, 19/35-36 Soi 19, Sukhumvit Rd. (☎253 35 56), near Asok Station. Good prices, great location, and quiet rooms. Reserve in high season. All rooms have A/C. Singles with shared bath 350฿; doubles 400฿, with bath 450฿. ❷

P.B. Hotel, 40 Sukhumvit Soi 3 (☎651 1525). From Sukhumvit Rd., head up Soi 3, also called Soi Nana, and turn down the alley across from Bumrungrad Hospital; it's on the left. Very nice hotel-style rooms with TV, fridge, and marble baths at lower prices than you would expect, but not many other hotel-type luxuries. Close to happening Q-Bar and trendy Bed Supperclub. Doubles 700฿. ❹

LONG-TERM ACCOMMODATION

It is not difficult to find long-term accommodation in Bangkok. Sukhumvit contains many guesthouses offering weekly and monthly rates, and the area has a thriving expat community. The **YWCA** (p. 109) in the Silom Rd. area also has monthly rates.

Thuang Thong House, 21 Sukhumvit Soi 11 (☎255 4610), in a small courtyard off Soi 11, past Suk 11. Homey rooms are spacious and quiet. 2-room suite with bedroom and combined sitting room and kitchen 15,000฿ per month. ❹

P.S. Guest House, 26/1 Sukhumvit Soi 8 (☎255 2309; psguesthouse@hotmail.com). This clean, quiet guesthouse has smart rooms and suites with hardwood floors. Bedroom with kitchen 17,000฿ per month, not including utilities. Bedroom with balcony 22,000฿, utilities included. ❹

Bright City Tower Service Apartments, 21/4 Sukhumvit Soi 11 (☎651 0159). All rooms have A/C, satellite TV, microwaves, and refrigerators. Rooms cleaned 6 days per week; 120 pieces of laundry included in monthly rent. Studio 18,000฿ per month, junior suite 20,000฿ per month. ❹

⚑ FOOD

Thai cuisine is world-renowned, but no one is more obsessed with and proud of it than the Thais themselves. Thus, they become visibly excited by travelers who venture away from the Thai-Western fare of *farang*-friendly restaurants to eat food the way the natives do—right from the street. While most guesthouses connect to overpriced Thai and Western cafes, the most authentic, best-tasting, and cheapest Thai victuals are served from carts and no-name restaurants lining back alleys. Close your eyes and lose your fears.

FOOD BY TYPE

THAI		Crepes and Co.	Sukh
Bussaracum	Silom	Dick's Cafe	Silom
Cabbages & Condoms	Sukh	Sphinx	Silom
Coca Noodles	Siam		
Forest Tea House	Siam	**INTERNATIONAL**	
KP Suki	China	Cha Cha An	Siam
Krna Nappharat Restaurant	Bang	Daidomon	Siam
Nameless Noodle Place	China	▨ Eat Me!	Silom
O! Hungry	Bang	Hoon Kuang	China
Sam Tam Paradise	Siam	La Casa	Bang
Si Amnouai	Dusit	Moghul Room	Sukh
The Noodle Corner	Siam	▨ Roti Mataba	Bang
Witthyakit Building Food Court	Siam	Royal India Restaurant	China
Yum Saap	Siam	Shoshana	Bang
		White Orchid Restaurant	China
FUSION (WESTERN AND THAI)			
▨ Anna's Cafe	Silom	**VEGETARIAN**	
Bangkok Youth Hostel Cafe	Dusit	May Kaidee's Vegetarian Restaurant	Bang

BANGLAMPHU AND KO RATTANAKOSIN

For good food stalls, stroll down **Soi Rambuttri, Krai Si Road** (in the evening), or **Phra Chan Road** (during the day) opposite **Thammasat University.** The university's **cafeteria** has good cheap grub. During the weekday lunch hour, vendors catering to Thai professionals serve a diverse selection of food. On weekends, hawkers hang out in the area around **Sanam Luang. Khaosan Road** bursts with overpriced Thai and Western cuisine. One or two blocks north on **Tani Road** and at **Wat Chai Chanasongkram,** food stalls fry noodles and rice dishes all day and into the night.

▨ **Roti Mataba,** at the bend in Phra Athit Rd. where it becomes Phra Sumen Rd. This roadside corner is home to some of the best Muslim Thai food in the area; the tender chicken curry *roti* (41฿) is delicious, and the beef-stuffed *mataba* (25฿) will have you eating seconds. Abundant breakfast *roti* options (8-20฿). Open Tu-Su 7am-10pm. ❶

May Kaidee's Vegetarian Restaurant (☎282 5702). Walk to Tanao Rd. at the end of Khaosan Rd. Take a right, a quick left, and left again down the first *soi;* it's 50m down. Sit on a street-side stool and suck on sweet Thai specialties: black sticky rice with coconut milk and fruit (35฿). May Kaidee has a book of recipes (350฿) and offers cooking classes (1000฿) that focus on healthy vegetarian cooking. Open daily 9am-11pm. ❷

SWEET STREET EATS

With the overwhelming abundance of sidewalk vendors, indoor and outdoor markets, and restaurants in Thailand, it's easy to understand the popular saying, "Half of Thailand is cooking, and the other half is eating." Streetside vendors, who pay for their little spot of concrete, are not only fast and cheap, but often provide fresher, not to mention better, eats than what you'll find at twice the price in your guesthouse.

The communication difficulties, piles of raw pork (*moo*) and chicken (*kai*), and simple novelty of eating meals from a street vendor might make some travelers hesitate, but there is often less risk of getting ill from stalls on the street than from restaurants, which carry ten times the quantity of food in order to serve a larger menu. Language difficulties with vendors are easily overcome; vendors usually specialize in just a few dishes (and sometimes only one), and by taking note of the ingredients or simply by watching, you can order with the confidence that you'll receive something you'll enjoy. Vendors are very courteous about cutting down on spice, and if you want spicy *(pet)*, you'll most likely have to ask for it.

Below are some specialties that you'll frequently find on the street (meats optional).

Pad thai: the national dish, it is made of pan-fried rice noodles, [Cont'd on next page...]

Shoshana, on Chakrapong Rd. Facing the temple at the end of Khaosan Rd., turn right and right again at the first alley. This guesthouse restaurant specializes in delicious Israeli and Middle Eastern cuisine such as *falafel* (50฿), *shawarma* (60฿), and salads. Plenty of vegetarian options. Open daily 11am-11pm. ❷

La Casa, 210 Khaosan Rd. (☎629 1627). Fresh pastas (150฿), salads (100-130฿), and creamy gelato are good reasons to stop by this popular Italian restaurant. The extensive menu also includes pizza, risotto, seafood, and meat. Open daily noon-midnight. ❸

Krua Noppharat Restaurant, 130-132 Phra Athit Rd. (☎281 7578). Thai professionals pack in at lunch to enjoy the authentic Thai food at this award-winning restaurant. Fried rice with pork 30฿. Chicken with cashew nuts 60฿. Open M-Sa 10:30am-9pm. ❷

O! Hungry, 45 Soi Chana Songkram (☎629 1412). Next to My House Guest House. This conveniently located restaurant serves Thai and Western options (50-70฿) and has a nightly seafood grill at 6pm. Beer 50฿. Cocktails 70-100฿. Open daily 7am-2am. ❷

DUSIT AND THEWET

The pavement opposite the guesthouses on **Si Ayutthaya Road** bustles with food stalls, as does the market at the end of the road by Thewet pier. With just about every Thai rice, noodle, and curry dish available at rock-bottom prices (30-40฿) these stalls are the best dining option for visitors in this area, especially as there are very few restaurants. Shanti Lodge, Tavee Guesthouse, and Sri Ayuttaya (p. 107) all serve quality Thai food at reasonable prices. With no English sign, **Si Amnouai ❶**, on Si Ayutthaya Rd. at the intersection with Samsen Rd. opposite the National Library, serves the same dishes as the stalls outside at the same prices (20฿)—only indoors. (Open daily 5am-late.) **Bangkok Youth Hostel Cafe,** 25/2 Phitsanulok Rd., has a mostly Thai clientele despite international flags. The menu features noodles, curries, and Western treats (60-130฿). Open daily 11am-10:30pm. ❷

CHINATOWN, PAHURAT, AND HUALAMPHONG

The center of **Yaowarat Road** is a treasure of outdoor dining, and the *sois* that branch off it overflow with culinary delights prepared right on the street. Roasted chestnuts and translucent, succulent lychees abound by the kilo. This area requires more adventurous tastes: shark-fin soups and abalone dishes are specialties. Sampling these delicacies on the street is much cheaper than trying them in a restaurant (sharkfin soup in a restaurant runs 2000฿ and up; on the street it's 300-600฿). As you move down Yaowarat it shifts from Chinese to Indian; excellent Indian restaurants are plentiful near where **Chakraphet Road** meets **Pahurat Road.**

Royal India Restaurant, 392/1 Chakraphet Rd. (☎221 6565), near the river; look for the sign on the left as you come from Yaowarat Rd. Menu features delicious Indian dishes (some vegetarian) at 50-100฿. The *thali*—curry, *masala,* and *naan* set menu (150-190฿)—saves you from making a difficult choice. Open daily 10am-10pm. ❸

Hoon Kuang (☎623 0640), on Yaowarat Rd. a block west of the White Orchid Hotel. Delicious Chinese classics in the heart of Chinatown. Extensive vegetarian and seafood options. Sweet-and-sour tofu 100฿. Prawn with asparagus 200฿. Open 11am-10pm. ❸

White Orchid Restaurant and Coffee Shop, 415 Yaowarat Rd., in the White Orchid Hotel. Famed *dim sum* (30฿ per dish, buy 5 get 1 free) and Friday night all-you-can-eat dinner buffet (6-10pm, 160฿) are reliably delicious. The upstairs restaurant specializes in expensive delicacies like sharkfin soup (2,200฿) and bird's nest soup with seafood (135฿). Open **24hr.** for late-night snacking. ❷

Nameless Noodle Place, on Yaowarat Rd., across from the White Orchid Hotel. Popular eatery serves up a mean noodle soup (30-50฿) and simple rice dishes. Stainless steel furniture and garage doors that open onto the street set it one notch higher than its food-cart neighbors. Similar establishments are scattered all along Yaowarat Rd. Try rice with braised pork rump (30฿); wash it down with a cold chrysanthemum juice (10฿). ❷

KP Suki, 233 Yaowarat Rd. (☎222 6573), at the intersection with Ratchawong Rd. This clean, bright restaurant serves a sanitized, *farang*-friendly version of the noodle and soup dishes found on the street. Their specialty is a chicken broth soup you cook at your table and add meat, dumplings, and veggies to. Friendly, attentive service and nice bathrooms. Most noodle and rice dishes 35-70฿. Open 10:30am-10pm. ❷

SILOM ROAD

Silom Road brims with delicious, expensive restaurants, particularly near Silom Center. Small tourist cafes set up at night on **Surawong Road** opposite Patpong. Look for local fare along **Convent Road** and inside **Soi Ngam Duphli.** If you feel invincible, try the food cart opposite Dick's Cafe—it serves fried scorpions, grasshoppers, and milky white grubs. For some power protein, try the worm salad.

▨ **Eat Me!,** 1/6 Soi Piphat 2 (☎238 0931), off Convent Rd. to the left. Creativity and food collide in this stylish

bean sprouts, peanuts, lime, bean curd, scallion, dried red chili, egg, and the meat of your choice.
Pad ka-phrao: meat with chilis and basil, usually on rice.
Pad kee mow: stir-fried vegetables with chilis and meat (this is a spicy one).
Pad see iew: wide noodles with oyster sauce, vegetables, and meat.
Khao pad: fried rice flavored with meat, egg, and a few veggies.
Kuaitaio nam: ubiquitous and delicious noodle soup with meat or fish balls, bean sprouts, and green onions. Soup stalls are recognizable by the little white fish balls and balls of white noodles in the window.
Papia thot: spring rolls, usually containing bean sprouts, pork, crabmeat and shredded jelly; common on Khaosan Rd. at night.
Satay: meat grilled on a stick. Choose from pork, squid, sausage or any part of the chicken.
Gai thot: fried chicken.
Pla thot: fried fish—don't eat the fins.
Khai chiao: omelette, available with a wide variety of meat and vegetable fillings.
Khanon pang na moo: minced pork on bread, fried.
Som tam: raw, unripe papaya salad; also available with unripe mangoes.
Khao niaw mamuang: mangoes with sticky rice.
Banana pancakes: needs no translation.

restaurant. Photography and sculpture downstairs, delicious entrees upstairs (300-500฿). Live jazz F-Su 8-11pm complements shots of chocolate vodka. As luxurious as a Thai massage. Open daily 3pm-1am. AmEx/MC/V. ❺

Anna's Cafe (☎632 0619; reservations at www.annascafes.com), toward the end of Saladaeng Rd. heading away from Silom Rd. Named after Anna Leonowens, the English governess to the children of King Rama IV (made famous first in the book *Anna and the King*, and then in *The King and I*), this restaurant has some of the best dining in Silom for some of the lowest prices. Extremely popular with Thai families for its Western fusion and authentic Thai dishes as well as the complimentary birthday cake. Look for the twinkling lights draped in the garden outside. Entrees 75-200฿. Open 11:30am-10pm. ❹

Sphinx, 100 Soi 4 Silom Rd. (☎234 7249; www.sphinxthai.com). This trendy, award-winning, and gay-friendly (though not exclusive) restaurant and bar serves Thai and Western dishes (150-375฿) by candlelight. The bar picks up around 11pm and doesn't let up until closing. Cocktails 150฿. Open daily 6pm-2am. AmEx/MC/V. ❺

Dick's Cafe, 894/7-8 Soi Pratoochai (☎637 0078; www.dickscafe.com). From Patpong, cross Surawong Rd. and walk two *sois* to the right. This classy gay cafe and bar draws a *farang* male clientele of all ages. Well-lit with wicker chairs, sofas, and modern-art decor, it's perfect for lunch or late-night socializing. Thai and Western food 60-130฿. Beer from 70฿. Cocktails 140฿. Open 11am-2am. ❸

Bussaracum, 139 Sethiwan Tower, Pan Rd. (☎266 6312), next to the Burmese Embassy. The best time to go to this slightly upscale Thai restaurant is for lunch, when they have an all-you-can-eat buffet of noodle, rice, and meat entrees. Spicy salads, soups and desserts for 170฿. Open 11am-2pm and 5-10:30pm. ❹

SIAM SQUARE

Siam Square is bursting with great restaurants—if you like American fast food. If not, in the afternoon and evening, vendors grill up juicy meats in front of the **National Stadium** on Rama I Rd., at the mouth of **Soi Kasem 1,** and along the *soi* weaving through Siam Sq. Cafes punctuate the *soi* around the square while fast-food chains and Ramen shops pop up in the shopping centers. The **MBK** has an inexpensive Asian food court on the sixth floor. Sidewalk restaurants dot **Ratchaprarop Road** and **Soi Wattanasin** opposite the Indra Regent Hotel.

Sam Tam Paradise, 392/14 Siam Sq. Soi 5 (☎251 4880). Young university students come here in droves to enjoy exotic salads in this hip new restaurant. No English menu, but waiters will help you pick out a good selection of dishes. Usually includes a mango or papaya salad (55฿), a meat dish (70฿), and soup (50฿). Open 11:15am-9pm. ❸

Sizzler, 4th fl., Siam Center Mall, Siam Sq. (☎251 2959). Take a break from the noodles, rice, and deep-fried everything on the street and get your weekly fill of fruits and vegetables at the 99฿ all-you-can-eat salad bar. Meat or seafood entrees 200-500฿, salad bar included. Open daily 11am-9pm. ❹

Cha Cha An, 484 Siam Sq. (☎252 5038), across from the Novotel Hotel in the parking lot at the end of Soi 6. As lively as a karaoke bar, but without the discordant singing, Cha Cha An serves up steaming hot *yakitori* (50-200฿), finger foods, and well-portioned pieces of sushi (set dinners 200-350฿). Open daily 11am-10:30pm. AmEx/MC/V. ❹

Forest Tea House, 400 Siam Sq. Soi 6 (☎251 2417), at the bottom of Siam Sq. Skytrain exit. As much nature as Siam Sq. can handle. Enjoy papaya salad, fried chicken, and sticky rice (80฿) in faux stone booths, among jungle decor. Satisfying spicy meal and large pearl milk tea 140฿. Open daily 11am-11:30pm. ❸

The Noodle Corner, on Soi Kasem Son 1, between Wendy House and the Reno Hotel. This nameless noodle spot features all your street-side favorites with a place to sit, an

English menu, and HBO blaring in the background. Combine soup, noodles, rice, or rice porridge with seafood (40฿) or chicken or pork (30฿). Open daily 9am-9pm. ❷

Coca Noodles (☎251 6337), at the corner of Henry Dunant Rd. and Soi 10 in Siam Sq. This popular ramen chain allows you to pick out meats, dumplings, and veggies to put in the soup you cook for yourself—or save yourself the time and embarrassment and order a pre-made soup (shrimp wonton soup 37฿). Open 11am-11pm. ❷

Witthyakit Building Food Court. Walk down Siam Sq. Soi 4, cross Soi 10, and at the next intersection, enter the basement of the tall building resembling a parking structure. Students and faculty from nearby Chulalongkorn University pack this food court for dozens of Thai dishes at 15฿ per plate. Open daily 11:15am-12:45pm. ❶

Daidomon, 2nd fl., Siam Center. Do away with "atmosphere," get down to business, and eat at this fast-food-esque all-you-can-eat Japanese buffet. Lunch 129฿. Dinner and all-day weekends 149฿. Open daily 10am-9pm. ❸

SUKHUMVIT ROAD

Sukhumvit Rd. brims with expensive quality restaurants and tourist cafes for wealthier travelers. If you want to burn *baht* for a fancy meal and get your money's worth, this is where to do it. The usual food stalls set up on many *soi* at lunchtime to sell Thai dishes for 20-40฿. **Soi 3/1** specializes in Middle Eastern cuisine.

Cabbages & Condoms, 10 Sukhumvit Rd., Soi 12 (☎229 4632). Whether you eat the exceptional Thai food in the beautiful garden or in the A/C restaurant, it is guaranteed not to cause pregnancy. Free condom with the bill. See feature, p. 127. Basil and chili chicken 130฿. Most dishes 80-250฿. Reserve on weekends. Open daily 11am-10pm. AmEx/V. ❷

Crepes and Co., 18/1 Sukhumvit Rd., Soi 12 (☎653 3990), past Cabbages & Condoms. Every type of crepe imaginable: sweet, rich, Western, Thai—or design your own (80-250฿, most around 150฿). Spanish-style *tapas* 90-130฿. Incredibly friendly and service-oriented staff. Open daily 9am-midnight. AmEx/MC/V. ❷

Moghul Room, 1/16 Sukhumvit Rd., Soi 11 (☎253 4465), down the *soi* opposite "Sea Food Center." One of Bangkok's best Indian restaurants. Muslim and Indian curries. Vegetarian dishes 80-90฿. Vegetarian set menu 180฿, with meat 220฿. Open daily 11am-11pm. AmEx/MC/V. ❷

◎ SIGHTS

BANGLAMPHU AND KO RATTANAKOSIN

With its many points of interest, Ko Rattanakosin requires at least an entire day to explore fully. Although extremely touristed, **Wat Phra Kaew** and the **Grand Palace** remain two of the most impressive sights in Bangkok. Chao Phraya River Express (Tha Chang) and buses (#1, 25, 47, 82; A/C #543, 544) stop near the compound. History and art lovers will be glued to the treasures in the nearby **National Museum.** A circuit of **monasteries** is also nearby.

▨**WAT PHRA KAEW (TEMPLE OF THE EMERALD BUDDHA) AND THE GRAND PALACE.** The Temple of the Emerald Buddha was initially the Royal Chapel of the Chakri Dynasty. Inside the *bot* is the actual **Emerald Buddha,** Thailand's most sacred Buddha figure. The Emerald Buddha was discovered in 1434, when lightning shattered a *chedi* in Chiang Rai and an abbot found a stucco Buddha inside. He removed all the stucco and found the glorious Emerald Buddha, made of precious jade, hidden underneath. The figure stayed in Lampang until 1468 before being carted off to Vientiane, Laos. Two hundred and fourteen years later, General Chao Phraya Chakri captured Vientiane and reclaimed the statue. In 1782, King Rama I ascended the throne, moved the capital to Bangkok, and built the Royal Chapel—Wat Phra Kaew—for the Buddha. The frescos on the walls inside the temple portray scenes from Buddha's life; the impressive back wall shows the Lord Buddha attaining Enlightenment and subduing man. Surrounding the temple of the Emerald Buddha are temples of lesser religious import but impressive beauty. Take a look at the frescoes that encircle the compound; the scenes are taken from the ancient Indian epic *Ramayana*.

Next door to the Temple of the Emerald Buddha is the **Grand Palace,** accessible through a gate connecting the two compounds. Inside the gate, look left; the building behind the gate is **Barom Phiman Hall,** still used to house visiting dignitaries. Queen Elizabeth and Bill Clinton have been recent guests. From this point, turn right and stroll down the path past royal buildings on the left. The first is **Amarinda Vinichai Hall,** which once held court ceremonies. Next, **Chakri Mahaprasad Hall,** the residence of King Chulalongkorn, is a hybrid of European and Thai design. Today, the reception areas and central throne hall are used for royal ceremonies and are off-limits to mere mortal backpackers. Farther on, **Dusit Hall** is a symmetrical Thai building with a mother-of-pearl throne.

The **Wat Phra Kaew Museum** is inside the Grand Palace (take a right after the gift shop). The first floor displays relics and parts from original buildings that have been replaced. The second floor contains hundreds of Buddhas and enamel and crystal wares. (☎ 623 5500. *No pictures allowed inside Wat Phra Kaew, although they are allowed elsewhere in the complex. Polite dress required: full shoes, pants, and shirts with sleeves. Shirts, long pants, and shoes are available at the entrance. Complex open daily 8:30am-3:30pm. Museum open daily 8:30am-4pm. 200฿. Admission to Wat Phra Kaew and the Grand Palace includes admission to the Royal Thai Decorations and Coins Pavilion and the Vimanmek Palace in Dusit within 7 days of purchase. Audio guide 100฿ for 2hr.)*

> **✦TIP✦** **GRAND PALACE, PLEASE.** The area around the Grand Palace is full of would-be scam artists who approach tourists, telling them that Wat Phra Kaew is closed for some reason, instructing them to come back in two hours. **Do not listen to these men.** Though they are often well-dressed and speak English well, they are lying. The *wat* is not closed and they are looking to earn commissions on the overpriced goods that they hope you will buy at their shops.

WAT PHO (THE TEMPLE OF THE RECLINING BUDDHA). Wat Pho is the oldest (technically, although it was completely renovated by Rama I), largest, and most architecturally spectacular temple in Bangkok. Its grounds are divided by Soi Chetuphon: one side is home to the monastery, while the other contains temple buildings. Wat Pho was built in the 16th century during the Ayutthaya period and expanded by King Rama I. His grandson, King Rama III, built the *wihaan* that houses the spectacular Reclining Buddha, 46m long and 15m high. Wat Pho is also home to Thailand's first university, a monastery that taught medicine a century before Bangkok was founded. A world-famous **Thai massage school** (p. 122) is its latest achievement. *(From Wat Phra Kaew, walk around the block and take 3 left turns from entrance. ☎ 225 9595. Open daily 9am-5pm. 20฿.)*

WAT MAHATHAT. Also known as the Temple of the Great Relic, this *wat* houses a large sitting Buddha and was home to King Rama I, who was an abbot before he took up military campaigning. Today, the temple is a famous center of Buddhist teaching and home to one of Thailand's two Buddhist colleges. The southern part of the complex offers daily English instruction in Buddhist meditation 7-10am, 1-4, and 6-8pm. *(Between Silpakorn University and Thammasat University on Na Phra That Rd., opposite Sanam Luang. For more info on meditation call ☎ 222 6011. Open daily 9am-5pm.)*

SANAM LUANG. Sanam Luang is the "national common" of Thailand. Once, criminals were lined up and shot here. Although public executions have been discontinued, summer soccer matches and kite-fighting contests—in which the large "male" kites *(chula)* pursue fleeing smaller "female" kites *(pukpao)*—have not (see **Traditional Pastimes,** p. 31). Food stalls ring the park in the daytime. *(On Na Phra That Rd.)*

NATIONAL MUSEUM. As Southeast Asia's largest museum, it is the crown jewel of Thailand's national system. King Chulalongkorn (Rama V) founded it in 1874 with the opening of a public showroom inside the Grand Palace to exhibit collections from the reign of his father. The museum has three permanent exhibition galleries: the Thai History Gallery, the Archaeology and Art History Collection, and the Decorative Arts and Ethnological Collection. The Thai History building was recently renovated and there is now extensive info in English. The section on the monarchy gives great insight into the modernization pressures the Thai kings have faced from the West. The other two collections have an impressive array of artifacts but have not yet been renovated; the galleries are aged and poorly lit, and there is little info in English. *(On Na Phra That Rd. past Thammasat University. ☎ 224 1333. Open W-Su 9am-4pm, tickets sold until 3:30pm. Free tours in English W and Th 9:30am. 40฿.)*

NATIONAL GALLERY. The National Gallery contains a very small collection of classical and contemporary Thai artwork. Rooms upstairs display paintings of scenes from epics and classical plays. Downstairs, works by the novice artist King Rama VI and the considerably more talented King Rama IX are on display. *(On Chao Fa Rd. opposite the National Theater. ☎ 282 2639. Open W-Su 9am-4pm. 30฿.)*

DEMOCRACY MONUMENT. Commemorating Thailand's transition from absolute to constitutional monarchy after the Revolution of 1932, the monument is built on the site of the bloody demonstrations of May 1992, when students and citizens protested the dictatorial rule of General Suchinda Kraprayoon. *(At the intersection of Ratchadamnoen and Dinso Rd.)*

WAT SAKET. Notable for its Golden Mount (an artificial hill topped with a gilded pagoda) soaring 80m high, this popular mount was once the highest point in the city. Today, Wat Saket's 360° panoramic view and golden *chedi* reward those fit enough to make the trek to the top. *(On Worachak Rd. Open daily 7:30am-5:30pm. 10฿.)*

WAT SUTHAT. This *wat* is famous for its association with the Sao Ching Cha (Giant Swing) directly in front of the temple and for housing Thailand's largest cast-bronze Buddha. In the past, Sao Ching Cha was the scene of several of the more curious Brahmin rituals, including one in which a priest would swing on a rope and use his teeth to try to catch money suspended 25m high. Many priests lost their lives performing this feat until a law passed during the reign of King Rama VII prohibited the ritual. The best part of the complex is the main *wihaan* compound, with marble floors, ornate statues, and impressive murals. The surrounding streets are filled with shops selling religious items like Buddha images and votive candles. *(On Tithong Rd. near the Giant Swing. Open daily 8:30am-9pm. 20฿.)*

WAT BOWONNIWET. Through tourists tend to overlook Wat Bowonniwet, it has historically received much attention from the monarchy. King Rama IV spent 27 years as chief abbot here, and the current king, King Bhumibol Adulyadej, spent several months as a monk here in 1956 shortly after his marriage and coronation. The *wat* is home to Thailand's second Buddhist college, Mahamakut University. Come admire the chapel's gorgeous ornamental borders and Chinese-style statues or observe the Western monks who live here. Be polite and discreet. *(On the corner of Phra Sawn and Bowon Nivet Rd. in Banglamphu, near Khaosan Rd. Open daily 9am-5pm.)*

DUSIT AND THEWET

The sights of Dusit and Thewet are quieter than those in the heart of the city and make for a relaxing morning or afternoon of sightseeing.

▨**VIMANMEK PALACE.** Built of golden teak during the reign of King Chulalongkorn (Rama V), the palace is the largest teak mansion in the world. Held together with wooden pegs, the 72-room structure was the king's favorite palace from 1902 to 1906. The palace displays many items from his reign, and the tour gives great insight into the life of this pivotal and long-ruling king. The museum in Aphisek Dusit Hall houses an impressive collection of silver jewelry, silk, and soapstone carvings. *(Entrance is on the left on U Thong Nai Rd. Bus #70 stops nearby. Shorts and sleeveless shirts not allowed. Open daily 9:30am-4pm, last admission 3pm. 45min. tours in English every 30min. 9:30am-3:15pm. Thai dancing daily 10:30am, 2pm. 100฿, students 20฿, under age 5 free, with a Wat Phra Kaew and Grand Palace admission ticket free. Admission to the palace includes a visit to the museum, open daily 10am-4pm.)*

DUSIT ZOO. Once part of the gardens of the Chitralada Palace, Thailand's largest zoo hosts a collection of regional animals, as well as rare species, including white-handed gibbons and white bengal tigers. *(On the right on U Thong Nai Rd. Entrances also on Rama V and Ratchavithi Rd. ☎ 282 9245. Open daily 9am-6pm. 30฿, under age 10 5฿.)*

WAT BENCHAMABOPHIT (MARBLE TEMPLE). This *wat*'s symmetrical architecture and white Carrara marble walls were built in 1899 by King Chulalongkorn. The courtyard is lined with 52 bronze Buddhas that represent styles from different periods, while the garden contains sacred turtles given to the temple by worshipers. Early in the morning (6-7:30am), the monks line the streets to accept donations of food and incense. In February and May, the *wat* hosts Buddhist festivals and candlelight processions around the *bot*. *(On the right of Si Ayutthaya after the Ratchadamnoen Nok Rd. intersection. Take bus #72. Open daily 8:30am-5:30pm. 20฿.)*

OTHER SIGHTS. Past the Si Ayutthaya Rd. traffic light, Ratchadamnoen Nok Rd. opens into Suan Amphon, site of the revered **statue of King Chulalongkorn (Rama V).** This beloved king, who ruled from 1868 to 1910, is remembered for abolishing slavery, modernizing Thai society (he introduced the first indoor bathroom, among other things), and fending off power-hungry British and French colonialists. On October 23, the anniversary of his death, patriotic citizens pay homage here.

Behind the statue, guarded by an iron fence and a well-kept garden, stands the former **National Assembly** (Parliament Building). This domed building was commissioned as a Royal Palace by King Chulalongkorn in 1908 to replace his old residence. Originally called Anantasamakhom, it was patterned after St. Peter's Basilica in Rome. Following the 1932 coup, the palace became the National Assembly building, but the Assembly has since been moved to Dusit. Past Wat Benchamabophit and Rama V Rd. on the left is **Chitralada Palace,** the official home of the Royal Family. The walled compound is protected by a moat and specially trained soldiers. The palace is closed to the public and, unfortunately, it is impossible to get a glimpse of it through the trees surrounding the compound.

CHINATOWN, PAHURAT, AND HUALAMPHONG

Chinese immigrants first settled southeast of the royal center along the Chao Phraya River in the 18th century, just after construction of the Grand Palace evicted them from Bangkok's first Chinatown. Today, this area is called **Yaowarat,**

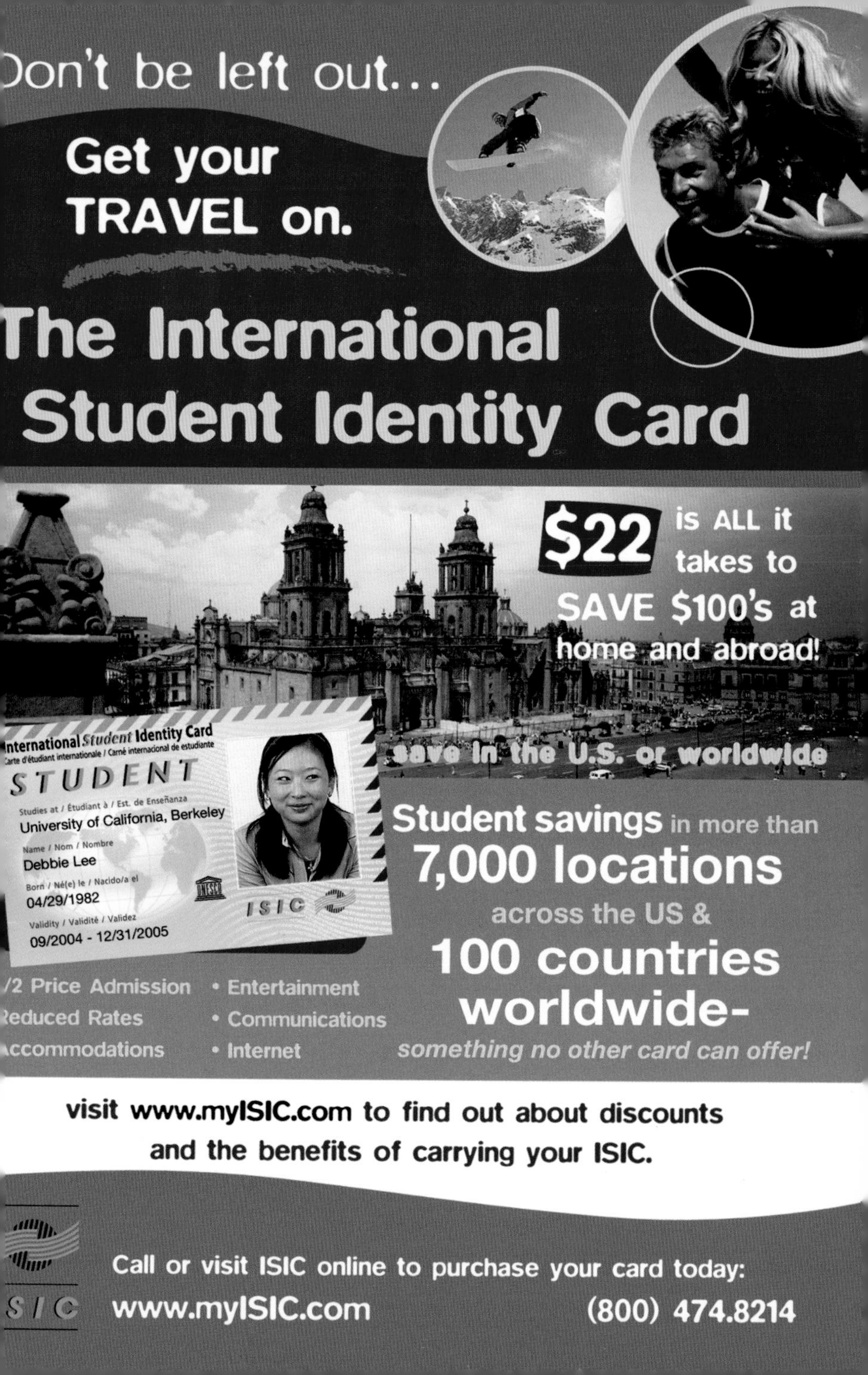

on't be left out...
Get your TRAVEL on.
The International Student Identity Card
$22 is ALL it takes to SAVE $100's at home and abroad!
save in the U.S. or worldwide
nternational Student Identity Card
arte d'étudiant internationale / Carné internacional de estudiante
STUDENT
Studies at / Étudiant à / Est. de Enseñanza
University of California, Berkeley
Name / Nom / Nombre
Debbie Lee
Born / Né(e) le / Nacido/a el
04/29/1982
Validity / Validité / Validez
09/2004 - 12/31/2005
ISIC
Student savings in more than 7,000 locations across the US & 100 countries worldwide-
something no other card can offer!
/2 Price Admission
educed Rates
ccommodations
• Entertainment
• Communications
• Internet
visit www.myISIC.com to find out about discounts and the benefits of carrying your ISIC.
Call or visit ISIC online to purchase your card today:
www.myISIC.com
(800) 474.8214

eTravel

exploration

education

excitement

experience

Good to go.

STA TRAVEL

www.statravel.com

CST #1017560-40

(800) 351.3214

WE'VE BEEN PLANNING ONE TRIP FOR **25** YEARS. **YOURS.**

STUDENT TRAVEL & BEYOND

after the road that runs through Chinatown, or **Sampaeng,** after the smaller road that runs parallel to Yaowarat one block south. Sampaeng has the densest concentration of market stalls in Bangkok. The neighborhood's narrow *sois* and vibrant street life make it worth exploring, especially at night, when the area comes alive. On the western edge of Chinatown is the Pahurat District where the population abruptly turns from Chinese to Indian and textiles take over as the main ware. In the area between Pahurat Rd. and Chakraphet Rd. lies the Pahurat Cloth District. The small *sois* are filled with fabric stores and retail shops selling cheap clothing.

■ **WAT TRAIMIT.** The only major temple in this area is home to the Giant Golden Buddha—a 3m, five-ton, 700-year-old Sukhothai-style gold statue. It is the largest pure-gold Buddha image in the world. When the Burmese sacked Ayutthaya, residents saved the statue by covering it with stucco. Its identity remained secret until 1955, when the statue slipped from a crane while being transported to Wat Traimit. Cracks developed in the plaster, the stucco was removed, and the Golden Buddha was rediscovered. *(Main entrance on Yaowarat Rd. near Charoen Krung Rd.; a smaller entrance on Traimit Rd., accessible by bus #73. ☎ 225 9775. Open daily 8am-5pm. 20฿.)*

SILOM ROAD

M.R. KUKRIT'S HERITAGE HOME. M.R. Kukrit is one of the most colorful characters of 20th-century Thailand. Born in 1911 to a princely family descended from Rama I and II, Kukrit was of the last generation to be raised in the Grand Palace during the time of the absolute monarchy, which made him a revered authority on Thai culture and the traditional lifestyle of the Thai upper class. A Renaissance man of sorts, Kukrit was an influential political leader, founder of Thailand's first political party, prime minister, and amateur actor, dancer, and author (see **Literature,** p. 28). He died in 1995. The home consists of five traditional Thai houses set on two beautiful acres and preserved largely as they were during Kukrit's lifetime. *(19 Soi Phra Pinit. From BTS: Chong Nonsi, walk south down Norathiwat Rajanakarin, cross busy Sathon Rd. and take the 2nd left; the house is 100m down on the right. ☎ 286 6185. Open Sa-Su and holidays 10am-5pm. 50฿. Free 30min. guided tour in English.)*

LUMPHINI PARK. Lumphini Park, the largest park in Bangkok and an oasis in its glass and steel, makes for some of the best people-watching in the city. In the mornings, the Chinese practice *tai chi* while others rent paddle boats and cruise the park's lakes. During the day, locals and expats relax at cafes along Ratchadamri Rd. The early evening sees a virtual carnival of runners, jazzercisers, and sports enthusiasts crowding the paths. *(The park is bordered by Ratchadamri, Rama IV, Sarasin, and Witthayu Rd. and is accessible from Silom by regular bus #15, 77, or 115, or from Siam Sq. and Banglamphu by regular bus #15. Skytrain: Sala Daeng. Open daily 5:30am-7pm.)*

ORIENTAL HOTEL. Founded by two Danish sea captains, the Oriental is one of the world's most famous hotels. H.N. Andersen built the grand Italianate building in 1887, which still stands as the "Authors' Residence" wing and shelters some of the hotel's finest, most expensive rooms. Some suites are available "on application" only. *(48 Oriental Ave. along the Chao Phraya River. Chao Phraya River Express: Tha Oriental.)*

SIAM SQUARE

Famed for its shopping malls, Siam Sq. has some sights and easy Skytrain access.

■ **JIM THOMPSON'S HOUSE.** This elegant house was home to American Jim Thompson, who revitalized the Thai silk industry after World War II and later disappeared in 1967 during a trip to Malaysia. Actually a combination of six teak buildings, the house is home to one of Thailand's best collections of Ayutthaya-

THE LOCAL STORY

THE MYSTERY OF JIM THOMPSON

On Easter Sunday in 1967, Jim Thompson went for a walk and never returned. His disappearance remains unsolved. Neither credible evidence of foul play nor Thompson's body have ever turned up, leading to continued conjecture about what happened 38 years ago to the expat who single-handedly built Thailand's silk trade into a multi-million-dollar industry.

Long before his disappearance gripped the public imagination, Thompson was famous, especially in Thailand. He fell in love with the country during World War II, while training as a member of the Office of Strategic Services (OSS), the clandestine US wartime intelligence service. When the war ended two days before his scheduled mission, Thompson decided to stay in Thailand for good.

Although he had no business experience, he was fascinated by the possibility of opening up Thailand to Western visitors. At the time, Thai silk was a cottage industry on the verge of extinction. Textile manufacturing had made the time-consuming traditional methods of hand-weaving almost obsolete. Thompson founded the Thai Silk Company in 1948, using only a handful of local weavers to supply his small business.

Although Thompson never learned more than a few words of Thai, through his uncanny busi-

[Cont'd on next page...]

and Rattanakosin-period art. Admission includes a tour in English, during which guides discuss ingenious architectural oddities in Thai houses. Like Jim Thompson's exquisite silk products, the house is a tasteful blend of traditional Thai art and modern Western luxury. A shop and restaurant are on the premises. Jim Thompson's flagship store, 9 Surawong Rd., is open daily 9am-9pm. (*Soi Kasem San 2, opposite the National Stadium. Take any Rama I Rd. bus. Skytrain: National Stadium.* ☎ *612 3744. Tours required; every 10min. Open daily 9am-4:30pm. 100₿, students 50₿.*)

SUAN PAKKAD PALACE MUSEUM. Suan Pakkad's eight traditional Thai houses hold the private collections of their Royal Highnesses Prince and Princess Chumbhot of Wagara Svarga. A very comprehensive and informative guided tour takes visitors through rooms filled with artifacts from the Ban Chiang civilization and the Sukhothai, Ayutthayan, and Bangkok Periods. (*352 Si Ayutthaya Rd. Take regular bus #54, 73, or 204 from Siam Sq. past the Indra Regent on Ratchaprarop Rd. Get off near the corner of Ratchaprarop and Si Ayutthaya Rd. and turn down Si Ayutthaya Rd.; it's on the left. Skytrain: Phayathai.* ☎ *245 4934; www.suanpakkad.com. 40min. guided tours in English leave frequently. Open M-Sa 9am-4pm. 100₿, students 50₿.*)

CHULALONGKORN UNIVERSITY. Thailand's most prestigious academic institution is worth a visit. The buildings are an architectural representation of Thai classicism, and the bookstore contains a fine selection of English books. (*On the eastern side of Phayathai Rd., south of Siam Sq. From MBK, cross Phayathai Rd. on the footbridge or take any bus heading south on Phayathai Rd. until you see the campus on the left.*)

OTHER SIGHTS. Opposite Jim Thompson's House is the **National Stadium,** the most noticeable landmark on Rama I Rd. aside from the Mahboonkrong Shopping Complex and the Siam Sq. Shopping Center. Used mostly for sporting events, the stadium holds 65,000. The famous **Erawan Shrine** is farther along Rama I Rd., where it becomes Ploenchit Rd. After accidents causing the deaths of several workers, the Erawan Hotel built this memorial. The shrine was intended to correct the hotel's karma, as it was determined that the original foundation stone had been laid at an inauspicious hour. Dancers hired by grateful worshippers often perform around the shrine.

SUKHUMVIT ROAD AREA

When Rama I/Ploenchit Blvd. crosses Witthaya Rd., it becomes Sukhumvit Rd., stretching southeast out of the city. This area hosts trendy nightlife, upper-crust travelers, red light districts, and nice restaurants, but few traditional tourist sights.

KAMTHIENG HOUSE. This ethnological museum is home to the Siam Society, a cultural society supported by the royals. The museum reconstructs daily life in 19th-century Thailand for people of the matriarchal Lanna culture. Videos and exhibits in English help to explain rituals, cooking, courtship, rice-farming, and water sharing in Lanna villages. The exhibit area is small and takes only an hour to visit. *(131 Soi 21 Asoke, on the left as you walk from Sukhumvit Rd. Near Asok Skytrain station. ☎661 6470. 100฿, students 50฿, age 18 and under 20฿. Open daily 9am-5pm.)*

THONBURI: WEST OF THE RIVER

◪ WAT ARUN (TEMPLE OF DAWN). Named for Aruna, the Hindu god of dawn, this *wat* was built in the Ayutthaya period and embellished during the reigns of Kings Rama II and III into its present Khmer-style form. The distinctive 79m *prang* is inlaid with ceramic tiles and porcelain. The best view of the *wat* is from the Bangkok side of the Chao Phraya River in the early morning or in the evening; the top of the *prang* affords beautiful views as well. *(In Thonburi, from Wat Pho, take a right from Chetupon Rd. onto Maharat Rd. and a left at Tani Wang Rd. This path goes to Tha Tien pier. From an adjacent pier, ferries cross to the wat for 2฿. ☎465 5640. Open daily 7am-6pm. 20฿.)*

ROYAL BARGE MUSEUM. The museum displays seven long, glittering royal barges and their ceremonial accoutrements. The most impressive barge in the museum is the Suphannahongsa, a 46m-long vessel requiring 50 oarsmen, reserved for the king when he makes his annual offering of robes to the monks during the Kathin Ceremony. *(On Arun Amarin Rd., under the bridge over Klong Bangkok Noi. Take a river ferry to Tha Pra Pinklao and walk down river, then follow the signs through the narrow sois to the museum. ☎424 0004. Open daily 9am-5pm. 30฿. 100฿ camera fee.)*

♫ ENTERTAINMENT

NATIONAL THEATER

Dedicated in 1965, the National Theater, on Na Phra That Rd. past the national museum, has regular drama and dance shows. The performance program changes monthly but usually includes at least one *lakhon* dance-drama performance and a concert by the Thai National Orchestra every Friday (see **Drama,** p. 27). Contact the theater for the month's schedule. (☎224 1342. Open M-F 9am-

ness sense and sheer charm, he was able to expand his business into one of Thailand's most lucrative exporters. By exposing wealthy tourists to Thai silk, Thompson turned silk into a high-end fashion trend and was soon filling orders for Broadway shows.

Not simply a successful businessman, Thompson was also respected for his genuine passion for the preservation of Thai arts and culture. In 1962, he restored a traditional Thai teak house on a Bangkok *klong.*

The Cameron Highlands, the area of dense jungle where Thompson disappeared, provide the setting for a disappearance that remains shrouded in mystery. As his friends napped, Thompson apparently left for a walk. Did he fall down a ravine? Was he killed by aborigines or caught in one of their animal traps? Did he take his own life?

These explanations were rejected after an exhaustive search failed to turn up a single shred of evidence, not to mention a body. The failure of the search only led to more speculation. Was Thompson, the former government agent, actually on a covert mission that went awry? Was he kidnapped by Communist agents from neighboring Cambodia?

For years, private investigators turned up nothing, local seers and European psychics offered revelations, and newspapers continued to wonder, while Thailand simply waited for its adopted son to come home. She's still waiting.

3:30pm and 1hr. prior to performances. Tickets 40-100฿ for government-sponsored shows.)

THAI CLASSICAL DANCE DINNERS

Missed the National Theater show? Don't worry, many restaurants offer Thai classical dance dinners with half a dozen traditional dances in an hour-long show. Shows usually include *khon* dances from the *Ramakien* (see **Dance**, p. 27). No shorts, sandals, or tank tops are allowed. Reserve at least a day in advance. At **Ruen Thep,** Silom Village, 286 Silom Rd., enjoy a dance dinner in a garden of turtle pools. Performances begin at 8:30pm and include seven dance styles that change monthly. (☎234 4581; www.silomvillage.co.th. Opens at 7pm; set Thai dinner at 7:30pm. Tickets 450฿. AmEx/MC/V.)

TRADITIONAL THAI MASSAGE

Quality among massage parlors varies tremendously, and many are fronts for prostitution. Pictures of women in the window are giveaways for the latter. Ask other backpackers about their favorites, in addition to using the following listings.

At Wat Pho, **The Traditional Massage School** (p. 116) offers massages for 300฿ per hr., as well as a 10-day, 30hr. course for 7400฿. (☎221 2974. Open daily 8am-6pm.) **Bann Phuan,** 25 Sukhumvit Soi 11, offers the traditional triumvirate of Thai, foot, and oil massage (☎253 5963. 1hr. 200฿, 300฿, and 400฿, respectively. Open noon-2am.) **Marble House,** 37/18-19 Soi Surawong Plaza, one *soi* up Surawong Rd. from Patpong 2, is one of the few massage parlors in Patpong that doesn't have a VIP room. It even has some blind masseurs, who are reputed to be the best in the business. (2hr. Thai massage 330฿. 1hr. head and shoulder massage 280฿.) A popular standby in the Banglamphu area is **Pian Massage Center and Beauty Salon,** 108/15 Soi Rambuttri, Khaosan Rd., down the tiny *soi* next to Nat Guest House on Khaosan Rd. (☎629 0924. Massage 80฿ per 30min., 140฿ per hr. 30hr. certification course 4000฿. Open daily 7am-3am.)

MUAY THAI (THAI BOXING)

One of the world's more brutal sports, Thai kickboxing is generally fought with opponents close together, constantly defending against a kick to the head, which would entail not only a concussion but also a sure knockout. For those who don't mind the actual fighting, the rituals and fervor that surround these matches are fascinating aspects of Thai culture (p. 30) which occur daily at one of two venues.

On Mondays, Wednesdays, Thursdays, and Sundays, the action is at **Ratchadamnoen Boxing Stadium,** on Ratchadamnoen Nok Rd. near the TAT office. Take regular bus #70 from Sanam Luang. (☎01 317 9917 or 629 9856. Fights begin at 6:30pm. Open 9am-11pm. Foreigner tickets 500-800฿, ringside 1500฿.)

On Tuesdays, Fridays, or Saturdays, head for **Lumphini Boxing Stadium** on Rama IV Rd. near Lumphini Park and the night market, which stages better fights—the top card is on Friday. (☎247 5385. M: Lumphini. Take regular bus #115 from Silom Rd. Fights Tu 6:30pm; Sa 5, 6:30, 8:30pm. Same prices as above.)

▣ SHOPPING

After a while in the Bangkok sun, the **Siam Square** and **Silom Road** areas begin to look like one big air-conditioned shopping mall. Siam Sq. houses five immense shopping centers, four movie complexes, 200 restaurants, and a few discos. (Most open daily 10am-10pm.) The area is a hangout for Bangkok teenagers and college students trickling in from Thailand's prestigious Chulalongkorn University.

The undisputed heavyweight of Bangkok's shopping centers is **Mahboonkrong Center (MBK),** on the corner of Rama I and Phayathai Rd. in the Siam Sq. area. With seven floors of department stores, arcades, electronics, music stores, fast-food joints, and a cinema, MBK puts most Western shopping malls to shame. MBK is also by far the cheapest of the Siam malls. Second-hand cell phones and fake designer purses and sunglasses abound in the mall's thousands of tiny shops. Outside MBK, the malls are name-brand and pricey. Connected by a skyway across Phayathai Rd. is the crowded and more upscale **Siam Discovery Center and Siam Square.** Spread over several *soi* are outdoor clothing and music stores, restaurants, two movie theaters, and a hotel. **Amarin Plaza,** at the intersection of Rama I and Ratchadamri Rd., and MBK's main competitor for the largest mall, the **Zen World Trade Center,** up Ratchadamri Rd. toward Phetchaburi Rd., have the same shops as Siam Center but are a little less busy.

⌂ MARKETS

Talat (street markets) all over the city are sources for knock-off designer watches, clothing (from Ralph Lauren to "Ralph Levis"), and pirated CDs.

▦ CHATUCHAK MARKET. This weekend market is a bargain-hunter's dream and a great example of market culture in Southeast Asia. The bustle is unmistakable and addictive as thousands of vendors sell everything from dalmatians to incense, although the main focus is clothing and plants. Chatuchak has a reputation for being the cheapest of all the markets, but come armed with plenty of free time and patience to navigate the crowds, hone your wallet preservation skills, and bargain ruthlessly with relentless vendors. Even the stingiest shopper will be hard-pressed to go home empty-handed. *(Skytrain: Mo Chit. Open Sa-Su 7am-6pm.)*

BANGLAMPHU MARKET. This frenzied market branches onto Chakrapong, Krai Si, and Tani Rd., but the tourist-oriented section is along Khaosan Rd. A late-afternoon affair, the market includes food, souvenirs, leather products, and fake designer clothing. Everything is overpriced, but the feel of the market is priceless.

SUAN LUM NIGHT BAZAAR. Between Lumphini Park and Lumphini Boxing Stadium, the Suan Lum night bazaar is one of the best markets in Bangkok. Search for clothing, gifts, souvenirs, and plants, or enjoy an evening stroll amid the bustling but pleasant stalls. Suan Lum houses several nice restaurants, beer gardens, and a food court where live music plays nightly beginning at 8pm. The best time to go is 6-10pm. *(Entrances on Wireless Rd. and Rama IV Rd. M: Lumphini.)* At the market, the Hun Lakhon Lek Joe Louis Troupe (p. 29) performs daily puppetry shows in the Joe Louis Theater. *(600฿, children 300฿.)*

OTHER MARKETS. Thewet Market is on Krung Kasem Rd. along the Chao Phraya River. The selection is not as diverse, but it's the one-stop shopping center for food or garden landscaping. *(Chao Phraya River Express: Thewet.)* A sweet and brilliant sight is **Pakklong Market,** southwest of Pahurat District over Triphet Ave. Take a river taxi to Tha Rachini and a relaxing stroll through this wholesale flower market. The best time to go is early in the morning or late at night.

In Chinatown the **Sampaeng Lane Market** runs through the heart of Chinatown one block south of Yaowarat Rd. If you need cutlery, jewelry, socks, monk supplies, hats, or fishing equipment, this lengthy alley is the place to go. Extending northwest from the corner of Yaowarat and Chakrawat Rd. is the **Nakhon Kasea (Thieves Market**—so called because stolen goods used to frequently turn up here), best known for its machinery, ice cream makers, and ninja weaponry.

The **Pratunam Market** operates during the day along Ratchaprarop Rd., oppo-site the Indra Hotel. Clothes are the main event, although there is also a wide selection of knick-knacks. In the **Silom** area, vendors set up along **Patpong 1 Road** after nightfall. This is *the* place to buy overpriced fake designer watches, clothing, or soap carvings.

▩ NIGHTLIFE

Bangkok's entertainment and nightlife need little introduction. The city's reputa-tion as the epicenter of Southeast Asia's internationalism is rooted in its effortless mix of traditional art and culture with the hip, connected youth who want to party until dawn. Like other global metropolises, Bangkok offers a wealth of activities, from sophisticated bars and shady massage parlors to dance shows and kickbox-ing—something to entertain and enlighten every type of traveler.

Check out the free *BK Magazine* (available at many bars and restaurants) or the *Metro* (100฿ at newsstands) for the latest in "cool." Places listed here are not associated with the skin trade (see **Red Light, Green Light**, p. 101).

BANGLAMPHU

Perhaps the best part of nightlife on Khaosan Rd. is the urban carnival that takes place on the street nightly after the road is closed to cars. Market stalls, *pad thai* and spring roll vendors, hair braiders, and impromptu street bars selling 60฿ "very strong cocktails" cover the sidewalks. While Khaosan used to be a scene limited to *farang*, the area is growing increasingly popular with edgy Thais and curious expats, drawn by upscale new bars. For a more artsy experience, head to one of the small bar/restaurants on **Phra Athit Road** near the river. Many have live music, and most are open daily 6pm-1am.

Banana Leaf Cafe, 34/1 Khaosan Rd. (☎629 3343), 50m from Gullivers. One of the best bars on Khaosan Rd., and the tourists haven't quite discovered it yet. Comprehen-sive Thai/Western menu 60-120฿. Drinks 60-140฿. Open daily 10am-2am.

Commé Café (☎01 329 8151), in the thick of it on Phra Athit Rd. Earth tones, R&B and jazz, and understated art won't get your pulse racing, but this cafe/gallery/restaurant is a relaxing place to chill with Thais and the occasional *farang*. Open daily 4pm-1am.

Hemlock, at 56 Phra Athit Rd., has a similar atmosphere to Commé Café, with a Greek twist. Open daily 5pm-midnight.

Gulliver's, 3 Khaosan Rd., at the corner of Chakrapong Rd. with a life-size *tuk-tuk* over the door. One of the most popular bars on Khaosan Rd., its specializes in Western food and beer in a dark tavern atmosphere. Pool tables and taps that won't stop until every-one's forced to go home. Beers 60-65฿ per bottle. Open daily 11am-2am.

Ad Here, 13 Samsen Rd. (☎629 2897). Right before Samsen Rd. changes into Chakrapong Rd. Old soul, jazz, and Beatles tunes soothe patrons. Beer 60-70฿. Cock-tails 90-120฿. Live music starts between 9 and 10pm. Open daily 4pm-1am.

Joy Luck Club, 8 Phra Sumen Rd. (☎629 4128). One of the many small, hip bar/restau-rants on chic Phra Athit Rd. that combine art and atmosphere. Thai food 70-90฿. Beer 60฿. Vodka 50฿. Johnnie Walker Black Label 1200฿. Open daily noon-1am.

Boh, Tha Tien pier, near Wat Pho. Though the area quiets down after the big sights close, Boh remains a popular place to enjoy the river view of the nearby temples at night and get tipsy with Thammasat University students. Singha 50฿. Open daily 6pm-1am.

SILOM

Silom Square quiets down after the malls close, but the area is home to six cine-mas and one very notable club. Silom Soi 4 is ground zero for nightlife in Bangkok;

great bars, restaurants, and clubs abound in the area. Sois 2 and 4 are centers for gay nightlife, but gay establishments are scattered all over the area. Patpong 1 and 2 are the infamous red light district. Patpong 1 also hosts a lively night market.

Tapas, 114/7 Silom Soi 4 (☎632 7982). Resident DJs spin house in this "room club" bar. Sink into a couch or get up and groove wherever there's space. Outdoor seating for fresh air. No cover downstairs. 300฿ cover upstairs. Beer 120฿. Open daily 8pm-2am.

Home, next door to Tapas. 3 floors of darkness weakly lit by candles constitute this new and popular bar. Great booty-shaking music—the young crowd gets up and dances in every inch of room. Beer 100-175฿. Cocktails 145-165฿. Open daily 6pm-2am.

DJ Station (☎235 1227), on Silom Soi 2, is awarded "Best Gay Disco" every year by *Metro*. With the metal decor, great house/techno, and a full range of openness, it's no wonder. Also features a nightly cabaret (11:30pm). Cover F-Sa 200฿, includes 2 drinks; Su-Th 100฿, includes 1 drink. No shorts or sandals. 20+. Open daily 11pm-2:30am.

Lucifer, on Patpong 1 Rd., next to Radio City, is delightfully and elaborately designed to look like hell; the club surely takes in its share of devils from the street and bars below. Regardless, this venue still gets kicking around midnight with dance remixes and happy house. Drinks 120฿. Cover F-Sa 130฿, includes 1 drink. Open daily 10pm-2am.

O'Reilly's Irish Pub, 62/1-4 Silom Rd. (☎632 7515), at the corner of Silom Rd. and Soi Thaniyon. A classic Irish pub in the Thai-style madness of Patpong. Live music 9:30pm-12:30am. Pints 99฿. Happy hour 4-7pm; buy-one-get-one free. Open daily 11am-2am.

Telephone Pub and Restaurant, 114/11-13 Silom Soi 4 (☎234 3279; www.telephone-pub.com). All orientations welcome, but caters to a gay crowd, both Thai and foreign. Signature fixture of numbered telephones at tables provides fiber-optic flirting options. Drinks 55-125฿. Western and Thai dishes 100-190฿. Open daily 6pm-2am.

Radio City and **Muzzik Café,** on the south end of Patpong 1 Rd. on opposite sides of the street. After 9pm these colorful, popular bars fill with *farang* seeking either refuge from the madness outside or the nightly live music. Check out the Elvis Presley (11pm) and Tom Jones (midnight) shows at Radio City, or rock out with live bands at Muzzik (starting 9:30pm). Cocktails 140-160฿. Both open daily 6pm-2am.

Concept CM² (☎255 6888), as in "Siam Squared," in the basement of the Novotel Hotel on Soi 6, is as classy as it gets. The city's most recognizable "club" features postmodern decor and talented bartenders. Dance to the beat of Thai and Western techno or dine in the restaurant area 6:30-10pm. Beer 170฿. Food 150-600฿. No shorts or sandals. 20+. Cover F-Sa 550฿, includes 2 drinks; Su-Th 220฿, includes 1 drink. Live music F-W. Officially open daily 7pm-2am, but the doors sometimes don't open until after 10pm.

SUKHUMVIT

Oft-neglected by tourists, Sukhumvit hosts some of the trendiest nightlife around. The Soi Nana area hosts a red light scene, although it's not quite as intense as the one in Patpong. Soi Cowboy (off Soi 21) is the gay Patpong. Most places get busy around 11pm.

Q Bar, 34 Sukhumvit, Soi 11 (☎252 3274; www.qbarbangkok.com). At the end of Soi 11 take a left. Well-to-do expats and even wealthier Thais mix and mingle in this classic institution of the Bangkok social scene. An upscale place, but the darkness and black-lights give it a relaxed feel. Food 150-200฿. Cocktails 200-260฿. Singha 150฿. Strict ID policy—20+. Cover F-Su 600฿, M-Th 400฿ includes 2 drinks. Open daily 8pm-2am.

Bed Supperclub, (☎651 3537), at the end of Sukhumvit Soi 11. This all-white, futuristic club is perhaps the hottest new thing in Bangkok. One side has the beds and supper (supper served in bed F-Sa 9pm, 1190฿; Su-Th 7:30-10:30pm, 990฿; reserve ahead); the other, the bar and DJs. No shorts or flip-flops. Strict ID policy—20+. Cover (Tu, F, Sa

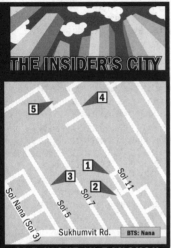

THE INSIDER'S CITY

ONE NIGHT IN BANGKOK

Savvy tourists often head to Silom and Patpong at night in search of something more sophisticated than the 60฿ street cocktails and hair-braiding stalls of Khaosan Rd. Those truly in the know (and willing to spend some *baht*), however, visit oft overlooked Sukhumvit for the best of Bangkok after dark. Cover prices can be steep, so bar-hopping may not be feasible for those on a budget, but the area is well worth visiting for a taste of the hottest nightlife Thailand has to offer.

1. **Suk II Guest House** is the perfect base for your Sukhumvit adventure. Prices are low—save up now so you can party later.

2. Fuel up with a delicious Indian dish from **Moghul Room.**

3. Warm up at **Gulliver's**—no cover and happy hour until 9pm.

4. Dine in bed or rock to the music of the hottest DJs at ultra-trendy **Bed Supperclub.**

5. Sip martinis with the beautiful and privileged at Bangkok's standard of nightlife excellence, **Q Bar**.

500฿; Su-M, W-Th 400฿) includes 2 drinks. Open daily 7:30pm-1:45am.

Mystique, 71/8 Sukhumvit Soi 31 (☎662 2374; www.mystiquebangkok.com). Difficult to find except for those in-the-know (make sure to get a cab driver who knows the way down tricky Soi 31 or ask for directions), talented DJs at Mystique keep 3 levels of sleek dance floors, plush booths and blacklight-struck aquariums throbbing, especially on F nights. Cocktails 280฿. Cover F-Sa 650฿, includes 2 drinks. Open daily 6pm-2am.

Witch's Tavern, 306/1 Sukhumvit Soi 55 (☎391 9791; www.witch-tavern.com). BTS: Thung Lo. Sukhumvit Soi 55 appears more like prosperous Southern California than Bangkok, and though it purports to be a British pub, it makes the very American claim of having the best burgers in town (250฿). The rollicking restaurant/bar boasts good food and a lively crowd. Live music M-Sa 9:30pm-2am. Open daily 10am-2am.

Gulliver's, 6 Sukhumvit Soi 5 (☎655 5340). The bigger, newer sister of the Khaosan institution. A playground of sorts for older white men with pool tables, a big screen TV showing British sports, a foosball table, and lots of Thai women. Happy hour (day really) runs noon-9pm, when shots are 59฿. Burger 115฿. Singha 70฿. Open daily 11am-2am.

LIVE MUSIC

Bangkok's most rewarding nightlife centers on jazz establishments with live music and classy Thai and foreign clientele. Off Ratchadamri Rd., **Soi Sarasin,** just north of Lumphini Rd., has restaurant/bars that play live music nightly. Bands generally start around 8pm, but things get cooking after 11pm.

Brown Sugar Jazz Pub and Restaurant, 231/20 Sarasin Rd. (☎250 1826), opposite Lumphini Park, is regarded as one of the best in the city, with jazz bands every night that draw well-dressed patrons. Food 90-360฿. Beer 120฿. Cocktails 150฿. Live music 9:45pm-1am. Open daily 5pm-1am.

Saxophone Pub and Restaurant, 3/8 Phayathai Rd. (☎246 5472; www.saxophonepub.com), away from Siam Sq., at the southeast corner of the Victory Monument. Another of the city's best jazz clubs. Several bands play nightly, mostly a funk/jazz/blues rotation; check the website for an exact schedule. Try to get a table downstairs. Thai and Western food is delicious (100฿). Beer from 120฿. Open daily 6pm-2am.

Tokyo Joe's, 9-11 Sivaporn Plaza, Sukhumvit Soi 24 (☎02 667 0359), opposite the Artisan Hotel. BTS: Phrom Phong. The most intimate of the jazz clubs, with a soulful Sunday blues special. Generally a whis-

The Story of Thailand's AIDS Fight

Mechai Viravaidya is Thailand's knight in shining armor. The only thing he may have more of than accolades is causes. In 1974, he founded the Population and Community Development Association (PDA), which initially ran family-planning programs in rural areas of Thailand. There are now 16 regional centers and branch offices throughout Thailand. Recently, he's started programs aimed at teenagers, factory workers, and hill-tribe villagers. The modern PDA is focused on the community, tending to every element of the larger picture. Mechai has been a senator, a cabinet member in the Prime Minister's administration, a visiting scholar at Harvard University, and a senior economist for the Southeast Asia region. In 1997, he was given the United Nations Population Award for outstanding contribution to population solutions and questions. He sits on the board of the Narcotics Control Foundation, is a trustee of the International Rice Research Institute, and is the Chairman of the Society for the Prevention of Cruelty to Animals. He is now the "Condom King," a symbol for activism and for, of course, safe sex.

Thailand's first AIDS case was discovered in 1984. By the late 1980s, one-third of Thailand's 200,000-400,000 injecting drug users had been infected with HIV. A thriving sex industry had facilitated the disease's rapid spread through the general population. In 1987, using techniques perfected during his family-planning campaign of the 1970s, Mechai Viravaidya and his PDA launched an AIDS prevention campaign.

At an international AIDS conference in Montreal in 1989, Mechai used his speech to sound the alarm about AIDS in Thailand. He called for a massive public education campaign. While the government stalled, Mechai continued anti-AIDS activism. PDA staff awarded t-shirts to the winners of condom-blowing contests. They opened popular Cabbages & Condoms restaurants with condom decor and appropriately named dishes. Captain Condom cruised the go-gos in Patpong, Bangkok's red light district, urging customers to practice safe sex. Mechai even crowned a queen in the Miss Condom beauty contest.

The epidemic in Thailand reached a crucial turning point in 1991, when Prime Minister Anand Panyarachun made AIDS prevention a national priority at the highest level. The Prime Minister chaired a National AIDS Committee. The media, government, and non-government organizations (NGOs) promoted 100% condom use in commercial sex. The campaign reduced visits to prostitutes by half, raised condom usage, cut cases of STDs dramatically, and achieved significant reductions in HIV transmission.

In 1991, the number of new HIV infections was almost 150,000 annually. In 2000, that number was less than 30,000. All government ministries participated in AIDS prevention. Public education led Thais to change unsafe behavior. The Ministry of Public Health's epidemiological surveillance system (used to track the progression of a communicable disease) proved a critical tool in generating public awareness and political commitment. Effective pilot projects helped ensure that policy led to the right outcome, and the NGO community played an important role in non-discrimination, respect for human rights, and a political dialogue on AIDS. All segments of society were involved: government officials, monks, prostitutes, and drug addicts.

With one million infected since the start of the pandemic, Thailand is still one of the world's hardest-hit countries. Today, over 700,000 Thais live with HIV or AIDS—approximately 2% of Thai men and 1% of Thai women. Each year until at least 2006, over 50,000 Thais will die from AIDS-related causes. Without heroes like the Condom King, the tragedy would be far worse.

For over a decade, the United States Armed Forces Research for Medical Science and the Atlanta-based Centers for Disease Control have collaborated with colleagues in the Armed Forces in Thailand and the Ministry of Public Health, as well as the private sector, to fight HIV/AIDS. Their projects range from vaccine trials to studies of mother to child transmission. International collaboration has been especially important since the 1997 Asian financial crisis, when Thailand cut its budget for HIV/AIDS by nearly 30%. HIV prevalence among injecting drug users is approaching 50%, demonstrating that the education campaign has yet to take hold in that population. Some Buddhist monasteries take in sick and dying AIDS sufferers who have run out of money and have nowhere else to go. The monumental task of prevention and care is far from complete and, unless efforts are sustained and sources of infection addressed, the achievements in controlling the epidemic could be at risk. Still, Thailand's response to the epidemic is one of the world's few examples of an effective national AIDS prevention program. Mechai Viravaidya's condom crusade has helped save millions of lives, both Thai and foreign. One man can make a difference.

The PDA (www.pda.or.th) is devoted not just to fighting the AIDS epidemic, but to community involvement and activism as well. To learn more, volunteer, make a donation, attend an event, or read Tom Agnes' biography about Mechai, entitled From Condoms to Cabbages. See Alternatives to Tourism, p. 81, for more information.

Ted Osius edited and contributed to various Let's Go guides from 1980 to 1984. In 1997, he opened the US Consulate General in Ho Chi Minh City. From 1998 to 2001, he served as Senior Advisor on International Affairs to former Vice President Al Gore. He is now a Regional Environmental Affairs Officer in Southeast Asia for the US Embassy and a published author.

key joint (160-180฿) but also has a smattering of *sake* (200฿) and beer (100฿). Heineken 75฿. Open daily 5pm-1am.

🔢 DAYTRIPS FROM BANGKOK

Travel agencies offer pricey daytrips to attractions outside Bangkok, but these sights can be seen more cheaply independently.

NONTHABURI

The best way to get to Wat Chalerm is by the Chao Phraya River Express ferry, which ends at the Nonthaburi Pier. From here, take another ferry to the west bank (2฿) and hire a motorcycle to Wat Chalerm (10฿). Open daily 9am-5pm.

Nonthaburi province straddles the Chao Phraya River 20km north of Bangkok. The town of Nonthaburi, on the east bank, is known for its fruit and earthenware. On the west bank of the river, in Amphoe Bangkluai, stands **Wat Chalerm Phra Kliad Wora Wihaan,** known to locals simply as Wat Chalerm. Chinese design influences the statues around the grounds as well as the ceramics and flowering decorations. Set in a grove, the monastery grounds are as pleasant as the breezy boat ride. Both the eastern and western piers are bordered by **fruit markets,** where a greater variety and better quality of fruits is available than anywhere in Bangkok.

SAMUT PRAKAN

A/C bus #511 runs by Tanao Rd., at the base of Khaosan Rd. and by the Gaysorn Central Chiatlum shopping plaza on Rama UIV Rd. (stop at the base of Chitlom BTS station) on the way to Samut Prakan. Take a songthaew from the center of Samut Prakan to Muang Boran or the Crocodile Farm (shared 5฿, one person 20฿). Tuk-tuks and taxis run between the 2 parks (50-60฿). Muang Boran: ☎323 9253. Open daily 8am-6pm, last entry 5pm. 100฿, children 50฿. Crocodile Farm: ☎703 4891. Crocodile shows every hr. 9-11am and 1-4pm; additional shows on weekends and holidays at noon and 5pm. Elephant shows 9:30, 10:30, 11:30am, 1:30, 2:30, 4:30pm. Open daily 7am-6pm. 300฿.

The center of Thailand's leather industry, Samut Prakan is 30km south of Bangkok toward the Gulf of Thailand. The main reason to come to Samut Prakan, however, is to see two main attractions: ▨**Muang Boran** and the **Crocodile Farm**. Muang Boran, the "Ancient City," is an open-air museum in the shape of Thailand that contains replicas of monuments and sights from around the kingdom, scaled to one-sixth of the size of the originals. Highlights include the Ayutthaya-style **Saphet Prasat Palace,** the **Dusit Maha Prasat Palace,** and **Khao Phra Wihaan,** which sits atop a hill and affords a spectacular view. The best way to explore the park is to rent a bicycle (50฿) and leisurely cruise the park's 15km of paths. The Crocodile Farm houses over 100,000 crocodiles, including the largest crocodile in captivity. At the "Crocodile Wrestling" show, trainers taunt the toothy behemoths. At the elephant show, the clever animals pluck 20฿ from spectators' hands and place them directly into their trainer's pocket. Other attractions include an aviary, snake pits, a dinosaur museum, and go-carts.

DAMNOEN SADUAK

Buses leave from Bangkok's Southern Bus Terminal for Damnoen Saduak and drop off passengers in the thick of the action (2hr., every 20min. 6am-9pm, 52฿). Upon arrival, locals approach, offering 1hr. boat tours for 300฿. The best time to visit is 8-10am. The market is open daily 6am-2pm. To return to Bangkok, take a yellow songthaew (5฿) into the center of Damnoen Saduak and wave down one of the buses as it turns around.

Only 109km from Bangkok, this **floating market,** though touristy, captures a quick snapshot of a transient canal economy. A boat tour (300฿ per hr.) is a must; there are several vendors, so try to find an English-speaking driver and a motorboat. A ride through the actual market is included in any tour. Boats pass on either side, filled with tourists or Thai women selling exotic fruits like *champoo*, a red or greenish fruit resembling a bell pepper that is said to have a cooling effect when eaten (30฿ per kg). Browse through the woodcarvings and cowboy hats, then head to the sugar farm and sample some palm flower juice or fresh-from-the-hive honey. Depicted in paintings, postcards, and picture books, the bustling scene has become the poster child for traditional Thai life. Some visitors may find the not-so-picture-perfect reality—murky waters, swarming flies, and high-pressure sales techniques—disappointing, but it's a great place to practice bargaining. Bring plenty of cash as there are no ATMs in the area. Feeding the fish outside the Buddhist temple (5฿ per bag of food) is a popular show of respect for vegetarianism.

NAKHON PATHOM

Buses leave the Southern Bus Terminal for Nakhon Pathom (A/C buses 1hr., every 10min. 4:10am-9:30pm, 34฿; buy a ticket for the return bus 2 blocks north of the chedi on Thanon Phayaphan, the road bordering the northern side of the canal. If you want to visit both the floating market and Phra Pathom Chedi in the same day take a bus from Bangkok to Damnoen Saduak early, visit the market in the morning, and stop in Nakhon Pathom on the trip (1hr., every 20min.) back to Bangkok.

Historians speculate that Nakhon Pathom was first inhabited in the third century BC by Buddhist missionaries from India, which would make it one of the oldest cities in Thailand; the city's name comes from the Pali word *Nagara Pathama*, which means "first city." This claim to antiquity is disputed (archaeological evidence begins in the sixth century AD), but undisputed is the fact that Nakhon Pathom is home to one of the world's tallest Buddhist monument, **Phra Pathom Chedi,** which rises to 127m. The monument is the town's primary tourist draw; and while it's impossible to go inside the huge *chedi* itself (which, for religious reasons, cannot even be excavated to find the remains of the original 10th- and 11th-century temples), the extensive grounds hold enough caves, temples, corridors, and other features of interest to occupy hours. Of particular note are the stone reliefs of angels and demons on lions below the Chinese temple, the intriguingly narrow, winding Lab Lae Caves on the southeastern part of the grounds, and the temple's small museum, which is bursting with old amulets, statues, pottery, and other artifacts, but almost devoid of explanations. (*Chedi* open 9am-5pm. 20฿.)

Nakhon Pathom's other local attraction is the **Sabaan Chan Palace,** a 335-acre complex with several residences restored to their original Rama VI condition, open to tour. (☎03 424 4237. Open daily 9am-4pm, last entry 3:30pm. 50฿.) The culinary specialty is *khao lam*, rice with coconut milk steamed in bamboo; sold all around the *chedi*. There is also a fruit market three blocks north of the temple.

Nakhom Pathom holds several festivals. A **fruit fair** is held every year in conjunction with the Chinese New Year (Jan.-Feb.); the **suckling pig festival,** which notably includes a "Jumbo Queen" contest (humans, not elephants), is held every summer at the Samphon Elephant Zoo; and a nine-day-and-nine-night festival to pay homage to Phra Pathom Chedi is usually held late in the year (Nov.-Dec.).

CENTRAL THAILAND

From Bangkok to Trat, the coastal highway follows the progression of economic development. Shiny new refineries, power stations, and petrochemical plants dominate the coast from Si Racha to Rayong. East of Rayong, construction sites and highway traffic give way to groves of durians and mangosteens. Ko Chang is still a backpacker favorite despite an onslaught of upscale development, and its surrounding islands offer ample opportunity to escape the crowds. Farther west, Ko Samet is convenient to Bangkok and the best beaches on the east coast, while charming Ko Si Chang is overlooked by tourists. Beyond its notorious sex trade, Pattaya offers a wide array of tourist attractions and easily accessible water activities. Chanthaburi and Trat teem with mountains, jungles, and waterfalls, most of them completely untouched by backpackers. The fertile Chao Phraya River Basin stretches from Hua Hin in the south to Nakhon Sawan in the north. The region's attractions include the awe-inspiring ruins of Ayutthaya and the lush landscapes fanning west of Bangkok around Kanchanaburi, as well as the River Kwai and the province's national parks. Southbound buses and trains wind through the beginnings of peninsular Thailand, a teaser for the sandy playgrounds farther south.

SI RACHA ☎ 038

Thailand may be a culinary heaven, but few towns celebrate the taste buds like Si Racha does. The maritime heritage of this fishing-village-turned-bustling-town lives on in the restaurants and food stalls, whose blinking lights tempt visitors to sample Thailand's finest and most traditional seafood. Besides its culinary appeal, the town is also home to one of Thailand's best zoos. If neither fish nor caged animals strike your fancy, make sure to arrive early enough to catch the ferry to Ko Si Chang; there are few other reasons to dawdle in Si Racha (and few tourists do).

▐ TRANSPORTATION

Buses heading from Bangkok to Si Racha leave from the Eastern Bus Terminal accessible from the Skytrain's Ekamai Station (2hr.; every 20-40min. 5:40-9pm; 50-70฿). Be on the lookout for a large, glossy-white department store on the right, as the driver will not announce the stop. All transportation in Si Racha operates out of the de facto **bus stop,** the Laemthong Department Store, on Sukhumvit Rd., a 20min. walk from the city center. **Buses** to **Bangkok** (every 20-40min. 5am-6pm; 40-55฿) and **Rayong** (every 20min. 5am-10pm; 40-60฿) depart next to the department store. Infrequent buses to other eastern destinations stop across from the main entrance. To reach the **city center** and **ferry** to **Ko Si Chang,** take either a **tuk-tuk** or **motorcycle taxi** (30฿) from the department store or walk a few blocks north on Sukhumvit Rd. and down Surasak I Rd.

CENTRAL THAILAND

Central Thailand

ORIENTATION AND PRACTICAL INFORMATION

Si Racha's main street, **Jermjompol Road,** runs parallel to the coast, the town's western border. As Jermjompol Rd. heads north, away from **Sukhumvit Road,** it intersects busy **Surasak I Road** to the right and Soi 10 to the left, and then, a block later, restaurant-laden **Si Racha Nakhon Road 3** to the right. Jermjompol Rd. continues north past a white clock tower and the causeway to the small island Ko Loi, home of the floating island temple Wat Ko Loi.

Currency Exchange: Siam Commercial Bank, 98/9 Surasak I Rd. (☎311 313), halfway between Sukhumvit Rd. and Jermjompol Rd. Exchanges traveler's checks. **24hr. ATM.** Open daily 8:30am-3:30pm.

Police: (☎311 800), infrequently staffed **booth,** at Jermjompol Rd. and Soi 10.

Medical Services: Phayathai General Hospital, 90 Si Racha Nakhon Rd. 3 (☎770 200). English-speaking staff available. Open **24hr.**

Internet Access: Naoni Internet, 1/15 Surasak I Rd. (☎511 064; fax 333 894). 25฿ per hr. Fax services available (100฿ per page to the US). Open daily 8:30am-7pm.

ily Chronicle

IN RECENT NEWS

WHERE HAVE ALL THE TIGERS GONE?

They are some of the most majestic, powerful, and impressive creatures on earth. Feared as full-grown adults and adored as cuddly cubs, tigers make for great tourist attractions. Yet the same brilliant orange coats and powerful physiques that draw crowds also lure Thai poachers and dealers of animal materials, causing a great deal of concern from animal rights watch groups.

The poaching of tiger products is sadly indicative of a larger, woldwide trend toward using exotic animals for health, food, and novelty products. Speculative reports have ignited concern that tigers are being shipped to the lucrative Chinese market for tiger bone (to treat rheumatism), kidney fat (to prolong erections), and even tiger penis, which is soaked in liquor and served at high-end brothels.

Alarmingly, the use of tiger parts has become unabashedly mainstream in Thailand. Though Thailand has all the proper laws in place to protect tigers, failure to enforce these laws only increases Thailand's notoriety as an offender in wildlife trafficking.

Post Office: (☎311 202). Past the park near the road to Ko Loi at the north end of Jermjompol Rd., a 10min. walk from the city center. **International phones.** Open M-F 8:30am-4:30pm, Sa-Su 9am-noon.

Postal Code: 20110.

ACCOMMODATIONS

Hotels near the bus stop at the Laemthong Department Store tend to be on the expensive side. Budget rooms line the salty sea near the Ko Si Chang ferry, a 20min. walk or 30฿ *tuk-tuk* ride from the bus stop.

Siri Watana (☎311 037), off Jermjompol Rd. 1 block north of Soi 10, opposite Si Racha Nakhon Rd. 3. This 60-year-old guesthouse is perched precariously over the water. Let the sound of waves lull you to sleep. Rooms are plain but generally immaculate. Towels and ceiling fan. No Western-style bathrooms. Singles 160-200฿; doubles 300฿. ❷

Samchai Hotel (☎311 131), at the end of Soi 10 off of Jermjompol Rd., across from Surasak I Rd. Busier and more impersonal than Siri Watana, with similar amenities except that most rooms have a TV. No English spoken. Singles 200฿; doubles 400฿. ❷

Laemthong Hotel, 139-2/1 Sukhumvit Rd. (☎322 886), inconveniently located across Sukhumvit Rd. from downtown Si Racha. You can't miss the giant neon sign on the roof of this 20-story building. Geared more toward business executives than tourists, Laemthong has drab, well-furnished apartment-style rooms. Singles and doubles 963฿. ❺

FOOD

Si Racha is famous for its **seafood,** often prepared with Si Racha sauce, a spicy red dressing which appears as ซอสศรีราชา on Thai menus. The prime location for gorging oneself on local cuisine is on **Si Racha Nakhon Road 3** after it branches off Jermjompol Rd., one block north of Soi 10. This sizable section of road overflows with food stalls, small restaurants, and larger open-air eateries, allowing diners to stroll through and take their picks. The best place to go to sample a variety of fresh seafood is the **market ❶,** where you can peruse the exotic dishes of literally hundreds of vendors. To get to the market, turn right on Si Racha Nakhon Rd. 3 from Jermjompol Rd. Take the first left; the market is across from the end of the road.

Hanamoto, 7 Si Racha Nakhon Rd. 3 Soi 8 (☎322 274). From Jermjompol Rd., turn right on Si Racha Nakhon Rd. 3 and make the 1st left—Hanamoto is on the left. A clean, cool oasis in a strip of Japanese restaurants and karaoke clubs. Lightly battered, fried-to-perfection shrimp tempura 160฿. Food generally 50-180฿. Bar has extensive selection of Japanese liquors. Large Singha beer 110฿. Open daily 6-11:30pm. ❷

Tik Ka Tow (☎01 270 5404). From Jermjompol Rd. turn right into Si Racha Nakhon Rd. 3. At the 1st fork stay left; the festively lit, open-air restaurant is on the right, with a bright yellow sign in Thai. Buffet (79฿) of fresh seafood and vegetables that you cook at your table on your own grill. Open 6pm-midnight. ❷

Sri Racha Seafood Restaurant, 160-164 Si Racha Nakhon Rd. 3. Turn onto Si Racha Nakhon Rd. 3 from Jermjompol Rd.; veer left at the 1st fork and right at the next. Serves the basics of Si Racha's cuisine. Dishes 80-200฿. Open daily 9am-9pm. ❷

◎ SIGHTS

Si Racha's main attraction is unquestionably the **Si Racha Tiger Zoo,** a rather gimmicky, amusement-park-style affair 9km east of town. A *tuk-tuk* from anywhere in the city should take 25min. and cost 100฿. The zoo's shows (in Thai only) are quite entertaining; take your pick from elephant, crocodile, and tiger shows or the pig-racing extravaganza. There are several opportunities to get a close look at the animals, including taking a picture with a baby tiger (150฿). It's an unusual zoo and an interesting way to kill time while waiting for the ferry. (☎296 556; www.tiger-zoo.com. Open daily 8am-6pm. Several shows per hr. 300฿, children 150฿.)

Those with less time can head to the temples nearer to town. From Jermjompol Rd., **Wat Radniyomtum** is several blocks down Surasak I Rd. on the right. Near the market, Surasak Suguan leads to **Wat Mahasiracha,** on the corner of Tesabarn Rd. The town's most touristed temple is **Wat Ko Loi** (Floating Island Temple), reached via a pleasant walk to the causeway at the northern end of Jermjompol Rd. Release a pair of finches at the top (20฿), watch enormous **sea turtles** in the nearby moat, or just wander around the base of the *wat*, where food stalls and trinket shops create a lively backdrop to the picnicking Thais who flock here on weekends. A shady, well-landscaped park stretches along the waterfront on Jermjompol Rd., complete with balance beams and pull-up bars. During the late afternoon, the park fills up with locals, and you can race the adults around the track or see-saw with the kids.

KO SI CHANG   ☎038

Poor Ko Si Chang is all dressed up with no place to go. A tourist boom years back encouraged the residents of this 5000-person fishing village to spruce up their island with new bungalows and English signs and maps. But as the rest of Southeast Asia opened up, more and more visitors cut Ko Si Chang from their itineraries, heading to the more spectacular Ko Samet and Ko Chang. Accordingly, Ko Si Chang remains a pretty island with good tourist services, friendly locals, and hardly a trace of commercialism. The great problem facing Ko Si Chang is that its ocean views are full of huge tankers and barges to the east. Only two locales, the **Khao Kha Cliffs** and spectacular **Hat Tampang,** escape this shadow. Those seeking postcard-perfect scenes should keep heading east, but for a sandy respite from hot, dusty Bangkok, Ko Si Chang fits the bill.

▣ **TRANSPORTATION. Ferries** to Ko Si Chang depart from Si Racha's main pier at the end of Jermjompol Rd., Soi 14 (40min., every 2hr. 8am-6pm, 30฿). Boats returning to Si Racha leave from **Ta Lang Pier** or **Ta Bon Pier** depending on the tide; ask your guesthouse owner to verify which (6, 8, 11am, 2, 4, 6pm; 30฿).

⚡🏠 ORIENTATION AND PRACTICAL INFORMATION. **Assadang Road** runs north along the water past the two piers, curves past the Chinese temple on the hill, and finally doubles back onto itself 4km later next to the Tiew Pai Guest House. The road then runs south to **Hat Ta Wang** and **Hat Sai Kaew** and branches off to **Hat Tampang**, the island's best beach. To get there, take a right onto **Chakra Pong Road** up the hill, then follow the signs. Motorized *samlor* (a motorcycle-drawn variation unique to Ko Si Chang) go anywhere on the island for 20-50฿, but the best way to see the island is to hire a *tuk-tuk*, regular *samlor*, or motorcycle taxi to take you on an all-inclusive tour of the island sights. The **Tiew Pai Guest House** rents **motorbikes** (200฿ for 12hr., 250฿ for 24hr.), a pickup truck that seats up to 15 people (500฿), and a limo bike (an extended version of the local **samlor**, 250฿), and conducts **boat tours** (3-4hr., 1500฿ for a group of 10). Just 25m up Assadang Rd. from Tiew Pai Guest House to the right, a family (☎01 949 1819) rents **mountain bikes**, though be forewarned—Ko Si Chang is extremely hilly!

The **Thai Farmers Bank,** 9-9½ Assadang Rd., between the piers, exchanges traveler's checks and has a **24hr. ATM** (☎216 132. Open M-F 8:30am-3:30pm.) The local **police** can be reached at (☎216 218). Ko Si Chang also has a general **hospital** (☎261 000), to the right up Assadang Rd. from the pier. Very slow **Internet** access is available from a nameless shop. From the pier, make a left on Assadang Rd.; when the road curves sharply up to the right, the shop is on the left. (30฿ per hr. Open variable hours, usually 11am-5pm.) Across from the hospital, the **post office** has an **international phone.** (☎216 227. Open M-F 8:30am-4:30pm.) **Postal Code:** 20120.

🏠🍴 ACCOMMODATIONS AND FOOD. Ko Si Chang's only budget-minded guesthouse is **Tiew Pai Guest House ❷,** to the left of the pier on Assadang Rd. Fortunately, it's cheap and well-kept, and the owners are friendly and can help you arrange your itinerary while on the island. At night, the guesthouse's karaoke bar thumps to the latest Thai pop. (☎216 084. Singles with shared bath 150฿; doubles 350฿, with A/C and fridge 450฿; triples and family rooms 750-1000฿.) Pricier bungalows line the beach. The best of these is the **Sichang View Resort ❸,** next to the Khao Khat Cliffs in the northwestern corner of the island, 2km from town. It offers a quiet retreat in the midst of great natural beauty. (☎216 210. Comfortable rooms with TV. Singles with fan 200฿; doubles with fan 500฿, with A/C 800฿, with hot water 900฿; add 200฿ to turn any room into a triple.) Conveniently located near the ferry, the **Sichang Palace Resort ❺** has clean rooms with A/C and balconies, along with a swimming pool and restaurant. From the ferry pier, make the first right onto Assadang Rd.; it's 40m up on the left. (☎216 276. Rooms facing the pool 810฿; facing the ocean 1000-1200฿.) The most convenient option for those who want to spend a day at the beach is **Tampang Beach Resort ❷,** just above Hat Tampang. Rooms are the type that are easy to wash sand out of, but the location is unbeatable. (☎216 179. Dorm-style rooms for groups of 10 or more 150฿; doubles 450-700฿; triples 1200฿.) **Camping ❶** is free on the beach; bring your own tent.

Food vendors ❶ sell noodle and rice dishes along **Assadang Road.** Try the tasty breakfast (70฿) and entrees, which range from typical rice dishes (25-30฿) to "fish 'n' fixin's" (180-200฿) at Tiew Pai Guest House's **restaurant ❶.** (Open daily 7:30am-1am.) Munch on more rice dishes (40-50฿) and fresh fish (54-220฿) at the **Sichang View Resort ❸.** Their steamed fresh grouper in black bean sauce (60฿ per 100g) is simple and satisfying. (Open daily 8am-9pm.)

◻ SIGHTS. A tour of Ko Si Chang takes just a few hours by motorbike or *samlor* (200-250฿). From the pier, Assadang Rd. winds up and to the right to the Chinese Temple, a 163-step climb from the road. The temple houses a golden image of a Chinese god in a natural cave and has a pavilion with views of the ocean. Four hundred steps farther up is an enshrined **Buddha footprint,** whose size makes it a good match for the **Yellow Buddha** on the island's west side. Beneath this 10m-high statue are several caves accessible from the lower platform in front of the Buddha. On the road between the Chinese Temple and Yellow Buddha are the striking **Khao Khat Cliffs,** where Rama V built a pavilion to enjoy the horizon and write poetry. The view from the king's seat is stunning. At the bottom, a path by the Sichang View Resort leads down to the cliffs, which are best visited at sunset.

Toward the southern end of Assadang Rd., near the two eastern beaches, are the ruins of King Rama V's **summer palace.** The economic crisis halted the restoration of this royal residence, but you can still see pagodas, reservoirs, and European-influenced buildings. To get there, continue south on Assadang Rd. through the gate of the Marine Research Institute. Continue to ◪**Hat Tampang,** Ko Si Chang's most swimmable beach, by taking the right branch of the road next to the gate and climbing over a steep hill, then making a right on Chalerm Prakariat Rd. Beach chairs are available for rent (20฿ per day).

PATTAYA ☎038

The rumors are true: Pattaya is a city that was built on sex tourism. From the early days when American servicemen first came here for "rest and recuperation" during the Vietnam War, the city has been "hospitable" to *farang.* Beer bars and go-gos filled with Thai women and single—or single enough—foreign men pervade the city. For many years, Pattaya has had an increasingly poor reputation, as a result both of the skin trade and pollution from growing numbers of tourists. In recent years, efforts to clean up the city, including the Pattaya Rehabilitation Project, have made some headway. Diving and snorkeling trips, jet skis, and speedboats are welcome diversions for willing tourists, and Pattaya is even advertised as a family vacation spot. Remarkably, Pattaya does have its charms, but they are forced to coexist with the seedier aspects.

▐ TRANSPORTATION

Buses: Buses from Bangkok depart from Ekamai Station (2½hr., every 30min. 6am-10:30pm, 90฿) and Mo Chit Station (2½hr., every 30min. 6am-9pm, 90฿). Public buses run from Si Racha (1hr., every 10-12min., 40฿) and Rayong (1hr., every 30min. 3am-6:20pm, 50฿). In Pattaya, buses to Bangkok's Ekamai Station (2½hr., every 30min. 5:40am-9pm, 90฿) and Mo Chit Station (2½hr., every 30min. 5:40am-7pm, 90฿) depart from the station on North Pattaya Rd., 2 blocks from Sukhumvit Hwy. A/C buses to Si Racha (1hr., 40฿) and Rayong leave from the bus stop on Sukhumvit Rd., close to the intersection with Central Pattaya Rd.

Trains: Arrive and depart from the **train station** off Soi 45 on Sukhumvit Rd., north of the intersection between Sukhumvit Rd. and Central Pattaya Rd. From Hualamphong Station in Bangkok (3¾hr., 7:10am, 40฿). From Hualamphong (3¾hr., 2:50pm, 40฿).

Local Transportation: Songthaew (10-200฿) travel up Pattaya 2nd Rd. and down Beach Rd. **Motorcycle taxis** (20-50฿) also abound.

Rentals: Thanyamat Rent (☎415 892), in front of Kangaroo Bar on Central Pattaya Rd., close to Beach Rd. Automatic motorbikes 200฿ per day and jeeps 500฿ per day.

◼✦ ▐ ORIENTATION AND PRACTICAL INFORMATION

Pattaya's main strip, **Pattaya Beach Road** (Beach Road), runs north-south, parallel to the coast. Toward the southern end of the city, Beach Rd. turns into **Walking Street,** an area closed to traffic after 9pm and the center of the city's nightlife. **Pat-**

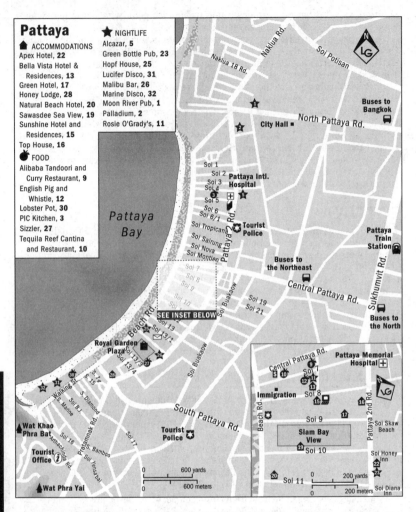

Pattaya

♠ ACCOMMODATIONS
Apex Hotel, **22**
Bella Vista Hotel &
    Residences, **13**
Green Hotel, **17**
Honey Lodge, **28**
Natural Beach Hotel, **20**
Sawasdee Sea View, **19**
Sunshine Hotel and
    Residences, **15**
Top House, **16**

★ NIGHTLIFE
Alcazar, **5**
Green Bottle Pub, **23**
Hopf House, **25**
Lucifer Disco, **31**
Malibu Bar, **26**
Marine Disco, **32**
Moon River Pub, **1**
Palladium, **2**
Rosie O'Grady's, **11**

♣ FOOD
Alibaba Tandoori and
    Curry Restaurant, **9**
English Pig and
    Whistle, **12**
Lobster Pot, **30**
PIC Kitchen, **3**
Sizzler, **27**
Tequila Reef Cantina
    and Restaurant, **10**

taya 2nd Road (2nd Rd.) runs parallel to Beach Rd.; between these two streets is the heart of Pattaya. They are intersected to the north by **North Pattaya Road** and in the south by **South Pattaya Road.** Small numbered *sois* also run between Beach and 2nd Rd., increasing in number as they go south. North Pattaya is the quiet neighborhood of Naklua; south is Jomtien Beach, a center for water sports.

Tourist Office: TAT, 609 Moo 10, Soi Pratamnak (☎428 750; fax 429 113), on the mountain near Big Buddha at the southern end of Pattaya. Open daily 8:30am-4:30pm.

Immigration Office: (☎410 240; http://pattaya-immigration.com). On Soi 8, close to Beach Rd. Extension of stay 1900฿, re-entry 1000฿.

Currency Exchange: Krung Thai Bank, on Central Pattaya Rd., 1 block from Beach Rd. Exchanges traveler's checks, 33฿ fee each. **ATM. Western Union** services at PS Plaza across the street. Open M-Sa 10am-8pm.

Books: Bookazine (☎710 472), on the 1st fl. of the Royal Garden Plaza. Carries English magazines, fiction, and travel guides. Open 10:30am-11pm.

Laundromat: On the small *soi* connecting Soi 7 and 8, across from the Bella Vista. Shirt 15฿, pants 15฿, shorts 10฿, underwear 5฿. Open 8am-8pm.

Tourist Police: 2 **24hr.** stations: one in north Pattaya on Pattaya 2nd Rd. just north of Soi Tropicena (☎425 957) and one in the south off of South Pattaya Rd. (☎425 937).

Medical Services: Pattaya Memorial Hospital, 328/1 Central Pattaya Rd. (☎422 741) is centrally located. **Pattaya International Hospital** (☎428 374) on Soi 8 in North Pattaya has a fantastic reputation and a **24hr. pharmacy** (☎428 374). Both hospitals have English-speaking staff and are open **24hr.** for emergencies.

Telephones: Many small shops advertise overseas calls. Most in central Pattaya charge 20฿ per min. to call America, Australia, or Europe, but a few blocks outside this area you will find 10฿ shops, like the one at the back of Mike's Shopping Center, facing Pattaya 2nd Rd., which is small but air-conditioned with comfy chairs (minimum 3min.).

Internet Access: Virtually identical Internet cafes can be found in the entrance courtyards at the Easting and Sunshine Hotels on Soi 8. 1฿ per min., 20฿ minimum. Printing 10฿ per page. Fax to USA, Europe, or Canada 50฿ per min. Open 8am-3am.

Post Office: (☎429 341). On Soi Post Office. **Western Union.** *Poste Restante.* Open M-F 8:30am-4:30pm, Sa-Su 9am-noon.

Postal Code: 20260.

> **🎯TIP**
>
> **MOTORBIKE BY-LAWS.** Riding a motorbike will probably be the most dangerous thing you do in Thailand. Many Thai rental shops will rent motorbikes to anyone, regardless of his or her ability to drive. Inexperience and motorbikes are a dangerous combination; add alcohol and you have a recipe for disaster. Each year, too many tourists are injured or die in motorbike-related accidents. Before you leave the rental shop, make sure you know how to ride your bike and that it is in good condition. Document any dents before you leave to avoid a hassle later. Whenever possible, *Let's Go* recommends seeking out alternate methods of transportation. But when there is no other choice, keeping a few things in mind will make your trip much safer. **Protect your eyes** by wearing goggle-style sunglasses, such as the designer knockoffs sold everywhere in Thailand. It's easy to get **turned around,** especially if you are used to driving on the right side of the road; force of habit often kicks in on the roundabouts and U-turns. **Stick to the shoulder.** On highways, motorbikes are expected only to occupy the far left shoulder so as to leave room for the other traffic. **Wear lots of clothing.** When skin hits asphalt at high rates of speed, the asphalt usually wins. You need at least jeans and closed-toed shoes. Always **be aware** of traffic which often jumps across to the other side of the road. **Wear your helmet.** They're required throughout Thailand, although most people seem to blatantly ignore this law. Nonetheless, given the mountains of evidence that prove time and again that they save lives, you'd have to be pretty hard-headed not to wear one.

CENTRAL THAILAND

🏠 ACCOMMODATIONS

Accommodations are easy to find in Pattaya, but, unfortunately, budget accommodations are another story altogether. One benefit of Pattaya's extreme tourism is that there are many hotels in the city, most of which are never full or only full during the high season. Many but not all hostels lower their prices significantly during the low season. Often, if you ask for a discount, slow summer hotels will be very accommodating. Usually, Pattaya's upscale hotels have websites where you can book online, and, if you plan ahead, you can get deals through Internet brokers.

Hotels in north Pattaya tend to be a bit quieter and more family-friendly, but also more expensive. Prices drop a bit in central and south Pattaya, and better deals can often be found on 2nd Rd., at hotels situated a block from the beach. Many travelers will feel uncomfortable staying in budget accommodations in south Pattaya, as they cater mostly to single European males. Unless otherwise noted, all hotels in Pattaya have air-conditioning, hot water, and ▨flushing toilets.

Sunshine Hotel and Residences, 217/1 Moo 10 Soi 8, Beach Rd. (☎429 247; www.sunshinepattaya.com). Large, pleasant rooms in a central location—one of the more social hotels in Pattaya. Rooms are situated around the hotel's 2 pools. Look for deals on the Internet. 1200฿; low-season 770฿. Ask for low-season discounts. ❺

Sawasdee Sea View, 327/1 Moo 10 Soi 10 (☎710 566). One of the cheapest options in Pattaya. The rooms are small and the shower is basically right over the toilet, but the hotel is still well-run. No hot water in fan rooms. Rooms with fan 280฿, with A/C 500฿; low-season 250฿/350฿. ❷

The Green Hotel, 217/10 Beach Rd. Soi 9 (☎423 555). Located on a surprisingly quiet stretch of Soi 9, the hotel has a peaceful feel and, in keeping with the name, a plant theme. A good value for the price. Doubles 650฿, low-season 500฿. ❹

Apex Hotel, 216/2 Soi 11 2nd Rd. (☎428 281; www.apexhotelpattaya.com). An incredibly popular budget hotel. Famous for its extensive breakfast (95฿) and dinner (160฿) buffets. The hotel has a pool and parking lot. In high season book 1-2 months in advance. 500-555฿; low-season 450-500฿. ❹

Top House, 382/29 Moo 9 Pattaya 2nd Rd. (☎423 979), opposite Caesar Hotel between Sois 8 and 9. Shaves down room prices (without sacrificing quality) by cutting down on some of the extras. No pool and no elevator. 500-600฿; low-season 400฿. ❹

Natural Beach Hotel, 216 Moo 10 Soi 11 (☎429 239; www.naturalbeach.com), on Beach Rd. at the corner of Soi 11. Well-kept rooms surround a small courtyard with a garden and pool. Standard 950฿, deluxe 1250฿; low-season 750฿/950฿. ❺

Honey Lodge, 597/8 South Pattaya Rd. (☎429 133). One of the more respectable budget options in southern Pattaya. The fluorescent lighting won't be flattering after a hard night out, but the rooms are basically clean and comfortable. Doubles 500฿. ❹

Bella Vista Hotel and Residence, 217/29-32 Moo 9 Soi 7 Beach Rd. (☎362 132), on a small street connecting Sois 7 and 8. A small, new hotel with immaculate rooms. Desk arranges tours to Phuket, Ko Samet, and Ko Chang. 750฿; low-season 600฿. ❺

⬡ FOOD

Unless you're looking for beer or meat on a stick, good food (especially good Thai food) can be hard to find in Pattaya. Many restaurants are in quieter northern Pattaya. Central Pattaya has notoriously few places to eat, though as you head south there is a cluster of restaurants, largely American chains, around the Royal Garden Plaza. Street vendors traverse Pattaya at all times, serving Westernized dishes as well as typical Thai offerings. If Western-style food isn't what you're in the mood for, stick to the carts and nameless restaurants peppering the streets.

Tequila Reef Cantina and Restaurant (☎414 035), 50m from Beach Rd. on Soi 7. Tex-Mex offers a clean, colorful atmosphere in which to enjoy a margarita (130-150฿) or two. The house specialty is the sizzling fajitas (295฿), but the Texas *chili con carne* (95-155฿) is award-winning. Extensive bar, selection of burgers (110฿), burritos (175-195฿), and Thai food (100-120฿). Open 11:30am-midnight. ❸

Sizzler (☎428 128), 2nd Rd., inside the Royal Garden Plaza. The all-you-can-eat salad bar (99฿) with fresh fruits, vegetables, salads, soups, and desserts is filling and a great deal. Add a meat or seafood entree to your salad for 220-555฿. Open 11am-11pm. ❸

PIC Kitchen (☎428 374), on Soi 5. An excellent Thai restaurant. The setting is lush and labyrinthine—choose from open gardens, air-conditioned rooms, or low tables with pillows on the floor. Prices vary depending on where you sit. Home to the **Jazz Pit**, an intimate, sophisticated garden piano bar, open 7pm-1am. Deep-fried stuffed crab claws 220฿. Mixed seafood with coconut milk and chili paste in a coconut shell (215฿) comes highly recommended. 20% off 8am-4pm. Restaurant open 8am-midnight. ●

Alibaba Tandoori and Curry Restaurant, 1/13-14 Central Pattaya Rd. (☎429 881), 2 blocks from Beach St. The most popular Indian restaurant in Pattaya, due to elegant decor and satisfying food. The Alibaba 20 Thieves, a tandoori platter of assorted meats, seafood, and vegetables for 2 people, is 450฿. Delivers. Open daily noon-midnight. ●

English Pig and Whistle, 217/34 Moo 9 Soi 7 (☎361 315). Very popular restaurant and pub with A/C in the midst of a sea of beer bars. Full English breakfast 135฿. Other English dishes 150-200฿. Also rents rooms for 600฿. Open 8:30am-2am. ●

Lobster Pot, 1 block down from the top of Walking St., on the right. It doesn't get any fresher than this. Pick your lobster, prawn, or fish out of the tank and savor it 20min. later. King lobster 195฿ per 100g, rock lobster 110฿ per 100g. Open noon-1am. ●

◉ SIGHTS

All sights in Pattaya are outside the city on the far side of Sukhumvit Rd. Pattaya's most popular attraction, the **Million Year Stone Park and Crocodile Farm,** has a collection of rock gardens and rare plants and animals on its 10 acres, as well as thousands of crocodiles. The park puts on several performances per day, including crocodile, monkey, magic, and fire-swallowing shows. For a couple extra *baht* you can ride an elephant or have your picture taken with tame tigers, bears, and lions. (22/2 Moo 1, Tamban Nong Pla Lai. Turn left at Km 140 on Sukhumvit Rd. ☎549 347. Open 8:30am-6:30pm. 300฿, children 150฿.) The principal event at the **Pattaya Elephant Village** is the elephant show, which takes place daily at 2:30pm (450฿). The village also offers two half-day elephant treks through the brush. Prices vary depending on where your hotel is, as they pick you up and drop you off at the end of the trek. (☎249 818. Off Siam Country Club Rd., 20min. from central Pattaya). If your trip to Thailand doesn't have enough sights for you, check out **Mini Siam** for recreations of famous landmarks from around the world. Alongside the River Kwai Bridge and the Emerald Buddha are icons like the Eiffel Tower, Statue of Liberty, and Leaning Tower of Pisa. Mini Siam is especially popular at night when the miniatures are lit up. (☎421 628. At Km 143 on Sukhumvit Hwy. 250฿.)

◉ BEACHES AND WATER SPORTS

The beach in central Pattaya tends to be disappointing to visitors. While it is not as polluted as it was a few years back, very little swimming goes on at Pattaya Beach. The sand is brown, the water a bit murky, and the bay clogged with boats. For a quieter beach experience, most people head north to Naklua. For water sports, Jomtien is the best spot to hit; while the water is still not clear, there are more swimmers bobbing around and families on the beach. A variety of jet skis (600฿ per 30min.), boats (600-1000฿ per 30min.), and sailboats (700฿ per hr.) are available for rent. Parasailing trips are also popular (500฿). Jomtien is also the only beach in Pattaya where windsurfing is available; renting a board costs 500฿ per hr. Another 100฿ will get you a 1hr. lesson.

Scuba diving and **snorkeling** are both popular activities in Pattaya. There are many dive shops in the area that offer both PADI certification courses in scuba diving and daily dive trips to one of Pattaya's islands or to one of the two shipwrecks offshore (Ko Larn and the HMS Khran are among the best dive destinations). Visibility is best during the high season, generally around 15m. During the low season visibility shrinks to 5-9m due to rain. **Paradise Scuba Divers,** on Beach Rd. behind the Siam Bayview Resort, offers 3-4 day PADI courses in English, German, Thai, and Dutch (☎710 567. 12,000฿) and organizes daily dive trips. (Snorkeling 800฿, scuba diving with equipment 2900฿.) Located midway between Beach and 2nd Rd. on the otherwise-deserted Soi 5, **Seafari Diving Center,** 359/2 Soi 5, offers award-winning certification classes. Their courses range from a one-day introductory course that includes guided reef dives to the full PADI instructor course. Seafari's trips offer pickup and drop off from guests' accommodations. (☎429 060; www.seafari.co.th. Snorkel 800฿, scuba 3000฿; prices include equipment.)

🎵 🎬 ENTERTAINMENT AND NIGHTLIFE

Nearly identical **massage** parlors line the streets of Pattaya. The standard offerings are foot massage (200฿ per hr.), Thai massage (200฿), and oil massage (250฿). The latter two are full body massages—a Thai massage requires you to change into loose-fitting garments provided by the establishment, while oil often requires you to disrobe completely (although it is possible to leave undergarments on if pre-ferred). For a slightly higher-quality experience, head to large massage houses like **Pothivej,** which specializes in 2hr. Thai massage for 500฿. (☎423 676. Located at the northern end of 2nd Rd. Open 11am-midnight.) Or, for an even more mystical experience, try a massage from a blind masseur at any of the many schools found in Pattaya, such as **The Blind Massage Institute,** 413/89 Thappraya Rd., in Jomtien. Blind masseurs allegedly have a more attuned sense of touch that increases their ability to read the body's muscles. (☎251 851. Open 10am-10pm. 1hr. Thai massage 150฿, 2hr. 300฿.)

Pattaya's nightlife is dominated by beer bars (open-air pickup joints) and go-go bars. The beer bars are all virtually indistinguishable from one another, although many name a country as their patron in order to attract male tourists from that region. Beer bars dominate Sois 7 and 8, and both beer bars and go-go bars can be found in great numbers along Walking St. and the *sois* that run off it.

Fortunately, not all of Pattaya's nightlife is focused (overtly) on commercial sex; classier bars and clubs dot the city. Gay nightlife is centered slightly north of Walk-ing St. on Pattayaland 2 (also known as Soi 3/4). One immensely popular form of entertainment in Pattaya is transvestite cabaret. The most famous of these is at **Alcazar,** 78/14 Moo 9, Pattaya 2nd Rd., which puts on choreographed shows nightly at 6:30, 8, and 9:30pm, plus an 11pm show every Saturday. (☎410 224. Tickets 500-600฿.) A less pricey and less professional cabaret is put on at **Malibu Bar,** on Soi Post Office at the corner of 2nd. Pattaya Rd. (Nightly 8pm-2am. Free.)

■ **Hopf House,** 219 Beach Rd. (☎710 650), between Soi Yamato and Soi Post Office. One of the best places to go to meet other tourists. Excellent food, home-brewed ale, nightly live music, and classy but comfortable interior. Pizza 160-220฿. Steak 400฿. Beer 75฿. Especially full on weekends—call ahead to reserve a table for dinner. Open Su-F 4pm-1am, Sa 4pm-2am.

■ **Lucifer Disco,** between Soi Diamond and Soi BJ on the beach side of Walking St. The amount of dancing varies at this multi-level disco, but Lucifer more than makes up for it with its devilishly cool faux-cavern atmosphere and young, lively crowd of tourists and locals. Big-screen TV upstairs. Bar upstairs more expensive than the one downstairs, where beer is 130฿. Live music nightly 10pm-1:30am. Open daily 6pm-3am.

Rosie O'Grady's Irish Pub and Restaurant, 217/36 Moo 9 Soi 7 (☎631 686), next door to the English Pig and Whistle, where (as in real life) the English and the Irish are close but separate. Patrons enjoy sports on the big-screen TV and Irish food as well as the requisite Guinness on tap. Irish stew 190฿. Drinks 80-150฿.

Green Bottle Pub, 216/3-9 Moo 10 2nd Rd. (☎429 675), between Sois 11 and 12, is a laid-back pub with a pretty good selection of food and nightly live music. Steak 400฿. Club sandwich 75฿. Thai food 100-230฿. Singha 80฿. Open daily 10am-3am.

The Moon River Pub, 179/168 Moo 5 North Pattaya Rd. (☎370 614), 2 blocks away from the beach. It's a bit comical to hear Thai bands singing about Lou'siana, but this country-western pub has a loyal following. Tropical drinks 165-175฿. Draft beer 120฿ and up. Happy hour daily 6-7:30pm. Live music Th-Su 9pm-2am. Open daily 6pm-2am.

Marine Disco, just past Soi Marine on the beach side of Walking St. The standard against which all other Pattaya discos are measured. One huge dance floor and pounding house and techno music draw crowds of *farang* and locals alike. The place heats up at 1am and pumps until early morn. Beer 140฿. Mixed drinks 230฿. Open 11pm-10am.

Palladium, on 2nd Rd. 2 blocks south of North Pattaya Rd. This huge club has a stage where professional groups perform nightly and better facilities than Marine disco, but because of its location away from the center of the action it tends to attract fewer crowds, except on weekend nights. Largely Thai clientele. Open nightly 9pm-2am.

⚡ DAYTRIP FROM PATTAYA: KO LARN

Ferries (40min.; 7, 10am, noon, 2, 5, 6pm; return 6:30, 7:30, 9:30am, noon, 2, 5, 6pm; 20฿) leave Pattaya from the pier at the southern end of Walking St. and land at Naban Port on Ko Larn. Ferries (50min.; 9:30, 11:30am, 1:30pm; return 3, 4, 5pm; round-trip 150฿, with lunch 300฿) also head straight from the pier of Pattaya to Thong Lang Beach.

> **TIP**
>
> **FERRY FAIR?** The only reason to take the more expensive ferry to Ko Larn is to avoid the motorcycle taxi (40฿) from Naban Port to Tawaen Beach, the only way to get across the island. The more expensive ferry drops off at Thong Lang Beach, a 5min. walk from Tawaen Beach. However, the free glass-bottomed boat ride advertised is a gimmick—the glass boat is nothing more than a transport boat from the big boat to the island and goes over nothing worth seeing.

Ko Larn is the largest of Pattaya's islands, with whiter beaches and clearer water than the mainland. Tiny Coral Island, just off Ko Larn's coast, has some of the best snorkeling in Pattaya. Ko Larn's biggest draw is Tawaen Beach, a wide expanse of white sand leading to turquoise water. Unfortunately, the beach fills up daily during the high season. A small area is roped off for swimmers, but most of the water is taken up by jet skis (600฿ per 30min.), banana boats (600฿ per 30min.), and speed boats (800฿ per 30min.). There are several other pretty beaches on Ko Larn, including Thieu Beach and Sanae Beach, but coral keeps people from swimming.

If you are going to stay overnight at the island, the best place to do so is at the **Sunrise Cafe and Bar ❷** (☎434 083), next to the pier at Naban Port. The owners are extremely friendly and rooms are clean and spacious. (Free Internet. Doubles with fan 350฿, with A/C 450฿.) The Sunrise also serves food (omelettes 30-70฿, sandwiches 30-50฿) whenever anyone wants it—a good alternative to the generic seafood places on the beach. Bring cash—there is no ATM on Ko Larn.

RAYONG ☎038

The city of Rayong, located on the east coast halfway between Bangkok and the Cambodian border, does not draw many tourists in its own right, but is a transportation hub, especially for those on their way to Ko Samet. The city's only claims to fame are its reputation for producing the succulent summer fruits pineapple and durian, and the dubious distinction of being the *naam plaa* (fish sauce) capital of Thailand. The time-intensive (and as one might imagine, smelly) process of producing *naam plaa* involves letting fish decompose for seven months—yum.

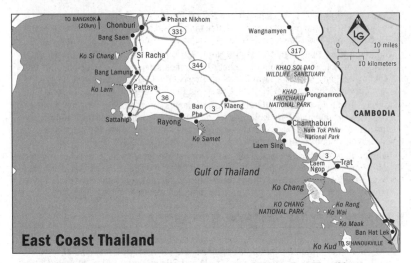

East Coast Thailand

Songthaew leave from **Rayong Bus Station** (☎611 379) for Ban Phe (20min., every 15min. 6:15am-6:45pm, 15฿). **Buses** go to: Bangkok (3½hr., every 30min. 3am-9:10pm, 117฿); Chanthaburi (2½hr., every 50min. 5am-7:30pm, 55฿); Khorat (6hr., every hr. 4:20am-9pm, 125-225฿); Nong Khan (13hr., every hr. 7am-8pm, 241-434฿); Pattaya (50min., every 30min. 3am-6:20pm, 50฿); Si Racha (2hr., every 20min. 5am-7pm, 55฿); Trat (7:30am-12:50pm, 91฿).

Rayong's main street, **Sukhumvit Road,** runs east-west through the center of town. The **bus station** is two blocks north of Sukhumvit Rd. The ocean lies to the south. Services include: **TAT Office** (☎655 420, tourist information line 1642), 7km west of Rayong; **currency exchange** and **24hr. ATM** at the Bank of Ayudhya, Sukhumvit Rd. (☎611 534; open M-F 8:30am-3:30pm); **Rayong Hospital** (☎611 104), on Sukhumvit Rd. east of the bus station; **Internet access** at Banana Computer, across from the Star Hotel (☎920 007; 30฿ per hr.; open 9am-8am); and the **post office** on Sukhumvit Rd., half a block east of the bus station. (Open M-F 8:30am-4:30pm, Sa-Su 9am-noon.) **Postal Code:** 21000.

Both hotels and restaurants are fairly scarce in Rayong. The **Burapa Palace Hotel ❸**, 69 Sukhumvit Rd., has large, bright, spartan rooms. (☎622 946. Rooms with fan 400฿, with A/C 600฿.) **The Star Hotel ❺**, 109 Rayong Trade Center, Soi 4, behind the bus station, is the luxury choice in Rayong, with plenty of activities to fill the time, including bowling, snooker, karaoke and two pools. (☎614 901. Doubles 1000-1500฿.) The Star also has a Japanese **restaurant ❸** with an excellent lunch buffet. (120฿. Open 6am-midnight.) The market behind the bus station is a good place to pick up fruit and dried fish. There is a **24hr. Tesco** grocery on Sukhumvit Rd., two blocks west of the bus station. Thaksinmajaraj Rd. has numerous noodle, curry and barbecue stands with small areas to sit down and eat in.

BAN PHE   ☎038

Ban Phe is a small coastal town that serves primarily as a jumping-off point to Ko Samet. Both Nuan Tip Pier and Tarua Phe Pier offer service to the island (p. 143).

Buses run from Bangkok's Ekamai terminal to Ban Phe (3½hr.; 15 per day 5am-8:30pm, return every hr. 4am-7pm; 124฿). The **Ban Phe Bus Station** is across from Nuan Tip Pier. To get elsewhere, take a **songthaew** from the street-side stop next to the bus station to Rayong (30min., every 10min. 6:15am-6pm, 15฿) and transfer there (see above). **Travel agencies** in Pattaya offer convenient direct service to Ban Phe for 150฿. Services in Ban Phe include: a **24hr. ATM** outside the 7-Eleven across from Tarua Phe Pier; the **police station** (☎651 111), midway between the two piers; and **Internet access** at Tan Tan Too, across from Tarua Pier. (☎653 671. 1฿ per min. Open 7:30am-6:30pm.)

If you miss the last ferry, there are several accommodations clustered around the piers. **Chareeya Court ❷**, on the small side street two blocks west of Tarua Phe Pier and across from Tadet Pier, offers adequate rooms at cheap prices. (☎652 432. Rooms with fan 200฿, with A/C 350฿.) **Diamond Hotel ❹**, 2 86/2 Moo 2, Tambol Phe, on the main road just west of Tarua Pier, has slightly more upscale rooms at higher prices. (☎651 826. Rooms with fan 700฿, with A/C 1000฿). Satisfy your waiting-for-the-ferry munchies at the **Stoney Monkey Pizza Company ❷**, next door to Tan Tan Too. (Cheese pizza 80-150฿. Hawaiian pizza 90-180฿. Open daily 8:30am-8pm.)

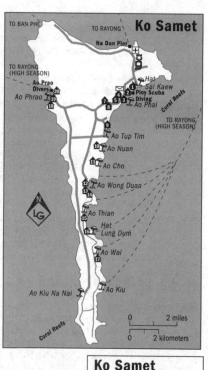

KO SAMET

☎038

Just four hours from Bangkok, Ko Samet is a popular vacation spot for Thais and foreigners alike. Over the past 20 years, beachside bungalows have slowly encroached on much of the shoreline, and loud *farang* pubs and Thai karaoke bars dominate the once-still nights. Development aside, however, Ko Samet delivers. With the best beaches and clearest water on the east coast, a dip in its tranquil waves or a nap on its clean, white sand will satisfy the traveler seeking good old-fashioned relaxation. Many travelers prefer Samet's low-key atmosphere to that of its rowdier and more developed island neighbors.

▣ TRANSPORTATION

Ferries: Nuan Tip Pier and **Tarua Phe Pier** in the town of Ban Phe serve Ko Samet. If you arrive via *songthaew* from Rayong, you will be let off at Tarua Phe Pier, opposite the 7-Eleven. Ferries here leave regularly and go to **Ao Wong Duan** (9:30am, 1:30, 5pm–not always available; one-way 60฿) and **Na Dan Pier** (every hr. 8am-5pm, one-way 50฿), regardless of the number of passengers. Buses from Bangkok stop in front of **Nuan Tip Pier** (☎651 508), 200m east of Tarua Phe Pier,

Ko Samet
see map above

🏠 BUNGALOWS AND RESORTS
Ao Phai Hut, 7
Ao Prao Resort, 20
Ploy Thalay, 2
Horizons Resort, 15
Le Vimarn Cottages, 18
Lima Coco Resort, 19
Lung Dum Bungalows, 16
Naga Bungalows, 4
Nice and Easy, 13
Nuan Bungalows, 10
Samet Cabana, 12
Samet Ville Resort, 17
Sea-Breeze Bungalows, 8
Sea Horse Bungalows, 14
Tok's Little Hut, 5
Tubtim Resort, 9
White Sands Resort, 3
Wonderland Resort, 11

🍎 FOOD
Jirawan, 1

CENTRAL THAILAND

which offers service to Na Dan Pier in northern Ko Samet (40min., 20-person min., round-trip 100฿). To get to Nuan Tip Pier, walk through the market toward the ocean. Additional boats with a 7-passenger min. are available during peak months to: **Ao Kiu/ Ao Pakarang** (200฿); **Ao Phrao** (45min., 120฿); **Ao Wai** (50min., 200฿); **Ao Wong Duan** (45min., 120฿).

Buses: Ban Phe Bus Station (☎651 528), opposite Nuan Tip Pier on the mainland. Buses go to **Bangkok** (3½hr., every hr. 4am-7pm, 124฿). If you're heading elsewhere, grab a *songthaew* to **Rayong** (30min., every 15min. 6:15am-6pm, 20฿) and transfer.

Local Transportation: Songthaew generally wait for 8-10 people before leaving. More remote destinations may require chartering the entire car—prices listed are per person and to charter. From Na Dan Pier to: **Ao Kiu** (50฿, 700฿); **Ao Phai** (20฿, 150฿); **Ao Phrao** (30฿, 300฿); **Ao Thian** (40฿, 300฿); **Ao Tup Tim** (20฿, 150฿); **Ao Wai** (40฿, 500฿); **Ao Wong Duan** (30฿, 300฿); **Hat Sai Kaew** (10฿, 100฿). *Songthaew* returning to the pier or offering taxi service wait at Ao Phai in front of Silver Sands Resort. The island is generally walkable—it's only a 500m stroll from Na Dan Pier to Hat Sai Kaew, and the walk from Ao Wong Duan to Ao Phai takes just 30min.

Rentals: Shops renting **motorbikes** cluster near Na Dan Pier and along the road to Hat Sai Kaew. 100-150฿ per hr., 300-400฿ per day with passport or 500฿ deposit. Open daily 8am-8pm. The only part of the island with paved roads is where the rental shops are; as soon as you leave the pier area the roads are extremely rutted and rocky.

✦ 🛈 ORIENTATION AND PRACTICAL INFORMATION

With only two roads stretching through its 16km, Ko Samet does not require much orientation. Boats disembark at **Na Dan Pier** on the island's northeast corner. A paved road runs south to the Park Service entrance booth, where you must pay a hefty **admission fee** to enter the island, technically a Thai national park (200฿, age 10 and under 100฿). Here, the path forks. Directly ahead is **Hat Sai Kaew,** while the right-hand fork continues south, behind the bungalows of the eastern beaches: **Ao Cho, Ao Hin Klong, Ao Kiu, Ao Nuan, Ao Phai, Ao Thian, Ao Tup Tim, Ao Wai, Ao Wong Duan,** and **Hat Lung Dum.** To get to these beaches, bear left at the fork after Ao Phai. Head straight to go to Ko Samet's only west-coast beach, **Ao Phrao.** Beachside paths and jungle trails link all the beaches except Ao Phrao and Ao Kiu.

Tourist Office: Visitors Center, next to the park entrance by Hat Sai Kaew, provides info on local wildlife. English-speaking Mr. Nan can be reached **24hr.** in case of emergency (☎01 663 5055). Open daily 8am-4pm, often much later in high season.

Tours: Many of Ko Samet's larger guesthouses offer air ticketing, domestic minibus service, and snorkeling tours.

Currency Exchange: Exchange as much money as you think you'll need at the banks in **Ban Phe,** west of the pier. Otherwise, the **post office** at Naga Bungalows offers the most competitive rates for currency, traveler's checks, and cash advances.

Books: Several accommodations, including Naga Bungalows and Sea-Breeze Bungalows at Ao Phai and Samet Ville Resort at Ao Wai, operate small English-language libraries.

Local Tourist Police: (☎651 669). On the mainland, a block east of the market at Nuan Tip Pier. English spoken. Open **24hr.**

Medical Services: Health Center (☎644 123), halfway between Na Dan Pier and the park entry. Some English spoken. Open M-Sa 8:30am-4:30pm. In emergencies, phone the **hospital** in Rayong (☎611 104); Ko Samet's emergency services are inadequate.

Telephones: Pay phones are near the Visitors Center and the pier. **Miss You Coffee Corner** offers international calls starting at 60฿ per min.

Internet Access: The large bungalows at Ao Phai, Ao Phrao, Ao Wong Duan, and Hat Sai Kaew all offer Internet access for 2฿ per min. Fast connections are available at **Miss You Coffee Corner,** just before the park entrance. (☎644 060. Internet 2฿ per min. Open 7:30am-midnight.)

Post Office: Naga Bungalows (☎353 257) operates a licensed **post office** next door to the hotel. Address *Poste Restante* to: "POSTE RESTANTE, Ko Samet, Ban Phe, Rayong 21160." Open daily 8:30am-9:30pm.

Postal Code: 21160.

ACCOMMODATIONS AND FOOD

All of Ko Samet's beaches offer some bungalow-type accommodation. In general, **Ao Cho** and **Ao Phai** offer the cheapest accommodations, while **Hat Sai Kaew** and **Ao Phrao** cater to older travelers with fatter wallets. Hat Sai Kaew, Ao Phai, and **Ao Wong Duan** are the most heavily touristed beaches; **Ao Kiu** and **Ao Nuan** the most secluded. Be prepared for major crowds on weekends and holidays, and expect prices to jump accordingly. **Camping** is available on all beaches, although your best bets are on secluded Ao Kiu, the rocks between Ao Phai and Ao Tup Tim, and the knoll behind the Visitors Center near Hat Sai Kaew. Prices fluctuate between high and low season, so call ahead for the most up-to-date figure.

AO PHAI. A 5min. walk from Hat Sai Kaew, Ao Phai is a backpacker haven—a more friendly and welcoming version of Bangkok's Khaosan Rd. Come here for cheap, quality lodging accompanied by a social atmosphere and great screenings of English-language flicks; don't come for romantic seclusion or quiet nights. Free of the litter and bobbing boats that sometimes plague Hat Sai Kaew and Ao Wong Duan, Ao Phai's white beaches are wide and its waters are good for swimming, despite the crowds. Accommodations, while plentiful, fill up quickly, so arrive before 3 or 4pm. At the northern end is the cheapest of the accommodations, **Naga Bungalows ❸,** a Ko Samet institution that remains the most popular spot on the island. The plain bamboo bungalows sit on stilts. (☎644 035. Book exchange and library. Internet 2฿ per min. Open 8:30am-9:30pm. Bungalows with fan 300฿, with private bath 400฿; low-season 200฿/400฿.) The **restaurant ❸** serves fresh bread, sundaes, tofu-veggie options, and more. (Entrees 30-250฿. Open 8am-10pm.) The **bar** is one the most popular hot spots on the beach—drinks are frequently discounted thanks to nightly themes and a "Tosser's Hour" 10pm to midnight (toss a coin and call it—if you guess correctly, the drink is free). **Tok's Little Hut ❸,** south of Naga and just as popular, but slightly more upscale, has wood-paneled bungalows with fans and baths. (☎644 072. Bungalows 300฿, with A/C 800฿; low-season 250฿/700฿.) Tok's **bar** rivals Naga for most popular—crowds usually depend on who has the better promotion that night. (Open until 2am). Newer **Jep's ❺** features clean, bright rooms and bungalows with added luxuries like extra-large beds. Their **restaurant** is one of the best on the beach. (Internet 2฿ per min., 10min. minimum. Open 9am-10pm. Bungalows 800฿, with A/C 1200-1500฿; low-season 600฿/1000-1200฿.) The hillside bungalows at **Ao Phai Hut ❹** are relatively clean wooden huts. All have private baths. (☎644 075. Electricity 5pm-7am only. Huts 600-1200฿; low-season 400-800฿.) **Sea-Breeze Bungalows ❹,** at the southern end of Ao Phai where the road branches off to Ao Phrao, has quiet bungalows with private baths and a book exchange—two of yours for one of theirs. (☎644 124. Bungalows with fan 500฿, with A/C 1200฿; low-season 300฿/500฿.)

AO KIU. With glistening white sand, good swimming, and a coral reef nearby, secluded Ao Kiu is Ko Samet's best beach. The beauty and seclusion come at a price, though; Ao Kiu is relatively hard to reach. A taxi from the pier will cost you a hefty 500฿, and from neighboring Ao Wai it's a 20-30min. walk along the back road. In 2004, Ao Prao Resorts bought and renovated the old bungalows on Ao Kiu. The new, luxurious complex is set to open in early 2005. While the gentrification of Ao Kiu largely prevents budget travelers from staying there, a trip down to the beach is still rewarding for those who want the best snorkeling on the island. For up-to-date information on the new resort, visit www.aopraoresort.com.

⚑ 🏠 AO PHRAO. Ko Samet's only western-facing beach is a smooth, white crescent of sand graced by sky-searing sunsets and the island's most luxurious accommodations and delectable fine dining. Bungalows line this long stretch of beach, punctuated by massage mats and ocean kayaks. Only three resorts line the uncrowded beach, making it perfect for a laid-back, romantic experience. But if you're looking for a cheap place to stay, lively backpackers, and beach frisbee, you're better off staying on the east coast. Make a right when the road forks just after the last resort; a 25min. hilly walk later, you will arrive at the pearly gates of **Le Vimarn Cottages ❺**, the island's ultra-expensive, nothing-but-luxury, 7000฿ bungalows. (40% low-season discount. Price includes transfer from Seree Ban Phe Pier.) Next up is **Lima Coco Resort ❺**, a newer establishment not as nice as its neighbors, but also slightly less expensive. (☎02 938 1811; www.limacoco.com. Rooms 2500฿ and up. Low-season discounts. Price includes transfer from Ban Phe.) If you can afford it, **Ao Prao Resort ❺**, at the southern end of the beach, mixes luxury with prices slightly lower than Le Vimarn's. (Ao Prao Resorts operates both resorts—make reservations through their Ban Phe office: ☎616 881; www.aopraoresort.com. Singles and doubles start at 4325฿, including speedboat transfers to and from Ban Phe. 35% low-season discount.) Their popular beachside **restaurant ❹** serves burgers (120-150฿), steaks (380฿), pasta (150฿), and Thai food (200-300฿).

⚑ AO NUAN. The best way to get to this beautiful, secluded spot is to ascend from the main road (take the next left after the turn-off for Ao Tup Tim) to a small hill overlooking the rocky beach below and then to descend upon the rustic 🏠 **Nuan Bungalows ❸**. Waves crash onto the rocks that make up the tiny beach. Behind it are immaculate wooden huts with mattresses on the floor and mosquito nets hanging from the ceiling—this place is like no other on the island. Usually full from November to April, so come early in case you have to go elsewhere. (No telephone or reservations. Small huts 250฿; doubles 500-700฿.)

⚑ HAT SAI KAEW. A 10min. walk from Na Dan Pier, Hat Sai Kaew caters mostly to package tours from Europe and Asia and is usually packed with sarong vendors, ferries, and seniors bobbing in the water. Consequently, the beach, though good for swimming, is usually crowded. Budget accommodations are scarce. Your best bet is the rather glum **Ploy Thalay Resort ❺**, halfway up the beach. The exterior is worn, but tiled rooms are tidy and come with private baths; the pillow seats that they put out are great to enjoy the evening ocean rolling by. (☎01 451 1387. Doubles with fan 600฿, with A/C 1000฿; low-season 500฿/800฿.) Farther south on the beach is the large **White Sands Resort ❹**. The sprawling complex has several convenience stores, a restaurant, and runs tours to the other islands. Electricity runs 5pm-9am only. (Rooms with fan 600฿, with A/C 1200฿; low-season 400฿/1000฿.) **Jirawan Restaurant ❸**, at Saikew Villa III, has many vegetarian options and slightly pricey seafood all night on the beach. (Seafood entrees 120-250฿. Open 7am-11pm.)

AO TUP TIM. This small, pretty, crescent-shaped beach is an easy 5min. walk along the coast from Ao Phai. Although it's usually less crowded than Ao Phai, it's fairly congested compared to the beaches farther south. **Tubtim Resort ➍**, on the southern end of the beach, offers the best deal on accommodations. The comfortable thatched bungalows all have private baths. (☎644 025. Doubles with fan and shower 500฿, with A/C 1200฿.) The **restaurant ➌** has an extensive menu of European and Thai options (40-300฿) in a green area with lots of large trees.

AO CHO. Small, secluded Ao Cho is the most whimsical of Ko Samet's beaches. The quaint pier on the shore is complemented by tree swings and flowered bushes on the grounds of the beach's only accommodation, **Wonderland Resort ➋**. (☎01 996 8477. Snorkel rental 50฿ per day. Motorbike rental 400฿ per day. Doubles with fan 150฿, with A/C 900-1200฿.) The **restaurant ➋** is open daily 7am-10pm.

AO WONG DUAN. "Half Moon Bay" is a spacious beach filled with restaurants, bars, and tour operators. Traffic and congestion makes it a noisy place to stay, and the constant roaring of jet skis and ferry departures make it a less than ideal atmosphere for swimming or sunbathing. The huge mother/daughter-owned **Nice and Easy** and **Sea Horse Bungalows ➎** complex offers not just a place to stay, but motorbike rental (100฿ per hr., 400฿ per day), jet ski rental (900฿ per 30min.), boat tours, and some of the best beachside dining on the island. (☎653 740. Doubles with fan 600฿, with A/C 800-1200฿; low-season 300฿/600฿. Extra person 100-150฿.) The **restaurant ➋** serves a greater range of food than most. (Entrees generally 40-100฿. Grilled seafood 200-300฿ or market price. Open 8am-1am.) The lowest-priced option on the beach is **Samet Cabana ➌**, at the north end of the beach, which has rooms in red bungalows, equipped with two small beds and shared baths. (☎01 838 4853. Rooms 400฿, with bath 700฿; low-season 300฿/600฿.)

AO THIAN (CANDLELIGHT BEACH) AND HAT LUNG DUM. Though these beaches have shorter stretches of sand broken up by longer intervals of rocks, they manage to strike a good balance between seclusion and accessibility, which makes them ideal for young couples who want to frolic in relative privacy. The short walk from Ao Wong Duan is enough to keep the mainstream masses out, but the good swimming, sunbathing, and reasonably priced accommodations draw slow-paced beach lovers. Stretching out across both beaches, **Lung Dum Bungalow ➌** is both remote and mellow, though quite busy. The well-priced but plain bungalows have private baths and patios facing the sea. Snorkeling gear can be rented for 50฿ per day. (☎01 652 8056. Doubles with fan 300-800฿; low-season 250-600฿.) Lung Dum's **restaurant ➌** offers inexpensive sandwiches and Thai food. (Entrees 60-200฿. Open 7am-10pm.) The slightly more expensive **Horizons Resort ➍**, on the Candlelight Beach side, offers hot water and TVs. (☎09 914 5585. Kayak rental 150฿ per hr. Snorkel gear 50฿ per day. Doubles with fan 600฿; low-season 400฿.)

AO WAI. Though remote, Ao Wai's clear water and clean, white sand backed by green vegetation make every second of the 25min. coastal hike from Ao Wong Duan to Ao Wai worth it. You'll have to charter a taxi from the pier (500฿), since few people venture so far south. The ride itself is a real off-road journey and is almost worth the high fare. Targeting package tourists, **Samet Ville Resort ➎** dominates the beach with pricey rooms. The **restaurant ➍** serves Thai dishes (40-300฿). Snorkeling gear rental is 100฿ per day. (☎651 681. Restaurant open daily 7:30am-9pm. Rooms with fan 900฿, with A/C 1300฿. 10% low-season discount.)

CENTRAL THAILAND

👁 🎵 SIGHTS AND ENTERTAINMENT

A thirst for sightseeing can be satisfied at the 14m-high **Sitting Buddha** and the smaller Buddha images at his knees. A gate next to the **Golden Buddha** abuts the road between Na Dan Pier and Hat Sai Kaew; follow the path to the statue.

Ko Samet boasts a lively **nightlife** scene on Ao Phai. The bar at **Naga Bungalows,** which occasionally features a free dancing show, battles **Tok's** next door to attract crowds with nightly promotions. Nearby **Silver Sands Resort,** at the southern end of the beach, offers a beachside bar that becomes an impromptu disco when crowds are large enough. The other beaches tend to quiet down when their restaurants close. The bars on Ao Phai are famous for serving ▊drinks by the bucket.

🏊 WATER SPORTS

With an abundance of coral reefs and clear water, it's no wonder that Ko Samet is popular for **snorkeling.** At Ao Phrao, Ao Kiu, and Ao Wai, reef communities are a 5min. swim from shore. Less-disturbed coral live in more remote reaches of the archipelago. Many establishments offer snorkeling tours of Ko Samet and the surrounding islets. There are now several **scuba diving** operations on the island, so it pays to shop around. **Ao Prao Divers,** based in the lobby of the Ao Prao Resort on Ao Phrao, runs a PADI-certified scuba diving school year-round. The school makes daytrips around Ko Samet and to Ko Thalu from November to May. (☎644 100. 2 dives 2500฿. 4- to 5-day certification courses 12,000฿. Specialty and more extensive dives 10-13,000฿. 3-4hr. introductory courses 2500฿. Open daily 8am-4pm.)

Ploy Scuba Diving (☎06 143 9318) on Hat Sai Kaew by Ploy Thalay, also offers certification courses (2-4 per day, 7000-10,500฿), dive trips for those already certified (2 dives 2500฿) and snorkel trips for 300฿ for a half day and 600฿ for a full day. (Open high season 8am-8pm; low season 8am-5pm.)

CHANTHABURI ☎039

Chanthaburi, the "City of the Moon," is famous for its waterfalls, fruit, and gemstones. Between May and July, the city's fruit market bulges with mouth-watering produce. Year-round, rubies and sapphires from all over the world are cut and sold right before your eyes in the city's gem district, before being distributed across the globe. These attractions, in addition to the neighboring national parks, make Chanthaburi a worthwhile visit.

📠 **TRANSPORTATION.** The **bus station** (☎311 299) on Saritidet Rd. sends buses to: Aranyaprathet (8hr., 15 per day 3am-10pm, 80-180฿); Bangkok (4hr., 12 per day 7:30am-11pm, 115฿); Khorat (6hr., every 2hr. 6am-10pm, 116-209฿); Mae Sot via Bangkok (10hr., 9am, 420฿); Pattaya/Si Racha (2½hr., 10 per day 5am-5pm, 90฿); Rayong (2hr., every 30min. 5am-7:30pm, 45-55฿); and Trat (1½hr., every hr. 9:30am-9:30pm, 30-42฿). **Taxis** go anywhere in town for 30฿.

🚩 **PRACTICAL INFORMATION.** To get downtown from the bus station, head left onto **Saritidet Road.** Saritidet Rd. ends at **Benchamarachuthis Road,** at the Kasemsarn 1 Hotel. The alley to the left of the hotel leads to **Sukhaphibal Road,** which runs parallel to Benchamarachuthis Rd. along the river. Heading right at the Kasemsarn 1 Hotel brings you to the commercial heart of town. Branching off Kasemsarn 1 to the right on **Si Rong Muan Road** leads to the **market.** The **gem district** is one block past Si Rong Muan Rd. on Kasemsarn 1; it is to the right down **Kwang Road** and left on **Si Chan Road.**

Services include: **Krung Thai Bank,** next to the post office on Benchamarachuthis Rd. (☎311 111; Cirrus/MC/V **24hr. ATM**; open daily M-F 8:30am-4:30pm); **24hr. police booth** at the bus station; a **clinic,** 20m to the left of the bus station on Saritidet Rd. (☎321 378; English spoken; credit cards accepted; open 8am-8pm; for emergencies, call Taksin Hospital, ☎351 467); **Chanthaburi Telecommunication Center,** next to the GPO on Thung Dondang Rd. near the Eastern Hotel, a 3km walk or a 30฿ taxi ride from town (☎325 916; open daily 7am-11pm); **Internet access** at **Perfect Net and Print,** on Saritidet Rd. 40m past the bus station toward town (☎351 403; 20฿ per hr.; open daily 8:30am-midnight); and the large **general post office,** inconveniently located on Thung Dondang Rd. near the Eastern Hotel. (☎311 013. *Poste Restante.* Open M-F 8:30am-4:30pm; Sa-Su 9am-noon.) **Postal Code:** 22000. The more conveniently located **Chantani Post Office** is on Benchamarachuthis Rd. across from the Kasemsarn 1 Hotel. (☎350 247. No *Poste Restante.* Open M-F 8:30am-4:30pm, Sa-Su 9am-noon.) **Postal Code:** 22001.

▐▜▐▟ ACCOMMODATIONS AND FOOD. Accommodations of any sort are scarce in tourist-free Chanthaburi. To reach two budget spots, continue down the alley at the end of Saritidet Rd. on Benchamarachuthis Rd., and turn left onto Sukhaphibal Rd. On the left is the **Arun Sawat Hotel ❷,** which features somewhat dingy rooms with fans and air-conditioning. (☎311 082. Doubles with fan 120-150฿, with A/C 250฿.) The **Chantra Hotel ❷,** 248 Sukhaphibal Rd., across the street, offers slightly more spartan accommodations. The clean rooms are a sterile white. Ask for the room by the river. (☎312 310. Doubles 120-150฿.) The **Eastern Hotel ❹,** 899 Thachalab Rd., is far from the bus station and market but offers mid-range hotel rooms with flushing toilets and air-conditioning. (☎312 218. Rooms 550฿.)

Take your grumbling stomach to Chanthaburi's immense **market ❶,** centered on the low-lying fountain one block west of Benchamarachuthis Rd., down Si Rong Muang Rd. The market is famous not only for its fruit, but also for its extensive selection of peppers. After sundown, hordes of food vendors dole out curries and noodle dishes. The **coffee shop and bakery ❶** at 33/4 Saritidet Rd. has some of the best pastries and cake anywhere. (Coffee 15฿. Sweets 10-20฿. Open M-F 6:30am-6pm, Sa-Su 7am-5pm.) For a classy dining experience, head to the **seafood restaurant ❷** around the corner from the Chantra Hotel on the river. The views are almost as impressive as the extensive menu. No English translations. (Dishes generally 60฿. Open daily 10am-midnight.) **Dream Restaurant ❷,** at 22/1 Saritidet Rd. by the bus station, is one of the few places in town that has both air-conditioning and English translations. Try the Thai salads (50-80฿), fried rice or noodles (35-45฿), or their specialty, milky crab spring rolls (75฿), which are satisfyingly creamy.

◪ SIGHTS. Chanthaburi's more spectacular sights are outside the city limits, but a few treasures within town keep travelers entertained for a day or two. On weekends, shoppers head to **Si Chan Road,** the heart of Chanthaburi's ▇**gem district.** Some 50-60% of the world's rubies and sapphires pass through Chanthaburi on their way from Cambodia, Laos, Myanmar, and even Africa. Though Chanthaburi's mines no longer produce as many gems as they used to, the city is still the center for cutting and buying. Tourists can see shops where mounds of gems are inspected and bought. Buyers are the people sitting at tables; brokers are usually the ones standing and circulating. Those who know what they are doing can get rubies and sapphires at a significant discount, but it is not recommended that tourists try to buy here, as they could be easily swindled into buying low-quality gems.

The 19th-century **Cathedral of the Immaculate Conception,** across the footbridge near the southern end of Sukhaphibal Rd., was built by French soldiers who occupied Chanthaburi from 1893 to 1905. It is the largest Catholic edifice in Thailand. On the southwest side of town, **Taksin Park** occupies many well-pruned acres.

Chanthaburians come here to relax for an evening or admire the sculpture of the Burmese-bashing King Taksin in the middle of the park. (Open daily 5am-9pm.)

Chanthaburi Province's tropical climate and fertile soil make it one of the best places in Thailand to grow fruit. In order to celebrate the area's renowned produce, Chanthaburi holds a 10-day **fruit festival** at the peak of the spring fruit season. Late May and early June sees the arrival of people from all over the country—and quite a few *farang*—to honor and, of course, enjoy mangosteens, rambutans, jackfruits, longans, and durians. Festivities include best fruit contests, fruit-eating competitions, a tour of local orchards, and a very popular beauty contest.

▌ NIGHTLIFE. Chanthaburi boasts a surprisingly happening nightlife scene. Its epicenter is at the enormous **Diamond Pub**, on the southwestern side of town. Live bands belt out Thai pop while a beautiful young crowd looks on. It rocks all week, but is packed Fridays and Saturdays. Bottles of soda go for 30฿, and Singhas are 120฿. Grab a taxi from the city center for 20฿. (Open daily 9pm-2am.)

▐ DAYTRIPS FROM CHANTHABURI. Although Chanthaburi may not be the largest city, surrounding national parks provide a welcome diversion.

▌ KHAO KHITCHAKUT NATIONAL PARK. Thirty kilometers north of town on Hwy. 3249 in **Khao Khitchakut National Park,** the **Chanthaburi River** churns down the 13 tiers of **Nam Tok Krathing** (Krathing Falls), the park's most popular attraction. A steep, rocky trail leads up from a Buddha at the mountain's base to tier 9; falls 10-13 are too dangerous to climb to. Falls #5-7 are great for swimming. Once you've bathed in cascades beneath enormous vines and golden butterflies, you'll understand why 2000 Thais flock to the falls every weekend. The climb is exhilarating and treacherous; come prepared with a swimsuit, good shoes, and lots of water.

A small **canteen ❶** stocks a few basic items and prepares simple rice dishes. (20-25฿. Open daily 6am-6pm.) **Food stalls ❶** set up on weekends and holidays. The **Visitors Center** has information in English. Bring your own tent to **camp ❶** on your own (30฿). Lodging options are limited to **bungalows ❹** for two (600฿), six (800฿), or eight people (2400฿). For weekend stays, call the ranger station at least one week in advance. *(Songthaew (20฿) depart from the corner of Prachaniyon Rd. and Benchamarachuthis Rd., opposite Krung Thai Bank, south of the post office. The songthaew drop you off at the 1.5km access road marked by the number 2511 and a white fleur-de-lis on a red fence post on the right side of the road. Tell your driver ahead of time that you are going to Khitchakut Park or Nam Tok Krathing, as the signpost is difficult to see coming up on a songthaew. The 24hr. park headquarters, ☎02 562 0760, is beyond the entrance booth. Open daily 6am-6pm. 200฿, 10 and under 100฿.)*

NAM TOK PHLIU NATIONAL PARK. Welcoming over 80,000 visitors per year, **Nam Tok Phliu** is one of Chanthaburi's best-known parks, although it's hardly the most spectacular. A trail cuts links the entrance to the park's namesake waterfalls **(Phliu Falls),** where Thai children gather to swim and catch fish in the nearby ponds. A 1km nature trail circles the falls and offers scenic views. The other falls, **Nam Tok Makok, Nam Tok Klong Nalai,** and **Nam Tok Nong,** offer more seclusion. The rest of the park's 135km² of rainforest are bereft of trails. The **Park Headquarters** and **Visitors Center,** on the road leading to the Phliu Falls, has maps in English with directions to the falls as well as information on renting a **bungalow ❺** for 800฿. *(From Chanthaburi, yellow songthaew (30min., 30฿) leave from the north side of the market's roundabout and stop at the park gate. When leaving, take a taxi to the highway intersection (100-160฿) and wait for a passing songthaew. Open daily 6am-6pm. 200฿, children 10 and under 100฿.)*

WAT KHAO SUKIM. On a mountainside 20km outside Chanthaburi, **Wat Khao Sukim** is the pride of local Buddhists. Built as a center for meditation, the temple

CENTRAL THAILAND

has drawn much attention due to several celebrity monks who have resided there. As a consequence, it has received impressive donations of Buddhist statues and artwork. Though the temple is not spectacular, the display halls, crammed with everything from trees made of colored glass to furniture inlaid with mother-of-pearl, are overwhelming. Amid all these riches, life-like wax replicas of monks sit in meditation. The roof offers panoramas of mountains, a waterfall, and fruit groves, providing a glimpse of Chanthaburi's natural beauty for those who don't have time for its parks. *(Take a taxi (round-trip 400฿), or catch a songthaew for Na Ya-am at Chanthaburi's market, get off at Sathorn, and catch a songthaew to the temple. Songthaew rarely make the trip to the temple, so a taxi may be your only hope. Open daily 6:30am-5pm.)*

TRAT
☎ 039

Trat, the least developed of the eastern provinces, has a population that subsists largely on fishing or growing fruit. Travelers who use Trat as a transit point to Ko Chang and the surrounding islands are now joined by travelers en route to Cambodia. For the adventurous backpacker, oft-overlooked Trat Province teems with jungles, waterfalls, temples, and beaches, few of them visited by *farang*.

▆ TRANSPORTATION

A/C buses from anywhere north or west of town stop on the east side of **Sukhumvit Road,** next to the cinema. Private bus companies offer A/C bus service to Bangkok (5hr., every hr. 7am-11:30pm, 189฿). **Suporat** (on the west side of Sukhumvit Rd. across from the market) buses to Bangkok stop at Chanthaburi (1hr., 6 per day 8:30am-7pm, 50฿), where you can transfer to all major destinations. All these companies cluster around the market. Blue **songthaew** heading to Laem Ngop (7am-6pm, 30฿) pull up one block south of the market, next to the pharmacy on Sukhumvit Rd. and leave when full. Blue *songthaew* going to Ban Hat Lek (1¾hr., 6am-6pm, 60฿) and Klong Yai (1½hr., every hr. 6am-6pm, 40฿) wait behind the market on Tat Mai Rd. Minibuses to Ban Hat Lek (1¼hr., every hr. 6am-6pm, 100฿) and Klong Yai (1½hr., every hr. 6am-6pm, 80฿), the recommended way to cross the border, wait on Sukhumvit Rd. two blocks north of the market. Near the pharmacy and market, **minibuses** depart when full for Chanthaburi (1hr., 6am-6pm, 60฿) and Pattaya (1½hr., 1:30 and 3pm, 250฿).

✈ ❓ ORIENTATION AND PRACTICAL INFORMATION

The main road in Trat is **Sukhumvit Road,** which runs north toward Bangkok and south toward Laem Ngop. Sukhumvit Rd. has two traffic signals, at both its northern and southern ends. Most services lie between or near them. At the northern traffic light, Sukhumvit intersects **Wiwattana Road,** where the post office, telecommunications office, and police station are clustered together.

> **Currency Exchange: Krung Thai Bank,** 59 Sukhumvit Rd. (☎520 542), opposite the pharmacy and next to the Trat Department Store. Exchanges traveler's checks (33฿ per check). **24hr. ATM.** Open M-F 8:30am-4:30pm.
>
> **Police:** 13 Samtersook Rd. (☎511 239). From Sukhumvit's northern traffic light, walk 3 blocks east on Wiwattana Rd. Open **24hr.**
>
> **Immigration Office:** There is no immigration office in Trat. The nearest immigration office (☎597 261) is in Laem Ngop (p. 153) and grants **visa extensions** (10-30 days, 500฿).
>
> **Pharmacy:** (☎512 312). South of the market and next to the *songthaew* bound for Laem Ngop. Open daily 7am-10pm.

Hospital: Trat Hospital (☎511 040), on Sukhumvit Rd., just past the north traffic light.

Telephones: Telecommunications Office, 315 Chaimongkol Rd. (☎/fax 512 617), marked by its radio tower. **International phones**/fax. Open M-F 8:30am-4:30pm.

Internet Access: There is a small Internet cafe at the corner of Sukhumvit Rd., at the southern traffic light. 1฿ per min., 10min. minimum.

Post Office: (☎511 175). Walk 3 blocks east on Wiwattana Rd. and make a left on Chaimongkol Rd. *Poste Restante.* Open M-F 8:30am-4:30pm, Sa-Su 9am-noon.

Postal Code: 23000.

ACCOMMODATIONS

There are plenty of guesthouses in Trat, and almost all of them are on **Thana Charoen Road** and **Lak Muang Road.** To get there from the buses and *songthaew* stops, walk about 5min. south on Sukhumvit Rd., and take a left at the traffic light onto Lak Muang Rd.; Thana Charoen Rd. is the next left after Lak Muang.

Pop Guest House, 1/1-1/2 Thana Charoen Rd. (☎512 392). Bamboo bungalows are simple, clean, and bright. Attractive garden and friendly staff are added bonuses. Breakfast 30฿. Rooms 80-400฿. ❶

Ban Jaidee Guest House, 69 Chaimongkol Rd. (☎520 678), make a left on Chaimongkol Rd. from Thana Charoen Rd. and follow the signs. The relaxing common areas and friendly staff give this beautiful guesthouse a social feel. Rooms 100฿. ❷

Windy Guest House, 64 Thana Charoen Rd. (☎524 419). Take a right down a small *soi* 25m from the Saritidet Rd. intersection. Rickety, traditional wooden Thai river house with decent, well-kept rooms. Plenty of travel info and a rowboat that guests can take on the river for free. Singles 80฿; doubles 100฿. ❶

Residang Guest House (☎530 103), near the end of Thana Charoen Rd. A real bargain, featuring enormous rooms with large windows. Some rooms have balconies. Bike rental 10฿ per hr. Singles with shared bath 100฿; doubles 150฿, with bath and TV 200฿. ❷

N. P. Guest House (☎01 578 7513), down the *soi* opposite Windy Guest House. Decent rooms. Owner speaks English well and has info on traveling to Cambodia. He can also arrange tours and border crossings. Internet 40฿ per hr. Singles 60฿; doubles 100฿. ❶

FOOD AND NIGHTLIFE

There's no excuse for not eating in the **market ❶**. During the day, food stalls set up on the first floor of the municipal market (elaborate soups with meat or fish 10-20฿). The **night market ❶** moves to the square, two blocks north of the municipal market building, behind the A/C bus terminal. (Open daily 7pm-midnight.)

Krua Rim Krong (☎524 919), off Thana Charoen Rd. before Residang Guest House, has great Thai food made with only the freshest ingredients. Stylish A/C restaurant and enclosed garden, almost too trendy for its surroundings. Open daily 11am-10pm. ❸

Cool Corner, 21-23 Thana Charoen Rd. (☎06 156 4129) also has great food and drinks. Friendly and informative owner. Open 7am-10pm. ❷

Sea House, at the southern traffic light on Sukhumvit Rd., serves a variety of drinks and rice dishes. Large Singha 80฿. Rice entrees 30-60฿. Open daily 8am-1am. ❷

SIGHTS

Most attractions lie in the province, not in the town. The travel-weary can relax with a **traditional Thai massage;** look for the sign outside a house on Thana Charoen

CENTRAL THAILAND

Rd., near the intersection with Sukhumvit Rd. (2hr. massage 250฿. Open daily 8am-8pm.) This may be enough to loosen your limbs for the 2.3km walk to **Wat Buppharam**. Walking south on Sukhumvit Rd., turn right down the little road before the Trat Department Store and follow it out of town to reach this mildly interesting *wat* on a little hill. Buppharam is the oldest temple in Trat, built during the Ayutthaya Period, circa 1648. The grounds contain buildings constructed in the traditional Thai wooden-house style, including monks' picturesque dwellings built on stilts in a little garden. During the day, you may catch the *wat's* monk school in session. Another option is to rent a bicycle from Residang Guest House.

▶ DAYTRIP FROM TRAT: LAEM NGOP

The last songthaew to Trat (30min., 30฿) leaves after the last boat arrives, usually around 6pm. The only other option is to take a taxi (150฿).

A sleepy village with a chaotic pier, Laem Ngop is the place to board ferries to **Ko Chang**. With Trat only a short *songthaew* ride away, there is no reason to dawdle here and certainly no reason to stay the night.

For **visa extensions** (10-30 days, 1900฿) and official information on visiting **Cambodia**, head for the **immigration office** on the ground floor of a white building about a 15min. stroll up the road from Laem Ngop to Trat, 300m beyond Thai Farmers Bank. (☎597 261. Open M-F 8:30-noon and 1-4:30pm.) **TAT**, 50m after the bank, has a friendly staff. (☎597 255. Open M-F 8:30am-4:30pm.) The **Thai Farmers Bank,** 500m from the pier on the Trat-Laem Ngop Rd., exchanges traveler's checks. (☎597 046. 33฿ per check. Open M-F 8:30am-3:30pm.) Laem Ngop's **hospital** (☎597 040), on Trat-Laem Ngop Rd., 2km toward Trat, has **malaria** medication (150mg doxycycline pills 2฿), recommended for travelers en route to Ko Chang, and a **malaria clinic.** (Open M-F 8:30am-noon and 1-4:30pm.) For info on the national park, head to the **National Marine Park Office.** From the pier, it's a 10min. walk down the first road on the left. (☎538 100. Open M-F 8:30am-noon and 1-4:30pm.)

> **BORDER CROSSING: BAN HAT LEK/SIHANOUKVILLE.** To enter Cambodia, you must have a Cambodian visa, available at the border at **Hat Lek** for 1200฿. To be on the safe side, it is best to obtain your visa at the Cambodian embassy in **Bangkok** (p. 103). Crossing the border takes 9-13hr. Depending on the departure time of the boat to **Sihanoukville**, an overnight stay may be necessary. Either way, it pays to get an early start. To get from Trat to **Ban Hat Lek,** take a blue *songthaew* from behind the market (1½hr., every hr. 6am-6pm, 35฿) or a minivan from 2 blocks north of the market (1½hr., every hr. 6am-6pm, 80-100฿). When you exit Thailand at the border, remember to obtain an exit stamp. After crossing the border, you can hire a taxi to cross the newly finished bridge to **Ko Kong,** where overnight accommodations can be found. Daily minibuses leave from outside the Cambodian immigration office at 9am for Phnom Penh (650฿) or Sihanoukville (550฿). Leave Trat by minibus by 7am to catch these minibuses. A boat departs daily at 8am (sometimes earlier) for Sihanoukville (3½-4hr., 600฿). To catch the boat, leave Trat at 6am. Stay the night in Sihanoukville or catch a bus to Phnom Penh (3½hr.; 10,000 *riels*).

KO CHANG ☎039

Ko Chang (Elephant Island) is rapidly going the way of its southern cousins. A steady stream of development with loads more on the way promises lots of tourists, high prices, piles of garbage, and resort commercialism. But for the moment,

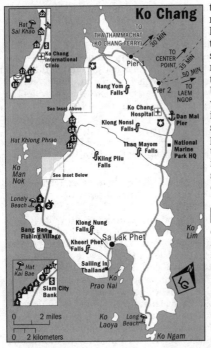

Ko Chang

see map above

🛏 ACCOMMODATIONS
Chokdee Bungalows, 12
Cookie Bungalows, 20
K.B. Bungalow, 7
K.P. Bungalows, 15
Kai Bae Beach Resort, 6
Kae Bae Hut, 8
KC Grande Resort, 22
Koh Chang Lagoon Resort, 19
Magic Bungalows, 13
Mam Kaibae Beach Resort, 5
Nature Beach Resort, 3
Paloma Cliff Resort, 17
Sea View Resort, 4
Treehouse Bungalows, 1

🍴 FOOD
Guitar House, 2
Hungry Elephant, 16
Invito, 18
Morgan Restaurant, 9
O₂ Bar, 10
Tropicana Restaurant, 14

⭐ NIGHTLIFE
Lek Bar and Diner, 11
Oodie's, 21

the island is still bursting with leafy rain forests, towering waterfalls, isolated beaches, and unexplored territory on its eastern coast. A new road skirting the border of the island makes it much easier to access even the most remote patches of sand. Unfortunately, the amount of trash washing up on beaches and coral increasingly renders the water less swimmable. During the low season, prices are often slashed by 40% and the beaches are almost empty. There is frequent ferry service year-round, so any time is perfect for a visit to this easternmost Thai island.

⌐ TRANSPORTATION

To reach Ko Chang, take a bus to **Trat,** then a *songthaew* (every 30min. or when full 6am-6pm, 30฿) from the front of the municipal market on Sukhumvit Rd. to whichever pier has a ferry leaving next, usually either **Laem Ngop Pier** or **Center Point Pier.** (Basic one-way tickets 30฿.) The ferry will arrive at one of the piers on Ko Chang's northern end (30-50min.). From Ko Chang, pickup-truck **taxis** run frequently to the west-coast beaches: **Hat Khlong Phrao** (30min., 40฿), **Hat Kai Bae** (50min., 40฿), **Hat Sai Khao** (15min., 30฿), and **Lonely Beach** (1¼hr., 70฿).

Ferries: Ferries run frequently from Pier 2 on Ko Chang to **Center Point Pier** (30min., every hr. 6am-7pm, 30฿) and **Laem Ngop Pier** (50min.; every hr. 6am-7pm, low season every 2hr. 7am-5pm; 30฿). Center Point is 5min. from Laem Ngop by *songthaew*; your driver will take you to whichever pier has the next ferry leaving. Ferries also go between **Ao Thammachat** (20min. from Laem Ngop) and Piers 1 and 3 on **Ko Chang** (25min., every hr. 7am-6:30pm, 30฿; high season only). Ao Thammachat and Center Point can accommodate vehicle crossings.

Local Transportation: Songthaew rule. A ride between beaches is 30-70฿. In theory, *songthaew* leave from Hat Kai Bae 1hr. before ferry departure, hit the other 2 beaches on the way up, and reach the pier just in time for departure.

Rentals: Motorbike rentals are available on any of the 4 beaches. A good rate is 150฿ per day for manual and 200฿ per day for automatic. The roads between Hat Sai Khao and the pier and Kai Bae and Lonely Beach are extremely steep and curvy, and very dangerous to ride on. Be sure your bike is in good condition before you leave and be very careful—insurance and contracts are uncommon to nonexistent. Usually a day rental will require a deposit of 500฿.

✦🛈 ORIENTATION AND PRACTICAL INFORMATION

Ko Chang's interior is a trackless rain forest. There is a well-paved road around the perimeter of the island, except for the very southern part. From the pier area at the island's northeast end, the road goes south to the east coast, passes waterfall trails, and branches into a western road that almost reaches Bang Bao and an eastern road that ends in the fishing village of Sa Lak Pet. A right turn at the pier leads past the west coast's four beaches: **Hat Sai Khao, Hat Khlong Phrao, Hat Kai Bae,** and **Lonely Beach.** The road ends in the picturesque fishing village of Bang Bao.

Tourist Office: Ko Chang National Park Headquarters (☎09 251 9244) in Than Mayom, at the midpoint of the east coast, 20km from Hat Sai Khao. Inconveniently located and understaffed. Open daily 8:30am-4:30pm. TAT is also in Laem Ngop.

Currency Exchange: Hat Sai Khao and Kai Bae have many banks and ATMs. **Siam City Bank,** on the main road at Kai Bae. Open daily 10am-6pm. **Siam Commercial Bank,** in the heart of Hat Sai Khao, exchanges traveler's checks for 33฿. Open 10am-8pm.

Books: The mini-market by the International Clinic at Hat Sai Khao sells English fiction, magazines, and guidebooks. Open 8am-9pm.

Laundromat: Laundromats are plentiful along the main roads at Hat Sai Khao and Kai Bae. Usually 30฿ per kg.

Police: (☎586 191). On the road just before Dan Mai. A police box is also on the main road in Hat Sai Khao, far north just before the road begins to climb the mountain.

Hospital: Ko Chang Hospital (☎586 131), on the eastern side of the island by Dan Mai Pier. Outpatient hours 8:30am-noon and 1:30-4:30pm. Open **24hr.** for emergencies. The more convenient **Ko Chang International Clinic** (☎551 151) is open 9am-8pm.

Telephones: Calls can be made at most bungalows and Internet cafes. A good rate is 60฿ per min. for calls to Australia, Canada, Europe, New Zealand, and the US. Service fees for collect calls are typically 10฿ per min. with a 15min. time limit.

Internet Access: Access becomes more sparse and expensive the further south you go. **Siam Huts** on Lonely Beach charges 3฿ per min. Access at Kai Bae, Hat Khlong Prao and Hat Sai Khao is 2฿ per min.; the occasional gem in Hat Sai Khao offers 1฿ per min.

Post Offices: (☎551 240) on the main road at the southern end of Hat Sai Khao. Address *Poste Restante* to: Post Office, Ko Chang Island, Thailand 23170, Western Union. Open M-F 8:30am-4:30pm, Sa-Su 9am-noon.

Postal Code: 23170.

🛏🍴 ACCOMMODATIONS AND FOOD

The northern end of the west coast is spiked with soaring cliffs, which soon level off to Ko Chang's celebrated beaches. Much of the new development is far pricier than the establishments that came before, squeezing budget travelers farther south. Of the coast's three principal beaches, **Hat Sai Khao (White Sand Beach)** is the closest to the pier and the most developed. **Hat Khlong Phrao** and **Hat Kai Bae,** 6km and 10km from Hat Sai Khao, respectively, offer more privacy. Farther south, **Lonely Beach,** of full-moon party fame, is the most laid-back. This stretch of sand is a 15min. walk through the jungle from Hat Kai Bae's southernmost cove. During the low season, guesthouses slash prices and are willing to negotiate.

◪ **HAT SAI KHAO.** Prices have skyrocketed in recent years at Hat Sai Khao. Oceanside huts have been renovated and made into luxury bungalows and large hotels are increasingly flanking the main road. While budget accommodations are virtually non-existent, Hat Sai Khao offers the most services. Dive shops, motorbike rentals, bars, restaurants, and Internet cafes are plentiful here, but for quiet and seclusion, keep heading south. At the southernmost point, **Paloma Cliff Resort** ❺ has a pool and bamboo huts overlooking the rocky point south of Hat Sai Khao. New Internet access promises to be one of the first 1฿ per min. operations on the island. (☎551 119. Rooms with fan 800฿, A/C 1500-2500฿. Up to 50% low-season discount.) The centrally located **Koh Chang Lagoon Resort** ❺ is more upscale, from bamboo bungalows to spacious rooms. All rooms include breakfast. (☎551 201; www.kohchanglagoonresort.com. Rooms and bungalows 2200฿; low-season 1600฿.) **Cookie Bungalows** ❺, 300m south, fits the pattern of renovated bungalows and brand-new hotel. (☎01 861 4227. Bungalows with fan 700฿, bungalows with A/C 1500฿; hotel rooms 1800฿. Low-season 300฿/500฿/1000฿.) **K.C. Grande Resort** ❺, at the north end of the beach, recently received a face-lift and went from budget to bank-breaking. Bungalows are neat and new, but on the edge of the action. (☎01 833 1010. Motorbike rental 150฿ per day. Bungalows 3300฿; low-season 1700฿.)

The **Hungry Elephant** ❸ has a reputation for great steaks and French food. Walk 10min. south from Hat Sai Khao; it's on the right. (☎09 985 8433. Steaks 175฿. Thai food 40-80฿. French food 70-200฿. Open daily 11:30am-11:30pm.) **Invito** ❹ serves oven-baked pizza and pasta in a romantic, intimate setting, just across from Paloma Cliff Resort. (☎551 326. Pizza 200-290฿. Pasta 160-280฿. Open daily 11am-11pm.) If you're looking for a little live music, **Oodie's** has it nightly, beginning at 10pm. (Cocktails 80-150฿. Small beer 40-60฿. Open daily 4pm-1am.)

◪ **HAT KHLONG PHRAO.** Although not the most remote, Hat Khlong Phrao is the most serene and sparsely settled of Ko Chang's three main beaches. Bunga-lows are widely spaced on broad expanses of sand punctuated by rock outcrop-pings and creeks from the interior. Each establishment has its own entrance, but all are connected by a walk along the beach. **K.P. Bungalows** ❷, toward the center of the beach, has cute, rustic, thatched bamboo huts. (☎01 863 7262. Doubles with fan 400฿, with private bath 600฿; low-season 200฿/400฿.) **Magic Bungalows** ❸ offers clean recently renovated rooms, and 3hr. snorkeling trips to Ko Yauk for 250฿ per person. (☎01 861 4829. Motorbike rentals 250฿ per day. Doubles 300฿, with private bath 500฿, with A/C 1300฿; low-season 150฿/300฿/700฿.) **Chokdee Bungalow** ❹, at the south end of the beach, has recently renovated bungalows with tidy toilets. (☎01 910 9052. 3hr. snorkeling outing to Ko Yuak 250฿. Huts with fan and private bath 500฿, with A/C 1500-1800฿; low-season 400฿/1000-1200฿.)

For a nice meal, head to one of the brand-new resorts on the beach. The **Tropi-cana** has a **beachside restaurant** ❸ with slightly pricey but well-prepared Thai food. (Seafood 150-250฿. European and Thai food 70-270฿. Open 6am-11pm.)

◪ **HAT KAI BAE.** Hat Kai Bae has a nice selection of restaurants, bars, Internet cafes, and bungalows without the overcrowding and conspicuous consumption characteristic of Hat Sai Khao. It also makes a good jumping-off point for explor-ing the island's south side. ▨**K.B. Bungalow** ❺ is a step above the typical mid-range accommodation, with well-appointed huts on nicely landscaped grounds, all with spacious full baths. There is a free lending library with English books. (☎01 862 8103. Doubles with fan 600฿, with A/C 1500฿; low-season 400฿/1200฿.) **Kai Bae Hut** ❹ is conveniently located right next to the *songthaew* stop and has nice, clean huts for reasonable prices. (☎01 062 8426. 2-person fan rooms 500฿; beachside 4-person bungalows 1500฿; low-season 300฿/800฿.) Snorkeling tours to Ko Yuak

(200฿) last half a day. The **restaurant ❷** serves plenty of fried Thai food, from pineapples to squid, plus a wide array of cashew dishes. (Dishes 60-100฿. Breakfast 40฿. Open daily 7am-10pm.) **Mam Kaibae Beach Resort ❹** is another good budget option, situated in the center of the beach in front of one of the less coral-ridden areas. (☎01 757 8570. Doubles with fan 500฿, with A/C 900฿; low-season 200฿/700฿.) A similar option with a slightly more upscale feel and a popular beachside restaurant is just north at **Kai Bae Beach Resort ❹.** (☎01 917 7704. Doubles with fan 500฿, with A/C 1500฿. Low-season 300฿/1000฿.) Kai Bae also now has its own upscale resort complex in **Sea View Resort ❺,** complete with a pool and fancy spa. (☎551 148. Standard room or cottage 2000฿. 40% low-season discount.)

The **O₂ Bar ❷** is a popular place to enjoy cheap and delicious Thai food in the relaxing open air. (Breakfast 40-70฿. Dishes 40-70฿. Beer 45฿. Cocktails 90-140฿. Open daily 8am-midnight.) **Morgan Restaurant ❷** has a varied menu of reasonably priced food and is especially popular for breakfast. (Breakfast 35-60฿. Veggie options. Open daily 7:30am-11pm.) **Lek Bar and Diner ❹** is a bit more expensive, but its loud pop music and festive lighting draw an energetic crowd. (☎07 131 0308. Thai food and grill 160-300฿. Heineken 65฿. Cocktails 70-140฿. Open 5pm-2am.)

> **TIP** If you want to escape the crowds but can't afford the boat transportation to its outlying islands, try walking to one. Off the southern part of Kai Bae, there is a small island where, at low tide, the waters recede enough so that it's possible to walk there and spend a couple hours on your own private island paradise. Mind the rising waters, though, or you'll be stranded out there until the next low tide.

◪ LONELY BEACH. The new road connects this once secluded beach to the rest of the world, but it remains one of the most chilled-out, tailor-made backpacker hideouts in Thailand. The best place to go to see fellow backpackers is the **Treehouse Bungalow ❶,** at the far southern end of the beach—still cheap and very rustic. (☎01 847 8215. Motorbikes 250฿ per day. Rooms 100-200฿. Low-season discount.) For a slightly more comfortable experience, the beachside bungalows at the **Nature Beach Resort ❸** are of the well-kept bamboo variety and have their own baths. (☎01 803 8933. Huts 300฿; bigger rooms 400-500฿. Low-season 150-300฿.) The **Guitar House ❶,** on the main road behind Treehouse, serves simple and cheap Thai food (open 11am-10pm). Ever since the demise of the beloved **Jah Bar,** the most consistent nightlife can be found at Treehouse's bar (open until 2am). During the high season, **Nature Bar** and **Monkey Bar,** on the beach by Nature Beach Resort, are popular nightspots.

◪ THE WEST COAST. Popular **Mama's Very Famous Snorkel Trips** (☎09 831 1059) is just north of the road's end on Hat Kai Bae. A trip to Ko Yuak costs 150฿; special three-island trips cost 450฿ and leave at 9am. Fishing boats can be rented for 500฿ per hour. Ko Chang's snorkeling outings are designed for high-season crowds. During the low season, you'll have to wait for smooth seas and rustle up a group. If you do come to Ko Chang in high season, check out the **Seahorse Dive Shop** (☎01 219 3844), behind Kaibae Hut. The friendly Swiss instructor offers four-day PADI courses (10,500฿). Dives cost 1200-1500฿, including equipment and food. The biggest dive conglomerate is **Ploy Diving;** they have outposts at every beach (☎01 155 1331). Diving and snorkeling tend to be very poor during the rainy season; many dive shops shut down entirely.

The west coast of Ko Chang also provides some opportunities to see the island's interior. **Khlong Pliu Falls** are massively popular and easily accessible. The 150m cascade has pools that are great for swimming. There is a 1km driveway leading up to the falls; the turn-off is on the main road behind Khlung Prao Beach. The falls are just 500m from the park entrance. (Open daily 8am-5pm. 200฿, students 100฿.) Just south of the main road, **Chutiman Chuayrum** offers tourists the chance to enjoy jungle treks while seated comfortably on top of an elephant. (☎09 939 6676. Open 8am-5pm. 1hr. 500฿, 2hr. 900฿.)

🅖 **THE EAST COAST.** The picturesque east coast is short on beaches but long on scenic beauty. Colonnades of rubber trees alternate with rambutan orchards, and several waterfalls are accessible by trails that begin along the road. While the falls themselves are nothing to write home about, the opportunity to catch a glimpse of the island's rugged interior shouldn't be missed. The town of **Dan Mai** hides a path to **Khlong Nonsi Falls,** a 30min. walk inland. **Than Mayom,** 4km to the south, is home to the **National Park Headquarters** (☎03 952 1122), with little to offer save a Visitors Center. Across the street, **Than Mayom Falls,** a favorite of King Rama V, still bears his initials. Clear mountain water gushes over a 7m-high rock into a jungle pool. (Only in rainy season, June-Dec. Accessible 8am-5pm. 200฿, 14 and under 100฿.)

Continuing straight when the road forks (the left branch) leads to the village of Sa Lek Phet, a decidedly untouristed area. Just before the road ends at the pier, there is a turn-off to the left (really only fit for motorbikes). This leads to the secluded, beautiful and swimmable **Long Beach** on the west coast of the island's southeast peninsula. There are 16 bungalows available, beginning at 100฿ per night. Call Tom, the owner (☎01 848 5052) ahead of time to make sure that someone will be there. A right at the fork and another quick right will lead to **Khlong Nung Waterfall;** a right at the fork and straight leads to **Kheeri Phet Waterfall.** Both are remote and difficult to access, but offer what might be some much-needed seclusion. The right fork ends at the homestay village and the pier where **Sailing in Thailand** can be found. From here, you can charter a sailboat from Frank the captain for a daytrip visiting islands (☎01 833 7673; www.sailing-in-thailand.com; 1800฿ per person), or you can charter a speedboat (800฿) or hire a local (around 300฿) to take you to one of the nearby islands to spend the day. One of the most beautiful islands is **Ko Wai,** home to the exceedingly popular Thai restaurant **Paradise.**

Getting to the east coast can be tricky. There are no motorbike rentals north or east of Hat Sai Khao, which means if you plan to take a motorbike you'll be traversing a very steep and curvy stretch of road. Alternatively, you can try to find a taxi or hire someone to drive you (400฿).

🏝 DAYTRIPS FROM KO CHANG:KO CHANG NATIONAL MARINE PARK

Forty-seven other islands besides Ko Chang make up the **Ko Chang National Marine Park.** Thirteen have accommodations, some of which cater only to package tourists; camping is free and legal anywhere. In the high season, many of these islands are easy to get to and have cheap lodgings. In the low season, most close up shop and head elsewhere. As the area becomes increasingly touristed, new operations pop up monthly. Food available in island guesthouses is overpriced but tasty.

KO MAAK

A ferry leaves Ko Maak from Ao Nid pier at 8am and Laem Ngop at 3pm (in high season daily, in low season on even-numbered days; 2½hr.; 210฿). Boats go to Ko Kham twice in the morning and return around 4pm (15min., 50฿).

The most accessible of the outer islands, Ko Maak offers the same travel amenities as Ko Chang, but with more solitude and better beaches. It is technically closed during the low season, but most guesthouses will offer lodging and food to anyone who shows up. There is a **clinic** and a **police box** on the road heading into the island from the pier. Expensive bottled water and toilet paper are available at the store at the base of the pier. Just north, a casual **post office** can periodically patch through **international phone** calls at high rates. (Open daily 7am-8pm.) The complex also has a **minimart** and **bicycle** and **motorbike rental.** There are no official taxi services, so on arrival, pick a truck waiting by the pier—each hotel and guesthouse usually sends one to meet every boat, free of charge. Parts of the narrow west beach have become very trashy, but it basks in the soft glow of splendid sunsets. The farthest accommodation south is **Lazy Days ❶,** with a relaxed party atmosphere. (Bungalows and teepees with shared bath 100฿.) Just up the beach, **Aukao Resort ❶** has bungalows (100฿, with fan and private bath 250฿).

The north side hosts a beach with unobtrusive bungalows and calm, coral-strewn waters, bordering a long bay. At the west end, **Fantasia ❶** (open Oct.-May) has great (though fan-less) A-frame bungalows tucked back on the hill in the coconut grove, with mosquito nets, floor mattresses, and shared baths (100฿). Beachfront bungalows with private baths, beach chairs, and fans go for 250฿. Up the beach, **Koh Mak Resort ❸** offers high-quality, spacious bungalows (300-600฿).

THE OUTER ISLANDS

To get to Ko Rang, charter a boat in Sa Lak Phet or check at Ko Chang bungalows for scuba or snorkeling tours. Sunsai Bungalows on Hat Sai Khao runs daytrips to the islands of Ko Loi, Ko Ngam, Ko Gia, and Ko Rang during the high season. Trips leave at 8:30am and return at sunset (350฿). In high season, a ferry leaves for Ko Wai daily at 3pm from Laem Ngop, returning from Ko Wai at 8am the following morning (2hr., 120฿). A banana boat leaves year-round from the river in Trat (W, Sa 11am) for Ko Kud, returning the next morning (4½hr., 150฿). In addition, a speedboat island-hopper service has started. Tickets cost 250฿. Check with guesthouses on the islands in Trat.

The islands off Ko Chang's southern coast are famous for fishing, coral, rock formations, bird nests, and bat guano. You can scuba dive at **Ko Rang,** home to an abundance of coral, fish, and toothy sharks. **Ko Wai,** a less-remote version of Ko Rang, is also surrounded by coral, and the fishing is legendary. From Ko Maak, there is a ferry to **Ko Kham,** which features a cheap **guesthouse** (open Oct.-June) and more sun and solitude. There are accommodations on far-flung **Ko Kud** (open Nov.-May), as well. **Bungalows ❶** on the islands range from 100฿ to 300฿ and package tours run 2000฿ per night. Ask at guesthouses in Trat.

ARANYAPRATHET ☎ 037

Aranyaprathet is the border town for the Cambodia-bound. A savvy traveler will arrive early enough to push straight on through without staying the night. The first train from Bangkok arrives with plenty of time for those heading to Siem Reap to reach it on the same day.

◪ **TRANSPORTATION.** In the center of town, **Mahadthai-Suwannasorn Road** and **Chaoprayabodin Road** intersect at a diminutive purple clock tower. The **railway station** sits nearby at the north end of **Suwannasorn Road.** Trains (☎ 231 698) leave Bangkok for Aranyaprathet at 5:55am and 1:05pm and depart Aranyaprathet for Bangkok at 6:40am and 1:40pm (5½hr., 48฿). The bus station is on the west side of town: walk three blocks straight out and one block to the right to reach the clock tower. **Buses** run to Bangkok (4hr.; 6:30, 10:30am, 1:30, 3pm; 164฿) and Sa Gaeo (every hr., 6am-6pm, 36฿). **Tuk-tuks** and **samlor** putter to hotels from the bus and train stations (20฿).

CENTRAL THAILAND

🔁 **PRACTICAL INFORMATION.** The border **market,** on Weruwan Rd., is colossal but mainly sells a dull mix of jeans, sunglasses, dresses, and other faux-Western items. (Open daily 6am-7pm.) Motorcycle rides to the market should cost 25-30฿; *tuk-tuks* run 40-50฿. Other services include: the **pharmacy,** one block north of the Aran Garden I Hotel (open M-Sa 6:30am-8pm); the **Telecommunications Office,** near the corner of Mahadthai and Raduthid Rd., 500m south of the clock tower, with **international phones** (open M-F 8:30am-4:30pm); and **Internet** access at I-net, 2 Raduthid Rd., one block before Aran Gardens (20฿ per hr.; open 10am-11pm). At the clock tower, the **general post office** has a **Lenso** phone card machine. (*Poste Restante.* Phone cards 300฿ and 500฿. Open M-F 8:30am-4:30pm, Sa 9am-noon.) **Postal Code:** 27120.

🏠🍴 **ACCOMMODATIONS AND FOOD.** Aranyaprathet has no guesthouses and few accommodations of any sort. Many travelers stay at the **Aran Garden I Hotel ❷,** 59/1-7 Raduthid Rd. Walk 500m south from the clock tower to Raduthid Rd. and then 600m east to Chitsuwarn Rd.; it's on the corner. Rooms are clean and plain. (☎231 105. Doubles 150฿, with TV 200฿.) Down Raduthid Rd. one block, **Aran Garden II ❸,** 110 Raduthid Rd., has much nicer, quieter rooms with Western toilets. (☎231 070. Singles 230฿, with A/C 370฿; doubles 300฿/450฿.) Another option, removed from the town's hubbub and equipped with a large pool table, is the **Great Inn House ❷,** 1km north of the train station. (☎223 432. All rooms have TV. Doubles with fan 200฿, with A/C 300฿.) The Great Inn also has a reasonably priced **restaurant ❷.** In the low season, many travelers crash for free on the office floor of their Siem Reap-bound tour company, which might even provide breakfast. Restaurants are dismal; it's best to enjoy noodles or rice at a street stall near the Aran Garden Hotels, or at the market at the end of Raduthid Rd. (Open daily 5am-8pm.) For those skipping straight to the border there is the **Star Grill ❷,** a fast-food joint with fried chicken. (Combo meal 55฿. Open daily 8:30am-5:30pm.)

> **BORDER CROSSING: ARANYAPRATHET/POIPET.** To enter Cambodia, you must have a Cambodian visa. Travelers can obtain visas either at the Cambodian embassy in **Bangkok** (p. 103) or quickly and conveniently at the border (1200฿). In Aranyaprathet, touts materialize at the train and bus stations offering trips to Siem Reap and Angkor Wat. They are helpful in navigating the chaotic bridge and boarding a public pick-up for the painful 5hr. ride ahead (in the cab 350฿, in the back 200฿). Trucks leave 500m beyond the Cambodian border on the left. Be sure to obtain an exit stamp from Thai immigration (open daily 7:30am-5:30pm) at the bridge. Border open daily 7am-8pm. A *tuk-tuk* from anywhere in town to the bridge costs 60฿.

AYUTTHAYA   ☎035

Entering the city of Ayutthaya is like walking into a time warp. For four centuries the city was the capital of Siam, raising 33 kings, withstanding 23 Burmese invasions, and extending its rule west to Myanmar and east to Cambodia. In 1767, however, good times turned bad when Ayutthaya was sacked by the Burmese, and the capital was moved to Bangkok, leaving the city a mere shadow of its former regal self. In 1991 UNESCO named Ayutthaya a World Heritage Site, but today *tuk-tuks* and motorbikes weave around the massive ruins that dot the city, and pedestrians walk by ancient royal palaces without so much as batting an eye. Perhaps most impressively, traffic routinely comes to a standstill as elephants bearing camera-toting tourists head from ruin to ruin. Ayutthaya's numerous sights, proximity to Bangkok, and comfortable guesthouses make it a worthwhile destination.

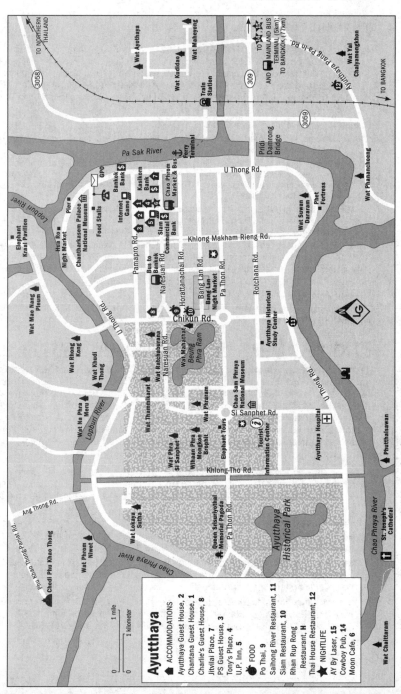

Ayutthaya

ACCOMMODATIONS
Ayutthaya Guest House, 2
Chantana Guest House, 1
Charlie's Guest House, 8
Jitvilai Place, 7
PS Guest House, 3
Tony's Place, 4
U.P. Inn, 5

FOOD
Po Thai, 9
Saihong River Restaurant, 11
Siam Restaurant, 10
Rhan Rup Rong Restaurant, H
Thai House Restaurant, 12

NIGHTLIFE
AY By Laser, 15
Cowboy Pub, 14
Moon Cafe, 6

0   1 mile
0   1 kilometer

TO NORTHERN THAILAND

Wat Ayothaya
Wat Kudidao
Wat Maheyong
Wat Kudidao

TO PAK KRET
AND MAINLAND BUS TERMINAL (5km);
TO BANGKOK (77km)
TO BANGKOK

Wat Yai Chaiyamongkhon

Ayutthaya Pang Pa-in Rd.

Train Station

Pa Sak River
Ferry Terminal
Pridi Damrong Bridge

GPO
Bangkok Bank $
Kasikorn Bank
Chao Phrom Market & Bus
Internet Game
Siam Commercial Bank $
Food Stails
Chanthankasem Palace National Museum
U Thong Rd.
Wat Phananchoeng
Khlong Makham Rieng Rd.
Wat Suwan Dararam
Phet Fortress

Pamapro Rd.
Bus to Bankok
Naresuan Rd.
Horattanachai Rd.
Bang Lan Rd.
Bang Lan Night Market
Pa Thon Rd.
Rotchana Rd.

Elephant Kraal Pavilion
Hua Ro Night Market
Wat Mae Nang Pleum
Wat Rhong Kong
Wat Khudi Thong
Wat Na Phra Meru

Lopburi River

U Thong Rd.
Chikun Rd.
Wat Mahathat
Beung Phra Ram
Ayutthaya Historical Study Center

Wat Ratchaburana Naresuan Rd.

Wat Thammikarat
Wat Pharam
Chao Sam Phraya National Museum
Si Sanphet Rd.

Wat Phra Si Sanphet
Wihaan Phra Mongkon Brophit
Elephant Tours
Tourist Information Center
Ayutthaya Hospital

Khlong-Tho Rd.

Ang Thong Rd.
Wat Lokaya Sutha
Queen Srisuriyothai Memorial Pagoda
Pa Thon Rd.
Ayutthaya Historical Park

Chao Phraya River
St. Joseph's Cathedral
Phutthaisawan

Phu Khao Thong Paniat Rd.
Chedi Phu Khao Thong
Wat Phrom Niwet
Chao Phraya River
Wat Chaittaram

☞ TRANSPORTATION

Trains: Ayutthaya Railway Station (☎241 521), on the mainland east of the island. Take the ferry from U Thong Rd. (2฿) and walk up the street. Otherwise, it's a long walk across **Pridi Damrong Bridge** and up your 1st left (*tuk-tuk* 30฿). Trains to: **Bangkok** (1 ½-2hr., 20 per day, 15-20฿); **Chiang Mai** via **Phitsanulok** (12-13hr., 4 per day, 161-1253฿); **Lopburi** (1½hr., 7 per day, 13฿); **Saraburi** (1hr., 15 per day, 9฿); **Udon Thani** (9hr., 5 per day, 145-306฿).

Buses: Ayutthaya has 3 bus stations.

Naresuan Rd. has a small station 1 block east of Chikum Rd., with buses that go to **Bangkok** (#901; 1½hr., every 20min. 4:30am-7:10pm, 41฿).

Chao Phrom Market, also on Naresuan Rd., has a chaotic mess of buses leaving from the west end of the market to **Saraburi** (#358; 2¼hr., every 30min. 6am-5pm, 30฿), connecting to destinations in the northeast, and **Suphanburi** (#703; 1¾hr., every 25min. 6am-5pm, 40฿), connecting with #411 to **Kanchanaburi.**

Mainland bus terminal, 5km east of the island (*tuk-tuk* 50฿). Buses go to: **Chiang Mai** (9½hr., 9 per day 6:30am-9pm, 283-625฿); **Phitsanulok** (5hr., 7 per day 7am–7pm, 140฿); and **Sukhothai** (6½hr.; 11 per day 7am-8:30pm, 169฿. VIP 11:30am, 10pm; 256฿.)

Ferries: Continuous **ferries** to the mainland (and the train station) leave from an alley off U Thong Rd. near the intersection with Horattanachai Rd. (2฿). **Longtail boats** and **cruisers** can be hired at the Chantharkasem Palace pier at the island's northeast tip for a 1hr. trip around the island (500฿, with 2 temple stops 600฿).

Local Transportation: Tuk-tuk/songthaew hybrids wheel around the island for 30-100฿. Rent by the hr. (100฿) or for a full day (500-700฿). Most guesthouses rent **bicycles** (50-60฿ per day).

▄✴ ⁊ ORIENTATION AND PRACTICAL INFORMATION

The Ayutthaya **city center** is an island at the intersection of the **Chao Phraya, Pa Sak,** and **Lopburi Rivers**. **U Thong Road** encircles the entire island. **Buses** from nearby cities stop next to the **Chao Phrom Market** at the corner of **Naresuan** and **U Thong Roads,** near **Khlong Makham Rieng Road** in the island's northeastern corner. Buses from northern Thailand arrive east of the island, 5km beyond the **Pridi Damrong Bridge.** Although *wats* are found all over the island, most tourist attractions cluster north of the **Tourist Information Center** on **Si Sanphet Road**. Guesthouses are concentrated in the eastern part of the island, north of the Chao Phrom Market.

Tourist Offices: Tourist Information Center (☎322 730), Si Sanphet Rd., a 5min. walk south of Wat Phra Si Sanphet. Sponsored by TAT. Carries timetables and large, handy maps. The Ayutthaya Historical Exhibition Hall on the 2nd fl. gives insight into the old capital. Office open M-Tu and Th-Su 8:30am-5pm.

Tours: KanKitti Travel (☎321 583), across from Tony's Place, right before Ayutthaya Guest House, has **Internet** (20฿ per hr.) and arranges bike tours (50฿) and nighttime *tuk-tuk* tours (100฿ per person) of the *wats.* Open daily 8am-10pm.

Currency Exchange: Many banks along the eastern stretch of Naresuan Rd. and the northeastern curve of U Thong Rd. have **24hr. ATMs.** Convenient to the guesthouses is **Siam Commercial Bank,** next to the bus station. Open M-F 8:30am-3:30pm.

Markets: Chao Phrom Market, at the corner of Naresuan and U Thong Rd. Open daily 7am-7pm. **Hua Ro Night Market,** farther north along U Thong Rd. from Chao Phrom. Open daily 4-10pm. **Bang Lan Night Market** is off Chikun Rd. Open daily 5-9pm.

Local Tourist Police: (☎241 446), on Si Sanphet Rd. Some English. Open **24hr.**

Medical Services: Ayutthaya Hospital, 46 U Thong Rd. (☎241 686), at the intersection of Si Sanphet and U Thong Rd. English spoken. Open **24hr.** No credit cards.

Telephones: International telephone booths outside GPO and at U.P. Inn

Internet Access: Internet Game, on Pamapro Rd., 30m from U Thong Rd., has fast connections and lots of gamers. 20฿ per hr. Open daily 9am-1am.

Post Offices: GPO, 123/11 U Thong Rd. (☎252 246), on the island's northeast corner. *Poste Restante.* Open M-F 8:30am-4:30pm, Sa 9am-noon.

Postal Code: 13000.

ACCOMMODATIONS

Budget accommodations cluster north of **Naresuan Road**, near Chao Phrom Market bus stop. Rates increase during festival season (Nov.-Dec.), and lodgings are harder to find. Most places have laundry and bike rental.

U.P. Inn, 20/1 Soi Thor Korsor (☎251 213). From Naresuan Rd., head up the *soi* opposite the bus station next to Chao Phrom Market, and make a left following the signs. Large, sunny, ultra-clean rooms, all with private toilet and shower. Plush common room with TV. Motorbike rental 250฿ per day. **Internet** 30฿ per hr., min. 15฿. Nighttime tours of ruins. International phone. Singles 200฿; doubles 250฿, with A/C 400-500฿. ❷

Tony's Place, 12/18 Naresuan Soi 1 Rd. (☎252 578), across from Ayutthaya Guest House. Clean rooms above a common garden have Western toilets. TV lounge, pool table, outdoor drinking area, and occasional live music round out the social atmosphere. Breakfast at 7am. Bar open until midnight. Motorbike rental 250฿ per day. Reserve ahead. Dorms 80-100฿; doubles 160฿, with bath 250฿, with A/C 400฿. ❶

Chantana Guest House, 12/22 Naresuan Rd. (☎323 200), next to Tony's Place. Quiet, simple, and clean. All rooms have Western toilets and shower. Reserve ahead. Singles and doubles with large bed 300฿, with A/C and hot shower 450฿. ❸

Jitvilai Place, 38/7 U Thong Rd. (☎328 177), 100m north of Naresuan Rd. A more upscale choice. Sparkling-bright rooms and floors to match. All rooms with private bath, A/C, and TV. Doubles 450฿, with hot water 500฿. ❹

PS Guest House. From Naresuan Rd., go north on Khlong Makham Rieng Rd. and then make a right onto Pamapro Rd.; it's on the right. Friendly, efficient owner. Rooms are large and fairly clean with wooden floors, but the shared bath is less than ideal. Singles 100฿; doubles 150฿. ❷

Charlie's Guest House (☎232 807), on Chikun Rd. opposite the entrance to Wat Ratchaburana. Large rooms overlooking the ruins. Seldom full and not as nice as guesthouses farther east—a last resort. Singles 140฿; doubles 200฿, with A/C 300฿. ❷

Ayutthaya Guest House, 16/2 Naresuan Soi 1 Rd. (☎232 658), on the *soi* across from the bus station. One of the largest guesthouses in Ayutthaya, with 3 main buildings and clean rooms. *Let's Go* does not recommend this guesthouse. Prices vary according to bath and A/C. Dorms 80฿, with A/C 100฿; singles 100-150฿; doubles 160-450฿. ❶

FOOD

Food stalls ❶ serving 20฿ chicken and rice are interspersed with tables of plastic toys, dried fish, and piles of fruit at **Chao Phrom Market,** one block east of the local bus stop. More stalls line U Thong Rd., particularly on the eastern side of the island, after the post office. For dinner, try the food stalls at the

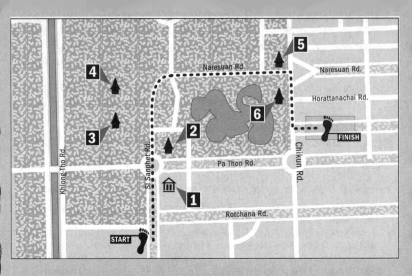

Ayutthaya is blessed with fascinating ruins left from its nearly 400-year period of prosperity and political power as capital of Thailand during the reign of 53 kings. Luckily for tourists, several of its most spectacular sights are within easy walking distance of the guesthouse area. Any walking tour should certainly be accompanied by a visit to the spectacular Wat Chaiwattanaram, on the mainland southwest of the city.

START: Tourist Information Center

FINISH: night market

DURATION: 4-5hr.

1 TOURIST INFORMATION CENTER. (p. 151) Start here for free information and maps. Then pique your interest for the sights to come with the historical exhibition on the 2nd fl.

2 CHAO SAM PHRAYA MUSEUM. (p. 152) This small museum is not as big a draw as the ruins but does hold the treasure found in Wat Ratchaburana, worth a look.

3 WAT PHRARAM. (p. 152) Built in 1369, an impressive *prang* and cloister, containing rows of stone images of Buddha, remain. Lotus flowers now surround the temple.

4 WIHAAN PHRA MONGKHON BROPHIT. (p. 151) Visit the largest Bronze Buddha in Thailand at this modern-looking *wat*. The Buddha once sat in the open air, but after several mishaps threatened the statue the *wat* was constructed to protect it.

5 WAT PHRA SI SANPHET AND THE ANCIENT PALACE. (p. 151) This spectacular *wat* replaced the original royal palace after it had been inhabited for over 100 years by 10 kings.

6 WAT RATCHABURANA. (p. 152) In 1957, when a crypt inside was looted and all 10 thieves later died mysteriously, rumors spread that the *wat* had a curse placed on it by the king himself. The remaining treasure is on display at Chao Sam Phraya Museum, stop #2.

7 WAT MAHATHAT. (p. 152) Come face-to-face with the giant stone Buddha head, entwined in the roots of a tree. This testament to the passage of time is one of the most photographed sights in Thailand; join the other tourists snapping their own picture or buy a postcard. Then wander through the rest of the *wat* next to the peaceful park.

8 NIGHT MARKET. (p. 150) End the walking tour with a well-deserved visit to the night market on Bang Lan Rd., full of delicious food and fruit options.

night markets such as the **Hua Ro Night Market** and the **Bang Lan Night Market**.

> **Saihong River Restaurant,** 45 Moo 1 U Thong Rd. (☎241 449), close to the intersection of U Thong Rd. and Chikun Rd. A local crowd enjoys the cool breeze and views of the *wat* across the river while sipping *tom yum*, a hot-and-sour soup with prawns (120฿). Dishes 50-120฿. Open daily 10am-9:30pm. ❷

> **Thai House Restaurant (Ruenthai Maisuay Restaurant),** 8/2 Moo 3 Klongsuanplu District, down the road from Wat Yai Chai Mongkhon and around the bend on the left. Tasty curry (80-120฿) spices up this quiet but elegant restaurant set in traditional Thai houses and mossy gardens. Entrees 80-250฿. Open daily 10am-10pm. ❷

> **Siam Restaurant** (☎211 070), on Chikun Rd. between Horattanachai and Bang Lan Rd. serves a Thai/Vietnamese menu. Vietnamese beef noodle soup (60฿) is filling, and a welcome change from green curry (100฿). Open daily 10am-10:30pm. MC/V. ❷

> **Po Thai** (☎322 020), at the intersection of Chikun and Horattanachai Rd. across from Wat Mahathat, combines 2 Thai favorites—food and massage—soothing both mouth and muscles. Basic Thai menu 50-100฿. 2hr. massage 360฿. Open daily 9am-10pm. ❷

> **Rhan Rup Rong Restaurant,** 13/112 Moo 2 U Thong Rd. (☎211 036). One of several restaurants on the river to offer dinner on land (entrees 100-300฿) or on a boat for groups of 8 and up. 1½-2hr.; 1000฿ per person. Open daily 11am-9pm. ❸

⬡ SIGHTS

Ayutthaya's crumbling ruins span several dozen kilometers; exploring them all takes several days. The **Tourist Information Center** has free maps that locate nearly every sight. An exhibit on the second floor showcases the city on slick touch screens (closed W). Make the best of your time by renting a bicycle or motorbike, an option at most guesthouses. Otherwise, *tuk-tuk* drivers will take you to the sights and wait while you visit. The "official" price is 200฿ per hr. or around 700-900฿ per day, but try to bargain for about half that (especially if traveling alone). The ruins are open until 6pm but usually allow visitors to stay until 6:30pm.

◪ WAT CHAIWATTHANARAM. This ancient royal monastery and cremation site is the most majestic and impressive of all the Ayutthaya ruins. The *wat* was built in ancient Khmer-style in 1630 by King Prasat Thong, during a period of great prosperity stemming from foreign trade. The 35m-high main *stupa*

ON THE MENU

THAI FUSION

Your backpacker instincts may tell you to avoid supermarkets for the more authentic—and cheaper—food stands and markets. But what is considered "authentic" today wasn't always so before, as the history of Thai culture attests. Like the culture and the language, Thai food is an amalgamation of foreign influences. While most Thais do eat at the market or food stalls, many of the Thai or Western brands offer hybrid varieties you probably can't find anywhere else, and in this sense, these products are authentically Thai.

Soups (many choices with "crab-flavoured" filaments) include **winter melon** and **fish maw** (air bladder). Familiar snacks like chips come in the less familiar seasonings of **green tea and basil** or **shrimp**. Why settle for plain vanilla ice cream when there are the more adventurous **durian, taro,** and **ruammit** (a mixture of lotus seeds, grass jelly, sweetened tapioca root, and sugar palm fruit)? Yogurt follows suit—look for varieties made with **aloe, carrots,** and an **apple and cucumber** soy substitute.

To create pandan juice pound cake, the leaves of the screw pine are pureed with water. Wash it down with corn milk and aloe vera juice (said to be good for digestion). Finish it all off by cleaning your teeth with some refreshing lychee with mint chewing gum.

represents Mount Meru, throne of the gods and center of the universe, and is surrounded by four mid-sized *stupas* and eight lesser *stupas*. The *wat* is believed to have originally been built to honor the king's mother or to celebrate a victory over Cambodia. It is particularly beautiful when lit up at night. *(Open daily 8am-6pm. 30β.)*

■ **ANCIENT PALACE AND WAT PHRA SI SANPHET.** Originally established in 1350, the ancient Royal Palace was here until 1448, when Wat Phra Si Sanphet was built on the grounds. As a royal monastery, the *wat* hosted important rituals and ceremonies. The site's three charred *chedis* once held the remains of the king, his father, and his brother, but are now empty. *(Open daily 7am-6pm. 30β.)*

WIHAAN PHRA MONGKHON BROPHIT. At 12.45m high and 9.5m wide, the 15th-century Buddha snuggled inside this *wat* is the largest bronze Buddha in Thailand. On display are photos and blurbs describing this restored Buddha's many incarnations. *(Just south of Wat Phra Si Sanphet. Open M-F 8am-4:30pm, Sa-Su 8am-5:30pm. Free.)*

WAT PHRARAM. Overshadowed by its more glamorous neighbors, this *wat* was built in 1369 by King Ramesan to commemorate the spot where his father and founder of the city, King U Thong, was cremated. Dozens of broken Buddha representations sit silently around the *wat*'s landmark *prang*. *(Across the street from Wihaan Phra Mongkhon Brophit. Open daily 8am-6pm. 30β.)*

WAT MAHATHAT. This impressive royal monastery was founded by King Borommarachathirat in 1374 and restored several times, most recently in the 18th century. Excavations done in the 1950s uncovered relics of the Buddha hidden deep in a seven-layered reliquary in the *stupa*. With those finds safely stored at the Chao Sam Phraya National Museum, the *wat*'s most famous attraction is a representation of the Buddha's face enshrouded in the roots of a tree. *(At the corner of Chikun Rd. and Naresuan Rd. Open daily 8am-6pm. 30β.)*

WAT RATCHABURANA. Wat Mahathat's most impressive neighbor was built by King Chao Sam Phraya in 1424. Legend has it that the king's two oldest brothers both coveted the throne and killed each other in a heated duel, allowing Chao Sam Phraya to ascend to the throne. To commemorate (or perhaps celebrate) his brothers' deaths, the king ordered the construction of Wat Ratchaburana over the site of their cremation. This *wat* is known for its wealth of gold artifacts and the mural paintings in its crypt. *(North of Wat Mahathat. Open daily 8am-6pm. 30β.)*

WAT YAI CHAIYAMONGKHON. This fabulous *wat* was founded in 1357 by King U Thong. In 1592, the giant *chedi* was built by King Naresuan the Great to commemorate a victory over the Burmese. The *wat*'s name, Chaiyamongkhon, meaning "Auspicious Victory," refers to this event. *(Southeast of the island on the mainland. 20min. bicycle ride from the island or a 40β tuk-tuk ride. Open daily 8am-5pm. 20β.)*

WAT PHANANCHOENG. This massive gold Buddha is the largest in Thailand and dates back to 1324, 26 years before Ayutthaya was founded. Legend has it that tears formed in its eyes when the city was sacked by the Burmese in 1767. *(West of Yai Chaiyamongkhon, about 2km farther down the road. Open daily 8am-5pm. 20β.)*

CHEDI PHU KHAO THONG. Though its distance from the island makes it difficult to reach, this *chedi* has an interesting history. The pedestal was actually built by the Burmese King Hongsawadi in order to commemorate the sacking of Ayutthaya in 1767. However, before the monument was completed, King Naresuan the Great won independence back for Ayutthaya in 1792. In classic victor fashion, King Naresuan ordered a Thai *chedi* built on top of the Burmese pedestal. *(Northwest of the island. Leave the island on Ang Thong Rd. and make a left on Phu Khao Thong-Pariat Rd. The chedi is behind the massive King Naresuan the Great Monument. Open daily 9am-6pm. Free.)*

AYUTTHAYA HISTORICAL STUDY CENTER. This US$8 million research institute funded by the Japanese government features displays on the ancient city's political, economic, and social practices. Scale models of villages during the Ayutthaya period give insight into daily life. Touring the surprisingly small upstairs exhibition hall shouldn't take more than 45min. *(On Rotchana Rd., 2 blocks east of the Chao Sam Phraya National Museum. Open M-F 9am-4:30pm, Sa-Su 9am-5pm. 100฿, with student ID 50฿.)*

CHAO SAM PHRAYA NATIONAL MUSEUM. An old-school presentation complete with wood-and-glass display cases, dusty artifacts, and missing labels, the Chao Sam Phraya Museum has little to recommend itself besides the splendid jewels taken from Wat Ratchaburana. *(On Rotchana Rd., near the intersection with Si Sanphet Rd. A 5min. walk from the Tourist Information Center. Open W-Su 9am-4pm. 30฿.)*

OTHER SIGHTS. A short bike ride north of the train station are the impressive **Wat Maheyong, Wat Kudidao,** and the smaller **Wat Ayothaya.** All three are devoid of tourists. *(Free.)* North of the island, the king used to watch his elephant army train at the **Elephant Kraal Pavilion.** The Kraal now serves as a home for abused elephants; it supports itself in part by making paper out of elephant dung and offering elephant tours of the city center. Visitors are welcome to the Kraal but they should not go up to the elephants without talking to the staff. *(☎ 321 982. On Pathon Rd. south of Wihaan Phra Mongkhom Brophit. 400฿ for 20min. elephant tour. Open daily 9am-4pm. Donations appreciated.)* Ayutthaya is also the site of one of the country's largest **Loi Krathong** festivals (p. 31), which usually takes place in November during the full moon. Thais gather around **Beung Phra Ram,** the lake in the center of the island, to see fireworks, watch *likay* (Thai folk dance), and chill out to live pop music. The *loi* (floating) of *krathong* (lotus-shaped paper boats with candles and incense) takes place at the **Chantharkasem Pier** opposite the Chantharkasem Palace Museum.

🎵 🍷 ENTERTAINMENT AND NIGHTLIFE

After a hard day *wat*-hopping, treat yourself to a **massage** at the Chao Phrom Market bus station. (From Naresuan Rd. it's the second building on the right. ☎244 582. 2hr. Thai massage 300฿. Foot massage 200฿ per hr. Open daily 10am-midnight.) From 7:30 to 9:30pm nightly, **Wat Phra Si Sanphet, Wat Mahathat, Wat Ratchaburana, Wat Phraram,** and **Wat Chiawatthanaram** are illuminated by floodlights. U.P. Inn and Kankitti Travel offer night tours of these *wats* beginning at 7pm (100฿). Note that entering the grounds of the *wats* after dark is illegal and dangerous. There is a limited amount of nightlife around the guesthouses—**Tony's Place** is always hopping—but to get to the real hot spots head to the mainland east of the island to the area around the Grand Hotel (*tuk-tuk* 60฿).

Moon Cafe (☎232 501), off Naresuan Rd., opposite Ayutthaya Guest House. A diverse crowd of travelers, A/C, and 400 jazz, blues, and classic rock CDs make it the best pub in town. Exchange travel stories and sing along to the Beatles. Large Singha 100฿. Live music F at 10:30pm. Open 4pm-1am; kitchen closes at 9:30pm.

AY By Laser (☎06 525 2742), east of the island next to the Grand Hotel. This massive discotheque features scantily clad Thai pop singers and dancers performing 3 45min. shows nightly (9, 10:20, 11:45pm). Watch the young Thai crowd dance while guzzling bottles of whiskey. 50฿ cover waived if you buy a bottle upon entry. Open 9am-1am.

Cowboy Pub, on Soi Grand, on the left before AY By Laser. A Thai cover band performs nightly—request all your favorite songs. Everybody drinks and has a slightly-out-of-tune good time. Heineken 50-90฿. Thai food 80฿. Band starts at 10pm. Open 4pm-1am.

CENTRAL THAILAND

LOPBURI
☎ **036**

From the moment you enter Old Lopburi, you can sense the town's rich history. Remarkably well-maintained ancient *wats* and traces of civilization that date back 4,500 years are found around virtually every corner. Modern stores and businesses blend together seamlessly with old stone temples and palaces, relics of Lopburi's past as a major cultural and political center during the Ayutthaya period. Continuing in this tradition, the new city is an important site for military training and higher education. Located 153km north of Bangkok, Lopburi makes for a captivating daytrip or a worthwhile stop on the train ride to Chiang Mai.

 TRANSPORTATION. Rail is the best way to get to Lopburi because the city is located away from the major north-south highways. The train station is in the heart of the old city, while the bus station is farther from the important hotels and sites. Frequent arrivals and departures to and from Ayutthaya and Bangkok, however, make Lopburi a very reachable destination by bus from the south.

The **train station** (☎ 411 022) is on Naphrakan Rd., in the old city across from Wat Phra Sri Rattanamahathat. **Trains** to Bangkok (3hr.; every hr. 1am-6:30pm, 9:35pm; 28-64฿) via Ayutthaya (1½hr., 14-48฿) and Chiang Mai (9-11hr., 7 per day 8:55am-12:30am, 146-212฿) via Phitsanulok (3-4hr., 28-64฿). Tickets to Bangkok on trains originating farther north can only be purchased within 30min. of departure.

The **bus station** is near New Lopburi on Narai Maharat Rd., the east-west road that connects the old and new cities, 2km from Old Lopburi. **A/C buses** go to Bangkok (2½hr., every 20min. 4:40am-8pm, 101฿). **Regular buses** make trips to Ayutthaya (2hr., every 20min. 4:50am-6:30pm, 28฿) and the closest town on the Bangkok-Chiang Mai route, Singburi (1hr., every 20min. 5:10am-6:40pm, 13฿). **A/C vans** leave for Bangkok (2½hr., every hr. 5am-7pm, 80฿) from Old Lopburi on Naphrakan Rd., a 2min. walk towards Narai Maharat Rd. from the train station.

Blue and green **city buses** ply Narai Maharat Rd. between the old and new cities (every 2min. 5am-8pm, 6฿). Blue **songthaew** handle north-south routes between Old and New Lopburi (every 5min. 5am-8pm, 5฿), but these are mostly walkable. Omnipresent yellow-vested **motorcycle taxi** drivers are good for rides within Old Lopburi (20-40฿). **Samlor** can be found at the rail station and on some streets in the old city (within Old Lopburi 10-20฿).

 PRACTICAL INFORMATION. Lopburi is actually two gradually converging cities, centered 2.5km apart along **Narai Maharat Road: Old** and **New Lopburi.** While New Lopburi, east of the old town, is the bustling epicenter of regional commerce, virtually everything of interest to tourists is in Old Lopburi. **Naphrakan Road** marks the eastern edge of the old city and is home to the train station, restaurants, the night market, Internet cafes, several sites of historical interest, and dozens of insufferable primates. **Surasongkhram Road** (also called Surasak Road), is the other major north-south road in the old city and has banks, hotels, police, day markets, King Narai's palace, and more ancient temples.

TAT recently moved to Rop Wat Pharthat Rd. in Old Lopburi, making it much more convenient for tourists. Exit the train station to the right, make the first left onto Rop Wat Pharthat Rd., and walk a block. Staff speaks decent English and dispenses maps, brochures, and transit information. (☎ 422 768; tatlobri@tat.or.th. Open daily 8:30am-4:30pm.) Other services include: **Krung Thai Bank,** at the corner of Narai Maharat Rd. and Surasongkhram Rd., with **currency exchange** services and a **24hr. ATM** in front (open M-F 8:30am-3:30pm, Sa 9:30am-12:30pm); the **police station,** at the corner of Narai Maharat and Naphrakan Rd. (☎ 411 013, open **24hr.**); the general **hospital,** in the new town on Phahol Yothin Hwy. (☎ 411 250; from the old city, follow Narai Maharat Rd., turn left at the provincial hall, and follow the road for a block; some English spoken; open **24hr.**); an **International telephone booth** at the CAT office next door to the main post office. (open daily 8:30am-8:30pm); **Internet access** at Online, with super-fast connections (on Ratchadamnoen Rd., halfway between the KFC and Naphrakan Rd.; 20฿ per hr., after 6pm 10฿ per hr; open daily 6am-midnight); and the **post office**, on Prang Sam Yod Rd., just past the temple of the same name on Narai Maharat Rd. The city's central post office is on Narai Maharat Rd. just before the bus station coming from the old city. (Central office ☎411 011. Both open M-F 8:30am-4:30pm.) **Postal Code:** 15000.

🄶🄲 ACCOMMODATIONS AND FOOD. Quality hotels in Old Lopburi are cheap, clean, comfortable, and within walking distance of the train station and sights. Most have reasonably priced Thai-Chinese restaurants on the ground floor.

The **Lopburi Asia Hotel ②**, 1/7-8 Surasongkhram Rd., with large, clean rooms and a professional staff, is located near King Narai's Palace in the old city. From Narai Maharat Rd. heading away from New Lopburi, turn left on Surasongkhram Rd. and walk two blocks. (☎618 893. A/C rooms have hot showers and big TVs. Rooms 200฿, with A/C 300฿.) Similar to the Lopburi Asia Hotel, but with cold showers and rooms that are a bit smaller, is the **Nett Hotel ②**, 17/1-2 Ratchadamnoen Rd. It is situated in an alley a block towards the train station from Lopburi Asia Hotel. (☎618 893. Rooms 140-160฿, with A/C 250฿.) The **Taipei Hotel ②**, 24/6-7 Surasongkhram Rd., is two blocks past Narai Maharat Rd. coming from the train station. The hotel has clean, straightforward rooms similar to others in town, but a bit larger. (☎411 523. A/C rooms have TV and hot showers. Singles 140฿, with A/C 290฿; doubles 170฿/350฿.) The **Lop Buri Inn ④**, 28/9 Narai Maharat Rd., is in the new city just before the Provincial Hall on the right. This large, upscale business hotel, convenient to the bus station, has 135 well-equipped A/C rooms, each with hot showers and satellite TV. (☎412 300. Rooms 500-600฿.)

There are excellent **day markets ❶** in the small alleys off Surasongkhram Rd. north of Narai Maharat Rd., going away from the train station, with plenty of fish and fresh produce. The smallish **night market ❶** sets up on Naphrakan Rd. near the train station. (Open nightly until 10 or 11pm.) The **food shop ②** next door to Lopburi Asia Hotel serves massive noodle dishes cooked to your specifications, but ask the price first or you may get gouged. **May Ka Mind ②**, on the corner of Naphrakan and Ratchadamnoen Rd., about a 5min. walk from the train station, is a favorite of local university students and offers tasty, reasonably priced Thai dishes in a comfy A/C setting. (Most dishes 45-85฿. Open daily 10am-8pm.) **White House Garden Restaurant ②**, is on Phraya Kamjad Rd. a block southwest of the intersection of Ratchadamnoen and Naphrakan Rd. From the rail station, turn right onto Naphrakan Rd., then take the second left, and walk a block. White House Garden offers decent Thai and Chinese dishes served in a pleasant garden atmosphere. The "Grilled White House Duck" (80฿) is their specialty. (Open daily 10am-10pm.)

🄶 SIGHTS. Formerly the second capital of Thailand, Lopburi has sights that display both Thai and Western influences.

WAT PHRA SRU RATTANAMAHATHAT. The age of ancient **Wat Phra Sru Rattanamahathat** is unknown, but it is nevertheless worth a visit, even if you just have time for a quick hop from the train station. The first thing you see upon entering is the **Sala Pluang Khruang,** a pavilion used by King Narai the Great to change into ritualistic garb for religious functions, located at the main assembly hall. Another assembly hall to the south features French doors and windows. Beyond this hall is the main pagoda, constructed around 1257. Due to frequent renovations since then, it features architectural styles from a number of different eras. *(Across from the train station on Naphrakan Rd. in Old Lopburi. Open W-Su 7am-5pm. Thais 10฿, foreigners 30฿.)*

CENTRAL THAILAND

KING NARAI'S PALACE. King Narai built his **palace** in 1666 when military and business affairs found him making frequent trips to Lopburi. The massive complex features intricate architectural designs that are intended to evoke lotuses at every turn. The walls of the middle and inner courts have 2000 lotus-shaped wedges in which candles were placed, lighting up the entire building spectacularly. The **Narai throne halls** are built in a fascinating fusion of French and Thai architectural styles.

King Rama IV renovated the palace in 1856, turning Lopburi into something of a second capital to Bangkok. Rama IV's four throne halls consist of **Phiman Mongkut,** where he resided; **Wisutthiwintchai,** where official business was conducted; **Chaiya-sattrakom,** which housed the primary stock of weaponry; and **Akson Sattrakhom,** where the king wrote letters, journals, and correspondence. Some of these writings are found in the adjacent **Somdet Phra Narai National Museum,** Thailand's third-largest museum, founded in 1923. The museum features artifacts dating back to prehistoric times, in addition to biographical artwork of King Narai and King Rama IV. Lastly, the shadow play section of the museum displays some of the puppetry that this region is known for. *(On Surasongkhram Rd., 2 blocks behind Wat Phra Sri Rattanamahathat. Open W-Su 9am-4pm. Thais 10฿, foreigners 30฿.)*

WAT PRANG KHAEK. Lopburi's oldest historical site, **Wat Prang Khaek** dates back to the 9th century AD. Three disconnected brick pagodas lie quietly on a triangular green lawn as traffic bustles by in all directions. The pagodas feature Khmer artwork in the centuries-old Phakho style. The assembly hall and water tank, located on opposite sides of the complex, were commissioned by King Narai the Great. *(On Surasongkhram Rd. at Narai Maharat Rd., in the center of Old Lopburi. Free.)*

PHRA PRANG SAM YOT. Phra Prang Sam Yot is a complex of three connected pagodas that dates back to the 11th century AD and is most significant as a well-maintained example of the Bayon style of Khmer artwork. It was originally a Khmer Buddhist temple of importance to members of the Mahayana sect. This group's faith had more overt ties to Hinduism, including *linga* features at the base of each of the pagodas, meant for worship of Shiva. King Narai the Great later converted it into a Thai Buddhist temple and constructed a brick assembly hall on the premises. The interior of this building contains architecture and a sandstone Buddha typical of the early Ayutthaya period.

Just across the railroad tracks is the **Phra Kan Shrine,** a large square pagoda from the 12th century AD. The pagoda is in ruins and two statues of the god Narai are mostly all that remains. A pavilion was constructed in front of the temple in 1951 and is home to several Narai statues and a pack of particularly vicious monkeys—protect your camera! *(On Narai Maharat Rd. at Naphrakan Rd. From the train station, follow the road toward the center of town to the major intersection 3 blocks away. Phra Prang Sam Yot open W-Su 7am-5pm. Thais 10฿, foreigners 30฿. Phra Kan Shrine open daily. Free.)*

KANCHANABURI ☎034

The Japanese invasion during WWII immortalized the otherwise undistinguished town of Kanchanaburi and the humble River Kwai. Backpackers now use the city—once of strategic importance in the overland route between Singapore and Yangon—as a base for exploring the surrounding waterfalls, caves, and jungles. They return in the evenings to their lively guesthouses beside the peaceful river to swap travel stories with Thai tourists hoping to escape hectic Bangkok life.

▐ TRANSPORTATION

Trains: Kanchanaburi Train Station, (☎511 285), on Saeng Chuto Rd. To **Namtok** via the **River Kwai Bridge** (2½hr.; 6:10, 10:50am, 4:30pm; 17฿) and Thonburi Station in

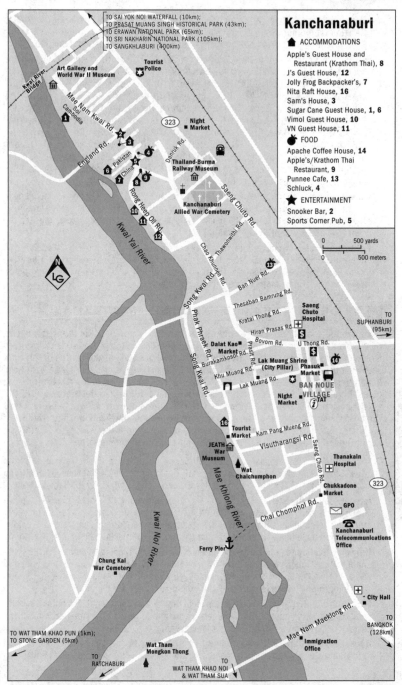

Kanchanaburi

ACCOMMODATIONS

Apple's Guest House and
  Restaurant (Krathom Thai), **8**
J's Guest House, **12**
Jolly Frog Backpacker's, **7**
Nita Raft House, **16**
Sam's House, **3**
Sugar Cane Guest House, **1, 6**
Vimol Guest House, **10**
VN Guest House, **11**

FOOD

Apache Coffee House, **14**
Apple's/Krathom Thai
  Restaurant, **9**
Punnee Cafe, **13**
Schluck, **4**

ENTERTAINMENT

Snooker Bar, **2**
Sports Corner Pub, **5**

TO SAI YOK NOI WATERFALL (10km);
TO PRASAT MUANG SINGH HISTORICAL PARK (43km);
TO ERAWAN NATIONAL PARK (65km);
TO SRI NAKHARIN NATIONAL PARK (105km);
TO SANGKHLABURI (400km)

Art Gallery and
World War II Museum

Tourist
Police

Kwai River Bridge

Mae Nam Kwai Rd.

Soi Cambodia

England Rd.

Night
Market

323

Daeruk Rd.

Pakistan

China

Thailand-Burma
Railway Museum

Rong Heep Oil Rd.

Kwai Yai River

Kanchanaburi
Allied War Cemetery

Saeng Chuto Rd.

0   500 yards
0   500 meters

Chao Khunnen Rd.

Thawonwithi Rd.

Ban Nuer Rd.

Thesaban Bamrung Rd.

Kratai Thong Rd.

Song Kwai Rd.

Phak Phraek Rd.

Hiran Prasas Rd.

Saeng
Chuto
Hospital

TO
SUPHANBURI
(95km)

Bovorn Rd.

U Thong Rd.

Dalat Kao
Market

Burakamkosof Rd.

Prasit Rd.

Lak Muang Shrine
(City Pillar)

Phasuk
Market

Song Kwai Rd.

Khu Muang Rd.

Lak Muang Rd.

BAN NOUE
VILLAGE

TAT

Night
Market

Tourist
Market

Kam Pang Mueng Rd.

Visutharangsi Rd.

JEATH
War
Museum

Wat
Chaichumphon

Mae Khlong River

Saeng Chuto Rd.

Thanakain
Hospital

Chukkadone
Market

323

Chai Chomphol Rd.

GPO

Kanchanaburi
Telecommunications
Office

Kwai Noi River

Ferry Pier

Chung Kai
War Cemetery

City Hall

TO WAT THAM KHAO PUN (1km);
TO STONE GARDEN (5km)

TO
RATCHABURI

Wat Tham
Mongkon Thong

TO
WAT THAM KHAO NOI
& WAT THAM SUA

Mae Nam Maeklong Rd.

Immigration
Office

TO
BANGKOK
(128km)

Bangkok (3hr.; 7:25am, 2:50pm; 25฿). Call (☎561 052) for info on weekend trains to **Bangkok** and other destinations (2hr., Sa-Su 5pm, 28฿). For short trips, such as the River Kwai Bridge, it is more convenient to take a bus, as they depart more frequently.

Buses: The **Kanchanaburi Bus Station,** (☎511 182), is in Ban Noue Village at the southern end of Kanchanaburi. To: **Bangkok** (#81; 2nd-class with A/C: 2hr., every 20min. 3:50am-6:50pm, 62฿; 1st-class with A/C: 2hr., every 15min. 4am-7pm, 79฿) via **Nakhon Pathom** (1½hr., 40฿); **Erawan National Park** (#8170, 1½hr., every 50min. 8am-5:20pm, 26฿); **Ratchaburi** with connections to **Cha Am, Hua Hin,** and **Phetchaburi** (#461, 2hr., every 15min. 5:10am-6:20pm, 36฿); **Sangkhlaburi** (#8203: 5hr.; 6, 8:40, 10:20am, noon; 84฿. VIP bus #8203: 4hr.; 9:30am, 1:30, 3:30pm; 151฿. A/C Van #8203: 3 hr., every hr. 7:30am-4:30pm, 118฿, departs across from main bus terminal); **Suphanburi** (#411, 1½-2hr., every 20min. 5am-5:45pm, 35฿) with connections to **Ayutthaya** and **Nakhon Sawan** (last connecting bus to these destinations leaves at 5pm).

Local Transportation: Orange **songthaew** run up and down Saeng Chuto Rd. including in their route the River Kwai Bridge (10฿). **Samlor** cost 10-20฿ from the railway station to TAT. **Motorcycle taxis** to guesthouses from bus station cost 30฿. A **ferry** crosses the river (5฿) at the end of Chai Chumphol Rd.

Rentals: Bicycles available from almost all guesthouses and on Mae Nam Kwai Rd. with deposit of some form of ID. 20-50฿ per day. **Motorbikes** are permitted on Mae Nam Kwai Rd. with passport deposit. 200฿ for 24hr., 150฿ for 9am-5pm. Cruising motorbikes 500฿ per day. Motocross bikes are difficult to find.

✦ ⁊ ORIENTATION AND PRACTICAL INFORMATION

Kanchanaburi is 129km from Bangkok and stretches roughly 4km along the banks of the **Kwai River,** which flows parallel to **Saeng Chuto Road,** the city's main drag. North of town is the famous **River Kwai Bridge;** 2km south of the bridge is the **train station** and the riverside **guesthouse area,** where *farang* congregate. **Mae Nam Kwai Road** connects the guesthouses to the River Kwai Bridge and is lined with Internet cafes, bike rentals, tour companies, and bars. Two kilometers farther south of the guesthouse area is **Ban Noue Village,** the city's main commercial area and home to the **bus station.** West of the bus station are the **city gate, day markets,** and **river wharf area.** Because Kanchanaburi is quite spread out, consider renting a bicycle to avoid the long, dusty walks between one part of town and the other.

▨ Tourist Office: TAT, (☎/fax 511 200), on Saeng Chuto Rd., a 5min. walk south of the bus station. Friendly, English-speaking staff deals out leaflets. Excellent regional map (20฿ donation). Bus and train schedules. Lenso phone. Open daily 8:30am-4:30pm.

Immigration Office: (☎513 325). On Mae Nam Maeklong Rd., 4km from TAT. Follow Saeng Chuto Rd. south away from Ban Noue Village and turn right at City Hall, 1km past the GPO. 1-month visa extension 500฿, 1-day processing. Bring 1 photo and 2 copies of passport including visa and departure card. Open M-F 8:30am-noon and 1-4:30pm.

Currency Exchange: Banks are common on the roads fanning out from the Kanchanaburi Bus Station. Several have **24hr. ATMs. Thai Farmers Bank** is 1 block from Saeng Chuto Rd. on Lak Muang Rd., heading toward the bus station. Open M-F 8:30am-3:30pm. **Punnee Cafe** (see below) can exchange money after hours.

Work Opportunity: Teach English at the local private Catholic school. 1-month, 3-month, and 1-year commitments. Teachers receive room and board plus stipend. Contact the school directly (☎09 889 0050, ask for Orawan).

Books: Punnee Cafe, 2/15 Ban Nuer Rd. (☎513 503), off Saeng Chuto Rd. Cafe with full bar features an English-language used bookstore, along with fish and chips (150฿).

Markets: The **Dalat Kao Market,** bounded by Chao Khunnen and Burakamkosol Rd., offers fresh produce and meat. **Phasuk Market,** across from the bus station near Lak Muang Rd. in Ban Noue Village, sells clothing and accessories. Both open daily dawn-dusk. The closest **night market** to guesthouses is the haphazard roadside affair just north of the train station on Saeng Chuto Rd. Open M, Th, Sa, Su 5-10pm. There is also a night market by the bus station on Tu, W, F nights. 10min. walk.

Tourist Police: (☎512 795), 1.5km north of train station on Saeng Chuto Rd. on the right. Free **luggage storage.** English spoken. Open **24hr.** 3 helpful **booths** at the foot of the Kwai River Bridge, on Song Kwai Rd. at Burakamkosol Rd., and on Mae Nam Kwai Rd. 50m past Apple's Guest House toward cemetery. Open daily 8:30am-6pm.

Medical Services: Saeng Chuto Hospital (☎621 129), 500m north of TAT on Saeng Chuto Rd. English spoken. Hospital and **pharmacy** open **24hr.** MC/V.

Telephones: Kanchanaburi Telecommunications Office, on Saeng Chuto Rd., Soi 38. Turn left at the post office; it's 200m on the right. International calls, phone cards, and **CATNET.** 1st min. 3฿, each subsequent min. 0.50฿. **24hr.** Open daily 8:30am-10pm.

Internet: Available all over the city, especially on Mae Nam Kwai Rd. (25-40฿ per hr.)

Post Office: GPO (☎511 131), on Saeng Chuto Rd., 1km south of TAT on the left. *Poste Restante.* Open M-F 8:30am-4:30pm, Sa-Su 9am-noon.

Postal Code: 71000.

⌧ ACCOMMODATIONS

Most of Kanchanaburi's best budget accommodations sit along (or in) the River Kwai in the northern part of the city, a 10min. walk from the train station or a 25min. walk from the bus station. Taxi rides from the bus station are 30฿, although some guesthouses will arrange for free pick-up if you call upon arrival. Guest-houses on Rong Heep Oil Rd. are quieter, while the ones on Mae Nam Kwai Rd. are always flooded with *farang.* All establishments listed serve Thai and Western food and help arrange tours. A hot shower is not a necessity in Kanchanaburi's steamy heat. As a result, hot water costs extra or is nonexistent in most establishments. Many of the guesthouses will do laundry for a small charge.

One of the disadvantages to staying on the river is the raucous noise from the floating discos, which boom until the wee hours of the morning on the weekends. The farther north one gets from the bus station, the less bothersome the disco noise becomes. Also, it is painfully obvious that some guesthouses pump water into and out of the river. Check the color and smell of the bathroom and its running water before agreeing on a room.

Jolly Frog Backpacker's, 28 Soi China, Mae Nam Kwai Rd. (☎514 579). Clean, attractive rooms overlook a beautiful courtyard and the river. Has a livelier and younger clientele than most of the other guesthouses. Nightly guest-picked movies. Singles 70฿; doubles 150฿, on-raft portion 150฿, with bath 200฿, with A/C 290฿. ❶

Sugar Cane Guest House in 2 locations. **22 Soi Pakistan ❷** (☎624 520), off Mae Nam Kwai Rd., turn-off 1 block north from turn-off to Jolly Frog Backpacker's. Impressive restaurant and lounge overlooking river. Bungalows with bath around manicured riverfront garden 150-250฿; raft house with A/C and hot shower 550฿. **7 Soi Cambodia ❷** (☎514 988), off Mae Nam Kwai Rd., 1km farther north toward the bridge, is quieter, if not as upscale. Laundry 20฿ per kg. Bamboo bungalows, singles 150฿; doubles 200฿; huge concrete bungalow with TV and A/C 400-550฿, depending on proximity to river.

Apple's Guest House and Restaurant (Krathom Thai), 52 Rong Heep Oil Rd. (☎512 017), at the juncture with Mae Nam Kwai Rd. Clean rooms surround a peaceful courtyard but lack riverside real-estate. Hospitable co-owner Apple leads an excellent cook-

THE LOCAL STORY

POWS

During WWII, few men left the POW camps between Kanchanaburi and Thanbyuzayat (Three Pagoda Pass) without coming under the care of Edward "Weary" Dunlop. As one of the Senior Medical Officers in the region, known to the men as "King of the River," Dunlop inspired hope during a torturous war. He was even dubbed "No. 1 Doctor" by the Japanese for his miraculous surgical successes.

This soft-spoken gentleman, towering at 6'4", toiled tirelessly in work camps. Like his fellow POWs, he suffered from dysentery, tropical ulcers, and recurring malaria and cholera. He had a reputation for toughness from his days of playing rugby for Australia, and he was just as driven to help his fellow POWs. Dunlop bravely and persistently confronted Japanese commanders about the appalling conditions of the camp.

In the wet season of 1943, Dunlop was instructed to force one third of his patients—some 00 sick men—to work. Dunlop's solution was what came to be known as the "log sitting game," having his sick patients simply sit on a log despite Japanese orders to work. The subsequent beatings resulted in more POWs landing in the hospital, and fewer being able to work. Dunlop's rebellion boosted morale among the prisoners and forced the Japanese to back down and let him keep as

[Cont'd on next page...]

ing course (750฿). Free pickup from the bus and train station. Info on Kanchanaburi and tourist sites is available. Singles 200฿, with A/C 500฿; doubles 250฿/500฿. ❷

Vimol Guest House (formerly Rick's Lodge), 48/5 Rong Heep Oil Rd. (☎514 831). Pleasant river-view restaurant. 1-seater speedboat 250฿ per hr. Fishing rod 50฿ per day. Bungalows with attic sleeping, fly-screen door ventilation, and bath 150฿ (not on river). Gorgeous wood-paneled floating raft rooms with A/C and bath 500-600฿. ❷

Sam's House, 14/2 Moo 1(☎515 956), a left off Mae Nam Kwai Rd. Tidy rooms set in garden courtyard or out on the river. Friendly staff and open-air riverside restaurant. Rooms in courtyard 150฿, on river 450฿, with A/C 350-600฿. The best option of three Sam's Guesthouses, which also include Sam's Place on Song Kwai Rd. and Sam's River Raft House on Rong Heep Oil Rd. ❷

VN Guest House, 44 Rong Heep Oil Rd. (☎514 082). The friendly staff welcomes a crew of easygoing backpackers. The cheaper rooms take prime position next to the river. Singles 50-60฿, with bath 100฿; doubles 70-80฿, with bath 150฿, with A/C 250-300฿. ❶

Nita Raft House, 27/1 Pakpraek (☎514 521). An easy 10min. walk from the bus station (100m north of JEATH museum) and 20 min. south of the main guesthouse area. Floating discos rock on nearby. Clean but simple rooms, set on a delightfully rambling group of rafts. Singles 80฿; doubles 120฿, with Western toilet and shower 180฿. ❶

J's Guest House, 32/4 Rong Heep Oil Rd. (☎620 307). Rock-bottom accommodations. Rooms float over a still inlet from the river and come with mosquito netting and a hammock. Singles 50฿, with bath 100฿; doubles 80฿/120฿. ❶

🍴 FOOD

From May to July, be sure to try the *khanun* (jackfruit), a Thai delicacy. This and other tasty victuals can be found in the cheap food stalls and open-air eateries that line the streets around the bus station. The markets in town, including two night markets on Saeng Chuto Rd. (one north of the train station, one north of TAT), make for cheap and authentic Thai eats. If market eating is not your style, head for **Song Kwai Road,** where dozens of indistinguishable restaurants cater almost exclusively to locals. Most tourists get meals at the guesthouse they are staying at, where convenience and location make up for average quality and value.

One of the best guesthouse restaurants is **Apple's Thai Restaurant ❷** (p. 173), which offers fabulous food (dishes 30-60฿). For a Thai-style Indian dish, try chicken massaman curry (65฿). Tofu can be substituted in all meat dishes. **Schluck ❷**, on Mae Nam Kwai Rd., stands out from the rest, offering A/C dining comfort. The delicious chicken schnitzel baguette (45฿) is drenched in mayonnaise dressing. (Open daily 4pm-1am.) Western food at **Snooker Bar ❶** isn't the greatest value, but Thai dishes prove worthwhile. (*Pad thai* with chicken 25฿. Open daily 9am-2am.) By the bus station, **Apache Coffee House ❸** provides a quiet meal in air-conditioned comfort. Though a bit expensive, the food is some of the best in town. Try the delicious pork chop (95฿). Entrees cost 80-120฿, coffee and desserts 40-60฿.

SIGHTS

Today, World War II's Allies and their old opponents join forces, packing into A/C buses to see the Death Railway Bridge and the graves of thousands of Allied soldiers. Several interesting museums quickly dispel (or confirm) myths associated with the war, and all stand as testament to the strength of the POWs.

Kanchanaburi's attractions are spread over 6km. To take it all in over a couple of days, rent a bicycle or motorbike—it's infinitely faster and easier than walking, cheaper than taking a taxi, and more convenient than trying to catch a bus.

▨ KWAI RIVER BRIDGE (DEATH RAILWAY BRIDGE).

Constructed between 1941 and 1942, the original Kwai River Bridge was the Japanese army's final attempt at completing the 415km Thai-Myanmar railway line (the "Death Railway") for transporting war materials to military camps in Myanmar. Roughly 16,000 POWs and 96,000 Asians died building the bridge, which was subsequently destroyed by British air raids in 1945. Engineers predicted that it would take five years to construct the bridge, but the Japanese forced POWs and local laborers to complete this vital section of the railway in 16 months. The bridge you see, although impressive, is a reconstruction built as a memorial to those who lost their lives. Kanchanaburi celebrates the **Kwai River Bridge Week** during the first week of December. Activities include archaeological and historical exhibitions, performances, musical events, and a spectacular light and sound show. *(3km northwest of train station. Orange minibus #2 runs from Focus Optic shop, 2 traffic lights from TAT (10min., 6am-7pm, 6฿). Approx. 2.5km walk north of guesthouses on Mae Nam Kwai Rd. Songthaew to bridge 10-20฿. Many local tour companies arrange rides on a train that crosses the River Kwai Bridge.)*

many patients in the hospital as he wanted. His newfound authority even allowed him to secure luxuries like duck eggs for them.

When Dunlop returned to Australia after the war, he made sure the Thais who risked their lives to help the POWs were recognized. Boon Pong, a Thai trader who spearheaded an underground system via the Kwai River, was singled out for commendation.

After the war, Dunlop became an internationally recognized surgeon, pioneering new techniques in thoracic cancer treatment. Ever devoted, he returned to Asia to train doctors in India, Vietnam, and Thailand. The Edward "Weary" Dunlop-Boon Pong Fellowship now brings Thai nationals to Australia to study medicine at Melbourne University.

A companion of the Order of Australia, a fellow of the prestigious Royal College of Surgeons in London, and the recipient of honorary fellowships and doctorates, Dunlop was also knighted in Britain by Her Majesty, given the Knight Grand Cross of the Most Noble Order of the Royal Crown of Thailand, and made an order of the White Elephant, Dunlop died in 1993 just before turning 86. He wished that his ashes be returned to the Hellfire Pass with the following epitaph, a fitting end for the man known as "The Surgeon of the Railway."

"When you go home,
tell them of us and say
We gave our tomorrow
For your today"

THAILAND-BURMA RAILWAY CENTER. This fairly new museum (opened in 2003) tells the bitter story of the 415km Death Railway, which was crucial to Japanese expansion into Asia during WWII. The museum has a 3-D model of the railway, video displays, historic artifacts, and details on the POWs. *(73 Chao Kunnen Rd., across from the Allied War Cemetery. www.tbrconline.com. Open daily 9am-5pm. 60฿.)*

ART GALLERY AND WORLD WAR II MUSEUM. Luring bridge visitors with claims of World War II exhibitions, the museum is actually a bizarre collection of odd, dusty exhibits. Everything from Thai stamps to dresses of former Miss Thailands can be found here. Follow the "toilet" signs to the basement, where cobwebs hide life-sized portrayals of the bridge construction, as well as automobiles and motorbikes used in the war. It's mildly interesting and very unusual, but skip it if you're pressed for time. *(50m toward town from the bridge. ☎ 512 596. Signs imply this is the JEATH museum; do not be confused, the JEATH museum is in town. Open daily 8am-6pm. 30฿.)*

JEATH WAR MUSEUM. Established in 1977 by the abbot of Wat Chaichumphon to honor victims of the Death Railway Bridge, JEATH (Japan, England, America/Australia, Thailand, and Holland) sits in a bamboo hut like those used to house POWs. The collection of pictures, artifacts, and drawings is modest but nevertheless intriguing. Newspaper articles posted on the walls highlight the accomplishments of famous POWs and their efforts to raise awareness of wartime events. *(500m south of the town gate on Phak Phraek Rd. ☎ 515 203. Open daily 8:30am-4:30pm. 30฿.)*

KANCHANABURI ALLIED WAR CEMETERY. This is the final resting place of 7000 Allied POWs, mostly British and Dutch, who died working on the Death Railway Bridge. Western tour groups often seem to outnumber the headstones. *(2km north of the bus station on Saeng Chuto Rd., a 5min. walk from the train station. Free.)*

CHUNG KAI WAR CEMETERY. Farther afield, Chung Kai holds the remains of 1700 Death Railway POWs in a setting more peaceful and pleasant than its larger counterpart in town, although the tranquility is often broken by the ruckus from the party boats. The trip makes a nice escape from the congestion of Kanchanaburi City. *(4km across the bridge at Song Kwai Rd.'s northern end. Free.)*

STONE GARDEN. Grassed oases sit among barren rocks in the Stone Garden, where the rock formations supposedly look like animals. This takes a bit of imagination, but the Stone Garden is nonetheless ideal for a picnic. *(On the same road as Chung Kai War Cemetery and Wat Tham Kao Pun, 5km farther than the cemetery and 4km farther than the wat.)*

WATS. Wat Chaichumphon (also called **Wat Dai**), next to JEATH, is most often frequented by townspeople. **Wat Tham Khao Pun,** 1km beyond Chung Kai War Cemetery, has a cave full of Buddhist shrines (5-20฿ donation suggested). Four kilometers across the river, Chinese-influenced **Wat Tham Mongkon Thong,** (Cave Temple of the Golden Dragon) is renowned for its "floating nun," a woman who can lie on water without sinking. Early weekend mornings are the best time to catch her in action. Private shows are 200฿, or 10฿ per person with a minimum of 20 people, to see her 10-15min. performance (which might be worth 10฿ but is probably not worth 200฿). The temple also features a small **museum** of Kanchanaburi's history. Behind the museum, dragon-shaped steps lead up the mountain and into a **limestone cave** that affords views of the surrounding mountains and valleys. Motorcycle taxis make the trip for 30฿; by motorbike, follow the road out over the bridge past immigration.

♪ ENTERTAINMENT

At night, most *farang* stick to bars, discos, and restaurants in the well-trodden area around the guesthouses along Mae Nam Kwai Rd. The small but popular **Sports Corner Pub**, at the corner of China Rd. and Mae Nam Kwai Rd., entertains Commonwealth folk with nightly showings of football, rugby, and cricket. (Open daily 9am-late.) Farther north on Mae Nam Kwai Rd. toward the bridge, **Snooker Bar** has three recent movie releases per night starting at 6pm. The staff is more than happy to let you sit and watch with just the purchase of a drink. (Large Singha 55฿. Open daily 9am-2am.) Though some report the atmosphere is inhospitable to *farang*, head to the **karaoke** and **live music bars** that line the east side of Song Kwai Rd. to experience a more authentic Thai night out. For dives that float, check out the tacky and charmingly mobile floating discos that launch from the west side of Song Kwai Rd. and cruise merrily down the river toward the bridge. You'll probably have to talk (or motion) your way onto these, as they're mainly for Thai tour groups, but it might be worth the effort.

⚑ DAYTRIPS FROM KANCHANABURI

Kanchanaburi is an ideal base for exploring the waterfalls, caves, and parks that stretch all the way to Sangkhlaburi and the Thai-Myanmar border. **Routes 3199** and **323** bisect the province at the northern end of Kanchanaburi and make good points of reference. 3199 is a well-paved passage to the Erawan waterfalls. 323 heads west to Sangkhlaburi and the Thai-Myanmar border (Three Pagoda Pass), passing Sai Yok National Park and Hellfire Pass. Independent travelers can take public transportation (bus or train), but this may limit them to visiting only one or two attractions per day. Motorbikes are an efficient way to see the sites; however, novice riders would be better off using other means of transportation. While the roads are generally excellent, the places of interest are separated by long stretches of highway driving. In between Kanchanaburi and Sangkhlaburi, gas must be obtained in Sai Yok and Thong Pha Phum. The scenic and paved 221km to Sangkhlaburi along route 323 (3-4hr. non-stop) has a steep final ascent that is tiring for both bike and body—make sure you're well rested and have the bike serviced before leaving. Pick up the excellent regional map from TAT for any independent exploration (20฿ donation).

A very reasonable alternative for a few extra *baht* is to use a tour agency. Most guesthouses guide or arrange tours for 150-1000฿, with a minimum of 3-5 people. While there are numerous tour companies in Kanchanaburi clamoring for your money, only 13 are certified by TAT. **A.S. Mixed Travel** (☎512 017), at Apple's Guest House, and **B.T. Travel Center**, 44/3 Rong Heep Oil Rd. (☎624 630), 50m down the *soi* opposite VN Guest House, can pack in one-day sightseeing tours to Erawan Waterfall, Hellfire Pass, and the Death Railway (650฿ at Mixed Travel, 580฿ at Travel Center). Adding bamboo rafting and elephant riding cuts one attraction and brings the price to 850฿/750฿. As always, ensure that your agency has a TAT license and that you know exactly what is included in the price; for example, whether the tour includes national park entrance fees and an English-speaking guide, or just transportation. Mixed Travel's package includes only transportation and national park entrance fees; Travel Center's includes an English-speaking guide and transportation. The companies also do 2- to 3-day treks (1500-2000฿).

A third way to see many of the sites is to charter a boat, as several sites are clustered along the Kwai River. Contact **Vimol Guest House** (p. 174) or **Safarine Travel** (☎624 140) for more info. Some of the travel companies arrange boat tours.

ALONG ROUTE 3199

ERAWAN NATIONAL PARK. The foremost tourist destination near Kanchanaburi is **Erawan** ("Three-Headed Elephant") **Waterfall.** The seven-tiered waterfalls may not be the biggest cascades, but they're certainly the most accessible. It's best to arrive early to beat the crowd of locals and *farang.* The first three levels are a 5-10min. walk from the trailhead. The challenging 2.2km trail to the top (1hr.) leads past enticing, clear-water swimming holes, rewarding the intrepid with greater seclusion. But watch out—the trail at the seventh tier is slippery. Sturdy shoes are recommended. Monkeys and other interesting wildlife are constant companions along the trail. Another persistent friend is the mosquito, who bites all the way to the top—bring repellent. The **Visitors Center,** next to where the Kanchanaburi bus stops, has maps, photos, and a slide show. **Accommodations ❶** range from camping (30฿ per person, 100฿ per tent) to dorms (mattresses 10฿; dorms 30฿) and bunga-lows (4 beds and bath 250฿ per person or 800฿ per bungalow). **National Park Head-quarters,** opposite the Visitors Center, handles accommodations and emergencies. *(65km from Kanchanaburi. Take public bus #8170 (1½hr.; every 50min. 8am-5:20pm, last bus back at 4pm; 26฿). Open daily 8am-4:30pm. 200฿; motorbikes 20฿; cars 30฿.)*

Phrathat Cave, also in the national park, 9km from Erawan Waterfall, has impres-sive stalagmites and stalactites which remain undisturbed by *farang* due to their remote location. For 20฿, a guide at the park office will take you on a 1hr. tour of the caves. *(From the market at Erawan Waterfall, turn left and follow the signs to Huay Mae Khamin Waterfall and Phrathat. The journey is over a rough dirt road. It may be possible to charter transport from the market (300-400฿), but it's easier and cheaper if you have your own wheels. Open daily 8am-4pm, but arrive by 3pm to see the caves.)*

SRI NAKHARIN NATIONAL PARK. Sri Nakharin has more animals and fewer tour-ists than Erawan, but getting there demands considerable time, money, and effort. About 105km from Kanchanaburi, **Huay Mae Khamin Waterfall's** nine tiers are best reached from **Erawan.** Only motocross bikes and 4WD vehicles can traverse the 42km dirt road, parallel to the reservoir, that leads from Erawan (about 2hr.). If you insist on taking your Honda Dream into this area, be advised that it may turn into your Nightmare: the first few kilometers of dirt track are a good indication of the roughness of the road. Service facilities are available along the way, so you won't run out of gas. A romantic alternative is to charter a boat (1-2hr., up to 10 people, 1000-1500฿) from **Tha (Pier) Kraden,** 13km northeast of the Sri Nakharin Dam, 5km past Mongatet Village. The pier is accessible over dirt road from Ban Kradan, but boat options may be limited. Continue the rough journey to Sisawat if this is the case. The National Park at Huay Mae Khamin has **accommodation ❶** options ranging from camping (30฿ per person) to bungalows with restaurant. *(Park open daily 8am-4:30pm. 200฿, children 100฿. Motorbikes 20฿, cars 30฿.)*

ALONG ROUTE 323: BAN KAO AREA

PRASAT MUANG SINGH HISTORICAL PARK. Muang Singh (City of the Lion) is an ancient city dating back to the 13th century. Once part of the Angkor Empire, the city features Khmer design and artwork. The ruins sprawl across almost 74 hectares, surrounded by moats, city walls, and the Kwae Nai River. The most notable structure in the park is Monument No. 1 (Prasat Muang Singh), which sits at the center of the city and towers above the rest of the park. An interesting exhibition hall near the park office has Buddhist sculp-tures found at the site. There is also an ancient burial site dating back 2000 years. The park is a worthwhile stop, especially for those interested in the Ankgor Empire but not able to go to Cambodia. *(Located 43km northwest of Kan-chanaburi. If driving, take Rte. 323, then turn off onto Rte. 3455; turn is about 40km* from Kanchanaburi. The park is a 7km drive southwest on 3455 and well posted. Trains (1¼ hr.; leave Kanchanaburi 6:10, 10:50am, 4:35pm; return 6:20am, 1:50, 4:30pm; 10฿) come closer to the park than buses. Get off at Thakilen; from the train station, walk 1km to the main road, then 1km to the right. Bus #8203 stops 7km from the park; transportation for the final leg may be hard to find. Return buses are best caught before 4pm. ☎591 122. Open daily 8:30am-4:30pm. 40฿, motorbikes 20฿, cars 30฿.)

BAN KAO NEOLITHIC MUSEUM. A small museum that houses artifacts and findings from the Thai-Danish excavations in the Ban Kao area in the 1960s. They discovered a Neolithic era settlement, including a burial site with 44 human skeletons and evidence of rituals and social stratification. While the museum is an interesting example of the Southeast Asian Neolithic culture of 3000-4000 years ago, its small exhibits can be easily seen in an hour. (Ban Khao is 6km south of Muang Singh, on 3455. See Muang Singh for directions.)

WAT LUANGTA-MAHABUA FOUNDATION. This foundation runs a tiger conservation project and wild animal rescue park. The grounds of the wat contain Indo-Chinese tigers, a leopard, water buffalo, deer, gibbon monkeys, and all types of farm animals. The best time to visit is in the late afternoon, when the tigers are brought out of their cages for feeding. If you arrive in the morning, the monks will gladly bring the tigers out for photo ops (suggested donation 20-40฿). The tigers are very tame, having been raised by the monks since birth; however, a few large scars on the shoulders of the monks suggest that they sometimes misbehave. (Take 323, and turn off for the Muang Singh Historical Park. After 5km a large billboard marks the next turn-off onto a 1.5km dirt road leading to the wat's impressive green gated entrance.)

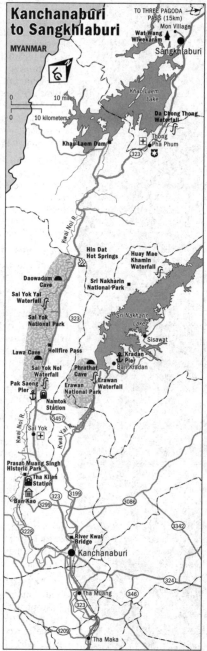

Kanchanaburi to Sangkhlaburi

MYANMAR

TO THREE PAGODA PASS (15km)
Wat Wang Wiwekaram
Mon Village
Sangkhlaburi
Khao Laem Lake
Da Chong Thong Waterfall
Thong Pha Phum
323
Khao Laem Dam
Kwai Noi R.
Hin Dat Hot Springs
Huay Mae Khamin Waterfall
Daowadum Cave
Sri Nakharin National Park
Sai Yok Yai Waterfall
Sai Yok National Park
323
Sri Nakharin Lake
Lawa Cave
Hellfire Pass
Sai Yok Noi Waterfall
Phrathat Cave
Pak Saeng Pier
Erawan National Park
Erawan Waterfall
Sisawat
Kradan Pier
Ban Kradan
Namtok Station
3457
Kwai Noi R.
Sai Yok
Kwai Yai
Prasat Muang Singh Historic Park
Tha Kilen Station
Ban Kao
3199
323
3299
3086
3228
3342
River Kwai Bridge
Kanchanaburi
324
Tha Muang
346
323
3209
Tha Maka

CENTRAL THAILAND

THE LOCAL STORY

WEAVING WONDERS

Wandering through the streets of Sangkhlaburi, you're bound to stumble upon a beautiful store showcasing fine handcrafted hill-tribe weaving. The store "Women for Weaving," run by the indomitable and affectionate Daisy Dwe and her daughter, provides the desperately poor Karen and Mon refugees with a valuable outlet for their skills.

"It didn't work for the first two years, but now we have eight weavers and eight setters," Daisy says with triumph. Her path to Sangkhlaburi was filled with tragedy, perseverance, and hope, and it has inextricably tied her to the plight of her fellow refugees.

"My father was an exiled Karen democratic leader. Frightened for our lives, we followed him to Thailand." Daisy and her husband, a doctor, had established a healthcare service for displaced people. While planning to apply for visas to Australia, Daisy's husband came down with malaria, most likely caught from one of his patients. Though not officially recognized as a citizen by the Thai government, Daisy's husband was so valuable to his community that the Thai government air-lifted him to Kanchanaburi for the best medical attention. Unfortunately, he died nevertheless.

Without a husband, Daisy felt Australia would not give her a visa. "Australia only needs doctors, not women...he was looking after so many poor people and he [Cont'd on next page...]

ALONG ROUTE 323: SAI YOK NATIONAL PARK

Sai Yok National Park is a 500km² park that stretches for almost 70km alongside Route 323 and the Mae Nam Kwai River. The first attraction is the Sai Yok Noi Waterfall, 60km from Kanchanaburi; and the last attraction is the Hin Dat Hot Springs, 130km from Kanchanaburi. All of the sights, with the exception of Lawa, are easily accessible from 323. (*Public bus #8203 to Sangkhlaburi leaves Kanchanaburi every 30 min., 6am-6:30pm and returns at similar intervals for 25-40฿. The National Park is open daily 6am-6pm. 200฿, children 100฿. Motorbikes 20฿, cars 30฿.*)

SAI YOK NOI WATERFALL. The "little" (*noi*) Sai Yok Falls are fairly decent, but they offer only food stalls and concrete paths instead of scenery or hiking trails. Tours stop here for quick photographs, and that's probably about enough. (*60km from Kanchanaburi. Bus #8203 to Sai Yok Noi runs every 30min. 6am-6:30pm, last return 5pm; the 1hr. ride costs 25฿. The waterfall is free.*)

LAWA CAVE. The electrically lit 200m cavern is the region's largest. Unfortunately, the user-friendly features do not extend to geographical accessibility. Hire a longtail boat (45min. one-way, up to 10 people 800฿; landing is 350m from caves) from Pak Saeng Pier, 2km southwest of Sai Yok Noi. Boats can continue up the river to Sai Yok Yai Waterfall and National Park. Alternatively, complete the 30min. trip on motorbike. After crossing the bridge next to Pak Saeng Pier, turn right just past the 3km marker and follow the partially sealed road to the caves. (*Open daily 6am-6pm. National Park entrance fee 200฿, children 100฿.*)

SAI YOK YAI WATERFALL AND NATIONAL PARK

ENTRANCE. Celebrated in poetry and song, the Sai Yok Yai Waterfall dribbles unimpressively, except between July and September, when it gushes unimpressively. One of the world's smallest mammal species, Kitti's Hog-Nosed Bats (p. 13), lives in the park's Bat Cave, 2km from the Visitors Center and accessible by trails. You can pick up maps and leave gear at the Visitors Center (3km off 323). Accommodations include **camping ❶** (30฿) and **rooms ❹** for two to twelve over the river for 500-1000฿. (*Open daily 6am-6pm. 200฿, children 100฿. Motorbikes 20฿, cars 30฿.*)

HIN DAT HOT SPRINGS. The two springs are rather small, but are popular with Thai tourists. One stays a constant 40°C, while the other fluctuates between 35 and 38°C. (*1km off 323. Pools have no English road signs, but the turn-off is 127km from Kanchanaburi and 15km before Thong Pha Phum. Bus #8203 goes from Kancha-*

naburi 2¾hr; every 30min. 6am-6:30pm, last return bus 4pm; 54฿. Hot springs 5฿, private room 20฿.)

ALONG ROUTE 323: HELLFIRE PASS

In their quest to complete the Thai-Myanmar railway, the Japanese Imperial Army would not let a mere mountain stand in their way. Thousands of oppressed laborers worked for months, manually chipping away rock under grueling conditions, to create the **Hellfire Pass**, so named for the ghostly campfire shadows that would dance on the mountain walls at night. Today, the pass is a trail leading down the former railway on a stunning 3km circuit around the area. The adjoining **Hellfire Pass Memorial Museum** showcases pictures, articles, and personal stories of the POWs whose lives were sacrificed in the construction of the pass. When not busy shepherding tourist groups, the knowledgeable Aussie curators are eager to answer questions. The Konyu cutting (aka Hellfire Pass) is a 15min. walk from the museum. The 3km trail around the entire railway clearing is very worthwhile if you have the time. (Between Sai Yok Noi and Sai Yok Yai. Take bus #8203 from Kanchanaburi and tell the attendant where you want to get off (1½hr.; every 30min. 6am-6:30pm, last return bus at about 4:45pm; 38฿). Open daily 9am-4pm. Suggested donation 30-100฿.)

SANGKHLABURI ☎034

Unlike its neighbor Kanchanaburi, Sangkhlaburi relies mostly on its natural beauty to attract tourists. The few man-made sights in town pale in comparison to the fresh air, rugged mountains, and dense jungle that envelop it. Travelers are entranced by the relaxing views of Khao Laem Lake, the numerous jungle-trekking adventures, and the opportunity to mingle with the Karen and Mon migrants who now call this town home. In 1989 the border was closed due to fighting between Shan and Wa separatist troops. With the continued recent stability, travelers are beginning to trickle into the region. While the tiny city center offers little to visitors, its setting makes it a desirable destination.

TRANSPORTATION. Public transportation from Sangkhlaburi only runs to Kanchanaburi (bus #8203: 5hr; 6:45, 8:15, 10:15am, 1:15pm; 84฿; with A/C: 4hr.; 8:45, 10:45am, 2:30pm; 150฿; A/C van: 3hr.; 6:30, 7:30, 9:30, 11:30am, 3:30pm; 118฿) and to the Three Pagoda **Pass** by songthaew (30min., every 40min. 6am-6pm, 30-35฿). A/C buses and minibuses from Kanchanaburi drop passengers at the **market** in the middle of town. Regular buses and songthaew arrive

left me with four children." Daisy showed a picture of her family. "If I'm not a strong woman, my children are in trouble. Never give up. Women must be the same as men." She sent her children back to Burma to live with her sister so they could get an education while she set up a guesthouse at the Three Pagoda Pass. "Oh what fun we had!" she says. "I had a guide who dove in the pond, speared fish, and cooked it for my guests."

But when war broke out at Three Pagoda Pass in 1989 between Karen and Mon groups, it was impossible to keep the business. "I've seen so many killed," she says, referring to women and children. "I'm trying to help all minorities since that time. It's a big job for one person."

After moving to Sangkhlaburi and being reunited with her children, Daisy used her English skills to become an interpreter and worked with aid workers at the refugee camps. She then set up a weaving factory to employ and benefit Burmese refugees. "So many people came to me. I am not a rich woman, but I [have saved] a little money...now I'm working for my people—I don't do this for myself...I'm looking after people through my weaving."

Open every day, **Women for Weaving** (☎595 413) is a few blocks from the Burmese Inn, on the same road. Daisy or her daughter will be delighted to answer your questions. Souvenirs start at 30฿, pencil cases 50฿, strap shoulder bags 150฿.

at the end of the street at the **bus station,** where **motorcycle taxis** congregate, ready to take visitors to guesthouses (10-20฿) or Wat Wang Wiwekaram (50฿). The **city center** is a simple grid, bordered at each end by the two turn-offs from the highway to Kanchanaburi. Arriving from Kanchanaburi, take the first turn-off to get to the **police station** and **hospital,** and the second to go to the bus station, **post office,** and **guesthouses.** To get to the **wooden bridge** from the bus station, walk past the post office and turn right at the first paved intersection.

🔃 PRACTICAL INFORMATION. Other services include: **Siam Commercial Bank,** opposite the marketplace, with **currency exchange** and an **ATM** (☎595 263; open M-F 8:30am-3:30pm); the **immigration office** which deals with visa extensions (☎595 107; open daily 6am-5pm); the **police** station (☎595 300; open **24hr.**), past the immigration office; the **hospital** (☎595 058; open **24hr.**), across from the police station; and **Internet** access, available opposite and left of the market on the road, directly across from the motorcycle taxis. (30฿ per hr. Open daily 4-10pm). The **post office,** 25m right of the regular bus stop, has an **international telephone booth** and **CATNET.** (☎595 115. Open M-F 8:30am-4:30pm, Sa 9am-noon.) **Postal Code: 71240.**

🛏🍴 ACCOMMODATIONS AND FOOD. The **Burmese Inn ❶,** 52/3 Tambon Nong Loo, is 1km to the right of the bus station, if facing the Siam Bank. The open-air veranda offers stunning views of the bridge. Owner and amateur astronomer Armin is a veritable walking tourist office and can arrange two- and three-day jungle treks (1300-1750฿). His wife Meo runs a two-day, seven-dish cooking course for 500฿. (☎/fax 595 146; www.sangkhlaburi.com. Motorbike rental 200฿ per day. Singles with fan and mosquito net 80฿, with bath 120฿; doubles with fan, net, and bath 180฿; bungalows with bath 250฿; family bungalows with satellite TV 500฿.) **P. Guest House ❸,** 81/2 Tumbon Nong Loo, 300m beyond the turn-off to the Burmese Inn, is a fusion of a wooden ranch with a Swiss chalet. The large rooms are immaculate, and the shared baths boast some of the cleanest squat toilets in Thailand. There is a lush garden walk leading down to the lake. (☎595 061; www.pguest-house.com. Canoes 25฿ per hr. Motorbikes 200฿ per day. Bicycles 100฿ per day. Singles 150฿; doubles 200฿. Elephant riding, rafting, and 1-night accommodation 850฿.) Both guesthouses have maps of Sangkhlaburi and the surrounding area.

Dining is primarily limited to guesthouses. The **restaurant** at **P. Guest House ❷** can cater to large groups and has exquisite food, such as *panaeng* curry (red curry with a hint of coconut milk and lime leaves; 55฿). It also has a foosball table and a lovely view of the lake. **Burmese Inn ❷** also offers food. Around the market, several **open-air restaurants ❶** line up tasty curries in pots during the day (20฿ per plate).

◙ SIGHTS. Most attractions in Sangkhlaburi are far away from the town center. Arrange **trekking trips** through P. Guest House or the Burmese Inn. You can also arrange trips in Kanchanaburi, where more options exist. Inquire at Kanchanaburi TAT. Those looking to take it easy might consider a **boat trip** on beautiful **Lake Khao Laem,** which features a partially submerged *wat* from pre-dam Sangkhlaburi.

The **longest wooden bridge in Thailand,** the 400m bridge of the Reverend Auttamo, crosses the massive Lake Khao Laem and connects the city of Sangkhlaburi to the **Mon Village.** Although they don't possess Thai citizenship, the Mon people are not quite refugees, as they live under the protection of the elderly Luang Phaw Utama, who watches over households in the area. Luckily, Utama has plenty of money with which to help the Mon, thanks to the many Chinese and Thai who flock to him bearing offerings in tribute to his supposed healing powers. To get to his temple, walk uphill from the bridge to the stop sign. Turn left, follow the winding road, and take a left at the next stop sign. The red-and-gold **Wat Wang Wiwekaram** sits at the end of the road, 4km from Sangkhlaburi opposite the **handicrafts market**

(30min. walk from wooden bridge; 20₿ donation). The wooden bridge is open only to pedestrian traffic. If traveling by motorbike, head to the highway, turn left, and follow the road over the commuter bridge. At the police box turn left (right heads to Huay Malai village) and take another left at the stop sign 25km down.

⚡ DAYTRIPS FROM SANGKHLABURI. The border crossing to **Phayathonzu** in Myanmar is marked by three stunted pagodas—hence the name **Three Pagoda Pass.** The small and sedate **market** displays numerous teak products and boasts some of the best prices for jade in Thailand. During World War II, the Death Railway crossed into Myanmar at this point, but after the war it proved not to be viable and has since been dismantled. A third Allied war cemetery (two others in Kanchanaburi; p. 176) lies in **Phayathonzu** as testament to the railroad's existence. More recently, Shan and Wa troops fought for power over the black market trade, and the Burmese government, realizing the strategic importance of the pass, regained control of the region afterwards. Daytrips into Phayathonzu are possible, but travelers are not permitted to go farther. For the past decade the area has seen relative stability, but check for reports of border skirmishes. (Open daily 6am-6pm.)

Due to poaching, the elephants, tigers, tapirs, bears, gibbons, and peacocks that inhabit **Thung Yai Sanctuary Park,** Thailand's largest conservation area, have retreated deep into the forest. Many visitors make the trip to see Karen villages. Most areas are accessible only by 4WD vehicles, even during the dry season. **Takian Thong Waterfall** in Thung Yai Sanctuary Park is an anomaly, with fully paved access. The waterfalls, more accurately described as a river cascade, are a 20min. walk from the park office through dense jungle. Sign in at the park office before completing the trip. Ask at the Burmese Inn or the P. Guest House (p. 182) about accessibility, road conditions, and possible jeep rental to other parts of the sanctuary. (Dry season 1000₿, more in the wet season. Park open daily 8am-6pm.)

Songthaew travel the 22km from Sangkhlaburi to Three Pagoda Pass from 6am to 6pm (30min., 30-35₿). The clearly marked turn-off to Thung Yai Sanctuary Park and Takian Thong Waterfall is 18km from Sangkhlaburi along the road to Three Pagoda Pass. In general, it is possible to get to the pass without personal transportation, but the same is not true of Thung Yai Sanctuary Park. The turn-off to Three Pagoda Pass from the highway is 3km from Sangkhlaburi toward Kanchanaburi.

PHETCHABURI ☎ 032

Phetchaburi, commonly known as Phetburi, is a remarkable contrast to the endless bustle of Bangkok, a short bus ride to the north. With no popular beaches, Phetchaburi remains largely undiscovered, but might make for a worthwhile stop on the way south. Visitors enjoy a small-town atmosphere along with several outstanding cultural sights, including historic *wats* and a former royal palace that overlooks the city from Khao Wang Hill. Phetchaburi, halfway between Bangkok and the getaway of Hua Hin, offers a cultural welcome to the southern peninsula.

⌐ TRANSPORTATION

Trains: Phetchaburi Railway Station (☎ 425 211) is on the northern edge of town, a 15min. walk from the center. Head left from the station and, after 1km, take the 2nd right onto Damnernkasem Rd. To: **Bangkok** (4hr., 11 per day 7:15am-10:30pm, 74₿); **Hua Hin** (1hr., 13-54₿ depending on train); and other destinations in the south. Buses are more convenient.

Buses: There are three bus stations in town. Most **A/C buses** from **Bangkok** (3hr., every 30min. 4am-8:30pm, 90₿) arrive at the intersection of Damnernkasem Rd. and Rot Fai,

BORDER CROSSING: THREE PAGODA PASS. About 24km from Sangkhlaburi, the Three Pagoda Pass is an anticlimax for those with visions of border intrigue. The border crossing from Three Pagoda Pass to Phayathonzu, Myanmar is sporadically open to foreigners, with several caveats. Prior authorization and a permit from the immigration office in Sangkhlaburi are required. Two passport-sized photos, photocopies of the front page of your passport and Thai visa, and US$10 are required for a permit. Return to immigration by 5pm to collect your passport. The US$10 is paid at the Myanmar border, and this allows you to enter 2km into the country. Remember, as this is not an official border crossing, you do not get your passport stamped and thus cannot get your Thai visa extended for another 30 days. Myanmar time is 30min. behind Thailand's. Immigration office open daily 8:30am-6pm.

Recent tensions between Thailand and Myanmar have resulted in frequent closings of the border. Be sure to check with the Thai embassy for the most current information. The area is also occasionally considered dangerous (see **Thai-Burmese Relations,** p. 23)—yet another reason to get the latest update from the Thai embassy or from your home nation's embassy; both keep close tabs on the border situation. *Songthaew* leaving from Sangkhlaburi's bus station make the trip (30min., every 40min. 6am-6pm, 30-35฿). If you're making the trip for a rich, historical experience, you'll be disappointed. The diminutive Three Pagoda communicates little of the place's turbulent past. According to one story, as the Burma Wars came to an end in the mid-1700s, the King of Thailand laid down three stones (representing Siam, Burma, and peaceful unity) to mark the border between the two countries. Villagers constructed three pagodas *(Chedi Sam Ong)* over the stones, and monks have used the middle shrine to pray for peace. To make the trip worthwhile, consider backtracking to the **Sawan Bundarn Cave,** located on the way to the Three Pagoda Pass. From Three Pagoda, walk 2km back toward Sangkhlaburi and turn left. Follow the dirt road for 700m and turn right onto a smaller track for 500m. A monk will give you a flashlight tour of the cave—for a donation, of course. (See **Myanmar, To Go or Not To Go?,** p. 300.)

the road that leads to the train station. Some private lines may arrive at one of the other 2 stations. The **regular bus station,** on Phetkasem Hwy., about 300m before the entrance to the Khao Wang cable car, has non-A/C buses to **Bangkok** (3hr., every 20min. 5am-5pm, 70฿) and A/C buses to **Hua Hin** (1hr., frequent, 30-50฿). Finally, orange (non-A/C) buses to **Cha Am** (1hr., 20฿) and **Hua Hin** (1½hr., 30฿) depart frequently from Matayawong Rd., around the corner from Wat Kamphaeng Laeng.

Local Transportation: The whole city can be traversed on foot, but for longer distances, **samlor** and **songthaew** are also options. Hard bargaining will be rewarded: no trip inside town should cost more than 20฿; trips outside of town run about 30฿. Alternatively, Rabieng Guest House (p. 186) rents out serviceable **bicycles** for 120฿ per day.

◀★▶ ORIENTATION AND PRACTICAL INFORMATION

Lying 160km south of Bangkok, Phetchaburi is best navigated with reference to the murky brown waters of the ever-creeping **Phetchaburi River. Damnernkasem Road** runs parallel to the river. Downstream and to the north, the road veers off to the left and away from the river, leading to the hospital and train station. Upstream, it intersects with **Ratchavidhi Road,** heading westward (away from the river) to Khao Wang Hill, and **Phongsuriya Road,** leading eastward to several hotels,

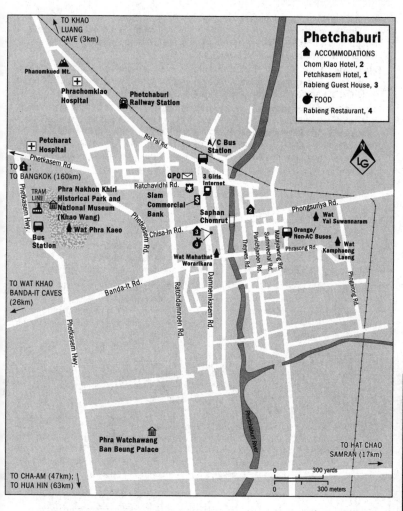

Phetchaburi

🏠 ACCOMMODATIONS
Chom Klao Hotel, **2**
Petchkasem Hotel, **1**
Rabieng Guest House, **3**

🍎 FOOD
Rabieng Restaurant, **4**

CENTRAL THAILAND

wats, and the **Saphan Chomrut** (Chomrut Bridge) across the Phetchaburi River. Another main road is **Panichjaroen Road,** the first right after the bridge, with an all-purpose market.

Tourist Office: There is a small, generally unstaffed tourist booth at the corner of Ratchavidhi and Phetkasem Rd.

Currency Exchange: Siam Commercial Bank, 2 Damnernkasem Rd. (☎ 425 303). Halfway between the bridge and the Ratchavidhi Rd. intersection. **24hr. ATM.** Open M-F 8:30am-3:30pm.

Police: Phetchaburi Police Station (☎ 425 500), on Ratchavidhi Rd. opposite the GPO. Very little English spoken.

Medical Services: Phrachomklao Hospital (☎ 401 125), 50m from the train station on the left. Some English spoken. No credit cards. Open **24hr.** Farther out is the **Petcharat Hospital** (☎ 417 029), on Phetkasem Hwy. north of town, close to the Khao Wong cable car stop. No credit cards. **24hr. emergency** care.

Telephones: 2nd fl. of GPO. **International phone** station and fax. Open M-F 8:30am-6pm, Sa-Su 9am-5pm. International pay phones are also found in front of **7-Eleven,** including the one on Phongsuriya Rd. between Surinvechai and Matayawong Rd.

Internet Access: Playnet, on Phongsuriya Rd. between Surinvechai and Matayawong Rd., offers new computers and the lowest rates in town. 20฿ per hr. Open daily 8am-midnight. **3 Girls Internet,** on Damnernkasem Rd. near Ratchavidhi Rd., offers services more convenient to the town's municipal center. 30฿ per hr. Open daily 9:30am-9pm.

Post Office: GPO (☎ 425 146), at the intersection of Ratchavidhi and Damnernkasem Rd. *Poste Restante.* Open M-F 8:30am-4:30pm, Sa-Su 9am-noon.

Postal Code: 76000.

ACCOMMODATIONS

When it comes to budget accommodations in Phetchaburi, you get what you pay for—meaning not very much. Rooms are cheap, small, and offer a bare minimum of amenities. Several accommodations cluster around **Chomrut Bridge,** a few minutes from the A/C bus station or a 15-20min. walk from the railway station.

Rabieng Guest House (☎ 425 707), at the foot of the Chomrut Bridge on the west bank, diagonally across from the Chom Klao Hotel. Tiny green rooms and street racket (bring earplugs) are concessions for the laid-back atmosphere. You'll probably spend most of your time in the excellent adjoining backpacker restaurant (see below). Friendly staff. Clean shared baths. Singles 120฿; doubles 240฿. ❷

Petchkasem Hotel, 86/1 Phetkasem Hwy. (☎ 425 581), behind Khao Wang Hill at the foot of the highway interchange, a 20min. walk from the town center. *Samlor* should cost 20฿. The best option for those interested primarily in Khao Wang and the Banda-It caves. Large, spotless rooms offer color TV and Western toilets. Good views from the upper floors. Rooms in the rear avoid highway noise. Singles 250฿, with A/C 300฿; doubles 350฿/400฿. ❸

Chom Klao Hotel (☎ 425 398), on Theywes Rd., across the street and bridge from Rabieng Guest House. It's the 4-story cream-colored building with blue trim overlooking the river on the left as you cross the bridge; look for its satellite dishes. The modest-sized, clean rooms show signs of age. Some with balcony, private bath, and Western toilet. Shared baths have squat toilets. Singles 30฿, with bath 70฿; doubles 260฿. ❶

FOOD

By far the best place to eat is the **Rabieng Restaurant** ❷, on the premises of the Rabieng Guest House. After 11pm, the bustling Rabieng is about the only source of non-canine activity in town. The absurdly extensive, reasonably priced menu (30-70฿) offers everything under the Thai sun. From serpent heads to spicy banana blossom salads to fish intestines, the opportunities for palate expansion are limitless. Fun mixes of 50s and 60s rock and a clear view of the river complete the experience. (American-style breakfast 70฿. Open daily 8:30am-1am.) There are several **food vendors** ❶ on Panichjaroen Rd., the first right after crossing the bridge, that serve noodles and some seafood specialities. One of Phetchaburi's best-known desserts is a delicious egg custard (35฿). Follow your nose to the nearest vendor. There is also a number of small family-style restaurants behind Khao Wang on Phetkasem Rd., near the Petchkasem Hotel. (12-15฿ per dish.)

👁 SIGHTS

With the exception of the Banda-It and Khao Luang caves, all sights are within walking distance of the town center.

PHRA NAKHON KHIRI HISTORICAL PARK AND NATIONAL MUSEUM (KHAO WANG). In the 1850s, King Rama IV, tired of the heat and exhaustion of Central Thailand, looked south to build a new royal retreat. His search ended on the hilltops overlooking Phetchaburi, where in 1858 he built **Phra Nakhon Khiri** (or Khao Wang). A unique mixture of Chinese and Western architecture, it spreads across the hill's three peaks. The westernmost peak houses the **royal residence**, a collection of halls and pavilions, where Rama IV and his son relaxed and entertained guests. The palace's original furnishings are still on display. **Phra That Chom Phet,** a 49m-tall *chedi*, sits on the middle peak. On the eastern peak is **Wat Phra Kaew,** which Rama IV ordered to be constructed in the same style as the Temple of the Emerald Buddha in Bangkok's Grand Palace. The park is accessible by a cable car that runs up to the royal residence. Your other option is the steep but short footpath (whose trailhead is guarded by monkeys) from the end of Ratchavidhi Rd. In early February, the town celebrates the **Phra Nakhon Khiri Fair** (see **Festivals,** p. 31), which features local art shows, cultural performances, and cart races. *(To reach the cable car, located on the opposite side of the hill town, take a samlor for 20฿ from the town center. Cable car runs 8:30am-5:15pm; one-way 30฿, children 10฿. ☎ 401 006. Museum open daily 9am-4pm. 40฿. Park open M-F 8:15am-5pm, Sa-Su 8:15am-5:15pm.)*

WAT YAI SUWANNARAM. This 17th-century religious compound features outstanding examples of art and architecture from the Ayutthaya period. Try asking one of the monks to open the two wooden buildings that contain well-preserved 18th-century murals. *(On Phongsuriya Rd., about a 10min. walk east from Chomrut Bridge, away from Khai Wang.)*

WAT KAMPHAENG LAENG. These five impressive laterite-block structures hold Buddha images that were originally part of a 12th-century Khmer Hindu shrine. Each of the five *prangs* is thought to be dedicated to one of the five major Hindu deities. In the Ayutthaya period, the temple was reconsecrated to Buddhism, and images of Buddha replaced the Hindu sculptures within five *prangs*. Currently, the temple is the residence of **Phra Khruu Yanwitmon,** Phetchaburi's most revered monk. *(Follow Phongsuriya Rd. past Wat Yai Suwannaram and turn right on Phogarong Rd., about 500m down. The wat will be on the right after about 500m. If the front gate is locked, turn right on the road just after the wat and enter at the gate on the right.)*

WAT MAHATHAT WORARIHARA. With its giant white *prang* dominating the Phetchaburi skyline, Wat Mahathat Worarihara is understandably one of the most popular religious sites in the area. The dozens of Buddha images surrounding the main *prang* and the stuccos on the *prang* pedestals draw crowds. The *bot* contains several gorgeous carvings. Ask a monk to access the cloisters (through a small door on the right of the *bot*) to see its endless rows of peaceful Buddhas. *(On Damnernkasem Rd., about a 10min. walk south of its intersection with the bridge.)*

WAT KHAO BANDA-IT. A set of steps between two elephant statues leads to several caves, which, in terms of sheer Buddha quantity, are impressive. A flashlight will help illuminate the "Thousand Buddhas" tucked into the crevices. *(From town, take Banda-It Rd. west, away from the river, past Khao Wang. The entrance is on the right side of the road at the group of 3 ornate shelters. Go through the right archway and up the short road. Motorcycle taxis from town run 30-40฿, samlor 50-60฿. Helpful English guides available, 40-80฿ tip suggested. Open daily 9am-4pm.)*

CENTRAL THAILAND

OVERCOMING THE VEGGIE WOES

Thailand is known the world over for its delicious fresh cuisine. For a vegetarian, however, many of the most delicious dishes can seem inaccessible. This is especially true in the coastal areas because of these regions' natural dependency on seafood as a staple.

On the beach in Cha Am, carefully avoiding the ever-present seafood, I order the most innocuous thing I can find on the menu—pineapple fried rice. Can't go wrong, right? Rice. Pineapple. No room for miscommunication. Right? Wrong. My rice contains very little pineapple. But it does have a whole lot of weird rubbery chicken (I think?) and an unidentified round pinkish meat that at first glance appeared to be overboiled carrots. Gross.

After eating around the various meats and still finding myself hungry, I move on to a restaurant a few doors down, one that declares itself to be "pure veg happy friendly." Playing it super-safe, I decide to order a green mango and papaya salad. Lettuce covers my plate, with green mango and bright orange papaya scattered throughout, making for a delightful and colorful assortment. I lift a large piece of lettuce with my fork, and am bringing it up to my mouth when I notice that it has revealed a metallic gleam of something underneath all the greens. With my fork, I shuffle

[Cont'd on next page...]

KHAO LUANG CAVE. This underground religious cave, about 4km north of town, is a bizarre and mildly interesting mix of Buddhist imagery, ill-tempered monkeys, and touristy gimmicks. The cave is best seen between 11am and 2pm, when sunlight illuminates the golden Buddhas and the red-tiled floor. For the adventurous, local entrepreneurs offer flashlight tours of the darker recesses, but the most detailed statues are out in front. *(Motorcycle taxis charge 40-50฿ from the town center, 100-150฿ round-trip. Buses can also stop here on the way to or from Bangkok.)*

🔳 DAYTRIPS FROM PHETCHABURI

KAENG KRACHAN NATIONAL PARK.
To get to the park, take a dark blue songthaew to Tha Yong, 20฿. There, switch to a Koeng Krachan songthaew to park headquarters, 20฿.

Thailand's largest national park envelops 3000km² of rain forest in the western half of Phetchaburi Province. Since the park's opening in 1981, four white elephants, long considered symbols of royal prestige and good fortune, have been captured here and presented to the king. The **Phetchaburi** and **Phanburi Rivers** entice rafters, and rangers lead three-day hikes in the high season for four people (200฿ per day, with food 352฿). Inquire at the visitor station near the park entrance. To reach the park's center and the waterfalls, get to the park by 9:30am, as the 68km road becomes one-way in the wrong direction at 10am. Car rental is 1000฿, and though *Let's Go* doesn't recommend it, hitchhiking is the preferred method of transportation among many park visitors. The alternative, spending the night at **Kaeng Krachan Lake** near park headquarters, gets old quickly. Four-person **bungalows ❶** are 100฿; **tents ❶** can be pitched for 10-30฿.

CHAO SAMRAN BEACH.
Minibuses leave from the station on Matayawong Rd., and songthaew run to the beach until 5pm, 10฿.

A good place for a picnic, the beach is virtually deserted during the week, although a larger number of Bangkok tourists make it down on weekends. Chao Samran used to be a favorite spot of the royal family. Plan to bring your own provisions.

CHA AM   ☎ 032

During the week, Cha Am looks like someone built an elaborate beach town but forgot to tell anybody. The beach is deserted, save the obligatory stray dogs and a few stray tourists, and hotels are empty. Come late Friday, however, upper-middle-class Thais begin to pour in, invading the hotels and resorts and driving roaring motorboats within inches of seemingly oblivious fellow Thai tourists resting on the white sand. For peace, relaxation, and a beautiful beach all to yourself, arrive sometime between Monday and Thursday and get out before the weekend rush.

⊑ TRANSPORTATION. The **Cha Am Railway Station** at the end of Narathip Rd. has **trains** to Bangkok (3½hr., 6 per day, 49฿) and Chumphon (4½hr., 6 per day, 53฿). The best place to catch a **bus** out of town is on Phetkasem Hwy. at Narathip Rd. Regular and A/C buses stop here on the way to Hua Hin (30min., every 20min., 20-30฿) and Bangkok (3½hr., every 20min., 95-113฿). A/C buses for Hua Hin and Bangkok also leave from the station at the intersection of Chaolai and Ratchaplhi Rd., one block south of Narathip Rd. Note that only buses whose origin or terminus is Cha Am stop here, so the frequency of service is relatively low. For Phetchaburi, take a Bangkok-bound bus (40min., 20-30฿).

Motorcycle taxis will take you from the town center to the beach or anywhere else in town for 20฿. **Shared taxis**, which regularly travel up and down Narathip Rd., cost 5฿. Cook Travel and Tours, on the northern part of Ruamjit Rd. just south of Jolly & Jumper, arranges **bicycle rentals** for 30฿ per hr. or 150฿ per day.

▄ PRACTICAL INFORMATION. Ruamjit Road is home to most of the hotels and restaurants in town. The road runs north-south adjacent to the beach. When going north, the beach is to the right. **Chaolai Road** runs parallel to Ruamjit Rd. and has some food and lodging offerings, particularly in the area south of **Narathip Road,** which meets Ruamjit Rd. on the southern end of Cha Am Beach and leads to the railway station, town center, and **Phetkasem Highway.** More information on the city, accommodations, and nearby sights is available at www.chaam-beach.com.

The regional **TAT** office (☎471 005), inconveniently located on Phetkasem Hwy. about 500m south of Narathip Rd., is open daily 8:30am-4:30pm. At the **24hr. tourist information booth,** inside the tourist police station on the beach side of Ruamjit Rd. at Narathip Rd., friendly officers speak more English than the people at TAT. **Siam Commercial Bank,** on Ruamjit Rd. just north of Narathip Rd., exchanges currency and has a **24hr. ATM.** (Open M-F 8:30am-3:30pm.) Other services include: **local tourist police,** in the small booth on Ruamjit Rd. at the intersection with Narathip Rd., who speak some English and are open **24hr.; Cha Am Hospital** (☎471 007), on Klongtien

aside all the other lettuce, and what do I see? A titanic silver fish occupies the central part of my plate. This beast, still whole, eyes and mouth wide open, with a spine sticking out the front of its head about the size of a small cell phone tower, seems about as surprised to see me as I am to see it. I eat the papaya and mango, and use the remaining lettuce to cover up the big fella. This is as close as he'll get to a proper burial. R.I.P., Fish. We almost ate ye.

These horror stories are not meant to imply, however, that vegetarians have to subsist on bread and jam from the nearest 7-Eleven. There are vegetarian options to be had, if one looks in the right places. The best place to start is at the local day and night markets, found in almost every city. There, a variety of fresh local fruits, vegetables, and nuts are available for your ready (and inexpensive) consumption. Food stalls at these markets are also good bets because the food is usually cooked right in front of you, so you can observe the ingredients used and even direct your meal's preparation. (For more information on special diets, see **Dietary Concerns**, p. 78.)

Perhaps the most important thing is to keep in mind that you can always try asking for any dish, appending your order with the phrase *phom* (for men) or *dii-chan* (for women) plus *kin jeh* (adding *ka* or *krap*)—meaning, all together, "I eat vegetarian food only."
—*Nitin Shah*

Rd. northwest of the beach, with very little English but **24hr. emergency** service; **International phones** at the **post office** and in front of each of the three **7-Elevens** on Ruamjit Rd.; and **Internet access,** at **Peggy's Pub** in the Long Beach Cha Am Hotel complex on the far northern end of Ruamjit Rd., or **Cook Travel and Tours**, just south of Jolly & Jumper (1฿ per min., 30฿ min.). The **post office,** on Ruamjit Rd., is equidistant from the Cha Am Villa Hotel and the Jolly & Jumper. (Open M-F 8:30am-4:30pm, Sa 9am-noon.) **Postal Code:** 76120.

⚑ ACCOMMODATIONS. With just a couple exceptions, you can divide the accommodations in Cha Am into two groups: middle-class hotels and exorbitant luxury resorts. While the resorts are extremely expensive and unnervingly antiseptic, the middle-class hotels are clean, comfortable, and reasonably priced, if a bit bland. Through bargaining, mid-week discounts of up to 50% can be obtained. Most rooms in town have two beds, and rates are the same for one or two guests. **🎖 Jolly & Jumper ❸,** 274/3 Ruamjit Rd. in the middle of town, just north of the post office and just south of Gems Hotel, is a massive white beast of a building that towers over the beach. Expat-owned and -operated, Jolly & Jumper is an exception to the aforementioned rule and is *the* backpacker dive in Cha Am. With the cheapest rooms, you lose some of the amenities of the middle-class hotels, but enjoy good vibes and save some *baht.* (☎433 887. Free 🚲bicycle use for guests. Basic rooms with fan and shared bathrooms 150฿, with amenities up to 450฿.) The well-established **Cha Am Villa Hotel ❷,** 241/1 Ruamjit Rd., about four blocks north of Narathip Rd. and a block south of the post office, offers large, clean, cable-TV-equipped rooms and a swimming pool free for guests. (☎471 241; www.chaam-villa.com. Rooms 250฿, with A/C 300-500฿.) Newer and larger rooms are available two doors down at the affiliated **Cha Am Villa Beach Hotel ❸.** (☎471 595. Rooms with A/C 400฿; prices increase up to 700฿ as you add amenities such as cable TV, refrigerators, and hot water.)

Prathanchok House ❷, on Rumajit Rd. three blocks north of Narathip Rd., offers the cheapest A/C rooms in town, plus flowers in the rooms, in the halls, and everywhere else you can think of. Clean, well-run, and with a friendly, poodle-loving owner. (☎471 215. Rooms 200฿, with A/C or TV 250฿, with both 300฿.) At **Kaenchan Beach Hotel ❺,** just north of center on Ruamjit Rd., between the two tallest buildings on the Cha Am skyline—the Gems Hotel to the south and the Mark-Land Hotel to the north—you pay more, but you get more. It has the feel of a luxury hotel at less than half the price of the behemoths that surround it. (☎471 314. Great bar downstairs. Breakfast included. Rooms with A/C, cable TV, and hot water 800-1500฿.) **Nirundorn Resort ❷,** 247/7 Ruamjit Rd., just south of Narathip Rd., is one of the newer and nicer middle-class lodges on the beach. Large, well-equipped, well-maintained rooms have standard competitive pricing. (☎471 038. With fan and cable 250฿, with A/C and cable 350฿, add a fridge 400฿.)

◖ FOOD. It should come as little surprise that seafood is the catch of the day in beachside Cha Am. Most tourist-oriented restaurants have menus in English featuring just about anything you can catch with a net. A few also offer good Western-style food. **🍴Poom ❸,** 274/1 Ruamjit Rd., in front of Gems and just north of Jolly & Jumper, offers a fantastic, enormous seafood menu and very friendly service. Those with a little extra cash can consider the "charcoaled shrimp" or the white prawn, each 900฿. (Dishes 40-200฿. Open daily 9am-10pm.) **Da Vinci's ❸,** 274/5 Ruamjit Rd., just north of Jolly & Jumper, serves up authentic-tasting Western cuisine in a classy, low-key, wood-paneled setting. The spaghetti bolognese, five-cheese pizza, and steak (80-400฿) are top menu choices. Some, however, head straight for the elegant bar, featuring Mai Tais, Singapore Slings, and the best Long Island Iced Tea this side of the Pacific. (Cocktails 110-240฿. Open daily 10am-midnight.) **Max ❸,** 222/57 Ruamjit Rd., beneath the Mark-Land Hotel and a block north of Da Vinci's, offers a good mix of Thai and Western dishes, sure to satisfy those homesick for burgers, pizza, and "select Scandinavian meat dishes." (Most offerings 80-130฿. Well-stocked bar in rear. Open daily 10am-midnight.) **Jolly & Jumper's restaurant ❸,** in the hotel of the same name, is, not surprisingly the biggest hangout for Westerners in town. It has a lively atmosphere and enormous Thai and Western menus, as well as a great dessert and drink selection. (Entrees 60-150฿. Open daily 8am-1am.)

◢ BEACHES. The mile-long stretch of sand that makes up **Hat Cha Am** (Cha Am Beach) is clean, white, and wide. During the week, when the town is deserted, you need only compete with dogs for control of the beach. Mondays through Thursdays are unquestionably the best days for those seeking a peaceful vacation.

There are a number of ways to enjoy the surf and sand. Beach chairs (rented for 5฿ per hr.) line the strand—just find one and sit, and its owner will come around to you. The same is true for motorboats, which are generally rented for 100฿ per 30min., although price varies by demand. Multi-person flotation devices and one-, two-, and three-person bicycles are also available on the beach.

▷ DAYTRIP FROM CHA AM: PHRA RATCHANIWET MARUKKHATHAI-YAWAN. This beachside palace, located about 10km south of Cha Am, marks the historical birth site of both Hua Hin and Cha Am. After being constructed in the 1920s for King Rama VI, it helped to popularize the area as a major vacation destination. What remains is an ornate wooden palace that sits in relative solitude beside the ocean. To get there, take a Hua Hin-bound bus and ask to be dropped off at the palace. You will be let off at a fairly easy 2km walk from the palace. The surrounding area is now the regional Border Patrol headquarters; you may need to obtain permission (which is easily granted) to proceed to the palace.

HUA HIN ☎032

Long before Phuket and Pattaya were catapulted into jet-set stardom, Hua Hin (Head Rock) catered to the Thai upper crust. Following the example of King Rama VI, wealthy Thai families vacationed on this long stretch of clean sand, mingling with local fishermen and squid vendors. Today, affluent Europeans have joined the Thais, and towering resorts share the waterfront with the fishermen. Still, there's something about this grand dame of beach resorts that remains unchanged: the night market still bustles with activity, the seafood still tantalizes the palate, and the beach remains as beautiful and spotless as ever. Hua Hin may look different, but new faces and facades only complement its aging grace.

◰ TRANSPORTATION

Flights: Hua Hin Airport (☎522 305), on the north side of the city, is served by **Bangkok Airways.** 4 flights per week (Su-M, W, F) to **Bangkok** (40min., 7:20pm, 950฿) and **Ko Samui** (1hr., 9am, 2080฿).

Trains: Railway Station (☎511 073), at the end of Damnernkasem Rd. A 10min. walk from town center. To: **Bangkok** (4hr., 16 per day, 54฿); **Chumphon** (4hr., 16 per day, 48฿); **Phetchaburi** (1hr., 12 per day, 34฿); **Surat Thani** (7hr., 12 per day, 73฿).

Buses: VIP bus station (☎511 654), 1st fl. of the Siripetchkasem Hotel on Srasong Rd. near Decharnuchit Rd. A/C buses to **Bangkok** (3½hr., every 40min. 3am-9pm, 120฿) via **Cha Am** (20min., 30฿). Southbound A/C buses and everything else depart from the **regular bus station** (☎511 230), a dusty roundabout at the end of Liab Tang Rodfai

TO KLAI KANG WON PALACE (100m);
TO ✈ (150m);
TO ➕ HUA HIN HOSPITAL (4km)
TO CHA-AM (26km);
TO PHETCHABURI (64km);
TO BANGKOK (224km)

Regular Bus Station

TO KAENG KRACHAN NATIONAL PARK (55km)

Chomsinthu Rd.

Chatchai Market

Naeb Kehardt Rd.

Phetkasem Hwy.

Fishing Pier

Leung Lom Soi

Naresdamri Rd.

Decharnuchit Rd.

Night Market

VIP Bus Station

Khao Hin Lekfai Viewpoint

Liab Tang Rodfai Rd.

Srasong Rd.

Amnuaysin Rd.

Sunshine Internet Cafe

Selakam Rd.

Hilton Hotel ■

Soi Bintaban

Poolsuk Rd.

Naresdamri Rd.

Kamnoadvitee Rd.

Phetkasem Hwy.

Soi Kanjanomai

Tourist Police

Srasong Rd.

Damnernkasem Rd.

GPO

Municipal Building

Siam Commercial Bank

■ Bookazine

Sofitel Central Hotel

Gulf of Thailand

0 50 yards
0 50 meters

San Pau Lo Hospital

TO SUAN SAN BEACH, KHAO TAKIEB, AND KHAO KAI LAS (6km); TO KHAO TAO & KHAO SAM ROI YOD NATIONAL PARK (63km)

Hua Hin

🛏 ACCOMMODATIONS
All Nations Guest House, **2**
Banpak Hua-Hin Hotel, **11**
HI-Hua-Hin/Euro Hua-Hin City Hotel, **12**
Fulay Guest House, **6**
Memory Guest House, **5**
Pattana Guest House, **1**

🍴 FOOD
Amadeus, **3**
Hua Hin Brewery, **10**
Maharaja, **4**
Siam Restaurant, **8**
Vassana Restaurant, **9**

⭐ NIGHTLIFE
Coconuts, **7**
Star Planet Pub, **13**

CENTRAL THAILAND

Rd., about 500m north of the railway station. To: **Bangkok** (4hr., every 20min., 100฿) via **Cha Am** (20min., 15฿); **Chumphon** (4hr., 12 per day, 120฿); **Phuket** (12hr., 6 per day 10am-11pm, 305-486฿); **Prachuap Khiri Khan** (1½hr., every hr. 6:30am-4pm, 50฿); **Surat Thani** (8hr.; 10am, 210฿; 11pm, 340฿).

Local Transportation: Samlor go round-trip to **Khao Krailas** and **Khao Takieb** (every 15min. 6am-7pm, 7฿). Green **songthaew** leave from the motorcycle shop at Decharnuchit and Srasong Rd. (every 15min. 6am-7pm, 7฿). **Tuk-tuks** and **motorcycle taxis** can be found on most street corners. No trip within town should cost more than 30฿ by *tuk-tuk* or 20฿ by motorcycle.

✈ 🛈 ORIENTATION AND PRACTICAL INFORMATION

Despite its immense popularity as a tourist destination, Hua Hin is surprisingly small and generally walkable. **Phetkasem Highway** and the train tracks run north-south through town. **Damnernkasem Road** leads from the train station to the beach and forms the southern boundary of the town proper, although the beach and resort area extends far beyond. To the north and running parallel to each other are **Decharnuchit Road** and **Chomsinthu Road,** both of which lead from the beach to Phetkasem Hwy. Most hotels, restaurants, and bars cluster around **Naresdamri**

Road, which branches off Damnernkasem Rd. close to the beach and passes by the Hilton. Free maps are available at the tourist office and many restaurants and bars.

Tourist Office: Tourist Information Service Center, 114 Phetkasem Hwy. (☎532 433), on the ground floor of the municipal building, at the Damnernkasem Rd. intersection. Helpful maps and decent English. The free *Hua Hin Observer*, a monthly English journal available at the tourist office and a number of hotels and restaurants, provides tourist information, listings, and amusing news articles. Open daily 8:30am-4:30pm.

Currency Exchange: Banks and **exchange booths** line Naresdamri and Damnernkasem Rd. near the Hilton. Most open daily 11am-7pm. **Siam Commercial Bank** (☎532 420), is next to the post office. Open M-F 8:30am-4:30pm; window open daily 11am-7pm.

Books: Bookazine, 166 Naresdamri Rd., opposite Sofitel Hotel. Open daily 9am-10pm.

Markets: The **night market,** on Donamuchit Rd. between Srasong Rd. and Phetkasem Hwy., is a bit touristy but has excellent Thai food. **Chatchai Market,** between Srasong Rd. and Phetkasem Hwy., is a great place to sample local street culture during the day.

Local Tourist Police: (☎515 995), in the little white building on the left side of Damnernkasem Rd. just before the beach. English spoken. Open **24hr.**

Medical Services: All services listed provide **24hr.** care. **San Pau Lo Hospital** (☎532 576), on Phetkasem Hwy., 400m south of the Tourist Center. Credit cards accepted. **Hua Hin Hospital** (☎520 371), 4km north of town on Phetkasem Hwy. A **Red Cross station,** next door to the municipal building, provides basic services.

Telephones: Next to the GPO. **International phone**/fax. Open daily 8am-midnight.

Internet Access: Sunshine Internet Cafe, beneath Hotel Thanawit in a *soi* off Amnuaysin Rd. near Phetkasem Hwy. Very fast access for 20฿ per hr. Open daily 9am-midnight.

Post Office: GPO (☎511 063), opposite the police station on Damnernkasem Rd., as soon as you turn off Phetkasem Hwy. toward the beach. *Poste Restante.* Open M-F 8:30am-4:30pm, Sa-Su and holidays 9am-noon.

Postal Code: 77110.

ACCOMMODATIONS

Most budget hotels cluster around Naresdamri Rd. and on the alleys that branch off it. While prices are similar, style varies, so shop around. Reservations are recommended during the high season, which is late November to mid-March.

All Nations Guest House, 10-10/1 Decharnuchit Rd. (☎512 747; cybercafehuahin@hotmail.com), on the left about 100m from the beach. All Nations offers clean rooms, shared baths with hot water, private balconies overlooking the sea, and a bar area downstairs. Friendly Canadian owner Tim, his wife, and the cheerful staff add to the pleasant mood. Upper-level rooms have less noise and better views. Rooms 150-250฿, with A/C 350-450฿; triples with A/C and cable TV 600฿. ❷ Just around the corner on Leung Lom Soi is **All Nations 2** (☎531 240), offering quieter surroundings. Smaller rooms have no hot water. Singles and doubles 150฿. ❷

HI-Hua-Hin/Euro Hua-Hin City Hotel, 5/15 Srasong Rd. (☎513 130), a half block from the train station towards Phetkasem Hwy. This recent addition to the Hostelling International family features spotless rooms that still have that new-paint smell. All rooms have private bath and A/C, and many have hot water and TV. 8-bed dorms 130฿; 6-bed dorms 160฿; 4-bed rooms 200฿ per person; 3-bed rooms 250฿ per person; singles and doubles 700-800฿. ❷

Pattana Guest House, 52 Naresdamri Rd. (☎513 393). Look for the sign pointing down an alley off Naresdamri Rd. 10m to the left of the pier. Serene, enchanting, traditional

200-year-old Thai home with clean rooms and teak furnishings. Personable staff and relaxed clientele. Rooms 240฿, with private bath 375฿. ❸

Memory Guest House, 108 Naresdamri Rd. (☎511 816), on the ocean, about 25m to the right of the pier. The deluxe rooms are nice and clean, but claustrophobes beware: the smaller ones make you feel like you're staying in someone's shoe closet. Rooms with fan 150-350฿, with A/C 500฿, with fridge 600฿. ❷

Fulay Guest House, 110/1 Naresdamri Rd. (☎513 145; www.fulay-huahin.com), across from Memory. You've always wanted to sleep by the sea, so why not over it? Breaking waves, comfortable patios, friendly staff. Rooms are simple and clean. All have private baths. Great breakfast menu 30-70฿. Rooms 250-350฿, with A/C and TV 750-1500฿, depending on size of room. ❸

Banpak Hua-Hin Hotel, 5/1 Poolsuk Rd. (☎511 653), near the intersection with Soi Bintaban opposite the temple. Large and slightly impersonal, the rooms are comfortable and have private baths, although the view from the windows (generally of neighbors' laundry) isn't ideal. Singles and doubles 250฿, with A/C 350฿. ❸

FOOD

Though Western-style restaurants are moving in, seafood reigns here, and for good reason. Every morning, Hua Hin's fishing fleet returns to the pier with a fresh catch. The lively **night market** ❶ is the best place to sample authentic Thai seafood, which is cooked right in front of you. (Dishes 10-50฿. Open daily 5pm-midnight.) **Chatchai Market** ❶ sets up during the day. For something sit-down, head to Naresdamri Rd., where quality restaurants line the entire length of the street.

Amadeus, 23 Naresdamri Rd., across from Memory Guest House, serves delicious *pad thai* (85-95฿) and offers an extensive Western menu (with an Austrian emphasis) that includes 8 kinds of steak. Most dishes 95-140฿. Open daily 9am-midnight. ❸

Maharaja, 25 Naresdamri Rd. between Amadeus and Fulay Guest House. A classy atmosphere and great Indian food for less than most restaurants near the Hilton. Save room for the delicious *ras malai* dessert (60฿). Extensive vegetarian menu. Most dishes 90-160฿. Open daily 11am-11pm. ❸

Siam Restaurant, on Poolsuk Rd., offers cheap Western and Thai dishes in a relaxed setting. Great drink specials. Entrees 40-100฿. Drinks 25-110฿. ❷

Vassana Restaurant, 154 Naresdamri Rd., just past the Hilton coming from the guesthouses. Very tasteful atmosphere with an impressive imported wine list. Western and Thai dishes average 80-145฿. Open daily 9am-midnight. ❸

Hua Hin Brewery, 33 Naresdamri Rd., in the Hilton. Western-style bar and restaurant serves up delicious seafood to go with the brew. Grilled fresh fish with baked potato 150฿. Seafood skewer 180฿. Open daily 10am-2am, full menu offered until 10pm. ❸

NIGHTLIFE

Notorious "girlie bars" dot the Hua Hin nightlife landscape, and it isn't hard to tell when you've happened upon one. There are, however, a number of bars that cater to Westerners on Damnernkasem Rd. and adjacent Selekam Rd. Several, including **Coconuts** (also called the Hard Kok Cafe), 85 Selekam Rd., are expat-run and have pool tables and televisions tuned to soccer games at any time of day. (Open daily until 1am.) For non-sporting entertainment, **Hua Hin Brewery** inside the Hilton offers overpriced drinks and nightly live performances of Thai bands covering Western hits which are entertaining, at the very least. (Beers 125-215฿. Generally starts getting crowded around 9:30-10pm.) The **Star Planet Pub** inside the City

Beach Hotel is similar but more reasonably priced and offers more Thai-themed live music acts. (Open daily until 2am.)

🔍 SIGHTS

Hua Hin's major attraction is the **Hua Hin Beach,** which rolls along for kilometers in either direction. While more scenic beaches can be found farther south, Hua Hin's is clean, with soft white sand. The fishing pier, at the base of Chomsinthu Rd., dominates one area; the prettier part of the beach begins just past the entrance to the Sofitel Hotel. Farther south, vendors wander the sand offering massages, food, and pony rides (100-400฿ for 30min.).

The **Sofitel Central Hotel,** 1.5km south of the pier, recreates a bygone era. Originally the Railway Hotel, it was built by Prince Purachatra, the former Director General of State Railways; it also had a brief stint in cinema as Phnom Penh's leading hotel in the film *The Killing Fields.* One of Southeast Asia's grandest five-star hotels (rooms start at 6000฿), Sofitel has beautiful grounds worthy of a stroll. Tourists on a budget can come for high tea (130฿) and meander through the green elephant herds in the topiary gardens.

If you head north past the Hilton Hotel and the pier, you can see **Klai Kang Won (Far From Worries) Palace.** A royal summer residence in the 1920s, the palace now houses the ailing king, and the grounds are closed to visitors.

The twin hills of **Khao Takieb** (Chopstick Hill) and **Khao Krailas,** 6km south of Hua Hin on Phetkasem Hwy., are accessible by motorbike or *songthaew* (7฿). Khao Takieb features a temple, hundreds of friendly monkeys (monkey grub sold on the spot for 120฿), and an excellent view of Hua Hin. Khao Krailas has a small lighthouse and a decent view of Hua Hin. Pine-tree-lined **Suan San Beach** is farther south and has unbeatable swimming. Charter a *songthaew* or *tuk-tuk* (150฿). Still farther south is **Khao Tao** (Turtle Hill).

🗺 DAYTRIPS FROM HUA HIN

TANAO SRI AND PA LA-U.

Take a taxi from outside Chatchai Market in Hua Hin (up to 1200฿; it will wait for you). A more affordable but dangerous option is to rent a motorbike (200฿) in Hua Hin and travel the 63km alone. From Hua Hin, follow local Hwy. 3218 until it meets Hwy. 3219, then follow signs. The route is well paved up to the park entrance and the scenery is inspiring. Past the checkpoint, the road turns to dirt and can be treacherous. Walk the last few kilometers to the waterfall and trailhead. It's a short hike (30min.) to the first cascade and swimming hole.

The region between Hua Hin and the Burmese border has spectacular natural sights. The **Tanao Sri Range** forms the border and backdrop for the **Pa La-u Forest** in Kaeng Krachan National Park (p. 188). Deep in the jungle, the twin waterfalls La-u Yai and La-u Noi merge to become **Pa La-u Falls,** an 11-tier cascade. It's best to visit between November and April. While three days are required to reach the source, trekkers can explore the first few levels in a day's hike. Longer stays require a guide and camping equipment. During high season, the park rents **tents ❶** and **bungalows ❸**. A **small eatery ❶** on the left-hand side of the road (look for a "Food & Beverages" sign) sells Thai staples (fried rice 20฿). Overnight trekkers should contact the **Sub-Forestry Office** one week in advance by writing to Kaeng Krachan National Park, Pa La Hua Hin, Prachuap Khiri Khan 77110. The office is past the checkpoint at the entrance. Try spelunking in the three **caves** on the way to Pa La-u on Hwy. 3219, 30km from Hua Hin near Nongphlab Village. At the main intersection in town, make a right onto Rte. 3301 and look for signs advertising the **Daow**

Lap Lae and **Kallon** caves, which are simultaneously spectacular caves and the standard Buddha brigade.

KHAO SAM ROI YOD NATIONAL PARK.

Take a southbound bus from Hua Hin, get off at Pranburi Market, and hire a taxi or songthaew to park headquarters. Park open M-F 8:30am-4:30pm.

Stunning limestone hills (the "Three Hundred Peaks") rise from the surrounding sea and marshland. The park is 63km south of Hua Hin off Hwy. 4. Park **bungalows** ❷ accommodate up to 20; reserve in advance (☎02 579 0529). There are some excellent **hikes** from headquarters for daytrippers, as well as extensive **caves** and canals for overnight visitors to explore. Insect repellent is a must.

PRACHUAP KHIRI KHAN ☎032

Flanked by verdant rock formations jutting sharply out from its bay, Prachuap Khiri Khan is an unassuming fishing town. Fishing boats and seafood restaurants meet along the pleasant waterfront promenade, and hip teens gather in small groups for an evening beer by the pier. Prachuap's easygoing attitude and mere handful of tourists mean that visitors will have two outstanding sights to themselves: the nearby caves, which hide a pair of magnificent reclining Buddhas, and the hilltop *wat*, which overlooks the bay.

▐▀ TRANSPORTATION

Trains: The **railway station** (☎611 175), on the corner of Maharat Rd. and Kong Kiat Rd., has frequent trains to **Bangkok** via **Hua Hin**. To: **Bangkok** (5hr., 175-235฿); **Chumphon** (3hr., 1:45pm, 140-200฿); **Hua Hin** (1½hr., 59฿); **Phetchaburi** (3½hr., 102฿); **Surat Thani** (5-6hr., 181฿).

Buses: A/C buses to **Bangkok** (4-5hr., every 30min., 140-176฿) leave from Phitak Chat Rd., between Kong Kiat Rd. and Maitri Ngam Rd. Most Bangkok-bound buses stop at **Hua Hin** (1½hr., 50฿). The **regular bus station**, on Phitak Chat Rd. across from the Inthira Hotel, runs buses to **Chumphon** (4-5hr., every hr., 100฿). For **Surat Thani,** catch a southbound bus from Bangkok on the highway 3km from Prachuap (taxi 30฿), or take a bus to Chumphon and transfer there.

Local Transportation: Downtown can be traversed on foot. For longer distances, look for **tuk-tuks.** Any trip around town should be no more than 20฿. *Tuk-tuks* to **Ao Manao** 20฿ one-way; to **Khao Khan Krad Cave** 30-40฿ per person one-way.

Rentals: Hipperock, (☎611 126) on Kong Kiat Rd., nearly opposite Yuttichai Hotel, rents bikes and motorbikes (200฿ per day). Open daily 8am-9pm.

✈ ⬛ ORIENTATION AND PRACTICAL INFORMATION

Prachuap Khiri Khan is extremely easy to navigate and can be traversed on foot in 15 min. It roughly follows a grid layout. The waterfront, **Chai Thaleh**, runs north-south on the eastern edge of town. **Khao Chong Krajok,** Prachuap's impressive, *wat*-topped mountain, rises on the northern edge of the waterfront. Between the railway tracks and the waterfront (and running parallel to them), are (from west to east) **Phitak Chat Road, Sarachip Road,** and **Suseuk Road.** Perpendicular to these is **Kong Kiat Road,** running from the **train station** in the west to the **pier** in the east. **Maitri Ngam Road,** south of Kong Kiat Rd., is home to the fruit and vegetable **market.**

The **Tourist Information Office** is on the waterfront 200m north of the pier, gives out maps, and is mildly helpful. (☎611 591. Open daily 8:30am-4:30pm.) The **Govern-**

CENTRAL THAILAND

ment **Savings Bank,** on Kong Kiat Rd. between Sarachip Rd. and Suseuk Rd., offers currency exchange and has a **24hr. ATM** outside. (Open M-F 8:30am-3:30pm.) Other services include: **police** (☎611 148), at the corner of Kong Kiat and Sarachip Rd.; **Prachuap Hospital** (☎602 060), four long blocks down Phitak Chat Rd. from Kong Kiat Rd., on the left; an **Internet** cafe on Sarachip Rd., near the day market (40฿ per hr.; open daily 8am-9:30pm); and the **GPO** (☎611 035), on Suseuk Rd., at the intersection with Maitri Ngam Rd. by the market. (**Telephones** and **Internet** on the 2nd fl. Open M-F 8:30am-4:30pm, Sa-Su 9am-noon.) **Postal Code:** 77000.

ACCOMMODATIONS

Although there are no exceptional backpacker accommodations, there is a small but sufficient selection of budget-friendly options, and almost nothing beyond medium-range. The **Yuttichai Hotel ❷,** a 2min. walk from the train station along Kong Kiat Rd.,

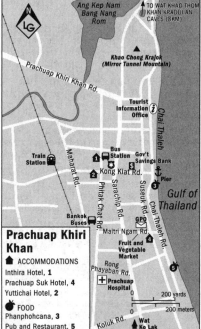

Prachuap Khiri Khan

▲ ACCOMMODATIONS
Inthira Hotel, 1
Prachuap Suk Hotel, 4
Yuttichai Hotel, 2

🍴 FOOD
Phanphohcana, 3
Pub and Restaurant, 5

on the right, is similar in style and amenities to other hotels. A simple breakfast is available for 20฿. (☎611 055. Boiling pots of duck soup 20฿. Free maps of Prachuap Khiri Khan. Singles 160฿, with bath 200฿; doubles 200฿/240฿.) From the train station, go down Kong Kiat Rd., turn onto Suseuk Rd. and walk for three long blocks; the **Prachuap Suk Hotel ❷,** 69-71 Suseuk Rd., past the market on the left, is a small, well-maintained hotel. (☎611 019. Singles with fan 150฿; doubles with fan 200฿, with A/C 350฿.) The **Inthira Hotel ❷,** on Phitak Chat Rd., has clean rooms, but no restaurant, and the lounge TV often blares late at night. (☎611 418. From the train station, go down Kong Kiat Rd. and take the first left. Rooms have bath with cold water. TVs 50฿. Singles 200฿; doubles 250฿.)

FOOD

With fleets of fishing boats just offshore, it's not surprising that seafood is cheap in Prachuap Khiri Khan. **Phanphohcana ❸,** past the pier to the south, has an extensive menu in English and serves good seafood. (Dishes 70-120฿. American breakfast 70฿. Grilled fish 120฿. Open daily 8am-10pm.) On the waterfront, a 5min. walk south past the pier, is the **⬛Pub and Restaurant ❷,** which serves vegetarian options such as mixed vegetable coconut curry (70฿). With live music, great decor, and dim lighting, it's also a pleasant place to grab a drink in the evening. (Open daily 5pm-midnight.) The **fruit and vegetable market ❶** is on Maitri Ngam, close to the post office. In the evenings, the **night food stalls ❶** opposite the police station serve excellent seafood, as well as typical entrees. (Open 5pm-midnight.)

CENTRAL THAILAND

👁 🏖 SIGHTS AND BEACHES

For a small town, Pratchuap Khiri Khan affords two remarkable sights that in themselves are worth the trip. What makes them even more exhilarating is their complete seclusion—you'll have them all to yourself. Ao Manao is devoid of *farang*, but is still very popular with local Thais.

KHAO CHONG KRAJOK (MIRROR TUNNEL MOUNTAIN). It's 421 steps to the golden *chedi* of this hilltop's **wat**, which offers a glorious 360° panorama of the surrounding bay and province. Its height allows for a lighthouse perspective of beachwalkers, approaching trains, and the general activity of the town. In addition, monkeys are given free rein of the hill and *wat*. Travelers should not approach or make contact with the monkeys. *(On the northern tip of town overlooking the bay. The steps start on Sarachip Rd. opposite the wat. Open 24hr. Free.)*

WAT KHAO THAM KHAN KRADAI AND CAVES. Overlooking the Ao Khan Kradai Bay are two impressive complexes of caves. A shiny, shell-paved set of steps leads to the first and smaller cave. On the hill to the left is the larger and superior complex, which holds two spectacular **reclining Buddhas.** Though the cave is lit, you may still want to bring a flashlight. *(8km north of town. Tuk-tuk 30-40฿ one-way. If driving, head north of Prachuap, into Ao Noi District, turn right at the sign for Ao Noi Seaview Resort, and follow that road until its end. There are no signs for the cave. Free.)*

🏖 **AO MANAO (MANAO BEACH).** Ao Manao is a scenic 2km beach enclosed by cliffs. It is necessary to pass through the adjoining Thai airforce base before reaching the beach. There is also a golf course, campground, and shooting range in the vicinity. Tubes are available for visitors, and excellent seafood stalls line the beach. *(6km south of Prachuap Khiri Khan. Tuk-tuk 20-30฿ one-way.)*

NORTHEAST THAILAND

Encompassing nearly one third of Thailand's landmass, and supporting an equal proportion of the nation's population, this plateau is called *Isaan*, meaning "vastness and prosperity." Ironically, largely agrarian Isaan is one of the country's poorest regions, and 10% of village children are severely malnourished. In contrast, the northeast's four largest cities, where the US set up airforce bases during the Vietnam War, are bustling centers of transportation, commerce, and education. Historically, the region has had stronger ties to Laos and the Khmer across the Mekong River than to the central plains, as the centuries-old Khmer ruins and Lao *chedis* of the region affirm. So close is this relationship culturally that the Isaan dialect carries striking similarities to Lao, and in some areas Thai is spoken as a second language. Aside from the national parks in Loei and Khmer ruins in Si Saket and Buriram provinces, the region lacks many awe-inspiring sights; however, travelers

are drawn to the region for its lack of large tour groups, fiery foods, captivating hospitality, and intoxicatingly slow pace of life. For skeptics who hold that any statement containing both "Thailand" and "off the beaten path" is oxymoronic, Isaan emerges as a buried treasure.

KHAO YAI NATIONAL PARK

Khao Yai National Park

For travelers hoping to rescue their lungs from the fumes of Bangkok, Khao Yai National Park offers salvation. Only 160km from Bangkok, Khao Yai, Thailand's first (and perhaps best) national park, opened in 1962. The humbling 2168km² of park ranges from stark prairie to thick evergreens, and boasts one of the world's largest monsoon rain forests. Wild elephants, tigers, and bears (oh my!) and more than 300 species of birds, including the great hornbill, also make their home in Khao Yai, though it's more likely you'll be swatting insects and peeling off leeches than coming face to face with a leopard or Asiatic black bear. Khao Yai is most conveniently reached via Pak Chong, an urban strip featuring little more than basic lodging and supplies.

PAK CHONG ☎044

Primarily a market town, Pak Chong is of little interest to travelers except as a base for Khao Yai National Park. The surrounding region, however, is being developed as a weekend retreat for wealthy Thais seeking a break from the madness and concrete of Bangkok. Developers draw upon the region's particularly short heritage as an agricultural and cattle-raising area with names like Khao Yai Cowboy City, Bonanza, and the OK Corral. Alongside themed attractions, housing developments, spas, and vineyards line the road from Pak Chong to Khao Yai. Since the construction of the rail line and the Mittaphap Hwy. connecting Bangkok to Khorat, Pak Chong has developed as a center of the region.

■ **TRANSPORTATION.** **Songthaew** leave for Khao Yai National Park around the corner from the 7-Eleven on Tesabarn 19 (every 20min. 6am-3pm, every 30min. 3pm-5pm; 20฿). The **train station** (☎311 534) lies at the end of Tesabarn 15. Trains go to Bangkok via Ayutthaya (3½-4hr., 9 per day 10am-2:30am, from 36-262฿) and Khorat (1-1½hr., 11 per day 9am-4am, from 18฿). At the first **bus station,** beside the Thai Farmers Bank just after Tesabarn 19, you can catch A/C buses en route from Bangkok to Khorat (1½hr., every 20min. 5am-9pm, 46฿) and make connections to northern and northeastern destinations. An **A/C bus station** is between Tesabarn 18 and the overpass, with service to Bangkok (3hr.; newer orange and red bus 74฿, blue bus 110฿). A second **A/C bus terminal** between Tesabarn 21 and 23 has service to Nakhon Sawan via Lopburi (6hr., 4 per hr. 7:20am-12:20pm, 150-180฿) Ordinary buses for Khorat also leave from this terminal (2hr., every hr., 34฿). A third **A/C bus station** next to the Shell station serves Chayaphurn (2½hr., 10 per hr. 9:30am-7:30pm, 83฿).

⁊ PRACTICAL INFORMATION. Pak Chong's development along transport lines explains its layout, which extends approximately 2km along the main strip, **Mittaphap (Friendship) Highway** paralleling the railway. Side streets are designated "Tesabarn Rd.," followed by a number. Odd-numbered Tesabarns generally parallel even-numbered Tesabarns on either side of the strip. The four major landmarks are the stoplight at Tesabarn 16/17, the 7-Eleven store, the pedestrian overpass, and the Shell gas station at Tesabarn 25.

The **Bank of Ayudhya,** centrally located between Tesabarn 18 and the overpass, gives cash advances, cashes traveler's checks, and has a MC/Plus/V **24hr. ATM.** (☎311 411. Open M-F 8:30am-3:30pm.) Other services include: the **day market,** which starts near Tesabarn 21 and extends one block uphill from the main road (open daily 6am-4:30pm); the **supermarket,** at the corner of Tesabarn 16, with flashlights, batteries and toiletries for Khao Yai treks (open daily 8:30am-9:30pm); the **night market,** between Tesabarn 17 and 19, with rows of food carts and young Thais on motorbikes; **CAT,** on the corner of Tesabarn 24, which handles faxes, receives **Internet,** receives collect calls, and places domestic and international phone calls (☎312 209; Internet 15฿ 1st hr., 12฿ every hr. after; collect calls 50฿; open M-F 8:30am-4:30pm); **Internet access,** between Tesabarn 15 and 17 (20฿ per hr.; open daily 9am-11pm); and the **post office,** directly across from CAT, which handles telegrams and money and postal orders. (☎311 736. Open M-F 8:30am-4:30pm.) **Postal Code:** 30130.

⌂ ACCOMMODATIONS AND FOOD. Khao Yai Garden Lodge ❶, Thanon Thanarat Km 7, on the left side of the road from Pak Chong to Khao Yai (Rte. 2090). A pleasant garden with an eclectic collection of small pools and Lamyai trees weaves through a series of charming houses and an artificial waterfall cascades into the swimming pool. The quality of rooms varies from decent to spectacular. (☎365 167; www.khaoyai-garden-lodge.com. Also runs park tours; see p. 202. Singles 100฿; doubles with bath 500฿; suites with marble bath and A/C 1800฿. Discounts for suites are negotiable.) Along the 30km stretch of road between Pak Chong and the park are luxury resorts, such as **Juldi's Khao Yai Resort and Spa ❸,** Thanarat Rd., Km 17. A swimming pool and tennis courts sit amid beautifully landscaped grounds. The spa offers Thai herbal steam saunas for 300-450฿, rice and tumeric scrubs for 600-900฿, or a traditional 90min. Thai massage for 500-750฿. (☎297 297; www.khaoyai.com. Great choice for a group. Breakfast included. 4-person bungalows Su-Th Nov.-Apr. 3630฿; low-season 3267฿. AmEx/MC/V.) **Phu Phaya Hotel ❹,** 733 Mittaphap Rd., on the left before the Shell station, is convenient with conventional modern rooms, but low on charm. Luxury rooms are well maintained and clean. All rooms have A/C, TV, and telephone. (☎313 490. Breakfast included. Standard rooms with private shower 490฿; deluxe rooms with private tub 690฿. MC/V.) **Jungle Guest House ❶** is at 63 Kongvaccin Soi 3, 1 Rd. Head on to Tesabarn 16 at the stoplight; when the road forks, veer left onto Thanon Kong Vaccine Soi 1; the guesthouse is 50m on the right. Jungle is run by an amiable family which organizes expeditions to the park; reservations recommended. (☎09 917 6044; malivan65@yahoo.com. Coffee included. Breakfast 25฿. 200฿ for 2-day excursion. Basic dorms with mattresses on wooden floors and no fan 100฿; private singles/ doubles with limited hot water shower and fan 150฿.)

NORTHEAST THAILAND

The **night market** has many food stalls, and some of the guesthouses have restaurants. Khao Yai Garden Lodge's restaurant serves both Thai and Western dishes.

SIGHTS. Located at Khao Si Siat in Tambon Klang, the main highlight of **Wat Thep Phithak Punnarum** is a steel and reinforced concrete 45m Buddha statue crowning a hill at an elevation of 56wa (112m; 1wa=2m), representing the 56 merits of Buddha. The statue's height symbolizes the number of years the Exalted One spent teaching people after he attained enlightenment. The 1280-step stairway up to the statue is the number of monks that gathered on Makha Buddha Day. From Pak Chong, take a Bangkok-bound bus to Km 150 then go 3km down the asphalt road.

THE PARK

Home to one of the last wild elephant herds and some of the world's few remaining wild tigers, the park has over 40km of **hiking** and **biking** trails through rainforest and grasslands. The **Visitors Center** rents bikes for 40฿ per hr. To avoid leeches, don't trek in sandals and steer clear of salty water. Leech-guards (70฿ to buy, 20฿ to rent) are available at the souvenir shop near Park Headquarters. The waterfalls alone are worth the trek. **Haew Narok** ("awful cliff"), a three-tiered cascade, is the tallest waterfall in the park. Its impressive 150m height can be deadly; elephants have been known to slip and fall from the surrounding cliffs. **Haew Suwat Falls** and **Pha Kluai Mai Falls** (named for the surrounding red orchids) are also noteworthy. **Nong Pak Chi Watch Tower** (11km from the north entrance) is the place to observe deer, and **Elephant Crossing** is the spot to view—you guessed it—elephants.

For a more convenient tour of the park, try **Jungle Adventure**—a 1½-day tour operated by the Jungle Guest House in Pak Chong. The tour, which includes Buddhist meditation caves, waterfall swims, elephant-trail treks, and a night safari, moves at a blistering pace and costs 950฿. Trips leave at 3pm and end the next evening. Khao Yai Garden Lodge offers similar tours for 950฿ plus entrance fee.

Leisurely 2hr. family **rafting** trips on Lam Tak Hong are offered May to September. Contact the Khao Yai Elephant Camp, Thanarat Rd. Km 19.5 (☎297 183). *Songthaew* leave the north park entrance for Pak Chong every hour 7am-4pm.

After stepping off the *songthaew* at the northern park entrance (☎04 429 7406), it's another 14km to Park Headquarters and the Visitors Center. You can arrange a pickup at the entrance to headquarters (☎04 429 7406). Although *Let's Go* does not recommend it, most travelers find they have to hitchhike to headquarters. (Park Headquarters and Visitors Center open daily 8am-6pm. Park map is free, although not detailed enough to use as a trail map. For longer treks, a guide is recommended; usually around 300-800฿. Park open daily 6am-9pm. 200฿, students 100฿, vehicles 50฿.)

To stay overnight in the park call the Royal Forest Department in Bangkok (☎02 506 2076) for permission—bookings must be made by 6pm. Two campgrounds, **Lamtakong ❶**, 6km from the Visitors Center, and **Orchid ❶** *(Pha Kluai Mai)*, 9km from the Visitors Center, offer campsites for 30฿ as well as tent rentals (1-person tent 80฿, 3-person 150฿). Alternatively, **Suratsawadee Lodge ❷**, 1km from the Visitors Center, offers dorm beds for 100฿ a night. Accommodations in lodges are also available at **Thanarat**, 6km from the Visitors Center, and **Kong Kaew ❹**, 0.2km from the Visitors Center (2-person lodges 500฿, 8-person 2400฿). Hardwood floor space is also available at **Kong Kaew Camp ❶** (50฿).

NAKHON RATCHASIMA (KHORAT)　　☎044

Known locally as Khorat, the name of the plateau on which it rests, Nakhon Ratchasima straddles the main corridor to all other destinations in Isaan. Although it's one of Thailand's largest cities, the texture of urban life found here is worlds away from the manic snarls of Bangkok. Designed by French engineers for Ayutthayan King Narai, the city was once fortified by a wall and surrounded by a moat (the

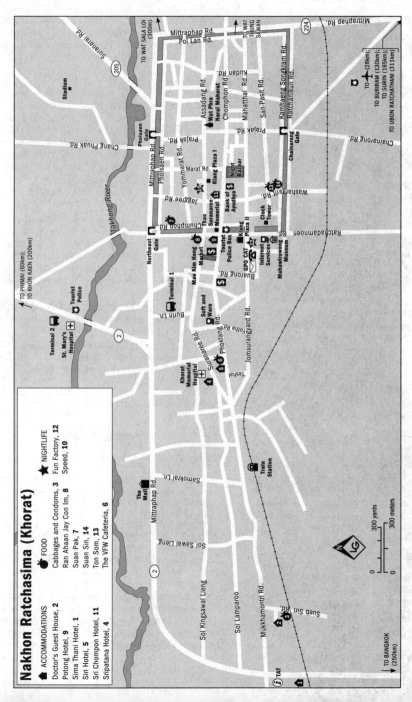

Nakhon Ratchasima (Khorat)

▲ ACCOMMODATIONS
Doctor's Guest House, **2**
Potong Hotel, **9**
Sima Thani Hotel, **1**
Siri Hotel, **5**
Sri Chompon Hotel, **11**
Sripatana Hotel, **4**

🍴 FOOD
Cabbages and Condoms, **3**
Ran Ahaan Jay Con Im, **8**
Suan Pak, **7**
Suan Sin, **14**
Ton Som, **13**
The VFW Cafeteria, **6**

★ NIGHTLIFE
Fun Factory, **12**
Speed, **10**

remains of which are still visible). Khorat enjoys close proximity to the silk-weaving of Pak Thong Chai, the pottery manufacturers of Dan Kwian, and the ruins of Phimai and Phanom Rung.

THE LOCAL STORY

KHORAT'S LEGENDARY HEROINE

Embodying the spirit of Khorat like no other symbol, the Thao Suranaree Memorial in the town center commemorates the heroic Khun Ying Mo, wife of Khorat's deputy governor during the reign of King Rama III. According to stories, Thao Suranaree (as she became known) feigned cooperation with the invading Lao army, while persuading the women of Khorat to seduce, intoxicate, and then murder the troops. She later rallied the women to fight alongside the men in a battle that led to the defeat of King Anuwong of Vientiane. Locals affectionately refer to her as "Yah Mo" (Grandmother Mo), wrap her shrine in ribbons, burn incense, and give offerings of bananas and coconuts. When she answers people's prayers, they sing thanks in the local Khorat dialect or hire young women to dance in her honor.

Despite this reverence for Thao Suranaree, two events cast doubt not only on her historical importance, but also her very existence. In 1996, Saphin Kaew-Ngaarn-Prasert published a master's thesis in which she proposed that the 1932 revolution that transformed Thailand from an absolute to a constitutional monarchy elevated Thao Suranaree from a forgotten historical footnote to a cult figure of national importance. The monument commemorated a legend who symbolized the rising power of the common citizen and ...

[Cont'd on next page...]

▣ TRANSPORTATION

Flights: Airport (☎259 534), 28km east of town. Catch a **Buriram**-bound bus (10฿) at **Bus Terminal 2**, or a **shuttle bus** (70฿) with pickup at your hotels. A van to the airport is also available on Asadang Rd. in front of Klang Plaza I (30min., 2-3pm, 50฿). **Thai Airways** (☎257 211), at the corner of Suranaree and Buarong Rd., has at least 1 flight to Bangkok per day. Open M-F 8:30am-4:30pm. **Air Asia** flies to Bangkok daily (4:50pm, 590฿ including taxes and fees).

Trains: Nakhon Ratchasima Train Station (☎242 044), on Mukkhamontri Rd. From the center of town, the station is 500m west on Mukkhamontri Rd., with an old locomotive out front. For a complete list of fares and departures, ask for an English timetable at the ticket booth. To: **Bangkok** (5-6hr.; 11 per day 6:50am-11:25pm; 50-315฿).

Buses: The easiest way to find your bus is to inquire which platform it departs from. Purchase tickets on the platform or on the bus.

Terminal 1 (☎245 443), on Burin Lane. To: **Bangkok** (3hr., every 30min., 157฿); **Nakhon Sawan** (#572; 6hr., every hr. 5am-11pm, 95-113฿); **Pak Thong Chai** (#1303; 1½hr., every 30min. 5:30am-8:30pm, 12฿); and numerous stops within the province.

Terminal 2 (☎268 899), is on Rte. 2 north of town beyond Takhong River. Take a motorcycle, *tuk-tuk* (40-50฿), or *songthaew* from in front of the Mae Kim Heng Market on Suranaree Rd. To: **Bangkok** (#21; 4hr., every 30min., 157฿); **Buriram** (#273; 3hr., every 30min., 57-80฿); **Chiang Mai** (#635; 12hr., 11 per day 3:30-9:45am and 2-8:30pm, 437-510฿); **Chiang Rai** (#651; 13hr., 6 per day 5am-6pm, 472฿-550฿); **Nong Khai** (#22; 3½hr., every 2hr. 9am-3pm and 10pm-3am, 215฿) via **Khon Kaen** (2hr., every hr., 104฿) and **Udon Thani** (3hr., every hr., 184฿); **Phimai** (#1305; 1½hr., every 30min. 5am-10pm, 36-40฿); **Surin** (#274; 4hr., every 30min., 70-97฿); **Ubon Ratchathani** (#25; 4½hr., 6 per day 8am-4pm, 250฿).

Local Transportation: Samlor and **tuk-tuks** are omnipresent. From TAT to the Thao Suranaree Memorial should cost no more than 50฿. City buses are just as convenient (6am-8pm, 5-7฿). Buses #1, 2, and 3 start on Mukkhamontri Rd. near TAT and all go into the center of town. They split where Mukkhamontri forks into Phoklang Rd. (#1), Suranaree Rd. (#2), and Jomsurangyard Rd. (#3). **Songthaew** run routes more frequently and coincide with bus-route numbering.

✦ ⓘ ORIENTATION AND PRACTICAL INFORMATION

Khorat is enclosed on the west and north by **Mittraphap Road,** on the east by **Pol Lan Road,** and on the south by the railroad. **Ratachadamnoen Road** and **Chumphon Road,** separated by a narrow park, divide the city into two halves, a quieter western half and a more commercial eastern one. In the middle of this divider, marking the center of the city, stands the dramatic **Thao Suranaree Memorial.** A rectangular moat, a remnant of the city's old fortifications, circumscribes the city's east half. **Chomphon Road,** not to be confused with Chumphon Rd., begins behind Thao Suranaree Memorial and cuts east-west through the center of the old city.

Tourist Offices: TAT, 2102-2104 Mittraphap Rd. (☎213 666; tatsima@tat.or.th), near the intersection with Mukkhamontri Rd. next to the Sima Thani Hotel. English spoken. Free brochures and a useful map. Info on cultural events and the Cambodian border. Open daily 8:30am-4:30pm.

Tours: Supatha Tour, 138 Chainarong Rd. (☎242 758).

Currency Exchange: Bank of Ayudhya, 168 Chomphon Rd. (☎242 388). MC/V cash advances and traveler's check exchange M-F 8:30am-3:30pm. **24hr. ATM.** Cirrus/MC/PLUS/V. Other ATMs line Chomphon Rd.

Markets: Mae Kim Heng Market, between Suranaree and Phoklang Rd. about 1 block beyond the city gate. **Supermarket** on ground fl. of Klang Plaza II department store, Jomsurangyard Rd. Open daily 10am-9pm. The 2nd and 3rd floors have the English-language section of a bookstore, with limited magazines. **The Mall,** on Mittraphap Rd., is one of northeast Thailand's largest shopping plazas, featuring an indoor Olympic-sized swimming pool, bowling alley, and cinema. The **night bazaar** fills 2 blocks of Marat Rd., between Chomphon and Mahatthai Rds. Open daily 6-10pm.

Local Tourist Police: (☎341 777). To the right of the Thao Suranaree memorial. Additional location across Mittraphap Rd., across from Bus Terminal 2.

Pharmacy: Amarin, 122 Chumphon Rd. (☎242 741), behind the memorial to the left. "Rx" on the glass doors. Adequate English. Open daily 8:30am-8:30pm. Also on the lower level of Klang Plaza II, on Jomsurangyard Rd., just off Ratchadamnoen Rd.

Medical Services: St. Mary's Hospital, 307 Mittraphap Rd./Rte. 2 (☎261 261), 50m south of Bus Terminal 2. Private hospital with excellent English-speaking staff. **Khorat Memorial Hospital,** 348 Suranaree Rd. (☎265

the modern patriotic woman, models the new government wished to promote. Thao Suranaree's legend reinforces the region's loyalty to Thailand—once uncertain, due to the large ethnically Lao and Cambodian populations.

Locals felt that the thesis attacked not only their revered figure, but their region's allegiance to Thailand as well. During protests of nearly 50,000 people, Kaew-Ngaam-Prasert's house was attacked, effigies of the academic were burned, and local politicians demanded the book destroyed and her master's degree withdrawn.

In 2001, a proposed film about Thao Suranaree again threatened the legend, this time within the framework of Thai-Lao relations. Laotians revere Thao Suranaree's opponent, King Anuwong. Fearing an unflattering portrayal of the king, Laotian authorities said the film would amount to an insult to Laos' former king, and by extension, the Lao people.

In spite of these accusations, Thao Suranaree's legend continues to represent ideals of democracy, feminism, and patriotism. An annual festival (March 23-April 3) draws thousands. While you won't see effigies of Kaew-Ngaam-Prasert, you will see folk songs and dances, a parade of knife-wielding women, and the Ms. Nakhon Ratchasima beauty contest, all in honor of the city's legendary heroine.

777). From the Thao Suranaree memorial, it's past the Sri Pattana Hotel on the right. Look for the new white building proclaiming "KMH." English spoken. Open daily **24hr.** Accepts Visa.

Telephones: CAT (☎259 707), next to the post office on Jomsurangyard Rd. Overseas calls, fax, and telex. Open daily 8:30am-4:30pm.

Internet Access: Internet Services, 768 Ratchadamnoen Rd., near the clock tower. Open daily 10am-midnight. 20฿ per hr. **Soft and Ware,** 438/2 Phoklang Rd. (☎267 766), near Yotha Rd. 1st hr. 20฿, each additional hr. 15฿. Open daily 10am-9pm.

Post Office: 48 Jomsurangyard Rd. (☎256 670). Facing the memorial, go right on Ratchadamnoen Rd. until Jomsurangyard Rd. Turn right and pass Klang Plaza II; it's on the right. Open M-F 8:30am-4:30pm, Sa 9am-noon.

Postal Code: 30000.

ACCOMMODATIONS

Budget digs in Khorat are generally dingy and run-down. Cheap and pleasant do not necessarily go together here, so if you are sick of grimy squat toilets and have a few extra *baht* saved up, this is one place to splurge on nicer accommodations.

Doctor's Guest House, 75 Sueb Siri Rd. Soi 4 (☎255 846). On the western edge of the city, past the train station and near TAT. The oldest and only real guesthouse in town. Distant location, but quiet. The best place in its price range. Laundry service 5-15฿ per item. Strict 10pm lockout. Small, clean rooms with fans 180฿. ❷

Sripatana Hotel, 346 Suranaree Rd. (☎251 652-4; www.sripatana.com). Clean rooms in an impersonal hotel. The curved hallways makes you feel like you're in a 70s futuristic movie. All rooms have A/C and TV. Internet and coffee shop. 460-615฿. MC/V. ❸

Sima Thani Hotel (☎213 100; sales@simathani,co.th), on Mittraphap Rd. Khorat's most luxurious hotel, miles above the rest. Traditional Thai dancing, pool, gym, spa, cafe. Enjoy it while it lasts. Deluxe rooms 2500-3000฿. MC/V. ❺

Siri Hotel, 688-690 Phoklang Rd. (☎241 556), 200m down Phoklang Rd. next to the VFW cafeteria. Run-down rooms but cheap. Singles with fan 120-140฿; doubles 180฿, with A/C 280฿; special room for 2 with TV, A/C, and fridge 380฿. ❷

Sri Chompon Hotel, 133 Chomphon Rd. (☎252 829), a short walk down Chomphon Rd. from the memorial. Small stark rooms. Singles with toilet and fan 160฿, with A/C 240฿; doubles 240฿/350฿. ❷

Muang Thong Hotel, 46 Chumphon Rd. (☎242 090). Look for the light-green wooden building with flags, to the right of the 7-Eleven. As you walk into the courtyard, the lobby will be on your left. Outwardly exudes old world Asian charm; inside, a real developing-world experience awaits—only for the hard-core. Rooms 120฿, with A/C 350฿. ❷

Potong Hotel, 658 Ratchadamnoen Rd. (☎251 962), at the corner of Phoklang Rd. Popular, with a central (albeit raucous) location. A last resort. Western toilets. Singles with fan 170฿, with TV and A/C 300฿; doubles with fan 220฿. ❷

FOOD

Mouth-watering cuisine is plentiful. The **markets** ❶ are fine places to sample regional specialties, such as *sai klog* (grilled pork sausages stuffed with rice; 5฿) and *kanom bueng* (small, taco-shaped, coconut-stuffed crepes; 1฿). An alternative is the **food courts** ❶ in the basement and fifth floor of the Klang Plaza II shopping center on Jomsurangyard Rd. Besides KFC and Dairy Queen, the food court offers cheap Chinese-Thai dishes (20-35฿) and hybrid pizza crepes (20฿). Purchase food coupons before ordering. (Open daily 10am-9pm.)

Ran Ahaan Jay Con Im, 191/2 Suranaree Rd., serves vegetarian entrees (10-20฿). Open daily 8am-midnight. ❶

Suan Sin, 163 Washasarit Rd. Heading south on Chumphon Rd. behind Thao Suranaree shrine, take a left onto Mahatthai Rd. and then a right onto Washarsarit Rd. Open air storefront serves Isaan specialties like cow-tail soup (65฿), pig's neck salad (40฿), and *yam dua diao un diao,* cooked bull penis in hot sauce. Dishes around 60฿. Open daily 10am-8pm. Next door is **Samram Lap,** which serves similar food outdoors (10am-11pm). ❷

Ton Som, 125-129 Washarasrit Rd. (☎252 275). From Chumphon Rd., take a left onto Mahatthai Rd. and a right onto Washarsarit Rd. Popular Thai and Western food. Spicy shrimp salad with lemongrass 85฿. Open daily 11am-11pm. AmEx/MC/V. ❸

Suan Pak (SPK), 154-158 Chumphon Rd., behind the shrine and to the left, past Dok Som. Sweet cafe serving cakes and an extensive menu (13 pages) of Thai, Chinese, and Western food. Entrees 45-120฿. Open daily 4pm-12:30am. ❷

Cabbages & Condoms (C&C Restaurant), 86/1 Sueb Siri Rd., just past Soi 4 and before the train tracks near Doctor's Guest House. Same food as its Bangkok sibling (p. 115). C&C is a nutritious meal away from the lead-laden air of Khorat. Vegetarian options 55-65฿. "Chicken in herb leaf bikinis" 65฿. Open daily 10am-10pm. ❷

The VFW Cafeteria, adjacent to Siri Hotel on Phoklang Rd. A slice of displaced Americana straight from the silver screen, exemplifying the "bar-and-grill" G.I. hangout in every Vietnam War flick. Cheeseburger 30฿. Fries 10฿. Open daily 8am-9:30pm. ❶

👁 SIGHTS

Khorat's handful of sights can be visited in a single afternoon. A good starting point is the **Thao Suranaree Memorial.** Constructed in 1934, the memorial is a source of identity and inspiration for generations of Khorat citizens. Shaped like a Chinese ship, **Wat Sala Loi's** unique symbolism adds to its appeal. Look for its sign on Mittraphap Rd., at the old moat's northeast corner. Its architecturally acclaimed inner sanctuary symbolizes the passage of the devoted to nirvana. Every Thai city has a sacred pillar from which distances are measured. Khorat's is enshrined at **Wat Phra Narai Maharat** on Prajak Rd., between Assadang and Chompon Rd. inside the city moat. This *wat* contains a sandstone image of the Hindu god Narayana as well as a *shiva linga* (phallus-shaped pillar). The **Mahawirawong Museum,** Khorat's branch of the National Museum, is on Ratchadamnoen Rd., one block past the clock tower from the shrine. Its small collection contains artifacts from the Angkor and Ayutthaya periods. (☎242 958. W-Su 9am-4:30pm. 10฿.)

🎵💺 ENTERTAINMENT AND NIGHTLIFE

The karaoke plague has reached epidemic proportions here. For temporary relief, the **Sima Thani Hotel,** next to TAT, occasionally holds dinner shows of Thai dance. Call ahead for availability. (☎213 100. 7-8pm. Free with *à la carte* dinner, about 250฿.) Performances of *phleng khoraat,* a traditional folk song, sporadically occur next to the clock tower. Lyrics are improvised and the drama depends on the wit of the singer. **Muay Thai** kicks off sporadically at the stadium; inquire at TAT. Khorat also has movie theaters on the sixth floor of Klang Plaza II, with Thai movies for 60฿ (10:30am-6:30pm) and a bowling alley on the eighth floor of the Plaza (40-70฿ per game; M-F 11:30am-1am, Sa-Su 10am-1am) on Mittraphap Rd.

Dance clubs rule the nightlife in Khorat. **Speed,** 191 Assadang Rd., next to the K Stars Hotel, has a full house of dance floors, live music, private karaoke rooms, and a cocktail lounge. Set the mood with some slow dancing (8-11pm), then get down to glittering disco until 2am. (☎248 944. No cover. Karaoke rooms 1000฿ per

NORTHEAST THAILAND

night.) **The Fun Factory,** on Jomsurangyard Rd. across from the Klang Plaza II, also celebrates the great age of disco. There is a one-drink minimum. (Live music. Hip hop dance floor F-Sa. 20+. Beer 80฿. Whiskey 290-1350฿. Open daily 9pm-2am.)

▶ DAYTRIPS FROM KHORAT

DAN KWIAN VILLAGE

From Khorat, follow Chomphon Rd. behind the Thao Suranaree memorial and turn right on Chainarong Rd. Turn left onto Kamhaeng Songkhram Rd., and walk past the vendors. On the right, you should see a small blue-striped bus (#1307; every 30min., 5฿). Indicate destination to the driver. Alternatively, catch the bus from Terminal 2. Disembark when the small road forks into 3 lanes lined with little shops. To return, wait on the left side of the road back to Khorat. When the bus comes, gesticulate wildly (last one at 6pm).

Tiny Dan Kwian Village, 15km southeast of Khorat, was the crossroads for traders traveling in bull-cart caravans between Khorat and Khmer. Villagers have collected the dark clay from the Moon River for years, giving the pottery its distinctive rusty color. The geometric-patterned work is beautiful but heavy and fragile.

PAK THONG CHAI

Take bus #1303 from Khorat's Bus Terminal 1 (every 30min. 8am-4pm, 16฿).

Pak Thong Chai, 32km south of Khorat, was once a traditional silk-producing village, but is now dominated by factories. Two of these, **Matchada,** 118/1 Moo Suebsiri Rd. (☎441 684), and **Radtree,** 442/1 Pak Thong Chai Rd., can arrange free tours through their facilities and allow visitors to observe the silk production cycle. Both factories are open 9am-5pm. Call and arrange ahead of time, as these tours are not a regular offering.

PHIMAI   ☎044

Since the fall of Angkor in 1432, Phimai has morphed from an important cultural center to an idyllic satellite of Khorat, 60km to the southeast. Roosters provide free wake-up calls at dawn in the shadow of Thailand's largest stone ruins, and the town's peaceful day lethargically unfolds where a great city once bustled. At one time, a laterite highway linked Phimai, along with nearby Muang Tham and Phanom Rung, to the Khmer empire's magnificent capital, Angkor Thom, 225km to the south. With only three things to see, all within walking distance of each other, you won't be pressed for time in Phimai.

⊏ TRANSPORTATION. Buses to Phimai depart from Khorat's Bus Terminal 2 (#1305; 1½-2hr., every 30min. 5am-10pm, 34฿). They first drop passengers off at the center of town, once you cross the Moon River. Be sure to get off here, because buses continue on to the **Phimai Town bus station** in a tacky housing development outside of Phimai proper. To get to the center of town from the Phimai Town bus station, take a red *songthaew* (5฿) or take a right from the bus station and walk down Sra Kaew Rd. for 1km. Bus #1305 leaves Phimai for Khorat (every 30min. 5:30am-7pm, 34฿). For those headed north to Khon Kaen, Nong Khai, or Udon Thani, get off at Talad Khae, 10km away from Phimai, and ask someone where to wait. Those moving on to Surin may bypass Khorat and save considerable time by taking a *songthaew* from the Phimai Bus Station to the train station at Hin Dat (30min., 8am, 20฿). From here, catch a Surin-bound train (2hr., 22฿).

▰ PRACTICAL INFORMATION. The Khmer ruins crown the northern end of the town's main thoroughfare, **Chomsudasaget Road.** Here, Chomsudasaget meets

Anantajinda Road, which runs along the front of the park. Services include: the **Thai Military Bank,** 222 Anantajinda Rd., which has an **ATM** (AmEx/Cirrus/MC/V) and exchanges traveler's checks (☎471 334; open M-F 8:30am-3:30pm); a **tourist police** booth (☎341 777) located across from the bank; the **police** pavilion and the compact **night market,** to the right of this intersection in a clock tower on Anantajinda Rd.; **Internet** (30฿ per hr.) at the Old Phimai Guesthouse; and a **post office,** 123 Wonprang Rd. (☎471 342). When facing the gate to the park, take a left onto Anantajinda Rd. Wonprang Rd. is the first right, and the post office is 150m down on the left. (Open M-F 8:30am-4:30pm, Sa-Su 9am-noon.) **Postal Code:** 30110.

WHERE'S THE BE IN BC? You may wonder why many Thai historical markers date the fall of Angkor to the same year as the end of the Vietnam War. Many Thai brochures and historical markers use the traditional Buddhist Era (BE) calendar, marking year 1 as the year of Buddha's death. To convert from Buddhist (BE) to Gregorian calendars (BC), subtract 544 from the BE year.

ACCOMMODATIONS AND FOOD. Phimai boasts three first-rate guesthouses and an excellent restaurant, making overnight stays quite rewarding. ⬛**Old Phimai Guest House ❶,** 214 Moo 1 Chomsudasaget Rd., two and a half blocks down Chomsudasaget from the bus terminal on a small *soi* to the right (look for the sign), has palatial rooms in an airy wooden house overseen by an English-speaking family. (☎471 918. Dorms 80฿; singles 130฿, with A/C 300-350฿; doubles 160฿.) The same family runs the **S+P New Phimai Guest House ❷,** 213 Moo 1 Chomsudasaget Rd., right across the alley. Their cosmopolitan graffiti, created by guests from around the world, keeps boredom at bay. (Bike rental 20฿ per hr. Laundry service 5-15฿. Huge singles 100฿; doubles 160฿.) **Boonsiri Guest House ❸,** 228 Moo 2 Chomsudasaget Rd., across the street from Baitiey Restaurant toward the park, has clean rooms overlooking the second-floor patio and rooftops of Phimai. (☎471 159. Dorms with fan 150฿; singles with A/C 350฿; doubles with A/C 550฿.)

⬛**Baitiey Restaurant ❷,** 246/1 Chomsudasaget Rd., is a block before the *soi* leading to the guesthouses. It doubles as an informal tourist info center, distributes free maps of Phimai, and rents bikes (15฿). The menu features a variety of Thai dishes (35-120฿), but the specialty is *pad mee,* cooked with fresh noodles made in Phimai (30฿). An English menu is available. (☎471 725. Open daily 7am-midnight.)

SIGHTS. Phimai's main attraction is the stately Khmer ruin smack in the middle of town within the ⬛**Prasat Hin Phimai Historical Park.** At its zenith, the Khmer empire covered much of mainland Southeast Asia, and evidence of its power and wealth remains in the hundreds of temples that still dot the region. The central white sandstone tower and surrounding red sandstone and laterite antechambers and walls that remain of the Khmer temple in Phimai were built in the late 11th century in a style similar to Angkor Wat, probably during the reign of Suriyavarman I. Certain architectural traits create the illusion that the 28m central tower is taller than it actually is. Archaeologists went a bit overboard with their "restoration"—hence the abundance of cement and the incongruous plaster ceiling in the central sanctuary. On the right of the stone causeway with *naga* balustrades is a collection of faded sandstone lintels. Although the temple is dedicated to Buddhism, many of the lintels depict Hindu gods and myths or scenes from the epic *Ramayana,* evidence of the Hindu tradition that preceded the spread of Buddhism. (☎471 568. Open daily 7:30am-6pm. 40฿.)

THE LOCAL STORY

COMING OUT ON OTOP

Modernization and economic growth are holy grails for developing countries like Thailand, and it is difficult to argue that the achievement of these goals will not be beneficial to the people of Thailand. Being a "late developer" has its costs and impediments to growth, but it also means that Thailand has been able to observe and learn from the growing pains of those who went before. Too often, modernization and economic growth have brought with them growing class inequality, too-rapid urban growth brought on by a mass exodus from rural areas, and the loss of traditional knowledge, culture, crafts, and ways of life. While Thailand has doubtless already begun to suffer some of these side-effects, it has also begun to take steps in rural areas to ease the transition from an agricultural economy to an industrial one.

One of the most successful programs implemented to help rural areas so far is One Tambon, One Product (OTOP). Using a concept borrowed from a similar program in Japan, OTOP seeks to promote the economic development of Thai villages while preserving each one's unique Thai heritage. OTOP works to achieve these goals (paradoxical in nature, according to some skeptics) by helping villages turn their native raw materials and local skills into export-quality goods that appeal both to Western tourists and foreign markets. The government assists locals in the process of forming a company, helping them learn about production, distribution, markets, and pricing.

[Cont'd on next page...]

The ⬛**Phimai National Museum** (in a white building with a red-tiled roof) is 500m down Songkhran Rd., which runs past the eastern perimeter of the temple complex. Facing the park, take a right onto Anantajinda Rd. and then take the first left. The museum includes an extensive collection of Khmer and Dvaravati art from all over the lower northeast of Thailand, as well as exhibits documenting the social, political, and economic history of the Isaan region. Those who miss the museum's opening hours can explore the pond in front and the outdoor displays of numerous lintels depicting Hindu gods. (☎471 167. Open daily 8:30am-4pm. 40฿.)

For a less cerebral diversion, **Sai Ngam,** the largest banyan tree in Thailand, stands on the banks of the Moon River 2km east of town. It's about a 10min. bike ride or 20-30฿ motorcycle jaunt from town, also on Anantajinda Rd. past the clock tower; stick to the main road and follow the signs. Walking under Sai Ngam's thick green canopy is like entering a J.R.R. Tolkien-inspired netherworld. Wizened old men will read your palm for a few *baht*. At the center, a small pagoda houses the spirit of this 360-year-old miracle. Other attractions include a traditional Isaan house built on stilts and a statue of **Sook Prasat Hin Phimai,** a famous Phimai boxer.

BURIRAM   ☎044

The capital of one of the most populated provinces in the northeast, Buriram is a soundscape of urban Isaan life, where the constant din of motorbike engines and chattering students masks the quiet decay of the surrounding Khmer-era ruins. Buriram serves as a regional transportation hub for northeastern Thailand, and, surprisingly, sports an active nightlife complete with on-the-prowl youth. At night, the pumping beats of Buriram's many dance clubs bring a lively end to a day spent on the city's southern moat listening to the beating wings of dragonflies.

▐ TRANSPORTATION

Trains: Buriram Railway Station (☎ 611 202), across from the clock towers at the end of Romburi Rd. To: **Bangkok** (3-8hr., 10 per day, 57-285฿) via **Khorat** (1½-2½hr., 10 per day, 24-185฿); **Ubon Ratchathani** (2-4hr., 14 per day, 40-291฿).

Buses: (☎ 615 081). Purchase tickets on board the bus. To: **Bangkok** (5hr.; 6 per day 8-9am and 8-10:30pm; 227฿); **Khon Kaen** (5hr., 1 per hr. 4:45am-4:15pm, 109฿); **Khorat** (2hr., every 20-

40min. 4am-5:30pm, 58-80฿); **Surin** (1hr., 8am-6:45pm, 15-20฿); **Ubon Ratchathani** (5hr.; every 30min. 1-5, 7am, 4pm; 45-55฿).

Local Transportation: Tuk-tuks (40-60฿) congregate at the bus station and in the center of town around Romburi Rd. **Motorbikes** (30-40฿) are more common than *tuk-tuks* and are the most convenient way to get around. There are no city buses in Buriram. Any transportation is hard to get at night or when it is raining.

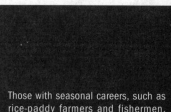 ORIENTATION AND PRACTICAL INFORMATION

Most of the activity in Buriram centers on the train station and **Romburi Road**. The railway station and train tracks bound the city on the northern and western edges. An oval-shaped moat to the east of Romburi Rd. encompasses an area that includes the **post office** and **police station**. Two upscale **hotels** flank the city on the eastern and western edges off **Jira Road**.

Tourist Offices: A lot of information is available at **TAT** in Khorat. The **Buriram Cultural Center** (☎611 221), behind the gates of Rajabhat University on Jira Rd., offers some assistance, but not much English. Exhibits on the province's geological and cultural history are on display. Open M-F 8:30am-7pm, Sa-Su 9am-4pm.

Currency Exchange: Banks line Romburi and Sunthorn Thep Rd. **Bangkok Bank** (☎612 718) is on the corner of Sunthorn Thep and Thani Rds. Open M-F 8:30am-3:30pm. **ATM** AmEx/Cirrus/MC/PLUS/V.

Markets: On Phitak Rd. between Romburi Rd. and Sunthorn Thep Rd.

Police: Buriram Police Station (☎611 234), on Jira Rd., 50m east of Romburi Rd.

Medical Services: Buriram Hospital (☎615 001), on Na Sathanee Rd. Exiting the train station, take a left. The hospital will be on your right.

Internet Access: MP.COM (☎613 206), on Bulamduang Rd. between Honchana and Jira Rd., has Internet access (15฿ per hr.). From the bus station take a left on Bulamduang Rd.; it will be on your right. Open daily 8:30am-10pm.

Post Office: Buriram Post Office (☎611 142) on Lak Maung Rd. From the train station, walk down Romburi Rd. and take a left onto Jira Rd. Walk past the police and make a left onto Lak Muang Rd.; it's 1 block up. Open M-F 8:30am-4:30pm, Sa-Su 9am-noon.

Postal Code: 31000.

Those with seasonal careers, such as rice-paddy farmers and fishermen, are encouraged to spend their off-seasons learning local handicrafts and joining the OTOP company.

OTOP products now include silver jewelry made by the Karen people from hill-tribe villages, ceramic dolls and carved elephants from Chiang Mai, woven bamboo baskets from the Po Thong district, mango wood vases from Si Saket, black onyx jewelry from Kanchanaburi, fresh, canned, frozen, and dried fruits from Chanthaburi, and hundreds of other products from villages all over Thailand.

Whether preserving Thai heritage through adaptation to Western consumer markets is problematic or genius remains to be seen. OTOP companies have seen considerable financial success thus far, and tourists seem to enjoy snatching up one-of-a-kind-but-actually-ubiquitous hand-carved mango wood products in markets all over Thailand. The economic growth of Bangkok, however, continues to outstrip that of the villages, and the uneven balance of power and wealth in urban and rural areas is plain to see. Hand-carved chopstick sets alone will not sustain the needy economies of Thailand's poorest villages.

ACCOMMODATIONS

There is a wide quality gap between Buriram's low-end digs and the classier choices farther out of town. The more convenient—but also sparser—options cluster around the railway station off Niwas Rd.

Thai Hotel, 38/1 Niwas Rd. (☎611 112), diagonally across from the train station on Romburi Rd. (despite mailing address). A few decent rooms close to the action. Singles 180฿, with A/C and hot water 300฿; doubles with A/C 320฿. ❷

Phanompiman, 439 Jira Rd. (☎621 205). From the train station, walk to the end of Romburi Rd. Take a right onto Jira Rd. At the traffic circle walk 200m toward the Rama I Monument. It's the white 5-story building with a magenta awning on the campus of Rajabhat University. Clean rooms usually occupied by professors and university guests. Singles and doubles with TV and A/C 400฿. ❸

Thepnakorn Hotel, 139 Jira Rd. (☎613 401), about 2km east of town. One of the 2 posh hotels in Buriram. Cafe and snooker bar on the premises. Singles and doubles 570฿; suites 700฿; VIP room 1320฿. ❹

Vongthong Hotel, 512/1 Jira Rd. (☎620 860), is the closest guesthouse to the bus station. Take a left onto Bulamduang Rd., the 2nd right onto Honchana Rd. and it's on the right. A real old-world charmer, this place is like an Alpine lodge, only oriental. Standard singles and doubles 540฿; gigantic deluxe rooms—like a Cadillac—800฿. ❹

Grand Hotel, 137 Niwas Rd. (☎611 089). At the end of Romburi Rd., take a left onto Niwas; it is 50m down on the left. Look for the turquoise building. Rooms are decent, but definitely wear sandals into the shower. Singles with fan 210฿; doubles 250฿. ❷

FOOD AND NIGHTLIFE

Buriram has an array of good restaurant choices. **Paladmuang Road,** between Thani, Niwas, and Bulamduang Rds., is loaded with open-air restaurants frequented by locals, most lacking English signs. The day market on **Phitak Road** behind the large pond is overflowing with mangosteens (a deliciously fragrant fruit, 20฿ per kg) and fatty pork leg over rice (25฿). On the left hand side of Paladmuang Rd. 70m south of Niwas Rd. is **Ok, My Milk ❶,** a happy place to enjoy milk products. (☎01 547 9138. Iced milk drinks 15-20฿. Ice cream 10-40฿. Thick toast with flavored jams 7-10฿. Open daily 7:30am-9pm.) **Bamboo Beer Bar ❶,** 14/13 Romburi Rd., is on the corner of Romburi and Thani Rd. Drink a beer while sitting on cushioned bamboo furniture and add your can to the growing wall in back. Popular with the local expat community, this may be the only place in Isaan to flex your English muscles and reconnect with Khaosan Rd. (☎625 577. Western breakfast 85฿. Thai food 25-40฿. Most importantly, large Chang beer 50฿.)

Within Buriram city proper lies a raging nightlife scene in a large parking lot off **Romburi Road,** near the train station. **Speed,** 24/4 Romburi Rd. (☎612 124), is a zany, two-floored, outer space extravaganza. Get cosmic with a live band and float among the glowing stars. (Singha or Heineken 70฿. No cover. Open daily 9pm-2am.) Next door is the **Cybork Discoteque,** surrounded by snooker and other bars.

SIGHTS

Buriram serves as a convenient base for daytrips to the Khmer ruins at Phanom Rung, about 120km south of the city. The most worthwhile sights closer to the city are the **Khao Kradung Park** and the **Kradong Reservoir.** To get to the park, catch a *songthaew* or bus heading toward Prak Hon Chai. The centerpiece of the park is a large white statue of Phra Suphatbohit Buddha, sacred to the Buriram people. It sits atop Khao Kradung, an extinct volcano, and can be reached via a 265m staircase or a concrete road lined with Buddha statues. The reservoir below provides an ideal picnicking spot.

PHANOM RUNG AND MUANG THAM

The ancient Khmer temples of Phanom Rung and Muang Tham are the tourist magnets of lower Isaan. While transportation is not too difficult to find, set out early to avoid getting stranded. From Khorat (Bus Terminal 2) or Surin, catch bus #274 or 98 and get off at Ban Ta-Ko (2hr., 37฿), which is clearly marked as the turn-off for Phanom Rung (16km) and Muang Tham (24km). If you're just going to Phanom Rung, you can catch a songthaew (around 30฿) via Ban Don Nong Nai (which is 6km closer to Phanom Rung), but the return trip is more difficult to arrange, especially during the low season. Alternatively, a bus from Buriram heading to Chanthaburi passes by Ban Don Nong Nai (#522; 1½hr., every hr. 5:30am-2pm, 30฿). From Ban Don Nong Nai, motorcycle taxis will take you to Phanom Rung and back (12km) for 100฿, which includes 1½hr. at the ruins. To go to Muang Tham, 8km farther, is an additional 50฿. This option is recommended during the low season and on weekdays, when transportation is unpredictable. To return to Surin or Khorat, get back to Ban Ta-Ko before 5pm, as buses run less frequently after that. Returning to Ban Ta-Ko by motorbike is an additional 30฿. From Ban Don Nong Nai you can pick up the Buriram-bound bus if you arrive before 2pm. If you want to head to Muang Tham first, take a bus from Buriram to Prak Hon Chai (25฿) and hire a motorbike from there (8km). Another option is to book a full-day tour (380฿, 4-person minimum) to both temples at the Old Phimai Guest House in Phimai. Tours also visit Prasat Hin Khau Praviharn, a magnificent temple just across the Cambodian border (625฿, 4-person minimum).

■**Prasat Hin Khao Phanom Rung Historical Park,** is home to one of the largest surviving Khmer monuments. This majestic temple was built between the 10th and 13th centuries. Standing atop an extinct volcano 383m above sea level, the temple commands dramatic vistas of the surrounding plain, broken in the southeast by the Dongrek Mountains of Cambodia. Inside the complex, three terraced platforms lead up to the robing room, a partially reconstructed stone structure on the right, where the king prepared himself before performing religious ceremonies. The 160m promenade lined with lotus-bud-shaped pillars leads to the main complex and its stairway, guarded by five-headed *nagas* (mythical snakes). The stairs that follow lead to the main temple; at the top is a second bridge and the main gallery. Once you're through the hallway of the gallery, you'll be standing in daylight on the third bridge, facing a portico of the chamber leading to the main sanctuary. The lintel above this entrance, the **Phrai Narai Lintel,** depicts a Hindu creation myth featuring Lord Narayana, an *avatar* (incarnation) of Vishnu. It was once stolen, resurfaced in the Art Institute of Chicago, and returned in 1988. (☎631 746. Open daily 6am-6pm. 40฿. Tourist information center open daily 9am-4pm.)

Dating from the 10th century, **Wat Muang Tham** is situated in a low valley 8km from Phanom Rung. Though fresh from an overhaul at the hands of the Thai Fine Arts Department, Muang Tham cannot match the splendor of Phanom Rung. Still, it provides a detailed picture of a Khmer temple in its present incarnation. (Open daily 7:30am-6pm. 30฿.)

SURIN ☎044

For one week each November, hordes of Thai and *farang* flood Surin to watch dancing, bejeweled, soccer-playing pachyderms on parade in the Surin Elephant roundup. The other 51 weeks of the year, Surin remains a rare stop on itineraries, as most travelers press on to the Mekong River. Their loss is your gain; this peaceful town, boasting one of the niftiest night markets around, is a jumping-off point for the many small Khmer ruins and traditional villages dotting the surrounding countryside. Only 50km from the Cambodian border, Surin reflects the province's unique mixture of Lao, Khmer, Thai, and indigenous Suay cultures.

▐ TRANSPORTATION

Trains: Surin Railway Station (☎511 295), beside the elephant statue on Tanasan Rd. Trains to: **Bangkok** (4½-9hr., 9 per day, 299฿) via **Khorat** (2-3hr., 32-204฿); **Ubon Ratchathani** (3hr., 11 per day, 31-150฿).

Buses: Surin Bus Terminal (☎511 756), on Chit Bam Rung Rd. From the traffic circle, go 1 block east past Mr. Donut, and then 2 blocks to the left; it's on the right. Buses to: **Bangkok** (7-8hr., 10 per day 7:30am-10pm, 280-380฿); **Chiang Mai** (15hr., 6 per day 2:45-10:45pm, 275-685฿); **Khorat** (4hr., about every 30min. 4am-6pm, 64-97฿); **Pattaya** (9hr., 9 per day 9am-10:30pm, 170-300฿); and **Ubon Ratchathani** (4hr., 9 per day 7:30am-9:30pm, 60-110฿) via **Si Saket** (40฿).

Local Transportation: Samlor around town 20-25฿; **tuk-tuk** 30-40฿.

✈ ❓ ORIENTATION AND PRACTICAL INFORMATION

The provincial capital Surin is 452km from Bangkok and is easily reached by bus or train from Bangkok, Khorat, or Ubon Ratchathani. Surin has few English street signs. The main street, **Tanasan Road,** runs north-south. At its north end is the **train station,** which faces an elephant statue. Several blocks down Tanasan Rd. from the train station is a **traffic circle.** To reach the traffic circle from the bus station, exit to the left, pass the *soi* with the sign for the Petchkason Hotel, and take the next right. Tanasan Rd. is the first intersection. One block past the traffic circle on Tanasan is the intersection with **Krung Sri Nai Road,** which offers **day** and **night markets, the post office** (on the right past the traffic circle), **banks,** and a **hotel.**

Tourist Offices: Brochure and Surin map available at TAT in Khorat. The **Surin City Hall** (☎516 075), on Lakmuang Rd., can also offer tourist info. Open M-F 8:30am-3:30pm. Mr. Pirom at **Pirom's House** (p. 215) is an invaluable English-speaking resource.

Currency Exchange: Bangkok Bank, 252 Tanasan Rd. (☎512 013), just past the traffic circle on the right. **24hr. ATM** AmEx/MC/PLUS/V. Open M-F 8:30am-3:30pm. Several other banks and ATMs also lie along Tanasan Rd.

Markets: Day and **night markets** are in the same location along Krung Sri Nai Rd. From the train station, walk 1 block past the traffic circle. The permanent market is on the right; the left side of the street comes to life at dusk.

Police: Surin Police Station (☎511 007), on Lakmuang Rd. Walking from the train station down Tanasan Rd., take a left. It's on the 2nd block on your left.

Pharmacy: Kayang Chelan Pesat, 294 Tanasan Rd. (☎513 055). Near Krung Sri Nai Rd. Open daily 8:30am-9pm.

Medical Services: Ruam Paet, Tesabarn 1 Rd. (☎513 192), a tall building with a blue and white sign. Facing the train station at the traffic circle, turn right; it's after 2nd stoplight on the right. English-speaking doctor. **Surin Hospital** (☎511 757), on Lakmuang Rd. From the traffic circle, head away from the train and take a left; it's on the left.

Internet Access: Internet is available on Krung Sri Nai Rd., between Tesabarn 3 and Tanasan Rd., across from the day market. 15฿ per hr.

Post Office/Telephones: Surin Post Office (☎511 009), on the corner of Tanasan and Tesabarn 1 Rd. at the traffic circle. **Phone** and **fax** available 7am-10pm. Open M-F 8:30am-4:30pm, Sa-Su 9am-noon.

Postal Code: 32000.

IT'S AS EASY AS

one, two, three

uno, dos, tres

un, deux, trois

один, два, три

일 , 이 , 삼

Immerse yourself in a language.

Rosetta Stone® software is hands-down the fastest, easiest way to learn a new language — and that goes for any of the 27 we offer. The reason is our award-winning Dynamic Immersion™ method. Thousands of real-life images and the voices of native speakers teach you faster than you ever thought possible. And you'll amaze yourself at how effortlessly you learn.

Don't force-feed yourself endless grammar exercises and agonizing memory drills. Learn your next language the way you learned your first — the natural way. Order the language of your choice and get free overnight shipping in the United States!

The guaranteed way to learn.

Rosetta Stone will teach you a language faster and easier than other language-learning methods. We guarantee it. If you are not satisfied for any reason, simply return the program within six months for a full refund!

Learn what NASA, the Peace Corps, thousands of schools, and millions around the world already know: Rosetta Stone is the most effective way to learn a new language!

FREE OVERNIGHT SHIPPING
In the United States
(Use promotion code lge005s)
1-800-788-0822
www.RosettaStone.com/lge005s

Available for learning:
Arabic • Chinese • Danish • Dutch • English
French • German • Hebrew • Hindi • Indonesian
Italian • Japanese • Korean • Latin • Pashto
Polish • Portuguese • Russian • Swahili • Swedish
Spanish • Thai • Turkish • Vietnamese • Welsh

Personal Edition. Solutions for Organizations also available.

Meet Dumbo...

he lives in Thailand and loves Pad Thai.

Destinations

Join one of our 1 to 24 week volunteer projects in over 20 countries worldwide that need your help with conservation, care work, media, teaching, building, and health care.

Immersion

Live and work among locals for an experience like no other. Touch a child's life at a Brazilian Youth Outreach Center or feed a recovering penguin in South Africa - the options are endless.

Impact

In Thailand, i-to-i volunteers work with disadvantaged kids, teach life and literacy skills, and support the local economy by helping collect and breed fish - a primary source of income

i-to-i Volunteer Travel

Extraordinary people
Amazing places
Meaningful travel

i-to-i

Request a free brochure
www.i-to-i.com/lg
800.985.7527

⬛ ACCOMMODATIONS

Except for one superb guesthouse, accommodations are uninspiring. During the elephant roundup, rates can soar 50% and finding a room is nearly impossible.

⬛ Pirom's House, 242 Krung Sri Nai Rd. (☎515 140). From the traffic circle head away from the train station on Tanasan Rd. Make a right onto Krung Sri Nai Rd.; it is 2 blocks down when the road bends a sharp left. Beautiful teak-wood house. Mr. Pirom offers several tours in his SUV (from 750฿ per day). At the time of this write-up, Mr. Pirom is in the process of moving to a new location. If his guesthouse on Krung Sri Nai Rd. is empty don't fret. To get to his new one, take a right when exiting the train station, and walk to the end of the road. Take another right over the train tracks and the 1st left onto Muangleng Rd. Look for **Pirom's Guesthouse No. 2** on the left at the end of the dirt driveway. Laundry 5-20฿. Strict 11pm lockout. All rooms have shared baths. Dorms 70฿; singles 100฿; doubles 150฿. ❶

Santhong Hotel (Nid Diew Hotel), 279-281 Tanasan Rd. (☎512 009). From the train station, it's on the left just after the traffic circle, opposite Bangkok Bank. Rustic rooftop rooms with shared toilet 80฿. Singles 150฿, with A/C 330฿; doubles 250-410฿. ❶

New Hotel, 6-8 Tanasan Rd. (☎511 322), outside the train station beside the minimart. It's convenient, but toilets are subpar. Singles 120-160฿; doubles 280฿; A/C rooms 330-500฿. ❷

🍴 FOOD

Surin has some of the best Isaan food around, especially at the market. Try the Hoi Hut, fried river oysters in a crispy batter over bean sprouts, flavored with sweet- and-sour sauce (20-30฿). On opposite sides of Krung Sri Nai Rd., at the intersection of Tesabarn 3, the day and night markets stay open **24hr.** From the train station, take the second left onto Sanitnikhomrat Rd. and **Wai Wan Restaurant ❷,** 44-46 Sanitnikhomrat Rd., is on the right. (☎511 614. *Khao num phrik goong nam sand*—rice topped with shrimp in a red curry coconut milk sauce—40฿. Open daily 8am-10pm.) Inside Surin Plaza, across from the suspension bridge, **Hot Pot: Suki Shabu Restaurant ❹** is a Pan Asian chain serving *dim sum* and hot pot combinations of pork, seafood, and beef for 199-219฿. From the traffic circle, walk west toward the KFC sign; take a right and enter Surin Plaza on the left. (Open daily 11am-9:30pm. AmEx/MC/V.)

👁🎵 SIGHTS AND ENTERTAINMENT

Surin is a pleasant place to relax and enjoy Isaan life, but there aren't many "official" sights unless you're there for the annual **Elephant Roundup,** in mid-November (check with TAT for exact dates). The stars of this two-day festival honoring the national animal are the 200 pachyderms who awe audiences with feats of strength and skill. Highlights include a battle reenactment, a staged "elephant hunt" exhibiting traditional Suay techniques, and a tug of war between man and beast. The finale features a soccer match played by the agile beasts.

For those whose idea of fun involves a good beat and a dance floor, **Sparks** is the place. From the traffic circle, head down Tesabarn Rd. toward the Mr. Donut sign. Take a left at Sirirat Rd. and proceed 300m—look up high for the red sign, next to the Thong Tarin Hotel. Sparks is packed on weekends, when locals gather to get their groove on. (☎514 088. Cover 70฿. Open daily 9pm-2am.)

🔲 DAYTRIP FROM SURIN: SILK WEAVING VILLAGES

To visit the villages solo, walk toward the train station on Tanasan Rd. After the traffic circle, enter the second alley on the left. From here, trucks (approx. every hr. 7-9am) ferry

NORTHEAST THAILAND

visitors the 20km or so. Return early to avoid a wait or an overnight stay in the village. To reach Ban Ta Klang take a Roi Et-bound bus until Km 36. Make sure you tell the bus driver your destination before boarding. There are two bus routes to Roi Et. Transfer to a songthaew or, although Let's Go doesn't recommend it, hitchhike for 22km on the road to the left.

Anyone can visit the local **silk-weaving villages,** but the communication barrier and sometimes-wary villagers make learning the silk-making process difficult for the average traveler. Luckily, Mr. Pirom can act as a go-between. His tours go to places like **Ban Ta Klang,** a Suay village featuring elephants that are trained and kept as pets; an elephant show is held on Saturdays 9:30-11am at the **Elephant Education Center** (200฿.) Contact the Surin Elephant Village (☎01 966 5285) or the Ban Ta Klang headman, Tambon Krapho (☎01 999 1910), for more information.

Other sights include **Ban Khaosinarin,** a group of traditional silk-weaving villages, and numerous Khmer ruins and temples including **Prasat Srikhoraphum,** which are similar to the ruins of Muang Tham near Phimai.

> **BORDER CROSSING: CHONG JIAM/CAMBODIA.** To enter Cambodia, you must have a Cambodian visa; best obtained at the Cambodian embassy in Bangkok (p. 103). The border crossing is about 70km from Surin and only open during the weekends 8am-4pm. Buses from Surin depart 5 per day 5:50am-1:40pm. The crossing opened in 2002 and now welcomes Thais to a Cambodian casino.

SI SAKET   ☎045

Vignettes of daily Isaan life abound in this small provincial capital: customers leave money for the shopkeeper who fell asleep behind his counter, mechanics inadvertently construct obstacle courses of motorbikes, wrenches, and oil cans on the sidewalks, and more people peddle bicycles than motorbikes. This daily routine is briefly interrupted by the **Lamduan festival,** usually held on the first weekend of March, celebrating the blooming season of the province's official flower, and the **Rambutan-Durian Fair** in May or June, where lines of Ram Danawasi dancers don elaborately carved golden headdresses amid fruit stands permeated by the odor of the fragrant fruit. Besides these festivals, the thing to do in Si Saket is to appreciate that there is little to do. Sit back and enjoy.

TRANSPORTATION. Trains leave from the **railway station** (☎611 525), in the center of town on Konrotfai Rd., to: Bangkok (10hr., 6 per day 7:40am-8:20pm, 361-621฿) via Surin (1½hr., 20-126฿) and Khorat (3½hr., 48-171฿); Ubon Ratchathani (45min., 11 per day 3am-7:30pm, 13฿); Surin (9:25am, 2pm); Khorat (7:40am, 6pm) via Surin. Buses depart from Si Saket Bus Terminal (☎612 500) in the south of town. From the train station, walk down Kwangheng Rd. for four blocks, toward the city hall. The bus terminal will be on your right. Buses go to: Bangkok (8-9hr.; 10 per day 6:45am-8pm; 244-475฿); Chiang Mai (15hr., 6 per day 1:35-7:40pm, 350-685฿); Rayong (13hr.; 9 per day 7:40am, 4:50-8:50pm; 220-550฿) via Khorat (5hr., 340฿); Ubon Ratchathani (1½hr.; 5am-noon, 4-6:30pm; 25-160฿). **Samlor** around town cost 10-25฿, **tuk-tuks** cost 20-40฿.

PRACTICAL INFORMATION. The provincial capital of Si Saket is 571km from Bangkok and can be easily reached by bus or train from Bangkok, Khorat, or Ubon Ratchathani. The city is laid out in an irregular grid pattern; the railway runs from the west to east and divides the city in two north-south sections. The main street, **Khunkhan Road,** runs north-south. On its northern end, it changes its name to **Wijit-**

nakhon Road. The **tourist service center, post office,** and **police station** are all located on **Tepa Road,** which runs east-west and intersects Wijitnakhon Rd. in the north. South of the railway, Kwangheng Rd. parallels Khunkhan Rd. until they intersect one block past the bus terminal. Brochures and maps of Si Saket are available at TAT in Khorat. The **Tourist Service Center** (☎611 574), at the intersection of Tepa and Lakmuang Rds., can offer some information about the province. (Limited English. Open M-F 8:30am-4:30pm.) **Bangkok Bank** is on Khunkhan Rd. across from the Kessiri Hotel. (**ATM** AmEx/MC/Plus/V. Open M-F 8:30am-3:30pm.) Several other banks and ATMs also line Khunkhan Rd. Other services include: a **day market** at the intersection of Khunkhan and Konrotfai Rds.; a bustling **night market** along the railway, east of the train station, toward Khunkhan Rd.; the **police station** (☎612 732) on Thepa Rd; several **pharmacies** on Khunkhan Rd.; and **Si Saket Hospital** (☎611 503), at the intersection of Ubon and Kasikam Rd. From Khunkhan Rd. walk past Kwangheng Rd. on Ubon Rd. for 1km.

Pooh Pooh, on a side road between Khunkhan and Kwangheng Rd., offers **Internet** access. From the KFC, walk south on Kwangheng Rd. toward the bus station. The side road will be on your left; look for the Tutsaya sign. (15฿ per hr. Open 9am-midnight.) **CAT** is located on Tepa Rd. between Lakmuang and Paladmonthol Rd. (Open M-F 8:30am-noon and 1-4:30pm.). The **post office** is next door. (Open M-F 8:30am-4:30pm, Sa-Su 9am-noon.) **Postal Code:** 33000.

ACCOMMODATIONS AND FOOD. After the reopening of the Khmer Ruins at Khao Praviharn, the guesthouses in the area expected droves of visitors. Unfortunately, they are still waiting for the influx and many have gone under in the meanwhile. Perhaps the best budget option is the **Thai Siem Thai Hotel ❷**, 147/5 Si Saket Rd., which offers clean rooms not too far from the train station. From the station walk past the traffic circle on Si Saket Rd., and it's on your right before the intersection with Tepa Rd. (☎611 458. Singles 180฿, with A/C 220฿; doubles with A/C and TV 260-280฿.) Another option is the **Prompinam Hotel ❸**, 849/1 Lakmuang Rd. From the train station, cross the train tracks and turn right. It's the five-story white building on the left. Hallways are centered around circular light wells. (☎612 757. Singles and doubles 300฿, with A/C and TV 490฿.) At the **Kessiri Hotel ❹**, 1102-05 Khunkhan Rd., a curious Thai bungalow (which once housed a rooftop swimming pool and restaurant overlooking the city) crowns this 11-story tower. It now lies abandoned, and a similar lack of upkeep is found in some of the rooms. (☎614 006. Singles 550฿; doubles 750฿; suites 1600฿.) Taking the second left from the train station will bring you northeast to the **Santisuk Hotel ❷**, 573 Soi Wat Phra To, with lumpy beds. (☎611 496. Singles 120฿; doubles 150฿.) As a last resort check out the **Si Saket Hotel ❷**, 348 Si Saket Rd. From the train station it's on the first block on the left. A budget option, you get what you pay for (or don't). (☎612 582. Singles 120฿, with fan 200฿; doubles 180฿, with A/C 300฿.)

Most restaurants outside of hotels serve the usual fare of curry or noodles. The night market has some tasty and inexpensive treats; try the *tom yum kung* (spicy prawn and lemon grass soup with mushrooms; 60฿).

SIGHTS AND ENTERTAINMENT. While there's little to do within town, *wats* and waterfalls dot the surrounding landscape. Those who want to have some Khmer ruins all to themselves should visit the numerous, albeit small, ruins such as **Prasart Srakamhaeng Yai.** These 11th-century ruins consist of three towers erected on the same base. The tops of the towers have collapsed, but the lintels over the doorways remain, displaying intricately carved images of Hanuman giving a ring to Sita, or the God Indra riding the Airavata, his elephant. To get here from Si Saket, take a bus or *songthaew* heading to Surin via Uthumpornphisai (26km,

#4186, every hr. 9:30am-4:40pm, 13฿). They are also accessible by train from Uthumpornphisai, where it's 2km from the station. Look for signs to the turnoff.

Huai Chan Falls is a popular waterfall for weekenders. To get there take a bus to Kunhan (49km, every hr. 6am-6pm, 25฿) and then hire a motorcycle taxi (50฿) to take you the other 24km to Huai Chan. The 8m-high **Sum Rong Khiat Falls** (also known as Pisat Falls) is 26km from Kunhan. Hiring a motorbike will cost 100฿ one-way. The waterfalls are best seen during their peak flows (Sept.-Feb.); otherwise, they're timid trickles. Also in Kunhan is **Wat Lan Khuad,** or the Wat of a 1000 Bottles—a product of religious inspiration, grassroots environmentalism, and thousands of beer bottles. After seeing local drunks litter the roadsides with beer bottles, a monk was inspired to build a temple out of them. Local citizens donated their own bottles, emptied of liquid, of course. (Located 50m from town.)

⚑ DAYTRIP FROM SI SAKET: KHAO PHRA WIHAAN NATIONAL PARK. A kilometer over Thailand's contested southern border, one of Thailand's best monuments is actually in Cambodia. Khao Phra Wihaan is a temple complex built by the Angkor kings, probably as a retreat for Hindu priests and a pilgrimage site. The complex rises 800m up a steep grade overlooking the Cambodian plains to the south; its principal chapel is on the peak of a great cliff 600m high.

A contemporary of Angkor Wat, it was built between the 10th and the 12th century by King Rajendravarman. Large steps lead past four pavilions and tourist markets. Although officially opened to the public in 1991, it was closed two years later because of violent hill skirmishes between the Khmer Rouge and the Cambodian government. In August 1998, it was reopened. Today, a ripped-up helicopter pays homage to the last government siege in 1998 that captured the mount. As of April 2000, the region appears to have stabilized; however, **don't stray from the well-trodden path. The area may still contain live land mines.**

During the week, the grounds are empty, and transportation requires some creativity. Whenever you go, start the 98km southern haul early to facilitate a smooth trip. Catch one of the buses or songthaew to Katharalak (1½hr., every hr. 6am-6pm, 25฿) from Warin Chamrap. From Katharalak, tell locals where you want to go. On weekends they may put you on a bus directly to the site, but on weekdays they will direct you to another songthaew that goes to the Phumsalon turn-off (1hr., leaves when full, 15฿). From there, some travelers ignore the motorcycle taxis (round-trip 200฿) and try to hitch a ride for the remaining 10km south on the highway, although *Let's Go* does not recommend hitchhiking. From Ubon (platform #19) buses leave from 5:30am-6pm (30฿) to Kantaralak (2hr.). From Si Saket, Bus #523 leaves for Kantaralak (2hr., every hr. 5am-6pm, 28฿). An infrequent songthaew goes from Si Saket to Phumsalon (31฿), only 10km north of the site. Park open daily 8am-5pm. Admission is 200฿ to enter the part in Thailand and another 200฿ to enter the ruins, which are actually in Cambodia.

UBON RATCHATHANI ☎ 045

The trading and communications hub for the northeast corner of Thailand, Ubon Ratchathani (or simply "Ubon"), attracts few travelers except during the Candle Festival in July. This festival features processions of beeswax serpents, saints, and Buddhas—some larger than the monks that carry them. This "royal city of lotuses," has a fine museum and is famed for its silk and cotton cloth. Those interested in monastic Buddhism can visit many of the region's secluded forest monasteries. Not far downstream, the Moon River flows into the "emerald triangle," where Laos, Cambodia, and Thailand converge in the lush jungle.

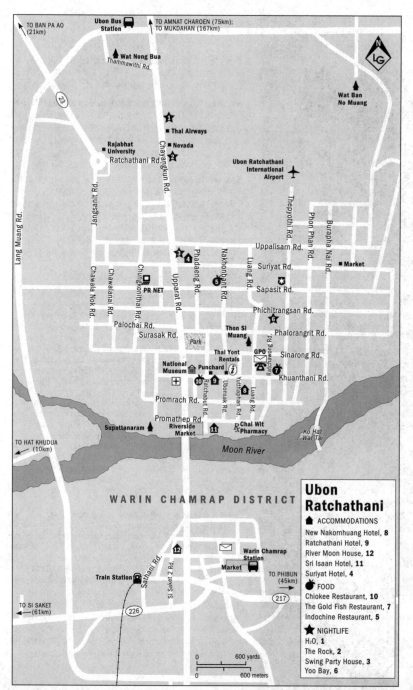

TO BAN PA AO (21km)

Ubon Bus Station

TO AMNAT CHAROEN (75km); TO MUKDAHAN (167km)

Wat Nong Bua
Thammawithi Rd.

Wat Ban No Muang

Rajabhat University
Ratchathani Rd.

Thai Airways

Nevada

Ubon Ratchathani International Airport

Lang Muang Rd.

Chawala Nok Rd.

Chawalanai Rd.

Chungkonthai Rd.

PR NET

Palochai Rd.

Surasak Rd.

Chayangkun Rd.

Upparat Rd.

Phadaeng Rd.

Nakhonbpit Rd.

Luang Rd.

Uppalisarn Rd.

Suriyat Rd.

Sapasit Rd.

Phichitrangsan Rd.

Phalorangrit Rd.

Sinarong Rd.

Khuanthani Rd.

Thepyothi Rd.

Phon Phan Rd.

Burapha Nai Rd.

Market

Park

Thon Si Muang

Thai Yont Rentals

GPO

National Museum

Punchard

Promrach Rd.

Ratchabut Rd.

Ubonsak Rd.

Yuttidphan Rd.

Luang Rd.

Promathep Rd.

Supattanaram

Riverside Market

Chai Wit Pharmacy

Ko Hat Wat Tai

Moon River

TO HAT KHUDUA (10km)

WARIN CHAMRAP DISTRICT

River Moon House

Train Station

Sathani Rd.

Si Saket 2 Rd.

Warin Chamrap Station

Market

TO PHIBUN (45km)

TO SI SAKET (61km)

0   600 yards

0   600 meters

Ubon Ratchathani

ACCOMMODATIONS
New Nakornhuang Hotel, **8**
Ratchathani Hotel, **9**
River Moon House, **12**
Sri Isaan Hotel, **11**
Suriyat Hotel, **4**

FOOD
Chiokee Restaurant, **10**
The Gold Fish Restaurant, **7**
Indochine Restaurant, **5**

NIGHTLIFE
H₂O, **1**
The Rock, **2**
Swing Party House, **3**
Yoo Bay, **6**

THE LOCAL STORY

FOREST RETREAT

Wat Pah Nanachat is unlike any other forest monastery in Thailand. Its name, meaning "International Forest Monastery," refers to its mission to train non-Thai monks—most from Australia, Germany, and the US. English is spoken, although students are expected to learn Thai to obtain an in-depth Buddhist education. Backpackers, hippies, and other "fringe" members of society were drawn to the opportunity the monastic life provides to seek liberation from "unsatisfactoriness" *(dukkha)*, which Buddhists believe to be one of the fundamental characteristics of existence. Recently, the monastery has attracted 20-somethings, academics, and millionaires, reflecting the growing appeal of Buddhism in Western societies.

The *wat* emphasizes individual meditation and communal work in an environment free from distractions. Daily life consists of chanting, meditation, and chores like sweeping and cleaning. Monks wake up at 3am and eat only one meal per day. On the weekly Buddhist holy days *(wan phra)*, the community tries to meditate throughout the evening without lying down. Isolated among acres of trees, life can be directed toward meditation and self-reflection. Social conversation is limited to talking about Dhamma practice, and the few MP3 players are used only to listen to Dhamma talks.

[Cont'd on next page...]

▐ TRANSPORTATION

Readily accessible by air, bus, or train, Ubon is the last stop on the northeastern branch of the national rail network. To go farther east or north, travelers must rely on the sometimes-daunting bus system.

Flights: Ubon Ratchathani International Airport (☎245 612), on Thepyothi Rd. **Thai Airways,** 364 Chayangkun Rd. (☎313 340), 2km north of the river on the right. Open M-F 8am-4pm. Flights to **Bangkok** (2 per day 8:30am, 7:45pm; 1405-2205฿). **Air Asia** also flies to Bangkok (6:45am, 6:25pm; 600฿).

Trains: Railway Station (☎321 276, advance ticketing 321 004), on Sathani Rd., Warin Chamrap District. Buses #2 and 6 run to the station from Upparat Rd. (5฿). Trains go to: **Bangkok** (9-12hr., 6 departures 7:05am-7:15pm, 301-641฿) via **Si Saket** (13-50฿), **Surin** (31-152฿), and **Khorat** (58-313฿). Additional trains head to **Khorat** (6:25am, 4:45pm) via **Si Saket** and **Surin.**

Buses: Ubon has 2 main bus stations.

Ubon bus station (☎316 089), at the far north end of town: take city bus #2, 3, or 11. To: **Bangkok** (10-12hr., every 20-30min. 4am-9:30pm, 267-431฿); **Chiang Mai** (17hr., 2 departures 12:15-6:20pm, 325-685฿) via **Surin** (3hr.; 60-160฿); **Nakhon Phanom** (4½-6hr., 5 departures 6am-2pm, 91-164฿) via **Mukdahan** (2½hr., 9 departures 5:45am-5pm, 60-108฿) and **That Phanom** (3½hr.); **Pattaya** (12hr., 9 departures 6:30am-7:30pm, 215-455฿) via **Khorat** (6hr., 115-340฿); **Udon Thani** (6hr., 6 departures 5:45am-1pm, 140-232฿) via **Khon Kaen** (4hr., 169฿) and **Yasothon** (1hr., 68฿). Tickets for all above buses can be purchased at the kiosks in the terminal. For destinations within the province, buy tickets on the bus. To: **Det Udon** (platform #23, 25, and 27; 6:30am-5pm; 20฿); **Kantaralak** (platform #19; 5:30am-6pm, 30฿); **Khong Chiam** (platform #26, 28; 8, 9am, 12:30, 4:30pm; 30฿); **Na Cha Luai** (platform #25; 9:30, 10:30, 11:30am; 30฿); **Phibun** (platform #22, 24; 6:30am-4:30pm; 25฿). Local tour companies have booths at the bus terminal, making it easy to shop around and compare prices.

Warin Chamrap station, south of the Moon River, has more frequent buses to provincial locations: take *songthaew* #1, 3, 6, or 7 (5฿). Buses to: **Na Cha Luai** (every hr. 10am-1pm, 30฿); **Phibun** (every 20min. 5am-7:40pm, 20฿); **Si Saket** (every 30min. 6am-6pm, 22฿); **Surin** (every 30min. 7am-5pm, 43฿). From Phibun, *songthaew* run to **Chong Mek** (every hr. 6:30am-5:30pm, 25฿) and **Khong Chiam** (every 30min. 8am-4:30pm, 20฿).

Local Transportation: City buses (numbered *songthaew*) run 5am-6pm (5฿). From Upparat Rd., buses #2 and 6 run to the train station and buses #2, 3, and 11 go to the Ubon bus station. Buses #1, 3, and 9 go near the Warin bus station. **Tuk-tuks** and **samlor** roam the streets (up to 60₿ from the Moon River to Sahamit bus station).

Rentals: Thai Yont, 300-316 Khuanthani Rd. (☎243 547), across from the Ratchathani Hotel. Reliable, well maintained and well serviced. **Motorbikes** 300₿ per day. Open M-Sa 8am-5pm, Su 8am-noon. **Ubon Rental Cycle,** 115 Sinarong Rd. (☎242 813), across from the Krungtong Hotel. **Bicycles** 20₿ per hr. 100₿ for 5-24hr. Overnight rental available. Open M-Sa 8am-3pm.

✦ 🎵 ORIENTATION AND PRACTICAL INFORMATION

Ubon's main thoroughfare, **Upparat Road,** stretches north-south for 12km; at its north end it is called **Chayangkun Road.** To the south, it crosses the **Moon River** into the **Warin Chamrap District,** where the train station is. Buses #1, 2, 3, and 6 go there from Ubon proper. North of the river, Upparat Rd. passes the riverside **market** and intersects **Khuanthani Road,** two blocks up. The **hospital** and **museum** are here, and **TAT** is several blocks to the right.

Tourist Offices: TAT, 264/1 Khuanthani Rd. (☎243 770). Turn right onto Khuanthani Rd. at the National Museum; TAT is on the left, 2 blocks down. Free, useful maps. Fluent English spoken. Open daily 8:30am-4:30pm.

Currency Exchange: Bangkok Bank, 13 Ratchabut Rd. (☎262 453). **ATM.** AmEx/MC/Plus/V. Open M-F 8:30am-3:30pm. Banks line Upparat Rd.

Markets: The **riverside market** is a round-the-clock affair. As you cross the bridge into Ubon, the market is immediately to the right of Upparat Rd.

Local Tourist Police: (☎244 941), at the corner of Suriyat and Thepyothi Rd., near the airport. English spoken.

Pharmacy: Chai Wit, 87 Promathep Rd. (☎254 077). From TAT, walk 2 blocks toward the river. Chai Wit is 1 block to the left—look for the yellow and green sign across the street. Open M-F 7am-7:30pm, Sa 7am-noon.

Medical Services: Rom Klao, 123 Upparat Rd. (☎244 658), 2 blocks north on Upparat Rd. From the bridge, it's on the left before Khuanthani Rd. English spoken. Open **24hr.**

Internet Access: One of the fastest and cheapest places to surf the web is **PR Net.Com,** 100/1 Chung Konnithan Rd. From Upparat Rd. with your back towards the river, take a left onto Sapasit Rd. Walk 2 blocks and take a right. 10₿ per hr. Open daily 8am-9pm.

Post Offices/Telephones: GPO, 145 Sinarong Rd. (☎254 001). From the museum, walk past TAT and

Many monks recognize that theirs is a tough life—and locals who worship here do as well. Locals donate food and money to the monastery, perhaps in the hope that in another life, they too will receive the opportunity to free themselves from *dukkha*. It takes 6½ years to be considered a fully trained monk, and another 5 to become a teacher. About half leave the monastery before then.

Because the monastery's primary mission is to train future monks, only a few committed guests are able to stay here, ranging from overnight to several weeks. Guests are expected to participate in most monk activities. Men on longer stays must shave all their facial hair—including their eyebrows—as a sign of their commitment.

Because accommodations are limited, write several weeks in advance to request a stay. Only those who have done meditation retreats before are accepted. Write to "The Guest-monk," Wat Pah Nanachat, Ban Bung Wai, Amphoe Warrin, Ubon Ratchathani, 34310. The monks also welcome visitors with questions and a genuine interest in Buddhism from 10am-noon. The monastery is 12km south of Ubon Ratchathani on the road to Si Saket (Rte. 226). Take a songthaew or Si Saket-bound bus from around Warim Chamrap bus station (7-8₿); ask locals for the right vehicle. The monastery is situated within walls, a ¼km walk from the road. From March to mid-May, the monks are away on retreat.

turn left on Luang Rd. *Poste Restante* behind the office. Open M-F 8:30am-4:30pm, Sa-Su 9am-noon. AmEx/MC/V. **Telephone** service available M-F 8:30am-4:30pm at a 2nd post office at 159-163 Phadaeng Rd., between Suriyat and Sapasit Rd. The **Warim Chamrap** postal branch (☎324 333) is at 88 Tahar Rd.

Postal Code: 34000.

ACCOMMODATIONS

Sri Isaan Hotel, 62 Ratchabut Rd. (☎261 011), across from the riverside market. Clean but small rooms are strung along a mosaic-tiled staircase and bright sky-lit atrium. Not the miser's choice. Laundry service 5-20฿. Singles 550฿; doubles 600฿. ❹

Ratchathani Hotel (☎244 388), on Khuanthani Rd. 1 block over from the National Museum. Bright, clean rooms with tiled floors and comfortable sitting chairs. Singles 330฿, with A/C 500฿; doubles 450฿/650฿. AmEx/MC/V. ❸

River Moon House, 21 Si Saket 2 Rd., Warin Chamrap (☎286 096). Walk straight out from the train station past the golden horse statue and take the 2nd left. It's on your right, across from the fire station. Pan, the owner, gives excellent travel advice and offers 1-day tours to Khao Pravihaan (350฿ plus admission fee). Breakfast 50฿. All rooms have shared baths. Singles 120฿; doubles with twin beds 150฿. ❷

Suriyat Hotel, 302 Suriyat Rd. (☎241 144), walking towards the bus terminal, 30m to the right of Upparat Rd. Not much to look at from the outside, but inside it's pristine. Singles 200฿, with A/C and hot water 400฿; doubles 350฿/450฿. ❷

New Nakornhuang Hotel, 84-88 Yutthaphan Rd. (☎254 768). From TAT, head past the 7-Eleven towards the river. It's on the 1st block to the left. Decent rooms, decent prices. Singles 160฿, with TV 190฿, with A/C 270฿; doubles with fan 240฿, with TV 270฿. ❷

FOOD

The **market,** off Promathep Rd. east of Upparat Rd., serves duck salad, *kuay chap*, and other Isaan and Vietnamese dishes around the clock. At night, **vendors** also gather on Ratchabut Rd. off Khuanthani Rd. near the Ratchathani Hotel.

Chiokee Restaurant, 307 Khuanthani Rd. (☎254 017), diagonally across from the National Museum. Wooden screens open onto the street for a breezy meal. Serves breakfast: porridge with fish (40฿). Most dishes 30-120฿. Open daily 6am-6pm. ❷

Indochine Restaurant (☎254 126), on Sapasit Rd. in between Phadaeng and Nakhonbant Rd. Grilled beef in wild betel leaves 60฿. Banana blossom salad 80฿. *Ban khao* (crispy pancakes filled with minced pork, shrimp, and bean sprouts) 40฿. Open daily 9am-6pm; upstairs lounge 6pm-midnight. ❷

Muang Buffet (Vegetarian Buffet) (☎323 360), at the corner of Prathumthepphakdi and Thetsuban 81 Rd. *Songthaew* often park in front. Run by schoolgirls affiliated with the Ratchathani Asok temple, the restaurant serves as part of a campaign to stop eating meat and live a healthier lifestyle. Meat is replaced with a soybean derivative. All dishes come with brown rice (10-20฿). Sweet herbal teas. Open M-Sa 6am-2pm. ❶

The Gold Fish Restaurant, 142/1-2 Khuanthani Rd. (☎242 394), 50m east of Ratchawong Rd. On the upscale side, serving some nice fish dishes. Thai menu only. Owner speaks English. Steamed catfish with vegetables in *isaan* sauce 120฿. Red ant eggs (in season) 80฿. Most dishes about 60-180฿. Open daily 10:30am-10pm. ❸

SIGHTS

The **Ubon Ratchathani National Museum** is considered one of the country's best.To get there, heading toward the bus terminal, take a right off Upparat Rd. It's on the left, on Khuanthani Rd. The museum documents the region's history and culture and features a 1500-year-old bronze kettle drum, a 9th-century Dvaravati boundary stone, Khmer lintels, and local crafts. (☎ 255 071. Open W-Su 9am-4pm. 30฿.)

Wat Thon Si Muang, on Luang Rd., has one of the best-preserved wooden scripture halls in Thailand. Raised on piers in the center of a pool, the hall was designed to prevent ants and termites from destroying the scriptures. In the convocation hall, wall paintings depict everyday life in the 19th century. Celebrating the Buddhist Lent, the July **Candle Festival** (p. 31) takes place in the park of the same name as the *wat*, encompassing an entire city block north of the National Museum.

Wat Nong Bua, off Thammawithi Rd. near the bus terminal, is a 56m-high replica of the Great *Chedi* of Buddhagaya in India, the site of Buddha's enlightenment. The exterior reliefs depict the four postures of Buddha: birth, achievement of enlightenment, first sermon, and passing. *Songthaew* (city buses) #2 and 3 will drop you off 0.6km away on Chayangkun Rd., while *songthaew* #10 will drop you off closer. **Wat Ban No Muang,** northeast of town, features a modern-style, 50m-tall, three-headed elephant. Pass underneath to view a giant *wihaan* being paddled away in a large sailing vessel. Take *songthaew* #8 to get there.

Two relaxing spots on the Moon River provide diversions for locals. **Ko Hat Wat Tai** is an island surrounded by huts on stilts above the water. Locals order food from restaurants on the island and picnic in the huts during the dry season (Jan.-Apr. 11am-6pm). Take *songthaew* #1 to the end of Khuanthani Rd. and walk toward the river and across the concrete bridge. More highly recommended, although more distant, is **Hat Khudua,** similar to Ko Hat Wat Tai and located 12km west of town. *Songthaew* #9 from Warin Chamrap bus terminal will take you there. (Open 8am-5pm, or depending on demand, as late as midnight.)

🎵 🎭 ENTERTAINMENT AND NIGHTLIFE

Ubon's nightlife is concentrated on Upparat Rd., a few kilometers north of the river. The **Nevada** multiplex, past the Ratchathani intersection on the right, shows the latest action flicks (60฿), but sadly, they are all dubbed into Thai.

Swing Party House, 140/1-2 Chayangkun Rd. (☎ 265 145), between Suriyat and Uppalisarn Rd. Facing the bus station, it's on the right. The best-decorated bar in town. Singha 100฿. Live music nightly at 9:30pm. Open daily 7pm-1am.

The Rock (☎ 280 999), in the basement of the Nevada Hotel on the northern end of Chayangkun Rd. A pumping disco. Large Singha 99฿. No cover. Open daily 9pm-2am.

H₂O, 488/1 Chayangkun Rd. (☎ 280 315), 100m north of the Nevada Hotel. Housed in a glass and metal box, this chic pub is Ubon's epicenter of trendy, with leopard-skinned bar stools and chrome chairs. Jug of Singha 140฿. No cover. Open daily 7pm-2am.

Yoo Bay, on Phichitrangsan Rd. between Thepyothi and Luang Rd. Ubon's most popular discotheque for the younger (20-something) crowd.

🏛 MARKETS

Ubon is famous for silk and *khit*-patterned cotton cloth. Two stores sell clothing made from the area's handwoven cotton. **Maybe Cotton Hut,** 124 Sinarong Rd., is near Ratchawong Rd. (☎ 254 932. Open daily 7:30am-9pm.) For **Peaceland,** 189 Thepyothi Rd., look beneath the bougainvillea. (☎ 244 028. Open daily 10am-8pm.)

Those looking for world-famous Isaan silk should try the **Women's Weaving Cooperative** in the village of **Ban Pa Ao,** 21km north of Ubon on Rte. 23. Ban Pa Ao is a 200-year-old village famous for its bronze and silk wares. Their traditional *mudmee* silk is available in an array of colors and patterns. Prices begin at 650฿ per meter, and run into the thousands. Weavers perform demonstrations on request.

The clothes, mostly women's blouses and skirts, sold in the showroom, start at 450฿. Buses to Yasothon or Roi Et can drop you off if you ask (10฿). For more info, contact the town leader, Apichat Phanngoen (☎313 505). (Open daily 8:30am-6:30pm.) From the main road, the cooperative is 3km east; motorcycle taxis can take you the rest of the way (20฿). To return to Ubon, flag down any bus heading south to the city, or catch a *songthaew* directly from the village (20฿).

For a more general selection of local handicrafts, try ■**Punchard,** 158 Ratchabut Rd., which sells local silk, *mawn khuan* (traditional axe pillows), fish traps, rice containers, and bronze trinkets. Exit and turn right from TAT and then turn right again at the first intersection; it's on the immediate right. (☎243 433; www.punchard.net. Open M-Sa 9am-8pm.)

BORDER CROSSING: CHONG MEK/VANG TAO. Travelers can enter Laos at the village of Chong Mek, 44km from Phibun. From the village of Vang Tao on the Lao side, it is 1hr. to Pakse, an excellent springboard for exploration of southern Laos. Other than the border crossing itself, there is little of interest for travelers here except on Saturday and Sunday, when a market featuring baskets, sarongs, frogs, and military fatigues springs up on both sides of the border. From Ubon, take a bus from the Warin Chamrap station to **Phibun** (1hr., 5am-6pm, 20฿). At the Phibun market, locals can direct you to *songthaew* heading to **Chong Mek** (1¼hr., 7am-5pm, 20฿).

Travelers can purchase a 15-day visa on arrival for $US30, or a heftier 1500฿ (1 passport photo required). 30-day visas are available from the Lao embassy in Bangkok or the consulate in Khon Kaen (3-day processing 1100฿, expedited processing up to 1400฿). Before crossing the border you must officially register your departure from Thailand at the **immigration office,** 30m before the fence on the right. Once in Laos, present visas to immigration, just beyond the border on the right. From Vang Tao, *songthaew* can drive you to **Pakse** (10฿). Border open daily 8:30am-4pm. The Lao entry tax varies, but currently stands at 50฿.

■ DAYTRIPS FROM UBON RATCHATHANI

FOREST MONASTERIES

Wat Pa Nanachat is behind a rice field off the highway to Si Saket, near Bung Wai village. Catch a Si Saket-bound bus or songthaew from Warin Chamrap Station, and ask to get off at Wat Pa Nanachat (13km, 7-8฿). It's located about 500m from the road, inside a walled forested compound. Wat Nong Pa Pong temple is 10km south of Ubon and off the road to Katharalak (ask for directions at Pa Nanachat).

Northeast Thailand is known for meditation. Forest *wats* became the home of *dudtong* (serious and ascetic) monks who keep strict vows—they limit food to one meal per day and ask for alms daily. Members of the Santi Asok sect are only allowed to walk barefoot. Ubon province has accessible monasteries. Visitors should wear proper dress and enter quietly, as silent meditation is often in session.

■**Wat Pa Nanachat** has the unique mission of training non-Thai monks. English is the main language, and those studying meditation and Buddhism are welcome to visit 10am-noon. Serious students may be able to arrange a stay lasting overnight or several weeks, but must write in advance (see **Forest Monastery,** p. 220). The *wat* is a branch of nearby **Wat Nong Pa Pong,** known principally for meditation teacher **Ajahn Chah,** famed for his discipline. Both *wats* have more than 20 acres of forest, providing a pleasant place to spend some time. A major branch of the controversial **Santi Asok** sect resides 6km to the east of town; ask in town for details.

PHU CHONG NAYOI NATIONAL PARK

From Warin, take a bus to Na Cha Luai (every hr. 10am-1pm, 30฿). From Ubon, buses run less frequently (Platform #25; 9:30, 10:30, 11:30am; 130฿). The park is another 15km from Na Cha Luai. You can hire a motorcycle taxi for 120฿ or a songthaew (200฿ round-trip.) Campsites 20฿ per person; bungalows 100฿ per person. Park admission 200฿. Open 6am-6pm. Although TAT states that the area has been de-mined, stay safe and do not venture off well-trodden paths.

Covering 686km² in the Emerald Triangle, this national park stretches through the forested region bordering Thailand, Cambodia, and Laos. Highlights of the park include the **Huay Luang Waterfall** (Bak Taey), which plunges 30m into a basin of emerald green water (3.5km south of headquarters), and **Phu Hin Dang,** a cliff offering views of the two neighboring countries (accessible only by car or motorbike).

KHONG CHIAM   ☎ 045

The tranquil hamlet of Khong Chiam is 60km east of Ubon, at the confluence of the Moon and Mekong Rivers. To local youths it's a provincial backwoods town, but to the metropolis-weary traveler, it's a paradise where the pace of life echoes the somnolent flow of the river.

🖳 TRANSPORTATION. Take a bus from the Warin or Ubon Ratchathani bus station to **Phibun Mangsahan** (platform #22, 24; 1hr., every 30min. 5am-6pm, 20-25฿). From the Phibun market, take a *samlor* to the *songthaew* station on the Moon River (10฿ at most). You can also walk. From the bus stop, head towards the market. Turn right onto Thiboon Rd. and walk 3 long blocks. At the traffic signal, take a left and walk until you reach the river. *Songthaew* are in a parking lot on your right and go to Khong Chiam (45min., every hr., 25฿). A direct bus runs infrequently from Ubon (platform #26, 28; 2hr.; 8, 9am, 12:30, 4:30pm; 50฿). It takes a similar route but doesn't require a bus change. There is also a bus from Khong Chiam to Bangkok (7:30am, 2:30pm; 392฿). If you get stuck in Phibun, **Hotel Phibun ❸,** 65/1 Thiboon Rd., opposite the Thai Farmers Bank, is on the way from the bus stop to the *songthaew* station along the river. This hotel, on the right, has immaculate singles and doubles. (☎441 201. Rooms with fan 200-250฿, with A/C 300-350฿.)

🔽 PRACTICAL INFORMATION. Khong Chiam is a peninsula shaped like a long acute triangle: its two main roads come together in a point as they jut out into the two rivers. **Klaewpradit Road** runs from the market and bus stop straight through the center of town, ending at a *wat*. **Rimkheng Road** runs along the Mekong River parallel to Klaewpradit Rd. Here, a stone tablet identifies Khong Chiam as the easternmost point in Thailand.

Services include: the **immigration office** on Klaewpradit Rd.; Khong Chiam's lone bank, **Krung Thai Bank,** on Klaewpradit Rd., which exchanges currency (☎351 123; open M-F 8:30am-4:30pm); the **police station** (☎351 023), located opposite the stone tablet on Rimkheng Rd.; **Khong Chaem Hospital** (☎351 083 or 351 2888), 1.5km out of town on the Khong Chiam-Phibun Rd; and the **post office,** on Klaewpradit Rd. across from the immigration office, with an **overseas phone.** (☎351 016. Open M-F 8:30am-4:30pm, Sa-Su 9am-noon.) **Postal Code:** 34220.

🛏🍴 ACCOMMODATIONS AND FOOD. Surprisingly, tiny Khong Chiam is packed with comfortable guesthouses. The **🏠Ban Kiang Nam Hotel ❹,** 89 Klaewpradit Rd., is 300m toward the *wat* from the bus station. The Martha Stewart of Khong Chiam, Ms. Yaovaluck Chompoo has created cozy rooms with peach-colored stone tiles, floral curtains, and wicker furniture sets. For the backpacking couple, not your backpacking buddies. (☎351 374. Rooms 600-900฿; 3-room suite 1500฿.)

Arraya Resort ❹, on Pookchamchai Rd., has bungalows situated among small concrete terraced water gardens, a site perhaps more appropriate for a minigolf course than a resort. (☎351 191. Singles and doubles 500-600฿.) The **Mongkhon Guest House ❷**, 595 Klaewpradit Rd., 30m up from the bus station, is newly renovated with shiny new wood and impeccably clean rooms, all with toilet and bath. (☎01 718 3182. Singles 150฿, with A/C 350฿.) The **Ban Rim Khong Resort ❺**, 37 Klaewpradit Rd., across from Ban Kiang Nam, is a micro-estate of small bungalows, some of which overlook the Mekong. The blue-car-peted interiors and tubside rock gardens add to the eclectic mix. (Affordable if you're traveling in a group. A/C bungalows 1000฿.) The **Apple Guest House ❷**, 267 Klaewpradit Rd., past the bank and opposite the post office, is slightly less charming than Mongkhon. Motorbikes are available for 150-200฿ per day. (☎351 160. Singles and doubles 150฿, with A/C 300฿.) The **Khong Chiam Hotel ❷**, 355 Pakumchai Rd., offers lackluster rooms in a green concrete building. Walking away from the bus station on Klaewpradit Rd., take a right at the sign for the hotel, before the Apple Guest House. (☎351 074. Rooms with bath 150฿, with TV 250฿, with A/C 300฿. A few good **restaurants ❷** line Rimkhong Rd. by the river—menus and prices are similar at all of them. (Fried fish 80-200฿. Spicy fish soup 120฿. Fried rice 30฿.

> **⚠ ENDANGERED ANIMALS.** Restaurants in Thailand serve up many varied and delicious meals—but some may contain the meat of endangered animals. Look out for any restaurant serving Mekong Giant Catfish (*Plaa Buek*, p. 331), softshell turtle, barking deer, clouded leopard, and certain species of bear, among other animals (p. 13). Check out the Thailand page of www.anima-linfo.org or www.wwfthai.org for updated information on endangered species and environmental concerns.

◙ SIGHTS. Khong Chiam is known for the *mae nam song si*, or convergence of the "Two-Color" river, an effect created by the different levels of silt suspension from the blue Moon and brown Mekong Rivers. In the dry season, this effect is not as stunning, but the low water level creates a dry mud moonscape from which travelers can almost touch Laos. At the end of Klaewpradit Rd., walking through the temple grounds leads to a pavilion with an excellent view of the two rivers.

About 20km north of Khong Chiam is **Pha Taem National Park,** housing a 200m stretch of prehistoric rock paintings. (☎249 780. Open 6am-6pm. 200฿.) Two kilometers before the cliffs at Sao Chaliang, erosion has created chantral-shaped rock formations. During the high season, two or three *songthaew* may depart to Nawng Pu Poi (15฿). It's a 2km walk from the road. Inquire about departures and private transportation rentals at Apple Guest House. A motorbike can be hired for 100฿ one-way. Once at Pha Taem, it's a 500m walk to the paintings.

Tana Rapids National Park, 3km south of Khong Chiam, is named after a cataract on the Moon River. Accommodations in the park include bungalows (100฿ per person) and campsites (20฿ per person). Tent rental (20฿) is also available. A *tuk-tuk* can be hired one-way from Khong Chiam for 50฿. (☎243 120. Open 6am-6pm. 200฿.) Both parks can be reached via the Mekong by hiring a boat from Khong Chiam to **Pha Taem** (800฿), **Kaeng Tana** (400฿), or **"Two-Color" river** (200฿).

Traveling 17km to Khong Chiam from Phibun will bring you to the village of **Ban Sai Mun** (any *songthaew* from Phibun will drop you off there for 5-7฿), where forging gongs for temples and classical Thai music groups is the major industry. You can contact Mr. Bunrak, a gong maker and seller, at ☎318 181.

MUKDAHAN
☎ 042

Although the 1893 demarcation of the Mekong River as an international boundary politically separated Mukdahan from Savannakhet, Laos, the region remains unified by its culture, food, and lifestyle, as evidenced by the golden baguettes sold in shops and the annual boat races in October enjoyed from both sides of the river. The Indochine market in the center of the city, which sells Chinese goods transported via Laos, and a bridge (expected to open in 2006) spanning the Mekong will further strengthen the economic links between the two sides. The provincial capital is easily walkable and is a convenient border crossing with Savannakhet.

📧 **TRANSPORTATION.** The main **bus station,** 33 Chayangkong Rd. (☎671 478), is 3km away on the side of the highway opposite the town. To walk into town, take a left out of the terminal and a right at Wiwitsurakan Rd., the first major intersection, 500m ahead. Follow this street as it merges to the right. Make a left at Phitak Phanomket Rd. and walk 0.5km into the heart of town. *Tuk-tuks* to the river are 20-40฿. **Buses** run to Bangkok (platform #1; 10-12hr.; 8, 8:30, 8:50am, 2:40pm; every 30min. 3:30-8:30pm; 202-590฿) via Khorat (6hr., 175-243฿). Prices depend on routing. To: Khon Kaen (platform #3; 4½hr., every 30min. 3:30am-4:30pm, 115฿); Nakhon Phanom (platform #8; 2½hr., 6 departures 5am-5pm, 40-56฿); That Phanom (1hr., 22฿); Ubon Ratchathani (platform #2; 2½hr., 10 per day 6:15am-5:20pm, 60-108฿); and Udon Thani (5½hr., 7 per day 8:30am-3:30pm, 93-167฿). With a 30-day Lao visa, obtainable at the Lao embassy in Bangkok or the consulate in Khon Kaen, you can take a **ferry** to Savannakhet. You can also obtain a 14-day visa on arrival for US$30 (p. 228).

📧📧 **ORIENTATION AND PRACTICAL INFORMATION.** The town is laid out on a grid, with streets running roughly parallel (north-south) and perpendicular (east-west) to the Mekong, the town's east border. Along the river bank is **Samron Chaikhong Road,** site of the **Indochine Market,** the *wat,* and the pier. Parallel to Samron Chaikhong, heading from the river, are **Samut Sakdarak (Mukdahan-Domton) Road** and **Phitak Santirad Road.** Perpendicular to these are **Song Nang Sathit Road,** which runs from the pier past the Huanum Hotel to the night market, and, one road south, **Phitak Phanomket Road,** where the **post office** is. The **traffic circle** is located at the intersection of Phitak Phanomket and Phitak Santirad Rd. The **bus terminal** is on the main highway **Chayangkong Road (Route 212),** 3km northwest.

  Thai Farmers Bank, 191 Song Nang Sathit Rd., two blocks up the road from the pier and one block past Huanum Hotel, has a **24hr. ATM** and exchanges currency. (☎611 056. Open M-F 8:30am-3:30pm except holidays. AmEx/MC/V.) Other services include: the **Indochine market,** which sets up every day at the waterfront and sells trinkets like mini disco balls, Buddha images, and dinnerware; the **day market,** off Phitak Phanomket Rd., 500m west of the traffic circle, heading away from the river; the **night market,** four blocks from the river on Song Nang Sathit Rd.; **bike rentals** at the Huanum Hotel (100฿ per day); the **police station** (☎611 333), on Phitak Santirad Rd. between the traffic circle and Song Nang Sathit Rd.; **Huan Hong Osoth Pharmacy,** at 38 Samut Sakdarak Rd., opposite Huanum Hotel (☎612 002; open M-Sa 6am-8pm, Su 6am-noon); **Mukdahan International Hospital** (☎611 983), 1km south of downtown on Samut Sakdarak Rd. past Mukdahan Hotel; **Internet** at 44 Phitak Phanomket Rd., 400m from the traffic circle heading away from the river, past the Ploy Palace Hotel (15฿ per hr.; open daily 9am-11pm); and the **post office,** 18 Phitak Phanomket Rd. (☎611 065. Open M-F 8:30am-4:30pm, Sa-Su 9am-noon.) The **Telekom office** is downstairs. **Lenso** phones accept DC/MC/V and Access AT&T. (☎611 697. Open M-F 8:30am-4:30pm.) **Postal Code:** 49000.

NORTHEAST THAILAND

ACCOMMODATIONS AND FOOD. Saensuk Bungalows ❸, 136 Phitak Santi-rad Rd. Heading towards the river on Phitak Phanomket, take a right on Phitak Santirad Rd.; it's two blocks down on the right with a Thai sign. It offers clean, air-conditioned rooms, with TV, set around a stone parking lot. (☎611 214. Rooms 300-350฿.) **Huanum Hotel ❷**, 36 Samut Sakdarak Rd., is on the corner of Samut Sak-darak and Song Nang Sathit Rd., one block from the pier. It is a labyrinth of stair-cases and fairly clean rooms. The A/C rooms with hot water and TV are cleaner. (☎611 137. Singles 120฿, with bath 220฿, with A/C 280฿; doubles 300฿, with A/C 320฿.) Next to Pith Bakery, **Hong Kong Hotel ❷**, 108 Phithaksantirat Rd., provides clean, worn rooms with firm beds and Western toilets. From the traffic circle fac-ing the river, make a left; it's on the left. (☎611 143. Rooms 160฿.)

The **night market ❶** along Song Nong Sathit Rd. is especially good. Clean and well-organized stalls serve up spicy *som tam* (papaya salad) and *larb sod* (a tangy and very spicy minced pork). *Paw pia thawt* (Vietnamese spring rolls) come *sot* (fresh) or *thawt* (fried). Also, many French-Lao bakeries vend rolls, cakes, eclairs, and more. Packed in single-serving plastic bags, an entire meal totals 20-30฿. **Fore-most Restaurant ❸** is on 74/1 Samut Sakdarak Rd. From Huanum Hotel, walk one block past the pharmacy; it's at the next intersection, diagonally across from the 7-Eleven. It serves the obligatory noodle soup as well as a more substantial Thai and Western meal. (☎612 251. Prawns in hot pot with vermicelli and garlic 150฿. Pine-apple tart 6฿. Other entrees 40-150฿. Open daily 7am-10pm.) The small **Mumsabai Restaurant ❷** has good food. Walking toward the river on Song Nong Sathit Rd., it is on the right one block before the river. (☎633 616. Fried noodles with kale and egg 30฿. Mixed vegetables in oyster sauce 60฿. Vegetables in coconut soup 60฿. Open daily 10am-10pm.) **Pith Bakery ❷**, 703 Phithaksantirat Rd., serves Western breakfasts (35-45฿) and the only brownies this side of the Mekong. The owner speaks English and can offer travel advice. (☎611 990. Open daily 8:30am-9pm.) Next to the bakery, a food stand serves Vietnamese rice flour dumplings.

SIGHTS. A larger-than-life golden Buddha contemplates the Mekong from **Wat Si Mongkan Tai,** on Samron Chaikhong Rd. **Chao Fa Mung Shrine,** far up Song Nang Sathit Rd., houses the city pillar. If you happen to arrive at the end of Buddhist Lent (in late fall), you'll catch boat races on the Mekong.

> **BORDER CROSSING: MUKDAHAN/SAVANNAKHET.** Purchase a 15-day visa on arrival for $US30, or a heftier 1500฿ (1 passport photo required). 30-day visas are available from the Lao embassy in Bangkok or the consulate in Khon Kaen (3-day processing 1100฿, expedited processing up to 1400฿). From Mukdahan, take a **ferry** to Savannakhet. (M-F 7 per day 9am-4:30pm, Sa 6 per day 9am-2:30pm. 50฿ ferry fare, 50฿ surcharge for Sa arriv-als, and 50฿ if only staying one night.) The Lao entry tax varies (currently 50฿).

DAYTRIP FROM MUKDAHAN: MUKDAHAN NATIONAL PARK. Known for its rock formations and caves, **Mukdahan National Park** also boasts prehistoric rock art, wildlife, and cliff-top views of the Mekong. The collection of huge, oddly shaped rocks at the main entrance is the chief crowd-pleaser. The undersides of many overhanging rocks are decorated with now-faded prehistoric paintings. Trail maps are available from the park office at the entrance. Trails are marked in Thai; arrows pointing straight ahead direct hikers along the main 2km hike to the **Buddha Cave Waterfall.** During the dry season, the falls shrink to a trickle. Rickety wooden stairs lead to the **Buddha Cave,** lined with thousands of Buddha images.

The park can be reached from Mukdahan by buses and *songthaew* leaving town on Samut Sakdarak Rd. towards Dontan (Rte. 2034), past Mukdahan Hotel on the right (2 per hr. 6am-6pm, leaves when full; 10-15฿). The entrance is a 15min. walk down a small paved road on the right. (200฿. Camping fee 20฿. Open daily 8am-6pm.)

THAT PHANOM ☎042

Although That Phanom overlooks the Mekong, many travelers would overlook this tranquil town if it was not home to one of Thailand's most sacred pilgrimage sites, Wat That Phanom. Towering nearly 60m, the Lao-style (gem-encrusted, gold-gilded) *chedi* is revered by Thais and Laos alike. This seamless melding of Thai and Lao cultures is mirrored in the presence of both Lao and Vietnamese cuisine. Given That Phanom's pleasing aesthetics and backwater pace of life, it is not surprising that many enchanted travelers linger here longer than planned.

TRANSPORTATION. That Phanom, midway between Nakhon Phanom and Mukdahan, is easily reached from either town by bus or *songthaew* (20฿), which stop along **Chayangkun Road (Highway 212)** and at a small **bus station** (☎547 247) south of town. **Buses** leave for Ubon Ratchathani (3½hr., 14 per day 7:10am-2:30pm, 72-137฿) via Mukdahan (1½hr., 21-38฿) and Udon Thani (5hr., 9 per day 9:30am-6pm, 90-119฿) via Sakhon Nakhon (1½hr., 29-50฿). Several companies run to Bangkok, including government buses (11hr.; 8-9am, frequently 4-6:30pm; 400-620฿). **Thaisgoon Tour,** 158 Chayangkun Rd. (☎541 288), a block from the GPO toward the *wat*, has daily departures to Bangkok (11hr.; 8am, frequently 5-7:30pm; 200-358฿) via Khorat (7hr., 140-245฿). *Songthaew* and buses to Nakhon Phanom (1½hr., every 10min., 20-34฿) leave from a stop 150m north of Thai Military Bank, across from the gas station.

PRACTICAL INFORMATION. Wat That Phanom is on Chayangkun Rd. **Siam Commercial Bank,** 359 Chayangkun Rd., diagonally across from the *wat*, has a **24hr. ATM.** (☎525 784. Open M-F 8:30am-3:30pm. Amex/Cirrus/MC/V.) The **Lao Market,** on the far end of Rimkhong Rd. toward the police station, sells wood products from Laos. (M and Th 6am-noon.) Other services include: the **police station** (☎541 266), in the north end of town on Phanom Phanarak Rd.; the **That Phanom Hospital** (☎541 255), 2km on the highway towards Mukdahan; and **Internet** access, 116 Chayangkun Rd., on the second block before the bus station, on the left. (15฿ per hr. Open daily 8am-10pm.) The **GPO,** 322 Chayangkun Rd., past the bank and songthaew stop, has **international** phones. (☎541 169. Open M-F 8:30am-4:30pm, Sa-Su 9am-noon.) **Postal Code:** 48110.

ACCOMMODATIONS AND FOOD. Accommodations fill during the February festivals. Expansive suites with fridge, TV, and A/C are available at ▨**Kritsada Rimkhong Resort ❹,** 90-93 Rimkhong Rd. From the pier, walk past Niyana toward the Lao market; it's six *sois* on the left, across from the *wat*. (☎540 088; www.geocities.com/ksdresort. Suites 500฿.) Another good choice is **Niyana Guest House ❶,** 110 Moo 14, Rimkhong Rd. From the victory arch, head to the pier and turn left onto Rimkhong. It's on the second *soi* to the left. Niyana serves food and rents bicycles for 40฿ per day. (☎541 450. Singles 100฿; doubles 140฿.) **Rimkhong Bungalow ❸,** 130 Soi Prempoochanee, one *soi* north of Niyana Guest House, is musty and pricey. (☎541 634. Singles 250฿, with A/C 350฿; doubles 300฿/500฿.)

At **food stalls ❶** on Chayangkun Rd., 20฿ buys savory roast chicken, sticky rice, or a bowl of Vietnamese *pho*. Several restaurants line Rimkhong Rd. A good **night market** sets up off Chayangkun Rd., across from the school, and dishes up tantalizing cuisine, like *pad mun sen* (pork and bean vermicelli). Most dishes are 10-20฿. (Open until around 9pm.)

NORTHEAST THAILAND

◙ **SIGHTS. Wat That Phanom** is the most sacred religious structure in northeast Thailand. Legend says it was built to house one of the Buddha's clavicle bones, transported from India. Topped by a 110kg gold spire, the shrine has been restored seven times since its initial construction. The most recent reconstruction occurred in 1978, after heavy rains in 1975 collapsed the 57m *chedi*. The *wat* is surrounded by a cloister housing dozens of golden Buddha images. Depending on whom you ask, it's between 12 and 26 centuries old. At the beginning of February, thousands come to pay their respects during the annual **Phra That Phanom Homage Fair.**

About 15km northwest of That Phanom is the silk-weaving village of **Renu Nakhon.** Travelers can enjoy Isaan music and dance at the **Renu Nakhon Wat,** sporadically performed during the winter and holidays; contact TAT in Nakhon Phanom for more information. Take any Nakhon Phanom-bound *songthaew* to the Renu Nakhon junction 8km north of town; from there, hire a *tuk-tuk*.

NAKHON PHANOM ☎042

Nakhon Phanom, the city of mountains, is named for its view of the jagged green limestone outcroppings across the river in Laos. Indeed, the picturesque vista dominates the city and creates a dramatic backdrop for ordinary life here; around sundown, the riverside promenade comes alive with women sweating to an aerobics workout and young teens gossiping, while the occasional elephant, a light reflector attached to its tail, traces a flashing red line in its wake.

▐ **TRANSPORTATION. Nakhon Phanom Airport** (☎587 444), 15km out of town, has flights to Bangkok (M and Sa 7:30am, Tu-Fr 10:20am, Su 11am, 2455฿). **PBAir** (☎511 265) is on Aphibanuncha Rd. From Fuang Nakhon Rd. with your back to the river, take a left. It's one long block on the right. The **Nakhon Phanom Bus Terminal** (☎513 444), on Piya Rd., is in the southwest corner of town. **Buses** go to Bangkok (11-12hr., 8 per day 7:20am-6pm, 319-635฿); Khon Kaen (4hr., 6 per day 6:10am-4pm, 97-175฿); Mukdahan (2½hr., 13 per day 5:45am-5am, 40-56฿) via That Phanom (1hr., 26-30฿); Sakhon Nakhon (1½hr., every hr. 7am-5pm, 36-50฿); Udon Thani (4½hr., 13 per day 5:15am-3pm; 87-120฿). **Tuk-tuks** hang out near the night market on Apibanbuncha Rd. Getting around town costs about 20฿.

▐ **PRACTICAL INFORMATION.** Two main roads run parallel to the river; smaller roads perpendicular to the river connect the two. **Sunthon Wichit Road** is adjacent to the river and lined with a promenade. From north to south on Sunthon Wichit are TAT, post office, and police station. Farther south, past the intersection with **Fuang Nakhon Road,** is the **clock tower** and the immigration office. **Aphibanuncha Road** runs parallel to Sunthon Wichit. At the end of Fuang Nakhon Rd. is **Piya Road,** where the **bus terminal** is located.

The local **TAT** is one block north of the post office at 184/1 Sunthon Wichit Rd. (☎513 490. Open daily 8:30am-4:30pm.) The **Bangkok Bank,** on Srithep Rd. behind the Indochine market, exchanges currency and has an **ATM.** (☎511 209. Open M-F 8:30am-3:30pm.) Other services include: a **day market** off of Aphibanuncha Rd.; a **night market** on Fuang Nakhon Rd., three blocks inland from the river (opens around 6pm); **Nakhon Phanom Police Station** (☎511 266), on Sunthon Wichit Rd., one long block north of the clock tower; **pharmacy** Sawang Fhama, 478/80 Aphibanuncha Rd., where it intersects with Fuang Nakhon Rd. (☎511 141; open daily 7am-8pm); **Nakhon Phanom Hospital** (☎511 424), on Aphibanuncha Rd., a few blocks north of the intersection with Fuang Nakhon; **overseas calling** at the **CAT** office on Salaklang Rd., two blocks north of the post office on the left (open M-F 8:30am-4:30pm); **Internet Access** (15฿ per hr.) at Cybernet, 37 Sunthon Wichit Rd., 50m off of Fuang Nakhon Rd. (☎513 633; open daily 8:30am-10pm); and **Nakhon**

Phanom Post Office, 341 Sunthon Wichit Rd., next to the police station. (☎512 945. *Poste Restante.* Open M-F 8:30am-4:30pm, Sa-Su 9am-noon.) **Postal Code:** 48000.

▐▐ ACCOMMODATIONS AND FOOD. There isn't really a guesthouse scene in Nakhon Phanom. Generally, accommodations are mid-sized hotels showing signs of age. The hotel heavyweight of Nakhon Phanom—in terms of price and quality— is ▨**Nakhon Phanom River View Hotel ❺,** 9 Nakhon Phanom-That Phanom Rd., about 2km south of town on the road toward That Phanom. (☎522 333. Standard rooms 900฿. Amex/MC/V.) Some rooms at the **Windsor Hotel ❸,** 272 Bamrungmuang Rd., have a view of the Lao mountains. From Aphibanbuncha Rd., walk toward the river on Fuang Nakhon Rd. and take a right; the hotel is on your right. Many of the "renovated" rooms require repairs. (☎511 946. Singles with TV 250฿, with A/C 350฿; doubles with A/C 400฿.) **Grand Hotel ❸,** 2210 Si Thep Rd., is a few blocks south of the clock tower. The A/C rooms are better-kept than the fan rooms. (☎511 526. Singles 180฿, with A/C 320฿; doubles 280฿/380฿.) Beside the clock tower, away from the river, is the **First Hotel ❷,** 16 Si Thep Rd. Built around a volleyball court, the rooms are fairly clean and the toilets are very squat. (☎511 253. Singles and doubles 190฿, with A/C 300฿.)

As in other towns along the Mekong, riverfront restaurants dominate Nakhon Phanom's culinary scene. A few open-air restaurants line Sunthon Wichit Rd. south of the immigration office, and you can always get a 20฿ bowl of noodles at the **night market ❶** on Fuang Nakhon Rd. The **Golden Giant Catfish Restaurant ❷,** 257-261 Sunthon Wichit Rd., is on the riverside beside the clock tower, toward the immigration office. (☎09 421 8491. Most dishes 60-120฿. Open daily 7am-10pm.) Another good choice is the Vietnamese restaurant **Sweet Home ❸,** 281 Buangrungmuang Rd. From Fuang Nakhon Rd. with your back to the river, take a left onto Buangrungmuang Rd. It'll be on your left right before the intersection with Nittayo Rd. Although serving only three dishes, this eatery is famous for its *nam neung*— pork, starfruit, green bananas, garlic, and chilis on rice-paper wrappers, all for 60-100฿. (☎511 654. No English sign. Open daily 9am-4pm.)

◉ ▐ SIGHTS AND ENTERTAINMENT. Wat Okatsribuaban, adjacent to the promenade south of the clock tower, houses two highly revered images of the Buddha. Tourists come to Nakhon Phanom for the view and you can enjoy it, too, as you take relaxing evening strolls along the **riverfront promenade.** And if all this *wat*-hunting and pleasure-strolling has worn you down, recharge with pumping MP3s and an ice-cold Heineken (small 50฿) at the **Duck Pub,** Piya Rd., one block toward the city center from the bus terminal. (No cover. Open daily 8pm-1:30am.)

BORDER CROSSING: NAKHON PHANOM/THA KHAEK. Travelers can purchase a 15-day visa on arrival for $US30, or a heftier 1500฿ (1 passport photo required). 30-day visas are available from the Lao embassy in Bangkok or the consulate in Khon Kaen (3-day processing 1100฿, expedited processing up to 1400฿). Before crossing the border, obtain an exit stamp from the **immigration office** just opposite the Indochine market on Sunthon Wichit Rd. (☎511 235. Open M-F 8:30am-4:30pm.) A **boat** behind the office shuttles passengers to Tha Khaek (14 per day 8am-4pm, 60฿). The Lao entry tax varies, but currently stands at 50฿.

SAKHON NAKHON ☎042

Marking the entrance to Sakhon Nakhon is the city shrine, a giant bowl of golden *naga* (mythical snake) heads above a small pond. This shrine is meant to symbol-

OCCUPATION: FOREIGNER'S WIFE

Try asking any three-year-old girl in a rural village what she would like to be when she grows up, and you would be surprised to hear how many of them reply *mia farang* ("foreigner's wife")," states Adul Jankaew, headman of Ban Nonngarm village in Udon Thani province. As in many Isaan villages, foreign marriage has become an aspiration for young girls. "[Parents] teach their kids that if someone asks them about what they want with their future, they should reply *mia farang*." As a ninth-grader succinctly puts it: "Why not marry a foreigner? It's good money."

Although Thai-*farang* marriages often carry a social stigma, in parts of the northeast where many *mia farang* come from this once-taboo subject is becoming an accepted social norm. In Ban Nonngarm, 25 of the 180 families have *farang* among their in-laws.

"[Mia farang] are mostly typical Isaan women, rather dark skin, quite strong and healthy, and not the type to attract typical Thai men," says Decha Vanichvarod, director of the National Economic and Social Development Board's northeastern division. The organization's February 2004 report named economic security as the main reason for marrying, or in many cases, remarrying. Nearly 80% of the 15,284 *mia farang* interviewed had formerly been married to Thai...

[Cont'd on next page...]

ize an ancient mythical war against the *naga* who turned the city into water, thereby forcing its relocation. Now located near the shores of Nong Han lake, the largest lake in northeastern Thailand, the city's crooked *sois* have survived despite the implementation of wide-avenued—albeit rather warped—city planning. The industrial cousin of rice paddies and thatched roofs, the city is a marketplace for all sorts of mechanical beasts of burden. Nonetheless, home to the revered Buddhist shrine of Phra That Choeng Chum and the royal residence Phu Phan Raja Nivej, it is a pleasant stop between Nakhon Phanom and Udon Thani.

TRANSPORTATION. Sakhon Nakhon Airport (☎ 713 919), 6km northwest of town, has flights to Bangkok (10am, 2140฿). **PB Air,** 399 Kumuang Rd., inside the Majestic Hotel, also has flights to Bangkok (1¼hr., 2295฿) daily. (☎ 715 245. Open M-F 8am-5pm.) **Sakhon Nakhon Bus Terminal** (☎ 712 860) is at the southern end of Ratpatana Rd. From the post office, take a left onto Ratpatana Rd.; the terminal is about 1km down on the left. **Buses** run to: Bangkok (11hr., 6 per day 8:30am-7:15pm, 200-420฿) via Maha Sarakham (3½hr., 84฿); Kalasin (2½hr., 8 per day 7:30am-3:30pm, 45-63฿); Khon Kaen (3½hr.; 8, 9, 11am, 5:30pm; 69-125฿); Nakhon Phanom (1½hr., 10 per day 8:30am-6pm, 35-50฿); and Udon Thani (2½hr., 25 per day 5am-6:30pm, 60-80฿). **Tuk-tuks** are hard to find, but **samlor** are everywhere and will take you around town (20-40฿).

ORIENTATION AND PRACTICAL INFORMATION. Sakhon Nakhon is 647km from Bangkok and 93km from the Mekong River. Most buses traveling from the northeastern edge of Thailand will pass through the city on their way to Bangkok in the south or Udon Thani in the west. The streets are laid out in a rebellious grid with twisted connecting *sois* that add character as well as confusion. The western border of town is marked by **Ratpatana Road,** with the bus station at its southern end. To the north, **Charoenmuang Road** runs east-west, with the post office at its western end; a few hotels line this street. **Sookkasem Road** connects these two roads and forms the eastern boundary, making a truncated trapezoid within which most of the city clusters.

Services include: **Bangkok Bank,** 1324/20 Sookkasem Rd., at the intersection with Premprida Rd., with a currency exchange and **24hr. ATM** (☎ 711 501; open M-F 8:30am-3:30pm); a **day market,** off of Sookkasem Rd. west of the bus station; a **night market,** across from the Majestic Hotel, down Kumuang Rd.; the **Sakhon Nakhon Police Station,** 75 Jaiphasook

Rd. (☎716 409), two blocks north of the traffic circle; **Sakhon Nakhon Hospital** (☎711 615) on Charoenmuang Rd. east of the traffic circle; the **pharmacy**, 1891/2 Sookkasem Rd., near the night market (☎732 678; open daily 8am-9pm); **Internet access**, across from the Sakhon shopping plaza, off of Robmuang Rd., between Premprida and Sookkasem Rd. (15฿ per hr.; open daily 8:30am-midnight); and the Sakhon Nakhon **post office**, 224 Charoenmuang Rd., at the intersection with Ratpatana Rd. (☎711 049. *Poste Restante.* Open M-F 8:30am-4:30pm, Sa-Su 9am-noon.) **Postal Code:** 47000.

⌂◨ ACCOMMODATIONS AND FOOD. The nicest hotel in town is **The Majestic Hotel (M.J.)** ➍, 399 Kumuang Rd., off Sookkasem Rd. near the market. (☎733 771. Breakfast included. Rooms 540฿; superior 840฿.) Near the intersection with Robmuang Rd., the **Dusit Hotel** ➌, 1784 Yuwapatana Rd., has economy rooms with hot water, A/C, and TV. The rooms are well kept and there's access to a swimming pool, but don't be deceived by the luxurious lobby; most rooms have not been renovated. (☎711 198. Singles and doubles 350฿. MC/V.) The **Petchsakol Hotel** ➌, 448/1 Sookkasem Rd., at the intersection with Mankhalai Rd., may not be as well kept as some of the hotels in Sakhon Nakhon, but it certainly has character. The hallways are covered in pebbled mosaics, while rooms are plastered with floor-to-ceiling posters of pastoral scenes. All rooms have hot water, A/C, TV, and fridge. (Rooms 350฿.) **Chareonsook Hotel** ➋, 635 Charoenmuang Rd., at the intersection with Jaiphasook Rd., has clean and spacious rooms, but the baths are slightly less appealing. (☎712 916. Singles 150฿, with A/C 200฿, with TV 250฿; doubles 200฿/300฿/350฿.) A slight step down the ladder from the Chareonsook Hotel, **Kusuma Hotel** ➋ is on 316/1-2 Charoenmuang Rd., two blocks past the traffic circle toward the post office. (☎711 112. Singles 150฿, with A/C 250฿.)

For a good steak, check out **Tongdee Steak House** ➋, 1310 Sookkasem Rd., which offers large steaks for 220-450฿ in an intimate setting. (☎711 817. Thai dishes 60-100฿. Open daily 10:30am-2:30pm and 5-9pm.) Across from the bus station, **Green Corner Restaurant** ➋, 1773 Ratpatana Rd., is a family restaurant serving breakfast (100฿), Isaan salads (75-95฿), rice dishes (30-50฿), and desserts. (☎711 073. Mao berry juice 30฿. Open daily 7am-10pm.) North of Wat Jaeng, head to **Willy Nam Nueng** ➊, 1301/6 Sookkasem Rd., for 20฿ sweet-and-spicy cold Vietnamese noodles. (☎731 120. Pork spring rolls 88฿. Open daily 7am-8pm.) A superb noodle and rice joint on Jaipha-

men. The women send an average of 8000฿ a month back to their families, amounting to an annual sum of 1.4 billion *baht* in foreign currency, or 6% of the region's GDP.

Some governors also recognized the economic benefits of these unions. Nopporn Janthornthong, governor of Roi Et province, established the *Mae Ban Ruam Ja* ("Housewives Come Together" Club, a group of *mia farang* who promote local products abroad, as well as encourage tourism to Isaan among their husbands' family and friends. "These women have been viewed in a negative light for too long...they bring in foreign currency and have boosted the province's economy for decades. Why shouldn't they be recognized positively?"

Despite this recognition by the local government, many *farang* husbands feel that it has done little to deal with the substantive issues concerning official recognition. Currently, a foreign husband cannot inherit his Thai wife's property. Others find that the recent governmental recognition simply reinforces the stereotype that these marriages are simply about money, and glosses over other reasons Thai women want to marry *farang*, such as the tendency for wealthy Thai males to womanize, gamble, and drink. Prasit Boonchoob, the headman of Ban Jaan, said that he recognizes that *farang* often take good care of their wives. He says, "If I was still single now, I don't think I could get a wife from this village."

sook Rd. next to the Chareonsook Hotel, **Clearwon ❶** serves a generous portion of noodles with pork strips for 20฿. (Open daily 8am-7pm.) Outside Wat Phra That Choeng Chum on Charoenmuang Rd. are a few 50-gallon drums of red-hot embers grilling up whole salted catfish (30฿). **Pang Pong ❷**, 1658/5 Premprida Rd., north of Robmuang Rd., serves frothy milkshakes to cool the soul and dry the sweat. (☎01 262 1444. Shakes 10-20฿. Open daily 10am-10pm.)

🔆 **SIGHTS. Wat Phra That Choeng Chum** is Sakhon Nakhon's most sacred shrine. Located on Reuang Sawat Rd. at the intersection with Charoenmuang Rd., it houses a 24m gold and white Lao-style square *chedi*. The annual **wax castle procession**, featuring a collection of miniature beeswax Buddhist temples and shrines, celebrates the end of Buddhist Lent (usually in mid-October) and takes place at the *wat*. Behind the *wat* is the Somdej Phra Srinakarin's **garden**, made in honor of the king's mother. It's located on the shores of **Nong Han Lake**. Unfortunately, the lake is infested with liver flukes, freshwater parasites that infect fish and treat human skin as if it were an amusement park. **Don't swim in the lake, and don't eat undercooked fish, especially in Sakhon Nakhon.**

🎵 **NIGHTLIFE.** Several open-air bars line Tor Patana Rd., off of Ratpatana Rd., a local favorite being **Suan Rak**. (Small Singha 50฿. Open daily noon-midnight.) Next door, **Golden Pond** offers daily live rock and pop bands starting at 10:30pm. A **cinema** is located on Premprida Rd., between Sookkasem and Robmuang Rd.

🔁 **DAYTRIP FROM SAKHON NAKHON: PHU PHAAN NATIONAL PARK.** Once a hideout for communist guerilla forces in the 1970s, the 645km² of low-lying mountains and forests are now home to deer and monkeys, as well as the occasional black bear and elephant. While there are only a few short hiking trails, the park is a respite from the dusty Isaan towns. (30฿ camping fee; 50฿ tent rental. Bungalows 500-600฿.) The incomplete Khmer sanctuary of **Phra Thad Phu Phek**, located on a hill 544m high, offers one of the best viewpoints in the park. The **park headquarters** is located 25km from Sakhon Nakhon on Rte. 213 to Kalasin. (☎703 044. Open daily 8am-6am.) Most of the small waterfalls and viewpoints are only 3km off the road. To get to the park from Sakhon Nakhon, take an Udon-bound bus for 15km to Nong Mek. From Nong Mek, it's another 14km walk along the road. Although *Let's Go* does not recommend hitchhiking, some travelers do so along this road.

UDON THANI ☎042

Home to a six-digit population, Udon Thani is one the most prosperous cities in the northeast and Isaan's chief agricultural, commercial, and transportation center. The city was the site of a US Air Force base during the Vietnam War, and the American presence can still be felt in its Western restaurants and expatriate community. Also, don't miss Ban Chiang's UNESCO World Heritage Site.

📋 **TRANSPORTATION**

Flights: Udon Thani Airport (☎246 567), on the Udon Thani-Loei Hwy., 5km southwest of town. **Air Asia** (☎02 515 9999), flies to **Bangkok** (3:45, 8:20pm; 459-850฿). Open daily 8am-9pm. **Thai Airways,** 60 Makkhaeng Rd. (☎243 222), also has flights to **Bangkok** (8:20am, 2:45, 8:25pm; 1890฿). Open M-F 8-11:30am and 1-4:30pm.

Trains: Train station (☎222 061), at the east end of Prajak Rd. Booking office open daily 6am-8pm. To: **Bangkok** (10-11hr.; 8:16am, 6:40, 8:03pm; 175฿-1077฿) via **Khon Kaen** (3hr., 25-50฿); **Nong Khai** (1hr., 7 per day 5am-8:50pm, 11฿).

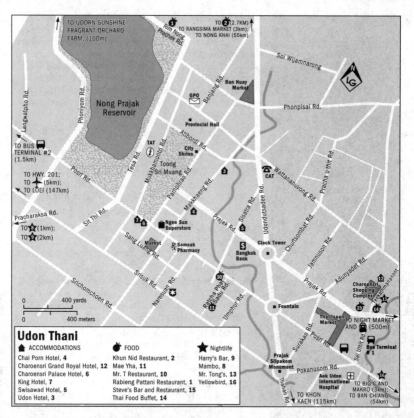

Udon Thani

▲ ACCOMMODATIONS	● FOOD	★ Nightlife
Chai Porn Hotel, **4**	Khun Nid Restaurant, **2**	Harry's Bar, **9**
Charoensri Grand Royal Hotel, **12**	Mae Yha, **11**	Mambo, **8**
Charoensri Palace Hotel, **6**	Mr. T Restaurant, **10**	Mr. Tong's, **13**
King Hotel, **7**	Rabieng Pattani Restaurant, **1**	Yellowbird, **16**
Swisawad Hotel, **5**	Steve's Bar and Restaurant, **15**	
Udon Hotel, **3**	Thai Food Buffet, **14**	

Buses: Buses to **Ban Phu** (1½hr., 20 per day 6:30am-5:30pm, 25฿) leave from Rangsima Market, as do buses to **Nong Khai** (every 20min. 5:20am-8pm).

Bus terminal #1 (☎222 916), near Charoensri Shopping Complex off of Sai Uthit Rd. To: **Ban Chiang/Sakhon Nakhon** (#230; 3hr., every 30min. 4am-7pm, 58-80฿); **Bangkok** (#407; 9-10hr., every hr. 6am-11pm, 179-500฿) via **Khorat** (4½hr., 102-184฿); **Khon Kaen** (2hr., every 30min. 7am-5pm, 44-79฿); **Ubon Ratchathani** (#268; 6hr., 8 per day 5:15am-1:15pm, 141-230฿) via **Mukdahan** (4hr., 91-167฿).

Bus terminal #2 (☎247 788), 2km west of town on the ring road, has northbound buses to: **Chiang Mai** (11hr.; 8:15, 10:15am, 7, 8:30pm; 300-540฿); **Loei** (#220; 3½hr., every hr. 4am-5pm, 55฿); **Nong Khai** (#221; 1hr., every hr. 5:45am-3:45pm, 21฿).

Local Transportation: Songthaew #7 runs between bus terminals #1 and #2 as well as TAT (5฿); #6 along Udondutsadee Rd. from the fountain, north to Rangsima Market and bus station #2; #14 from the train station to TAT. Free *songthaew* route maps available from TAT. Plenty of **samlor** (20-30฿) and **tuk-tuk** (20-50฿) run around town.

✖ 🛈 ORIENTATION AND PRACTICAL INFORMATION

Udon Thani, 562km northeast of Bangkok, lies between Khon Kaen and Nong Khai along the railroad line and **Friendship Highway**. Navigating the city requires a decent map, flexibility in interpreting street signs, and an eternal awareness of the **Nong**

THE BIG SPLURGE

RIDING IN STYLE

From the stretch *samlor krueng* to the lopsided *samlor gai nai*, motorized transportation in Thailand has developed many regional variations. Although they are commonly known countrywide as *tuk-tuks*, for the chirping sound made by their exhaust pipes, in Udon Thani these road critters are also known by another name—Skylabs. Udon Thani is home to the company that started it all, Udon Ake Panich, now the largest Skylab factory in the northeast.

In 1978, Mr. Narong thought of attaching a motorcycle engine on a *amlor* frame. Inspired by the soaring achievement of the first US space station (hence their name), Narong saw his Skylabs as revolutionizing transportation in the northeast. Previously, most people in Isaan used bicycles and traditional *samlor*, or, for bulkier cargoes, ox-drawn carts and pickup trucks. The Skylab introduced a lighter, more affordable vehicle for mid-weight cargoes.

Despite the *samlor's* prevalence in cities, most of Udon Aek Panch's customers are farmers, who purchase Skylabs for personal use. Customers aren't limited to Thais, however. Two Germans exported their Skylab after they had it outfitted with a mobile coffee-shop unit. Another *farang* had a 550cc engine (the same as a pickup truck) attached to his to carry larger loads and to travel to mountainous parts of the country.

[Cont'd on next page...]

Prajak Reservoir, a large park on the town's west side and a good landmark. **Prajaksinlapacom Road** (commonly known as Prajak Rd.), **Posri Road,** and **Srisuk Road** run east-west. Each road sports a traffic circle where it diagonally intersects **Udondutsadee Road.** Away from the reservoir, Prajak Rd. ends at the **train station** near **bus terminal #1.** The **airport** and **bus terminal #2** are on the far side of the reservoir, west of the town center.

Tourist Office: TAT, 16/5 Mukkhamontri Rd. (☎325 406, ext. 27), at the edge of the reservoir. Look for the back door on Tesa Rd. Open daily 8:30am-4:30pm.

Currency Exchange: Bangkok Bank, 154 Prajak Rd. (☎221 505). Open M-F 8:30am-3:30pm; currency exchange open daily 8:30am-5pm. **24hr. ATM.**

Local Tourist Police: (☎240 616), in front of TAT.

Police: (☎328 515), at Srisuk and Naresuan Rd.

Pharmacy: Somsak, 194 Posri Rd. (☎222 478). Very well-stocked pharmacy carries gauzes and sports braces. Open daily 7am-8pm.

Medical Services: Aek Udon International Hospital, 555/5 Posri Rd. (☎342 555). One of the best hospitals in the northeast. English-speaking doctors. **24hr. pharmacy.** AmEx/MC/V.

Telephones: CAT, 108/2 Udondutsadee Rd. (☎222 805). North of the clock tower before Wattananuvong Rd. **Lenso international** phone. Open M-F 8:30am-4:30pm.

Internet Access: On virtually any street but Posri Rd. for 10-30฿ per hr. Try the nameless **Internet shop** at 56 Phonphisai Rd., near the Ban Huay market across the stream.10฿ per hr. Open daily 8am-midnight.

Post Office: GPO, 2 Wattananuvong Rd. (☎222 304), behind the provincial wall. *Poste Restante.* Open M-F 8:30am-4:30pm, Sa-Su 9am-noon.

Postal code: 41000.

ACCOMMODATIONS

If you're looking for a nice room at a good price, you've come to the wrong town. However, a number of hotels do exist and if you have the *baht*, luxury is just around the corner.

Charoensri Grand Royal Hotel, 277/1 Prajak Rd. (☎343 555), behind the Charoensri Shopping Complex. Nothing gritty or budget here; this is Udon's most luxurious hotel. Bar, garden, pool, gym. Breakfast included. Singles or doubles 1100฿. ⑤

Udon Hotel, 81-89 Makkhaeng Rd. (☎248 160). A good value with those little luxuries—A/C, hot water, tub, TV. Breakfast included. Singles in old wing 460฿, new wing 500฿; doubles 500฿/550฿. ❸

Charoensri Palace Hotel, 60 Posri Rd. (☎242 611), at the corner with Pamphrao Rd. Good choice in the semi-budget range, especially if you like bright red carpets. Singles or doubles 300฿, with fridge 360฿; VIP 600฿. ❸

King Hotel, 57 Posri Rd. (☎221 634), set back from the street on the same block as Charoensri Palace Hotel. Basic rooms on a stark corridor. Car park on the 1st floor; you sleep on the 2nd. Singles 190฿, with A/C 220฿; doubles 230฿/270฿. ❷

Srisawad Hotel, 123 Prajak Rd. (☎243 586), set back from the road, across from Bangkok Bank. Cheap basic rooms. Singles and doubles 160฿, with A/C 250฿. ❷

Chai Porn Hotel, 209-211 Makkhaeng Rd. (☎222 144), next to Mandarin Restaurant. Despite its name and appearance, Porn is not a house of ill repute. Communal TV room. Tidy singles 150฿, with A/C 200฿; doubles 200฿/250฿. ❷

◪ FOOD

Khun Nid Restaurant, 64 Udondutsadee Rd. (☎246 128). From Ban Huay market, walk 2km north toward Rangsima Market. After the overpass, take the 2nd left. Walk 700m past the *wat* on your right and a sign will direct you to the restaurant on your left. Locals praise Mr. Srichan's variety of Isaan food. *Miang gai* (stewed chicken served with raw green vegetables, herbs, garlic, and insects) 200฿. Seasonal dishes include *gaeng het kong* (stewed wild mushrooms with chilis) or *mok luuk aud* (tadpole souffle wrapped in banana leaves; 60฿). Open daily 9am-10pm. ❷

Mae Yha, 81 Ratcha Phat Sadu Rd. (☎223 889), 4 blocks south of Posri Rd. Walking toward the reservoir from the fountain, take the 2nd left; it's on the 2nd block on the left. Colossal local superstar. A multistory family restaurant bursting at the seams with a giant menu and yummy desserts. Seven-scoop sundae 75฿. Thai, Chinese, and Western food 40-150฿. Open daily 9:59am-10:59pm, sharp. V. ❷

Rabieng Pattani Restaurant, 53/1 Rim Nong Prachak (☎241 515). From Wattananuvong Rd., make a right on the path adjacent to the reservoir. Out of the way, but worth it. A local favorite with fabulous seafood (85-150฿). Open daily 9am-11pm. MC/V. ❸

Steve's Bar and Restaurant, 254/26 Prajak Rd. (☎244 523), about 30m east of the traffic light at Teekathmananont Rd. A British affair—cricket on the telly and proper pub food. Steak and kidney pudding

Despite its name, the Skylab Chopper, outfitted with 100-150cc engines, can barely lift off at its maximum speed of 60-70km per hr. (The smaller engines get about 40km per liter and the larger 35km.) If you want a fuel gauge, or any indication of what gear you're in, the next step up is the *Sing Dum* (Black Tiger), which is built from all new parts (Skylab Choppers are built from some Japanese used parts). But if you want the power of an automobile without the frame and the cost, there's the Jumbo, outfitted with a Daihatsu engine. Unlike the other Skylabs, it can go in reverse and up steep hills.

If you're looking for luxury, you can have your *tuk-tuk* custom-made. However, in your average Skylab, style choices are limited. Fuel tanks come in red, silver, blue, and gold, while the bench cushions on the back are in bright reds, yellows, and blues. While Skylabs are spray-painted with pastoral scenes of huts and rice fields, those who don't want to be mistaken for an ice cream truck or amusement park ride gone off the tracks can request a custom color palette. So forget your notions of "sport" in a utility vehicle and drive off in style with the Skylab.

Udon Ake Panich. 117/2-4 Prajak Rd. (☎242 290). Open M-Sa 7:30am-5pm, Su 7:30am-1pm. Skylabs with 110cc engines go for about 50,000฿ (US$1250).

150฿. Fish and chips 100฿. Steaks 180-220฿. Open daily 8am-11pm. ❸

Mr. T Restaurant, 254/7 Posri Rd. (☎327 506), at Sisatra Rd. This restaurant, bar, and coffee shop has a mellow atmosphere and acoustic guitar in the evenings. Breakfast 100-120฿. Steaks 120฿. Open **24hr.** ❸

Thai Food Buffet (☎01 965 3819), at the intersection of Teekathmananont and Prajak Rd. For starved stomachs and wallets: 50฿ buys all you can eat. Open **24hr.** ❷

👁 SIGHTS

About 2km northwest of town, the small **Udorn Sunshine Fragrant Orchid Farm** (☎242 475), 127 Nongsamrong Rd., is a botanical talent show. Mr. Pradit Kampermpool devoted a decade of his life to developing the first orchid perfume, aptly named "Miss Udorn Sunshine," which he markets on every possible occasion. The next enclosure over, where *Desmodium gyrant* makes its home, is even more fascinating. These unremarkable-looking plants perk up and shimmy to the vibes of music or human voice. Thanks to Mr. Kampermpool's years spent cross-breeding, the plants respond almost instantaneously, as opposed to their more lethargic wild counterparts. These plants are reputed to have psychological healing powers related to meditation: by focusing on the plants, patients are relieved of worry. Mr. Kampermpool's orchids boom from September to April, while the dancing plants thrive year-round. To get to the farm, take Posri Rd. past the reservoir and bear right on Phoniyom Rd. After the first stoplight, the turn-off for the farm is 100m ahead on the left and the farm is another 100m to your right. *Songthaew* #16 and #5 pass by the turn-off. (Open daily 7am-6:30pm. Suggested 30฿ donation, goes toward food and clothing for the poor and AIDS patients.)

Nong Prajak Reservoir, in the northwest section of town, is full of benches, pavilions, and footbridges. Join mothers, children, and sweethearts feeding the catfish.

🎵 🎭 ENTERTAINMENT AND NIGHTLIFE

The theater at the top of the Charoensri Shopping Complex screens Thai films (90฿ and up). Udon's nightlife revolves around two clubs: **Mambo** and **Yellowbird.** To get to Mambo in the Napalai Hotel, 572 Pracharaksa Rd. (☎347 444), head west toward the reservoir on Srisuk Rd. and walk left where Pracharaksa Rd. branches off Srisuk for 1km. Bathe yourself in fluorescent blue light to the pounding beats of Thai pop. (Open daily 9pm-2am.) Closer to town, but less popular, Yellowbird disco at the Charoen Hotel also plays Thai pop. (Open daily 10pm-1:30am.) About 200m past the discos, **Mr. Tong's** outdoor bar, on Teekathmananont Rd. across from the Charoensri Complex, is a great place to finish the evening if you don't mind incandescent color schemes. The town's expats and the locals who love them swear by **Harry's Bar,** 19/4 Banliam Bypass. Heading past the reservoir on Srisuk Rd., take a left on Pracharaksa Rd. and a right on Suk Rd. *Tuk-tuks* from the town center cost 80฿. (Both bars: beer 60-80฿, mixed drinks 100-110฿; no cover; open nightly until 1-2am.)

🏪 MARKETS

The real deal is **Ban Huay Market** at the north end of Udondutsadee Rd., where a network of vendor-lined *sois* surrounds a huge, covered area with tons of delicious goodies. The largest **night market** is located just outside the train station entrance at the east end of Prajak Rd. **Thai Isaan Market,** on Sai Uthit Rd., and **Rangsima Market,** north on Udondutsadee Rd., are both uninspiring.

NORTHEAST THAILAND

Makro and **Big C** supermarkets are located 3km out of town on the Ban Chiang Rd.; *songthaew* #2 and 10 go there. Within town, **Ngee Sun Superstore**, 119-123 Posri Rd., is between Makkhaeng and Parnphrao Rd. (Open daily 9am-9pm.)

▶ DAYTRIPS FROM UDON THANI

BAN CHIANG

Orange and blue songthaew leave from Posri Rd. for Ban Chiang (1½hr., every 30min., 25฿). On Sai Uthit Rd., walk past the bus station on your left and make a right onto Posri Rd. You will see the songthaew on the right side of the road opposite a small supermarket. The turn-off for Ban Chiang is on the left—and usually the bus driver will just drop you off here. If so, take a tuk-tuk for the remaining 6km (30-40฿). Buses and songthaew return to Udon from the museum entrance every 1½hr. until 2pm. If you miss these, hire a tuk-tuk to the main road; there are frequent buses from Sakhon Nakhon to Udon.

Ban Chiang, 54km east of Udon Thani, is one of Southeast Asia's most significant archaeological discoveries and was recognized as a UNESCO World Heritage Site in 1992. The story of its discovery begins in 1966, when Stephen Young, a Harvard University archaeology student, tripped over a large root. Catching himself, he found the rim of a partially unearthed pot staring him in the face. Upon closer scrutiny, he found that the area was littered with half-buried pottery. By the time excavation began in the mid-1970s, many valuable artifacts had been sold to collectors in trading centers worldwide. The skeletons and numerous bronze artifacts found here have shed light on the lives of the inhabitants of the area between 3000 and 1000 BC. They also indicate that the civilization possessed knowledge of metallurgy much earlier than originally estimated, casting doubt on the theory that metallurgy came to Thailand from China.

The **national museum** documents the unearthing of Ban Chiang. The second-floor exhibits have comprehensive captions in English. (☎208 340. Open daily 8:30am-5pm. 30฿.) At the other end of the village, **Wa Phosi Nai** displays a well-preserved burial site with intact artifacts. (Exit left from the museum; the **excavation site** is 600m down on the right.)

ERAWAN CAVE

Erawan Cave is just off the Udon Thani-Loei Hwy. (Hwy. 210). Any Loei-bound bus will drop you at the turn-off between Km 30 and 31 (93km, 30-35฿). From there, another tuk-tuk will transport you the additional 2km from the entrance to the cave.

Visible from several kilometers away, this towering limestone outcrop is pierced by a gaping crevice sheltering a large Buddha. While the few stalagmites in the cave aren't that impressive, the volume of the lunar landscape within is. At the base of the outcrop is a *wat* from which a series of stairs ascends to the cave entrance. Eventually the steps branch; take the flight to the left. A path with a view of the nearby peaks runs through the mountain to the other side.

NONG KHAI ☎042

If Khaosan Road is a noisy, spunky kid, then Nong Khai's riverfront is its calm, cool older brother. Drawn at first by the popular border crossing with Laos, travelers end up staying on to see one of Thailand's most unique Buddhist temples—Sala Kaew Ku. The large influx of foreigners, along with the greatest number of temples per capita, makes for one of Thailand's most authentic tourist towns, bringing Thais and *farang* alike.

NORTHEAST THAILAND

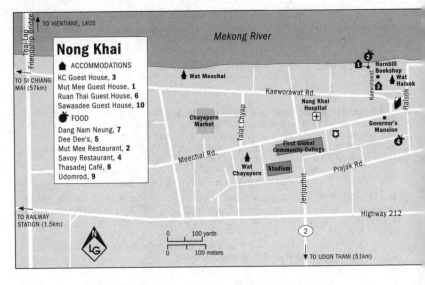

▣ TRANSPORTATION

Trains: Nong Khai Railway Station (☎411 592), on Hwy. 212, 1.5km west of town. *Tuk-tuk* ride from Rimkhong Rd. 30-50฿. Trains to **Bangkok** via **Khon Kaen** and **Udon Thani** (10-12hr.; 7:30am, 7:05pm; 183-1177฿) and **Khorat** (6hr., 1pm, 64฿). Booking office open daily 7am-7pm.

Buses: Nong Khai Bus Terminal, off of Prajak Rd. at the east end of town. To: **Bangkok** via **Khon Kaen, Khorat,** and **Udon Thani** (#23; 12hr., 12 per day 5:30am-5:30pm, 273-545฿); **Nakhon Phanom** (#224; 5-7hr., 6 per day 6:40-9:50am, 106-148฿) via **Beung Khan** (2hr., 50-70฿); **Udon Thani** (#221; 1hr., 16 per day 5:30am-4pm, 21฿). Green buses go to **Loei** (#507; 6-8hr., 5 per day 6-11:35am, 84฿) via **Si Chiangmai** (1hr., 22฿), **Sangkhom** (2-3hr., 37฿), and **Pak Chom** (5hr., 57฿). To get to **Chiang Khan,** switch buses at **Pak Chom.**

Local Transportation: For those who just want to walk, **tuk-tuks** are abundant to the point of distraction, as drivers assume all *farang* are desperately in need of their services. 20-50฿.

Rentals: Bicycle rental at Mut Mee Guest House (43฿ per day) or at the front of the *soi* leading to Mut Mee (30฿ per day). **Motorbike rental** 200฿ per day at **Nana Motor,** 1160 Meechai Rd. (☎411 998), opposite Chayaporn Market. Open daily 7:30am-6pm.

✳▣ ORIENTATION AND PRACTICAL INFORMATION

Nong Khai is a major border crossing to **Vientiane, Laos**—the **Friendship Bridge** joins the two countries. In the north, Nong Khai is bordered by the **Mekong River,** while **Highway 212** marks the town's southern boundary. Parallel to Hwy. 212, from south to north, are **Prajak Road, Meechai Road,** and **Rimkhong Road.** The **train station,** on Hwy. 212, 2.5km west of the town center, is a bit of a hike. The **bus station** is off of Prajak Rd., southeast of the main tourist area. Guesthouses are scattered to the northeast, and most have maps.

Currency Exchange: Bangkok Bank, 372 Soi Srisaket (☎412 675), in the ground fl. office next to the ATM. Open M-F 8:30am-3:30pm. For currency exchange only—open Sa-Su 8:30am-4pm.

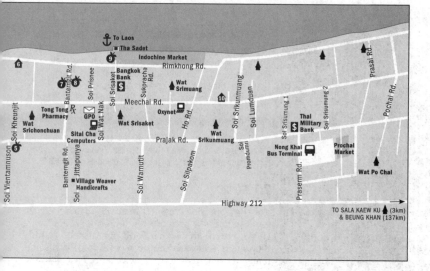

Markets: The **Indochine market,** along Rimkhong Rd. near the Mekong river, features a cornucopia of scented soaps, electronics, binoculars, and, of course, massive grilled fish. Open daily 9am-5:30pm. **Prochai Market,** adjacent to the bus terminal, and **Chayaporn Market,** to the west, sell the usual produce and meats.

Books: Hornbill Bookshop, 1121 Kaeworawat Rd. (☎460 272), on the *soi* to Mut Mee Guest House. Open daily 10am-7pm.

Police: (☎411 020), on Meechai Rd., facing the hospital.

Pharmacy: Tong Tong Pharmacy, 382/2 Meechai Rd. (☎411 690). Exit left from the post office; it's on the corner. Open daily 7:30am-9pm.

Medical Services: Nong Khai Hospital, 1158 Meechai Rd. (☎411 504), near City Hall and opposite the police station.

Internet Access: Sitai Cha Computers, 269/1 Soi Wat Nak, next to the Kiwi Cafe. If the owner, Malinee, challenges you to a game of Scrabble, let her win. 20฿ per hr. Open daily 9am-9pm. **Oxynet,** 569/2 Meechai Rd. 25฿ per hr. Open daily 9am-midnight.

Telephones: Lenso phones in the **GPO** and along Meechai Rd.

Post Office: GPO, 390 Meechai Rd. (☎411 521). **International phone.** *Poste Restante.* Open M-F 8:30am-4:30pm, Sa-Su 9am-noon.

Postal Code: 43000.

ACCOMMODATIONS

🛏 **Mut Mee Guest House,** 1111/4 Kaeworawat Rd. (☎460 717; www.mutmee.net). From the bus station, take a left onto Prajak Rd. for 1km. Take a right onto Haisok Rd. and a left before the *wat.* The guesthouse is around the corner, down a well-posted *soi.* Mut Mee offers a riverside patio, loads of information, and a steady stream of talkative travelers. *Tai chi,* meditation, and *reiki* classes offered in the high season or upon request. Dorms 90฿; singles with shared hot shower 130฿; doubles 150-450฿. ❷

🛏 **Sawasdee Guest House,** 402 Meechai Rd. (☎412 502). From the post office, 5 blocks toward the bus station behind Wat Srikunmuang. This rickety wooden guesthouse has

ON THE MENU

ISAAN CUISINE

Although you can find central cuisine throughout Thailand, there are many dishes that traditionally come from the northeast. Much of the food, like Isaan culture in general, has been influenced by neighboring Cambodian and especially Lao cuisine. The infertile soil of the region supports a glutinous variety of rice, *khao niaow*, or sticky rice. Served in covered baskets and eaten with fingers, it's the staple of any Isaan meal. The sticky quality is said to digest more slowly and hold off hunger pangs, helpful for farmers who spend many hours out in the fields. Many other essential ingredients—bamboo shoots, mushrooms, and leafy vegetables—are remnants of the days when locals had to forage in the forest to supplement the rice crop. Meals are traditionally eaten on bamboo mats and served on the floor.

Classic dishes include:

Larb: spiced minced meat generally served with a side plate of raw vegetables (basil, cabbage, and cucumbers), *gai* (chicken), *nua* (beef), *moo* (pork), *phet* (duck), or *plaa* (fish).

Sup nau mai: wet curry with bamboo shoots, squash, and mushrooms.

Bun plaa: minced fish mixed with fish sauce and *jiao* (chili paste).

Naam duk moo: grilled pork, chili, onions, and lemongrass.

[Cont'd on next page...]

very clean rooms and real flavor. Glowing courtyard is the cream-filled center. Singles 100฿; doubles 140฿, with A/C and hot water 300฿. ❷

Ruan Thai Guest House, 1126/2 Rimkhong Rd. (☎412 519; www.ruanthaihouse.com). From the Indochine market, walk 3 blocks toward Wat Hasok. Clean rooms in the white building; cleaner (and pricier) rooms in the wooden buildings. Singles 120฿; doubles 200฿, both with shared cold shower; rooms with private hot shower 300-400฿. ❷

KC Guest House, 1018 Kaeworawat Rd., on the same *soi* that leads to Mut Mee Guest House. Basic rooms, almost in view of the river. Singles 100฿; doubles 150฿. ❷

🔲 FOOD

For the homesick traveler, many co-*farang*-owned establishments provide some Western comfort. Good, inexpensive Thai food can also be found. **Chayaporn Market ❶** on the west side of town has loads of prepared eats available. More **food stalls ❶**, some offering fresh seafood, crowd the intersection of **Rimkhong** and **Haisok Road.** Two blocks south, where **Prajak Road** meets Haisok Rd., the smell of *pad thai* and skewered meats wafts down the street.

🔲 **Dang Nam Neung,** 1062/1-2 Banterngit Rd. (☎411 961), half a block toward the river from Mecchai Rd. Serves one thing and serves it well: nam neung, Vietnamese spring rolls you make yourself. 50฿ per person or 155฿ for 4 buys a platter of greens, starfruit, green banana, cucumber, sausages, and rice-paper wrappers. Open daily 6am-7pm. ❷

Savoy Restaurant, 242/2 Moo 3 Sri Lang Tuan (☎07 232 1091). From Prajak Rd., take a right onto Haisok Rd., then take the 1st left before the Pantawee Hotel. Co-owned by a French butcher, his signature green peppercorn sauce is served with steak, chicken, or duck. Assorted meat platter *(jambon, saucisson, rillettes, pâté)* 100฿. Entrees 80-140฿. Open daily 10am-10pm.

Dee Dee's, on the corner of Prajak Rd. and Soi Vientamnuson. Inexpensive Thai food that's popular among locals. Most dishes 25-100฿. Open daily noon-midnight.

Mut Mee Restaurant, 1111/4 Kaeworawat Rd. Great food matches great guesthouse. Thai, Western, and vegetarian menu. Most dishes 30-60฿. Open daily 8am-10pm. ❷

Udomrod, 423 Rimkhong Rd. (☎421 084), next to the immigration pier. Postcard-perfect views of Laos and the Mekong. Standard menu of fish and Thai food.

Most dishes 45-120฿. Fresh fish 80-180฿. Open daily 7am-9:30pm. ❸

Thasadej Café, 387/3 Banterngit Rd. (☎412 075). The antithesis of noodles and rice. Rotating specials highlight various Western foods. Transforms into a bar in the evening. English-speaking owners Carsten and Tum help tourists with rides and train tickets. Baguette with cheese 60฿, gyros 110฿, pizzas 100฿. Open daily 8am-1am. ❸

🔍 SIGHTS

▥ SALA KAEW KU (WAT KHAEK). The city with the most *wats* per capita, Nong Khai can boast another superlative, as it's home to one of Thailand's most unique temples. Towering concrete statues of Hindu and Buddhist figures represent various levels of Buddhist cosmology: the good and the evil, the mundane and the fantastic, the innocent and the freaky—all the brainchild of a Lao mystic, **Luang Poo Boun Leya Sourirat.** After building a park in Vientiane, Sourirat fled to Thailand when the Communists came to power in 1975. Most of the temple's gravity-defying figures are gods, goddesses, demons, and Buddhas found in the Indian pantheon of mythical deities. Enter the giant mouth in back to learn about *samsara,* the Buddhist belief in the endless life cycle of rebirth and suffering. A series of sculptures arrayed in a circle represents the events of one life cycle. Near the entrance of the circle is a statue of Buddha stepping over the enclosure walls, conveying the message that the way to step outside of this cycle is to follow the teachings of Buddha. *(Head east on Rte. 212, past "St. Paul Nong Khai School" on the right; Sala Kaew Ku is 2 turn-offs later. 4km outside of town. 15-20min. bike ride. Tuk-tuks can be hired for 100-120฿ round-trip. Open daily 8am-5pm. 10฿.)*

WAT PO CHAI. Another more sedate but equally famous statue is housed in Wat Po Chai. Murals in the *wat* illustrate the story of how this gold and bronze Buddha image, known as Luang Pho Phra Sai, sank into the Mekong after the raft that was transporting it from Laos capsized. Twenty-five years later, it resurfaced: many believed it to be a miracle. *(Off of Prajak Rd., down Prochai Rd. Open daily 7am-5pm.)*

▥ VILLAGE WEAVER HANDICRAFTS. Seekers of handwoven *mudmee* fabrics can visit Village Weaver Handicrafts, off Prajak Rd. near the Honda dealership. This 22-year-old project promotes local industry and offers lucrative work to Isaan women who are at risk of turning to brothels for their livelihood. Seamstresses tailor outfits at warp speed and ship

Gaeng tom gai: wet curry with chicken, eggplant, cabbage, and basil.

Sai krog isaan: sausages made with diced pork, garlic, lime juice, and rice.

Nua naam tok: grilled beef salad.

Nau mai dong: tangy baby bamboo shoots with chilis and scallions, fermented for a month.

Mook: pureed souffles wrapped in banana leaves (unlike in the central region, no coconut is used). *Mook nau mai* (bamboo shoots), *moot het* (mushrooms), *mook kai phlaa* (fish).

Rare dishes, considered delicacies:

Goi: shredded raw beef mixed with chilis and cow's blood, only served on special occasions.

Nam phrik mot som: red-ant egg dip.

Noo naa yang: barbecued field rat.

Gaeng tookay: gecko curry.

Gaeng phak waan khai mot daeng: sweet vegetable curry with red-ant eggs.

Nguak wua thod: deep fried beef gum.

The best places to sample Isaan food are the roadside stalls or restaurants that have most dishes pre-cooked. Watch out for stalls that have lots of flies, or food that has been sunbathing the entire afternoon. There are few formal restaurants that serve Isaan food.

them everywhere in the world. (*1151 Soi Jittapunya.* ☎*411 236; village@udon.ksc.co.th. Open daily 8am-5pm. Weaving demos M-F.)*

DAYTRIPS FROM NONG KHAI

■ PHU PHRA BAT HISTORICAL PARK

To have enough time to see the park and get back, catch a bus to Ban Phu (#294; 1½hr., 7:15am, 30฿) from the Nong Khai Bus Terminal. Take a left from the Ban Phu station and walk 100m over the bridge to where songthaew (15min., every 15min., 5฿) take you Ban Tiu. From here, hike 4km to park headquarters or grab a motorcycle taxi (50฿). Leave the park by 2pm, as the last bus back to Nong Khai leaves Ban Phu at 3pm. If you have a motorbike, you can take Hwy. 2266 from Si Chiangmai to Ban Tiu via Ban Klang Yai (32km). See Si Chiangmai (p. 245) for more information.

Some 85km southwest of Nong Khai, not far from the dusty village of Ban Phu, the eerie wizardry of prehistoric hunter-gatherers lingers at Phu Phra Bat Historical Park. On 5.5km² of forested mountains in the Phu Pan Range, the park boasts a fine collection of prehistoric cave paintings and rock shelters that date back to 1500 BC. Over a dozen excavations lie scattered along a shady, well-marked path. Buddhas abound in **Tham Phra** (Cave of Buddha Images). At the top of the mountain, the 800m path yields an astounding vista of **Pha Sadet Cliff,** which has a perfect picnic area overlooking the Lao mountains. (☎910 107. Open daily 8:30am-sunset. Admission 30฿. Camping fee 20฿, tent rental 50฿. 1-2 person bungalows 300฿; each additional person 100฿.)

■ WAT PHU TOK AND BUENG KHAN

From the Nong Khai Bus Terminal, take bus #224 to Bueng Khan (2hr., every hr. 6am-3pm, 45฿). From the Bueng Khan bus stop (across from the Kasikorn Bank), catch a bus to Ban Similai (40min., 12฿). Hire a motorcycle taxi (30min., 40-50฿) or a tuk-tuk (100฿) for the remaining 20km to Phu Tok.

Although it's one of northeast Thailand's most spectacular sights, ■**Wat Phu Tok** (meaning "single mountain") remains untouristed because of its remote location. The shrine stands on a red sandstone outcropping, rising to seven levels, each representing a stage of enlightenment. Level five has a sanctuary built into the cliff. Thick bamboo groves cover the paths at level seven. On the opposite side of the mountain is a hermitage built on a pinnacle nestled under a boulder. Along the way, huts and platforms are used for meditation. Reaching the top involves climbing stairs into a maze of paths that cut into the rock and wooden platforms. When traversing the platforms, be careful of the gaps between the lower planks. The view of the Isaan plains makes the sweaty ascent more than worth it, though climbing the stairs isn't recommended in windy weather.

The sheer isolation of Wat Phu Thawk makes tackling it in one day difficult. If you're coming from Nakhon Phanom, heading to Nong Khai, you'll probably want to spend the night in Beung Khan, the largest town between Nakhon Phanom and Nong Khai on Hwy. 212, and the only place between Nong Khai and Phu Tok for overnight stays. Hwy. 212 becomes **Thaisamok Road,** home to a small bus stop, a rotary, and a clock tower. To reach the guesthouses from the bus stop, head toward the rotary, turn right onto **Maesongnang Road,** and left onto **Prasatchai Road.** Two hotels are 100m down at the first intersection. **Santisuk Hotel ❷,** 21/2 Prasatchai Rd., is on the right. (☎491 114. Singles with TV and Thai-style bath 150฿, with A/C 280฿.) **Samanmit Hotel ❷,** 34/3 Prasatchai Rd., is directly across from Santisuk. (☎491 078. Singles with shared bath 100-140฿, with A/C 200฿.)

NORTHEAST THAILAND

PHU WUA WILDLIFE SANCTUARY

From Beung Khan, take a bus to Nakhon Phanom. At Ban Chaiyaporn (24km from Bueng Khan), get off the bus. Take a right at the turn-off for Ban Phu Sawat (5km from the turn-off); turn right and continue on for 2.5km to the park office. The waterfalls are a further 3km from this point (8km from the bus drop-off).

Jungle and evergreen forest protect the elephants, bears, palm civets, monkeys, and gibbons that call the park's 187km² home. Visit **Tham Fun Waterfall,** or check out the more impressive waterfalls, like the 50m **Tham Phra (Chanaen) Waterfall,** with its first tier cascading over one large boulder, and the **Chet Si Waterfall** ("Seven Colors Waterfall"), so named because it often reflects the colors of the rainbow. The latter two are accessible by car or motorbike (at 30km, the distance is too far to walk) and difficult to reach during the late rainy season. All the waterfalls are best seen from August to September, when they are at their full strength.

BORDER CROSSING: NONG KHAI/VIENTIANE. 15-day Lao tourist visas are issued on the **Friendship Bridge** for US$30 or a heftier 1500฿ (1 passport photo required). 30-day visas are available from the Lao embassy in Bangkok or the consulate in Khon Kaen (3-day processing 1100฿, expedited processing up to 1400฿). Ask at Mut Mee Guest House for the latest info. A *tuk-tuk* from Nong Khai to the bridge should cost 30-50฿. A bus shuttles people across the bridge for 10฿. On the other side, public buses run the 25km to Vientiane (50฿), or you can take a taxi (100-150฿). The Lao entry tax varies, but currently stands at 50฿.

SI CHIANGMAI ☎042

The founding of Si Chiangmai is a tale of two cities. After battling several wars, the king of Chiang Mai led his people to seek refuge in Vientiane. Just before crossing the Mekong, his daughter fell sick and died. Devastated, the king could go no further, and his people settled here, naming the town Si Chiangmai, or "prosperous new city." The city still looks over the back streets of the Lao capital, and it upholds its name with a booming rice-paper wrapper industry, producing 200,000 pieces per day. Si Chiangmai also boasts Thailand's largest ketchup factory, and the tomato is accordingly celebrated in a February festival, complete with tomato-eating contests and the crowning of Ms. Tomato. While there's little to do in town, the surrounding rice fields, waterfalls, and *wats* make for leisurely side trips.

TRANSPORTATION. Buses stop on the highway, on Sois 17 and 18, on their way to Sangkhom (1hr., every hr. 5am-6pm, 25฿) or to Nong Khai (2hr., every hr. 5am-5pm, 40฿). Rent **motorbikes** (200฿ per day) at a store on the highway at Soi 17.

PRACTICAL INFORMATION. Three main streets run parallel to the Mekong. Running along the shore of the river is **Rimkhong Road,** followed by an unnamed street and then the main highway, **Ming Muang Road. Sois 1-30** connect the three. Services include: currency exchange at **Kasikorn Bank,** 125 Moo 2, on the main highway at Soi 19 (☎451 447; open M-F 8:30am-3:30pm); **24hr. ATM** access across the street at Krung Thai Bank (Cirrus/MC/V); the **market,** behind the main highway and away from the river, between Sois 17 and 18; the **hospital** (☎451 125), on the main highway across from Soi 23; **police** (☎451 035), also on the main highway, to the right of the hospital; **Internet** at Manareet Resort (30฿ per hr); and a **post office,** 337 Ming Muang Rd., across from Soi 25 on the main highway. (☎451 095. Open M-F 8:30am-4:30pm, Sa-Su 9am-noon.) **Postal Code:** 43130.

NORTHEAST THAILAND

⌐⌐ ACCOMMODATIONS AND FOOD. Anne's Guesthouse ❷, 686 Moo 1 Ming Muang Rd., between Sois 22 and 23, has huge, clean rooms with tiled floors in its newer section. Rooms in the older wooden section are neither as clean nor as large. (☎451 201; wijittra_saenyan@hotmail.com. Bike rentals 30฿ per day. Massage 150฿ per hr. Laundry 10-15฿. Singles 200฿, with A/C 350฿; each additional person 50฿.) Tim no longer runs the place at **Tim's Guesthouse ❷**, 553 Moo 2 Rhimkhong Rd., between Sois 16 and 17, but new owner Wimonrat provides loads of information and can arrange motorbike rentals for 200฿ per day. (☎451 072; blackjack132@hotmail.com. Squat toilet and cold shower. Rooms with fan 150฿.) The downstairs **restaurant** serves noodles (30฿) and curries (40-50฿). Spicy Isaan salads are 45฿. (Open daily 7am-10pm.) **Maneerat Resort ❸**, 74 Rimkhong Rd., between Sois 23 and 24, has an attached restaurant, serving chicken with cashews for 90฿ and entrees for around 90-150฿. (☎451 311. Restaurant open daily 6am-midnight. A/C singles 300฿; doubles 350฿.) In between Sois 29 and 30, a **bakery** brings out hot baguettes at around 2:30pm.

◙ SIGHTS. Si Chiangmai serves as a base for trips to **Phu Phra Bat Historical Park.** The 36km journey passes through rice and pineapple fields, as well as several villages. There's no public transportation, and if you bike there, it would be wise to spend the night at the park: watching the sunrise from atop one of the rock formations is recommended. Take Rte. 2266 next to the post office. At Ban Klang Yai (29km), head towards Ban Tiu for 3km. Signs will direct you along the remaining 4km to Phu Phra Bat. **Wat Hin Maak Peng** (20km) is halfway between Si Chiangmai and Sangkhom (p. 247). Along the main highway, 5km towards Nong Khai, is a small park along the river with pachydermic topiary. Between Nong Khai and Si Chiangmai is **Wat Nam Mong,** housing the sacred Phra Chao Ong Tue, a 4m golden Buddha image in the style of northern Laos. It is said that it shed tears when the Buddha's hand was cut off by thieves. To get to the *wat,* take a Nong Khai- and Tha Bo-bound *songthaew* or bus to Km 31. It's 2.2km down the road to your right.

Within town, there are no official tourist sites; walk around and observe shop owners drying their rice wrappers. Occasional cockfights (Nov.-Feb.) and violent fish fights (May-Aug.) are held on street corners and in backyards. Things also liven up during the **tomato festival** in May, where locals sometimes dress up as the red bulbous fruit, teenagers compete in singing contests, and visitors can witness the splendor of the Ms. Tomato beauty pageant. The view across the river is uninspiring; it's mostly flat, and you can see the tops of some of Vientiane's concrete buildings. **Biking** along the town's three roads can be relaxing.

SANGKHOM ☎042

Sangkhom's lush surroundings, waterfalls, cliffs, and stunning vistas of the Mekong are a good reason to stay a day or two. While the town has retained its jungle-village charm, wooden and concrete-block houses have replaced most of the bamboo and straw-thatched huts, now confined only to tourist bungalows. As you stroll along streets filled with the savory aroma of frying banana chips (a local specialty), the town's drowsy pace may lull you into staying longer than you planned.

▐ TRANSPORTATION. Sangkhom lies on the river road (Rte. 211) between Nong Khai and Pak Chom. **Buses** go to: Loei (3-4hr., every hr. 8:30am-4:30pm, 37฿) via Pak Chom (1½hr., 25฿) and Nong Khai (3-3½hr., every hr. 8:30am-4:30pm, 40฿) via Si Chiangmai (1hr., 18฿). To go onwards to Chiang Khan, transfer to **songthaew** at Pak Chom (an additional 1½hr., 4 per day, 20฿).

🔢 PRACTICAL INFORMATION. Sangkhom is essentially a one-street town, with the **Pak Chom-Ming Muang Road** as its spine and numbered *sois* branching off. Entering Sangkhom from Nong Khai, you'll pass by the **hospital** on the left and the first bridge; 2km farther is the center of town, where the **police station** and the **market** are located. From the market, it's another 1.5km to the **post office,** located after a second bridge.

Services include: the **police** (☎ 441 080); a **pharmacy,** 203 Pak Chom-Ming Muang Rd., diagonally across from Buoy's Guesthouse, toward the market (open daily 7am-6pm); **Sangkhom Hospital,** 72 Moo 3 Pak Chom-Ming Muang Rd. (☎441 051); sporadic **Internet access** in a convenience store near Soi 5, across from the motorbike shop (30฿ per hr.; open daily 8am-8pm); and the **post office,** 43 Moo 1. (☎441 069. Open M-F 8:30am-4:40pm, Sa-Su 8:30am-noon.) **Postal Code:** 43160.

🏠🍴 ACCOMMODATIONS AND FOOD. 🔲**River Huts Guest House ❷**, 239 Soi 4, on the river behind the large iron gate, has clean, standard, riverside bungalows. (☎441 012; riverhuts@hotmail.com. Bike rental 30฿ per day. Singles and doubles with private hot shower 200฿.) The 🔲**Bungalow Cake Resort ❷**, 116 Moo 2, has— in addition to a charming name—small white cottages, some with a river view. It is located beyond the second bridge, 50m before the GPO. (☎441 400. Singles and doubles with fan 250฿; with A/C, TV, and hot water 500฿.) An attached **restaurant ❷** has vegetarian dishes available on request. (Entrees 50-80฿. Open daily 7am-11pm.) The **Buoy Guest House ❷**, between Soi 3 and 4, ½ mi. before the GPO, offers romantic bungalows along the river. (☎441 065. Singles 100฿; doubles with private bath 200฿.) Mr. and Mrs. Toy, owners and chefs of the guesthouse's **restaurant ❷** (only open during the high season), prepare Thai and Lao specialties (jungle curry 50฿) and have tons of information—ask about rentals, local tours, and boat trips. (Motorbike rental 200฿ per day. Boat tours 150฿.) Maps of the area are also available. **Poo Pae Guest House ❷**, on the river, diagonally across from the police station, has clean wooden rooms, only one of which faces the river. (☎441 088. Singles and doubles 150฿, with A/C 300฿; doubles with 2 twin beds and A/C 400฿.) Below is a popular **restaurant ❷** with Thai-Chinese dishes for 50-100฿. (Open daily 7:30am-10pm.) **TXK Guest House's restaurant ❸** is famous for 100฿ Thai and Lao feasts.

🔲 SIGHTS. The surrounding jungle is dotted with caves, *wats*, and **waterfalls.** The impressive **Than Thip Falls** are a 30min. motorbike ride west of town. Take any bus or *songthaew* heading toward Pak Chom or Loei for 13km (between Km 97 and 98). Take a left and go down the road for 3km. Bring your bathing suit—the second tier (of three) has a swimming hole.

Just as relaxing, but not as impressive, are the **Than Thong Falls,** just off the road (between Km 72 and 73), 12km east of town. *Songthaew* heading to Si Chiangmai will drop you there for 8฿. Than Thong is a road leading 4km up to **Wat Pha Tak Seu,** a temple with a commanding view of the Mekong. Wat Pha Tak Seu can also be reached via a 2km series of steps and trails leading up from the river road, 4km east of town. It is not advisable to take this path during the rainy season.

Wat Hin Maak Peng, located 2km east of Sangkhom, is halfway between Sangkhom and Si Chiangmai, at Km 64. Any Si Chiangmai-bound bus or *songthaew* will drop you off for 10฿. In sharp contrast to the ascetic vows taken by these monks of the Thammayut sect, the exteriors of the grand modern buildings are set among richly landscaped grounds and bamboo groves. The river pavilion faces a much less opulent Lao *wat* across the Mekong. (Gates open daily 6am-7pm.)

CHIANG KHAN
☎ 042

Tucked behind the Mekong River, north of Loei and west of Nong Khai, Chiang Khan is not to be missed. It offers the same beautiful scenery and slow afternoons of other frontier towns, but relative seclusion, few tourists, and spectacular guesthouses make it a great rest spot. Life remains fairly slow and isolated here, along the meandering Mekong. With a soothing atmosphere and few sights to distract you, you're free to kick back, enjoy the cultural enrichment, and be rejuvenated.

▣ **TRANSPORTATION.** Pak Chom and Loei serve as Chiang Khan's connection to the rest of the world. **Songthaew** leave from Rte. 201, between Sois 6 and 7, for Loei (1hr., every 30min. 5:30am-5pm, 20฿). and from Chiang Khan Rd. between Sois 7 and 10 for Pak Chom (1hr., every 30-60min. 6am-4pm, 20฿). From Pak Chom, **buses** run to Nong Khai (#507; 4½hr. total, 2hr. to Sangkhom; last bus 3pm; 50฿). Buses to Bangkok leave from Soi 9, next to the market. (6pm, 197฿. A/C 8am, 6:30pm; 270-347฿. VIP 6:30pm, 540฿.)

Motorbike rental is available at Friendship, Chiang Khan, and Rimkhong and Ton Khong Guest House (p. 248) for 200-300฿ per day.

▣ **PRACTICAL INFORMATION.** Resting on the muddy Mekong River, Chiang Khan is in northern **Loei Province,** 50km from the provincial capital. The two main roads, parallel to each other and the river, are **Chai Khong Road,** closer to the water, and **Chiang Khan Road,** the highway through town. **Sois 1-28** connect the two roads.

Services in Chiang Khan include: the **immigration office,** past the hospital down Soi 28 on the riverfront (☎ 821 911; 30-day visa extensions 1900฿; open M-F 8am-8pm); a **day market** two blocks away from the river on Soi 9; a small **night market** between Sois 17 and 18; the **police** (☎ 821 181), down Soi 28, around the corner from the immigration office; **Ruammith Osoth Pharmacy,** on Chiang Khan Rd. at Soi 9 (☎ 821 168; open daily 6am-9pm); the **Chiang Khan Hospital** (☎ 821 101), on Chiang Khan Rd. across from Soi 25; **Internet access** on Soi 10 (30฿ per hr.; open daily noon-10pm); and the **Chiang Khan Post and Telegraph Office,** 50 Chai Khong Rd., on Soi 26. (☎ 821 011. **International phone.** *Poste Restante.* Open M-F 8:30am-4:30pm, Sa-Su 9am-noon.) **Postal Code:** 42110.

▣▣ **ACCOMMODATIONS AND FOOD.** Unlike other backpacker havens where supply and demand are balanced, Chiang Khan's great guesthouses far outnumber sweaty *farang.* All guesthouses have English-speaking owners. ⬛**Friendship Guest House ❷,** 300 Chai Khong Rd., between Sois 5 and 6, has large, simple teak rooms. (☎ 01 263 9068. Bicycle rental 50฿ per day, motorbikes 200-300฿ per day. Singles 150฿; doubles 200฿.) **Loogmai Guest House ❸,** 112 Chai Khong Rd., Soi 5, is modern and chic. The minimalist aesthetic created by the white walls, abstract paintings by the owner (noted artist Somboon Hormtientong), and wood floors and furniture make this one of the best-designed guesthouses in the northeast. All rooms have a fan. (☎ 06 234 0011; loogmaiguest@thaimail.com. Small rooms 300฿; large rooms 400฿. Only one room has private bath, 400฿.) **Chiang Khan Guest House ❷,** 282 Chai Khong Rd. between Sois 19 and 20, has homey wooden rooms with shared baths. (☎ 821 691; http://welcome.to/chiangkhan. Bicycle rentals 50฿ per day, motorbikes 200฿ per day. Singles 150฿; doubles 200฿.) The guesthouse serves up **family-style dinners ❷** for guests (70-100฿), and also arranges Isaan music and dance performances (1300฿). **Rimkhong Guest House ❷,** 294 Chai Khong Rd., Soi 8, is a fragrant wooden guesthouse with squat toilets. English, French, and Thai are spoken, and maps and loads of information on local daytrips are available. (☎ 821 125. Motorbike rental 200฿ per day. Singles 150฿; doubles 170-340฿.) **Ton Khong Guest House ❷,** on 299/3 Chai Khong Rd., at Soi 10, has snug and spotless rooms. (☎05 112 2028. Bicycle rentals 50฿ per day, motorbikes 200฿ per day. Singles 100฿; doubles 150฿, with private bath 200฿, with A/C 300฿.) **Mekong Culture and Nature Tours ❺**, 1.5km west of town on Chiang Khan Rd. away from Nong Khai, offers secluded bungalows by the river with shared baths. Only those really looking to get away from it all and armed with strong bug repellent need apply. (☎821 457. River kayaking tours 1590฿ per person, bike tours 1390฿ per person; min. 4 people. All bungalows 900฿; low-season 600฿. 15% *Let's Go* discount.)

Chiang Khan does not have many restaurants, but the guesthouses usually do a good job of satisfying growling stomachs. While most guesthouses don't have restaurants, most will cook a dish for you. Along the river by the **Kaeng Khut Khu Rapids** are a few **food stands ❶** serving local specialty *kung den*, tiny live shrimp that dance around your plate (around 40฿). **Rabieng ❷**, between Sois 9 and 10, churns out tasty Chinese food. (Dishes 50-80฿. Open daily 9am-10pm.) **The Look Kosana ❶**, on Chiang Khan Rd., Soi 19, serves *pad thai* (25฿) and morning glory vine in garlic bean sauce (50฿) to satisfy even the pickiest taste buds. (Open daily 9am-10pm.)

⬛ SIGHTS. About 3km east of town, towards Nong Khai, a turn-off leads left to **Kaeng Khut Khu Rapids**, where picturesque rock piles interrupt the Mekong's seaward journey. Follow the sign to **Wat Thakhaek** and continue for 1km. A row of covered picnic areas are great for watching the rapids from February to May. *Songthaew* (10฿) and *tuk-tuks* (round-trip 50฿) make the trip from Chiang Khan Rd. On weekends, and occasionally during the week, vendors set up stalls selling local goods and cook up fresh fish and shrimp dishes.

Some guesthouses can arrange **boat trips** to Kaeng Khut Khu (200฿ per person) or help you charter a boat to go farther downstream to Pak Chom (4-5hr., 1800฿) and Nong Khai (8hr., 8500฿). Upstream trips to the **Hoong River** (3hr., 100฿) often visit **Phra Yai (Phu Khok Ngra)**, a 19m Buddha statue located on a 315m hill overlooking the Mekong, about 23m from Chiang Khan.

A more convenient viewpoint is at **Phu Tok.** About 3.5km in the direction of Nong Khai, a further 0.5km past the Wat Thakhaek turn-off, another turn-off leads right. Follow the narrow paved road for 2km until the road forks. Bear right. You'll probably have to walk your bike up the hill. Before you go, **make sure your bike's brakes are in superior condition; it's a steep descent.**

LOEI
☎042

A big billboard on Hwy. 201 greets visitors to Loei with, "Welcome to Loei, Land of the Sea of Mountains and Coldest in All Siam." Grammar aside, the sign captures the essence of this seldom-visited but appealing province. It is the only base from which to venture into the cloud-frosted mountains in search of hermit caves and Thailand's version of the vineyards of southern France—the Chateau de Loei Vineyards. At the end of June, the three-day rain-making **Phi Ta Khon Festival** in Dan Sai transforms the western district into a shamanistic orgy of brightly colored costumes and masks, parading spirits, and dancing fueled by drinking shots of *lao khao* ("white spirit"), culminating in a final day of Buddhist sermon at the *wat.* Those who make the trip to Loei find a perfect place to unwind after a day exploring the countryside and national parks.

NORTHEAST THAILAND

▐▀ TRANSPORTATION

Buses: All buses leave from the **main bus terminal** (☎833 586), off Maliwan Rd., south of the city center. Green buses go to **Nong Khai** via **Pak Chom, Sangkhom,** and **Si Chiangmai** (#507; 7hr., every hr. 5:40-10:40am, 84฿). If you're going to Nong Khai, take a bus to **Udon Thani** (platform #2; 3hr., every 20min. 4am-8pm, 55฿) and then

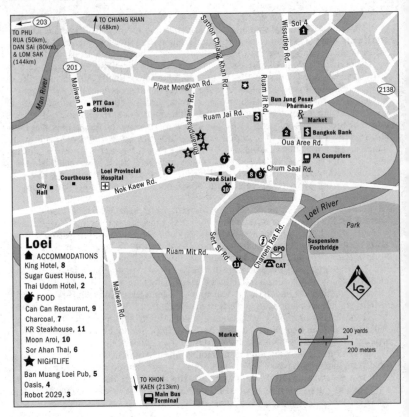

Loei

♠ ACCOMMODATIONS
King Hotel, **8**
Sugar Guest House, **1**
Thai Udom Hotel, **2**

🍴 FOOD
Can Can Restaurant, **9**
Charcoal, **7**
KR Steakhouse, **11**
Moon Aroi, **10**
Sor Ahan Thai, **6**

★ NIGHTLIFE
Ban Muang Loei Pub, **5**
Oasis, **4**
Robot 2029, **3**

catch a bus to Nong Khai; it's at least 2hr. faster. Buses also run to: **Bangkok** (9-10hr., every hr. 6am-8pm, 200-495฿); **Chiang Mai** (10hr., 5 per day 10:15am-10:30pm, 184-410฿); **Chiang Rai** (11hr., 5 per day 6:30-10:30pm, 286-367฿). Chiang Mai and Chiang Rai buses travel via **Phitsanulok** (5hr.) and **Lom Sak** (4hr., 6 per day 5am-5pm, 58฿). **Long-distance buses** may be full upon arrival; guarantee a seat by buying a ticket at the bus terminal counter. *Songthaew* go to **Chiang Khan** (1hr., every 30min. 5:30am-5:30pm, 20฿).

Local Transportation: Samlor and **tuk-tuk** 20-40฿. **Motorbike** rental (200฿ per day) at the **bike shop,** between Chum Saai and Ruam Jai Rd., 20m north of the traffic circle.

🔾 🛈 ORIENTATION AND PRACTICAL INFORMATION

Loei town is a tangled mess of streets on the Loei River's western bank. **Charoen Rat Road** runs the length of the river, beginning near the bus terminal at the **market**. Moving north into town on Charoen Rat Rd., you'll see the **post office** and a white suspension footbridge, followed by **Chum Saai Road,** which becomes **Nok Kaew Road** three blocks down at a busy traffic circle. Continuing up Charoen Rat Rd., you reach **Ruam Jai Road,** a major east-west thoroughfare. **Maliwan Road (Highway 201),** forms the town's western border.

NORTHEAST
THAILAND

Tourist Office: Loei Tourism Co-ordination Center (☎812 812), on Charoen Rat Rd., opposite the GPO. Maps and brochures of Loei province. Open M-F 8:30am-4:30pm.

Currency Exchange: Bangkok Bank, at the intersection of Oua Aree and Charoen Rat Rd. Open M-F 8:30am-3:30pm. **24hr. ATM.** AmEx/MC/PLUS/V.

Police: (☎811 254), on Pipat Mongkon Rd., the city's northern border.

Pharmacy: Bun Jung Pesat Pharmacy, 83 Charoen Rat Rd. (☎830 634), on the corner of Ruam Jai Rd. Open daily 3am-8pm.

Medical Services: Loei Provincial Hospital (☎811 541), at the intersection of Maliwan Rd. and Nok Kaew Rd., opposite provincial offices. Some English spoken. Cash only.

Internet Access: PA Computers (☎814 761), on Charoen Rat Rd. between Chum Saai and Oua Aree Rd. 20฿ per hr. Open daily 9am-8pm. Internet available between Chum Saai and Ruan Jai Rd. 15฿ per hr. Open daily 10am-10pm.

Telephones: International calls from **CAT,** next door to the GPO on Charoen Rat Rd.

Post Office: GPO (☎812 0222), on Charoen Rat Rd., between the footbridge and night market. Open M-F 8:30am-4:30pm, Sa-Su 9am-noon.

Postal Code: 42000.

▐ ACCOMMODATIONS

Sugar Guest House, 4/1 Wisuttiep Rd. (☎09 711 1975), down Soi 4 on the right. Clean rooms with white-tiled floors in a new house. Bike rental 30฿ per day, motorbikes 200฿ per day. English spoken. Singles 150฿; doubles 200฿. ❷

King Hotel, 11/9-12 Chum Saai Rd. (☎811 701), has the cleanest rooms in town—decked out in tile with phone, TV, A/C, and hot shower. Singles 380฿; doubles 399฿; VIP rooms with fridge 1200฿. ❹

Thai Udom Hotel, 122/1 Charoen Rat Rd. (☎811 763), on Oua Aree Rd., has decent, clean rooms. Slightly worn down, and furnished with a desk, phone, and TV. Singles 240฿, with A/C 350฿; doubles 320฿/500฿; VIP rooms 600฿. ❸

▐ FOOD

Some of the best places to eat are the **open-air restaurants ❷** in front of the movie theater just off Oua Aree Rd., opposite Thai Farmers Bank, and at the main bus terminal. Pyromaniacs can order *pak boong fai daeng* (flaming morning glory vine), leafy water spinach that the chef sets on fire before hurling towards your plate. A couple of **food stalls ❶** line Chum Saai Rd. where it turns into Nok Kaew Rd., just after the traffic circle. All of them serve fine noodle and rice dishes for about 30฿.

Charcoal, at the traffic circle at the intersection of Sathon Chiang Khan Rd. and Chum Saai Rd., has a patio and serves heaps of Thai classics. Chicken with cashews 80฿. Most dishes 40-90฿. Open daily 5pm-midnight. ❷

Sor Ahan Thai, 32/106 Nok Kaew Rd. (☎813 436). 2 large blocks west of the traffic circle, away from the river. Garden restaurant has an extensive Thai and English menu. Most dishes 40-100฿. Tasty noodles with shrimp 40฿. Open M-Sa 9am-10pm. ❷

Moon Aroi, 22/1 Sert Si Rd. (☎833 660). A great late-night option. Vegetarian dishes upon request. Fried river oysters with bean sprouts 60฿. Open daily 4pm-5am. ❷

Can Can Restaurant (☎815 180), on Chum Saai Rd., next to the King Hotel. Not exactly budget, but its delicious food makes it one of the most popular restaurants in town. Most dishes 35-80฿. Fresh fish and juicy steaks 120-200฿. Open daily 7am-10pm. ❷

K.R. Steakhouse, 58/1 Sert Si Rd. (☎06 677 8955), near the intersection with Charoen Rat Rd. Serves Korean barbecue and Thai and Chinese dishes. Spicy green mango with fried shrimp 100฿. Most dishes 60-150฿. Open daily 10am-midnight. ❸

🎵 ENTERTAINMENT

There is a **cinema** on Sathon Chiang Khan Rd. between Ruam Jai Rd. and the traffic circle. Western-style pubs line **Rhuamphattana Road.** As you walk west on Nok Kaew Rd., toward the highway, Rhuamphattana Rd. is the first right after the traffic circle. Halfway down on the left is **Ban Muang Loei Pub,** and directly across the street, its twin, **Oasis.** Both bars offer live music after 8:30pm (small Singha 50฿); Ban Muang has Thai country music. Continuing down the street, you'll see two robot statues on your right; a large, glowing spaceship marks the entrance to **Robot 2029.** Rock bands play nightly at 10:15pm in a neon-lit hall. (Large Singha 90฿.)

🏺 MARKETS

Loei has two **day/night markets.** One, at the northern end of Charoen Rat Rd., opposite the 7-Eleven, has grilled meats and largely useless plastic items ranging from combs to space guns. The night market gets going around 6pm and closes between 9 and 10pm. The second market sets up at the southern end of Charoen Rat Rd. Six rows under tin roofs offer the usual meat and produce. (Open daily 10am-9pm.)

🗺 DAYTRIPS FROM LOEI

▨ CHATEAU DE LOEI VINEYARDS

Take a bus bound for Lom Sak (1½hr., 60km, 30฿) and get off when you see the blue metal sign in English on your left, and the Km 60 marker on your right. The cream-colored vineyard shop sells fresh grapes, organic produce, local crafts, and, of course, bottles of wine (300-1100฿). The actual vineyard is another 1km down the road beneath the sign. (☎809 521. Open daily 8am-5pm.)

One of Thailand's first wine-producing vineyards (there are now multiple wine producers), Chateau de Loei is amazingly large by any standard. After a long process of securing permits to import foreign grapevines into Thailand amid general skepticism, a thriving vineyard now stands in the middle of Loei's mountains. The wine itself is not for the connoisseur (nor really the avid novice), but a walk through the vineyards is pleasurable. The rolling landscape offers views of marching rows of grapes, a small reservoir, and a private runway.

▨ PHU KRADUNG NATIONAL PARK

Buses (70km, 25฿) to Khon Kaen drop you off at the Amphoe Phu Kradung Administrative Office. From here, catch a minibus (15฿) to the National Park Office. The park is packed on weekends and holidays, but closes from June to Sept. You'll probably want to spend a night at the park. The camping fee runs 30฿ per person. Tents are available for 100-200฿. Mountaintop lodging 5 starts at 2000฿ per bungalow. Reservations should be made weeks in advance with the National Park Division of the Forestry Department in Bangkok. (☎02 561 4292, ext. 724.) Park admission 200฿.

The bell ringing that could be heard every weekly Buddhist day inspired the name of this popular sanctuary ("Bell Mountain"). Trails criss-cross the 60km² plateau's pine forests and grassy meadows. The 5km hike (2-6hr.) from the mountain base to park headquarters on the plateau rim is facilitated by bamboo stairways. Porters can tote your gear (10฿ per kg). Visitors who reach **Pha Lom Sak** or **Pha Daeng** are rewarded with views of the sunset.

NORTHEAST THAILAND

Willing explorers can bid the Khon Kaen bus adieu at Nong Hin, 4.3km from Loei, the turn-off for ■Suan Hin Pha Ngam, a stone forest where limestone outcroppings form a natural labyrinth. Guides promise not to lose you for 100฿ per group. The 18km to Ban Pha Ngarm are traversed only by chartered *songthaew* for 500฿. (☎801 900. Suan Hin Pha Ngam open M-F 9am-4:30pm, Sa-Su 8am-5pm.)

PHU RUA NATIONAL PARK

To get to the park, catch bus #14 to Lom Sak (1hr., every hr. 5am-5pm, 25฿) via Phu Rua; watch for the large English sign on the right. Although Let's Go doesn't recommend hitchhiking, the easiest way to get to the park headquarters, 3.5km away, is to hike up the road and try to snag a lift. Otherwise, songthaew charge an outrageous 300฿. Park open year-round. Park admission 200฿.

Small nurseries cultivate a rainbow of flowers along the road, culminating in a January flower show near the turn-off to **Phu Rua National Park,** 50km from the city center. The majestic centerpiece of this park is a 1375m **mountain.** Personal vehicles can travel to the top, where a large Buddha surveys the scene below. Routes include a 2km trek to a **waterfall,** from which it's 5.5km to the peak.

It is possible to complete the circuit in a day, but an overnight stay at the park is recommended. (Camping fee 30฿ per person. Tents 100-200฿. Lodging for 3-6 people 250-500฿.) Large groups should contact the **National Parks Division** in Bangkok (☎02 561 4836). Alternative accommodations are available at the **Song Pee Nong Bungalow ❹** (☎899 399), about 2km away from the park entrance on the right, if you are heading toward Loei. Bungalows are simple and clean, with decent shared Western toilets. (Wooden bungalows 500฿; larger concrete bungalows 700฿.)

NAM NAO NATIONAL PARK

A daytrip to the park is possible but inadequate, especially if you are using public transportation. From Loei, catch a bus to Lom Sak (runs regularly 6am-5pm, 63฿). At the Lom Sak bus terminal take a Khon Kaen-bound bus and get off at park headquarters on the left. Hwy. 12 (connecting Lom Sak and Khon Kaen) cuts through the park. As most trailheads start from this road, buses to Lom Sak or Khon Kaen can help traverse the long distances between trailheads. Park headquarters is 55km from Lom Sak, and 103km from Khon Kaen. (☎05 672 9002.) Park admission 20฿.

Nam Nao, meaning "cold water," stretches for 1000km^2 at the junction of Loei and Phetchabun provinces. Its sandstone hills and sandy plains make it ideal for hiking. During the 6-7hr. ascent to the park's highest peak, **Phu Pha Chit** (1271m), a landscape of low shrubs and small yellow flowers, rolls down the mountain. The park also has verdant bamboo forests and the obligatory waterfall and cave. The camping fee is 30฿ per person. Tent rental for 1 to 3 people is 250฿. **Resorts** line Hwy. 12 near the park, but these are more expensive choices.

HIGHWAY 203

Transportation is somewhat difficult to arrange as there are no songthaew that travel that far out of the city, and distances are impractical for a tuk-tuk. However, a bus to Lom Sak runs along Hwy. 203, from which the sights are accessible. Between the Km 13 and 14 white markers on the right side of the highway, there is a grey sign in Thai for the Huay Nam Man reservoir on the left, marking the turn-off on the right. It's another 3.5km walk to the reservoir. Songthaew travel the 18km to the Phu Luang Wildlife Sanctuary's park checkpoint when it's open.

Loei's real attractions lie outside the provincial capital in the surrounding mountains. The first is **Huay Nam Man Reservoir,** about 20km from the city center. Rent a raft (100฿) for a lazy afternoon of floating about; a small flag is provided to signal to the boats filled with food to come serve you a bowl of noodles or a bag of fruit.

Further along the highway, 35km from Loei on the left, is the turn-off for the **Phu Luang Wildlife Sanctuary** (☎841 566), containing thick jungles, grasslands, and pine forests. It is closed from June to December. The sanctuary is best traversed with 4WD vehicles; however, minivans are available for rent.

LOM SAK   ☎056

Located between the Phang Hoei and Luan Prabange mountains, Lom Sak serves as a transit point between Khon Kaen and Phitsanulok. For those heading to Nam Nao National Park (50km), or Phu Hin Rong Khla National Park (60km), this small town could serve as a base to purchase supplies, or as an overnight stop from the scenic mountain road from Loei.

⊑ TRANSPORTATION. The **bus terminal** is located 2km west of town, at the intersection of Samakeechai Rd. and Rte. 12. All buses stop at Soi Suriyat, between Kotchasanee and Wajee Rd., just one block away from the main intersection adjacent to the municipal grounds. **Buses** to: Khon Kaen (4.5hr., 21 per day, 73-102฿); Loei (4hr., 6 per day 5am-5pm, 63฿) via Dan Sai and Phu Reua; Phitsanaluk (2.5hr., 16 per day 5:20am-5:10pm, 50-70฿). **Phet Tours** (☎701 164), on Soi Suriyat across from the police station, runs buses to Bangkok (6hr., 16 per day, 179-230฿). **Thin Siam Tours,** next to the New Sawan Hotel, also runs buses to Bangkok (7 per day 8:30am-midnight, 230฿). **Songthaew** direct to Khao Khoa leave from behind the market on Soi 3 irregularly (25฿).

⃗ PRACTICAL INFORMATION. The town's main intersection is where north-south **Kotchasanee Road** meets **Ronnakij Road** to the east and the multilane **Samakeechai Road** to the west. **Wajee Road** runs parallel to Kotchasanee, and *sois* run off both these roads. The fenced municipal grounds are two blocks north of Ronnakij Rd., between Kotchasanee and Wajee Rd.

Services include: currency exchange at **Bangkok Bank,** across from the New Sawan Hotel on Samakachai Rd. with a **24hr. ATM** (☎720 413; open M-F 8:30am-3:30pm); a **day market,** hidden behind buildings fronting Soi 3 and Ronnakig Rd., between Kotchasanee and Wagee Rd.; the **police** (☎701 102), in the municipal complex, adjacent to the bus stop; a **pharmacy**, Chan Bin, at the corner of Soi 3 and Wachee Rd. (☎705 022; open daily 6am-8pm); **Lom Sak Hospital,** 15 Samanachee Rd., 1km from the main intersection, past the overpass and a further 300m down the road to your right (☎702 001; English-speaking doctor); **Internet** at 134 Ronnakij Rd., in the middle of the second block to your left, walking away from the main intersection (20฿ per hr.; open daily 10am-10pm); telephones at **CAT,** behind the post office; and a **post office,** on Wajee Rd past Soi 20. (☎701 103. Open M-F 8:30am-4:30pm, Sa-Su 9am-noon.) **Postal Code:** 67110.

⃘⃗ ACCOMMODATIONS AND FOOD. Stay overnight in style at the **Lom Sak Nattirat Grand Hotel ❹**, 63/10 Kotchasanee Rd., about 1km from the main intersection, past Soi 18. In front, balustrades and plush curtains decorate Lom Sak's most luxurious hotel. An eerie fiberglass cowboy peers over the swimming pool. (☎745 022. Singles and doubles 700฿. V.) The **New Sawan Hotel ❷**, 147/6 Samakeechai Rd., is one building away from the main—and somewhat loud—intersection. (☎746 316. Singles with TV 200฿, with A/C and hot water 300฿; doubles 300-400฿.) **Baan Kaew Guesthouse ❸**, 18/4 Soi Wajee 3, boasts clean rooms, fresh-smelling sheets, and a very quiet location. From the market, on Soi 3, walk past Wajee Rd. for one block; Baan Kaew is set around a parking lot behind the wooden pub. (☎702 005. Singles and doubles with TV and squat toilet 280฿, with A/C 380฿.)

At night, food stalls set up on Wajee Rd. in front of the municipal grounds. (Delicious grilled pork chops 20฿, with sticky rice 5฿.) Downstairs from the Grand Hotel, the **Puang Choom Restaurant ❸** serves Thai, Chinese, and Western dishes. ("Fried Chicken Maryland" 120฿. Flame Be-Fried Water Mimosa Watercress 60฿. Most dishes 80-120฿. Open daily 6:30am-1am.) **Drai Woh ❸**, 17/1 Kotchasanee Rd., next to the Thai Military Bank one block towards the municipal grounds from the main intersection, is known for its Chinese dishes. (☎702 129. Five-spice duck 80฿. Spicy fish soup 150฿. Most entrees 20-150฿. Open daily 9:30am-9pm.) **Muang Lome ❸**, 22/13 Samakeechai Rd., the brown building after the Caltex gas station, specializes in Chinese and Thai food. (☎701 105. Frog with garlic and pepper 70฿. Fried spring greens in oyster sauce 50฿. Most entrees 70-200฿. Open daily 4:30am-10pm.) Expats flock to **Duang Ta ❷**, located in the small *soi* before Soi Suriyat from the main intersection towards the municipal grounds. The English-speaking owner serves up both Thai and Western dishes. (☎701 781. Thai curries 50฿. Spaghetti with meat sauce 35฿. Beefsteak 100฿. Most entrees 25-40฿. Open daily 7am-8pm.)

KHON KAEN ☎043

Like other Isaan cities, Khon Kaen lacks a "big" tourist attraction. Nevertheless, its festive nightlife, open-air markets, and efficient transportation system give visitors the means to enjoy themselves. The high concentration of bookstores serve the affiliates of Khon Kaen University, northeastern Thailand's largest. The 7200 students, a vibrant young crowd, make for a hip evening scene. The city also serves as a base for interesting daytrips to the rest of the province.

▐ TRANSPORTATION

Flights: Khon Kaen Airport (☎246 305), 8km west of town off Maliwan Rd. **Air Asia** (☎02 515 9999), has flights to **Bangkok** (daily, 2:30pm, 399-850฿). Open daily 8am-9pm. **Thai Airways,** 9/9 Prachasamran Rd. (☎227 701), inside the Hotel Sofitel, flies to **Bangkok** (3 per day, 1605฿).

Trains: Khon Kaen Railway Station (☎221 112), where Ruen Rom Rd. ends at Darunsamran Rd. To: **Bangkok** (8hr.; 9:43am, 8:13, 9:56pm; 259-978฿); **Khorat** (3-4hr.; 1:40, 8:13pm; 38฿); **Nong Khai** (3hr.; 3:36, 4:14, 5:50, 9:50am, 2:33pm; 35฿) via **Udon Thani** (25฿); **Udon Thani** (2hr., 7 per day 3:36am-6:44pm, 25฿).

Buses:

Bus terminal (☎237 472), on Pracha Samoson Rd., by the pedestrian overpass. Buses to: **Bangkok** (7hr., every 25min. 6:30am-9:30pm, 129฿); **Khorat** (3hr., every 30min. 5:20am-7pm, 95฿); **Mukdahan** (5hr., every 30min. 4am-6:30pm, 115฿); **Nakhon Phanom** (6hr., 6 per day 7:30am-4:30pm, 175฿) via **Kalasin** (1½hr., 80฿) and **Sakhon Nakhon** (4hr., 124฿); **Nakhon Sawan** (7hr., 6 per day 5:30am-1:30pm, 72฿); **Phitsanulok** (6hr., 3 per day 9am-3pm, 150฿); **Ubon Ratchathani** (4½hr., every hr. 5:40am-2pm, 115฿); **Udon Thani** (2hr., every 20min. 5:20am-7pm, 65฿).

A/C bus terminal (☎239 910), on Glang Muang Rd. Buses to: **Bangkok** (7hr., every hr., 259-400฿) via **Khorat** (3hr., 121฿); **Chiang Mai** (12hr.; 8, 9pm; 394฿) via **Phitsanulok** (5hr., 203฿); **Loei** (5hr.; 11:30am, 3:30pm; 139฿); **Nakhon Phanom** (5hr.; 7:30, 10am, 4pm; 175฿) via **Sakhon Nakhon** (4hr., 124฿); **Nong Khai** (3hr.; 5:30am, 1, 3, 5pm; 110฿); **Ubon Ratchathani** (5hr., every 2hr. 9am-5pm, 169฿).

Local Transportation: Look for **samlor** (20-30฿), **tuk-tuks** (20-50฿), and **songthaew** (5฿). TAT lists all 20 *songthaew* routes. *Songthaew* #4 runs along Nah Muang Rd.; #11 from Khon Kaen Railway Station to TAT; #17 from TAT to the National Museum.

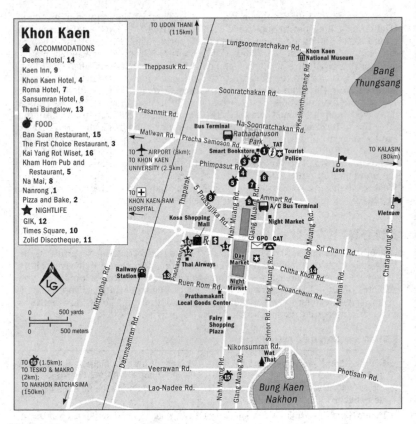

Khon Kaen

🔺 **ACCOMMODATIONS**
Deema Hotel, **14**
Kaen Inn, **9**
Khon Kaen Hotel, **4**
Roma Hotel, **7**
Sansumran Hotel, **6**
Thani Bungalow, **13**

🍴 **FOOD**
Ban Suan Restaurant, **15**
The First Choice Restaurant, **3**
Kai Yang Rot Wiset, **16**
Kham Horn Pub and
    Restaurant, **5**
Na Mai, **8**
Nanrong ,**1**
Pizza and Bake, **2**

⭐ **NIGHTLIFE**
GIK, **12**
Times Square, **10**
Zolid Discotheque, **11**

➕🛈 ORIENTATION AND PRACTICAL INFORMATION

Khon Kaen, 450km from Bangkok, is easily accessible by plane, bus, or train. The main north-south thoroughfares, **Nah Muang Road** and **Glang Muang Road**, are lined with hotels, restaurants, and the A/C bus terminal. Farther south, the parallel Muangs cross **Sri Chant Road,** home to the best nightspots. Past Sri Chant Rd. on Glang Muang Rd. are the post office, police station, and day market, leading to **Ruen Rom Road.** A right turn onto Ruen Rom Rd. from Nah Muang Rd. leads to the train station. The **regular bus terminal** and **TAT office** are on **Pracha Samoson Road.**

> **Tourist Office: TAT,** 15/5 Pracha Samoson Rd. (☎244 498). A brown and white building several blocks from the regular bus terminal. Maps and guides of Khon Kaen and surrounding provinces. Open daily 8:30am-4:30pm.
>
> **Consulates: Laos,** 171 Pracha Samoson Rd. (☎242 856). 30-day visas US$40 (1600฿); available same-day if you come early. Open M-F 8:30am-noon and 1-4pm. **Vietnam,** 65/6 Chatapadung Rd. (☎235 264). 15-day visas about US$40 (1600฿); 2-3 working days to process. Open M-F 8-11:30am and 1:30-4:30pm. Light-blue *songthaew* #10 runs to both consulates.

Currency Exchange: Banks and ATMs on Sri Chant Rd. **Bangkok Bank,** 254 Sri Chant Rd. (☎225 144), next to Charoen Thani Princess Hotel entrance. After-hours exchange during the high season. Open M-F 8:30am-7pm, Sa-Su 9am-5pm. **24hr. ATM.**

Markets: Sizeable **day market** hides behind storefronts along Nah Muang and Glang Muang Rd., stretching south to Ruen Rom Rd. Fruits, vegetables, and pig heads on sale. Popular items include *mudmee* silks and triangular pillows. Open daily 5am-6pm. When other shops shut down, the **night market** gets going along Ruen Rom Rd. at the south end of the day market. Roadside eateries stretch into the horizon. **Tesco Lotus** and **Makro** supermarkets are located 4km south of the city center on Mittraphap Rd. Light blue *songthaew* #10 goes to both.

Books: Smart Bookstore, 23 Pracha Samoson Rd. (☎237 005), on the corner of Glang Muang Rd. Open M-Sa 7:30am-8pm, Su 7:30am-6pm.

Local Tourist Police: 15/5 Pracha Samoson Rd. (☎236 937), left of TAT. Open **24hr.**

Pharmacy: Phon Phesad (☎228 260), just off Sri Chant Rd. near the Bangkok Bank. Open daily 8am-midnight.

Medical Services: Khon Kaen-Ram Hospital, 193 Sri Chant Rd. (☎333 800), on the side of the tracks away from town. English-speaking doctors. Open **24hr.**

Internet Access: Places on Glang Muang Rd. north of Ammart Rd. for 10-15฿ per hr.

Post Office: GPO, 153/8 Glang Muang Rd., just south of Sri Chant Rd. *Poste Restante* on ground floor. Open M-F 8:30am-4:30pm, Sa-Su 9am-noon. **CAT** (☎236 097), next door, has **international** calling and Internet service. Open M-F 8:30am-4:30pm.

Postal Code: 40000.

ACCOMMODATIONS

Sansumran Hotel, 55-59 Glang Muang Rd. (☎239 611), between the giant plastic tusks, near Phimpasut Rd. Spacious rooms with baths and lots of those carved lions so popular in Isaan hotels. Khon Kaen's best value. Singles and doubles 150-250฿. ❷

Kaen Inn, 56 Glang Muang Rd. (☎245 420; kaeninn@yahoo.com), at the intersection with Ammart Rd. Standard rooms are the best value—clean, comfortable, and perfectly located in the middle of town. Karaoke, restaurant, and free airport transfers. Standard singles and doubles 500฿; deluxe 800฿. ❹

Khon Kaen Hotel, 43/2 Phimpasut Rd. (☎333 222; www.khonkaen-hotel.com). A block up from Kaen Inn but a step down in upkeep. Singles and doubles 550฿. MC/V. ❹

Deema Hotel, 113 Chitha Khon Rd. (☎321 562). Very clean and comfortable, but a bit out of the way. Frequented by locals. Singles and doubles 200฿, with A/C 320฿. ❷

Roma Hotel, 50/2 Glang Muang Rd. (☎334 444), around the block from its upscale sister, Khon Kaen Hotel. A bit pricey for budget accommodations, but in a central location. Singles 230฿, with A/C 350฿; doubles 250฿/400฿. MC/V. ❷

Thani Bungalow, 222 Ruen Rom Rd. (☎221 428), at the intersection of Ruen Rom and Prachasamran Rd., next to the Nissan dealership. Large wooden bungalows are just about all it's got going for it. A/C bungalows have TV and hot water. Singles and doubles 250฿, with A/C 500฿. ❷

FOOD

Sidewalk **eateries** ❶ cluster on Phimpasut and Ammart Rd. Cheap Isaan meals like *sup nau mai* (shredded bamboo-shoot salad) tempt hungry passersby at **night markets** on Lang Muang and Ruen Rom Rd. Korean BBQ restaurants surround Bung Kaen Nakhon.

Ban Suan, 539/3 Nah Muang Rd. (☎227 811). Exiting Fairy Plaza, take a left and walk for 1km. Look for the tall Kawasaki sign on your left; the restaurant is immediately before it. Chinese, Thai, Isaan, and outdoor Korean BBQ. Stir-fried asparagus with shrimp 80฿. BBQ platter 150฿. 5% *Let's Go* discount. Open daily 4pm-2am. ❷

Kai Yang Rot Wiset, 177 Mittraphap Rd. Take blue *songthaew* #10 toward Tesco Lotus (5฿); it's just beyond the PTT gas station on the left. Buffet is easy for the linguistically challenged as well as for the taste buds. Dishes 20฿. Open daily 7am-10pm. ❶

Kham Horm Pub & Restaurant, 38 Nah Muang Rd. (☎243 252), between Phimpasut and Ammart Rd. Outdoor BBQ. Nightly live music. Stir-fried chicken with baby corn 60฿. Most dishes 40-120฿. Open daily 10am-2am. ❷

Pizza and Bake (☎258 883), on Glang Muang Rd. across from the Nanrong Hotel. Vietnamese, Thai, and international food. *Nam nueng* (fresh spring rolls; 99฿). Vietnamese pork pizza 65฿. Most dishes 50-100฿. Open daily 7:30am-11pm. AmEx/MC/V. ❷

Na Mai, 42/14 Ammarat Rd. (☎239 958), 2 blocks west of Kaen Inn. From the outside it's a gentle, pink European cottage—on the inside it's spicy Thai food all the way. Try the asparagus, baby corn, and cabbage or the curried seafood in coconut shell (either one 80฿). Open daily 11:30am-10pm. ❷

The First Choice Restaurant, 18/8 Phimpasut Rd., opposite Khon Kaen Hotel. Numerous vegetarian choices. Set breakfast 70฿. Thai dishes 50-100฿. Pizza 160฿. Steaks 150-250฿. Open daily 7:30am-11pm. ❷

Nanrong (☎243 610), on Glang Muang Rd., near the intersection with Pracha Samoson Rd. Serves a simple menu in a simple wooden house. Curry noodles 20฿. Pork stew 30฿. Open daily 8am-8pm. ❶

◎ SIGHTS

The only noteworthy sight here is the well-presented **Khon Kaen National Museum,** at the Lungsoomratchakan and Kasikonthungsang Rd. intersection. Lime-green *songthaew* #14 stops here. The museum documents the history of central northeast Thailand. The second floor has articles from the olden days (Lopburi period) while the first floor is devoted to the really olden days (Ban Chiang period and earlier). Particularly impressive are the *semas*, or carved boundary stones. (☎246 170. Open W-Su 9am-4pm. 30฿.)

In the southeast corner of Khon Kaen is **Bung Kaen Nakhon,** a lakeside recreational area enclosed by four *wats* and numerous food stalls. Every April it hosts the **Dok Khoon Song Kran Festival,** featuring Isaan music, floral processions, and dances. On the southeast shores of the lake is **Wat Nong Waeng,** where you can climb to the top of the 9-story *chedi* for panoramic views of the city.

About 4km northwest of town, **Khon Kaen University** is home to a small art and cultural **museum** (☎332 035), near the university gate on Maliwan Rd., displaying temporary exhibits. There's also a fine arts department on campus and, if you're lucky, friendly students may give you a tour and show you their artwork. *Songthaew* #8 makes the trip through campus from town, passing the museum.

Prathamakant Local Goods Center, 79/2-3 Ruen Rom Rd., is 30m from the Nah Muang Rd. intersection. Those unable to visit **Chonabot** (p. 259) can enjoy silk handicrafts here. Lots of *mudmee* silks, classy and funky shirts and skirts, wooden carvings, and instruments for sale. (☎224 080. Open daily 9am-8:30pm.)

◪ ◱ NIGHTLIFE AND SHOPPING

The arcade near The First Choice Restaurant is packed with karaoke bars, beer gardens, and pubs. All the major hotels behind Sri Chant Road have some sort of nightlife, like the **GIK** discotheque at the Hotel Sofitel. Across the street is the Kosa Shopping Center, a generic mall showing Hollywood **movies** (dubbed in Thai, 80฿). There's also a **cinema** at the more popular Fairy Plaza Shopping Center, on Nah Muang Rd. Adjacent to the Sofitel Hotel on Prachasamran Rd. is the **Times Square** complex with six small bars. (Small Singha 50฿. Open 9pm-1am.) The **Zolid Discotheque,** on the bottom floor of the Charoen Thani Princess Hotel, off Nah Muang Rd., has three levels of dancing and huge screens showing music videos. (☎240 400. Small Singha 80฿. No cover. Open daily 9pm-2am.)

⚡ DAYTRIPS FROM KHON KAEN

PHUWIANG NATIONAL PARK

Buses to Phuwiang (25฿) leave daily before 1:30pm from the regular bus terminal. From Phuwiang Station, hire a tuk-tuk for the remaining 20km (100฿). Open daily 8:30am-4:40pm. Park admission 200฿.

Those interested in ancient reptiles should swing by Phuwiang, home to the largest dinosaur fossils in the country. Fossils dug up from the nine quarries located in the area have added weight to the theory that *Tyrannosaurus Rex* existed first in Asia Minor before crossing the Bering Straight to North America. (30฿ camping fee, 120฿ 2-person tent; bungalows 300฿ per person.)

CHONABOT

Catch a bus to Nakhon Sawan (1hr., every hr. until 1:30pm, 22฿) from Khon Kaen's regular bus terminal and ask to be let off at Chonabot police station. Facing the station, walk right to the 1st intersection and turn left. The 1st silk factory is on the right after the post office. The last bus back to Khon Kaen leaves at 5pm. Most factories open M-Sa 8am-5pm.

Chonabot's livelihood comes from hand-woven silk. Besides the small factories peppering the town, the **Sala Mai Thai,** located 3km from town toward Nakhon Sawan on the left, sells local wares and presents exhibits on the silk-making process. (☎286 160. Prices vary depending on the thickness and weight of the material. *Mudmee* silk runs 1300฿ for 4 yards. Open daily 9am-5pm.)

BAN KOK SA-NGA

45km from Khon Kaen. From the regular bus station, take a bus to Kra Nuan (1½hr.; every 30min., last return 6pm; 15฿) on Rte. 2039. Get off at Km 14 and ride a tuk-tuk to the village (30฿) or walk the 2km. Snake-breeding center open to the public (20฿).

Villagers in "King Cobra Village" have been taming deadly king cobras since 1951, using them as attention-getters for their herbal medicine businesses. Villagers stage "boxing" exhibitions: after tempting the snakes to strike, the masters skillfully sidestep death. Performances must be scheduled in advance. Contact Mr. Prayoon Yongla (☎06 219 0428).

ROI ET ☎043

Peering above Roi Et's busy streets and concrete roofscapes is the tranquil gaze of the world's tallest blessing Buddha. The Buddha is not the only hyperbolic symbol; the town's name "101," refers to Roi Et's former prosperity, when it boasted 11 gates and 11 vassal townships but was frequently ravished by floods. Rebuilt in another area, this growing provincial capital commemorates its illustrious past with a new city gate adjacent to one of the northeast's best-manicured urban parks. Situated in the heart of Isaan, the town is a great place to sample regional staples like *sup nau mai* (bamboo shoot curry), browse *mudmee* (tie-dyed silks) and *khaens* (Isaan panpipes), and visit the province's *wats*.

NORTHEAST THAILAND

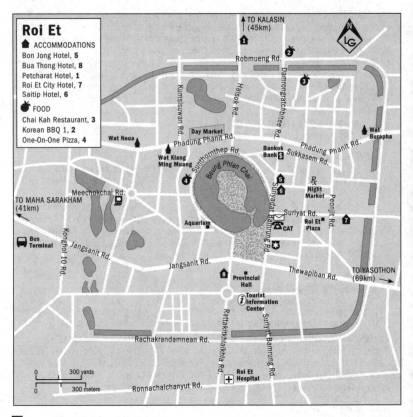

Roi Et

🏠 ACCOMMODATIONS
Bon Jong Hotel, **5**
Bua Thong Hotel, **8**
Petcharat Hotel, **1**
Roi Et City Hotel, **7**
Saitip Hotel, **6**

🍴 FOOD
Chai Kah Restaurant, **3**
Korean BBQ 1, **2**
One-On-One Pizza, **4**

🚆 **TRANSPORTATION.** The **airport** (☎518 246), is 13km from town on the Roi Et-Pon Thong Rd. **PB Air** (☎518 572; office open daily 9am-4pm) flies to Bangkok (M 8:30am, Tu-Sa 4:50pm; 1980฿).

The Roi Et **bus terminal** (☎511 939) is 2km west of town towards Maha Sarakham on Jangsanit Rd. From the post office, take a right onto Jangsanit Rd. for 2km. **Buses** run to: Bangkok (8hr.; every hr. 5:30am-1:30pm, 5-9:30pm; 228-455฿) via Khorat (4hr., 120-155฿); Don Tan (3hr.; 7am, 10, 12:40pm; 59฿); Kalasin (1hr., every 30min. 5:30am-4:30pm, 20฿); Surin (3hr., every hr. 5:30am-4:30pm, 70฿); Ubon Ratchathani (3hr., every hr. 11pm-8pm, 60-110฿) via Yasothon (1½hr., 20฿); Udon Thani (4hr., every hr. 8:30am-3:30pm, 61-140฿) via Khon Kaen (2hr., 74฿). **Samlor** will take you around town for 20-30฿.

🛈 **PRACTICAL INFORMATION.** Roi Et is centered around the Beung Phlan Chai Lake. **Sunthornthep Road** encircles the lake, until it joins with **Suriyadet Bamrung Road** in the east. Most stores and hotels are east of the lake, on **Peonjit Road. Rattakitkhlaikhla Road** to the south and **Haisok Road** to the north bisect the city north-south. The bus terminal is located on the western end of the main east-west artery, **Jangsanit Road.** Jangsanit Rd. becomes **Thewapiban Road** in the east. The hospital, tourist center, and other provincial government buildings are centered around a **traffic circle** where Rattakitkhlaikhla and **Rachakran-damnean Road** intersect, south of the lake.

The **tourist information center** is on Rachakrandamnean Rd., near the traffic circle. Only limited English is spoken. (☎511 055. Open M-F 8:30am-4pm.) **Bangkok Bank,** 27 Suriyadet Bamrung Rd., at the intersection of Sukkasem Rd., **exchanges currency** and has a **24hr. ATM.** (☎514 591. Open M-F 8:30am-3:30pm. Cirrus/MC/V.) The **day market** is at the intersection of Haisok and Phadung Phanit Rd., north of the lake. The **night market,** one of the largest in Isaan, sets up off of Peonjit Rd., between Sukkasem and Suriyat Rd. Other services include: **police,** 123 Suriyadet Bamrung Rd. (☎511 777), next to CAT; Bhasucha-kornchumchan (**community pharmacy**), 56-58 Prame Pracharaj Rd., opposite the night market, diagonally across from the 7-Eleven (☎575 451; open daily 8am-8pm); the **Roi Et Hospital** (☎518 200), on Ronnachaichanyut Rd., away from the lake, past the traffic circle and moat on Rattakitkhlaikhla Rd., on the left across from the 7-Eleven; **Internet** access, 27/2 Meechokchai Rd., past the traffic circle on Meechokchai Rd. coming from the lake, on the left (15฿ per hr.; open daily 9am-midnight); **international calls** and faxes at CAT, 119 Suriyadet Bamrung Rd., next to the post office (☎511 500; **Internet** 7.20฿ per hr.; min. 100฿; open M-F 8am-4:30pm); and the **GPO,** 117 Suriyadet Bamrung Rd., at the intersection with Suriyat Rd. (☎520 505. Open M-F 8:30am-4:30pm, Sa-Su 9am-noon.) **Postal Code:** 45000.

⌜⌐⌐⌐ ACCOMMODATIONS AND FOOD. Roi Et City Hotel ❺, 78 Peonjit Rd., across from the Roi Et Shopping Plaza, is Roi Et's classiest hotel, located in the heart of the commercial area. (☎520 387. Breakfast included. Singles and doubles 980฿. MC/V.) **Petcharat Hotel ❷,** 66-80 Haisok Rd., is past the moat, across from the Mai Thai Hotel. There are cheap and musty rooms on the first floor; the second floor is a step up in cleanliness and value. VIP rooms are decked out in gold satin bed coverings and thin purple curtains. All rooms have A/C, TV, hot water, and a Western toilet. (☎511 741. Singles and doubles 250-300฿; VIP rooms 600฿.) The **Saitip Hotel ❷,** 95 Suriyadet Bamrung Rd., is situated around a large parking lot. Firm mattresses and clean air-conditioned rooms compensate for knee-busting squat toilets. (☎511 742. Singles and doubles 250฿, with A/C 300฿.) **Bua Thong Hotel ❷,** 40-46 Rattakitkhlaikhla Rd., is near the lake facing the park; look for the sign that says "hotel." You can't beat the price, but you can beat the quality. (☎511 142. Singles and doubles 120฿, with TV 180฿, with A/C 270฿.) **Bon Jong Hotel ❷,** 81-83 Suriyadet Bamrung Rd., has powerful fans that luckily blow away the fumes from the squat toilet. (☎511 235. Singles and doubles 150฿.)

The best Isaan food can be found in roadside take-away stalls throughout the city. **Korean BBQ 1** (Ngeu Yang Kao Lee Rim Beung 1) ❹, 13/14 Robmueng Rd., is across the moat, one street over from Haisok Rd. Boasting over 200 tables, it's one of the largest restaurants in Isaan. Numerous meat, seafood, and vegetarian items are available to cook yourself over the grill or hot pot. One of the most popular dishes is *plaa chon loei suan* (fish with vegetables), 180฿. Request your favorite Thai pop tune from the DJ. (☎513 407. Open daily noon-midnight). **Chai Kah Restaurant ❷,** 67 Damrongratchbitee Rd., along the northern moat, serves Isaan, Thai, and Chinese food. (Fried chicken 60฿. Fish salad 100฿. Fried vegetables 50฿.) **One-Oh-One Pizza ❷,** 98/5 Sunthornthep Rd., near Meechokchai Rd. on the lake, has a simple decor and menu. The schnitzel steak with green salad is 75฿. (☎514 070. Burgers 50฿. Spaghetti 90฿. Pizzas 90-210฿. Delivery within ring road; free if order is over 250฿. Open daily 10:30am-midnight.)

⬛ **SIGHTS. Wat Burapha,** off of Phadung Phanit Rd., in the northeast corner of town. From Peonjit Rd., turn right onto Phadung Phanit. Wat Burapha is 500m to the left—keep looking up; you can't miss it. The largest structure at this *wat* isn't a pagoda; it's the world's tallest Buddha in a blessing posture, towering over the city at 67.8m. A set of stairs runs up behind the Buddha until about its hands. A small **aquarium** featuring northeast aquatic wildlife is located on the shores of the lake. (☎511 286. Open W-Su 8:30am-4:30pm. Admission 30฿.) The 200-year-old monastic hall at **Wat Klang Ming Muang,** on Phadung Phanit Rd., houses mural paintings and has a three-story bell tower you can climb up. From the lake, take a left onto Phadung Phanit Rd.; the *wat* is on the left. Two blocks past Wat Klang Ming Muang on Phadung Phanit Rd., **Wat Neua** boasts a 1200-year-old *chedi* set in a quiet courtyard dotted with *semaa*, ancient marker stones. Also on Phadung Phanit Rd., between Haisok and Peonjit Rds., are craft stores selling **silk** at cheaper prices than in Khon Kaen.

▶ **DAYTRIPS FROM ROI ET. Khu Phra Khona** is a set of three 12th- and 13th-century Khmer towers in the Bapuan style; the middle tower was restored in the 1920s. Take any Surin-bound bus to Suwannaphum (25฿). From there, it's an additional 12km. Your best bet is to hire a motorbike—the trip is 57km from Roi Et.

Costing seven billion *baht,* **Phra Maha Chai Mongkol Chedi** ("the great, victorious, and auspicious pagoda"), lives up to its name. It's on 101 *rai* of land, 101m in width, length, and height—further references to the town's name. You can walk along the wall that encloses a 7000m² forest. Located 80km from Roi Et, any Don Tan-bound bus that passes through Nong Phok will pass the temple.

Along Yasothon Rd. is **Wat Pha Noan Sawan.** With two towers resembling pinecones, and two giant tortoises welcoming you to this temple's entrance, shaped like the mouth of Hanuman (from the *Ramayana*), you may feel like you're in an acid-tripped 1950s theme park. Yasothon-bound buses will drop you off (15฿). From the drop-off point, the *wat* is another 4km down the road on your right. Farther away from Roi Et on Yasothon Rd. is **Beung Khla,** a reservoir with food stalls. Take any bus to Yasothon; the reservoir is about 10km past Selaphum.

YASOTHON ☎045

If all Isaan is off the beaten path, Yasothon is another two steps off; the only *farang* you'll meet here are holding a Bible or their Thai wife's hand. The only time tourists flock here is during the *Boon Bang Fai,* northeast Thailand's largest rocket festival. Commencing during the end of the dry season over a weekend in mid-May, the rituals summon the rain god Phaya Thaen to ensure plentiful water for the planting season. The festival begins with parades and bamboo-rocket launches during the day, and ends with fireworks at night. As the festival is a fertility rite, those men whose rockets fail to launch or explode midway up are appropriately slung with mud. Besides the festival, Yasothon has little to hold tourists' interests except for a few small mosques on the outskirts of town, providing a respite for those *wat*-ted out.

📧 **TRANSPORTATION.** Located on the highway between Roi Et and Ubon Ratchathani, frequent **buses** to these cities pass through town along Rte. 23 (Chaeng Sanit Rd); there's a **bus stop** in front of the district office, near the intersection of Wariratchadet Rd. The **bus terminal** (☎712 965) on Rattanaket Rd. mostly serves buses within the province; however, there are buses to Roi Et (1½hr., 9 per day 7:10am-4pm, 38-49฿) and Ubon (1½hr., 8 per day 11:20am-5:50pm, 53-68฿).

🛈 PRACTICAL INFORMATION. Chaeng Sanit Road (Route 23) is the main artery through town. Paralleling Chaeng Sanit to its east are **Prachasamphan** and **Rattana-ket Roads,** where most of the shops, restaurants, and the bus terminal are. **War-iratchadet Road** and **Wittayathamrong Road** are the main cross streets, demarcated by traffic signals on Chaeng Sanit Rd. Paralleling Wittayathamrong Rd. one block north is **Uthairamrit Road.**

Services include: **Bangkok Bank,** 241 Chaeng Sanit Rd., which exchanges **currency** and has a **24hr. ATM** (☎711 443; open M-F 8:30am-3:30pm; Cirrus/MC/V); the **police** (☎711 572), on Chaeng Sanit Rd., on the right when exiting the provincial hall; **Yasothon Hospital,** 26 Chaeng Sanit Rd. (☎714 042), about 1km outside of town towards Ubon, at the corner of the Rte. 202 junction; and the **pharmacy,** 193 Chaeng Sanit Rd., near the intersection with Wittayathamrong Rd. (☎714 567. Open daily 8am-8pm.) The only **Internet** access in town is at Cool Bytes, 72-74 Soi Nanapan. From Chaeng Sanit Rd., take a left on War-iratchadet Rd.; it's down a *soi* across from the market. (15฿ per hr. Open daily 8:30am-9pm.) The **post office** (☎711 761) is located on 216 Chaeng Sanit Rd., between the provincial hall and Wariratchadet Rd. (Open M-F 8:30am-4:30pm, Sa-Su 9am-noon.) **Postal Code:** 35000.

🛏🍴 ACCOMMODATIONS AND FOOD. Surprisingly for such a small town, Yasothon's accommodations are all at mid-range prices. These prices, however, nearly double during the Rocket festival; it's best to book early. **JP Emerald Hotel ❺,** 36 Prapa Rd., is down the road across from the provincial hall. It's Yasothon's most luxurious and expensive hotel. (☎724 848. Breakfast included. Singles and doubles start at 800฿. MC/V.) **Yasothon Orchid Garden Hotel ❸,** 219 Rattanaket Rd., extends the entire block to Prachasamphan Rd. From the bus station, it's on the first block on the left. This Mediterranean-yellow hotel is Yasothon's newest and brightest hotel. Large white rooms come with TV, A/C, and hot water. (☎721 000. Singles and doubles 400฿. MC/V.) **RP Mansion Park 1994 ❸,** 275 Prachasamphan Rd., is only one block away from Yasothon Orchid Garden Hotel with your back facing Wittayathamrong Rd. Although more dated, rooms and prices are identical. (☎712 235. Singles and doubles 400฿. MC/V.) **Yodnakhon Hotel ❷** is at 143/1 Uthairamrit Rd. From Bangkok Bank, turn left onto Uthairamrit Rd.; it's on the left two blocks down. All rooms have TV, fan, cold water, and that's about it. (☎712 662. Singles 250฿, with A/C 300; doubles 280฿/330฿.) In the rare chance that all of the above are full, the **Varathon Hotel ❷,** 600-12 Chaeng Sanit Rd., has budget rooms at mid-range prices. On the main highway to Ubon, it's about 1km from Wittayathamrong Rd. on the right. (☎712 736. Singles and doubles 250฿, with A/C 300฿.)

Most restaurants in Yasothon serve standard Isaan fare like *sup nau mai* (bam-boo-shoot curry), as well as the Isaan triad: *gai yang* (grilled chicken, 30฿), *som tam* (papaya salad, 10฿), and *khao niaw* (sticky rice, 5฿). The best food is at the roadside **food stalls ❶** throughout town, although there are some "formal" eating establishments as well. **Chai Bakery ❷,** 257/4 Rattanaket Rd., specializes in Isaan salads (60฿), as well as ice cream. It occasionally offers delicious cream puffs in the shape of a swan (5฿). From the bus terminal, it's located one block to the right. (☎712 370. Pizza 130฿. Steak 80-160฿. Open daily 8am-9pm.) **Cool Bytes ❷,** 72-74 Soi Nannapan, on the first floor of the Internet cafe (p. 263), serves up fried chicken (20฿ per piece), spaghetti (40฿), and pizza (59฿).

◐ **SIGHTS. Wat Mahathat,** off Wariratchadet Rd., is home to the highly revered **Phra That Anon,** a Lao-style *chedi* that houses the relics of Phra Anon, Lord Buddha's first disciple. According to legend, two monks, Phra Voh and Phra Tad, were banished from Vientiane after trying to build a *chedi* there. Undaunted, they built it here instead. Adjacent to the *chedi* is a 19th-century wooden scripture hall built above a pond. Exiting the post office, take a right onto Chaeng Sanit Rd. and another right on Wariratchadet Rd.; the temple is on the left.

The nearby village of **Ban Si Than** is famous for producing *mawn khwan,* triangular pillows found throughout Isaan, as well as *mudmee* silk and cotton fabrics. To get here, take a bus heading to Amnat Charoen and get off at the right turn-off between Km markers 18 and 19; it's another 3km down the road.

NORTHERN THAILAND

Northern Thailand's mountains constitute the lowest crags of the Himalayan foothills. Its Salawin River flirts with Myanmar before flooding into the Bay of Bengal, and its northeastern border is formed by none other than the mighty Mekong. Central Chiang Mai, formerly the capital of the prosperous Lanna Kingdom, serves as the first stop for many visitors. The magnificent historical ruins of Sukhothai break up the journey from Bangkok. The hill-tribe haven of Mae Hong Son is to the west. Many just choose to savor a peaceful piece of Pai, accessible by the renowned Mae Hong Son Loop. Chiang Rai, in the north, harbors poppy fields and the Golden Triangle. To the east, Nan, which borders Laos, is a good place for *wat*-lovers, as well as those seeking locales off the beaten path. Throughout the region, Chinese immigrants display pictures of the Thai Royal Family, tribal minorities inhabit remote mountainsides, and refugee camps swell with Burmese escaping their government. The dialect, cuisine, dance, and *wat* architecture of northern Thailand owe much to this fusion of cultures, reflecting the myriad influences of the region.

CHIANG MAI ☎ 053

The sighting of several good omens convinced King Mengrai to establish the seat of his great Lanna Kingdom in Chiang Mai in 1296—an auspicious beginning for a city that has become Thailand's second-largest, both in population and in tourist crowds. Thousands of *farang*, drawn by the promise of adventure and a cooler climate, clog the narrow streets of this ancient city. Some have long since surrendered to its charm, making the city their home and adding to the small expatriate community. The beautiful "Rose of the North" bustles with a big-city gait around the ancient ruins, largely oblivious of their presence. The increased stampede of tourists raises concerns that both hill-tribe culture and the natural environment are quickly eroding. Nonetheless, Chiang Mai seems to have retained its cultural autonomy. The distinctive dialect, Burmese-influenced art and architecture, and an abundance of sticky rice (a northern specialty) prove that the city is not about to surrender its heritage.

✈ INTERCITY TRANSPORTATION

The monthly magazines *Welcome to Chiang Mai and Chiang Rai* and *Guidelines Chiang Mai*, available at travel agencies, guesthouses, and hotels throughout the city, have comprehensive transportation schedules.

BY PLANE

Chiang Mai International Airport (☎270 222), on Sanambin (Airport) Rd., 3km southwest of the city center, is accessible by **taxi** (100฿), *tuk-tuk* (50฿), or *songthaew* (20฿). **Thai Airways,** 240 Phra Pokklao Rd., has branches around the city. (☎211 044. Open daily 8am-5pm.) It flies to: Bangkok (11 per day 7am-9:15pm, 2170฿); Mae Hong Son (5 per day, 10am-4:10pm, 765฿); Phuket (daily 11:15am, 4640฿); Kunming, China (Tu, Su 2:30pm). **Bangkok Airways,** at the airport (☎281 519), flies to:

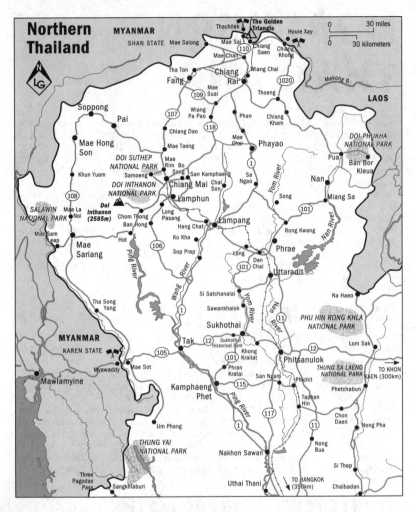

Bangkok (1-2 per day, 2170฿) via Sukhothai (940฿); Jinghong (Tu, Th 4:10pm; 4540฿); **Xian** (W, Su 7:50pm; 10,910฿). **Lao Airlines** (☎ 223 401) flies to Vientiane (Tu, F, Su 1:30pm; 3360฿) via Luang Prabang. **Air Mandalay,** 148 Charoen Prathet Rd. (☎ 818 049), flies to Mandalay (Th 2:55pm; 3200฿) and Yangon (Tu, Su 2:55pm; 2895฿). **Mandarin Airlines** (☎ 201 268), 2nd floor at the airport, flies to Taipei (Tu, Sa 10:45am). **Silk Air,** 153 Sri Donchai Rd., at the Imperial Maeping Hotel, flies to Singapore. (Tu, Th, F 10:55am; Su 5:30pm; 7000฿. ☎ 276 459. Open M-F 8:30am-5pm, Sa-Su 8:30am-1pm.) A branch of STA Travel is **Trans World Travel Service Co., Ltd.,** 259/61 Tha Pae Rd. (☎ 272 416), which may offer cheaper student tickets than carriers do. You'll need a student card (200฿ with passport and proof of student status). All international flights are subject to a 500฿ departure tax (cash only).

BY TRAIN

The **Chiang Mai Railway Station,** 27 Charoen Muang Rd. (☎244 795), on the eastern outskirts of the city, is accessible by *songthaew* (10-20฿) and *tuk-tuk* (40-50฿). Trains run daily to Bangkok (11-14hr., 7 per day 6:55am-9:50pm, 161-1193฿). Most Bangkok-bound trains also stop in Lampang (2hr., 23-53฿) and Phitsanulok (6-7hr., 105-190฿). Many options are available for an extra charge. Reserve sleeper tickets well in advance (this must be done in person); lower berths are pricier. (Refunds: 80% 3 days before travel. Ticket window open daily 6am-8pm.)

BY BUS

Tuk-tuks (30-50฿) and *songthaew* (20฿) shuttle between the old city and **Arcade Bus Station** (☎242 664), 3km to the northeast. **Chang Phuak Bus Station** (☎211 586), on Chang Phuak Rd., 1km north of the old city, runs buses within the province.

DESTINATION, BUS#	DUR.	FREQUENCY/TIME	PRICE
ARCADE BUS STATION			
Bangkok, 18	10hr.	19 per day 6:30am-9pm	224-625฿
Chiang Rai, 166	3hr.	17 per day 6am-5:30pm	77-139฿
Chiang Khong, 671	6hr.	6:30, 8am, 12:30pm	121-169฿
Khon Kaen, 633 or 175	12hr.	11 per day 5am-9pm	219-437฿
Khorat, 635 (Nakhon Ratchasima)	12hr.	10 per day 3:30am-8:30pm	243-510฿
Lampang, 152	2hr.	every 30min. 6am-4pm	29฿
Mae Hong Son, 170	8hr.	6:30, 8, 11am, 8, 9pm	143-257฿
via Mae Sariang	5hr.	1:30, 3pm (Mae Sariang only)	78-140฿
Mae Hong Son, 612	7hr.	7, 9, 10:30am, 12:30pm	105-147฿
via Pai	4hr.	4pm (Pai only)	60฿
Mae Sai, 619	4hr.	8 per day 6am-5pm	95-171฿
Mae Sot, 672	6hr.	11am, 1:10pm	134-241฿
Nan, 169 or 113	6hr.	15 per day 6:15am-10:30pm	117-230฿
Phitsanulok, 155, 132, or 623	6hr.	11 per day 6:30am-8pm	120-196฿
Sukhothai	5hr.	13 per day 5am-8pm	122-171฿
Ubon Ratchathani, 587	17hr.	6 per day 12:15-6pm	325-685฿
CHANG PHUAK BUS STATION			
Chom Thong	1¼hr.	every 20min. 6:30am-6pm	23฿
Lamphun	1hr.	every 10min. 6:20am-6pm	12฿
Tha Ton	4hr.	6 per day 6am-3:30pm	70฿
via Fang	3½hr.	every 30min. 5:30am-5:30pm	60฿

■ ORIENTATION

Chiang Mai is 720km north of Bangkok. The primary area of interest is within the old city and the area to its east, which stretches 1.5km to the **Ping River.** A square moat delineates the old city; within it, the east-west *soi* numbers increase as you go north. **Phra Pokklao Road** (north-south) and **Ratchadamnoen Road** (east-west) divide the city. **Moon Muang Road** follows the inside of the moat and intersects Ratchadamnoen Rd. at **Tha Pae Gate,** the center of backpacker activity. **Tha Pae Road** runs east from Tha Pae Gate, crossing the river on **Nawarat Bridge.** Along the way, it intersects **Chang Klan Road,** home to the night bazaar, and **Charoen Prathet Road,** which flanks the Ping's west bank. TAT is on **Chiang Mai-Lamphun Road,**

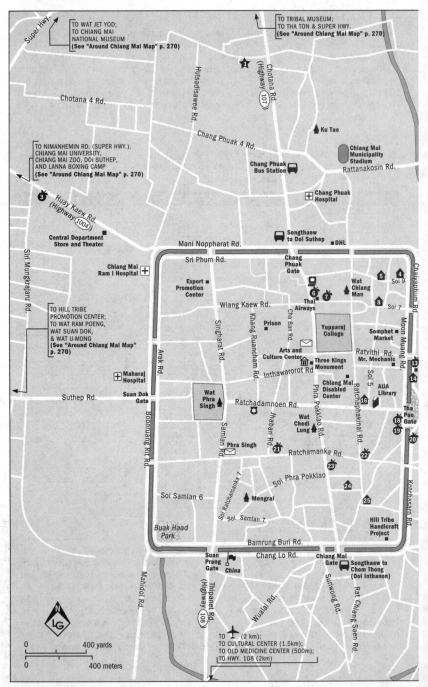

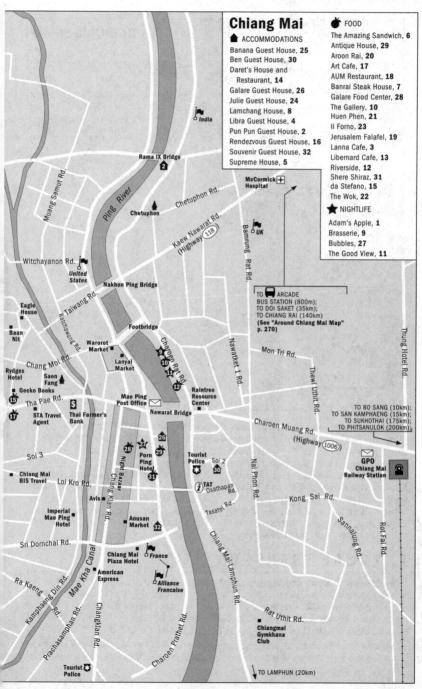

Chiang Mai

🏠 ACCOMMODATIONS

Banana Guest House, 25
Ben Guest House, 30
Daret's House and
 Restaurant, 14
Galare Guest House, 26
Julie Guest House, 24
Lamchang House, 8
Libra Guest House, 4
Pun Pun Guest House, 2
Rendezvous Guest House, 16
Souvenir Guest House, 32
Supreme House, 5

🍴 FOOD

The Amazing Sandwich, 6
Antique House, 29
Aroon Rai, 20
Art Cafe, 17
AUM Restaurant, 18
Banrai Steak House, 7
Galare Food Center, 28
The Gallery, 10
Huen Phen, 21
Il Forno, 23
Jerusalem Falafel, 19
Lanna Cafe, 3
Libernard Cafe, 13
Riverside, 12
Shere Shiraz, 31
da Stefano, 15
The Wok, 22

⭐ NIGHTLIFE

Adam's Apple, 1
Brasserie, 9
Bubbles, 27
The Good View, 11

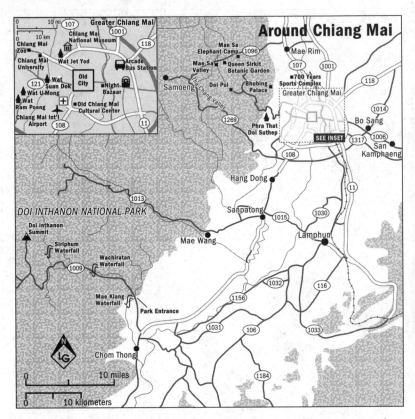

which hugs the Ping River's east bank. The circuitous nature of the one-way roads is quite straightforward once you've mastered the pattern. Fortunately, there's no need, as walking is easy (15min. from Tha Pae Gate to the night bazaar) and *tuk-tuk* and *songthaew* flood the streets for longer trips.

Guesthouses, TAT, and other tourist-geared establishments stock free copies of *Guidelines Chiang Mai* and *What's on Chiang Mai*, which offer occasionally useful and often amusing practical info. Watch out for *City Life Chiang Mai*, the closest thing the expatriate community has to a local paper, with announcements, classifieds, and expatriate horror stories. Tough to find, it may be easiest to read online at www.chiangmainews.com.

⌐ LOCAL TRANSPORTATION

Songthaew, Tuk-tuk, and Samlor: *Songthaew* (10-20฿) go anywhere in the city except along special routes, to the airport, or to the bus station. They don't run at night. Don't pay more than 40฿. Already occupied *songthaew* are cheaper than empty ones. *Tuk-tuks* and *samlor* cost 20-30฿ within the old city, 40-60฿ for trips across the city, and 400-500฿ per day. **Taxi** service (☎ 201 307) can also be arranged.

Bike Rentals: Bicycle and motorbike rental shops litter the Tha Pae Gate area; all require a deposit, a photocopy of passport, or both. Bicycles 30-60฿ per day. Motorbike rental is typically 150฿ per day for 100cc and 200฿ for 125cc, with an additional 50฿ for insurance. Discounts for long-term rental. With similar pricing throughout Chiang Mai, the quality of a shop's bikes and the service they provide in the event of a breakdown sets them apart. High in both respects, **Mr. Mechanic**, 4 Moon Muang Rd. Soi 5 (☎214 708), also has comprehensive insurance. Motorbike 120฿, with insurance 170฿, and a full range of options 300-700฿ per day. **The Chiang Mai Disabled Center**, 133/1 Ratchaphakhinai Rd., rents mountain bikes (40฿ per day).

Car Rentals: Avis, Royal Princess Hotel, 112 Chang Klan Rd. (☎281 033), and the airport (☎201 574) rents Toyota Corollas (1790฿ per day) and Suzuki 4WD (1290฿ per day). Open daily 8am-5pm. In the Old City, **North Wheels**, 127/2 Moon Muang Rd. (☎216 189).

⁊ PRACTICAL INFORMATION

TOURIST AND FINANCIAL SERVICES

Tourist Office: TAT, 105/1 Chiang Mai-Lamphun Rd. (☎248 604), across from the first bridge 500m south of Nawarat Bridge. On the 2nd fl. Chock-full of maps, current transportation schedules and brochures. English spoken. Open daily 8:30am-4:30pm.

Consulates: Australia, Canada, China, France, India, UK, and the **US** offer visas and consular services. See **Embassies and Consulates,** p. 35, for contact info.

Visa Services: Travel agents around town can organize visas. **Laos** (same price as in Bangkok). 4-day processing 750฿ for 15-day visa, 2-day wait 1050฿. **Vietnam** (slightly more expensive than in Bangkok): 4-day processing 2400฿ for a 1-month visa.

Immigration Office: 97 Sanambin (Airport) Rd. (☎277 510). **Visa extensions:** 1-day processing 500฿. Bring 2 passport photos, 2 copies of passport photo page, visa, and arrival/departure card. Open M-F 8:30am-noon and 1-4:30pm.

Currency Exchange: Banks line Tha Pae Rd. **Thai Farmers Bank,** 169-171 Tha Pae Rd. (☎270 151). **24hr. ATM** Cirrus/MC/PLUS/V. Open M-F 8:30am-3:30pm. Currency exchange booths in the night bazaar on Chang Klan Rd. Open daily until 10pm.

American Express: Sea Tours Company, 2/3 Prachasamphan Rd. (☎271 441). The only AmEx affiliate in Northern Thailand. Will replace American Express Traveler's Cheques. Open M-F 8:30am-4:30pm, Sa 8:30-11:30am.

Work Opportunities: Australia Center, 75/1 Moo 14, Suthep Rd. (☎810 552), on a *soi* after the turn-off to Wat U-Mong, provides a leaflet on working in Chiang Mai as an English teacher. **Rejoice Urban Development** (☎806 227; www.rejoicecharity.com) on Canal Rd. Take Suthep Rd. to Canal Rd., the next major intersection after the turn-off to the super-highway. Turn left; it's 7 bridges down on the right. For more opportunities, see **Alternatives to Tourism,** p. 84.

LOCAL SERVICES

Luggage Storage: At the **train station** (☎245 363) 10฿ per piece per day for the first 5 days, 15฿ per additional day, 20-day max. Open daily 4:50am-8:45pm. At the **airport** 30฿ per day, 14-day max. Open daily 6am-10pm. Most guesthouses store luggage for free, although security is questionable; never leave passports or credit cards in luggage.

Books: The best used bookstores, **Gecko Books** (☎874 066), open daily 10am-7pm, and **Backstreet Book** (☎871 413), open daily 9am-10pm, sit next to each other on Chang Moi Kao Rd. at the Tha Pae Gate. The **American University Alumni Language Center (AUA);** (☎211 973) offers library service with a large selection of English books and videos. 1-day pass if you want to sit in A/C and read the paper. Visitor membership 140฿ per month. Resident 400฿ per year. Open M-F 8:30am-6pm, Sa 9am-1pm.

THROW WATER AT MONKS—EVERYONE'S DOING IT

t's impossible to hit the streets during ◆**Songkran** (Thai New Year Festival) without being hit with streams of water. Originally, water symbolized cleansing—literally washing away the previous year. The more traditional aspect of the festival involves pouring scented water over the shoulders and hands of elders in a request for blessing.

Most of the time, however, you'll be dodging masterfully aimed beams of water, shot from pump action water guns, and having your cheeks smeared with a mix of baby powder and water. If it seems somewhat dangerous, that's because it is. In 2002, three people drowned in Chiang Mai, while the national death toll stood at 564, with 37,473 injuries, most from drunk driving but some related to vision-impaired accidents. A few visitors gripe that the three-day festival lasts too long, but most find themselves joining in on the fun.

The traditional home of Songkran is in the villages. An exodus from the cities to family reunions in the country leads to logistical nightmares reminiscent of airports on Christmas Eve. Reunited families participate in cleansing and merry-making. The first day corresponds to the last day of the Old Year; nothing impure should be brought forward. Instead it is a time to bless elders and cleanse

[Cont'd on next page...]

Markets: The **night bazaar** (p. 281), a must-see of Chiang Mai, dominates Chang Klan Rd. 6pm-midnight and is stocked with hill-tribe handicrafts, expensive furniture, and designer rip-offs. The southern end leads to sit-down food joints at Anusan Market where the English dishes may be up to double the price. Head north to the **nightly food stalls** at Warorot Market for a cheap and quick bite.

EMERGENCY AND COMMUNICATIONS

Ambulance: ☎ 1669.

Tourist Police: (☎ 248 130), on Chiang Mai-Lamphun Rd. Open **24hr.**

Pharmacy: Pharma Choice 2 (☎ 280 136), in Suriwong Plaza at Tha Pae Gate. Open daily 9am-7pm.

Medical Services: McCormick Hospital, 133 Kaew Nawarat Rd. (☎ 241 010), has ambulance service and a **24hr. pharmacy.** English-speaking doctors. MC/V. On the other side of town, the plush **Chiang Mai Ram I Hospital,** 9 Boonruang Rit Rd. (☎ 224 861), has the same services.

Telephones: Overseas calls at post offices. Internet cafes around town offer collect (30฿) and overseas calls. The cheapest overseas rates calls placed via the Internet.

Internet Access: Internet cafes line the northern half of Ratchaphakhinai Rd. 20฿ per hr. Around Tha Pae Gate 30฿ per hr. **The Chiang Mai Disabled Center,** 133/1 Ratchaphakhinai Rd., 20฿ per hr. Open daily 8am-8pm, Internet until approx. 10pm.

Post Offices: GPO (☎ 245 376), on Charoen Muang Rd., 150m toward the old city from the train station. *Poste Restante.* Open M-F 8:30am-4:30pm, Sa-Su 9am-noon. **Mae Ping Post Office** (☎ 252 037), on Charoen Prathet Rd., just north of Nawarat Bridge. Open M-F 8:30am-4:30pm, Sa 9am-noon. **Phra Singh Post Office** (☎ 814 062), on Samlan Rd., south of Wat Phra Singh. Open M-F 8:30am-4:30pm, Sa 9am-noon. All 3 provide **CATNET** with PIN or card. GPO and Phra Singh have **international phone/fax. DHL Worldwide Express,** 160/1 Mani Noppharat Rd. (☎ 418 501), east of the Chang Phuak Gate. Open M-F 8:30am-6pm, Sa 8:30am-5pm.

Postal Code: 50000.

▐ ACCOMMODATIONS

Guesthouse signs sprout from almost every *soi* entrance within a 1km radius of **Tha Pae Gate.** Reservations are recommended during festival periods (p. 31), the largest of which are the three-day **Flower Festival** in early February and the four-day **Songkran Water Festi-**

val (Thai New Year) in mid-April (see **Throw Water at Monks**, p. 272), when certain guesthouses inflate their prices. The easiest way to choose an accommodation is to pick a neighborhood. The area around Tha Pae Gate is in close proximity to everything, although the drone of traffic and bar tunes is unnerving. Heading north from Tha Pae Gate on Moon Muang Rd. (with the traffic) leads to Soi 7 and 9 in the Old City, blissfully quiet at night and packed with budget choices. The pace at the Ping River is frenetic, and it's difficult to find budget lodgings as upmarket hotels clog the area. Many guesthouses make their money from treks. In the high season, if you don't sign up for your guesthouse's trek, you may be asked to sign out. Many of the guesthouses listed have motorbike rentals, restaurants, and laundry service, and some will pick you up from the bus and train station if you call in advance. Beware of louts who tell you that the guesthouse you're interested in is closed or full—all they want is a competitor's commission.

THA PAE GATE AREA

Libra Guest House, 28 Moon Muang Rd. Soi 9 (☎/fax 210 687). Tidy, small rooms, a nice garden, and attentive service. Some backpackers may be annoyed by the rules and pressure to use Libra's services. Consistently praised treks (3-day, 1600฿, max. 12 people). Cooking school 700฿ per day. Laundry service 25฿ per kg. Check-out 10am. Reservations recommended. Doubles with bath 100฿, with hot water 150฿. ❶

Rendezvous Guest House, 3/1 Ratchadamnoen Rd. Soi 5 (☎213 763), 50m left off Ratchadamnoen Rd. Superb value with bath, TV, cable, and fridge in every room. Laundry service 30฿ per kg. Safety deposit box. Rooms 280฿, with A/C 380฿. ❹

Lamchang House, 24 Moon Muang Rd. Soi 7 (☎210 586). Charming house in a concrete jungle. The handful of comfy 1st-floor bamboo rooms are always full. All rooms with shared bath. Singles 90฿; doubles 160฿; 3-person private outdoor house 300฿. ❶

Supreme House, 44/1 Moon Muang Rd. Soi 9 (☎222 480), 100m from Libra Guest House. Helpful owner. No-hassle accommodation with flexible check-out time. 4000+ multi-language books, free for guest use. Singles with hot water 100฿, with A/C 200฿; doubles 150฿/250฿; triples and quads 200฿/300฿. ❶

Julie Guest House, 7/1 Soi 5 Phra Pokklao Rd. (www.julieguesthouse.com), best reached by walking down Ratchaphakhinai Rd., following the signs. Cheap rooms and rooftop hammocks are the big draws here. Pool table, TV, and VCR. Dorm 50฿; singles 130฿; doubles with hot shower 140฿; triples with hot shower 180฿. ❶

oneself. Not even the *muangs* (Buddha images) are spared a thorough scrub; the most important ones are paraded through the streets before receiving their bath at the temple. The second day is the transitional period into the New Year. Typically, sand is made into *chedis* outside temples in order to represent the sacred soil a lay person tramples upon during the year. The final day is the start of the New Year. In 2005, the year in Thailand will be 2548 (years after the death of Lord Buddha).

While every day has its associated customs, if you're just looking for some *sanuk* ("love of life" or "fun-loving"), you'll love the water fights of Songkran. If you can be in Thailand at the time, it's an unforgettable experience.

Bangkok's parades are the most elaborate, while Chiang Mai appears to have been designed with Songkran in mind—the moat serves as a constant reloading source for pickups packed with water assassins. But the villages are the place for a more traditionally Thai Songkran experience.

If you're planning to be in any of the major cities during Songrkan, book transportation and accommodations early. As with every national holiday, a lack of vacancies and gross inflation of prices are the norm. Also keep in mind that banks, museums, stores, and offices will be closed for those three days. One last warning—don't wear anything white (it will be transparent in 2min.).

Daret's House and Restaurant, 4/5 Chaiyaphum Rd. (☎235 440), opposite Tha Phae Gate's north end. Central location and top-notch restaurant make up for unimpressive rooms. Small bookstore. **International phone.** Internet 30฿ per hr. Check-out 10am. All rooms have bath. Singles 120฿; doubles and twins 140฿, with hot water 160฿. ❷

NEAR THE PING RIVER

Ben Guest House, 4/11 Chiang Mai-Lamphun Rd. Soi 2 (☎244 103, soiphet99@hotmail.com), down a *soi* adjacent to the tourist police, signposted for Ben's. Large beds, hot showers, and fans. Nice garden. Laundry service 40฿ per kg. Check-out 10am. Motorcycle rental 150฿, with insurance 200฿. Internet 30฿ per hr. All rooms 150฿. ❷

Pun Pun Guest House, 321 Charoen Rat Rd. (☎243 362; www.armms.com), at Rama IX Bridge. The only budget accommodation by the river, though a bit far from city center (about a 30min. walk). Small restaurant/bar with cable TV and pool table. Carlsberg 30฿. Bungalows by the river 175฿; rooms with hot water and Western toilet 225฿. ❷

Souvenir Guest House (☎818 786; www.souvenir-guesthouse.com), on Charoen Prathet Rd., at the intersection with Sri Donchai Rd. Nice rooms on a busy road. Table tennis and weight room, 2hr. 30฿. Best-value rooms are A3 and A4 with shared bath and patio. Singles 170฿, with bath 220฿, with A/C 370฿; doubles 200฿/260฿/410฿. ❷

Galare Guest House, Charoen Prathet Rd. Soi 2 (☎818 887; www.galare.com), last right turn before Nawarat Bridge. Nice rooms in manicured garden on the riverfront. Best rooms are downstairs. Singles with A/C 450฿; doubles with TV and fridge 860฿. ❹

Banana Guesthouse (☎206 285), south end of Ratchaphakinai Rd. A true budget option in the southeast corner of the Old City. Basic rooms with a popular sitting area and friendly staff. Dorm beds 50฿; private rooms 150฿. ❶

🍴 FOOD

Nowhere else in Thailand has as wide a variety of restaurants as Chiang Mai. Diners can alternate between quick markets and elaborate dining rooms. All options have one thing in common: great value. Thanks to the large expat community, you can find Western dishes around Tha Pae Gate. The culinary highlight of Chiang Mai, however, is northern Thai food. Dishes are served with sticky rice, and regional curries, characterized by a lack of coconut milk, are generally spicier. The food connoisseur will love the *Chiang Mai Restaurant Guide Book* (40฿) available at the **Chiang Mai Restaurant Club,** 128/1 Rattanakosin Rd. (☎233 297; open M-F 10am-5pm), or at any of the member restaurants around town. Of the 54 places offering a 10% discount on Chef Recommendations, *Let's Go* lists the Chiang Mai Cultural Center, Huen Phen, The Good View, and Jerusalem Falafel.

MARKET FOOD. Somphet Market, on Moon Muang Rd. between Soi 6 and 7, serves banana pancakes (10-15฿), fried noodles (20-40฿), and *kuay tiaw lu chin plaa* (fishball noodle soup, 20฿). It's open all day, but food stalls don't get going until after 7pm. **Anusan Market,** between Chang Klan and Charoen Prathet Rd. north of Sri Dornchai Rd., is an overpriced nocturnal snack zone. Dining is cheaper at the **Galare Food Court** in the middle of the night bazaar, where a casual dinner is served with nightly entertainment. In the evening, the road that runs between **Warorot Market** and **Lanyai Market** on the west bank of the Ping River is crammed with food stalls offering Chiang Mai's best Thai take-out. Freshly sliced fruit (10฿) is available at all the markets. The mango season (Mar.-May) brings 🌟*khao niaw mamuang* (mangos and sweet sticky rice), a Thai delicacy.

TRADITIONAL FOOD. For a serious culinary experience, try a *khantoke* dinner. At this formal meal, diners sit on the floor and use their hands to eat rice, two meat dishes, and two vegetable dishes from bowls placed on a *khantoke*, a low tray table. The **Old Chiang Mai Cultural Center,** 185/3 Wualai Rd. (☎275 097), 1.5km south of the old city, also offers vegetarian and Muslim versions. State your preferences when calling ahead for the necessary reservation. The 3hr. affair, accompanied by traditional dancing, begins nightly at 7pm (270฿, transportation included).

WITHIN THE MOAT (THE OLD CITY)

🏠 **Huen Phen,** 112 Ratchamanka Rd., west of Phra Pokklao Rd. Northern Thai dining at its finest. Locals come here for the spicy *num phrik* (chili paste with meat, 35฿). *Farang* with soft palates may prefer the curries (50-60฿). Banana-flower and pork-rib curry 50฿. Banana in coconut milk 15฿. Portions are small, but have exquisite flavor and allow you to sample more. Open daily 8am-3pm and 5-10pm. ❷

The Wok, 44 Ratchamanka Rd., east of Ratchaphakhinai Rd. Owners run the Chiang Mai Thai Cookery School. Impeccable "special Northern style food." Spicy Chiang Mai sausage 60฿, Thai-style fishcakes 60฿, Chiang Mai curry 60฿, black sticky rice pudding 30฿, iced *panadanus* leaves drink 20฿. Open daily 11am-10pm. ❷

Banrai Steak House, Phra Pokklao Rd. Soi 13, around the corner from Thai Airways. This Chiang Mai institution lives up to its boast of having "the best steak in town." Steak and chicken barbecued in Thai marinades served up with veggies and baked potato 99฿. Coconut shake 20฿. Sandwich 50฿. Fried rice 50฿. Open daily noon-midnight. ❸

The Amazing Sandwich, 252/3 Phra Pokklao Rd., next to Thai Airways. Choose toppings from an extensive selection. Sandwich 60฿, baguette sandwich 70฿, sub 85฿. Salad platter 85฿. Open M-Sa 8:30am-7pm, Su 11am-3pm. ❸

Il Forno, 142 Phra Pokklao Rd., south of Ratchamanka Rd. intersection. Decorated in traditional Italian red, green, and white. Delivers fresh bread and pasta. Thin-crust pizza 110-150฿. Vegetable panini 45฿. Divine tiramisu 60฿. Open Su-F 9am-10:30pm. ❸

THA PAE GATE

Aroon Rai, 45 Kotchasarn Rd., south of Tha Pae Rd. and before Loi Kroa Rd. The multitude of *farang* and Thais who have dined under the portraits of His Majesty have left Aroon Rai looking well worn, and for good reason—the food is tasty and cheap. English menu highlights Northern specialties. Curries 40-50฿. Open daily 8:30am-10pm. ❷

da Stefano, 2/1-2 Chang Moi Kao Rd., off Tha Pae Rd. High-quality Italian restaurant with reasonable prices, considering the excellent service and elegant A/C dining room. Bruschetta 30฿. Gnocchi with asparagus pesto and ricotta cheese 120฿. Homemade pasta with eggplant, mushrooms, and tomato sauce 90฿. Spaghetti bolognese 90฿. Pizza margherita 110฿. Open daily 11am-11pm. ❸

AUM Restaurant, 65 Moon Muang Rd., just south of the Tha Pae Gate. Trendy vegetarian restaurant enhanced by convenient locale and second-hand bookstore. Cushioned seating area upstairs. Soups and stir-fry with Thai sauces 40-50฿. Vietnamese spring rolls with carrot sauce 40฿. Open daily 8am-2pm and 5-9pm. ❷

Art Cafe, 291 Tha Pae Rd., as central as you can get. Caters to those craving Western food. Beef burritos 90฿; tasty, crispy pizza 120-160฿; real gelato 20฿ per scoop. Open daily 10am to 10 or 11pm. ❸

Jerusalem Falafel, 35/3 Moon Muang Rd., near AUM Restaurant. Incredible falafel pita with hummus, tahini, and fries 80฿; feta salad 50฿. Open daily 10am-11pm. ❷

NEAR THE PING RIVER

⬛ Riverside, 9-11 Charoen Rat Rd. From Nawarat Bridge, take a left on Charoen Rat Rd.; it's the 1st building on the left. Attentive staff serves beef salad with mint leaves (60฿). Entrees 80-120฿. Romantic evening dinner on boat ride down the Ping River. Board 7:15pm and depart at 8pm; 70฿ minimum fee. Open daily 10am-1:30am. ❷

Antique House, 71 Charoen Prathet Rd., before the turn-off to Porn Ping Tower Hotel on the opposite side of the road. Fancy the chair you're sitting on? Take it home—most of the decor in this serene, 131-year-old teak house is for sale. *Som tam* (papaya salad with seafood) 60฿. Dishes 40-150฿. Open daily 11am-midnight. ❸

Shere Shiraz, 23-25 Charoen Prathet Rd. Soi 6, off Chang Klan Rd., down the *soi* south of Porn Ping Tower Hotel. Delicious South Asian restaurant serves Middle Eastern and Thai food, too. Tandoori chicken 200฿, chicken *tikka* 100฿, naan 15฿. 10% service charge. Open daily 10am-11pm. ❸

The Gallery, 25 Charoen Rat Rd. (☎241 866), next to The Good View (p. 282). Excellent Thai food in a classy, intimate setting—a 100-year-old teak house overlooking the Ping River. The restaurant also exhibits local artwork. Excellent chicken wrapped in banana leaves. Entrees 80-120฿. Open daily noon-midnight.

COFFEEHOUSES

The hills of Northern Thailand have proved ideal for coffee plantations. The **Royal Project** and other NGOs have promoted this cash crop as an alternative to opium among the hill tribes. The fruits of their labor are readily available in the city.

Libernard Cafe, 295-299 Chang Moi Rd., one block from the moat. It's Sunday every morning. Coffee is the highlight, but there are also breakfast options. Black coffee 30฿, latte 45฿, cappuccino 45฿. Scrambled eggs, toast, bacon, and coffee 75฿. Whole wheat banana pancake with cappuccino 80฿. Open daily 8am-5pm. ❷

Lanna Cafe, 81 Huay Kaew Rd. (www.lannacafe.org), before Siri Mangkhlachian Rd. Originally established by a Japanese NGO to export coffee beans grown by hill tribes to Japan, the cafe is the result of an expanding market. Coconut cappuccino 35฿, 250g. roasted coffee beans 110฿. Sandwiches 40-60฿. Open daily 8am-6pm. ❷

◉ SIGHTS

WITHIN THE MOAT

WAT CHIANG MAN. The oldest *wat* in the city, Chiang Man was built by King Mengrai in 1296. With its low-sloping roofs and intricate facade, the temple is a classic example of Northern Thai design. The *wihaan* on the right contains two Buddha images: **Phra Setangamani** (Crystal Buddha), thought to have come from Lopburi 1800 years ago, and **Phra Sila** (Stone Buddha), imported from India some 2500 years ago. *(At the north end of Ratchaphakhinai Rd. Open daily 9am-5pm.)*

WAT CHEDI LUANG. Built by King Saen Suang Ma in 1401, the temple walls hold the spectacular remains of Chiang Mai's largest *chedi*, which once spiraled 86m toward the sky before being destroyed by an earthquake in 1545. A *naga* staircase adorns the *wihaan*, which houses a **standing gold Buddha** and 32 *Jataka* story panels depicting scenes from the Buddha's life. Legend holds that Wat Chedi Luang was home to the Emerald Buddha during the statue's stay in Chiang Mai. On the east side of the *wat* (right side from entrance) is **Monk Chat,** a unique opportunity for tourists to talk to monks about Buddhism, the monk lifestyle, and more. *(From Tha Pae Gate head west on Ratchadamnoen Rd. and turn left onto Phra Pokklao Rd.; it's opposite the Yamaha music store. Monk Chat open M-Sa noon-6:30pm; free.)*

WAT PHRA SINGH. This *wat*'s chief attraction is the bronze **Phra Singh Buddha** in **Phra Wihaan Lai Kam,** left of and behind the main *wihaan*. Experts aren't sure if this is the genuine Phra Singh Buddha, as there are identical statues in Bangkok and Nakhon Si Thammarat. The image is the focus of Songkran festivities (see **Throw Water at Monks,** p. 272) when incense is lit and offerings are made to the Phra Singh Buddha, which is cleansed with holy water. *(On the western side of the old city, at the end of Ratchadamnoen Rd.)*

OUTSIDE THE MOAT

WAT JED YOT. Inspired by the Mahabodhi Temple in Bodhgaya, India, King Tilokaraja built this shrine in 1455. In 1477, the Eighth World Buddhist Council met here to revise the *Tripitaka* scriptures of Theravada Buddhism. The two Bodhi trees are said to be descendants of the one Gautama sat under during his enlightenment. *(On the superhighway, 1km from the Huay Kaew Rd. intersection.)*

WAT U-MONG. Another remnant of King Mengrai's building spree, this peaceful forest temple has serene footpaths that lead through the trees. Several sculptures dot the grounds, but perhaps the most notable is the emaciated image of "Our Lord Buddha before realizing that this wasn't the path to enlightenment." The sculpture is at the back of the confine before the pagoda representing the four noble truths (suffering, cause of suffering, path leading to cessation, cessation) and after the turn-off to the derelict farm. Tunnels leading into the hill at the site of the original *wat* are lined with niches housing Buddha figures. Other points of interest on the grounds are the **Herbal Medicine Garden,** a handicapped **vocational training center,** and the *wat*'s **library** (open daily until 4pm). On Sundays from 3 to 6pm, enjoy a *dhamma*'s lecture in English. *(Off Suthep Rd., on the outskirts of town. Following Suthep out of town, the turn-off is marked by a faded green sign and is the 3rd left after the super-highway. It's 2km farther down the road.)*

WAT SUAN DOK. King Ku Na constructed the "Temple of Flower Gardens" (also known as Wat Buppharam) in 1383. The enormous Chiang Saen-style bronze Buddha inside the *bot* dates from 1504. Inexpensive Buddhist amulets and literature are sold at nearly every *wihaan*. Originally, the grounds served as a pleasure garden for the first kings of Chiang Mai, but later became a cemetery for their remains. Today, *tai chi* is practiced in the gardens daily at 6:30am. Suan Dok hosts **Monk Chats** (www.monkchat.net); follow the signs to the building in the back. *(On Suthep Rd., after the Hill Tribe Products Promotion Center. Monk chats M,W, F 5-7pm.)*

CHIANG MAI NATIONAL MUSEUM. This museum features art and artifacts collected from Northern Thai royalty, commoners, and hill tribes. Chronological dioramas depict the rise and fall of the Lanna Kingdom (*Lanna*, referring to the region of Northern Thailand, literally means "a million rice fields"). At its peak in the 13th and 14th centuries, the kingdom, a contemporary of the Sukhotai Kingdom, encompassed modern-day Northern Thailand, eastern Myanmar, and western Laos. Lanna encompasses Phrae, Nan, Phayao, Mae Hong Son, Lamphun, Chiang Rai, and Chiang Mai. *(☎ 221 308. On the superhighway, 500m past Wat Jet Yod on the left side of the road if coming from Huay Kaew Rd. Open daily 9am-4pm. 30฿.)*

TRIBAL MUSEUM. The polished exhibits, collected by the Tribal Research Institute, explore daily life, language derivation, gender roles, and costumes of various hill tribes in Northern Thailand. The second floor documents the development of the hill tribes, most notably in introducing cash crops, new technology, and education. The nine-sided building—representing the nine hill tribes of Thailand—makes a great stop for those interested in hill-tribe culture and history, or for those about to go trekking to local villages. The museum also helps visitors interested in arranging a homestay in a hill-tribe village. (☎ *210 872. On Chotana Rd. in Ratcha-mangkhla Park, 4km north of Chang Phuak Gate, the same entrance as the Chiang Mai Shooting Club. Tuk-tuk from Chang Phuak Gate 30-50฿. Open M-F 9am-4pm. 20฿ suggested donation.)*

CHIANG MAI UNIVERSITY. Though architecturally uninspiring, the university's 725 park-like acres offer a pleasant break from the city's urban sprawl. The library is in the center of the grounds, just south of the central roundabout. The University's Art Museum often hosts major exhibits. (*Museum* ☎ *944 833. 6km northeast of the old city off Huay Kaew Rd.)*

CHIANG MAI ZOO AND ARBORETUM. You can find everything from black bears to zebras housed somewhere along the network of roads that crisscross the zoo. The paths are both confusing and exhausting to walk; pick up a map before heading into this civilized safari. The star attraction in the zoo is the Giant Panda exhibit, which was introduced in late 2003. The two pandas are a gift from China and advertised as a symbol of Thai-Chinese friendship. (☎ *358 166. On Huay Kaew Rd. at the base of Doi Suthep, after Chiang Mai University. Open daily 8am-6pm. Last ticket sold at 5pm. 30฿, children 5฿, an additional 100฿ to see the pandas. Bicycles 1฿, motorbikes 10฿, cars 30฿.)* Next door, the **Huay Kaew Arboretum** provides a shady respite or an invigorating workout (if you opt to use the fitness track).

CHIANG MAI ARTS AND CULTURE CENTER. Located in the old Provincial Hall, the museum has 13 rooms of permanent exhibits documenting the history and culture of Chiang Mai and Northern Thailand. The museum is geared more towards local youth, and while the building itself is remarkable, those interested in the art and history of the area would be better served by seeing the Chiang Mai National Museum (see above). (☎ *217 793. Located just behind the Three Kings Monument on Phra Pokklao Rd. Open Tu-Su 8:30am-5pm. 90฿ adults, 40฿ students)*

◪ TREKKING

Chiang Mai has over 200 companies itching to fulfill the trekking desires of eager *farang*. 3-day/2-night treks (4-person min.) run 1500-1800฿ per person to the **Maeteang, Phrao, Sameong, Doi Inthanon,** or **Chiang Dao** areas. Extra days can be negotiated. These five are the only legal trekking areas around Chiang Mai and with 200 companies tromping through them, there is no such thing as a non-touristed area. This doesn't mean you'll have to elbow your way through mobs of tourists, but some villages see more than they might care to. Many agencies guarantee "private areas" to which they have exclusive access, but there will invariably be overlap. Maeteang, with its bamboo rafting, hosts the most trekkers; Chiang Dao gets the fewest because it runs along the questionable Myanmar border. Chiang Mai's areas encompass Akha, Lisu, Karen, Meo, Yao, and Padong villages.

Some Chiang Mai-based companies also run treks to **Mae Hong Son** and **Pai.** If either of these locales tickles your fancy, it's better to hop on a bus and book from there, where a three-day trek will cost 1500-1800฿. Mae Hong Son and Pai see fewer trekkers because Pai's rivers are too low to raft in the hot season and the rivers around Mae Hong Son may become too fast to navigate in the rainy season. Mae Hong Son abuts the troubled border with Myanmar.

Pai has primarily Lisu and Karen villages; Mae Hong Son has almost exclusively Karen ones. During the low season, it's easier for solo travelers to join a trek in Chiang Mai. In Pai or Mae Hong Son, you might need to assemble your own group or you may end up paying more.

All guesthouses either run their own treks or have an affiliated partner (usually TAT-certified) that they recommend to guests. It is important to understand exactly what the trek price includes—such as sleeping bags and food. Treks run by **Libra Guest House** and **Eagle House,** 16 Chang Mai Gao Rd. Soi 3 (☎874 126), near Somphet market, opposite the old city, consistently receive rave reviews. **Chiang Mai Green Tour and Trekking,** 29/31 Chiang Mai-Lamphun Rd. (☎247 374), donates a portion of its proceeds to a conservation program and offers nature and bird-watching tours, as well as the more conventional "ethno-tourism" variety.

Travelers looking for extreme adventure can go **rock climbing,** regardless of experience. Most trips go to Crazy Horse Buttress. Two companies that run these trips are **The Peak Adventure** (☎516 529; www.thepeakadventure.com) and **Chiang Mai Rock Climbing Adventures** (☎111 470; www.thailandclimbing.com).

> **WELCOME TO THE JUNGLE**
>
> As of early 2004, less than half the trekking companies met TAT and **Northern Thailand Jungle Club** regulations, which include stipulations that guides have at least 10 years experience and speak both English and some hill-tribe dialects; that all costs (e.g. food, transportation, insurance, and elephants or bamboo rafts, if offered) be included in the stated price; that treks have no more than 12 participants; and that the company employ men from the villages they visit as porters and charge the prices set by the Northern Thailand Jungle Club. Not every company with a Jungle Club Plaque is actually a member; many have been expelled for having three or more lawsuits brought against them. For updated info on legitimate outfits, contact the tourist police or Sangduen Chailert, the president of the Northern Thailand Jungle Club and manager of **Gem Travel,** 29 Charoen Prathet Rd. Soi 6 (☎272 855), which also runs treks. The Jungle Club's website at www.thaifocus.com/jungle is an excellent source of info on trekking and the hill tribes.

⊠SPORTS

Chiang Mai has abundant opportunities to watch or participate in sports such as Muay Thai (Thai Boxing), bowling, ice skating, jogging, cycling, and tennis.

Lanna Muay Thai Boxing Camp (☎892 102; www.lannamuaythai.com), off Huay Kaew Rd., is Chiang Mai's premier boxing training center for both foreigners and Thais (p. 91). The **Bar Beer Center,** on Moon Muang Rd. at the Tha Pae Gate, lets you watch the So Anucha Thai Boxing School train from 4 to 7pm. Muay Thai matches are held every night in the same arena at 10:30pm. Galare II of the **Galare Food Center** (☎272 067) in the night bazaar has live Thai boxing from 9 to 11:30pm.

The fourth floor of the Central Department Store on Huay Kaew Rd. has both **Bully Bowling** and **Bully Ice Skating.** (Bowling open M-F 11am-1am, Sa-Su 10am-1am. 70-90฿ per game, shoes 30฿. Skating open M-F 11am-9pm, Sa-Su 10am-10pm. 70฿.)

A **fitness track** can be found at Huay Kaew Arboretum on Huay Kaew Rd. A better **fitness park** is on Nimonaha Min Rd. at the University Arts Museum. The track is set around a concrete moat (330m) with concrete logs and an archaic wooden bench press. (Open daily 5am-8pm.) **Buak Haad Park** in the southwestern corner of the Old City is a hidden oasis. (Open daily 5am-10pm.) Once you've worked up a sweat, cool off in one of the several hotel pools, which open up to public use for a price. The pool at Top North Hotel at Tha Pae Gate is a convenient option (50฿).

Golf and **tennis** can be played at the **Chiangmai Gymkhana Club,** in the southeastern corner of town off the Chiang Mai-Lamphun Rd. The club was founded in 1898 by 14 Englishmen who lived in Chiang Mai as traders, but whose true passions were racing, polo, and tennis. Today, club membership is 60% Thai. Nine holes on the monotonous course cost 150-200฿. Caddies (80฿) are compulsory. (☎241 035. Office open daily 9am-5pm. Golf club rental 300฿, driving range 25฿ for one

NORTHERN THAILAND

THE LOCAL STORY

LADY KILLER

The words Muay Thai conjure up images of a bloodbath; certainly no place for a drop-dead-gorgeous woman. Nong Toom tenaciously disproved these assumptions, forcing her opponents to drop at her pedicured feet. But when she burst onto the kickboxing scene at the age of 16, Nong Toom wasn't quite so feminine. A *katoey* (transvestite), she fought as a man, but dressed as a woman. Known to wear red lipstick and a bra in the ring, Nong Toom was anything but lady-like in her disposal of opponents, amassing a 50-3 record. At the beginning of one match, her opponent mockingly kissed her on the cheek. After Prinaya crushed him, she returned the kiss. As her celebrity grew, she assumed the name Prinaya Kiat-busaba, to honor her trainers at the Lanna Boxing Camp in Doi Suthep, Chiang Mai.

In 1999, Prinaya underwent a sex-change operation to become physically attuned to her inner gender. The operation officially ended her professional kickboxing career, however, as Muay Thai regulations do not allow men to fight women. Having retired from one stage, Prinaya ascended another. In 2002, she was singing at the Icon Club in Bangkok. Unsurprisingly, her incredible story of beating adversity and discrimination has been immortalized in film in 2003's *A Beautiful Boxer*.

bucket of balls. Tennis hard-courts 80฿ per hr., 40฿ extra per hr. for lighting. Open daily 6am-8pm.) The **Anantasiri Tennis Courts**, (☎222 210) located on Hwy. 11 across from the National Museum, are the best public option with lighted courts at night.

▤ COURSES AND FORUMS

Chiang Mai offers several popular courses to tourists, specifically Thai cooking, massage, meditation, and language. (For more detailed info on all courses, please see **Alternatives to Tourism**, p. 81.)

COOKING CLASSES

Most popular are the one- to five-day **cooking courses**, which usually cost around 700฿ per day, and include a trip to the market, materials, and a recipe book.

The Chiang Mai Cooking School, 1-3 Moon Muang Rd., Chiang Mai 50200 (☎05 320 6388; www.thaicookeryschool.com). Run out of The Wok (44 Ratamanka Rd., Chiang Mai 50200; ☎05 320 8287; p. 275), this school, established in 1993, is the most widely known in all of Thailand. The Chiang Mai Cooking School provides a comprehensive course: 1-day 900฿, 2-day 1800฿, 3-day 2600฿, 4-day 3400฿, 5-day 4200฿.

Gap's Thai Culinary Art, 3 Ratchadamnoen Rd. Soi 4 (☎278 140; http://thai-culinary-art.infothai.com).

Baan Thai Cooking School, 11 Ratchadamnoen Rd. Soi 5 (☎357 339; www.cookinthai.com).

Chili Club Cooking Academy, 26 Rathwithi Rd. Soi 2, run by Eagle House (☎874 126; www.eaglehouse.com).

MASSAGE CLASSES

Massage classes are also quite popular.

Old Medicine Hospital, 238/8 Wuolai Rd. (☎275 085), opposite the old Chiang Mai Cultural Center. 10-day certified course 4000฿.

Mama Nit, 1 Chaiyaphum Rd., Soi 2 (☎668 289) at Baan Nit. 2-day course 1000฿, 10-day course 3000฿.

International Training Massage, 17/7 Maraket Rd. (☎218 632; www.infothai.com/itm).

Thai Massage School, 238/8 Wualai Rd. (☎275 085; www.thaimassageschool.ac.th).

MEDITATION COURSES

Whether you'd like to stay for one day or for one month, there's a meditation program that fits your needs.

Northern Insight Meditation Center (☎278 620), at Wat Ram Poeng, near Wat U Mang. Offers 10-day retreats and 26-day meditation courses.

Voravihara Insight Meditation Center (☎826 869), at Wat Pratat Sri Chom Thong, 60km SW of Chiang Mai. 26-day course followed by suggested 10-day retreat.

Hatha Yoga, 129/79 Chiang Mai Villa 1, Pa Daed (☎271 555). Preksha meditation and other spirituality courses. Offers one-day classes as well as longer courses.

LANGUAGE COURSES

The final step toward cultural immersion is taking a **language course** such as the ones offered at the **AUA** or **Payap University.**

American University Alumni Language Center (AUA), 73 Ratchadamnoen Rd. (☎278 407; www.auathailand.org), offers a small variety of courses, including a 30hr. course in survival Thai and a more thorough 60hr. course.

Payap University (☎243 164; www.payap.ac.th) offers a similar menu of courses.

Chiang Mai Thai Language Center, 131 Ratchadamnoen Rd. (☎277 810; cmat@lox-info.co.th).

CULTURAL FORUMS

Insights into Buddhism are available through **informal discussions** about the Buddhist faith held in the **Chinese Pavilion** at Wat U-Mong (Su 3pm), and **Monk Chat** at Wat Suan Dok and Wat Chedi Luang (p. 276). Wat Suan Dok also has free **Tai Chi sessions** (daily 6:30am). A forum on cultural aspects of Asia is the **Northern Thai Discussion Group,** which meets the second Tuesday of each month (5:30pm) at the **Alliance Française.** Check the *Chiang Mai Newsletter* for upcoming speakers.

🔲 SHOPPING

Chiang Mai offers a wide selection of local handicrafts to avid shoppers. **Tha Pae Road** is one of the best daytime hunting grounds, but rampant consumerism takes off only after dark. The famed **night bazaar** on **Chang Klan Road** showcases a variety of antiques, silver jewelry, hill-tribe embroidery, Thai textiles, pottery, designer clothing knock-offs, and pirated DVDs. Haggle down the inflated tourist prices, which can be twice as high as the fee you finally settle on. The night bazaar may be Chiang Mai's top tourist destination: most nights, the crowds stretch shoulder to shoulder for several blocks. Bangkok is still the home of tailored fashion, but that doesn't mean there aren't options around the night bazaar. It is a spectacle to see even if you are not intending to buy anything.

Warorot Market is a multi-story expanse containing food, textiles, and clothing. The higher into the complex you go, the lower the prices. Next door in **Lanyai Market** on the river side, flower stalls are everywhere and spill out onto the road. Buy a *poung ma lai* (festive flower necklace; 5฿). Memorable Thai souvenirs include *morn sam laim* (triangular reclining pillows; approx. 200฿-1000฿ depending on quality). A popular choice is to have artists reproduce your photos in portrait-sized pieces on canvas. (Charcoal is the cheapest: 1 person approx. 1000฿, 2 people 1500฿, 3 people 2000฿.) Artists are primarily found in the center of the night bazaar near the Galare Food Center. There may be significant reductions in price if you buy multiple photos or if you're willing to wait longer for the reproduction.

The **Hill Tribe Handicraft Project,** 1 Moon Muang Rd., in a brick building at the southeastern corner of the old city, sells Karen, Lisu, Akha, Lahu, Yao, and Hmong village quilts, bags, pullovers, and sculptures. (☎274 877. Open M-F 9am-4:30pm.)

NORTHERN THAILAND

The better-known **Hill Tribe Promotion Center,** 21/17 Suthep Rd., next to Wat Suan Dok, has a greater selection of traditional and innovative crafts. (☎277 743. Embroidered bag 280฿, Karen dress 650฿. Open daily 9am-5pm. MC/V.) Both government-run stores seek to shift tribal economies away from opium cultivation by providing alternative means of income. The **Export Promotion Center,** 29/19 Singharat Rd., opposite Cathay Pacific Airways, showcases high-quality Thai products for export. The manufacturer's business card is with each display, so if you like what you see among the hundreds of displays, it's possible to track it down. (☎216 350. Open M-F 8:30am-noon and 1-4:30pm.)

If you are interested in high-end antiques, grab a copy of *Art & Culture-Lanna*, available in some guesthouses, at TAT, and online at www.artandcultureasia.com. The brochure lists and describes many of the studios and galleries in Chiang Mai.

▯ ▮ ENTERTAINMENT AND NIGHTLIFE

Major Cineplex, 2 Mahidon, in the Central Airport Plaza, is the largest and newest cinema. (☎283 989; www.movieseer.com for show listings. M-Th 80-100฿, F-Su 100-120฿.) The Central Department Store has a **Vista Movie Theater** on the fourth floor that shows newly released movies. (☎894 415. M-Th 70฿, F-Su 90฿.) The Alliance Française hosts **French films** with English subtitles; check *Guidelines* for upcoming screenings. (☎275 277. Tu 4:30pm, F 8pm; 30฿.) Movieline (☎262 661) is a recorded English announcement of what's playing around town. The **Galare Food Center,** 89/2 Chang Klan Rd. (☎272 067), in the night bazaar, features various acts on a rotating schedule between two stages. Galare I (sponsored by Chang Beer) has traditional dancing and music. Galare II alternates between a drag show and Thai boxing. (Cabaret 8-9pm, boxing 9-11:30pm.)

Several wildly popular **bars** and **clubs** lie on the Ping's east bank, just north of Nawarat Bridge. The 30฿ *tuk-tuk* from Tha Pae Gate is well worth it. *Farang* pubs line **Moon Muang Road.** Those immediately at Tha Pae Gate attract backpackers; those to the south on Loi Kro Rd. are sketchier. There are very few outright go-go bars in Chiang Mai; "karaoke" bars fill the void. The night bazaar hosts the most relaxed gay bars and attracts a mixed crowd. Other gay nightlife clusters in the *sois* west of Chang Phuak Bus Station, north of the old city.

Riverside, 9-11 Charoen Rat Rd. (☎243 239), has long been the most popular club. Live music nightly at 8pm. Screwdriver 110฿. Large Singha 95฿. Corona 140฿. Pitcher of beer 300฿. Open daily 10am-1:30am.

Bubbles, 46-48 Charoen Prathet Rd. (☎270 099), in the Porn Ping Tower Hotel. Chiang Mai's premier disco. Mixed gay and straight crowd. Cover Su-Th 100฿ includes 1 free drink, F-Sa and holidays 200฿ includes 2 drinks. Drinks 100฿ Open daily 9pm-2am.

Brasserie, 37 Charoen Rat Rd. (☎241 665). Croonin' tunes on an intimate stage start around 9:30pm. If you're lucky, the owner Took may take a turn himself. Whiskey and soda 90฿. Large Singha 90฿. Open daily 6pm-1:30am.

The Good View, 13 Charoen Rat Rd. (☎302 764), between Riverside and Brasserie. Music is like Riverside's—only louder. Great Japanese restaurant. Large Singha 120฿. Corona 150฿. Kamikaze 150฿. Open daily 6pm-1:45am.

Inter Bar, on Tha Pae Rd. near Art Cafe, always has a solid crowd, even when other places are dead. Chill atmosphere and pool table. Music nightly 7:30pm-1am. Small Singha 60฿. Screwdriver 110฿. Open daily 2pm-2am.

Adam's Apple, on Wiang Bua Rd. The turn-off from Chofana Rd. is 300m past the Novotel. Indisputably the most popular gay venue in Chiang Mai. Restaurant, bar, and karaoke downstairs; go-go boys upstairs. Raunchy cabaret (F-Sa 11pm). Singha 130฿.

◪ DAYTRIPS FROM CHIANG MAI

▨ DOI INTHANON NATIONAL PARK

To get from Chiang Mai to the summit of Doi Inthanon using public transportation, first go to Chom Thong, then to Mae Klang Waterfall, and then to the summit. To get to Chom Thong, take either a bus from Chang Phuak Station (1¼hr., every 20min. 6:30am-6pm, 23฿) or yellow songthaew from Chiang Mai Gate (leaves when full, 20฿). From Chom Thong, songthaew head to the national park and Mae Klang Waterfall, an 8km ride up Hwy. 1009 to the turn-off. Songthaew cost 10-20฿ and leave when full—which may take a while—6am-5pm. Catch another songthaew from Mae Klang to the summit (30฿). If using your own transportation, the turn-off to Hwy. 1009 and Doi Inthanon National Park lies before Chom Thong off Hwy. 108. Take either Triparet Rd. or Wualai Rd. out of Chiang Mai to get on Hwy 108. Chom Thong is 58km from Chiang Mai and the summit is another 47km from Chom Thong. Using private transportation to get to the summit is strongly advised, as it is much quicker—though the roads are steep and curvy. Even if using private transportation, you should leave early in the morning if attempting a daytrip. If relying on public transportation, you will need to make plans to stay overnight in the park. All inquiries (☎355 728). Office open M-F 8:30am-4:30pm. Park and facilities open daily 6am-6pm. Park admission 200฿, students 100฿. Motorbikes 20฿, cars 50฿.

Doi Inthanon National Park is 482km² and located about 60km southwest of Chiang Mai. It is one of Thailand's best national parks: it has the country's highest peak (2585m), the most bird species of any site in the country (400), several beautiful waterfalls, scenic vistas, and well-paved roads to the summit. It also has some of the best tourist information; pay the national park entrance fee and pick up a map from either the vehicle checkpoint (500m after the turn-off to Mae Klang Waterfall), the Visitors Center (1km from the vehicle entrance on Hwy. 1009), or park headquarters (at Km 31 of Hwy. 1009). **Mae Klang Waterfall** is the first stop for most visitors. The 1km path above the falls leads to the Visitors Center.

Just before the **Visitors Center** on Hwy. 1009, a 1km path leads to **Borichinda Cave.** Guided tours can be arranged at the Visitors Center, which also has exhibits on local animal life, notably the nocturnal pangolin, an armadillo-like creature.

The powerful **Wachiratan Waterfall** is the next stop at Km 20.8. At Km 31 is the elegant **Siriphum Waterfall.** The lane leading to it winds through the park's **Royal Project,** where hill tribes are encouraged to supplant opium production with strawberry and flower cultivation. The road bids farewell at Doi Inthanon's summit (usually obscured by mist), 48km from Chom Thong.

At the summit, there is a Vistors Center with info on the wildlife in the park. There are also two worthwhile trails at the summit, the brief **Aangka Nature Trail** and the 4km **Ki Mae Pan Nature Trail.** Mae Pan is closed during parts of the rainy season and you must get clearance at park headquarters (☎355 728) at Km 31.

The cool season (Oct.-Feb.) is the best time to visit. The average park temperature then is 12°C (50°F)—bring raingear and warm clothing, especially if you intend to hike. The park has **guesthouses** ❹ (500-2000฿), **camping** ❶ (30฿), **tents** ❶ (70฿), and a **restaurant** at park headquarters just past Siriphum Falls.

WAT DOI SUTHEP AND DOI SUTHEP NATIONAL PARK

The national park is 16km northwest of Chiang Mai. Songthaew leave when full from Chang Phuak Gate (6am-5pm, 30฿), and the Chiang Mai Zoo (6am-5pm, 30฿), located on Huay Kaew Rd. After Wat Suthep, the songthaew continue to Bhubing Palace (50฿) and Doi Pui, a Hmong village (80฿). Motorbikes make for an exhilarating trip up the mountain to see the wat (30min.). While the road is well-paved, however, it has numerous sharp turns and a steep descent. Past the Bhubing Palace, the last 4.5km of the ride to the Hmong village are unpaved. The park headquarters (☎295 117), 1km past Wat Phra That Doi Suthep, provides trail maps and accommodations. Camping ❶ in the national park costs 10฿ per night. 2-person (200฿) and 5-person (500฿) tents, and 2-person (200฿) and 10-person (2000฿) cabins ❸ are available for rental. Reserve at least a week in advance. National park admission 200฿.

If you only have time to visit one of Chiang Mai's 300 *wats*, Wat Phra That Doi Suthep, built in 1383 and one of Thailand's most sacred pilgrimage sights, should be it. *Phra that* refers to the Buddha's relics enshrined here, namely his *incus* (a tiny bone in the middle ear). *Doi* is a Northern Thai word for mountain, and *suthep* is derived from the Pali *Sudevoy*, the name of the hermit who inhabited the area before the shrine was constructed. While the glint of the brilliant gold *chedi* is visible from the city's limits, the sweeping survey of the city from the temple's observation deck (1676m high) is sublime. Upon reaching the *wat*, voyeurs have the option of ascending either via cable-car (round-trip 20฿) or the 297 steps. (30฿ admission for foreigners; does not require national park admission.)

Encompassing a 261km² area surrounding Wat Suthep, Doi Suthep National Park contains an amazing range of natural life. A project started in 1987 by a Chiang Mai University professor has thus far collected over 2000 species of plants in the park—more than in all of the UK. While the wildlife is regrettably being forced up the mountain as Chiang Mai proper expands, the park still offers much for wide-eyed wanderers. **Waterfalls** line Huay Kaew Rd. (Hwy. 1004), which leads up the mountain; keep an eye out for their turn-offs. A nature trail leads from the park headquarters passing **Sai Yok Waterfall** (2km) and **Monthatarn Waterfall** (3km). The standard national park fee applies even if you intend to only see one waterfall. After you reach Monthatarn Waterfall, follow the 2km access road to Huay Kaew Rd., where *songthaew* will shuttle you to Chiang Mai.

Bhubing Palace, 4km up the mountain from the *wat*, is the Royal Family's residence roughly from January to February. When they're not in residence, the palace and its lavish gardens are open to the public. (Open daily 8:30am-4:30pm; tickets sold until 3:30pm. 50฿.) **Doi Pui,** a Hmong Village 8km past the *wat*, suffers from tourist overcrowding. It is perhaps the only hill-tribe village in which the women pair high heels with traditional apparel. The trek to Doi Pui's summit (1685m), 7km up the road from Bhubing Palace, makes for a nice hike. The road splits 2km after Bhubing Palace: to the left lies Doi Bhubing Hmong Village, to the right is Doi Pui's summit. The lush garden of the **Hill Tribes Village Museum,** 150m uphill from the parking lot for the town, contrasts sharply with the squalid village itself. The museum's main attraction is its collection of tiny pink opium flowers. *(Open whenever there are visitors. 10฿.)*

LAMPHUN

Buses to Lamphun leave from the Chang Phuak Station in Chiang Mai and from just south of the footbridge near Warorot Market (1hr., every 10min. 6:20am-6pm, 12฿). Get off as the bus passes through the walled city; the Lamphun bus station is 2km south of town, where buses depart for Chiang Mai (every 30min. 6am-6pm). Electric blue songthaew leave from Chiang Mai-Lamphun Rd., south of TAT (every 20min. 5am-6pm, 15฿). Songthaew back to Chiang Mai depart just south of the museum, on Inthayongyot Rd. (15฿).

Tiny Lamphun, 26km southeast of Chiang Mai, offers a handful of worthwhile sights. The town's most exciting event of the year is the **Lum-Yai Festival** in August, celebrating the *lum-yai* (longan) season. **Wat Phra That Haribhunchai** is considered one of the seven most sacred temples in Thailand. The *wat*, Lamphun's chief landmark, sits on Inthayongyot Rd. in the town center; it's the first temple on the left after you enter the walled city from Chiang Mai. Grassy grounds and little *wihaan* surround the *chedi*, crowned with a nine-tier gold umbrella that reaches 46m in the air. Construction on the *wat* began in the

10th century, and the parasol at the top is rumored to be made of over 60kg of gold. When coming from Inthayongyot Rd., you should enter from the back. There is a loosely enforced 20฿ entrance fee. A block away is the **Haribhunchai National Museum,** with a small collection of Buddhas, bells, and other bric-a-brac. With your back to the *wat* on Inthayongyot Rd., it's to the left. (☎511 186. Open W-Su 9am-4pm. 30฿.) With your back to Chiang Mai, take a right after the museum onto Mukda Rd; when the road becomes Chamma Davi Rd., continue 2km to reach **Wat Chamma Davi.** This step pyramid *chedi* once had a gold coating, but thieves broke it off, giving the temple its other name, **Wat Ku Kat** ("pagoda without top"). There are several decent noodle restaurants just south of Wat Haribhunchai and a market next to Wat Chamma Davi.

Wat Phra Phut Ta Bat Tak Pah, 20km south of Lamphun, has views that rival Doi Suthep's. Except for the monks, you'll probably be the only one there. Before you reach the 472-step stairway, you'll pass some of the Buddha's footprints. Supposedly there is an imprint of the Buddha's robe on a cliff somewhere in the vicinity. Ask a monk for guidance—it's hard to find. To get to the *wat,* board a light blue *songthaew* to Pasang (5฿) south of the museum, just off Inthayongyot Rd. on the left. After everyone else gets off, the driver can take you the 9km to the *wat* for 15฿ more.

MAE SA VALLEY

Songthaew to Mae Rim, 17km north of Chiang Mai, leave from Chotana Rd. north of Chang Phuak Gate. Alternatively, take a bus headed toward Fang. Once in the Mae Rim district, transportation can be arranged to all the sights. Songthaew to Samoeng also leave from Chang Phuak Gate, (2½hr., 30฿). By car, head north out of Chiang Mai along Chotana Rd. (Hwy. 107) and pass through the tiny town of Mae Rim. After the town, take the turn-off to the left onto Mae Rim-Somoeng Rd. (Hwy. 1096). To get back from Chiang Mai, either return the way you came (52km from Samoeng) or take Hwy. 1269 through the Chang Valley (43km from Samoeng).

The scenic Mae Sa Valley stretches 30km from Mae Rim to Samoeng along the Mae Sa River on Hwy. 1096. The first 15km from the Mae Rim are littered with a variety of eccentric tourist attractions—poisonous snake farms, bungee jumping, ATV trails, and lavish spas. The final 15km is much more picturesque and peaceful, as the well-paved road weaves through rural villages and up stunning mountainsides.

Much of the Mae Sa Valley is also part of Doi Suthep National Park. The cascades in the park tumble down the 10-tier **Mae Sa Falls,** spread over 1.5km. While the waterfalls are mediocre and the only trails are concrete and boardwalk, the park's proximity to Chiang Mai attracts hundreds of locals, especially on the weekends. 7km past Mae Rim (24km from Chiang Mai), the entrance to the falls has a Visitors Center with maps of the area for further explorations. (National park entrance fee of 200฿, students 100฿. Open daily 6am-6pm.)

Another popular attraction is the **Mae Sa Elephant Training Center,** located 3km past the Doi Suthep National Park entrance. The elephants and their riders put on a 40min. show daily at 9 and 9:40am (Nov.-Apr. there is a 1:30pm show as well). The anything-but-clumsy elephants demonstrate their strength and grace by handling teak logs and reveal their balance by maneuvering their huge bodies into surprising positions. (☎206 247. Admission 80฿.) There are also daily **elephant-back jungle tours** from 7am to 2:30pm (600฿ per hr.).

Just 2km past the training center is the 2600-acre **Queen Sikrit Botanic Garden,** established by the Thai government in 1993 as a research and conservation center. There are three walking trails in the park—the best being the 600m trail alongside the Mae Sa River to the rock garden and orchid nursery. There is also a greenhouse complex and museum on the site. (☎298 171. 20฿. Motorbikes prohibited.)

NORTHERN THAILAND

BO SANG AND SAN KAMPHAENG

Located east of Chiang Mai on Route 1006, both Bo Sang and San Kamphaeng are extremely easy to reach. White songthaew at the market on the west bank of the Ping River make the 15-20min. trip regularly during the day (10฿), as do those at the Chang Phuak bus station (10฿).

Bo Sang, 9km east of Chiang Mai, is world-famous for its umbrella production. Hand-painted rain-repellers are made by stretching mulberry paper over bamboo frames. Silk and cotton parasols, sporting various bright floral, feral, and bucolic designs, are manufactured in Chiang Mai. Seeing the artisans at work in the umbrella, lacquer-ware, woodwork, glass, and silver factories is worth a trip, but prices are no better than those in established stores near the night bazaar in Chiang Mai. In the third week of January, Bo Sang hosts the colorful **Umbrella Festival,** which has a parade and a beauty pageant (see **Festivals,** p. 31).

San Kamphaeng, just 4km down the road from Bo Sang and 13km from Chiang Mai, is famous for cotton and silk weaving. One main road with workshops tucked out of sight is basically all there is to this village. Duck into a side street to catch a glimpse of production. Choose from a wide variety of plaids, brocades, stripes, and solid colors. Other handicrafts are available as well.

PAI   ☎053

An oasis halfway between Chiang Mai and Mae Hong Son, tiny Pai (pop. 3000) attracts both artists and trendy pilgrims, who draw inspiration from the astoundingly picturesque town and surrounding area. Adding to the city's charm are the best selection of budget accommodation in Northern Thailand and the greatest culinary diversity outside of Chiang Mai. The locals, a harmonious mélange of cultures and ethnicities, are particularly friendly. Such a combination makes it difficult for many tourists to leave, as evidenced by the numerous long-term visitors (both Thai and *farang*) found in Pai. Behind the scenes, however, a clandestine heroin and opium culture has come to the attention of local authorities, who are starting to crack down on nefarious activities in the area.

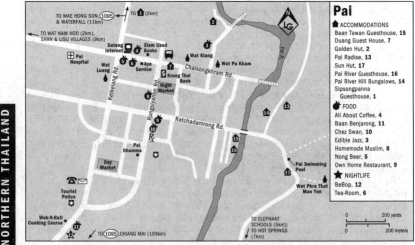

Pai

♦ ACCOMMODATIONS
Baan Tawan Guesthouse, **15**
Duang Guest House, **7**
Golden Hut, **2**
Pai Radise, **13**
Sun Hut, **17**
Pai River Guesthouse, **16**
Pai River Hill Bungalows, **14**
Sipsongpanna
  Guesthouse, **1**

● FOOD
All About Coffee, **4**
Baan Benjarong, **11**
Chez Swan, **10**
Edible Jazz, **3**
Homemade Muslim, **8**
Nong Beer, **5**
Own Home Restaurant, **9**

★ NIGHTLIFE
BeBop, **12**
Tea-Room, **6**

◻ TRANSPORTATION

Buses: The **station** is on Chaisongkhram Rd. To **Chiang Mai** (4hr.; 8:30, 10:30am, noon, 2, 4pm; 60฿) and **Mae Hong Son** (4hr.; 8:30, 10:30am, noon, 2, 4pm; 48฿, with A/C 67฿) via **Soppong** (2hr., 35฿). To go to **Tha Ton,** take a Chiang-Mai-bound bus to **Mae Malai** (3hr., 55฿), then take a bus to **Fang** (2½hr., every 30min. 6:30am-6pm, 45฿). Some buses continue to Tha Ton; otherwise, yellow *songthaew* make the trip from the main road in Fang (45min., 20฿). To reach Tha Ton by evening, it is necessary to leave Pai by noon at the latest.

Motorcycle Taxis: Found at the corner of Chaisongkhram and Rungsiyanon Rd. at Ban Pai, they travel to hot springs 50฿; waterfall 60฿; Tham Lot (2hr., 300฿). It's possible to arrange drop-off and pick-up.

Rentals: Many shops along Chaisongkhram Rd. and elsewhere rent **motorbikes** for 100-150฿ per day. **Aya Service,** 21 Chaisongkhram Rd. (☎699 940), offers 100cc for 100฿; 110cc 120฿. Turn left out of the bus station—it's 50m down on the left. Open daily 7:30am-10:30pm.

◼✳ ▢ ORIENTATION AND PRACTICAL INFORMATION

Pai is 136km northwest of Chiang Mai and 111km northeast of Mae Hong Son. **Highway 1095** cuts through town, turning into **Ketkelang Road,** which forms the town's western border. Parallel to the border and one block east is **Rungsiyanon Road,** where the market and numerous restaurants are located. The two main east-west roads are **Chaisongkhram Road,** home of the **bus station,** Internet cafes, and trekking shops, and (two blocks south) **Ratchadamrong Road,** which crosses the **Pai River** to the town's east side, a popular guesthouse area.

Currency Exchange: Krung Thai Bank, 90 Rungsiyanon Rd. (☎699 028). Open M-F 8:30am-3:30pm. **24hr. ATM.** Cirrus/MC/PLUS/V.

Markets: The **night market,** which oddly sets up at 3pm on Rungsiyanon Rd. between Chaisongkhram and Ratchadamrong Rd., has food carts and the occasional hill-tribe entrepreneur scattered among the regulars. The **day market** is on Ketkelang Rd., south of Ratchadamrong Rd.

Books: Siam Used Books. 2 locations—one on the west end of Chaisongkhram Rd. and the other on Rungsiyanon Rd., opposite the police station. Open daily 10am-8pm.

Local Tourist Police: Toward Chiang Mai, after Ketkelang and Rungsiyanon Rd. merge.

Police: 72 Rungsiyanon Rd. (☎699 217), 500m south of the bus station.

Medical Services: Pai Hospital (☎699 031), on Chaisongkhram Rd. 500m west of the bus station. English spoken. Open **24hr.**

Pharmacy: On Rungsiyanon Rd. near Chez Swan. Open daily 6am-9pm.

Internet Access: Connections abound on Chaisongkhram Rd., most 1฿ per min. and open until 11pm. **Satang Internet** is 100m west of the bus station.

Post Office: 76 Ketkelang Rd. (☎699 208), south of the day market. **International phone.** *Poste Restante.* Open M-F 8:30am-4:30pm, Sa 9am-noon.

Postal Code: 58130.

◣ ACCOMMODATIONS

The number of guesthouses in Pai has risen from 15 in 1994 to over 60 today, and the competition has resulted in some of the best deals in Thailand. To choose a place to stay decide on your area of preference—the center of town

THE LOCAL STORY

WHO ARE THE HILL TRIBES?

Basic Facts. The total population of hill tribes in Thailand is about 700,000. There are nine different ethnic groups—Akha, Hmong, H'tin, Karen, Khamu, Lahu, Lisu, Lua, and Yao. The Karen are by far the largest group, representing about half of the hill-tribe population; the Hmong are 18%, the Lahu 12%, and the rest are much smaller. Most have migrated to Thailand in the last 200 years, coming from Myanmar, China, and Laos; they live in the hills of northern Thailand.

Lifestyle. Each of the nine groups has its own unique history, culture, and language. The vast majority practice various forms of animism, with small pockets of Buddhist and Christian tribes. They are all subsistence farmers, using traditional slash-and-burn methods. Popular crops are rice, and corn. Tribes all have their own distinctive dress—often consisting of colorful headdresses and hand-woven garments. The leader of each village (often a hereditary position) is called the headman.

Change and Development. Since the 1960s, the Thai government, NGOs, and the United Nations have actively implemented projects aimed at improving the hill tribes' standard of living and further integrating them into Thai society. Modern agricultural methods, namely cash crops and crop rotation, have been introduced. This gives extra...

[Cont'd on next page...]

(Duang), the scenic countryside (Sun Hut, Pai Radise), or directly on the Pai River (the rest).

Sun Hut (☎699 730; thesunhut1999@yahoo.com), in the small town of Mae Yen. Follow the road to the hot springs. Once you cross the 2nd bridge, Sun Hut is on your right. Teak and bamboo huts set in a beautiful garden with pond. Free bananas and tea for guests. Restaurant open 8am-5pm. Very clean huts with towels, mosquito nets, and fan. Singles 150฿; doubles 200฿. Deluxe huts with bath and porch 350-400฿. ❷

Pai Radise, 98 Moo 1 Ban Mae Yen (☎09 38 7521; www.pairadise.com). Turn left after the bridge over Pai River; located 200m on right. Pai's best accommodations. Pristine rooms, all with bath, and wood floors. 450฿ for 1 or 2 people; 400฿ if staying 2 days or more. ❹

Baan Tawan Guesthouse (☎698 116), sits on the river's west bank; turn before the bridge. Clean rooms and bungalows, sitting areas along river, tubes for guests (50฿). Singles and doubles 150฿; larger bungalows with private bath 250-350฿. ❷

Sipsongpanna (☎698 259; sipsongpanna33@hotmail.com). Follow Ketkelang Rd. north past Nong Beer, turning right at the turn-off; it's on the left. Pai's most stunning location inspires artists at the onsite studio. Restaurant 8am-8pm. Entrees 40-70฿. Rooms and bungalows with bath 300฿; deluxe 500-600฿. Reserve several days in advance. ❹

Pai River Hill Bungalows (☎698 230), 100m before Pai Radise. Relaxed restaurant with scenic views. Cozy bamboo huts overlook the Pai River and rice fields. Friendly Ms. Prem will provide free pick-up from the bus station. Singles 100฿; doubles 120฿, all with shared open-air bath, some with porch and hammock. ❶

Golden Hut (☎699 949), off Chaisongkhram Rd. Turn left from the bus station, then left again onto a dirt road before the 2nd *wat;* it's on the left alongside the Pai River. Complex of huts and bungalows; the best huts overlook the river. Laundry 20฿ per kg. Dorms 60฿; rooms and bungalows 100฿, with toilet 120฿, with bath 250-300฿. ❶

Pai River Guesthouse sits next to Baan Tawan. Same location, but cheaper rooms with fewer frills. All rooms have shared bath. Singles 80฿; doubles 100฿. ❶

Duang Guest House (☎699 101), central location across from the bus station. Quality restaurant and good tourist info. Rooms are small and show signs of wear. Singles 70฿; doubles 130฿, with bath 300฿; VIP rooms with TV and fridge 400฿. ❶

FOOD

In the evenings, head to the **night market** on Rungsiy-anon Rd. Located just south of the tourist police next to BeBop, **Baan Benjarong ❷** serves the best Thai food in Pai. Pleasant dining area and soothing music. (Tasty chicken with local herbs 60฿. Entrees 40-80฿. Open daily 11am-10pm.) The tastiest of the Ketke-lang Rd. joints is the oddly named **Nong Beer ❷**, 39/1 Chaisongkhram Rd., at the somewhat noisy intersec-tion with Ketkelang Rd. (Panaeng curry pork and rice 30฿. Open daily 7am-10pm.) **Chez Swan ❷**, 13 Rung-siyanon Rd., just south of the Ratchadamrong Rd. intersection, is an authentic French transplant. (Quiche Lorraine 60฿. Creme caramel 35฿. *Patate au gratin dauphinois* 55฿. Open daily 8am-late.) At **All About Coffee ❷**, 100 Chaisongkhram Rd., the omelette with tomato, onion, and cheese is the big-gest and best item on the set breakfast menu (served with homemade bread and coffee; 65฿). Former Bangkok advertising execs founded the trendy cafe and love sharing info on their new residence of Pai. (Pai coffee 35฿. Sandwiches 35-40฿. Open daily 8:30am-6pm.) **Own Home Restaurant ❷**, 9/4 Ratchad-amrong Rd., east of the intersection with Rungsiy-anon Rd., serves a large variety of vegetarian options. The aubergine salad (40฿) is particularly tasty. (Fruit salad with muesli 25฿. Open daily 7:30am-11pm; kitchen closes 10pm.) **Edible Jazz ❷** doesn't offer much food but it does provide authentic New Orleans atmosphere. A variety of jazz CDs soothes your soul while you rest on mats laid across the floor. (Delicious cappuccinos and lattes 50-60฿. Small food menu, burritos 80฿. Open daily 1-11pm.) Don't miss the baked goodies at **Homemade Muslim ❶**, at the southern end of the night market. (Delicious coconut cream pie 15฿. Chocolate croissants 10฿. Chicken potato pie 15฿.) Locals also recommend the **noodle shop ❶** at the back left of the day market (*kuay tiaw gai;* noodle soup with chicken; 20฿).

SIGHTS

Wat Phra That Mae Yen has sublime views. To get there, head east on Ratchadamrong Rd. and cross the Pai River; the 360 steps to the *wat* are 1km up, or you can take the easier, paved route. Continuing past the Mae Yen River leads to the **hot springs,** 7km from town. For a more luxurious experience, the local resorts (2km before the hot springs) pump the spring water to their grounds. **Natural Hot Spring Bungalows** has individual baths (40฿), while nearby **Thapai Spa Camping** has larger pools for laz-

income to villagers, discourages the destructive slash-and-burn method, and diminishes opium production. Tourism has also pro-vided another source of income to villages, albeit a controversial one (see **The Plight of the Padong**, p 294). The Thai government has also attempted to assimilate hill tribes through the introduction of the Thai language, education, Buddhism, and a greater number of political rights. Any hill tribe member born after 1975 has the right to be a Thai citizen, and will need to carry a Thai identification card to distinguish them from ille-gal refugees.

While there is still much to be done, the projects have been quite successful. The UN has lauded Thailand for the best hill tribe village development record in Southeast Asia. Unfortunately this development has often resulted in the painful erosion of hill-tribe culture.

Take extra care when visiting villages to minimize unintended disrespect. Be sure to ask for per-mission before taking a photo, either by using sign language (the "OK" sign) or through a guide. Some villagers believe the photo captures the subject's soul and may say no. Be careful when entering villages and houses, as the entrance is often a spirit domain. While opium is used in some villages, it is illegal. If you wish to make a donation, it is bet-ter to do so through local schools or Hill Tribe Museums, rather than by giving directly to villagers.

ing (50฿). It's possible to pitch a tent for free at the hot springs, or for 100฿ at either of the resorts. About 2km before the hot springs (5km from town), there are three **elephant schools.** In the other direction, on the road to Mae Hong Song, is a popular but not spectacular **waterfall,** 11km out of town. To get there, turn left after the army base (5km); it's another 6km from there. The return trip can take you through Shan and Lisu villages. Returning to the paved road from the waterfall, the dirt road turn-off is 200m on the right. The dirt road will deposit you on the road leading out of town from the hospital. Also on this road, 2km from the hospital, **Wat Nam Hoo** houses **Muang Pai** (Buddha image of Pai). The inexplicable water deposit in the bronze Buddha's cranium is believed to be sacred. Beware of locals offering gifts, especially around the waterfall; a number of foreigners have been ripped off and/or arrested for carrying illegal drugs.

TREKKING AND RAFTING

Trekking outfitters in Pai offer everything from hiking and rafting to elephant rides (300฿ per hr.), so shop around to see what suits you. **Back Trax,** 27 Chaisongkhram Rd., leads groups around the Pai and Soppong areas, giving 15-20% of their proceeds to the villages. Owner Chao, a member of the Lahu tribe, speaks excellent English. (☎09 759 4840; trek@yahoo.com. 3 days 1500฿. Open daily 8am-8pm.) **Duang Trekking,** at Duang Guest House (p. 288), offers treks that visit Karen, Lisu, and Shan villages, along with several waterfalls. (2-day treks 1000฿, with rafting and elephants 1450฿; 3-day treks 1500฿, with rafting 1750฿.)

Bamboo rafting is usually only possible from November to May, since Pai's rivers get rather wild in the rainy season. Whitewater rafting in rubber boats fills the void in the wet season, although by February the water level again drops too low for whitewater rafting. **Thai Adventure Rafting** (☎699 111), next to Chez Swan (p. 289), and **Northern Green** (☎699 385), on Chaisongkhram Rd. next to Aya Service (p. 287), have similar adventures down the Khong and Pai rivers. By the time you've finished paddling, you're in Mae Hong Son. (2-day trips stay overnight in established campsites, 1800฿. 4-person minimum.)

ENTERTAINMENT

Pai also offers a variety of less strenuous activities. Plunge into the Pai Swimming Pool, located 500m east of the bridge, on the way to Sun Huts. (40฿; children 20฿, open daily 9am-6pm.) BeBe's **Wok-N-Roll** is Pai's recommended cooking course, located opposite Baan Benjarong Restaurant. (1 day, 750฿ for 4 dishes; includes trip to the market, breakfast, cookbook, and your tasty creations.) Pai is also the place to pamper your soul—**Pai Dhamma and Herbal House,** on Rungsiyanon Rd. opposite the police station, has Thai massage and aromatherapy. Three- to ten-day meditation and massage courses are available, while the "detox" course is best for those coming off Ko Phangan. (☎699 964. Meditation course with detox 1500฿ per day, includes accommodation; 3-day massage course 1000฿ per day. Note that it plans to move in the next year, so check with a tourist agency if it's not on Rungsiyanon Rd.) Across the road, **"Mam"** teaches yoga to those with or without experience. (☎09 954 4981. 2½hr. class 250฿.)

The town boogies nightly to blues at the regionally renowned **BeBop,** on Ketkelang Rd. (Hwy. 1095), just south of Baan Benjarong (p. 289). The house is packed every night—arrive by 10pm. (Open daily 6:30pm-12:30am. Music 9-10:30pm.) **Golden Triangle Bar and Restaurant,** at the eastern end of Chaisongkhram Rd., is a more relaxed option. (Open daily 4pm-midnight.) The "free-spirited" **Tea-Room** across from All About Coffee on Chaisongkhram Rd. has movies at 7pm. Every kind of tea except Lipton is available, along with art and photography for sale. The sign on the door says it all: "Open When We're Happy." The small "movie theater" next to Tea Room offers several rooms with DVD players and a large selection of DVDs to choose from. (1 person 150฿, 2-3 people 250฿. Closes midnight).

⚡ DAYTRIP FROM PAI: THAM PLAA AND HIGHWAY 1095

Best attempted with a motorbike. Take the turn-off from Hwy. 1095 to Nai Soi (also marked to Pha Sua); follow the road as it veers right at the turn-off 500m farther down. The return trip can be completed via Tham Plaa; at Mok Chom Pae, take the direct route to the highway. Be careful not to miss this unmarked turn-off. From there, signs lead to Tham Plaa.

Some of Thailand's most stunning, rugged scenery graces Hwy. 1095 between Pai and Mae Hong Son (111km). A well-planned trip to **Mae Aw** can cover most of the attractions. The KMT village of Mae Aw is on a mountaintop about 40km north of Mae Hong Son, straddling the Burmese border. The village entrance is marked by a gate emblazoned with Chinese script and the words "Ban Rak Thai," its Thai name. The breathtaking trip, including valley crossings and mountain panoramas, is best appreciated by Shan and Hmong villages dot the road, as well as **Pha Sua Waterfall,** approximately 27km from Mae Hong Son. Those with lunch can dine in natural splendor at the picnic tables.

The Fish Cave—**Tham Plaa**—sits next to Hyw 1095, 16km north of Mae Hong Son. The Shan villagers who look after the fish never catch them, believing that the spirit of the mountain guards the fish from harm. As a result of their protected status, the fish grow quite large (many more than 80cm long). Recently, a scuba-outfitted Australian camera crew penetrated the pool's depths and discovered a waterfall and an open-air cavern deep below the surface. Local lore has it that Japanese soldiers, retreating from Myanmar, buried treasure in such caverns. Visitors, however, are relegated to the circuitous nature trail that passes by the aquatic peepholes. (Free. Visitors Center open daily 8am-4pm.)

MAE HONG SON ☎053

Lush valleys, rocky streams, and forested mountains dotted with hill-tribe villages and temples—arguably the most picturesque scenery in northern Thailand—have visitors flocking to Mae Hong Son. *Farang* tourists come for some of Thailand's best trekking, and Thai tourists come to soak up the rural lifestyle. The best time to visit is during the Bua Tong Blossom Festival in the beginning of November, when the local wild sunflower turns hillsides golden. The revenue from tourism can be plainly seen in the manicured gardens and modern infrastructure. The *songthaew* driver with the "Keep Mae Hong Son Small" sticker on his windshield is clearly fighting a losing battle.

▬ TRANSPORTATION

Flights: Mae Hong Son Airport (☎611 367), on Nivit Pisan Rd. Turn left at the hospital at the east end of Singhanat Bumrung Rd. **Thai Airways,** 71 Singhanat Bumrung Rd. (☎612 220). Open M-F 8am-5pm. Flies to **Chiang Mai** (35min.; 12:45, 3:10, 5:30pm; 870฿). **Air Andaman** (☎620 451), with offices at the airport, flies to **Bangkok** (1¾hr., 4 per week, 2055฿).

NORTHERN THAILAND

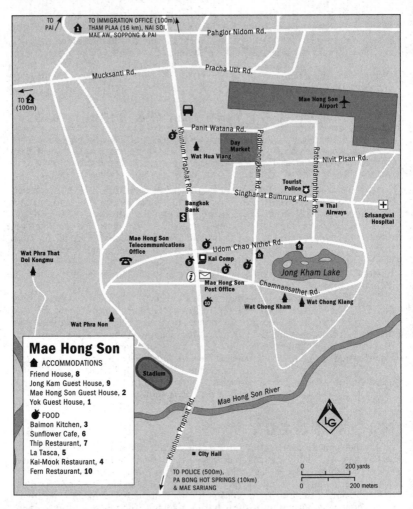

Mae Hong Son

⌂ ACCOMMODATIONS
Friend House, **8**
Jong Kam Guest House, **9**
Mae Hong Son Guest House, **2**
Yok Guest House, **1**

🍎 FOOD
Baimon Kitchen, **3**
Sunflower Cafe, **6**
Thip Restaurant, **7**
La Tasca, **5**
Kai-Mook Restaurant, **4**
Fern Restaurant, **10**

Buses: 33/3 Khunlum Praphat Rd. (☎611 318). To: **Chiang Mai** (7½-8½hr., 11 per day 6am-9pm, 105-261฿) via **Mae Sariang** (4hr., 4 per day 6am-9pm, 78฿; with A/C, 6, 10:30am, 9pm, 140฿) and **Khun Yuam** (2hr., 35฿); or via **Pai** (3½hr., 4 per day 7am-12:30pm, 53฿; with A/C, 8am, 105฿) and **Soppong** (2 hr., 33฿).

Local Transportation: Songthaew leave for points north of Mae Hong Son from the day market on Punit Watana Rd. **Motorcycle taxis** and **tuk-tuks** wait at the bus station and airport (10-40฿).

Rentals: Numerous places around the traffic light on Khunlum Praphat Rd. rent **motorcycles. Highway,** 67/2 Khunlum Praphat Rd. (☎611 620), opposite Thai Farmers Bank, south of the lights, has "as new" motorcycles with good service facilities. 150฿ per day; passport or 500฿ and passport photocopy required for deposit. Open daily 8am-7pm. **TN Tour,** 107/17 Khunlum Praphat Rd. (☎620 059), rents Suzuki 4WD.

✦❔ ORIENTATION AND PRACTICAL INFORMATION

Mae Hong Son is 348km from Chiang Mai via Mae Sariang (Hwy. 108, the southern route), and a meandering 274km via Pai (Hwy. 107 and 1095, the northern route). Buses stop on **Khunlum Praphat Road,** which is home to restaurants, trekking outfitters, and banks, and runs north-south through the center of town. As you turn left out of the bus station and head south, the second intersection is **Singhanat Bumrung Road.** Another block south, guesthouses dot **Udom Chao Nithet Road,** which borders the **Jong Kham Lake;** the water glistens with reflections of *wats* and *chedis.*

Tourist Office: TAT (☎612 982), on Khunlum Praphat Rd., 200m south of traffic light, opposite post office. Eager staff hands out tourist brochures and excellent maps. Open M-F 8:30am-noon and 1-4:30pm.

Immigration Office: 11 Khunlum Praphat Rd. (☎612 106), 1km north of the bus station. 10- or 30-day visa extensions depending on visa type. 2 photos and 2 copies of passport, departure card, and visa required. 1900฿. Open daily 8:30am-4:30pm.

Currency Exchange: Bangkok Bank, 68 Khunlum Praphat Rd. (☎611 275). Open M-F 8:30am-3:30pm. **24hr. ATM.** AmEx/MC/PLUS/V.

Books: Saksarin Tour, 88/5-6 Khunlum Praphat Rd. (☎612 124), next to La Tasca. Small selection of English fiction and travel books. Comprehensive map selection.

Markets: The **day market** is on Panit Watana Rd. next to Wat Hua Viang. Roadside stalls sell fruits and vegetables; the covered market sells mainly meat. Cookies mix with hill-tribe bags and cartoon-character umbrellas in the nearby *sois.*

Ambulance: ☎1669.

Local Tourist Police: (☎611 812). At the corner of Rachadamphitak and Singhanat Bumrung Rd. Helpful. Same excellent maps as TAT, and good English is spoken. Open daily 9am-9pm. **24hr. emergency.**

Pharmacy: 37 Singhanat Bumrung Rd. (☎611 380). Open daily 7am-8pm.

Medical Services: Srisangwal Hospital (☎611 378), at the end of Singhanat Bamrung Rd. English-speaking doctors. **24hr. emergency** care.

Telephones: Mae Hong Son Telecommunications Office, 26 Udom Chao Nithet Rd. (☎611 711), just west of Khunlum Praphat Rd. **International phones** and fax. **Lenso** phone at post office. **CATNET.** Open M-F 8:30am-4:30pm.

Internet Access: Cheapest (and slowest) is the **CATNET** at the Telecommunications Office. 11฿ per hr.; buy 100฿ card. Several places around the traffic light. **Kai Comp,** just north of the post office. 1฿ per min., 40฿ per hr. Open daily 8am-11pm.

Post Offices: Mae Hong Son Post Office, 79 Khunlum Praphat Rd. (☎611 223). Open M-F 8:30am-4:30pm, Sa-Su 9am-noon.

Postal Code: 58000.

⌂ ACCOMMODATIONS

Lakeside guesthouses are central, but loud renditions of the *Chang* beer jingle make for poor lullabies. Those venturing to Mae Hong Son from Pai may be disappointed with the budget options. All of the town's guesthouses are in two areas; the central area around the lake, and the less convenient but quieter northwest outskirts of the city. Standard hotels cluster along Khunlum Praphat Rd.

Friend House, 20 Paditchongkam Rd. (☎620 119). Turn left out of the bus station, take the 1st left after the traffic light, and then the 1st right; it's just off the intersection with Udom Chao Nithet Rd. Cleanest of the lakeside joints. Upstairs rooms have balcony

THE LOCAL STORY

THE PLIGHT OF THE PADONG

Perhaps the most ubiquitous of all Thailand's attractions are the Padong long-necked women. It is impossible to leave Bangkok without seeing them on postcards or hearing stories about them. In reality, the total number of Padong is only about 7,000, out of which a mere 300 live in Thailand, in Mae Hong Son Province.

The women are famous for the brass coils they wear around their necks. The coils—weighing 5kg or more—push down the woman's collarbone, which creates the illusion of a very long neck. Research shows that Padong women's necks are actually normally sized; if the brass coils were removed, the neck would revert from its elongated state.

Padong legend holds that in their golden age, a pack of tigers attacked a village and bit several tribal members on the neck, killing them. This so worried the village leader that he forced girls and unmarried women to wear neck coils. Originally, the coils were made of gold, but as that became too expensive, brass was substituted. Girls receive their first set of coils at age five , and three more are added every three years until the girl is 25 or is married. The tradition began dying out in Myanmar, but once groups fled to Thailand, entrepreneurs seized on the women as a tourist gold mine.

The Padong tourist villages are quite controversial, as critics see...
[Cont'd on next page...]

with view of the lake. Laundry 30฿ per kg. Rooms 100฿, with shower 250฿. ❷

Mae Hong Son Guest House, 295 Mucksanti Rd. (☎612 510). Turn right out of the bus station and left on the 1st street. Verdant garden and relaxed atmosphere. Singles 150฿; doubles 200฿, with bath 250-300฿. Private bungalow with bath 450-500฿. ❷

Yok Guest House, 14 Sirimongkol Rd. (☎611 532). Turn right out of the bus station, then take the 2nd left; it's 300m on the right after the *wat*. Quiet, residential surroundings set back from the main road. Free transportation from airport and bus station. Clean rooms with fan, towels, and bath 200฿, with carpet 300฿, with A/C 400฿. ❸

Jong Kam Guest House, 7 Udom Chao Nithet Rd. Turn left from the bus station, and take the 1st left after the traffic light; it's on the right. Breakfast 30-50฿. Laundry 30฿ per kg. 3-day/2-night walking treks to Karen village 600฿ per day. Only consider the 2 bungalows closest to the lake. Large rooms, but upkeep could be better. Singles 80฿, with bath 180฿; doubles 100฿/ 200฿. ❶

🍴 FOOD

In order to satisfy increasing demand, Mae Hong Son has diversified its food options. Most restaurants now offer Western specialties, but the best options are still the Northern Thai dishes. **Fern Restaurant ❷,** on Khunlum Praphat Rd. just south of the post office, serves what locals call the best Thai food in town. (Entrees 40-80฿. Local chicken with herb 70฿. Live Thai music nightly until 9pm. Open daily 10am-11pm.) **Baimon Kitchen ❶,** on Khunlum Praphat Rd. opposite and south of the bus station, has good, cheap Thai entrees. Try their specialty *khao soy,* a Northern Thai coconut curry noodle dish, for 20฿. (Pineapple chicken 25฿. Lots of tofu dishes 10-40฿. Open daily 7am-11pm.) **Kai-mook Restaurant ❷,** on Udom Chao Nithet Rd. just east of the intersection with Khunlum Rd., serves great Thai food in a pleasant, clean setting. (☎612 092. Tasty duck with gravy 70฿. Chicken curry 50฿. Large set menu for 3 people 350฿. Open daily 10am-2pm and 5pm-midnight.) Stop by the **Sunflower Cafe ❶,** Soi 3 Khunlum Praphat Rd., at 8am for oven-fresh bread and a delicious breakfast. To get there, face the post office and follow the road's left fork 100m; it's on the left. The cafe also offers treks and info on the region. The comfy cushioned seating is a great place to put together a trekking group or to trade secrets with fellow travelers. (☎620 549. Cheesecake 25฿. Papaya shake 15฿. Open daily 7:30am-11:30pm.) The tranquil view from **Thip**

Restaurant ❷, 23/11 Paditchongkam Rd., perfectly complements the food. (Crispy *hoi jou*—Chinese pork sausage—60฿. Chicken with oyster sauce 30฿. Open daily 9am-10pm.) **La Tasca ❸,** 88/4 Khunlum Praphat Rd., opposite and north of the post office, has terrific meals. Homemade gnocchi and fettuccine start at 95฿. (Pizza from 85฿. Tiramisu 35฿. Open daily noon-11pm.)

👁 SIGHTS

Wat Phra That Doi Kongmu, 474m above town, has a panoramic view of the city. Built in 1874, this Shan-influenced temple is Mae Hong Son's most important *wat.* Nearby **Wat Phra Non** houses a 12m Burmese-style reclining Buddha and the ashes of Mae Hong Son's kings. To get to either *wat,* head west on Udom Chao Nithet Rd. and turn left at the end. On the right is Wat Phra Non, and the road to the hilltop vista of Wat Phra That Doi Kongmu is the right before the stadium.

A jogging track circles **Jong Kham Lake.** Feed the fish (fish food 5฿) or visit the lake's south side to see two famed *wats.* **Wat Chong Klang** is on the right, with Buddhist glass paintings and wooden dolls brought from Myanmar over 100 years ago. (Open daily 8am-6pm.) **Wat Chong Kham,** built in 1827, shines with gold-leaf.

The **Pa Bong Hot Springs** offer a different type of soul-cleansing. The relaxation center, 10km south of town toward Mae Sariang, pipes spring water into private baths. (Small bath 40฿, large 200฿. Thai massage available. Open daily 9am-7pm.)

🎒 TREKKING

Mae Hong Son has some of the best trekking in Thailand—several Chiang Mai-based treks descend here. The surrounding hills support villages of Lisu, Lahu, Hmong, and Karen tribes, as well as Shan and Kuo Min Tang (KMT) zones. During the low season, putting together your own crew can lower prices, since Mae Hong Son draws fewer travelers than Chiang Mai and there aren't always organized groups. TAT can provide you with a list of the 28 licensed travel agents in Mae Hong Son. Once you decide on a company, it doesn't hurt to check their status with the tourist police. For those heading to the sights by themselves, TAT still has the best free regional map. Detailed trekking routes are found on the regional map produced by the **Pai Association for Travelers** (available at some restaurants and trekking agencies; 10฿). **Sunflower Tours,** run out of Sunflower Cafe (see above), offers consistently good butterfly- and bird-

them as exploitative. Proponents of the coils counter that the village has increased income. The biggest and most touristed of the Padong villages is Nai Soi, near Mae Hong Son. It is clear to anyone who has been there that the women do not lead an authentic village life. Instead, they pose for pictures, superficially play together in the river, and weave baskets for tourist souvenirs. Contradicting their detractors, the Padong women themselves say that they don't mind the photographs and that life in Thailand is much better than in Myanmar.

Indeed, the Padong don't have much more appealing alternatives. The Padong could live in intense poverty in Myanmar, under an oppressive government that persecutes them. They could flee to Thailand, perform taxing farm labor, and lead a life of bare subsistence. Or they could establish tourist villages in Thailand, where they strive to please photographers all day, all the while making more money than by traditional methods. While the tourist village is not a perfect way of life for the Padong, it surpasses their next-best option.

If you are interested in seeing the Padong, go to Hoy Sen Thao, Huay Ma Khen Som, or Noi Soi—all in Mae Hong Son Province. All of the villages can be reached by private transportation. The entrance fee is 250฿, some of which goes directly to villagers. Tour companies charge much more.

watching tours, as well as treks featuring elephants, bamboo rafts, and visits to hill tribes. Owner La leads most outings and can tailor trips to your interests (1- to 5-day trips 600฿ per person per day, 4-person min.). Treks with **Mae Hong Son Guest House** (p. 294) also receive favorable reports. (☎ 620 105. 3-day trek 1800฿; 4-person minimum.)

DAYTRIPS FROM MAE HONG SON

NAI SOI (LONG-NECKED KAREN VILLAGE)

Take a songthaew from Mae Hong Son's day market to the Shan town (leaves when full, 30฿); then walk or hail another for the 3km to Nai Soi. Returning can be tricky; a motorcycle taxi is your best bet (250฿). For those with their own transportation, the turn-off is Km 199 on the highway to Pai. Turn left at this point, and take the 1st left 500m down. There is a sign at this 2nd turn-off, but it is obscured. Entrance 250฿. Open daily 6am-6pm.

Travelers can't make it as far as Mae Hong Son Province without hearing about the Burmese refugees who make this village their home. At the age of five, the girls in this subset of the Karen tribe are fitted for their first brass neck rings. By adulthood, the rings have compressed the woman's collarbone and rib cage so that her neck appears stretched. Many visitors find the zoo-like atmosphere disturbing.

SOPPONG (PANG MA PHA)

Buses stop in Soppong on their way between Mae Hong Son (2hr., 4 per day 10am-5:30pm, 30฿) and Pai (1½hr., 4 per day 9am-6pm, 30฿). The last bus to Chiang Mai (5½hr.) is at 2:30pm. Soppong is 43km from Pai and 66km from Mae Hong Son.

Soppong stretches over 4km of Hwy. 1095; at the end closest to Pai is the turn-off to **Tham Lod** (Lod Cave). Follow the 9km road to its end to reach the entrance to the cave. Prehistoric remains have been found among its stalagmites and stalactites. Visitors must hire a guide at the entrance to take them through the three gigantic underground caverns (100฿ for 1-4 people). The highlight of the final chamber, where the burial remains lie, is the subterranean river crossing. Rafts can be chartered either at the beginning of the cave (round-trip 400฿ for 1-4 people) or before the subterranean river crossing (round-trip 200฿ for 1-4 people). The first stretch of the cave can be easily navigated by foot, so the raft is not necessary. During the lowest point of the dry season, even the subterranean river crossing can be waded. The best time to visit the cave is about 1½hr. before sunset, so that the tour will conclude with the aerial display put on by swifts as they return to the cave. Sunrise provides a clearer view of the vortex that forms in the cave before the birds' exit. A 20min. walk around the side of the cave leads to the viewing area. (☎ 617 218. Open daily 8am-5pm.)

To get to the cave from Soppong, catch a motorbike taxi (60฿) or rent your own transportation. **Jungle Guest House** (see below) offers a **jeep** service (round-trip 350฿, seats 5) and has motorcycles of varying quality (200฿ per day). The repair shop opposite Little Eden and Soppong River Inn also has motorcycles (200฿ per day). Other services include: a **police box** near the bus stop; the **police station** (☎ 617 173) about 2km from the bus station in the direction of Mae Hong Son; **Pangmapha Hospital** directly after the police station (☎ 617 154, limited English spoken); and **Soppong Post Office** between the bus station and Jungle Guest House, equipped with **CATNET**. (☎ 617 165. Open M-F 8:30am-4:30pm.) There is also **Internet** access at **Soppong River Inn** (2฿ per min., 100฿ per hr.).

Travelers intending only to see Tham Lod may find that the serene environs and attractive accommodations provide an incentive to stay longer. The nearby **coffin caves** can be explored from Soppong—inquire at guesthouses for directions and info on obtaining guides. **Jungle Guest House ❶,** 300m toward Mae Hong Son from the bus stop, has a range of rooms along with a good restaurant. (☎617 099. Rooms 80-100฿; bungalows with bath and hot shower 180-200฿.) The most luxurious lodgings are at **Soppong River Inn ❹**, across the street from Jungle Guest House. The intimate rooms overlooking the river are unparalleled. One night's sleep on the comfy beds may well be worth two nights' rest elsewhere. The riverside lounge serves breakfast, and the restaurant by the road is open for lunch and dinner. (☎617 107; www.soppong.com. Single bungalows 120฿; doubles 200฿. Very nice bungalows with private bath 500-700฿, depending on size and proximity to the river.) The posh **Little Eden ❸**, on the main road between the bus station and the turn-off to old Soppong and the cave, is a good family option, with comfy bungalows in a riverside garden and a swimming pool. (☎617 054; www.littleeden-guesthouse.com. High-season 350฿; low-season 250฿.)

Two places in the vicinity of the cave boast stunning, quiet settings well away from the main road. 500m before Lod Cave, the popular **Cave Lodge ❶** (☎617 203; www.cavelodge.com.), features a restaurant and reading room complete with campfire setting. The staff organizes hiking, caving, and kayaking trips (around 450฿ per trip). Old dorms are fanless but bug-netted. (Laundry service. Kitchen closes at 8pm. Old dorms 60฿; rooms 120฿; bungalows 150฿, with bath 280-350฿.) The oft-overlooked **Lang River Guest House ❶**, to the left before Tham Lod's parking lot, is a backpacker's dream. Many bathe in the river. Friendly owner Chalong mingles with guests in the evenings. (Superb partitioned dorms with mosquito nets 60฿; single bungalows with bath 100฿; doubles 150฿.)

MAE SARIANG ☎053

Mae Sariang, a small, peaceful town (pop. 8000), is a good base for exploring nearby hill-tribe villages. Trade of teak, rice, and heroin across the border with Myanmar has fueled a small building boom, and the town has long prepared for an overflow of tourism from Mae Hong Son: information markers clutter every street corner. But neither the construction nor the as-yet-to-materialize tourist flood has managed to disrupt Mae Sariang's drowsiness. Charming countryside and quiet nights await those willing to leave the beaten path connecting Chiang Mai, Pai, and Mae Hong Son. Visiting Mae Sariang is a worthwhile way to complete the loop, instead of merely backtracking.

▐ TRANSPORTATION. The **bus terminal** (☎681 347) is on Mae Sariang Rd., 100m north of the traffic light, opposite the PTT gas station. **Buses** run to Chiang Mai and Mae Hong Son (4hr., 5 per day 7am-1:30pm, 80฿-140฿). **Yan Yont Tours** (☎681 532), just south of the bus station, offers **VIP buses** to Bangkok (12hr.; 4, 7pm; 420฿). **Songthaew** head to Mae Sot (6hr., every hr. 7:30am-12:30pm, 150฿). **Motorcross-bike rental** is just south of the PTT gas station (250-400฿ per day).

▐ PRACTICAL INFORMATION. Mae Sariang is bordered by the **Yuam River** to the west and **Highway 108** to the east. The two main roads run north-south. **Mae Sariang Road** is the location of the bus station and numerous shops, and, one block to its west, **Langpanit Road** runs parallel to the river and hosts the best guesthouses. Perpendicular **Wiangmai Road** stretches from the river to Hwy. 108 and intersects Mae Sariang Rd. at the traffic light in the town center. **Saritpol Road,** site of the morning market, connects Mae Sariang and Langpanit Rd. one block south of the light. A second block south of the traffic light, **Wai Suksa Road** heads west out of town across the town's only bridge to Mae Sam Laep.

Services in Mae Sariang include: an **immigration office,** 200m north of the hospital on Hwy. 108, for visa extensions (☎681 339; open M-F 8:30am-4:30pm); **Thai Farmers Bank,** on Wiangmai Rd. west of Mae Sariang Rd., with **ATM** and **currency**

exchange (Cirrus/MC/PLUS/V; open M-F 8:30am-3:30pm); **police** (☎ 681 308), on Mae Sariang Rd. 150m south of the traffic light; a **pharmacy**, on the corner of Siritpol and Langpanit Rd. (open daily 8am-9pm); the **hospital** (☎ 681 027), on Hwy. 108, 200m toward Mae Hong Son from the intersection with Wiangmai Rd.; **Internet access** on Wiangmai Rd. east of the traffic light (30฿ per hr.; open daily 9am-10pm); and the **post office**, 31 Wiangmai Rd., which has an **international phone/fax**. (☎ 681 356. Open M-F 8:30am-4:30pm and Sa-Su 9am-noon.) **Postal Code:** 58110.

📷🖴 ACCOMMODATIONS AND FOOD. For a resplendent setting, try the **Riverside Guest House ❸**, 85 Langpanit Rd., 300m north of Wiangmai Rd. From the bus station, turn left onto Mae Sariang Rd., right at the first intersection, and right again on Langpanit Rd.; it's 100m down on the left. The cheapest rooms are in the damp, dark basement, while more expensive rooms have balconies overlooking the river. (☎ 681 188. Bicycles 50฿. Check-out 11:30am. Basic singles 100฿; doubles 180฿. Tiled-floor singles with private bath 280฿, with A/C 450฿; doubles 350฿/550฿. Across the street is the budget-friendly **Northwest Guesthouse ❷**, which sacrifices the river view for exceptionally clean rooms and modern fixtures in a cozy saloon setting. (Bicycle rental 50฿; motorbike rental 250฿. Singles with fan 100฿; doubles 150฿.) Next to the Riverside Guest House is the **Riverside Hotel ❹**, with the best rooms in town and a price tag to match. Beautiful wooden rooms, all with TV, private bath, and balcony. (☎ 621 201; riverhouse@hotmail.com. Internet 40฿ per hr. Singles and doubles with fan 550฿, with A/C 750฿.) The third budget choice is **See View Guesthouse ❷**, located on the west bank of the Yuam River. Just follow Wai Suksa Rd. across the bridge and take the first left. All the rooms are set in a sprawling yard, unnecessarily far from the river. A saloon-themed restaurant is on the premises. (☎ 681 556. Large, clean singles with bath 150฿; doubles 200฿. Small overpriced bungalow singles with bath 250฿; doubles 300฿.)

Of all the open-air eateries along Wiangmai Rd., the popular **Renu Restaurant ❷**, 174/2 Wiangmai Rd., 50m toward the highway from the traffic light, probably has the best eats. (Cashew nut with some chicken thrown in for good measure 60฿. Most entrees 40-50฿. Open daily 6am-midnight.) Across the street, **Intira Restaurant ❷**, offers good Thai and Chinese entrees for 25-60฿. (Chicken in oyster sauce 50฿. Open daily 8am-10pm.) On the west side of the bridge, overlooking the river and mountains, is **Mai Long Yee Bar ❷**. (No English sign. Basic food 30-60฿. Drinks 50-75฿. Live country music nightly at 8pm. Open daily 5pm-midnight.) The **stands** that set up on Mae Sariang Rd. around the bus station in the evening sell cheap and tasty food. Also, many guesthouses have their own restaurants.

📷 DAYTRIPS FROM MAE SARIANG. The country around town, dotted with hill-tribe villages, is perfect for walks or bike rides. The 6km to **Pha Maw Yaw** is particularly scenic and isolated. To get there, take Langpanit Rd. north and follow the left bend around the *wat*. This affluent Karen village is charmingly set among the green fields, and its fine temple, **Phra That Chom Mawn,** has a panoramic view over Mae Sariang. On the other side of town, on the road south to Mae Sot, the **Big Buddha** is an intriguing sight. Those intrepid enough to make the trip up the hill are rewarded with another magnificent panorama of Mae Sariang. Follow Wiangmai Rd. out of town. Just before the highway, turn right onto the road to Mae Sot. It's impossible to miss the 10m Buddha. The Riverside and See View Guesthouses and the Riverside Hotel have decent regional maps, and can organize day or overnight trekking, rafting, and elephant-riding trips (800-1200฿ per day, 4-person min.).

Salawin National Park is a 700km² protected reserve, located west of Mae Sariang and stretching to the Burmese border. The front entrance is 6km from

Mae Sariang. Take Wau Suksa Rd. across the bridge and turn off at the sign. However, there is very little to see in this area of the park—just dusty trails and sparse woods. The back entrance is along the Moei River, which separates Thailand from Myanmar. Take a boat upstream from Mae Sam Laep, and get off at the small beach (30min. boat trip). The path up the hillside leads to the ranger's headquarters—a friendly but uninformative stop. It's difficult to walk in the area without a guide, but the pleasant setting is reason enough to visit. It's possible to stay at Salawin National Park, next to the headquarters, in simple but pricey **lodgings** ❹ with a stunning ⬛**view** of the Moei River and the hills of Myanmar. (Doubles 400฿; lodge for 9 people 1200฿.) Alternatively, you can pitch **your own tent** ❶ on the sand for 30฿ per person. Either way, bring extra blankets for warmth at night. The national park is serviced only in the high season. With any chartered boat to the national park, be sure to negotiate a visit to the hillside Karen village of **Ta Tar Fan,** which is only 10min. farther upstream and overlooks a Myanmar army camp.

Points downstream are more scenic than those upstream. Check at guesthouses in town to ensure the safety of the area before leaving. Border skirmishes still occur, and the Myanmar side is scattered with land mines, so don't venture there.

To reach **Mae Sam Laep,** 46km west of Mae Sariang on the border, take *songthaew,* which leave Mae Sariang from just east of the bridge near the morning market. The first *songthaew* (1½hr., 50฿) leaves around 7am; others depart when full. The last comes back in the afternoon—ask your driver for a return time. If completing the journey by motorbike, you'll need a motorcross bike in the wet season—roads can be muddy and there are several creek crossings. (River boats from Mae Sam Laep depart by 9am, return 3pm; 100฿. Chartered boats 750-850฿.) All guesthouses can arrange trips to Mae Sam Laep and Salawin National Park.

On the route to Mae Hong Son are the **Mae Surin National Park** and **Mae Surin Waterfall**—Thailand's tallest cascade, located about 120km north of Mae Sariang and 45km northeast of Khun Yuam. To get to the park, hop off when the Mae Sariang/Mae Hong Son bus stops in Khun Yuam. Catch a *songthaew* for the remaining distance in front of Ban Farang, 100m toward Mae Sariang from the bus stop, at the curve in the main road. This less-traveled route might set you back 500-700฿ for a private *songthaew* ride or leave you waiting for days.

Worth a quick look if you're waiting for the bus in Khum Yuam is the **Japanese WWII Museum.** It's not much more than a collection of artifacts (guns, uniforms, photos, etc.), but the English-language articles provide an insightful look at Japanese occupation in the area. (100m toward Mae Sariang from Ban Farang. Open daily 8:30am-noon and 1-4:30pm. 10฿.) If overnighting, **Ban Farang** ❶ has suitable rooms for all budgets. (☎522 086. Open-air, clean, comfy dorms 50฿; rooms with cold shower 250฿; rooms with hot shower 350฿.)

MAE SOT ☎055

Mae Sot is a small, bustling city 7km east of Myanmar. The volatile border leads to an influx of Burmese refugees and black-market goods. All of the winding routes to Mae Sot (also called "Mae Sod") pass through police border checkpoints, in an attempt to curtail the influx of Burmese refugees and Internally Displaced Persons (IDPs). Mae Sot's vibrant day market is a sight to behold, where "Union of Myanmar" currency notes, hill-tribe headdresses, and precious gems mingle with the usual pig heads and mangos. While most travelers pass through Mae Sot en route to Um Phang or just to get a visa extension at the border, the refugee situation draws some back to offer their services to local NGOs.

MYANMAR: TO GO OR NOT TO GO? Tourism in Myanmar undoubtedly financially supports one of the world's worst military regimes, but reality for the people of Myanmar makes things more complex. In one of Southeast Asia's poorest countries, the fledgling tourist industry is, for many, the only alternative to state-sponsored slave labor. Increasingly relaxed tourist regulations mean that informed travelers can direct their money to Myanmar's people, not to its repressive government. Many Burmese hope that more travelers will visit their impoverished nation and bring money with them; some also want travelers to witness the political situation and tell others about it. The Burmese government's abuses are not a new story, yet they have only recently come to the attention of the world, after the country opened up to foreign investment and tourism in 1989. Many argue that responsible and informed tourism is a far more effective means to change than the tactic of isolating a military government, which then has no incentive to stop its abuse of power. **It is important to note that Burmese citizens have disappeared or been beaten severely for discussing politics with foreigners.** For the locals' sake, if you decide to travel to Myanmar, **avoid discussion of politics** and educate yourself about how to avoid empowering the military junta. The choice to travel to Myanmar is yours. *Let's Go* only asks that you make it an informed one.

▐ TRANSPORTATION

Flights: Mae Sot Airport (☎563 620), 3km west of town. Take a *songthaew* toward the Moei River Market (10฿). Minibus service from the airport daily (80฿). **Thai Airways,** 110 Prasatwithi Rd. (☎531 440), books flights with **Air Andaman** and **Phuket Air.** To **Bangkok** (Tu, Th, Sa 9:55am; F, Su 2:20pm; one-way 1915฿) and **Chiang Mai** (Su-M, W, F 3pm; one-way 1185฿).

Buses: There are 5 **bus stations** in town, within 200m of town center. The station (☎532 949) for trips to and from **Bangkok** (10hr.; 8per day 8-8:30am, 7-9:45pm; 211-420฿) is 2 blocks north of the police station. Ticket office open daily 9am-5pm. Orange *songthaew* to **Mae Sariang** (6hr., every hr. 6am-noon, 160฿) leave from

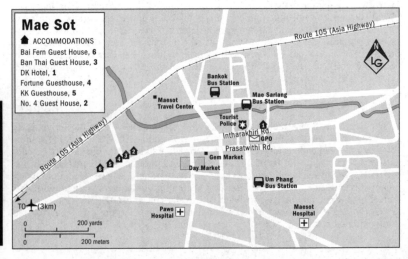

Mae Sot

⌂ ACCOMMODATIONS
Bai Fern Guest House, **6**
Ban Thai Guest House, **3**
DK Hotel, **1**
Fortune Guesthouse, **4**
KK Guesthouse, **5**
No. 4 Guest House, **2**

Route 105 (Asia Highway)

Route 105 (Asia Highway)

Bankok
Bus Station

Mae Sariang
Bus Station

Maesot
Travel Center

Tourist
Police

Intharakhiri Rd.
GPO
Prasatwithi Rd.

Gem Market
Day Market

Um Phang
Bus Station

TO ✈ (3km)

Pawo
Hospital

Maesot
Hospital

0   200 yards
0   200 meters

behind the covered market area south of the bus station for Bangkok. Orange-and-white **minivans** to **Tak** (1½hr., every 30min. 6am-5:30pm, 44฿) gather on the east side of the same market. The station (☎532 331) for green buses to **Chiang Mai** (6½hr.; 8am, 9am; 115-207฿) is 1 block east of the police station on Intharakhiri Rd. Head south from the police station and take the 1st left after the mosque and you'll see a cluster of blue *songthaew* to **Um Phang** (5hr., every hr. 7:30am-3:30pm, 100฿). White **vans** to **Phitsanulok** (4hr., 7 per day 7am-3pm, 125฿) via **Sukhothai** (2½hr., 100฿) leave from the station at the southern end of the main market.

Local Transportation: To go to the **Moei River Market** and the **border,** catch a blue **songthaew** (10฿) opposite Bank of Ayudhya near the west end of Prasatwithi Rd. Last one returns at 6pm.

Rentals: Guesthouses rent **bikes** (50฿). **Motorbike** rental (☎532 099) is next to Bangkok Bank on Prasatwithi Rd. 160฿ per day. Open daily 8am-5:30pm. To keep your passport for Myanmar, you must put down a 5000฿ deposit and take an old motorbike.

◪ 🛈 ORIENTATION AND PRACTICAL INFORMATION

Mae Sot is 165km west of Sukhothai and 7km east of Myanmar. The two main roads run east-west: **Intharakhiri Road,** with traffic heading east, runs parallel to **Prasatwithi Road,** with traffic heading west toward the Burmese border. **Asia Highway** bypasses town a few blocks north of these two major roads. The **police station** is on Intharakhiri Rd. in the center of town; guesthouses primarily lie on the same road to the west. The **market** sprawls south of Prasatwithi Rd. near the Siam Hotel. Free maps with varying degrees of accuracy are available at guesthouses.

Tours: For your wallet's sake, go to Um Phang to book a trek. To book in Mae Sot, try TAT-approved **Mae Sot Conservation Tours,** 415/17 Tang Kim Chiang Rd. (☎532 818; maestco@cscoms.com) 3 days/2 nights 5500฿ per person; min. 3 people.

Immigration Office: (☎563 003). Next to Friendship Bridge at Moei River. (For visa extension, see **Border Crossing: Moei-Myawaddy,** p. 302) Open daily 6am-6pm.

Currency Exchange: Banks line Prasatwithi Rd., most with **24hr. ATM.**

Markets: The **day market** stretches south from Prasatwithi Rd. on either side of the Siam Hotel. Remarkably large for small Mae Sot. Crowded *sois* full of frogs and vegetables bottleneck before opening into large covered areas selling every kind of shirt, from collared to tie-dye. The bustling **gem and jade market** on Prasatwithi Rd., stretching east from the Siam Hotel, heats up by noon and closes at 4pm. The casual buyer will feel intimidated without an eyepiece. The **night market** at the east end of Prasatwithi Rd. is mostly food stalls, making for good, cheap eats. The **Moei River market,** at the border 7km west of town, sells Burmese fabrics, foodstuffs, and gems, as well as French skin-care products and Sony Playstations.

Laundry: On both ends of Intharakhiri Rd.: next to the DK Hotel, and at the other end, next to Bai Fern Guest House (30฿ per kg).

Local Tourist Police: (☎533 523), near Asia Hwy. in the vicinity of the Bangkok bus station. With your back to the police station, head left, take the 1st left and follow it to the end; it's on the left. Ok city map and good bus schedules. Minimal English. Open **24hr.**

Medical Services: Pawo Hospital (☎544 397), south of town past the market, near the vans to Sukhothai. Some English spoken. Hospital and **pharmacy** open **24hr.** MC/V.

Telephones: Maesot Telecommunications Office, 784 Intharakhiri Rd. (☎533 364), 10min. walk west of guesthouses. Standard 33฿ for assisted collect call. Lenso phone and **CATNET.** Open M-F 8:30am-4:30pm.

NORTHERN THAILAND

Internet: 112/9 Prasatwithi Rd. (☎531 909), 2 doors west of Thai Airways. 25฿ per hr. Open daily 9am-8pm, but Internet access often until midnight.

Post Office: GPO (☎531 277), on Intharakhiri Rd. With your back to the police station, head left; it's 150m down the road on the right. *Poste Restante.* Lenso phone. Open M-F 8:30am-4:30pm, Sa-Su 9am-noon.

Postal Code: 63110.

BORDER CROSSING: MOEI-MYAWADDY A 7km *songthaew* ride away from Mae Sot, this Thai/Myanmar border crossing is a relatively hassle-free way to extend your Thai visa. Blue *songthaew* leave from Prasatwithi Rd., opposite the Bank of Ayudhya (10min., every 15min. 7am-5pm, 10฿). Show up at the Thai-Myanmar Friendship Bridge, present your passport to the Thai authorities to get an exit stamp, walk over the bridge, present US$10 or 500฿ and your passport to Burmese officials to be stamped, and then walk back over the bridge and receive your brand-new visa. If you intend to pay in US dollars, bring them with you to Mae Sot, as banks there don't have small bills and authorities are frequently out of change. If you want to see Myawaddy, just leave your passport with Burmese officials and be sure to return by 5pm. Myawaddy's main attractions are a temple called **Shwe Muay Wan** and a fairly typical market. Burmese touts are even more relentless than Thai ones—be prepared to have unwanted "guides" on your trip. Get updated on the political situation in Myanmar before crossing the border (see **Myanmar, To Go or Not To Go?**, p. 300).

ACCOMMODATIONS

The number of guesthouses in Mae Sot is growing by the day; travelers now have a nice list to choose from. Most are located at the west end of Intharakhiri Rd., about 0.5-1km from the police station.

KK Guesthouse, 668 Intharakhiri Rd.; just east of Bai Fern (☎737 101; glamax007@hotmail.com). This new guesthouse has very clean tiled rooms, all with bath and nice beds—specify your preference, hard or soft. Its innovative and artsy Bar Kong has a pool table and serves food and drinks. Singles 150฿; doubles 200฿. ❷

Bai Fern Guest House, 660/2 Intharakhiri Rd. (☎533 343). With your back to the police station, it's 400m to the right. Wonderfully friendly staff. All rooms with fans and shared hot-water bath. Small singles 100฿; large but noisy upstairs doubles 150฿. ❷

Ban Thai Guest House, 740 Intharakhiri Rd. (☎531 590; banthai_mth@hotmail.com), 25m farther west from No. 4 Guest House. Well off the main road, it's Mae Sot's nicest guesthouse. Beautifully decorated rooms, with comfy mattress, table, and cushioned seating. All rooms have shared bath. Bike rental 50฿. Singles 250฿; doubles 350฿. ❷

Fortune Guesthouse (☎536 392), on Intharakhiri Rd., next to Ban Thai. This new guesthouse has simple clean rooms, some with balcony. Living room has TV and movies. Singles 100฿; doubles 150฿; with bath 150฿/200฿. ❷

No. 4 Guest House, 736 Intharakhiri Rd. (☎/fax 544 976; www.geocities.com/no4guesthouse), 200m past Bai Fern, on the right. Fairly indifferent staff. Bicycle rental for guests 30฿. 11pm curfew. No food service. Futons on hardwood floors with nets and fans in dorm 50฿; singles 80฿; doubles 100฿. ❶

DK Hotel, 298/2 Intharakhiri Rd. (☎542 648), 50m east of post office. Multi-story hotel complete with marble floors. Large, impersonal rooms with Western toilet, hot water, and small balcony. Rooms with fan and telephone 250฿, with A/C and TV 450฿. ❷

🚽🍴 FOOD AND NIGHTLIFE

The day and night markets have a huge selection of cheap eats. Various other restaurants are scattered throughout the town.

Bai Fern Restaurant serves incredible *farang* fare. The "Bai Fern delight" pizza (ham, veggies, and pineapple, with bacon- and cheese-stuffed crust; 120฿) is delicious. Plenty of baked goods and espresso. Thai entrees 30-40฿. Open daily 7am-10pm. ❷

Tea Shop, opposite the mosque, has an English menu and serves up cheap and tasty samosas (2฿ each), *roti*, and curries. Open daily 8am-8pm. ❶

Khrua Canadian, on Tong Kim Chiang Rd., serves good *farang* and Thai food under the watchful eyes of the Toronto-born owner. Has satellite TV and fair-trade hill-tribe coffee. Chicken cheeseburger 50฿, fries 40฿. Open daily 7am-10pm. ❷

Bussarakum Restaurant, on Prasatrithi Rd., opposite the Siam Hotel, serves excellent Thai food and has an extensive menu. Thai-style sweet-and-sour chicken 30฿, soups 40-60฿. Open daily 7am-10pm. ❷

Crocodile Tear Pub & Restaurant, on Intharakhiri Rd. before the guesthouses, has live music daily from 9pm. The fabulous 2- to 3-man band will let you join their heart-wrenching Dylan covers if you feel inspired. Singha 60฿. Open daily 5pm-1am. ❷

UM PHANG   ☎055

If Um Phang's vistas from the 1500m-high peaks don't take your breath away, the speed of your *songthaew* on the hellish trip from Mae Sot will. Sitting on top is illegal and dangerous, but many travelers do it anyway in order to get a better glimpse of the unbelievable view. Surrounded by hill-tribe villages and dense forest, tiny Um Phang—whose name is derived from *Umpha*, the document Karen people show for identification—welcomed fewer than 2000 *farang* trekkers last year, compared with the tens of thousands stomping around Chiang Mai. This remote oasis is well known to Thais, however, who escape on weekends and holidays to see the world's sixth-largest, and arguably Thailand's most beautiful, waterfall—Thee Lor Su.

🚌 TRANSPORTATION. The main road from Mae Sot forks just before entering Um Phang: **Praveshphywan Road,** the left branch, leads into the center of town, and **Sukhomwattana Road,** downhill to the right, runs parallel to Praveshphywan Rd. Note that there are no street signs in Um Phang. The turn-off to the *songthaew* station lies halfway along Praveshphywan Rd., opposite the green-and-cream elementary school. It's a further 200m uphill on the left. The road with the sign to Ban Pa La Tha at the back side of the *wat* off Sukhomwattana Rd. leads to the river and several guesthouses. *Songthaew* drivers working on commission may deposit travelers on this road. *Songthaew* to Mae Sot depart every hour 8am-2pm (4hr., 100฿). If demand is high, there may be departures at 7am and 3pm. Your guide or hotel clerk can arrange for the *songthaew* to pick you up from your place of accommodation; notify him ahead of time.

📋 PRACTICAL INFORMATION. Services in town include: **bicycle rental** from Tu Ka Su Cottages, a 5min. walk farther out of town from Um Phang Hill Resort (☎561 295; 40฿ per day); the **police station** (☎561 001), on Sukhomwattana Rd., 600m into town from the fork; the **hospital,** a white, four-story building visible from almost anywhere in town, slightly farther uphill from the *songthaew* station (☎561 270; open **24hr.;** some English spoken); **Internet access,** at Dot Com, across from Gar-

THE LOCAL STORY

AUGUSTINE, BURMESE REFUGEE

Most people you encounter in Um Phang are Karen refugees from Burma, and almost all of them have harrowing tales of their escape. One particularly captivating story is that of Augustine, a guide at Um Phang Hill Resort.

Augustine's parents were well-off, educated members of the upper-middle class in Rangoon, Burma. But there was one problem: Augustine's father, a Shiite Muslim from Iran, was a member of an opposition political party, looked upon unfavorably by Burmese military rulers. In 1988, when Augustine was just 13, police arrested his father as part of a country-wide crackdown on dissidents. As so often happens with people arrested in Burma, he was never heard from again. Word eventually came through back channels that he had been killed during torture after refusing to give the names of his collaborators. Augustine's mother, a Karen woman who was also a baptized Christian, soon met a similar fate.

With no immediate family left, Augustine went to live with his grandmother. He enrolled in Rangoon University, where he received an excellent education, but always under intense supervision. "There was an Army man with a machine gun in every classroom," he says. "And the gun was always pointed at the lecturer—just in case he said something that the Army didn't like."

[Cont'd on next page...]

den Huts on Sukhomwattana Rd. just before the river (1฿ per min., 30฿ per hr.; open daily 8am-midnight); and the **post office** (☎561 127), on the left before the fork as you drive into town, with **international telephone** service and **CATNET**. (Cash and collect calls only. Open M-F 8:30am-noon and 1-4:30pm, Sa 9am-noon.) There are **no banks. Postal Code: 63170.**

☎ 🖂 ACCOMMODATIONS AND FOOD. There's been an explosion of guesthouses in Um Phang over the past few years. The system here is to draw visitors in with cheap, generic rooms and then hard-sell them into partaking of the hotel's trekking services. Beware of high-pressure tactics and make it clear that you only want accommodation, and will decide on a trek later. More important than where you stay is who your guide will be (see **Choosing Your Um Phang Guide,** p. 306).

❷Phudoi Guest House and Camp Site ❷, up a hill off to the left coming into town, is more than the name implies. While the older rooms, which overlook a small pond, are similar to others in town, the new rooms are spotless, well-equipped, and still have that new-paint smell. All rooms offer hot water and satellite TV. (☎561 619. Singles 200฿; each additional person 50฿.) **Um Phang Hill Resort ❷,** just across the river, has reasonably clean and reasonably priced rooms. The fan rooms are newer and less musty than some of the A/C rooms. If you want a shiver-free shower, make sure yours works before taking the room. (☎531 409; www.umphanghill.com. Singles with ostensibly hot showers and satellite TV 150฿, with A/C 200฿; each additional person 50฿.) **Garden Huts ❷** (☎561 093) has clean, basic bungalows with shared bath for 100฿ and overpriced private bungalows for 500฿. **Um Phang House ❷** (☎561 021), 50m toward the river from Sukhomwattana Rd., has elevated rooms and wooden bungalows for 200-300฿. Facing the *wat* on Pravesphywan Rd., follow the road down the right side to get to there and to the road headed to the river. The **Trekker Hill ❷** company is one of the biggest operations in town. Run by Mr. Jantawong (Mr. T), it has teak and stone shelters with futons and mosquito nets. The turn-off to Trekker Hill lies down the road from Phudoi Guest House and Campsite, just before Boonchuey Camping on Pravesphywan Rd.; the accommodation is 100m up the hill on the left. (☎561 090. Laundry 5฿ per piece. Small food service available. Bungalows 100-200฿ per person.)

Restaurants dot the main street beyond these last two accommodations. Only **Phudoi Restaurant ❷** (not connected to the Phudoi Guest House), on the left of

Pravesphywan Rd., 100m farther into town from the *songthaew* station turn-off, gets enough customers to keep the chef interested. (Standard Thai and Burmese fare 50฿. Open daily 7 or 8am-10pm) A small **morning market ❶** sets up next door at the crack of dawn to cater to your breakfast needs. **Tom's Restaurant ❶**, opposite the entrance to the *wat* on Pravesphywan Rd., serves plates of curries and noodles. (20-25฿. Open daily 6am-7pm.) **Um Phang House ❶** has a small restaurant that will whip up fresh simple Thai dishes. (Chicken with cashew nuts 30฿.)

🔰 **TREKKING.** Trekking to one or both of the waterfalls in the region is a great way to see the natural beauty of the Um Phang area and also develop a strong understanding of the way of life of Karen refugees and the political situation that drove them from Burma. Two standard treks through well-worn routes operate in the region. Visits are possible year-round to the spectacular **Thee Lor Su,** which plummets over 400m through several deep waterholes. It is the sixth-largest waterfall in the world and the largest in Thailand. The best viewing is in November after the wet season, when individual cascades span 300m across the cliff face. Treks to Thee Lor Su typically last three days/two nights. The second trek to **Thee Lor Lay** ("Waterfall over the Cliff") is only worth viewing May-December, when the water is flowing. The remoteness of this trek, coupled with the novelty of rafting past the waterfall, make it a popular choice. Treks to Thee Lor Lay take 2-days/1-night. There is a rather rushed 2-day/1-night Thee Lor Su option that requires taking a *songthaew* back to Um Phang from a road crossing. All treks include rafting, camping, food, and water. Government-set prices for two-day/one-night treks start at 2000฿, with the three-day/two-night treks costing 3000฿ and combined four-day/three-night treks to both waterfalls starting at 5000฿. Add-ons such as elephant rides and Karen hill-tribe village overnights cost extra. Additionally, some hill-tribe villagers may request money (often 20฿) for passing through; inform your guide ahead of time that you are not keen on paying such tolls.

It is possible to view Thee Lor Su in the dry season without going on a trek. The waterfall lies 47km from Um Phang. The first 25km to the turn-off to **Thee Lor Su Wildlife Sanctuary,** just past the Karen village of **Doei Lokei,** take 20min. The following 22km take 1½hr. over a rough dirt road that turns into a muddy stream during the wet season. From the car park, an informative 1.5km **nature trail** leads to the waterfall. You can camp here, but in the high season the

Finally, under intense pressure from the Burmese military, which suspected him of harboring resentment towards them for killing his parents, Augustine fled Rangoon, his education cut short. He settled near Um Phang, began work as a guide, and married a Karen woman. Today, they live as Buddhists in a small wooden house near the rice paddies that are the sole source of financial support for most villagers.

Augustine, now 29, and his wife have three children, between the ages of one and 10. The children, despite having been born in Thailand, are not legal citizens of any country and, like their parents, are only allowed to travel freely within a narrow strip of land in Thailand near the Burmese border. Like the other refugees, they are a family without a nation, accepted by none and only tolerated, partially and temporarily, by the Thai government.

Augustine last returned to Yangon (Rangoon) seven years ago to visit his aging grandmother, but he says that he was afraid to linger there more than a week, lest the Burmese Army discover his presence and bring him in for "questioning." Does he ever hope to be able to move back to his native land? "I dream that one day, I can," he says. But for now, he has found some level of peace with what he does have. "I have no family to return to in Burma. My family is all here. As long as we are free to live and free to speak, then I have to be happy with that."

grounds are a "tent city" as trekking groups clamor for space. (Camping 10฿ per person; tent rental 50฿.

TIP

CHOOSING YOUR UM PHANG GUIDE. During most of the year, guides in Um Phang outnumber would-be trekkers about two to one, leading to a very high-pressure sell that begins the instant you step off your *songthaew*. Drivers work on commission from local guesthouses and trekking companies, so they will drop you off at the place of their choice unless you emphatically specify otherwise. As convenient as it may seem just to pick the place where you land, it's important to choose wisely and carefully because you effectively place your life in your guide's hands during a trek.

Be sure to explore your options: ask around and converse extensively with your guide and make sure you are able to understand each other completely—several guides in town are fluent in English. Ask him about his background and language abilities. All guides in Um Phang claim to speak Karen (extremely important for dealing with the hill-tribe villages that you'll pass through), but their actual linguistic competence varies. Lastly, alcohol and drug abuse are serious problems among the Karen in Thailand, the unfortunate byproduct of the *anomie* of refugee life. Every village you visit will offer you and your guide a shot glass of traditional rice wine, an extremely potent locally distilled drink that tastes similar to vodka. Ask your guide how much he drinks and if he uses any drugs, especially opium, marijuana, and *ya ba,* a methamphetamine produced in mass quantities in Myanmar and regularly smuggled across the border (see **Crazy Medicine** p. 414). Carefully observe your guide before going on the trek with him and err on the side of caution in noting any questionable behavior.

Your prospective guide should be willing to take you out for a few hours to the villages near Um Phang so that you can get a feel for his travel style, communicative abilities, and attentiveness to your concerns. This is without question the surest way to vet out any problems and decide whether he is the right fit for you.

TAK   ☎ 055

All roads lead to Tak—thankfully, they also lead out. Whether your route is Bangkok-Chiang Mai, Sukhothai-Ayutthaya, or Khorat-Mae Sot, you'll pass through this provincial capital. Despite TAT's attempts to paint it as a destination in its own right, there's not much to do in town. As direct transportation to trekking destinations farther west becomes more common, more travelers will pass by Tak's smiling people and majestic mountains without bothering to get off the bus.

☐ TRANSPORTATION. The **bus station** (☎ 511 057), near the intersection of Hwy. 1 and 12, 500m northeast of town, serves: Bangkok (7hr., 17 per day 8:30am-10pm, 123-345฿); Chiang Mai (4hr., 5 per day 12:30-7pm, 122฿); Kamphaeng Phet (1hr., every hr. 6am-7pm, 25฿); Sukhothai (1½hr., every hr. 8:30am-5:30pm, 31-43฿). Orange-and-white **minibuses** go to Mae Sot (1½hr., every 30min. 6:30am-8pm, 44฿).

🚩 PRACTICAL INFORMATION. Tak's four main roads run parallel on the east side of the **Ping River**, which flows north to south. Closest to the river is **Kitticarjon Road**, then **Chompon Road** and its night market food stalls. Next are **Taksin Road** and **Mahattai Bamruang Road,** lined with hotels. On the town's eastern edge **Highway 1** crosses **Highway 12** before going to Chiang Mai.

NORTHERN THAILAND

Services in Tak include: **TAT,** 500m west of the bus station, with timetables, and maps (☎514 341; tattak@loxinfo.co.th; open daily 8:30am-4:30pm); **Bangkok Bank,** 683 Taksin Rd., near the Sa Nguan Thai Hotel, with a **24hr. ATM** (open M-F 8:30am-3:30pm; AmEx/MC/PLUS/V); the **market,** on Taksin Rd.; the **police station** (☎511 354), on Mahatthai Bamruang Rd., east of the footbridge over the river; a **pharmacy** next to Mae Ping Hotel (☎511 706; open daily 8am-8pm); **Taksin Hospital** (☎511 025), on Hwy. 1 in the south part of town; and the **post office,** across an athletic field left of TAT, with **international phones, CATNET,** and a **Lenso** phone outside. (☎511 140. Open M-F 8:30am-4:30pm, Sa-Su 9am-noon.) **Postal Code:** 63000.

᚛ᚚ ACCOMMODATIONS AND FOOD. Sa Nguan Thai Hotel ❷, 6/9 Taksin Rd., one block inland from the night market, is Tak's best value. It's tough to spot—look for the open-air sitting room and second-story veranda toward the bridge. (☎511 153. Old wing rooms with baths 180฿; new wing doubles with TV 220฿, with A/C 340฿; twins 400฿.) Cheaper, with squat toilets, the **Mae Ping Hotel ❷,** 231/4-5 Mahatthai Bamruang Rd., is another block inland from Sa Nguan Thai and 150m to the right. (☎511 807. Singles 110฿; doubles 140฿, with A/C 250฿.)

Tak doesn't have conventional restaurants. Instead, seek out **noodle shops** near the police station, the **day market** on Taksin Rd., the **night market** on Chompon Rd., or, best of all, the **food stalls** in the park between Kitticarjon Rd. and Chompon Rd.

⬛ SIGHTS. The paved riverside path and popular warped suspension footbridge offer views of the mountains to the west and, near sunset, billows of beautiful clouds. Continuing upstream leads to **Taksin Bridge.** Cutting east at this point, but before TAT, is the **shrine of King Taksin** (1734-1782). Thais make the pilgrimage to light incense (5฿) and pay their respects to their revered king.

Larn Sang National Park is 17km west of Tak on the road to Mae Sot. The buses drop you on the highway, 3km from headquarters and 5km from the **Visitors Center.** Although *Let's Go* does not recommend it, it's possible to hitch a ride. At **Larn Sang Waterfall,** 150m from the Visitors Center, clear water cascades down rocky ledges. Linger on the shady observation deck, or take a plunge. Thai tourists flood the lower falls on weekends, turning them into a makeshift water-park, but leave the upper falls, **Pha Peung** (750m walk) and **Pha Tae** (2.2km), deserted. **Camping ❶** in the park is permitted. (Park open daily 6am-6pm. 30฿, with a rented tent 250฿. Bungalows 200-500฿. Park admission 200฿, children 100฿.)

Taksin Maharat National Park, with the nine-tiered **Mae Ya Ma Waterfall** and huge Kabak trees, is 26km west of Tak on Hwy. 105. The entrance is 2km from the highway turn-off. (☎511 429. Campground ❶; rooms 200-300฿. Open daily 7am-6pm.)

Bhumibol Dam is the eighth-largest dam in the world; its reservoir is 100 mi. long. A 1½hr. bus ride (25฿) from Chompon Rd., near the night market, leads to its base; it's a 3.3km walk to the dam's crest. Try to finagle a tour of the dam's insides.

KAMPHAENG PHET ☎055

Kamphaeng Phet ("diamond wall"), 77km south of Sukhothai, attracts daytrippers wishing to see the three World Heritage Sites in northern Thailand (the other two being Sukhothai and Si Satchanalai National Parks). The history of this northern town begins with the Sukhothai period of the 14th century and the Ayutthaya period of the 15th century, when it was a principal northern city strategically located to defend against the northern kingdom of Lanna (Chiang Mai) and the western kingdom of Burma (Myanmar). Not only a military presence, Kamphaeng Phet also functioned as a commercial hub. As a gateway town to northern Thailand, it continues to thrive. Its religious sites, military past, commercialism, and

NORTHERN THAILAND

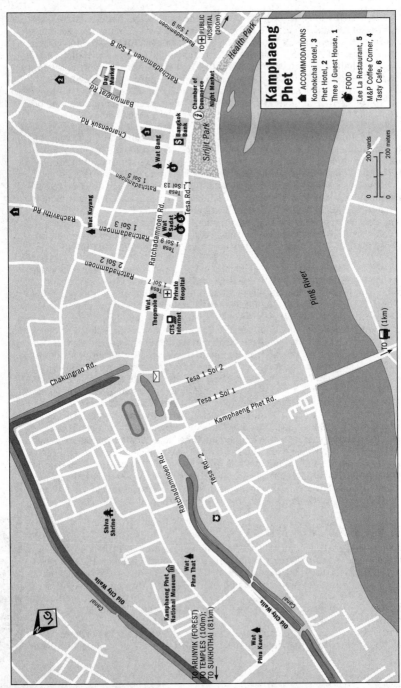

proximity to beautiful national parks only draw a trickle of *farang* compared to other popular northern towns, making Kamphaeng Phet all the more alluring.

TRANSPORTATION

The **bus station** is 2km west of Kamphaeng Phet, across the wide bridge. As the halfway point between Chiang Mai and Bangkok, Kamphaeng Phet is a transportation hub, and **buses** heading in both directions stop here frequently during the day. Buses go to Bangkok (6hr., 120-212฿), Chiang Mai (5hr., 134-220฿), and Phitsanulok (43฿). **Songthaew** run to Sukhothai (35฿) from the bus station. Upon arrival ask to be dropped off on the east side of the river, opposite the bus station, for convenience. Many hotels provide free or cheap transportation to the bus station; **samlor** will also take you there or anywhere else within town for 10-20฿.

ORIENTATION AND PRACTICAL INFORMATION

Kamphaeng Phet is situated 338km from Bangkok and 337km from Chiang Mai. A large bridge—**Kamphaeng Phet Road**—unites the west bank of the **Ping River,** the side on which the bus station is located, and the east bank, where the historical parks, accommodations, and restaurants sit. At the foot of the eastern entrance of the bridge is a rotary that intersects Kamphaeng Phet and **Tesa 1 Road,** which runs south from it into the busiest part of town. Running away from the town center from Kamphaeng Phet Rd. is **Tesa 2 Road.** Tesa 1 Rd., and **Ratchadamnoen Road,** which runs parallel to it, are one-way streets serving as backbones to the town. North of Kamphaeng Phet Rd. lie Wat Phra Kaew and Wat Phra That, both 5min. from the rotary, and the Ancient Forest Temples Site, a couple of kilometers away.

Although there is no official tourist office in Kamphaeng Phet, the Chamber of Commerce at the intersection of Tesa 1 and Bamrungrat Rd. provides a free map and answers general questions. Services include: **ATMs** and **currency exchange** at **Bangkok Bank,** at the southwest corner of Ratchadamnoen and Charoensuk Rd. (open daily 8:30am-3:30pm); the **police** on Tesa 2 Rd., 200m north of the rotary, in the direction of the historical park; a private **hospital** on Tesa 1 Rd., just north of Tesa 1 Soi 7.; a **hospital** on Ratchadamnoen Rd., south of Charoensuk Rd. (☎714 223; poor English); **CTS Internet,** on Tesa 1 Rd. just before Tesa 1 Soi 7, coming from the rotary, more

THE HIDDEN DEAL

THREE-J GUEST HOUSE

In a town full of historic, ornate pagodas, Three-J's charming architecture and landscaping make it a landmark unto itself. This beautiful guesthouse, which opened in March 2002, features 12 pristine rooms with exteriors that feel like a Postmodernist take on the Stone Age. Four of the rooms have air-conditioning and a private bath, while even the rooms sharing a common bath are spotless and have hot showers. The rooms cluster around a rainforest-like garden, replete with songbirds and fountains. The ebullient Mr. Charin and his lovely wife lavish heaps of personal attention on every single one of their guests. The abundant breakfast offerings, prepared with love and meticulous care by Mrs. Charin, seem enough to feed a family of four for a week. Mr. Charin also operates a resort in a nearby forest area; ask him for more details.

Go south on Ratchadamnoen Rd., take a left on Ratchadamnoen 1 Soi 3, go past a big temple on your left, and follow the road along for 500m. Car rental (1000฿ per day), motorbike rental (200฿ per day), bike rental (350฿ per day). Internet (30฿ per hr.), food, laundry, and free transportation to the bus station. Rooms with fan 200฿, with bath 300฿, with bath and A/C 400฿.

reliable than other places (15฿ per hr.); and a **post office** on Tesa 1 Rd., 200m south of the rotary. (Open M-F 8:30am-4:30pm, Sa-Su 9am-noon.)

ACCOMMODATIONS

For an oft overlooked budget option in Kamphaeng Phet check out ▨**Three J Guest House ❷**, 79 Rachavithi Rd. (☎713 129; see p. 309). One block east of Ratchadamnoen Rd., the **Kochokchai Hotel ❸** is a decent, middle-range hotel in the center of town. Basic rooms come with telephone, TV, and bath. (☎711 247. Rooms with fan 290฿, with A/C 330฿.) A few hundred meters from Ratchadamnoen Rd., across from the 7-Eleven, the **Phet Hotel ❹**, 189 Bamrungrat Rd., is the most popular *farang* choice. The hotel deserves high marks for its professional staff and luxurious amenities and facilities. The rooms, while spacious and well-equipped, do show their age, but the swimming pool, lounge, Internet, pub, and two restaurants on the premises help counteract this shortcoming. The deluxe rooms buy you little more than a few extra square meters of real estate. (☎712 810. American breakfast included. Singles 550฿, deluxe 650฿; doubles 650/700฿.)

FOOD

The town's **day market ❶**, off Bamrungrat Rd. at Vijit 1 Rd., features row after row of fresh produce and even fresher fish. For after-dark fare, Kamphaeng Phet's enclosed **night market ❶**, just south of the Chamber of Commerce on Tesa 1 Rd., is a particularly raucous good time. Local food offerings are limitless. With no English sign (look for the "Food, Ice Cream, Beverage" sign instead), **Tasty Cafe ❶**, between Tesa 1 Soi 9 and Tesa 1 Soi 13 on Tesa Rd., serves good food, although the portions tend to be small. (English-language menu available. Fried rice 25-35฿. Lychee sundae 35฿. Open daily 11am-midnight.) Two doors down, **Lee La Restaurant ❷**, 125 Tesa 1 Rd., is the place for a night out. It's classy and candle-lit, with live music most nights. (Dishes 50-120฿. Beer 60฿. Open daily 11am-midnight.) Across the street from Wat Bang, **M&P Coffee Corner ❷**, has a colorful feel and a large coffee menu. (Cappuccino 50฿. Thai dishes 35-80฿. Open daily 10am-10pm.)

SIGHTS

OLD CITY. A northern section of Kamphaeng Phet was once surrounded by a fort and a moat, some of which still remain visible. The main attractions of the Old City are **Wat Phra Kaew** and **Wat Phra That,** both situated in a beautifully maintained park. Hundreds of years ago, Wat Phra Kaew was the biggest (and therefore the most important) temple in Thailand, supposedly housing the Emerald Buddha (now in Bangkok) at one point. Much of the structure has been worn down over the years, but some of the remaining parts, like the Buddha images, columns, and bell-shaped *chedi*, still stand. The square faces, joined eyebrows, and almond-shaped eyes of the two sitting and one reclining Buddha images suggest that they are in the U-Thong style of the early Ayutthaya period. Wat Phra That, just southeast of Wat Phra Kaew, is a similarly preserved temple made of laterite and brick. *(Open daily 8am-4pm. 40฿ entrance fee gets you into both the Old City and Arunyik Temples.)*

KAMPHAENG PHET NATIONAL MUSEUM. This museum has an informative display explaining the significance of Buddha images. It also outlines the history of Kamphaeng Phet, and houses a 500-year-old, 2.1m bronze Shiva statue. The statue's original site, featuring an exact replica, is 300m on the left as you exit the museum. While Shiva is a Hindu deity, the locals treat the statue as if it were a Buddhist monument. *(Across from Wat Phra Kaew. Open W-Su 9am-5pm. 30฿.)*

ARUNYIK (FOREST) TEMPLES. This beautiful forested area only a couple hundred meters behind Wat Phra Kaew is home to more than a dozen temples built by Sukhothai-era monks. These temples were originally constructed in the relaxing environment of the woods to foster meditative practices for the monks, but today the area has become a peaceful, serene park suitable for a leisurely walk or bike ride. While the area is all beautiful, two temples are of special interest. **Wat Phra Non,** the first big site on the left, is supported by colossal laterite pillars several meters high and a few feet thick, still standing firmly today. A huge reclining Buddha once lay in the center of the temple, but today only its absence can be felt.

A little north of Wat Phra Non is **Wat Phra Si Iriyabot** with its better-preserved four Buddha images. The square structure in the middle was designed to support a roof, which, in turn, protected the four niches each containing a different Buddha: walking, reclining, sitting, and standing. Today, the standing figure is in the best condition. A few hundred meters down the road, 68 stucco sculptures of elephants surround the lower base of the temple. The uppermost section of the temple has been completely destroyed, but climbing up there offers a nice view of the area. *(Open daily 8am-4pm. 40฿ entrance fee gets you into both the Old City and Arunyik Temples.)*

SUKHOTHAI   ☎ 055

In 1238, the Thais established the new capital of the Lanna Kingdom near the Yom River and drove the Khmer to the east. Named "Sukhothai," or "Dawn of Happiness," the city marked the birth of the first Thai nation. Sukhothai's period of glory is preserved in its spectacular ruins. Old Sukhothai and Ayutthaya are Thailand's two premier—and most visited—ancient sites. Nearby Si Satchanalai, Old Sukhothai's twin city (with its own impressive ruins) remains untrafficked.

⊏ TRANSPORTATION

Flights: The **airport** (☎612 448) is 26km out of town. **Bangkok Airways** (☎613 075), at the Pailyn Hotel, nestled on the road to the old city, flies to: **Bangkok** (daily 12:50pm; Su-M, W, F 4:40pm; 1500฿); **Chiang Mai** (daily 10:40am, 1040฿); **Luang Prabang** (Su, M, W, F 1:10pm; 4300฿). 100฿ departure tax. Shuttle bus to the airport from Sukhothai Travel Service 90฿.

Buses: There is a brand new **bus station** (☎614 529) 1.5km north of town on Bypass Rd. It is possible to walk into town using the shortcut path behind the bus station (see map). White, pink, and blue *songthaew* run along Bypass Rd. into town (5฿ before 4pm). *Tuk-tuks* to town are 30฿. Buses go to: **Bangkok** (7hr., every hr. 7:50am-11pm, 199-256฿) via **Ayutthaya** (5hr., 169฿); **Chiang Mai** (6hr.; 1:30, 2:30am; 14 per day 7:15am-5:30pm; 171฿) via **Tak** (1hr., every hr. 7:30am-6:15pm, 31-43฿); **Chiang Rai** (6-7hr.; 6:40, 9, 11:30am, 190฿); **Phrae** (4hr.; 8:40, 11:40am, 1:40, 4:10pm; 92฿); **Phitsanulok** (1hr., every 30min. 6:20am-8pm, 23-32฿). **Minibuses** to **Mae Sot** (2½hr., 7 per day 8am-4pm, 100฿) leave from a traffic triangle off Charot Withi Thong Rd., 2 blocks north of the main traffic light.

Local Transportation: Tuk-tuks 20-30฿. **Samlor** 10-20฿. At the terminal on Charot Withi Thong Rd., 200m west of the bridge, red-, white-, and blue-striped **songthaew** run to Old Sukhothai (every 20min. 6am-6pm, 10฿). A **bus** to **Si Satchanalai** runs from the bus station (every 30min. 7am-4:30pm, 30฿).

Rentals: Lotus Village and **Ban Thai Guest House** rent **bicycles** for 30-50฿ per day. Bicycles cost 20-30฿ per day at the Historical Park and 20฿ per day at Si Satchanalai. **Thanin Motorbikes,** 112 Charot Withi Thong Rd. (☎613 402), 20m past Thai Farmers

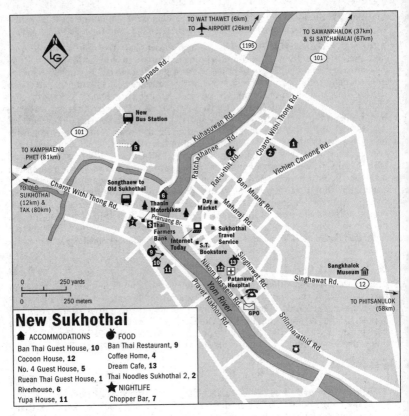

TO WAT THAWET (6km)
TO AIRPORT (26km)
TO SAWANKHALOK (37km)
& SI SATCHANALAI (67km)

New Sukhothai

🏠 ACCOMMODATIONS 🍴 FOOD

Ban Thai Guest House, **10**   Ban Thai Restaurant, **9**
Cocoon House, **12**   Coffee Home, **4**
No. 4 Guest House, **5**   Dream Cafe, **13**
Ruean Thai Guest House, **1**   Thai Noodles Sukhothai 2, **2**
Riverhouse, **6**   ⭐ NIGHTLIFE
Yupa House, **11**   Chopper Bar, **7**

Bank with **24hr.** bell service, rents **motorbikes.** (150฿ per day; open daily 7am-8pm). Guesthouses rent them for 200฿.

✦ 🛈 ORIENTATION AND PRACTICAL INFORMATION

New Sukhothai city, 12km east of the old city (*muang gao*) and 427km north of Bangkok, appears at an L-shaped bend in the Yom River. **Charot Withi Thong Road** and **Singhawat Road** each run parallel to the river (about three blocks east of it), and converge at Sukhothai's largest intersection, near the bend in the "L." From there, Charot Withi Thong Rd. crosses **Praruang Bridge** and continues into the old city, intersecting **Nikorn Kasaem** and **Pravet Nakhon Road** along the way. **Highway 101** bypasses the town at its northern end.

Tourist Offices: The small tourist office on the east side of Praruang Bridge gives out timetables and brochures. Open M-F 8am-4:30pm. The bus counter has the same info. The guesthouses—especially Ban Thai and No. 4—have the best tourist advice.

Tours: Sukhothai Travel Service, 327/6-7 Charot Withi Thong Rd. (☎ 613 075), books domestic and international flights. Open daily 8am-5pm.

Books: S.T. Bookstore, 41/2-3 Nikorn Kasaem Rd. (☎612 272), 100m from the bridge. Michael Map of Sukhothai is a practical, glossy souvenir (39฿). Open daily 8am-9pm.

Currency Exchange: Most banks change currency and traveler's checks. **Thai Farmers Bank,** 134 Charot Withi Thong Rd. (☎611 932), at the base of the bridge, has a **24hr. ATM.** Cirrus/MC/Plus/V. Open M-F 8:30am-3:30pm. Other banks on Singhawat Road.

Police: 263 Nikorn Kasaem Rd. (☎613 110), 250m beyond the post office.

Medical Services: Patanavej Hospital, 89/9 Singhawat Rd. (☎621 502), 200m from the intersection of Singhawat and Charot Withi Thong Rd., on the right. Some English spoken. Hospital and **pharmacy** open **24hr.** Visa.

Telephones: At the GPO. **International telephone,** fax, and **CATNET** upstairs. Open M-F 8:30am-4:30pm, Sa 9am-noon. Lenso telephone at 7-Eleven.

Internet: Cafes on Nikorn Kasaem Rd. near the bridge. **Internet Today,** on Charot Withi Thong Rd., 100m into town from the bridge. 1฿ per min., 40฿ per hr. Open until 11pm.

Post Office: GPO, 241 Nikorn Kasaem Rd. (☎611 645), 1km south of the bridge. *Poste Restante.* Open M-F 8:30am-4:30pm, Sa-Su 9am-noon.

Postal Code: 64000.

ACCOMMODATIONS

Sukhothai has the highest number of charming guesthouses in the region. From this convenient base, it's possible to explore the many provincial attractions or branch out into neighboring Tak and Phitsanulok. Most guesthouses lie near the centrally located, albeit unappealing, Yom River, and fill up during Sukhothai's long tourist season (June-Feb.)—call a few days in advance to guarantee a room.

▨ **Ban Thai Guest House,** 38 Pravet Nakhon Rd. (☎610 163; guesthouse_banthai@yahoo.com), on the west bank. Take a left after the bridge at Thai Farmers Bank and walk 150m. Friendly owners, with lots of tourist info. Rooms newly renovated. Singles 150฿, doubles 200฿; concrete rooms or bungalows with bath 200-250฿. ❷

▨ **No. 4 Guest House,** 140/4 Soi Klong Maelampan (☎610 165). From Charot Withi Thong Rd., turn at the *songthaew* lot. From the bus station, follow the path behind the station (400m). Take a *tuk-tuk* after dark. Tranquil bamboo bungalows with porch, sofa, open-air shower, and mosquito nets. Excellent tourist info. Thai cooking lessons 1500฿ (150฿ per dish). Singles 150฿; doubles 180฿; nice 3-room suites (1-4 people) 350฿. ❷

Riverhouse (☎620 396; riverhouse_7@hotmail.com), on Kuhasuwan Rd., 150m north of Thai Farmers Bank. Has a better view of the river, overlooking the *wat* and day market. Rooms upstairs in main house with floor mat and mosquito net: singles 150฿; doubles 200฿. New rooms with tiled floor and bath 200฿/250฿, with A/C 300฿/350฿. ❷

Cocoon House, 88/1 Singhawat Rd. (☎612 081), reception and check-in at Dream Cafe. A visual feast. Well-lit at night. Peaceful sitting area with selection of Thai classical music. Full breakfast 120฿. All rooms have A/C and hot bath. Singles and doubles 500฿. Bungalows to be completed by the end of 2004. ❹

Yupa House, 44/10 Pravet Nakhon Rd., Soi Mekapat (☎612 578). Turn-off 25m beyond Ban Thai Guest House. Wonderfully friendly Mr. Chuer and his wife, Yupa, run this traditional homestay. There's no patio, but top-floor rooms open onto balconies. Cheap laundry service. Dorms 60฿; rooms 100฿, with bath 150฿. ❶

Ruean Thai Guest House, 181/20 Soi Pracharuammitt (☎612 444; rt_guesthouse@hotmail.com), off Charot Withi Thong Rd., 1km from Praruang Bridge. Beautiful and breezy sitting area. Free bikes for guests, free pickup from bus station. Clean but overpriced rooms, all with bath. Singles 250฿, with A/C 500฿; doubles 300฿/600฿. ❸

🍴 FOOD

Daytime food stalls congregate on the sidestreets west of **Charot Withi Thong Road;** at night, the best bet is **Ramkhamhaeng Road,** the first cross street on the east side of the river or the stalls just east of the bridge. Try the *pad thai* here; it's a point of pride for the people of Sukhothai. **Food stalls ❶** on Charot Withi Thong Rd. leading up to the bridge have fantastic meals at great prices (20฿). Off the road to the north in front of the *wat* are a variety of **fruit stalls ❶** (watermelon 10฿).

Dream Cafe, 96/1 Singhawat Rd., next to Patanavej Hospital. The best restaurant in Sukhothai comes at a price, but it's worth it. The owner, Chaba, will gladly walk you through the extensive menu and explain the subtleties of Thai herbs. Ask her to brew a fruit tea (not on the menu) or take a stamina shot, which is said to improve everything from strength to sexual desire. Roasted eggplant and basil with shrimp 120฿. Entrees 100-150฿. Open daily 10am-midnight. MC/V. ❸

Coffee Home, on Rat-u-thit Rd., next to Lotus Village. Pleasant outdoor candlelit dining with elegantly presented food. *Kiao krop* (pork wonton in plum sauce) 65฿. Chicken sauté in oyster sauce 80฿. Coffee 20-50฿. Open daily 11am-11pm. ❷

Thai Noodles Sukhothai 2, 139 Charot Withi Thong Rd. It's 300m past the school on the right, at the turn-off to Ruean Thai. Look for a restaurant with small ivy-covered fountains and a 2 on the store sign in all-Thai script. The specialty is *kuay tiaw sukhothai* (noodle soup with pork, green beans, coriander, and chili; 15฿). Phenomenal *pad thai* (20฿). Top half of Thai menu is noodles, bottom half rice dishes. Open daily 10am-3pm. ❶

Ban Thai Restaurant, 38 Pravet Nakhon Rd., at Ban Thai Guest House. Serves great food on a nice patio. A great place to get tourist info and meet other travelers. Tofu can be substituted for meat. Sweet-and-sour pork with pineapple, papaya, and mango 60฿. Milk and fruit shakes 15฿. Open daily 7am-9pm. ❷

👁 🎵 SIGHTS AND ENTERTAINMENT

Not your typical temple grounds, **Wat Thawet**'s surroundings are a three-dimensional maze of brightly colored statues that furnish more than a few morbid illustrations of the punishments awaiting those who disobey Buddhist precepts. Inspired entirely by a single dream of the *wat*'s now-deceased monk, highlights include a woman with a rooster head (the head of the animal she killed) and a man being forced to eat his own intestines. To get there, ride northeast on Charot Withi Thong Rd. Turn left onto Bypass Rd. Go over the bridge, and take the first paved right. The turn-off is 6km down the highway on your right, 700m after the major intersection with another highway. Great fried bananas are sold along the highway for lunch.

The **Sangkhalok Museum** displays hundreds of artifacts detailing the daily lives of people who inhabited the nearby ruins. Ceramic masterpieces from the Lanna Kingdom, around 700 years old, are also on display. It's 1.5km outside of town. Follow Singhawat Rd. out of the city as it turns into Hwy. 12 (toward Phitsanulok). Turn left at the first major intersection (Hwy. 101); it's 100m on the left. (☎ 614 333. Open daily 8am-5pm. 100฿, children under age 17 50฿.)

The **day market ❶** is bordered by the river, Praponbamrung Rd. and Charot Withi Thong Rd. Poking your head in and around the area's *sois* will reveal the usual market produce, meat, and plastic sandals. The produce rolls into the market at all hours of the day due to Sukhothai's crossroad location between north and south; the 2am influx is surprisingly busy as locals bargain for the freshest produce.

A nightspot for *farang* and Thais alike is the **Chopper Bar,** 101 Charot Withi Thong Rd., on your left walking from the river to the old city bus stop. Transsexuality is not the theme—it's incidental—but adds flavor nonetheless. (Large Singha 65฿. Folk music 8-10pm. Open daily 1pm-midnight.)

⚔ OLD SUKHOTHAI HISTORICAL PARK

To reach the park, located 12km west of New Sukhothai, take the striped red, white, and blue songthaew that leave from the lot 200m west of Praruang Bridge (20min., every 20min. 6am-6pm, 10฿). Park ☎ 697 310, museum 612 167. Park open daily 6am-7pm; museum open daily 9am-4pm. Old City Entrance 40฿, Museum 30฿, North/West/South Entrances an additional 30฿ each. Bike 10฿, motorbike 20฿, car 50฿ extra fee. Combined pass, which includes all of Old Sukhothai's attractions, plus those of Si Satchanalai, is a great value at 150฿, and is good for visits within 30 days.

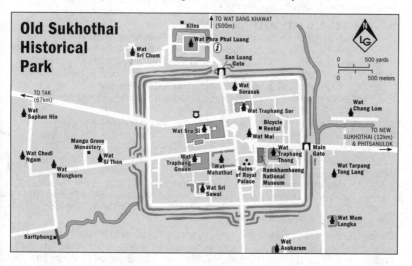

Old Sukhothai was the center of the first true Thai Kingdom. It peaked around AD 1300, and was soon annexed by the expanding Ayutthaya Kingdom. The Sukhothai period is considered Thailand's golden age, when King Ramkhamhaeng supposedly devised the first Thai script, and Thai arts and culture flourished.

MAIN ENTRANCE AND RAMKHAMHAENG NATIONAL MUSEUM. To the left of the east gate is the newly renovated ◪Ramkhamhaeng National Museum. The excellent museum should be every visitor's first stop. It has a chronology of ancient Sukhothai, various Buddha images found in the excavations, and replicas of ancient stone inscriptions, including the first Thai script. The centerpiece is the bronze Walking Buddha, one of the examples of Sukhothai-style sculpture. (*The east gate serves as the main entrance, and is where songthaew from Sukhothai arrive. This entrance sells excellent brochures for 3฿. Bikes can be rented close to the entrance for 20-30฿.*)

INSIDE THE OLD CITY WALL. The town centerpiece is **Wat Mahathat.** The main *chedi* is famed for its lotus shape, an architectural feature particular to the Sukhothai period. Also unique are several standing Buddha images in the Ceylonese style. Many of the ornate carvings around the *wat* remain in fantastic condition. Nearby **Wat Sri Sawai,** a south-facing Hindu shrine converted into a Buddhist temple, is the only Sukhothai ruin that doesn't face east. Its centerpiece is a set of three huge *prangs*, which shoot out of the temple.

NORTH OF THE OLD CITY WALL. North of **San Luang Gate** is **Wat Phra Phai Luang**, where there is more room to explore and fewer tourists. Situated on an island encircled by a moat, the *wat* has a magnificent Khmer-style *stupa* and plaster reliefs of Buddha. The *wat* is treasured by archaeologists for its traces of pre-Sukhothai period art. **Wat Sri Chum** sits just to the west. Its *mondop*, a cone-shaped structure, houses the must-see 15m "talking" Buddha. As the legend goes, the great King Ramkhamhaeng, assembling his troops for war, brought them in front of the massive Buddha image at the *wat*. In a terrifying supernatural display, he compelled the image to speak and urge the soldiers to fight bravely. (Since those days of yore, a hidden staircase has been discovered that leads to an opening behind the Buddha's mouth.) The tunnels on your right and left as you enter the temple were escape passages for the king.

WEST OF THE OLD CITY WALL. At **Wat Mungkorn,** with its distinctively circular *chedi,* the road splits. To the left lies **Saritphong (Phra Ruang Dam),** an earthen dam 487m long and 4m wide, which today can hold up to 400,000m³ of water. The water was necessary in Sukhothai's glory days to keep the moats full and the gardens green. The road to the right leads back to the main road between Sukhothai and Tak, but not before passing the entrance to **Wat Saphan Hin,** 200m up the hill. The *wat* contains a towering Buddha in standing position, known as **Phra Attharot.**

▶ DAYTRIP FROM SUKHOTHAI: SI SATCHANALAI AND CHALIANG

Old Si Satchanalai is 56km north of Sukhothai, and the park entrance is 1km west off Hwy. 101. Take a public bus from Sukhothai bus station (1hr., every 30min. 7am-4:30pm, 30฿). Make sure the driver knows you are getting off at the old city, as new Si Satchanalai is 8km farther north. Last bus returns before 5pm, from Hwy. 101. ☎679 211. Park open daily 8am-5pm. 40฿. Admission to Chaliang is included in Si Satchanalai admission, and park hours are the same. Kilns open daily 8am-4:30pm. 30฿.

During the 13th century, Thailand's golden age, Si Satchanalai rivaled Sukhothai in wealth and sophistication. When Ayutthaya rose to preeminence in the late 14th century, however, Si Satchanalai sank into anonymity. A World Heritage Site, Si Satchanalai has excellent tourist facilities, including a **Visitors Information Center** marked by signs from the roads entering the park. The park entrance has free brochures and maps. Near the entrance, you can rent bikes for 20฿, tents for 80฿, and sleeping bags for 20฿. Despite its historical significance and impressive ruins, Si Satchanalai does not receive many visitors; at times, it will feel like you have the massive park all to yourself. Locals like to say that Old Si Satchanalai and Old Sukhothai are two beautiful women—but only Sukhothai is dressed up.

After a left at the entrance, ahead on the right is **Wat Chang Lom,** the city's central *wat.* According to ancient inscriptions, King Ramkhamhaeng ordered the temple's construction in 1287. Across the road, **Wat Chedi Chet Thaew** combines northern, southern, and local styles. Farther on, **Wat Nang Phaya** is notable for its magnificent stucco reliefs on one wall of the *wihaan.* On the hill overlooking Wat Chang Lom is Wat Khao Phanom Phloeng, with a nice *chedi* and seated Buddha.

Two kilometers to the southeast of Si Satchanalai, also along the Yon River, is what remains of the ancient city of Chaliang, which is actually older than Si Satchanalai. To reach the ruins, take a right just before the bridge that leaves the park. Its main structure is **Wat Phra Si Rattana Mahathat.** The distinctive square *stupa* actually encloses a smaller one. A turn-off 500m before the *wat* leads to **Wat**

Chom Chuen Archaeology Site Museum, where 15 excavated human burial remains confirm the existence of communities before the Sukhothai period.

The unearthing of 200 kilns at **Ban Ko Noi,** 5km beyond the park, challenged conceptions of ancient Siam as isolated and technologically simple. The city's kilns produced advanced celadons (ceramics known today as *sawankhalok* or *sangkhalok*) for export to countries as far away as the Philippines. The Siam Cement Company has spent 2-3 million *baht* making a few of these kilns accessible to tourists. Kiln #61 is located in Chaliang and has an adjacent museum. Kilns #42 and 123 (together) are northwest of Si Satchanalai, along the river, and are covered for protection from the elements. Only one ticket is necessary to see both kiln sites.

LAMPANG ☎054

Lampang's history dates back to the 7th-century Dvaravati period, when it played an integral role in the Lanna Kingdom. Like other northern cities, it clings to its heritage; unlike other northern cities, it has little to cling to. The sprawling city isn't too impressive—its swampy concrete-banked Wang River, congested streets, and mediocre sights don't do much to attract visitors. The few tourists who do wander through will agree that Lampang's friendly and hospitable citizens are its redemption.

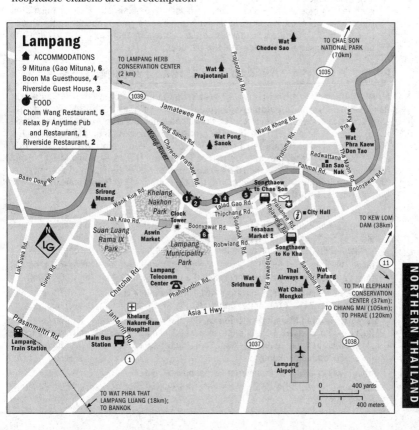

NORTHERN THAILAND

▐ TRANSPORTATION

Flights: The **airport** is on Sanambin Rd. 2km south of town center. **Thai Airways,** 236 Sanambin Rd. (☎217 078). Open daily 8:30am-5:30pm. To **Bangkok** (M, Sa 11:15am; 2055฿). **PB Air** at the airport (☎226 238; open daily 8am-6pm) flies to Bangkok (Su-F 9:55am, 5:10pm; 2055฿). Departure and insurance tax 105฿.

Trains: Lampang Railroad Station (☎318 648), on Prasanmaitri Rd. 2km SW of the clock tower. To reach the station, flag down a westbound *songthaew* (10-20฿). Trains to: **Bangkok** (10-12hr., 6 per day, 146-284฿) via **Phitsanulok** (5hr., 88-151฿) and **Ayutthaya** (9hr., 135-261฿); **Chiang Mai** (2hr., 9 per day, 23-53฿).

Buses: The **bus station** (☎227 410) is off Asia 1 Hwy., 2km southwest of the clock tower. All prices listed are with A/C. To: **Bangkok** (8hr., 7:30am-9pm, 193-540฿); **Chiang Mai** (2hr., every 30min. 2am-9pm, 39-70฿); **Chiang Rai** (5hr., every 45min. 5am-5pm, 81-113฿); **Khorat** (10hr.; 9:30, 11:30am, 8pm; 212-382฿); **Nan** (4hr., 11 per day 8am-midnight, 86-154฿); **Sukhothai** (4-5hr., every hr. 6:30am-4:30pm, 91-164฿) via **Phitsanulok** (4hr., 91-196฿); **Udon Thani** (2, 8, 9-9:45pm; 219-355฿) via **Loei** (8½hr., 145-277฿).

Local Transportation: Blue **songthaew** go anywhere in town (10฿)—flag one down on any major street. Trips to and from the bus and train stations cost 10฿ more (for no good reason except that you're a captive customer). **Samlor** usually cost around 50฿. Lampang is one of the last cities in Thailand to use **horse carts** for public transportation (see **Tours,** p. 318). The guesthouses on the river rent **motorbikes** (200฿ per day with passport deposit) and **bicycles** (30-40฿ per day).

▐▐ ORIENTATION AND PRACTICAL INFORMATION

Most roads radiate from the **clock-tower rotary** near the town center. **Boonyawat Road,** the town's main commercial road, heads east, passing hotels, banks, and shops. In the opposite direction, **Tah Krao Road** runs past the **Aswin Market. Suren Road,** off the west end of Tah Krao Rd., runs to the **train station. Thipchang Road,** a commercial avenue parallel to Boonyawat Rd., lies one block north of the clock tower. **Talad Gao Road,** one block north of Thipchang Rd., runs alongside the **Wang River** and is the location of the town's most popular guesthouses and restaurants. The bus station, on **Jantsurin Road,** and the train station, on **Prasanmaitri Road,** are both about 2km southwest of the clock tower.

Tourist Office: (☎218 823), on Boonyawat Rd., just past Praisanee Rd. Go in the gate where the horse carriages line up. Set back 50m from the road. Not to be confused with either of the "tourist info" places by the clock tower. Free tourist brochure, which is also available from guesthouses or the bus station. Open daily 8:30am-4:30pm.

Tours: The horse-cart stand opposite the police station on Boonyawat Rd. arranges tours—a unique but expensive way to see the town (30min. 200฿; 1hr. 200-300฿).

Currency Exchange: Banks line Boonyawat Rd. **Bangkok Bank,** 36-44 Thipchang Rd. (☎228 135). **24hr. ATM.** AmEx/Cirrus/MC/PLUS/V. Open M-F 8:30am-3:30pm.

Markets: Tesaban Market 1 sets up near City Hall at the intersection of Boonyawat and Rajawang Rd. Dresses, fruit, and underwear in abundance. **Aswin Market** is next to the clock tower. Both are open daily 6am-7pm. **Night food stalls** move in at 7pm and supply cheap food until midnight.

Police: (☎217 017), on Boonyawat Rd., opposite City Hall.

Pharmacy: (☎223 869), on the corner of Boonyawat and Praisanee Rd. Open daily 8am-10pm.

NORTHERN THAILAND

Medical Services: Khelang Nakorn-Ram Hospital, 79/12 Phaholyothin Rd. (☎225 100). Open **24hr.** AmEx/MC/V.

Telephones: Lampang Telecommunication Center, 99 Phaholyothin Rd. (☎221 700), 500m before the hospital, heading to the bus station. **Overseas calls, CATNET,** and fax. Open daily 7am-8pm.

Internet Access: CATNET at the GPO or Lampang Telecommunications Center is the best bet (11฿ per hr.). At night, computer gamers crowd out 'net surfers at Lampang.

Post Office: GPO (☎224 069), on Thipchang Rd. Follow Boonyawat Rd. to City Hall and then turn left on Praisanee Rd. *Poste Restante.* **Lenso** telephone. Open M-F 8:30am-4:30pm, Sa-Su 9am-noon.

Postal Code: 52000.

ACCOMMODATIONS

There is a sparse selection of quality accommodations in Lampang. Hotels are clustered along Boonyawat Rd., and the few guesthouses are near the Wang River.

Boon Ma Guesthouse, 256 Talad Gao Rd. (☎322 653), 100m east of Riverside Guest House (away from the clock tower). Its enormous, clean rooms are Lampang's best value—though the atmosphere and scenery are lacking, as in the rest of Lampang. Ms. Boon Ma has a small restaurant. Motorbike rental 200฿. Singles 100฿, larger rooms with hot bath 150฿; doubles 150฿/200฿. ❷

Riverside Guest House, 286 Talad Gao Rd. (☎227 005). From the clock tower, walk along Boonyawat Rd. with the river on your left, then turn left onto the *soi* with the sign to the guesthouse. It's 2 blocks down, where the *soi* curves. Relaxing veranda over the river. Laundry. Motorbike rental 200฿ per day. Tours of surrounding sights 350฿ each, 800฿ min. Doubles 250฿, riverside 350฿; suites 600฿. ❷

9 Mituna (Gao Mituna), 285 Boonyawat Rd. (☎222 261), on the 1st block from the clock tower on the right. Clean rooms with hot water and fan. A/C rooms have bathtubs and Western toilets. Singles 143฿, with A/C 286฿; doubles 204฿/306฿. ❷

FOOD

Riverside Restaurant, on Thipchang Rd. From the clock tower, walk to the river; it's 250m to the right. Serves up strongly flavored Thai dishes (40-80฿) in a cozy benched patio. Pizza on W and Sa-Su. Band starts at 7:30pm. Open daily 10am-midnight. ❷

Relax By Anytime Pub and Restaurant, adjacent to the Riverside Restaurant. The current hotspot for young and trendy locals. Thai entrees, including fried rice with meat (45฿), and seafood soups (60-80฿). Band starts at 9pm. Open daily 6am-1pm. ❷

Chom Wang Restaurant, 276 Talad Gao Rd., across from Riverside Guest House (no English sign). Delicious Thai favorites on an outdoor deck. Fried chicken in banana leaves 60฿. Open daily 6pm-midnight. ❷

SIGHTS

Wat Phra Kaew Don Tao, in the northeastern corner of town, housed the Emerald Buddha during the reign of King Anantayot (r. 1436-68). The 50m-high *chedi* supposedly contains the hair of the Lord Buddha. A building to its left holds a large golden reclining Buddha. The *wihaan* is open to visitors on Buddhist holidays only. (*Wat* open daily 6am-6:30pm. 20฿.)

Ban Sao Nak, the "House of Many Pillars," is a large teak structure that sits north of the Wang River. Mentioning this restored masterpiece conjures up a lot of pride for the people of Lampang, as the Crown Prince and Princess Consort honored this spot by having lunch here on a bright day in 1977. The owner at that time, Khunying Valai Leelanuj, whose grandfather built the house in 1895, has since passed away, and the house is now open to the public as a museum. The engaging history of the house is as strong as its pillars, but a visit may only be memorable to those interested in traditional Lanna architecture. Most artifacts and exhibits are labeled solely in Thai, but there is a small English brochure. (Open daily 10am-5pm. 30฿.)

Despite the rather stodgy name, the ◼**Lampang Herb Conservation Center** (☎350 787; www.herblpg.com) is one of the most fascinating places in Lampang. Though it's only a few kilometers outside of town, its off-the-beaten-path location makes private transportation the best option. To get there, drive west on Jamatawee Rd. (Hwy. 1039) for approximately 2km. When you see signs for the center, hang a right on the street across from the 7/11, go down it for 400m, and then turn left on the dirt road just before the bridge; the center is 200m down on your left. Set in a lush garden, this spa and research center has the remedy for whatever ails you—there are over 100 herbal products for sale, designed to do everything from promoting appetite to improving sexual potency. A catalogue in English explains properties of the products. The prices in the English catalogue are twice those in the Thai catalogue, so make sure to use the Thai catalogue (product numbers in the two catalogues are identical) when making purchases. This place is sitting on a gold mine if the "medicinal plant for AIDS immunity" works—but *Let's Go* begs you not to count on it. A practical buy is *Porng Karn Yoong Tar Klai Hom* (#104), an insect repellent (20-40฿). The body-cleansing options are soothingly indulgent (herbal vapor bath 80฿, herbal bath 150฿, face scrub 50฿, body scrub with herbs 200฿), as are the massages (100฿ per hr., with herbal oil 300฿). Fancy organic shampoo is available in the vapor rooms and should be enjoyed after the free barefoot health walk around the gardens. (Open daily 8am-8pm.)

▶ DAYTRIPS FROM LAMPANG

WAT PHRA THAT LAMPANG LUANG

Songthaew to Ko Kha leave from Robwiang Rd., 1 block west of Praisanee Rd. (20฿). The wat is about 3km north of Ko Kha—negotiate with a driver in Ko Kha (20-30฿) or catch a songthaew bound for Hang Chat and tell the driver to stop at the wat (10฿). If driving from Lampang, take Asia Hwy. 1 south and take the exit for Ko Kha, then look for signs to the wat. If arriving with private transportation from the Thai Elephant Conservation Center or Chiang Mai, there's no need to backtrack all the way to Lampang; look for signs to the wat and Ko Kha from the highway.

About 18km southwest of Lampang in the town of Ko Kha sits **Wat Phra That Lampang Luang,** one of northern Thailand's finest displays of religious architecture. Its giant *chedi* and low wooden buildings also hold Lampang's most sacred Buddha. Through the main gate, the central *wihaan* is an open-air Lanna-style structure, supported by 46 laterite columns. Constructed in 1486, the chapel houses two important Buddha images: **Phra Jao Lan Tang,** cast in 1563, is enclosed in a golden *mondop* near the rear of the temple, and **Phra Jao Tan Jai** sits behind the *mondop*. Directly behind the *wihaan*, the *chedi* houses relics of the Buddha. Wihaan Naamtaen, to the right of the *chedi*, displays murals dating from 1501, while a 700-year-old Buddha image rests inside Phra Phuttha Wihaan to the left of the *chedi*. A Buddha footprint lies behind Haw Phra Phutthabat, a white building constructed in 1149. Only men can enter, whereupon they'll discover a puzzling white sheet before the indistinct Buddha footprint. Close the door and a mesmerizing optical illusion results: sunlight reflects off the golden *chedi*, is inverted by the small slit in the door, and finally reaches the makeshift screen.

Beyond the back wall, a shrine showcases the temple's most valuable Buddha image, a **jade Buddha** from the Chiang Saen period (1057-1757). In April, during the Thai New Year, the image takes the limelight in a procession through the streets of Lampang. To the south of the complex are several small but interesting museums.

THAI ELEPHANT CONSERVATION CENTER

Take a Chiang Mai-bound bus; ask to be let off at the Center (35min., 20฿). The show ground is 2km farther on foot. If driving, the center is located on Hwy. 11, 37km west from Lampang. (☎ 229 042). Shows daily 9:30, 11am; weekends 1pm. 80฿.

The Thai Elephant Conservation Center, 37km west of Lampang, is on the highway between Chiang Mai and Lampang, outside the Thung Kwian Forest. Elephants begin training here at age three and continue under one master until they are 61 years old, when they retire from their elephant obligations. The center was established to employ elephants and their *mahouts* (handlers) in other pursuits to preserve the species, given their decreasing importance in traditional labors such as logging and construction. Shows feature the animals walking in procession, skillfully maneuvering teak logs, and *wai*-ing the crowd. It's amusing to watch these pachyderms with black-and-white vision create modern masterpieces as the mahouts pass them brushes dipped in brightly colored paint. Bundles of sugar cane or bananas are for sale (10฿), while an extra 50฿ buys a 10min. elephant ride. A 30min. ride through the forest costs 400฿. (Rides daily 8am-3:30pm.) The center has a homestay program that lets you stay and work with *mahouts*.

The site is also home to the **Hang Chat Elephant Hospital,** set up by the Friends of the Asian Elephant. Foundress Soraida Salawala helps treat injured and sick elephants from the region. The hospital's most famous patient was the three-ton Motola. In August 1999, on a break from her job at a Lampang timber camp, Motola stepped on a landmine (planted during the on-going guerrilla war between the Karen hill tribe and the Burmese military) and blew off her left front foot. After an agonizing three-day trek to safety, Motola arrived at the hospital, where doctors immediately pumped her full of elephant-strength painkillers. Thai and international donors contributed over US$125,000 for the three-hour operation to amputate the shredded limb. Within a day she was awake and playful, being fed bananas and sugar cane by hospital staff. Vets later fitted Motola with a metal prosthesis.

Thung Kwian Market is on the same highway as the Elephant Conservation Center and 5km closer to Lampang. The souvenir facade hides great food options—if you can handle the sight of fried bugs, disemboweled lizards, and cow placentae.

CHAE SON (JAE SORN) NATIONAL PARK AND KEW LOM DAM

To get a songthaew to Chae Son Falls, 70km from Lampang, look for the dirt parking lot 100m down the soi running between Thipchang and Talad Gao Rd., 1 block toward the GPO from Bangkok Bank (1½hr., 50฿). Returning will be difficult; Let's Go does not recommend hitchhiking, but families visiting on the weekend may offer rides. If driving, take Pratum Rd. (Hwy. 1035) north from Lampang. Park open daily 6am-6pm. Park admission 200฿, students 100฿. Waterfall 200฿. Camping permitted (30฿). Tent rental 180฿ for 2 people, 250฿ 3. 3- to 15-person bungalows 600-3000฿ (☎229 000). Songthaew to Kew Lom Dam do not run regularly—you will have to charter one or use private transportation. Take Asia Hwy. 1 north, then follow the signs for the turn-off. Kew Lom Dam is 38km north of Lampang. Boat from Lampang 50฿. Open daily 6am-6pm.

This award-winning national park boasts modern facilities and **hot springs.** The springs' main draw is not the **bubbling sulfurous pools** reaching 82°C, but rather the luxurious **private baths** (20฿; 5฿ for shower). A less private, but similar, option is to plunge into the **river** where the water from the hot spring merges pleasantly with the river water. **Chae Son Waterfall,** plummeting 150m over six tiers, lies 1km farther up the road. An engineering feat, the concrete staircase leading to the fall's origin is more imposing than the waterfall itself. An easy 3km nature trail along the river links the two sites (fish food 10฿). The **Kew Lom Dam** is a relaxation spot favored by Thai and *farang* alike. Packed during the holidays, the island can be reached by boat (50฿). Make **bungalow** reservations with the Royal Irrigation Department (☎02 241 4806) or Kew Lom Resort (☎223 772).

THA TON   ☎053

The scenic boat trip down the Kok River to Chiang Rai is reason enough to visit tiny, idyllic Tha Ton. Although few visitors stay long enough to explore the ethnic villages nearby, they come in droves to spend the night. Arriving from Chiang Mai before noon allows travelers to soak up the scenery over lunch, ascend the surrounding hills, and stroll among life-size Chinese, Hindu, and Buddhist figures at Wat Tha Ton—all before hopping onto a chartered longtail boat the next morning. A white 30-ft. Buddha surveys the quiet town from his hilltop perch, and his smiling face suggests he is content with the valley below.

▐ TRANSPORTATION. Route 1089, which continues northeast across the river to Mae Chan 62km away, is Tha Ton's main road. Mae Salong is 43km away, Chiang Rai 92km, and Chiang Mai 175km. **Buses** leave from the north side of the bridge toward Mae Salong and Mae Chan. Those to Chiang Mai (4hr., 6 per day 6:25am-2:25pm, 70฿) depart from a lot 100m north of the river. Buses to Mae Sai (2½hr., 3pm, 35฿) stop near the police box just beyond the bus lot. For Chiang Rai, take a Mae-Sai-bound bus to Mae Chan (1hr., 20฿) and wait for a connecting bus (45min., 10-15฿). Yellow *songthaew* head to Fang (45min., every 10min. 5:30am-3pm, 20฿) and to Mae Salong (1½hr., every 30min. 7:30am-4pm, 50฿) from a lot north of the bus station around the bend. **Longtail boats** leave from the pier on the river's south bank for Chiang Rai (4hr., 12:30pm, 250฿; the boat stops for 20min. in Ruammit). Reserve a seat at the **Tha Ton Boat Office** by the pier. (☎459 427. Open daily 9am-3pm.) Chartered private craft (seats 6-8 depending on season, 1600฿ including guide) won't leave after 3pm—the ride is dangerous in the dark. In the high season it is preferable to put together your own group of 6; this way, it's possible to make both the enticing plunge into the Kok River and stops in the villages.

▐ PRACTICAL INFORMATION. While there are no banks or exchange booths, **Tha Ton Tour** at Chankasem Guest House, near the pier, might exchange small sums. The nearest **ATM** is in Fang. A **morning market** sets up 200m south of the bridge and leaves a fruit stand behind for the rest of the day. (Open daily 5:30-7:30am.) The closest **hospital** (☎459 036) is in Mae Ai, 7km south. In an emergency, call your guesthouse for transportation—ambulances are slower. Others services include: a **tourist police box,** just before the pier (open 8:30am-4:30pm; **24hr. emergency**); a **pharmacy,** next to the morning market (open daily 8am-8pm); **international calls** at ABC Amsterdam Restaurant, north of the bridge next to the bus station (60฿ per min.); **Tha Ton Internet** (1฿ per min.) across the street from the pier on the south side of the bridge; and the **post office,** on the main road opposite the entrance to Wat Tha Ton. (Basic postcard and letter service only. Open M-F 8am-noon and 1-4:30pm.) **Postal Code:** 50280.

⚡⚡ ACCOMMODATIONS AND FOOD. Tha Ton has a wide range of quality accommodations, all clustered along the Kok River, near the bridge. Affordable **Thip's Travelers House ❷,** just south of the bridge on the main road, is run by the lovable, English-speaking Mrs. Thip. (☎459 312. Restaurant open daily 7am-9pm. Laundry. Bicycle rental 80฿ per day. Singles with private cold showers 100฿; doubles 150฿.) **Tha Ton Garden Riverside ❷** has bungalows in a garden along the river. To get there, take the first left north of the river; it's past the Tha Ton Chalet. While you're there, try the *tom yum* soup with shrimp for 60฿. (☎459 286. Restaurant open daily 7am-10pm. English menu. Single rooms with cold shower 150฿; doubles 200฿. Nicer bungalows with hot bath 300฿, with A/C and TV 500฿.) Continue down the road from Tha Ton Garden Riverside to get to **Garden Home ❷.** This huge, shaded property has its own riverside beach and waterfront restaurant. (☎495 325. Basic rooms with fan and cold shower 150฿, bungalows with hot shower 300฿; larger bungalows closer to river with A/C, porch, and tiled floor 600฿; massive stone bungalows on river 1500฿. Prices increase Nov.-Dec.) **Apple Guest House ❷** has bungalows in two locations. To reach the more affordable ones, head south from the bridge and take the second left; they're on the right 150m down. These large, clean bungalows are Tha Ton's best value, though the guesthouse lacks atmosphere and river scenery. (☎459 315. Singles with cold shower 100฿; doubles 150฿, with hot shower 250฿; larger suites 400฿.)

Most food in Tha Ton is at the guesthouses—there are few separate restaurants. Quality, upmarket restaurants are located at **Tha Ton Chalet** on the river's north side and **Apple Guesthouse** on its south side. Food stalls are just south of the river, with the vendors in front of Thip's specializing in Indian and Thai *roti* for 15฿ each.

◙ SIGHTS. Wat Tha Ton dominates the hillside above Thip's Travelers House. The temple features life-size representations of figures from Hindu, Buddhist, and Chinese mythology in man-made caves, as well as fantastic views of the town and countryside. A visit to the two Buddhas is 20฿, but exploring the complex's other scenic areas costs nothing. The easiest route up the hill begins at the arch across the road from the post office. When you reach the fork in the path marked by a large figure, turn left for the golden dragon-headed Buddha, or right for the 12m-tall white Buddha. Follow the road from the golden dragon-headed Buddha all the way to the top to reach the stunning new temple complex.

The **Mae Kok River,** originating in the mountains of Myanmar's Shan states, enters Thailand above Tha Ton and flows 200km to meet the Mekong River in Chiang Saen. **Bamboo rafting** to Chiang Rai (a 3-day excursion) is a quiet, leisurely method of exploring villages along its banks. The Akha town of **Mae Salak** is the biggest you'll pass; it serves as a starting point for journeys south into the Wawi area, home to numerous Lahu, Lisu, Hmong, Akha, Karen, and Yao hamlets. **Phatai** is a Black Lahu village on the north bank. **Jakue** has a Catholic missionary school and numerous Lahu products for sale. **Pha Khang** has picturesque mountains, and **Pha Keau** has steep cliffs. The stop everyone makes is **Ruammit,** 45min. from Chiang Rai, a large Karen village that now resembles a traveling circus, complete with elephant rides (400฿ per hr.), photos with boa constrictors (10฿), and endless rows of souvenirs. From there, it's another 20min. to the **Temple Cave. Tha Ton Tour** (☎373 143), before Chankasem Guest House, offers treks to Chiang Rai. (2-day raft and boat trek 1500฿ per person, 3-day Akha and Lalu village trek and boating 1800฿ per person; elephant rides and longneck village extra. Open daily 10am-

8:30pm.) **Thip's Travelers House** leads bamboo raft trips down the Mae Kok. (☎459 312; thiptravel@hotmail.com. 3 days, including an elephant trek. 6-8 people 250฿ per person, 4 people 350฿ per person. Will also arrange 1-, 2-, and 3-day treks.) All prices assume at least four participants. Be sure to understand what any chartered trip entitles you to and be aware that in the dry season the shallow waters can be difficult to navigate and trips take longer than planned.

MAE SAI   ☎053

One of Thailand's main links with Myanmar, Mae Sai is a bustling border town during the day, but turns into a ghost town in the evening when the border shuts down. With an established opium trade and a burgeoning gem trade stemming from a recently discovered sapphire mine in the Shan State, Mae Sai's future as a trade center looked bright—until a full-scale three-way battle broke out in February 2001 among the Shan, Thai, and Burmese troops. Three Thai civilians died in the shelling, and the resulting tensions caused the border to close for four months. A similar situation erupted in early 2002, when Burmese officials accused the Thai military of aiding the Shan (see **Thai-Burmese Relations,** p. 23). While the trade of precious stones and antiques from Myanmar and China is no longer what it was, it's hard to tell this from the bustle in the streets. Aside from the border crossing, travelers can find impressive caves and national parks near Mae Sai.

▛ TRANSPORTATION

Buses and Songthaew: Mae Sai Bus Terminal, 4km south of bridge along Phahonyothin Rd. Red *songthaew* head there every 10min. (5฿). Buses to: **Bangkok** (14hr.; 7am, 5:30, 5:45pm; 481฿); **Chiang Mai** (5hr.; 8, 9, 11am, 2, 3:10pm; 95-171฿); **Chiang Rai** (1½hr., every 15min. 6am-6pm, 25฿) via **Ban Pasang** (45min., 15฿). From Chiang Rai, **songthaew** go to: **Mae Salong** (1hr., leave when full 7am-2pm, 50฿); **Nakhon Ratchasima** (14hr., 5 per day 5:15am-6pm, 281-590฿); **Pattaya** (14hr., 5 per day 5:15am-6pm, 530฿). South of Thai Farmers Bank, blue *songthaew* go to **Chiang Saen** (1hr., every hr. 7am-2pm, 30฿) via **Sop Ruak** (40min., 20฿).

Local Transportation: Motorcycle taxis and **samlor** pepper Mae Sai. Rides within the city 10-30฿. From guesthouses to bus terminal 30฿. Green *songthaew* go up and down Phahonyothin Rd. (5฿).

Rentals: The Honda Shop (☎731 113), on Phahonyothin Rd., nearly opposite the Bangkok Bank, rents 110cc motorbikes for 150฿ with passport deposit.

◼▟ ORIENTATION AND PRACTICAL INFORMATION

Mae Sai is 61km north of Chiang Rai, 68km northeast of Mae Salong, and 35km northwest of the Golden Triangle. Hwy. 110 turns into **Phahonyothin Road,** and runs north to the **border crossing** marked by the new gate and **Friendship Bridge.** Phahonyothin Rd. hosts a dusty carnival of *farang*, Thai, and Burmese who browse, bargain, and beg at street stalls, as well as numerous banks and shops. **Silamjoi Road** follows the river, heading west from the Friendship Bridge toward guesthouses.

Immigration Office (☎731 008), on Phahonyothin Rd., 2km south of bridge. 10-day visa extension 1900฿. 1-month visa extension for 60-day tourist visas. Bring 2 photos and 2 photocopies of passport. Open daily 8:30am-4:30pm. For a cheaper option, see **Border Crossing: Mae Sai/Thachilek,** p. 327. Immigration Office at the **border** (☎733 261). Border open daily 6:30am-6:30pm. Tourists are asked to cross back by 5pm.

Bank: All along Phahonyothin Rd. **Thai Farmers Bank,** 122/1 Phahonyothin Rd. (☎640 786). Open M-F 8:30am-3:30pm. **24hr. ATM.** Cirrus/MC/V.

Markets: During the day, stalls line Phahonyothin Rd.—check out the base of the bridge for herbs, gems, teak, and flowers. 200m south, level with and opposite the police station, is "ruby alley." Food stalls set up at night near the bridge. The market in **Thachilek,** immediately to the right of the bridge, peddles pirated CDs, cheap (in price and quality) cigarettes, and standard regional market fare, as well as numerous illegal items such as guns and jaguar skins. Thai *baht* is the accepted currency.

Ambulance: (☎731 300 or 731 301).

Local Tourist Police: (☎733 850), in a booth next to the bridge. Open daily 8am-5pm.

Police: (☎731 444), on Phahonyothin Rd. 200m south of bridge. Call tourist police first.

Pharmacy: Drugstore, next to and south of the police station. Owner speaks excellent English. Open daily 8am-8pm.

Medical Services: Mae Sai Hospital, 101 Moo 10 Pomaharat Rd. (☎751 300), off Phahonyothin Rd. 2km south, turn right after the overpass into the *soi*, 400m down.

Telephones: Mae Sai Telecommunications Center, next to the post office. Fax. **CAT-NET.** Open M-F 8:30am-4:30pm. LENSO phone at 7-Eleven south of the bridge.

Internet Access: Take the last right before the bridge, look for the sign leading to the 2nd fl. 20฿ per 30min., 30฿ per hr. Open daily 9am-9pm.

Post Office: Mae Sai Post and Telegraph Office, 230/40-41 Phahonyothin Rd. (☎731 402), 4km south of the bridge and, despite the address, not on the main road. *Poste Restante.* Open M-F 8:30am-4:30pm, Sa-Su 9am-noon.

Postal Code: 57130.

⌐ ACCOMMODATIONS

Mae Sai Guest House, 688 Wiengpangkam Rd. (☎732 021), 500m west of border gate; well signposted. Idyllic escape with thatched bungalows, restaurant overlooking Myanmar, and laundry service. Thailand's hottest showers. Best-value singles and doubles 100฿-150฿; doubles with bath 300฿; bungalows on the water 400-500฿. ❷

King Kobra Guest House, 135/5 Silamjoi Rd. (☎733 055), 200m west of border gate. Owner Joe and his friend John have travel info and can offer advice on motorbike treks to northern Thailand, Myanmar, and China. Restaurant, laundry service, and nightly movies. Singles 120฿, with bath 200฿; doubles 150฿/250฿; "VIP" room 350฿. ❷

Northern Guest House, 402 Timphajom Rd. (☎731 537), between King Kobra and Mae Sai Guest House. Follow Silamjoi Rd. along the river. Verdant garden on the riverfront. Rustic wooden huts with fan have most appeal (100฿). Rooms with cold shower 150฿; modern units at the edge of river with hot water and bathtub 250฿, with A/C 350฿. ❷

Chad Guest House, 52/1 Soi Wiengpan (☎732 054), off Phahonyothin Rd., 1km south of bridge. Cheap, quiet place run by friendly English-speaking family. Map available for guests. Rooms with shared toilet and shower. Singles 100฿; doubles 150-200฿. ❷

⌐ FOOD

The **night market ❶** along Phahonyothin Rd. has dishes on display, so a quick point will get you what you want. (Open daily 7-10pm.) Pamper your palate at **Jo Jo Coffee House ❷,** 233/1 Phahonyothin Rd., opposite the Thai Farmers Bank. Food tastes even better than it looks on the menu. Bitter melon soup with white gourd on rice is 35฿; a banana split is 40฿. Use the *a la carte* option to sample several flavors (Small 30฿; medium 40฿; large 50฿. Open daily 6am-5pm.) Going down the *soi* directly opposite Thai Farmers Bank leads to a series of stands with tables that specialize in *pad thai* (20฿). Restaurants open at night are limited, but **Rabieng Kaew Restaurant ❸,** 150m south of the bridge on Phahonyothin Rd., is a good option. Their minced pork and coconut in chili paste (50฿) is a spicy treat. (Specials 80-150฿. Coconut ice cream 20฿. Open daily 9am-10pm.)

▣ DAYTRIPS FROM MAE SAI

THAM LUANG (GREAT CAVE) NATIONAL PARK

There are two marked entrances to Tham Luang on Hwy. 110—be sure to take the well-paved one. After the three-headed dragon, continue straight for Khun Nam Nang Non (Sleeping Lady Lagoon) or take the first right and then the next left (about 1km) on paved roads to Tham Luang. It may be possible to find a motorcycle taxi or samlor at the entrance from the highway. There are no guides at the park, but locals at the park can sometimes be convinced to join you for a nominal fee.

The national park lies 8km south of Mae Sai, 2.5km off Hwy. 110. Its caverns burrow 200m into the mountain. Other caverns in the National Park include the very manageable **Buddha Cave** and the 7km-deep **Royal Luang Cave.** (Open daily 7am-5pm.) Maps of the area are available at the entrance. The office has small lanterns (30฿), though any extended exploration requires a flashlight and supplies.

Two more caves are inside **Wat Tham Plaa,** 12km south and 3km west of Mae Sai along Hwy. 110. *Samlor* along the highway will take you for 20฿. Fresh water surges through **Tham Plaa (Fish Cave),** also called "Monkey Cave" because of the gamboling primates. They're everywhere, so hold onto small children and belongings. Wear boots and long pants, and feed the monkeys at your own risk. The more adventurous can explore **Tham Gu Gaeo,** rumored to lead ultimately to Myanmar. The path to the right of the temple leads to attendants who take visitors to a Buddha village 2km away (50-70฿ per person). Bring a flashlight. You can buy incense and candles and dedicate them to Buddha for protection from cave spirits.

DOI TUNG

To reach Doi Tung, take a green songthaew to Mae Chan (15฿). At the turn-off from Hwy. 110, purple songthaew take visitors the other half of the trip.

The **Royal Villa,** located in Doi Tung, lies 32km from Mae Sai, and was the home of the Princess Mother (mother of King Rama VIII and King Rama IX) from 1988 until 1994, when she passed away at the age of 94. The palace, constructed of recycled pinewood crates at the request of the Princess Mother, has an exquisite carving of the zodiac in the grand reception hall. The warmth of the beloved King's mother can be seen in the pictures of her gardening in Switzerland that adorn the walls. Her chamber is preserved much as it was. Visitors to the royal palace are asked to dress conservatively. If a visitor's clothing is not appropriate—tank top, shorts, or miniskirt—officials will provide a denim garment, best left in the 80s. The **Mah Fah Luang Gardens,** a beautiful blend of Thai and European garden styles, flow down the hill from the Royal Villa. At least part of the peaceful setting is in bloom year-round. The brand-new **Princess Mother Commemorative Hall** is located at the entrance. While most of the signs are in Thai only, the Hall captures the deep respect and admiration that Thais have for the Royal Family. (All open 6:30am-5:30pm. Royal Villa 70฿, garden 80฿, Commemorative Hall 30฿, all three 150฿.)

About 8km past the Royal Villa is the peak of Doi Tung (1500m), with **Wat Phra That Doi Tung** and its twin *chedi.* The 300 steps along the staircase provide beautiful views over the valley. There is a stunning back route to Doi Tung from Mae Sai, which weaves its way along the border. The road, however, is extremely dangerous if you stray into Myanmar. Ask at your guesthouse for current info about the border situation. The route leading from Hwy. 110 to Doi Tung is heavily touristed and safe to travel.

BORDER CROSSING: MAE SAI/THACHILEK 30-day and 60-day visas can be renewed by crossing into Thachilek and returning to Mae Sai on the same day. First, go to passport control at the border gate and get a departure stamp. Then proceed across the bridge and hand over 250฿ or US$5 and your passport. The Burmese border control will stamp your passport and hold onto it until you exit the country. When you re-enter Thailand, you'll be able to stay another 30 or 60 days, depending on your visa. When you surrender your passport to the Burmese, they will give you a very thin **piece of paper.** That piece of paper is your passport, so hold onto it. The border is open daily 6:30am-6:30pm. Myanmar time is 30min. behind Thailand, so its border is open daily 6am-6pm. Thai immigration officials ask that you cross back by 5pm. (See **Myanmar, To Go or Not To Go?,** p. 300.)

MAE SALONG   ☎ 053

Fifty years after the Chinese Nationalists' 93rd Division fled China in the wake of the Communist victory and settled in this mountaintop village, Mae Salong maintains its Chinese identity. Chinese characters adorn door frames, red lanterns decorate tea houses, and the dialect of China's southern province, Yunnan, is more common than Thai. The steep slopes surrounding Mae Salong, once covered in thick jungle, now lie barren in order to accommodate the year-round harvest of tea. Pockets of natural beauty still exist, making Mae Salong an appealing daytrip. The best time to visit is in January, when the cherry blossoms are in bloom.

☐ TRANSPORTATION. *Songthaew* run frequently early in the morning and leave when full; if the wait is unbearable, you can pay the full fare (300฿). To get to **Chiang Rai,** take a light blue *songthaew* to **Ban Pasang** (1hr., 7am-2pm, 50฿), and then flag down a passing bus (1hr., every 30min. 6am-6pm, 20฿). To get to **Mae Sai,** take the light blue *songthaew* to Ban Pasang, then catch a bus heading north (45min., every 20min. 7am-7pm, 20฿). Yellow *songthaew* to **Tha Ton** (1½hr., 7am-2pm, 50฿) leave from the small **day market,** 1km toward Tha Ton from the town center. The market features Akha wares and Chinese herbs. The **main road** through Mae Salong stretches 2.5km and is a continuation of roads from Tha Ton (Rte. #1234) and Ban Pasang (Rte. #1130). The Khumnaipol Resort marks the Tha Ton end, and the Mae Salong Villa marks the Ban Pasang end.

⚐ PRACTICAL INFORMATION. The town center is near the guesthouses and has **food vendors** and a **mosque.** The **morning market** is off the road to Mae Salong Resort. Other services include: **Thai Military Bank,** opposite Khumnaipol Resort (☎765 159; open M-F 8:30am-3:30pm; AmEx/Cirrus/MC/PLUS/V; **ATM** open daily 6am-10pm); a **police booth** (☎767 7109) near the Mae Salong Villa; and **Internet** at the Golden Dragon. (60฿ per hr.) The nearest **hospital** is in Mae Chan and there are **no international phones.**

⚐☐ ACCOMMODATIONS AND FOOD. Since few travelers choose to stay the night in Mae Salong, the accommodation options are somewhat disappointing. **Golden Dragon ❷,** on the main road between the Mae Salong Resort and Akha Guest House, has clean rooms with hot shower and balcony. (☎765 009. Boasts coffee in a land of tea. Singles 200฿; doubles 300฿.) The family-style **Akha Mae**

NORTHERN THAILAND

Salong Guest House ❷, just off the main road near the mosque, has four huge rooms with wood floors and common bath. The owner sells Akha ware, distributes useful maps (10฿), arranges one-day horse treks or motorbike trips to hill-tribe villages (400฿), and speaks English. (☎765 103. Singles and doubles 130฿; triples 150฿.) Next door, **Shin Sane Guest House ❷** has bland bungalows, and cheaper rooms on the overhead bridge. The staff arranges horse treks to nearby villages for 600฿, and sell trekking map for 10฿. (☎765 026. Singles and doubles 100฿; bungalows with Western toilet and hot water 200-300฿.)

Yunnanese **noodle shops** and **vendors** abound (5฿ per serving). **Tea shops** provide a relaxing ambience; a kettle of Mae Salong tea soothes for 50฿. **Mini ❷,** 300m toward Tha Ton from the Golden Dragon, serves *kanom jiin naam ngiaw* (Yunnanese noodle soup, 25฿), the town specialty. Ask for vegetarian options. The store also rents motorbikes for 200฿ per day. (Lao beer 50฿. Open daily 7am-10:30pm.) **Sakura Restaurant ❸** is a popular Thai/Chinese restaurant in Mae Salong Resort. The translated menu may make you wish it wasn't, with items such as braised sea slugs (250-350฿). Sakura also has more standard fare (chicken with cashew nuts; small 80฿, large 120฿. Open daily 7am-10pm.)

◪ SIGHTS. For an awesome view, follow the road to the Mae Salong Resort and walk up the steps to the **pagoda** at the top of Doi Mae Salong. Do not scale the steps leading up the front of the *wat;* take the side road instead. From here, a road continues 4km through mountain scenery and finally curves back into town via the day market. Area hill tribes include **Akha, Lahu, Lisu,** and, in smaller numbers, **Hmong** and **Yao.** There aren't many organized trekking groups, although the intrepid can set off alone. Pick up a map at Akha Mae Salong or Shin Sane Guest House (10฿), but don't wander too far; in addition to hill-tribe villages, pockets of Shan and KMT groups line the Burmese border. Drug trade and clashes have erupted between Khun Sa's Shan United Army and the Wa National Army. Ask in town about the current situation. The footweary can inquire about 4hr. **horseback riding treks** at Akha Mae Salong or Shin Sane Guest House (400฿ per person).

For those who don't have the time and/or resources to overnight in a hill-tribe village, **Ban Lorcha** is more illuminating than a visit to a museum. The Akha village, with the help of the PDA, has established a **"Living Museum"** in order for the villagers to benefit from tourism without drastically changing their lifestyles. An entrance fee of 40฿ includes a guide who will walk you through the village. While the experience is contrived—the blacksmith doubles as the drum player for the welcoming dance—visitors are left for the most part to observe village life without being forced to buy handicrafts. There are also two other villages between Ban Lorcha and Tha Ton that travelers can visit. Ban Lorcha is on Rte. 1089 between Tha Ton and Mae Chan, 1km toward Tha Ton from the turn-off to Mae Salong. From Mae Salong, take yellow *songthaew* headed to Tha Ton (20min., 15฿).

CHIANG SAEN   ☎053

King Saen Phu founded this small town in 1328 as the capital of the Chiang Saen Kingdom. In 1803, Rama I destroyed the city to keep it from the Burmese, and the district did not recover until the 1880s, when Rama V turned out the remaining Burmese and repopulated the city with Thais. Remnants of Chiang Saen's former Lanna glory now border modern concrete creations. Today's city of over 50,000 people is only slightly more capable of hosting tourists than the crumbling ruined city it replaced—as evidenced by its meager supply of accommodation selections, transportation routes, and tourist sights. Travelers heading to Myanmar or Laos would do better to bypass Chiang Saen en route to Mae Sai or Chiang Khong.

TRANSPORTATION. From the river end of Phahonyothin Rd., **buses** go to: Bangkok (12½hr.; 3pm, 283฿; 4:20pm, with A/C 594฿); Chiang Mai (6hr., 8:20am, 150฿); Chiang Rai (1½hr., every 30min. 5:15am-5pm, 25฿) via Mae Chan (45min., 15฿). The booking office for Bangkok (☎650 822) is in an unmarked house set back from the street east of Siam Commercial Bank. Blue **songthaew** go to Mae Sai (1hr., every 40min. 7am-5pm, 25฿) via Sop Ruak (20min., 15฿) from across the main road. Green *songthaew* to Chiang Khong (2hr., 7am-3pm, 50฿) wait on Rimkhong Rd., 150m south of Phahonyothin Rd. **Longtail boats,** leaving from the "T" intersection, head up and down the Mekong to Chiang Khong (2hr., 1800฿ per boat, up to 6 people) and Sop Ruak (40min.; 400฿ per boat, round-trip 500฿; up to 6 people) from 8:30am to 6pm. **Samlor** wait at stands on the river (10-20฿).

PRACTICAL INFORMATION. Chiang Saen's two main roads intersect at the **Mekong River. Rimkhong Road** runs north-south along the river, which separates Thailand from Laos to the east. **Phahonyothin Road** runs east-west from the river and is where buses arrive. Heading north on Rimkhong Rd. leads to Sop Ruak and Mae Sai; heading south leads to Chiang Khong; going west on Phahonyothin Rd. leads to Chiang Rai. Chang Saen's facilities are scattered along Phahonyothin Rd., all within walking distance. Services include: **Siam Commercial Bank,** 773 Phahonyothin Rd., with a **24hr. ATM** (Cirrus/MC/PLUS/V) and currency exchange (☎777 041; open M-F 8:30am-3:30pm); the **day market, pharmacy** (☎651 108, open daily 8am-8pm), and **police station** (☎777 111) at the intersection of Rimkhong and Phahonythin Rd.; the **Chiang Saen Hospital** (☎777 017) 1km from the river; and the **immigration office** at the first crossroad on the left from the river on Phahonyothin Rd. (☎777 118. Open M-F 8:30am-4:30pm.) At the intersection, there is **Internet access** (30฿ per hr.; open daily 9am-6pm), **motorbike rental** (180฿, open daily 8am-5pm), and **international telephone** availability from vendors with cell phones. The **post office,** offering **CATNET,** is 600m from the river on Phahonyothin Rd. (☎777 116. Open M-F 8:30am-4:30pm, Sa-Su 9am-noon.) **Postal Code:** 57150.

ACCOMMODATIONS AND FOOD. With the river to your back, walk west for 500m on Phahonyothin Rd. and turn right before the post office. 100m down on the right, just past a bank, is **J.S. Guest House ❷,** with cozy, quiet rooms with fans and common bath—Chiang Saen's best deal. Stick to rooms in the house. (☎777 060. Bike rental 40฿. Singles and doubles 100฿.) **Gin Guest House ❷,** 1.5km upstream of Rimkhong Rd., is more upmarket, with large, clean rooms in and around the family's well-maintained house. It is a bit far from town, but fortunately offers motorbike (200฿) and mountain bike rentals (80฿). The music from nearby bars booms until 1am on most nights. Day hikes are pricey, including car and driver but not food, rafting, or elephant riding. (☎650 847. Mountain bikes 80฿. Motorbikes 200฿. Day hikes 2400฿ for 1-4 people. Bungalows with fan, bug nets, and hot showers 200฿; big tiled rooms with sitting room 300฿; family rooms 400฿.) **Chiang Saen Guest House ❶,** 45 Rimkhong Rd., north of the junction and just before the *wat*, has cheap rooms that could use more upkeep. The owner, an avid bird-watcher, can point out the many species in the area. (Concrete singles 80฿; doubles 120฿; twins with bath and view of Mekong 150฿; triples 200฿.)

At night try the **market ❶** on Phahonyothin Rd. (*Pad thai* 20฿.) **Food stalls** congregate on Rimkhong Rd. 300m south of the junction. *Paw pia thawt* (spring rolls) are great. Remember to order dishes *mai pet* unless you like burnt tongue.

SIGHTS. Chiang Saen National Museum is on Phahonyothin Rd. at the entrance to the city across from the post office. Along with a life-size model of a *plaa buek* (Giant Mekong Catfish), the small museum has impressive 15th- to 16th-century Lanna art and a well-done exhibit on hill-tribe cultures and costumes. (☎777 102.

NORTHERN THAILAND

Open W-Su 9am-5pm. 30฿.) Next door, a 13th-century brick *chedi*, the tallest Lanna Thai monument at 58m, dominates **Wat Chedi Luang. Wat Pasale** is outside the ancient city wall, 800m west of the river. The ornate *chedi* isn't as impressive, but its location (*pasale* means "of the teak forest") makes it a pleasant stop. (Open daily 8am-6pm. 30฿.) Following the road along the moat next to Wat Pasale leads to **Wat Chom Kitti,** 2km out of town. The hilltop offers compelling views of Laos and the Mekong, but is outdone by **Wat Phra That Pha-Ngao,** which includes Chiang Saen in the vista 4km southeast of town on the road to Chiang Khong. **Chiang Saen Lake,** a bird-watching site with the largest variety of water fowl in Southeast Asia, is a 7km ride southwest. The turn-off is marked on the route to Chiang Rai.

■ DAYTRIP FROM CHIANG SAEN: SOP RUAK (GOLDEN TRIANGLE). Sop Ruak may be its official name, but most refer to the confluence of the Sai River and the wider Mekong where Myanmar, Laos, and Thailand meet as **Sam Liam Tongkham** (Golden Triangle).

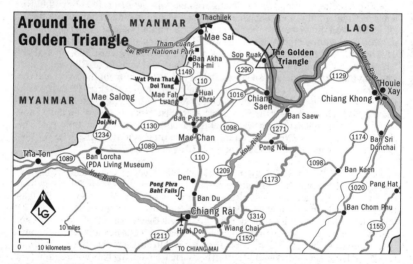

In the middle of town, the **House of Opium** features exhibits on the history and cultivation of opium, with pipe displays, info on drug warlords, and a diorama of a drugged-out old man. After showing how to grow opium, then how to smoke opium, it closes with a message about the dangers of drug addiction. Dioramas on the **Padong** (longneck villagers) and *plaa buek* (giant catfish) are thrown in for good measure. The museum does not have the quantity of info on opium nor quality of organization of the Hill Tribe Museums in Chiang Mai and Chiang Rai. (☎784 062. Open daily 7am-6pm. 20฿.) For a view capturing the three countries, head up the five-dragon-headed staircase next to the bank, then follow the road behind **Wat Phra That Doi Pu** up the hill to the viewpoint.

Just 2km north of Siam Bank, towards Mae Sai, is the world's largest opium research center. The massive state-of-the-art complex opened in 2004, and its **Hall of Opium** not only presents the history of opium, but also attempts to recreate the emotional experience that faces opium addicts—the highs, lows, peace, and pain—through its use of multimedia exhibits and sensory stimulation. (☎784 444; www.goldentrianglepark.com. Open Tu-Su 10am-3:30pm.)

Songthaew bound for Mae Sai (45min., 25฿) and Chiang Saen (20min., 15฿) pass through town between 7am and 2pm. Longtail **charter boats** seat up to six people and leave from various spots along the river for Chiang Khong (2hr., 1500฿); Chiang Saen (50min., 400฿); and Mae Sai (1hr., 500฿). Golden Triangle boats tour the area (300฿ for 30min., 400฿ for 1hr.; 1-6 people). Sop Ruak is just 8km north of Chiang Saen, and can be easily reached by bicycle or motorbike.

Next door to the House of Opium, **Siam Commercial Bank** runs a **currency exchange** booth that accepts all traveler's checks and has MC/V cash advances and a **24hr. ATM.** (☎ 784 191. Open daily 9am-5pm.) The guesthouses that once existed here have been bulldozed in anticipation of the boom expected to hit the region. The site is geared towards group tourists, who arrive on massive tour buses and wander around wondering exactly what it is they are supposed to see. Despite the site's lack of any significant natural or historic attractions, the developers seem convinced that the mere intersection of borders will be enough to attract tourists.

CHIANG KHONG ☎ 053

Chiang Khong (pop. 10,000) is the archetypal border town. There are no museums, parks, or interesting shops, but several banks line the interminable main street and wait for tourists transitioning between countries and currencies. The premier attractions of Chiang Khong are rest and relaxation. Many guesthouses overlook the majestic Mekong and afford alluring views of greener Laos. Quality accommodations and the engaging surroundings will please travelers during the wait.

▐ TRANSPORTATION

Buses go to Chiang Mai (6hr., 6am, 121฿; with A/C 8am, 218฿ and 11am, 169฿). Government buses through the Travel Company go to Bangkok (12-13hr.; 7am, 3:30, 4pm; 390-491฿). The **booking offices** for bus tickets to Chiang Mai (☎ 655 732) and Bangkok are next to each other, between the bridge and service station. Guesthouses also run a **minibus** to Chiang Mai (5hr.; 10:30am, 6pm; 220฿). Sombat Tours, opposite Chiang Mai booking office, runs private buses to Bangkok (☎ 791 644; 4pm, 491฿), as does Siam-First, opposite the Thai Farmers Bank (4pm, 491-573฿). Tickets go quickly; buy a seat in the morning to guarantee an afternoon bus. Buses to Chiang Rai leave from the market south of the bridge, across from the Esso Station (3hr., every hr. 5am-

THE LOCAL STORY

THE MEKONG GIANT CATFISH *(PLA BUEK)*

The Mekong Giant Catfish is believed to be the world's largest freshwater fish, growing as large as 300kg and 2.5m.

According to Chinese and Thai lore, the superhuman leader Kong Beng stationed his troops on the Mekong River during wartime. When food was nowhere to be found, Kong Beng created the giant fish in order to feed his starving troops and win the war.

Thai villagers along the Mekong still see the fish as sacred. Every April and May, the fish come to spawn from the mouth of the Mekong. Before catching the fish, the villagers must first obtain divine permission. They perform various rituals including animal sacrifice, in order to satisfy the deities and ensure a successful season. This practice is strongest in Ban Had Krai village, about 1km southeast of Chiang Khong's marketplace.

The fish is considered a delicacy and is highly valued. Villagers believe that eating the meat enables one to be as wise and as clever as Kong Beng himself. The meat sells for around 300฿ per kg., meaning an entire fish can fetch up to 100,000฿. Most of the few fish caught each year find their way to upscale Bangkok eateries. In late spring, it may be possible to find freshly caught *Pla Buek* in Ban Had Krai village. It is worth noting, however, that *Pla Buek* is currently on several endangered species lists.

5pm, 50฿). **Songthaew** to and from Chiang Saen (2½hr., 7am-noon, 50฿) gather near Soi 3, just south of the post office. @Net.com (see **Internet Access,** p. 332) has **motorbikes** for rent (200฿ per day).

■ ☑ ORIENTATION AND PRACTICAL INFORMATION

Chiang Khong is 144km northeast of Chiang Rai and 55km southeast of Chiang Saen. The main drag, **Saiklang Road,** runs northwest to southeast, parallel to the Mekong River. Numbered *soi* run perpendicular to the main road—odd-numbered *soi* head to the river. **Soi 13** is at the southeast end near the bridge and day market. **Soi 1,** home to several guesthouses, is a 25min. walk northwest from the market at the northwestern end of town. Continuing northwest past Soi 1 leads to the **cargo pier,** to the turn-off to **Chiang Saen** (Rte. 1129), and finally the **ferry pier** to Laos.

Tours: Traveler Corner, 17/3 Ban Wat Kaew T. Wiang (☎655 374), opposite Ann Travel near Soi 2. Run by friendly "Apple." Info, bookings, collect calls (30฿), and Laos visas (see **Border Crossing,** p. 334). Open daily 8am-9pm.

Immigration Office: The immigration office, next to the ferry pier to Laos, provides departure stamps and info on the border crossing (daily 7am-5pm). The main immigration office (☎791 322) is located next to Soi 13, and issues visa extensions for 1900฿. Open M-F 8:30am-noon, 1-4:30pm. See **Border Crossing,** p. 334.

Currency Exchange: Thai Farmers Bank, 20m south of Soi 7. **ATM.** Cirrus/MC/PLUS/V. Open M-F 8:30am-3:30pm. Other major banks line the main road.

Markets: Every Friday morning the **regional market** spills out onto the main road from the day market. Sa evening is the **night market,** on the main road around Soi 2.

Police: (☎791 426), next door to the immigration office, just north of the bridge.

Pharmacy: Boonchai Pharmacy (☎791 013), opposite Soi 7. Open daily 7am-8pm.

Medical Services: Chiang Khong Hospital, 354 Moo 10 (☎791 206), 3km outside of town. Go straight south on Hwy. 1020 toward Chiang Rai. Some English spoken. No credit cards. Open **24hr.**

Internet Access: @Net.com, across from Bamboo Riverside Guest House. 40฿ per hr.

Post Office: (☎791 555), near Soi 3. **International phone** in the compound and Lenso phone outside. **CATNET.** Open M-F 8:30am-4:30pm, Sa-Su 9am-noon.

Postal Code: 57140.

▐ ACCOMMODATIONS

Chiang Khong has a nice selection of quality budget accommodations, all located along the Mekong River. Some are near Soi 1, halfway between the bridge and the pier, and the others are past the Esso station, just south of the bridge, which is more secluded and quiet, though less convenient. The population of *farang* in Chiang Khong rises and falls sharply with each tour-bus load. By 5pm in the high season, the town's best accommodations are at saturation point, so try to call ahead to reserve your preferred digs.

■ **Bamboo Riverside Guest House,** 71 Huaviang Rd. (☎791 621; saweepatts@hotmail.com), 75m northwest of Soi 1. This fairly new guesthouse is the best place in town, and is very popular with backpackers. The guesthouse also offers a great **restaurant** with Mexican food, fresh-baked bread, and a guitar-playing proprietor. Laundry. Dorms 70฿; singles 100฿; bungalows 150฿; doubles with bath 200-250฿. ❶

Ban Tammila (☎/fax 791 234), by Soi 2. Has bungalows with private showers and sells a one-of-a-kind compact tent that can also function as a hammock (1350฿; www.siam-hammock.com). Restaurant. Laundry. Bicycle rental 150฿. Bungalow singles 200-400฿; doubles 300-400฿. ❸

Baan Rimtaling (☎791 613, www.geocities.com/baanrimtaling), just past River Guest House, offers a variety of rooms in a warm, intimate house. Massage and spa facilities. Charming Thai-Dutch owners also provide Thai language and cooking lessons, free rides to and from the bus station, and free bike rental for all guests. Dorms 50-80฿; singles 150฿; doubles 200฿; nice bungalows with hot bath 300-400฿.❶

Nomad's Guesthouse (☎655 537), next to Baan Rimtaling, is a new and very clean option. Offers a Western-influenced restaurant, Internet service, and views over a scenic bend in the Mekong. Breakfast 50฿. Bungalow singles 100฿; doubles 150฿; larger rooms in house with hot bath 250-300฿.❷

River Guest House (☎791 348). This is the closest place to the bus station—walk toward Chiang Rai from the bridge and turn left at the Esso, then left again onto Soi 15. Once at the river, turn right; it's 50m ahead on the left. An overlooked gem. Gorgeous bungalows, all with private balconies overlooking banana plantations and the Mekong. Dorms 60฿; bungalow singles 120฿; doubles 150฿; with bath 200฿. ❶

Hua Wiang Country Guest House (☎791 134), 150m past Bamboo Riverside Guest House toward the pier. Cheaper, bare-bones rooms. Free transportation to boat or bus. Laundry. Dorms with 3-5 beds 50฿; singles 60฿; doubles 80฿, with bath 150฿. ❶

◖ FOOD

Noodle-and-rice shops line Saiklang Rd. A morning treat from the **day market** ❶, south of the bridge, is *kanon ton kanon niaw* (rice flour balls with coconut filling; 5฿).

Bamboo Riverside Guest House's restaurant. Boasts the best Mexican food this side of the border, although it takes so long to prepare, you'll wonder if it actually came from there. *Pad thai* 30฿. Cheese quesadilla 65฿. Open daily 7:30am-noon and 6-9pm. ❷

Ban Tammila's restaurant. Good for midday fare, with an amazing view. Vegetarian menu. Small prices for large portions. Most entrees 25-40฿. Open daily 7am-4pm. ❷

Rimkhong, by the river between Soi 7 and 9. The freedom from *farang* comes at the price of an only partially translated menu. Green curry 50฿. Warmed spicy sausage salad 50฿. Open daily 7am-11pm. ❷

Teepee, by Soi 2 on Sarklang Rd. Plays Bob Marley by day, holds jam sessions by night, and serves fabulous tofu dishes. Fried tofu with cashews 60฿. Open daily lunchtime until late. ❷

◉ SIGHTS

The **KMT Cemetery** is 1km out of town on Hwy. 1129 at the top of the big hill on the left. The entrance is on a dirt road not visible from the highway. Although the gate is often locked, the caretaker lets visitors explore during daylight. Ask at guesthouses about bike rides to **Hmong villages,** though they may prove inaccessible in the rainy season (3hr., 3:30pm, 100฿ includes bike and guide). In April and May, **Ban Haadkhrai** hosts the annual giant catfish competition. Lao and Thai boats take turns trawling the river in search of the 2.5m, 200kg beasts (see **The Mekong Giant Catfish,** p. 331). Only a few are caught every year. The fishermen must ask permission of the spirits before catching the fish. To get here, head south out of town and take a left at the Esso service station with the police box in front, then walk 1km to Soi 31 and continue to the river. **Wat Haadkhrai** overlooks the pier where the fish are brought ashore. **See Don Chai,** a Lu handweaving village, is 14km south of the city. Showrooms are scarce and hours fickle, but politely poke your head into any house and ask if you can watch for a while. Take a motorcycle taxi or a blue *songthaew* (10฿) south out of town. Alternatively, take a Chiang Mai/Chiang Rai-bound bus and tell the driver where you want to get off.

BORDER CROSSING: CHIANG KHONG/HOUIE XAY. The ferry (20฿) across the Mekong leaves from the old pier and takes less than 15min. Frequent daily departures 8am-5pm. As of February 2004, 15-day visas are obtainable on arrival in Houie Xay for 1200฿. Just check in with the immigration office by the pier to get your Thai departure stamp, and then board the ferry. It is uncertain whether this will continue to be the case—check with the Laos Embassy or Chiang Khong immigration. The cheapest option is to get the visa in Bangkok or Chiang Mai (15-day visa with 2- to 3-day delay 700-800฿). If in Chiang Khong, try **Traveler Corner** (☎655 374; open daily 8am-9pm) or **Ann Tour** (☎655 198; open daily 7am-8pm), which both have offices on Saiklang Rd. near Soi 2. 15-day visas are 1500฿ for same-day service, and 900฿ with a 3-day wait. 30-day visas are 1900฿ with a 3-day wait and 1500฿ with a 4-day wait. Going through a guesthouse instead of a travel agency may raise the price by 100฿. Once in Houie Xay, catch a speedboat (6-9hr., 8am-1pm, 1100฿) or a slow boat (2 days, 10:30am, 650฿) to Luang Prabang. If you do the latter, pack food, water, and a good book; the boat will stop intermittently for cargo and stretching before overnighting in Pakbeng. As Lao currency fluctuates constantly, check current exchange rates next to immigration as you enter Laos. Special boats that make stops along the Mekong may be organized out of Chiang Khong for those who want to see more—ask at Traveler Corner for info. It is usually cheaper to cross the river and then buy your tickets, though the boats may fill up. The Lao entry tax varies, but currently stands at 50฿.

CHIANG RAI   ☎053

Chiang Rai has always played second fiddle to its southern neighbor, Chiang Mai. King Mengrai built Chiang Rai in 1262, using it as his central command post for three decades. The rivalry between the two cities began when the king switched allegiance to Chiang Mai, abandoning his original capital city. Besides offering stunning vistas and quality accommodations, Chiang Rai also features a hill-tribe museum and a night market, which stocks a wider array of tribal handicrafts than the larger one in Chiang Mai. Those overnighting in Chiang Rai leave feeling they've glimpsed authentic Thai city life without having to deal with the characteristic tourist traps of popular destinations. The city also serves as an ideal base for treks to villages in the mountains near the Burmese border.

▐ TRANSPORTATION

Flights: Chiang Rai International Airport (☎798 202), 9km out of town on Hwy. 110. To: **Bangkok** (1hr., 6 per day, 2645฿) and **Chiang Mai** (25min.; 8:40am, 8pm; 880฿). **Thai Airways,** 870 Phahonyothin Rd. (☎711 179), 1 block south of Teepee Bar. Open M-F 8am-noon and 1-5pm.

Buses: Chiang Rai Bus Station (☎711 224), on Prasopsuk Rd., 1 block east of the intersection with Phahonyothin Rd., next to the night market. To: **Bangkok** (12hr., 4pm, 264฿. A/C 10 per day 8am and 4:30-8pm; 351฿-370฿. VIP 8am, 6:30, 7pm; 700฿. Private companies 8am-7:15pm, 452฿); **Chiang Khong** (2½-3hr., every 30min. 6am-5:45pm, 42-54฿); **Chiang Mai** (3½hr., 6 per day 6:15am-5:30pm, 77฿; A/C 13 per

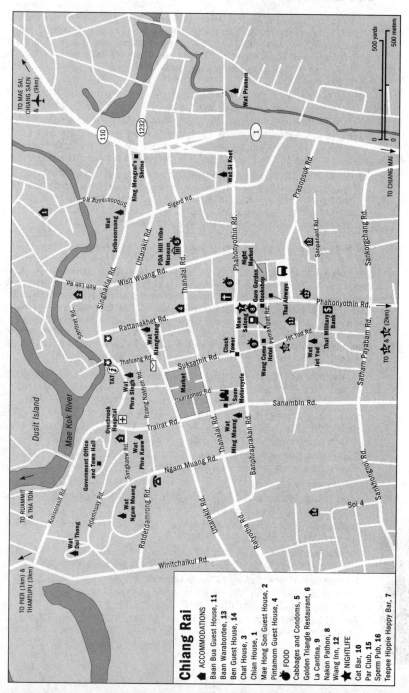

Chiang Rai

500 yards
500 meters

TO MAE SAI,
CHIANG SAEN &
(9km)

Wat Pranom

Wat Si Koet

King Mengrai's Shrine

Sigerd Rd.

Sriboonruang Rd.

Wat Sriboonruong

Uttarakit Rd.

Wisit Wuang Rd.

PDA Hill Tribe Museum

Thanalai Rd.

Phahonyothin Rd.

Night Market

Gare Garden Bookshop

Thai Airways

Prasopsuk Rd.

Sanpanad Rd.

Sankorgchang Rd.

TO CHIANG MAI

Phahonyothin Rd.

Singhaklai Rd.

Koh Loh Rd.

Rattanakhet Rd.

Wat Klangwiang

Mae Salong

Phahonyothin Rd.

Pamat Vat Rd.

Jet Yod Rd.

Thai Military Bank

Santirat Rd.

Clock Tower

Wang Come Hotel

Wat Jet Yod

TO ★ & ☆ (2km)

Satham Payabarn Rd.

Thaluang Rd.

TAT ⓘ

Wat Phra Singh

Suksathit Rd.

Ruang Nakhom Rd.

Market

Itsaraphan Rd.

Soon Motorcycle

Sanambin Rd.

Sankholngol Rd.

Dusit Island

Mae Kok River

Kaisorsait Rd.

Overbrook Hospital

Government Office and Town Hall

Sangkaew Rd.

Wat Phra Kaew

Trairat Rd.

Wat Ming Muang

Thanalai Rd.

Banphraprakan Rd.

TO RUAMMIT & THA TON

TO PIER (1km) & THAMTUPU (3km)

Adamnuay Rd.

Wat Ngam Muang

Ratdetdamrong Rd.

Ngam Muang Rd.

Uttarakit Rd.

Rayoha Rd.

Soi 4

Wat Doi Thong

Winitchaikul Rd.

ACCOMMODATIONS
Baan Bua Guest House, 11
Baan Warabordee, 13
Ben Guest House, 14
Chat House, 3
Chian House, 1
Mae Hong Son Guest House, 2
Pintamorn Guest House, 4

🍴 FOOD
Cabbages and Condoms, 5
Golden Triangle Restaurant, 6
La Cantina, 9
Nakon Pathon, 8
Wiang Inn, 12

★ NIGHTLIFE
Cat Bar, 10
Par Club, 15
Sperm Pub, 16
Teepee Hippie Happy Bar, 7

day 7:30am-5pm, 139฿); **Chiang Saen** (1½-2¼hr., every 15min. 6am-6pm, 25฿); **Mae Sai** (1½hr., every 15min. 6am-6pm, 25฿); **Mae Sot** (10hr., 7:20am, 200฿; A/C 9:20am, 360฿) via **Tak** (8hr., 165-297฿); **Nakhon Ratchasima** (12hr., 3:30pm, 262฿. A/C 6:15am, 1:15, 5:30pm; 472฿. VIP 7pm, 550฿) via **Phitsanulok** (6½hr., 139-292฿); **Nan** (6hr., 9:30am, 95฿); **Phitsanulok** (8hr., every hr. 7:30-10:30am, 214฿) via **Sukhothai** (6½hr., 190฿).

Boats: Leave from the pier (☎750 009) on the north bank of the Mae Kok river next to the Mae Fah Luang Bridge, 1km northwest of the city. To **Tha Ton** (4hr., 10:30am, 200฿) via **Ruammit** (45min., 50฿). Charter boats 1500฿ per day; max. 6 people.

Local Transportation: Songthaew, tuk-tuk, and **samlor** cluster on Uttarakit Rd. around the market and in the evening on Phahonyothin Rd. near the night bazaar. Fares in city 10-20฿. Within 10-15km radius, *songthaew* and *tuk-tuk* should cost under 50฿.

Rentals: Practically every guesthouse rents motorbikes through **Soon Motorcycle,** 197/2 Trairat Rd. (☎714 068), which offers a convenient drop-off and pickup service from guesthouses as well as free transportation to the bus station. New motorbikes 200฿, secondhand 150฿; 4WD Suzuki Jeep 1000฿, with insurance 1500฿. Reduced rates for longer rentals. Open daily 8am-7pm. **Avis** is at the airport (☎793 827).

◪ ⑦ ORIENTATION AND PRACTICAL INFORMATION

The **Mae Kok River** flows west to east, forming Chiang Rai's northern border. **Singhaklai Road,** site of TAT and guesthouses, skirts the river. The northern part of town lies between the river and **Banphraprakan Road,** which is 500m south and parallel to Singhaklai Rd. The most helpful landmark, the **Haw Nariga** (clock tower), stands in the middle of Banphraprakan Rd., forming a chaotic roundabout. **Jet Yod Road,** full of bars, leads south from there. One block east, a portion of **Phahonyothin Road** runs parallel to Jet Yod Rd., while the upper half curves around above the bus station. More info is available online at www.chiangraiprovince.com.

Tourist Offices: TAT, 448/16 Singhaklai Rd. (☎744 674). Receptive and organized office. Offers free maps (with bus schedules), brochures, a list of trekking outfits, and regional info. English spoken. Lenso phone outside. Open daily 8:30am-4:30pm.

Bank: Thai Military Bank, 897/7-8 Phahonyothin Rd. (☎715 657). Open daily 8:30am-9pm. **24hr. ATM.** AmEx/Cirrus/MC/PLUS/V. Thai Military Bank **currency exchange booth,** on Phahonyothin Rd., next to the night bazaar entrance. Open daily 6am-10pm.

Books: Gare Garden Bookshop, 869/18 Phahonyothin Rd., nearly opposite Thai Airways. Also has local art and handicrafts for sale. Open daily 10am-8pm.

Ambulance: (☎711 366).

Local Tourist Police: (☎717 779), downstairs from TAT. Will gladly give a background check on tour agencies. Open **24hr.**

Medical Services: Overbrooke Hospital, 444/3 Singhaklai Rd. (☎711 366), 250m west of TAT. **24hr. pharmacy.** AmEx/MC/V.

Telephones: Telecommunications Office (☎776 738), on Ngam Muang Rd. **CATNET,** fax, overseas calls. Open M-F 8am-8pm, Sa-Su 8:30am-4:30pm. AmEx/MC/V.

Internet Access: Mae Salong Coffee & Internet, on Phahonyothin Rd., opposite Thai Airways. Surf the net for 30฿ per hr. Energetic young staff will bring you local coffee (30฿) and fruit (20฿). Open daily 9am-10:30pm.

Post Office: 486/1 Moo 15 Uttarakit Rd. (☎711 421), 200m south of TAT and 300m north of the clock tower. *Poste Restante.* Open M-F 8:30am-4:30pm, Sa-Su and holidays 9am-noon.

Postal Code: 57000.

▐ ACCOMMODATIONS

Over 30 guesthouses and hotels have opened since the tourist boom hit Chiang Rai, and many boast excellent values. Most guesthouses are located near the river (though none sit directly on it) or in the vicinity of the town center (marked by the clock tower). The river guesthouses (Mae Hong Son, Chat, Chian) are quieter and closer to *wats*, though the mosquitoes are bad and the walk to the town center is over 1km. Centrally located guesthouses, though a bit more expensive, are within earshot of the night bazaar and numerous restaurants and shops. Call ahead in high season to reserve popular accommodations. All guesthouses have hot water and can arrange motorbike rental (150-500฿) and tours, and provide luggage storage. Check-out is usually between 11 and 11:30am.

Chat House, 3/2 Sangkaew Rd. (☎711 481), down the *soi* directly across from Overbrooke Hospital on Trairat Rd. Cheap and quiet, with comfortable patio and small garden. Very popular with backpackers. Laundry and trekking service. Bicycle rental 80฿ per day. It is possible to bargain during the low season. 3-bed dorms 70฿; singles 80฿; doubles 120฿, with bath 160-180฿, with A/C 250฿. ❶

Baan Bua Guest House, 879/2 Jet Yod Rd. (☎718 880; baanbua@yahoo.com). Heading south from the clock tower, the guesthouse is 3 blocks down on the left. Spacious and immaculately clean rooms in surprisingly quiet backstreet location, despite proximity to bars. All rooms sit near the garden, and have fan, Western toilet, and hot water. Tiled rooms with bath 200฿, with A/C 300฿; larger rooms 220฿/350฿. ❷

Mae Hong Son Guest House (☎715 367). From TAT, head east on Singhaklai Rd. and take the 2nd left (at the intersection with Rattanakhet Rd.) onto Santirat Rd. Follow the road 400m to the far end. Friendly manager Kuan keeps guests entertained as he works the bar in the garden cafe. All rooms have fans and mosquito nets (essential here). Laundry 45฿ per kg. Trekking service. Singles 80฿; doubles 100฿; triples 150฿. Rooms with bath and Western toilet cost 150฿ for a single, 200฿ for a double. ❶

Ben Guest House, 351/10 Sankhongnoi Rd., Soi 4 (☎716 775), 1.5km from the clock tower. Call ahead for free pickup, or head west on Banphraprakan Rd. from the clock tower, turn left at the first traffic signal onto Sanambin Rd., right on Sankhongnoi Rd., right again on Soi 4, and walk to the end. Charming teak mansion with veranda and adjacent brick wing. Rooms with bath are better value. Singles 100฿, with bath 160฿; doubles 120฿/200฿. New wing with fan 300฿, with carpet and A/C 350-400฿. ❷

Chian House, 172 Sriboonraung Rd. (☎/fax 713 388). From TAT, head east past the Rattanakhet Rd. intersection. Take the next left onto Koh Loh Rd., cross the bridge, and then follow the signs. From the bus station (2km.), take a *tuk-tuk* or call for pickup. Owner speaks excellent English. Family-oriented. Perks include restaurant with cable TV and salt-water swimming pool. Laundry 25฿ per kg. Internet access and overseas calls. Singles 80฿; doubles 150-250฿, with A/C 300฿; bungalows 250-300฿/350-450฿. ❶

Pintamorn Guest House, 509/1 Rattanakhet Rd. (☎714 161). A 10min. walk north on Phahonyothin Rd., then Rattanakhet Rd., from the bus station. 24hr. kitchen big on Western food. (Cheeseburger 50฿.) Cable TV, pool table, book exchange on the patio. Bland, worn rooms, all with hot bath. Singles 150฿; doubles 180; with A/C 250฿. ❷

Baan Warabordee, 59/1 Sanpanard Rd. (☎754 488). Turn off Phahonyothin Rd. onto Sanpanard Rd.; it's on the left. New pristine tiled rooms, all with balcony, TV, telephone, and hot bath. Singles and doubles with fan 300฿, with A/C 400-600฿. ❸

⬛ FOOD

Chiang Rai's culinary scene is concentrated in the neighborhood bounded by Jet Yod, Banphraprakan, and Phahonyothin Rd. Menus catering to Western palates cram the entrance to the night bazaar on Phahonyothin Rd. The best food, however, lies in open-air joints untouched by the Roman alphabet. The **day** and **night markets ❶** both serve a stellar variety of cheap food. At the night bazaar, try the Thai-style sweet-and-sour grilled fish from the back stall (60-80฿). Most guesthouses have restaurants. The elegant buffet feast at ⬛**Wiang Inn ❸**, 893 Phahonyothin Rd., seems too good to be true. (☎ 711 533. 100฿. Open M-F noon-2pm.)

⬛ **Nakon Pathon** (no English sign), 869/25-26 Phahonyothin Rd., just south of Teepee Bar, caters almost exclusively to the Thai working crowd. Small English menu. Run by an energetic husband-and-wife team. Unbeatable *khao moo dang* (barbecue pork with rice; 30฿) and Iced Milo (10฿). Noodle soups 30฿. Open daily 6am-3pm. ❶

Cabbages and Condoms, 620/25 Thanalai Rd., on the ground fl. of the Hill-Tribe Museum. Classy indoor dining area. Though the food is a bit expensive, it's for a good cause. *Tom-yam* 60-70฿. Grilled fish 140฿. Condoms are free and work better than cabbages. Other location in Bangkok (p. 115). Open daily 11am-midnight. AmEx/MC/V. ❸

Golden Triangle Restaurant, 590 Phahonyothin Rd., across from the night market. Informative English menu describing the local cuisine. Various curries, rice dishes, and noodles. Delicious *gaeng khao wan* (green sweet curry) 45-60฿. Open daily 7am-10pm. ❷

La Cantina, 1025/40 Jet Yod Rd. High-quality Italian food in a casual atmosphere. Extensive menu of homemade pasta served with unlimited bread and butter. 150-200฿ per person. Pizza 90-180฿. Open daily 8am-10pm. ❸

⬤ SIGHTS

According to local lore, the *stupa* of ⬛**Wat Phra Kaew,** originally known as Wat Pa Yier, was struck by lightning in 1434 and revealed an Emerald Buddha; the temple's name changed to "Wat of the Emerald Buddha" as a result. Today, the original is Thailand's most important Buddha image, and sits in Bangkok's Wat Phra Kaew (p. 115). A new image, commissioned in China in 1991 and carved from Canadian jade, sits in its place. The *wat* is a must-see. (At the west end of town on Trairat Rd., opposite Overbrooke Hospital. Open daily dawn-dusk.)

At the west end of town, walking from Trairat Rd. past Chat House on Sang Kaew Rd., rests **Wat Ngam Muang** atop the hill of the same name. Its *stupa* contains King Mengrai's ashes and relics. Directly east from Wat Ngam Muang, at the point where Phahonyothin Rd. merges with Hwy. 101, is **King Mengrai's shrine.** Many make the pilgrimage to the site and light incense and candles to pay their respect and draw strength from King Mengrai, their honored founder. **Wat Phra Singh,** on Singhaklai Rd. near TAT, dates from the 14th century and houses a copy of the famous Phra Singh Buddha image of Chiang Mai.

The **PDA Hill-Tribe Museum,** 620/25 Thanalai Rd., 300m east of Pintamorn Guest House, isn't nearly as informative as the one in Chiang Mai. The museum focuses on opium issues, and also sells local handicrafts and arranges treks (p. 339). The 25min. slide show on the region's different tribes will give you the basics, although the background music is distracting. (☎ 740 088. Open M-F 9am-6pm, Sa-Su 10am-6pm. 50฿ admission includes coffee. Slide show 50฿.)

Chiang Rai's city sights are all easily accessed by bicycle. The energetic can continue to **Thamtupu,** where Buddha images sit inside cliff caverns and are also carved on the limestone faces. The dirt road from Thamtupu is in good condition and makes for great, flat mountain-bike rides between jagged rocky peaks inter-

NORTHERN THAILAND

spersed with corn and banana plantations. The turn-off to Thamtupu is on the left, 700m after Mae Fah Luang Bridge (pier to Tha Ton), traveling north from Chiang Rai. The cave is a further 1km on a partially closed-off road.

ENTERTAINMENT

Teepee Hippie Happy Bar, 542/4 Phahonyothin Rd., just south of Banphaprakan Rd., offers a vegetarian menu and occasional acoustic blues band after 10pm in high season. (Open daily 11am-5pm and 6:30pm-1am.) Head to **Cat Bar,** 1013/1 Jet Yod Rd., for jamming sessions or a game of pool. (☎ 714 637. Small beer 50฿. Open daily noon-1am.) Next to Cat Bar on Jet Yod Rd. sits an endless row of bars with comparable music and atmosphere. The bars on the *soi* linking Jet Yod Rd.'s northern end with Banphaprakan Rd. drop the pretense of karaoke and go straight to go-go. The most popular disco in town is the **Par Club** in the Inn Come Hotel, 172/6 Rajbamrung Rd., accessible by *tuk-tuk*. (☎ 717 850. Cover 100-150฿, includes free drink. Open daily 9pm-1am.) Nearby **Sperm Pub**'s disco, in the Ruentip Hotel at the corner of Rajbamrung and Phahonyothin Rd., is more innocent than the name suggests. (☎ 754 179. No cover. Open daily 8pm-1am.)

MARKETS

The **day market ❶** is a massive affair encompassing an entire square block, the north-east corner of which borders the post office on Uttarakit Rd. Lots of vegetables and fresh fruit (pineapple 10฿) are on the north end along Uttarakit Rd. Inside is a winding maze of, well, everything. Bakeries sit next to tailors, next to pharmacies, next to wide selections of plastic combs. The only consistency can be found at the south end, which is clearly the meat section. **Food vendors ❶** move to the streets surrounding the market at night—go there for delicious and cheap dining before 10pm. The streets of the **night market ❶** are closed to all but pedestrian traffic, making it more manageable than its southern counterpart. The market contains a massive amount of hill-tribe products (including Akha ware) on the *soi* leading to the bus station off Phahonyothin Rd. Following it leads to a wider variety of tapestries, intricately carved boxes, handbags, instruments, headdresses, and Hello Kitty lights. A great selection of food (fruit shakes 15฿, papaya salad with seafood 30฿) surrounds a courtyard at the end of the *soi*. The focal point of the courtyard is a large stage that hosts performances of traditional hill-tribe music and Thai dancing. A smaller stage lies on the *soi* between Phahonyothin Rd. and the bus station. (Nightly performances on both stages 8-10pm.)

TREKKING

Chiang Rai's bucolic province—full of hill tribes—offers trekking routes less traveled than those around Chiang Mai. As always, trek prices should include food, transportation, and an informed guide. Typical treks run 3-days/2-nights (2-4 people around 2500฿ per person, 5-7 people around 2000฿ per person), but they can be as short as a day or as long as a week. Many companies have access to horses, elephants, rafts, and mountain bikes; consider which hill tribes you'd like to visit and mix and match your itinerary. Finally, make sure you like your guide, because your life is in his hands. If considering a company not listed below, check its status with TAT. Ben's Guest House, Chat House, Chian House, and Mae Hong Son Guest House all run flexible treks with guides who are registered with TAT.

Population and Community Development Association (PDA), 620/26 Thanalai Rd., which funds rural development, family planning, and AIDS education, treatment, and prevention programs among hill tribes, offers treks and one-day tours (p. 84).

NORTHERN THAILAND

The PDA has daytrips to Ruammit (the Karen elephant camp), which stop at a waterfall and some Yao and Akha villages. Company treks are pricier than those run out of guesthouses. PDA also accepts volunteers for many of its health-related projects. Most of the volunteers are selected through the Bangkok office, although occasionally the Chiang Rai office will accept applications directly. Thai language skills are strongly favored. If you're interested, bring a resume and plan to wait a week. (☎/fax 740 088; www.pda.or.th/chiangrai. 3-day/2-night trek to Lahu and Akha villages, including elephant and longtail boat rides, 3700฿ per person, 2-person min. Daytrips to the Golden Triangle 1500฿ per person, 2-person min. The more people, the lower the price. Max. group size is 12.)

If you don't mind paying for your volunteer experience, **Greenway** runs excellent work camps where volunteers live in a hill-tribe community (p. 83). To volunteer, you must complete an application in your home country. For more information on volunteer opportunities see Alternatives to Tourism (p. 81).

NAN   ☎054

Hidden amidst the mountains on the outskirts of the Lanna Kingdom, Nan (founded in 1369) developed a unique culture and history, remaining a semi-autonomous principality until 1931. The distinctive and beautiful architecture of the mural-bedecked *wats*, unlike that of any other region in Thailand, reflects this. During the 1960s and 1970s, Nan's isolation made it a haven for smugglers. Today, Nan's seclusion provokes nothing more threatening than frequent shouts of "I love you" from children unfamiliar with *farang*. Travelers who've been to Nan's mountainous back country are unlikely to tell you their favorite spot. They'd prefer to keep it to themselves while the mass of tourists falls over one another's heels on the Mae Hong Son Loop.

▐ TRANSPORTATION

Flights: Nan Airport (☎771 308), on Worawichai Rd., 4km north of town center. **Air Andaman** at the airport (☎711 222; open 10am-2pm) flies to **Bangkok** (daily 1:30pm, 2240฿) and **Chiang Mai** (M, W, F, Su 12:30pm; 1025฿).

Buses: The **bus station** is located just off Chao Fah Rd. (Hwy. 101), 200m north of the Nan River as you enter town. To: **Chiang Rai** (blue bus; 5hr., 9am, 90฿); **Phayo** (4hr., 1:30pm, 99฿); **Phitsanulok** (5hr.; 7:45, 9:45, 11:45am, 1:45pm; 146฿) via **Uttaradit** (101฿); **Phrae** (2hr., every 45min. 5am-5pm, 47฿); **Pua** (orange bus; 1½hr., every hr. 6am-6pm, 25฿). Across the street is a **booking office** (☎710 737) for **Chiang Mai** (6-7hr., 9 per day 7:30am-10:30pm, 117-211฿) via **Lampang** (4hr., 86-154฿). Buses to **Bangkok** (☎710 027; 10-13hr.; 8 per day 8-9am, 6-7pm; 236-600฿). **Sombat Tours** (☎710 122) and **Prae Tour** (☎710 348) also run buses to Bangkok. Book Bangkok buses in the morning to ensure an evening seat on the fastest route.

Rentals: Oversea, 490 Sumon Thewarat Rd. (☎710 258), at Mahawong Rd. **Mountain bikes** 30-50฿ per day; **motorbikes** 150-180฿ per day. Open daily 8am-5:30pm. Guesthouses will also arrange rentals for similar prices. Passport deposit required.

⊀ ▐ ORIENTATION AND PRACTICAL INFORMATION

The **Nan River** acts as the town's southern and eastern border. All buses arrive at the station off **Chao Fah Road,** in the southwestern corner of the city. About 400 meters north of the bus station, Chao Fah Rd. is intersected by **Suriyaphong Road,** which runs east-west and passes the **police station, City Hall,** museum, and *wats.* Two blocks north of Suriyaphong Rd., **Mahawong Road** passes the

Nan

🏠 ACCOMMODATIONS
Amazing Guest House, **3**
Nan Guest House, **7**
PK Guest House, **4**
Sukasem Hotel, **6**

🍎 FOOD
Rimkaew Restaurant, **1**
Ristorante Da Dario, **2**
Tanaya Kitchen, **5**

TO PUA (60km) &
DOI PHUKHA
NATIONAL PARK (85km)

TO ✈ AIRPORT
(200m)

Nan Provincial Hospital

Wat Satarod

Stadium

Telecomm Office

Rat Amnway St.

Worawichai Rd.

Premprachai Rd.

Mahayod Rd.

Aranyawat Soi 1

Nan Christian Suksa School

Sumon Thewarat Rd.

Premprida Rd.

Mahayod Rd.

Suan Tan Rd.

Pha Kong Rd.

Day Market

Night Food Stalls

Kamyod Rd.

Easy Internet

Khao Luang Rd.

Anonta Worarittidit Rd.

Mahawong Rd.

$

Dhevaraj Hotel

Produce Market

Nokham Rd.

Chompu Phuka Silverware Center

Rob Muang Rd.

TO PHAYAO (198km)

Nan Travel

Oversea Rental

Jettabut Rd.

River Dining

Mahaphrom Rd.

Nan Museum

Fhu Travel

Thai Payap Project

Suriyaphong Rd.

Suriyaphong Rd.

Wat Phra That Chang Kham

101

Wat Phumin

Wat Phaya Phu

Thali Rd.

Nan River

Bus Station

TO WAT PHRA THAT KHAO NOI (2km)

1025

Wat Phaya Wat

Thali Rd.

TO PHRAE (118km);
TO CHIANG MAI (318km)

TO WAT PHRA THAT CHAE HAENG (2.5km)

0   500 yards
0   500 meters

N

post office and goes over the town's bridge on the east side. Another block north, **Anonta Worarittidit Road** runs roughly east-west through the center of town. Intersecting all three of these is **Sumon Thewarat Road**, which runs north-south through the town center and is the primary thoroughfare. A useful point of reference, the **Dhevaraj Hotel** rests on this road, halfway between the intersections with Anonta Worarittidit and Mahawong Rd. Followed to its far northern end, Sumon Thewarat Rd. leads to **Worawichai Road**. Parallel to and one block east of Sumon Thewarat Rd. is **Khao Luang Road**. One block west of Sumon Thewarat lies **Mahayod Road**, which runs out the northern end of town via the turn-off to Pua; another block west is **Pha Kong Road**, with its small nightly food stalls.

Tourist Information: TAT (☎ 751 029), on Pha Kong Rd. across from Wat Phumin. No English spoken. Glossy pictures and free maps. Open daily 8:30am-5pm.

Currency Exchange: Thai Farmers Bank, 434 Sumon Thewarat Rd. (☎ 710 162), has a **24hr. ATM.** Cirrus/MC/PLUS/V. Open M-F 8:30am-3:30pm.

Police: 52 Suriyaphong Rd. (☎ 751 681), opposite City Hall.

Pharmacy: 347/5 Sumon Thewarat Rd. (☎ 710 452), opposite Thai Farmers Bank. Open daily 8am-7pm. Another pharmacy at Nan Provincial Hospital.

Medical Services: Nan Provincial Hospital (☎710 138), on Worawichai Rd. at the bend in Sumon Thewarat Rd. 3km north of downtown. Some English. *Songthaew* leave from the Nara department store, 1 block north of Dhevaraj Hotel (10฿). **24hr. emergency** care and **pharmacy.**

Telephones: Telecommunications Office (☎773 214), Mahayod Rd., 2km outside town, 200m past turn-off to Pua. Has **international phones, CATNET,** and fax. Open M-F 8am-6pm, Sa-Su 9am-4:30pm.

Internet Access: Easy Internet, 345/8 Sumon Thewarat Rd., opposite and north of Thai Farmers Bank. 20฿ per hr. Generally open daily 9am-10pm, but hours vary. **R&T Computer** on Sumon Thewarat Rd., across from Fhu Travel, also offers Internet access.

Post Office: GPO, 70 Mahawong Rd. (☎710 176), west of Sumon Thewarat Rd. *Poste Restante.* Open M-F 8:30am-4:30pm, Sa-Su 9am-noon.

Postal Code: 55000

ACCOMMODATIONS

Most of Nan's guesthouses are located about 4km northeast of the bus station and 2km northeast of the town center, making bicycle or motorbike rental very convenient. The Nan Guest House is the only guesthouse located in the center of town, where there are also a number of standard hotels.

PK Guest House, 33/12 Premphachraj Rd. (☎751 416). Walk north 1.5km on Sumon Thewarat Rd. and make a left after the school; it's down the 2nd *soi* on the right. Nice rooms and lounge set around a pond and garden. Bicycle and motorbike rental (30฿/150฿). Laundry. Shared bath and Western toilet. Wacky singles in oxcarts 100฿, larger singles 150฿; doubles 200฿; VIP suites 300-350฿. ❷

Nan Guest House, 57/16 Mahaphrom Rd. (☎771 849), a 15min. walk from the bus station. Follow Chao Fah Rd. for 4 blocks (500m), then take a right on Mahaprhom Rd.; it's on your left, about 500m away. Remodeled lounge and sitting area in main house. Centrally located. Great coffee. Laundry 5-10฿ per piece. Singles 150฿; doubles 230฿. More rustic and smaller rooms in back house: singles 80฿; doubles 150฿. ❷

Amazing Guest House, 25/7 Soi Snow White (☎710 893), 150m past the PK Guest House, on the left. Spacious rooms in the family's teak house. The friendly Thai owner speaks English well. Laundry 40฿ per kg. Massage 150฿ per hr. Singles 100-120฿; doubles 160-200฿; triples 210฿; new private bungalows with bath 200-250฿. Prices drop with longer stays (1 week 10% discount, 1 month 25% discount). ❷

Sukasem Hotel (☎710 141) on Anonta Worarittidit Rd., a half-block west of Mahayot Rd. Nan's best value; centrally located with basic, clean rooms. All rooms have TV, phone, and private bath. Singles and doubles with fan 180฿, with A/C 350฿. ❷

FOOD

Dining in Nan is an adventure. The region is known for its dog farms (and they're not breeding pets) as well as the famed **Nan River dining:** in an effort to keep cool during Nan's dry and exceptionally hot season (temperatures exceed 40°C), the locals sit up to their waists in the Nan River eating from the local **food stands** ❶ at firmly fixed tables. To get to the river dining, turn onto Nokham Rd., one block north of the produce market. The regional specialty is crispy fried dog—if you really want to try it, ask for *mah* or *soonahk.*

Tanaya Kitchen, 75/23-24 Anonta Worarittidit Rd., 1 block beyond Pha Kong Rd. from the bus station on the right. The friendly owner offers maps, an English menu with separate vegetarian options, delicious red curry for 50฿, and great potato bread for 10฿. Open daily 7am-8:30pm. ❷

Rimkaew Restaurant, on Sumon Thewarat Rd. at the bend 3km from town, just before the hospital. Perfectly located for fishing on the Nan River. It serves mostly Thai dishes from a simple English menu for 30-60฿. Open daily 10am-4pm and 7-10pm. ❷

Ristorante Da Dario (☎710 636), next to Amazing Guest House. A little piece of Italy. Spaghetti Pesto Genovese 100฿. Tasty small pizza 70-90฿, large 110-130฿. Open Tu-Sa noon-2pm and 3-10pm. ❸

👁 SIGHTS

The **Nan National Museum,** in the beautiful white palace at the intersection of Suriyaphong and Pha Kong Rd., features informative exhibits on Nan's history and Thailand's hill tribes. A revered black elephant tusk is on display. (☎710 561. Open daily 9am-4pm. 30฿.) Nan's ornate, detailed *wats* are among the most beautiful in northern Thailand. Across the street is **Wat Phra That Chang Kham,** which houses a walking Buddha made of gold. The 400-year-old **Wat Phumin,** on Pha Kong Rd. south of the museum, contains murals depicting Lanna culture. The distinctive golden *chedi* of **Wat Phra That Chae Haeng** shines 2km beyond the Nan River bridge. Constructed nearly 700 years ago, the *wat* is the oldest in the region. Southwest of town, **Wat Phra That Khao Noi** has a picturesque standing Buddha surveying the valley below. The attraction at **Wat Phaya Wat** is the slightly lopsided old pagoda that leans parallel to the bending coconut palm. Go west on Suriyaphong Rd. to Hwy. 101 and turn right after the bridge onto Hwy. 1095. Wat Phaya Wat is on the plain, while Wat Phra That Khao Noi is 2km up the road on top of a hill.

Back in town, the **Thai Payap Project** sells hill-tribe **handicrafts** from 15 villages in its showroom on Jettabut Rd. Follow the road directly opposite the Dhevaraj Hotel past the market; it's 400m down on the right. The project also arranges **homestays,** during which travelers may live and work with a family in one of two villages. All proceeds go to community development projects in the area. (☎772 520. Open daily 8:30am-5pm.) The project may move a few blocks north to Nokham Rd. in the near future. The best place to purchase **silver** is directly from the hill tribes (p. 344), but if you can't make the trip, **Chompu Phuka** has a showroom with hill-tribe silverware and fabrics. Follow Suriyaphong Rd. west out of town toward Phayao; the showroom is on the right opposite PT Gas Station. (Open daily 9am-5:30pm.)

🏴 MARKETS

A spacious **produce market** sets up on Jettabut Rd. directly opposite the Dhevaraj Hotel. Several counters serve over 20 dishes, which you can point at and buy by the bag (10-15฿). Along Anonta Worarittidit Rd., next to the northern bus station, is the **day market,** which is big on pineapples and really small turtles. The tiny **night market,** on Anonta Worarittidit Rd. outside the 7-Eleven, starts around 6pm. Cheap noodle and rice standards are 20฿. Food gets less appetizing around the corner on Pha Kong Rd., but don't miss the fabulous fruit stand at the end of the stalls.

🏴 DAYTRIPS FROM NAN

Few travelers get a glimpse of Nan's rugged backcountry. Nan is now almost entirely safe—some mines remain buried in the most remote areas, but risks are minor, especially on roads or trails. Getting lost is actually a greater danger, as English signs are sparse. Try to bring the name of your destination written in Thai. **Fhu Travel Service,** 453/4 Sumon Thewarat Rd., south of the intersection with Mahawong Rd., leads expeditions around the province. A **trek** with Mr. Fhu is the best way to visit the **Mrabi** (*Phi Tong Lueng,* "Spirit of the Yellow Leaves"), a tribe found only in Nan and Phrae provinces. Another option is **Nan Travel,** 324 Mahayod Rd., one block north of Wat Phra That Chang Kham. Year-round **rafting** on the Nan River through **Mae Charim National Park,** southeast of Nan, is also possible. (☎710 636. Price falls as group size increases. 1-day trek to Mrabi territory 1250฿ for 2 people, 700฿ for 5 or more; 3-day trek 2700฿/1500฿. 1-day rafting 2300฿/1200฿.)

DOI PHUKHA NATIONAL PARK AND ENVIRONS

Orange buses speed to Pua from the bus station in Nan (1½hr., every hr. 5am-6pm, 25฿). Songthaew, which leave from near Pua's market for Ban Bor Kleua, can drop you at the park office (first songthaew departs between 8 and 10am, and others leave infrequently throughout the day; 30฿). Once you're at the park, there's not much to do without private transportation. It's possible to loop your way back from Ban Bor Kleua to Nan taking back routes; pick up the regional map from TAT. If you're driving, take Hwy. 1080 from Nan (past an Esso station on the left) for 60km to Pua. Here, turn right just before the market (you'll have to loop back), then left 100m up the road at the English sign for the park (Hwy. 1256). The road stretches 47km over a mountain peak and through the park to Ban Bor Kleua. The road to Doi Phukha is steep and windy; check brakes before departing.

Dozens of waterfalls and caves dot **Doi Phukha National Park,** home to Hmong and Mien tribes. (Open daily 6am-6pm. 200฿.) The most easily accessed point from which to see the prized **Chomphu Phukha tree** (*Bretschneidera sinensis*) is 5km past the park office. Though not the world's only specimen (as locals tend to claim), it is still extremely rare. The slender tree blooms in February, and hordes of Thais come to see its foot-long clusters of red-veined, hibiscus-shaped flowers. Turn left off the highway and north from Ban Bor Kleua; a road leads to **Ban Sapan,** 10km away. After crossing the bridge just before the village, turn right onto a dirt road to reach the **Sapan Waterfall,** off the road to the right, marked by a red Thai sign and a smaller English one. The dry-season flow will probably leave you unimpressed, but it's worthwhile in the wet season.

If you have your own transportation, two attractions can easily be included in a daytrip to the area. **Silaphet Waterfall,** 9km from Pua, is more accurately described as a river cascade. Enjoy a picnic lunch watching tubing Thais bob through the white water. The hill-tribe village of **Phaklang** produces beautiful and inexpensive silverware. Several of the artisans work on site at the display rooms. To get to both places, take the same right before the market in Pua that you would take to get to Doi Phukha National Park. Instead of turning left, however, simply follow the road out of town. The turn-off to Silaphet Waterfall is marked in English from the road; the one to Phaklang is marked only in Thai and is on the right, 4km from Pua just before Doi Phukha Resort. It's 3km farther to the showrooms, next to a small lake.

The **park office** (☎701 000), 25km up the road from Pua, can sometimes provide **accommodations ❶;** call the National Park Division of the Forestry Service in Bangkok first to check. (☎02 579 0529. Tent rental 250฿. Camping 30฿; bungalows for 2 200฿.) A better choice is ◪**Bamboo Huts ❶,** nestled on the ridge of the mountain looking out to Laos. It features basic huts with shared facilities. The turn-off to Bamboo Huts is 1km before the park headquarters; it's a challenging 4km walk to the huts, passing the Thai Lue village that owner William grew up in. The mountain views along this walk are spectacular. Unfortunately, the huts themselves are situated on the mountain such that the views are merely "impressive." Huts have relaxed ambience, good food, and crisp mountain air. (3 meals per day 130฿. Great-value treks 1-day 500฿, 2-day 1000฿, 3-day 1500฿. Huts 100฿.)

PHRAE

☎ 054

Most often unnoticed by tourists on their way to Nan or Chiang Rai, Phrae is a quiet, peaceful town, the history and life of which are centered around the old city. Its main tourist attractions—a gorge that's billed as a mini Grand Canyon and Wat Phra Chaw Hae, a large temple structure—lie on the outskirts of town and may not be as appealing as other treasures in northern Thailand. For that exact reason, Phrae is a throwback to a more traditional Thai way of life, largely untouched by tourism. Travelers who decide to stay for a night or two will enjoy strolling through the old city, defined by quiet lanes, anchored with *wats*, and adorned with beautiful teak wood architecture.

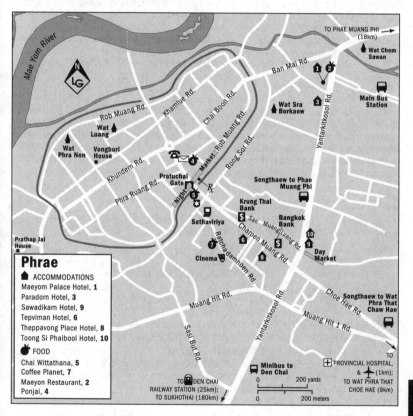

Phrae

▲ ACCOMMODATIONS
Maeyom Palace Hotel, **1**
Paradorn Hotel, **3**
Sawadikarn Hotel, **9**
Tepviman Hotel, **6**
Theppavong Place Hotel, **8**
Toong Si Phaibool Hotel, **10**

🍴 FOOD
Chai Wittathana, **5**
Coffee Planet, **7**
Maeyon Restaurant, **2**
Ponjai, **4**

TO DEN CHAI
RAILWAY STATION (25km);
TO SUKHOTHAI (180km)

Minibus to
Den Chai

0   200 yards
0   200 meters

TO PROVINCIAL HOSPITAL,
& (1km);
TO WAT PHRA THAT
CHOE HAE (9km)

TRANSPORTATION

Buses: Since Phrae is a gateway town to Nan and Chiang Rai on the route going north, its road transportation is frequent and convenient. The **bus station,** in the northeast corner of Phrae, just east of Yantarkitkosol Rd., runs buses to: **Bangkok** (9hr., every hr. 8am-5pm, 117-319฿); **Nan** (2½hr., every hr. 5am-7pm, 47-85฿); **Chiang Mai** (4½hr., every hr. 5am-7pm, 79-149฿) via **Lampang** (4½hr., 13 per day, 79-149฿); **Chiang Rai** (4hr., every hr. 5am-5pm, 80-150฿); **Phitsanulok** (3hr., every hr., 66-119฿); **Sukhothai** (4hr., every hr. 7am-5pm, 55-94฿).

Trains: The nearest **train station** is in Den Chai, about 25km away and on the **Bangkok-Chiang Mai** line. A **minibus** leaves from a stop on Yantarkitkosol Rd., 400m south of the intersection with Charoen Muang Rd. (45min., leaves when full 9am-6pm, 30฿).

Local Transportation: Blue and crimson **songthaew** (10฿) cruise Charoen Muang and Yantarkitkosol Rd. **Samlor** (10฿) do the same task. For the do-it-yourself type, **bicycles** can be rented at Maeyom Palace Hotel (100฿ per day).

■✳❼ ORIENTATION AND PRACTICAL INFORMATION

Phrae is situated 550km north of Bangkok and 200km southeast of Chiang Mai. There are two main roads in Phrae. The first is **Yantarkitkosol Road,** which runs north-south (the northern end forks to the bus station). The second is a road that is split by Yantarkitkosol Rd. into a western piece, **Charoen Muang Road,** which reaches the old city, and an eastern part, **Choe Hae Road,** which leads to the **hospital** and the **airport.** The old city is no longer demarcated by walls or forts, but a large rotary identifies the old town center. A **night market** brings life to **Rob Muang Road,** the first street as you enter the old city from the town center.

There is no official tourist office in Phrae. Services include: **Bangkok Bank,** on Charoen Muang Rd., which exchanges currency and has a **24hr. ATM** (open M-F 8:30am-3:30pm); the **police station,** open **24hr.,** at the intersection of Rong Sor and Ratchadamnoen Rd.; a **pharmacy** on Rob Muang Rd. near the entrance to the old city; a credit-card-operated **international phone** in front of the post office; **Internet access** at Sathaviriya, right near the police station (15฿ per hr.; open daily 9am-midnight); and a **post office** with telephone service, next to the central rotary in the old city. (Open M-F 8:30am-4:30pm, Sa-Su 9am-noon.) **Postal Code:** 54000.

♦ ACCOMMODATIONS

Accommodations options (particularly better-than-decent ones) in Phrae are limited—there may be more banks than hotels in town.

Tepviman Hotel, 226-228 Charoen Muang Rd. (☎511 003), in the center of town, is the best bet for budget travelers. The manager, a lady named Nuj, speaks excellent English and will happily provide tons of info. Basic rooms with bath 80-160฿. ❶

Theppavong Place Hotel, 346/2 Charoen Muang Rd. (☎521 985), about 100m from the Yantarkitkosol-Charoen Muang Rd. intersection toward the old city; take a left down the 1st alley. In the middle of a leafy garden are 30 clean, cozy rooms with satellite TV, private balconies, and hot showers. Lower-floor rooms are more modern, while the higher floors afford a better view. Rooms with fan 250฿, with A/C 350฿. ❸

Toong Si Phaibool Hotel, 84 Yantarkitkosol Rd. (☎511 011), at the intersection with San Muang Luang Rd. The 1st budget hotel as you enter town from the bus station. Its rooms are similar to Tepviman's, but show more wear and tear. Rooms have squat toilets and fans. Singles 130฿; doubles 180฿. ❷

Sawadikarn Hotel (☎511 032), 2 doors down from Toong Si Phaibool Hotel, has similar but cleaner rooms at better prices. Singles 100฿; doubles 150฿. ❷

Maeyom Palace Hotel, 181/6 Yantarkitkosol Rd. (☎521 028), directly across from the bus station. The best luxury hotel in Phrae, it has a pool and 2 restaurants. Bicycle rental 100฿ per day. All rooms have A/C, TV, and telephone. Singles 700-1000฿; doubles 900-1100฿. MC/V. ❹

Paradorn Hotel, 177 Yantarkitkosol Rd. (☎511 059). Go out of the bus station and follow Yantarkitkosol Rd. south for 200m. "Absolutely Clean," declare the signs and billboards posted around town, and it's no joke, though some of them feel a bit cavernous. Over 100 middle-range rooms between the main building and the satellite across the street, all with TV, telephone, and hot shower. Breakfast included. Singles with fan 290฿, with A/C 390฿; doubles 330฿/430฿. ❸

NORTHERN THAILAND

FOOD

The **day market** ❶ on San Muang Lang Rd. is a must-stop for fresh, cheap produce and fish in various stages of life and afterlife. The **night market** ❶ on Rob Muang Rd. is where locals flock for dinner.

■ **Ponjai,** behind the post office in the old city, serves excellent *kanom jiin*-style food (pick your own noodles and soup), as well as good old Thai dishes. Open-air, wooden terrace ideal for a relaxing lunch. Noodles 10฿. Soup 10฿. Open daily 7am-3pm. ❶

Chai Wittathana, on Charoen Muang Rd. just before Rob Muang, heading towards the old city; there are no English signs, but look for the bright yellow Thai menu boards on the wall. Owned by a man of Indian descent who speaks excellent English, Chai Wittathana offers cheap dishes similar to those at the nearby night market. Noodle and rice dishes 20-30฿ each. Fried chicken with cashew nuts 50฿. Open daily 5-11pm. ❶

Maeyon Restaurant, 181/6 Yantarkitkosol Rd., adjacent to the Maeyon Palace Hotel. The swankest hotel in town also has the fanciest restaurant. Thai favorites 60-120฿. The sky's the limit with Western dishes (150฿ and up). Open daily 7am-midnight. ❷

Coffee Planet, on Ratchadamnoen Rd. 100m from Rong Sor Rd., offers lattes, espressos, cappuccinos, and the like. Suitable for a morning or afternoon cup (25฿). ❶

SIGHTS

PHAE MUANG PHI. About 18km away from town on Hwy. 101, Phae Muang Phi presents strange rock formations and erosions, a miniature version of the Grand Canyon in the western United States. The mystery of its origin and location has superstitious locals convinced that phantoms haunt the area. A path runs through the park for a good 30min. walk, but it gets quite hot at midday. *(The best way to go is to charter a songthaew (200฿ round-trip)—they gather in front of the school on Yantarkitkosol Rd. Non-hired songthaew also make the trip from the school to Phae Muang Phi (35฿), but departures are sporadic. Open daily 7am-5pm.)*

WAT PHRA THAT CHAW HAE. Its 33m-high gilded pagoda and Phra Jao Than Jai Buddha image have established this *wat* as one of the most important pilgrimage sites in northern Thailand. Renovations of the area were completed in 2000. *(Songthaew, charging 20฿, leave from a stop in front of the provincial hospital roughly every hr. Otherwise, you can charter a songthaew for 200฿ round-trip. Open daily 7am-5pm.)*

WAT LUANG AND WAT PHRA NON. These two *wats*, situated in the northwest blocks of the old city, are one of the in-town tourist attractions. **Wat Luang** is the oldest temple in Phrae, built in 829, the same year the city was established. It was constructed to enshrine the city's Buddha image, which was originally covered in gold. A small museum with random antiques, Buddha images, and porcelain objects is next to the *wat*. **Wat Phra Non,** the building with the beautiful roof, is relatively new at about 100 years old. It houses an impressive reclining Buddha.

VONGBURI HOUSE AND PRATHAP JAI HOUSE. These houses—the former located in the old city and the latter about 1km from the old city—are examples of Phrae's famous teak architecture. Both the interior and exterior of the building are ornately decorated with wood carvings. *(Open daily 8am-5pm. 20฿.)*

WAT CHOM SAWAN. This *wat* features a fantastic Burmese/Shan-style temple built about 100 years ago. In addition to its structural beauty, two holy artifacts make the *wat* even more special: a 16-sheet ivory book with the teachings of Buddha written in Burmese and a bamboo basket covered in gold.

PHITSANULOK ☎055

A staging ground for Ayutthaya's campaigns against the Burmese and the station of the Third Army during Communist uprisings in the Nan hills, Phitsanulok ("Phitlok" or "Philok" to locals) retains its military tradition, hosting the annual Cobra Gold exercises between Thai and American forces. Despite its past martial prowess, Phitsanulok is an unthreatening gateway to northern Thailand. The busy metropolis welcomes travelers who overnight here while taking in Phra Buddha Chinnarat, one of the world's most famous Buddha images.

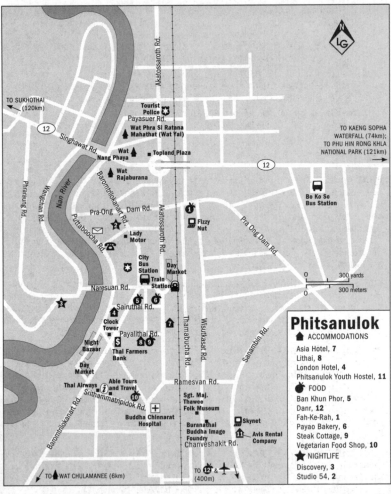

▣ TRANSPORTATION

Flights: Phitsanulok Domestic Airport (☎258 029), on Sanambin Rd. **Thai Airways,** 209/26-28 Srithammatripidok Rd. (☎242 971). With your back to TAT, it's 50m to the right. Open M-F 8am-5pm; open at the airport on weekends. Flies to **Bangkok** (4 per day, 1380฿). **Air Andaman,** booked through Thai Airways or at the airport, flies to **Chiang Mai** (Tu, Th, Sa 12:30pm; 1185฿).

Trains: Phitsanulok Train Station (☎258 005), on Akatossaroth Rd. To **Bangkok** (6-7hr., 11 per day, 129-479฿) via **Ayutthaya** (5-6hr., 8 per day, 108-185฿) and **Chiang Mai** (6-8hr., 11 per day, 125-210฿).

Buses: Bo Ko So Bus Station (☎242 430), on Phitsanulok-Lomsak Rd., east of town. City bus #1 shuttles between the train and bus stations. Buses to: **Bangkok** (6hr., 21 per day, 121-218฿); **Chiang Mai** (6-7hr., 26 per day, 120-216฿); **Chiang Rai** (6-7hr., 20 per day, 139-275฿); **Khon Kaen** (5hr., 13 per day, 113-203฿); **Mae Sot** (5hr., 8 per day 7am-4pm, 125฿); **Nakhon Ratchasima** (6-7hr., 15 per day, 137-247฿); **Phrae** (4hr., 14 per day, 66-119฿); **Sukhothai** (1hr., every 30min. 4:45am-6pm, 23-32฿); **Udon Thani** (7hr., 9 per day, 122-220฿) via **Loei** (4hr., 79-142฿). A/C is not available on all rides to all locations. For major destinations, buses have multiple routes; one route is often up to 1hr. quicker than another.

Local Transportation: City Bus Station, on Akatossaroth Rd., 1 block left of the train station. Buses run daily 5am-9pm. Bus #1 goes to Bo Ko So Bus Station, Wat Yai, and Naresuan University. Bus #4 goes to the airport. Regular buses 5฿, A/C 7฿.

Rentals: Lady Motor, 43/12 Baromtrilokanart Rd., 20m south of Studio 54. **Motorbikes** 150฿ for 9am-5pm, 200฿ for 24hr. Open M-Sa 8:30am-5:30pm. **Avis** at Phitsanulok Youth Hostel.

■✱■■ ORIENTATION AND PRACTICAL INFORMATION

Phitsanulok lies along the east bank of the **Nan River,** 377km north of Bangkok. **Puttaboocha Road** runs parallel to the river and hosts the beautifully lit night bazaar. One block east is **Baromtrilokanart Road,** which encompasses the financial district. The main thoroughfare, **Akatossaroth Road,** lies two blocks east of the river and also runs parallel to the railroad tracks. **Naresuan Road** shoots west from the **Phitsanulok Train Station** on Akatossaroth Rd., cutting through the busiest part of town, as well as through Baromtrilokanart and Puttaboocha Rd., before crossing the river. **Phra Buddha Chinnarat** is at **Wat Yai** at the northern end of Puttaboocha Rd. The **Bo Ko So Bus Station** is 2km east of the *wat* on the other side of the train tracks.

Tourist Office: TAT, 209/7-8 Surasi Trade Center, Srithammatripidok Rd. (☎/fax 252 742). Helpful staff. Info, maps, and timetables for Sukhothai and Phitsanulok. Open daily 8:30am-4:30pm.

Tours: Able Tours and Travel, 55/45 Srithammatripidok Rd. (☎243 851). With your back to TAT, it's 25m to the left. Books domestic and international flights. Open M-F 8am-6pm, Sa 8am-4:30pm.

Currency Exchange: Thai Farmers Bank, 144/1 Baromtrilokanart Rd. (☎241 497), at the clock tower. **24hr. ATM.** Cirrus/MC/PLUS/V. Open M-F 8:30am-3:30pm. Several **banks** are also on Naresuan Rd.

Luggage Storage: At the train station. 10฿ per piece per day. Open daily 7am-11pm.

Markets: Day market, north of the train station behind Akatossaroth Rd. One side has the standard collection of inane consumer goods, while the other is devoted to tasty and quick meals. Eventually, the two sides converge into 500m of fruits, vegetables, and meats. **Night bazaar,** on Puttaboocha Rd., 2 blocks south of the bridge. A plethora of great food stalls compensate for overpriced stone carvings. Another **day market** lies at the south end of Puttaboocha Rd., marking the end of the night bazaar.

Shopping: Topland Plaza, at the rotary on the north end of Akatossaroth Rd., is a multi-level department store selling everything from Guy Laroche to gadgetry. Open M-F 9:30am-9pm, Sa-Su 10am-9pm.

Tourist Police: 31/15 Akatossaroth Rd. (☎245 357), 200m past back entrance to Wat Yai. Little English spoken. Open **24hr.**

Medical Services: Buddha Chinnarat Hospital (☎219 844), on the southern extension of Akatossaroth Rd. at the turn-off to TAT. The official street address is on Srithammatripidok Rd. **24hr. emergency room** and **pharmacy.** 2 more hospitals are nearby.

Telephones: Phitsanulok Telecommunications Center (☎243 116), on Puttaboocha Rd. next to the GPO. International phone/fax. **CATNET.** Open daily 7am-10pm. AmEx/MC/V.

Internet Access: Fizzy Nut, just around the corner from Fah-Ke-Rah restaurant, offers the best deal in town. 15฿ per hr. Open daily 8am-11pm. **Skynet,** 108 Sanambin Rd. 30฿ per hr. Open daily 8am-midnight.

Post Office: GPO (☎258 313), on Puttaboocha Rd. 500m north of Naresuan Rd. *Poste Restante.* Open M-F 8:30am-4:30pm, Sa-Su 9am-noon.

Postal Code: 65000.

ACCOMMODATIONS

Phitsanulok Youth Hostel (HI), 38 Sanambin Rd. (☎242 060; www.tyha.org). About 2.5km from the train station. Take bus #4 toward the airport. Cross the train tracks, turn right on Sanambin Rd. and look for the hostel on the left. Clean rooms furnished with Thai antiques. Beautiful grounds include a lush garden with granite benches and a small waterfall. Laundry service. Lenso phone. Breakfast included. Open **24hr.** Dorms 120฿; elegant singles with bath 200฿; doubles 300฿; triples 450฿. ❷

London Hotel, 21-22 Soi 1 (☎225 145), off Puttaboocha Rd. From the train station, walk west on Naresuan Rd., take a left on Puttaboocha Rd., and it's 2 blocks down on the left. Retro downstairs sitting room. Yellow and green rooms with shared toilets. Singles 100฿; doubles 150฿. ❷

Lithai, 73/1-5 Payalithai Rd. (☎219 626). From the train station, walk left and take the 2nd road to the right. 50m down on the left side. Great-value, high-quality hotel rooms surround vine-draped inner courtyard, all with bath and TV. Breakfast included. Singles and doubles with fan 220฿, with A/C 330฿; doubles with A/C 440฿. ❷

Asia Hotel, 176/1 Akatossaroth Rd. (☎258 378). Take a left from the train station, walk 500m, and it will be on your left; or take bus #1 from the city bus station. Noisy location. Laundry 8฿ per piece. Immaculate singles with simple furnishings, Western toilet, and cold shower 200฿, with A/C 300฿; doubles 250฿/350฿. ❷

FOOD

Phitsanulok is famous for its open-air restaurants; **Payalithai Road** has the best and cheapest during the day. At night, the **night market's northern end** (p. 349) offers nearly a solid kilometer of eateries, beginning at the Naresuan Rd. bridge. All over the city (especially the night market), **flying-vegetable restaurants** ❶ hurl *pak boong fai deng* (flaming morning glory vine) from *woks* to distant plates.

Fah-Ke-Rah, 52/6 Pra Ong Dam Rd. Near the mosque, 35m past the train tracks away from town. Muslim restaurant with arguably the best food in Phitsanulok. *Lassi* 20฿. Chicken with yellow rice 25฿. *Roti gaeng* 20฿. Open daily 6am-2pm. ❶

Vegetarian Food Shop, 55/4 Srithammatripidok Rd. With your back to TAT, walk left 150m rounding the corner. Delicious, freshly squeezed orange juice 10฿. Veggie dish of the day with brown or white rice 10฿, 2 choices 15฿. Open daily 6am-2pm. ❶

Payao Bakery, 168 Akatossaroth Rd., opposite and left of train station. No English sign. Look for cakes in the window. A subdued student hangout with A/C comfort. Brownies (10฿), sundaes, and real food (club sandwich 45฿), too! Open daily 7am-10pm. ❷

Danr, 260/2-3 Sanambin Rd., 300m before airport. No English sign; look for glass windows with overhanging vines and palms. Popular for business lunches. The partially translated menu offers a mixture of Vietnamese and Thai dishes. Sour lemongrass soup 50฿. Open daily 10am-10pm. MC/V. ❷

Ban Khun Phor, on Chao Praya Rd., 1½ blocks north of Lithai hotel. Extensive and tasty Thai entrees (60-100฿), served in rustic atmosphere decorated with antiques. Fortunately, A/C has been added to the vintage setting. Marinated beefsteak 80฿. Salads 60-80฿. Open daily 11am-11pm. ❷

Steak Cottage, in Lithai Hotel. A carnivore's dream in this vegetarian town. Extensive steak list 80-120฿. Most salads have meat, too. Open daily 7am-2pm and 5-9pm. ❸

🗑 🎵 SIGHTS AND ENTERTAINMENT

Wat Phra Si Ratana Mahathat (Wat Yai), at the northern end of Puttaboocha Rd., shelters Phitsanulok's jewel. Cast in 1357, the spectacular **Phra Buddha Chinnarat** ("Victorious King") is one of the world's most commonly reproduced Buddha images. It can be seen glimmering from afar with a contemplative smile. The left wing of the *wat* (if you're facing Phra Buddha Chinnarat) has been turned into a mediocre museum. (Museum open W-Su 9am-4pm. *Wat* open daily 7am-6pm. Suggested 20฿ entrance donation includes brochure. Sarongs provided free of charge to the bare-legged.)

The **Sgt. Maj. Thawee Folk Museum,** 26/43 Wisutkasat Rd., is doing an incredible job trying to protect folk culture from being swept away in the sea of globalization. In an attempt to preserve local traditions, displays include items that are no longer in use. Detailed captions in English explain everything from bull-castration techniques to how the snake guillotine catches its prey. (☎212 749. Open Tu-Su 8:30am-4:30pm. Free, but donations accepted and deserved.) Across the street, Dr. Thawee also runs the **Buranathai Buddha Image Foundry,** where you can see handcrafted bronze Buddhas, from figurines to Goliaths, in different stages of creation. The house factory also has a gift shop; pick out your own bronzed Buddha. (☎258 715. Open daily 8am-5pm.) **Wat Chulamanee,** built in 1464, is 6km outside the city and is best reached by motorcycle taxi (100฿).

Pubs cluster at the far northern end of **Baromtrilokanart Road.** About the only thing **Studio 54,** at the Pailyn Hotel, has in common with its infamous New York namesake is that it hosts the "in" crowd. (Heineken and Carlsberg only, 100฿. Open daily 8am-2am.) For more bar options, head to the **Phitsanulok Bazaar** across the bridge on Naresuan Rd. Bars line the quadrangle around **Discovery,** a disco with live bands and a rebellious crowd. (Open daily 9pm-1am.)

🏃 DAYTRIP FROM PHITSANULOK: PHU HIN RONG KHLA

Park headquarters located 125km northeast of Phitsanulok. To reach the park, take a bus to Nakhon Thai (2hr., every hr. 6:30am-6pm, 28฿) and then grab a songthaew 32km to Phu Hin Rong Khla (1½hr., sporadic, 40฿). Private transportation is necessary to see much of the park. To charter a songthaew for the day will cost 1500฿ from Phitsanulok, less from Nakhon Thai. The direct drive from Phitsanulok takes 2hr. Take Rte. 12 from Phitsanulok and take a left onto Rte. 2013 to Nakhon Thai. Turn right onto Rte. 2331, follow signs to Nakhon Thai or National Park about 70km out on Rte. 12. Contact the Forestry Department in Bangkok (☎02 579 7223) or Phu Hin Rong Khla Park (☎05 523 3527) for more info. Park headquarters open daily 8am-4pm. 200฿, students 100฿.

NORTHERN THAILAND

The Thai army and the People's Liberation Army of Thailand (PLAT) clashed around Phitsanulok, on the land that this park now encompasses. From 1967-1982, PLAT survived in the Phu Hin Rong Khla forests near the Lao border. Recruits poured in after the crackdown on student demonstrators in Bangkok in 1976. The government then struck a decisive blow by offering amnesty to all students who joined the movement after 1976. In 1982, the area was declared a national park.

The most visited sight in the park is the **flagpole**, near the old Communist headquarters. A 3.2km **nature walk** leads to the flagpole, where the Thai flag now boldly flies. The flagpole stands on the ridge of the mountain range, offering a panoramic view of the valley below. The nature walk lies 2km from park headquarters along a marked and paved road. Pick up a map from park headquarters to explore the natural and historical attractions Phu Hin Rong Khla has to offer.

Phu Hin Rong Khla's park headquarters offers some **accommodations ❶**. (Tent rental 100฿. Camping 30฿; bungalows 600฿.) Those traveling with their own transportation will want to explore the many **waterfalls** that lie off Rte. 12. The best is the three-tiered, 40m drop of **Kaeng Sopha Waterfall,** 74km outside of Phitsanulok. The dry-season flow will leave you unsatisfied, but the large valley boulders entwined with trees warrant exploration. The turn-off to Kaeng Sopha Waterfall is 3km beyond the turn-off to Nakhon Thai. It's 2km from the main road to the waterfall. TAT has a regional map marking the relative positions of waterfalls along Rte. 12—all turn-offs are well marked, but it's reassuring nonetheless.

SOUTHERN THAILAND

One of the most famous international beach destinations, southern Thailand is a full-blown vacation mecca. With some of the world's best dive sites, thousands of kilometers of white sand beach, rock climbing, a steady nightlife, and well-developed tourist infrastructure, it's not surprising that millions of tourists visit every year. This steady stream of tourist dollars means that nearly every island is hospitable to visitors and English is an unofficial second language. While the tremendous development provides convenience it has also begun to overwhelm both the environment and Thai culture. Farther south, mosques gradually replace *wats* as the ethnic mix goes from Thai to Malay, and the number of tourists dwindles. Most travelers today enjoy the middle ground, balancing the extremes of the south.

CHUMPHON   ☎ 077

For most travelers, Chumphon is a stop en route to the tropical trinity of Ko Tao, Ko Phangan, and Ko Samui, and a gateway, both culturally and geographically, to the south. For those with extra time, however, Chumphon offers numerous local travel and ecotourism opportunities. With quality accommodations and tourist services, Chumphon is a fine stop for refueling, regrouping, or simply relaxing.

▆ TRANSPORTATION

Trains: Chumphon Railway Station (☎ 511 103), at the west end of Krumluang Chumphon Rd. Luggage storage 10฿ per day. To **Bangkok** and **Surat Thani** (3hr., 10 per day, rapid and express 243฿). To **Bangkok** (10hr., 7am, 80฿; rapid and express trains 7-10hr., every hr. 11:30am-10:30pm, 330-370฿) via **Hua Hin** (3-4hr.; 49฿, rapid and express 293฿) and **Phetchaburi** (4-5hr.; 62฿, rapid and express 308฿).

Buses: Tha Tapoa Road Terminal (☎ 502 725), opposite Tha Tapoa Hotel, runs A/C and non-A/C buses to **Bangkok** (8hr., every hr. 6am-2pm and 10pm, 211฿) and **Phuket** (6hr.; 4:30am, 4:30, 10pm; 196฿). Most buses to Bangkok stop in **Hua Hin** (5hr., 126฿) and **Phetchaburi** (6hr., 160฿). Orange buses leave from across the street, next to Tha Tapao Hotel, for **Hat Yai** via **Surat Thani** (3hr.; every 30-60min. 5:30-11am, 4:30pm; 65-102฿) and **Ranong** (3hr., 12 per day, 70฿). For **Krabi**, take a bus to Chumphon Mueng Mai bus station and change for a Krabi-bound bus.

Minivans: A useful alternative for **Ranong** (2hr., every hr., 90฿) because they are better able to navigate the winding roads; **minibuses** make the trip in 2hr. instead of the usual 3 by bus. Note, however, that the time saving comes through a blatant disregard for things like speed limits, lane markers, and Newton's law of opposing forces. Minibuses leave across from Infinity Travel.

Boats: 3 boats leave daily to **Ko Tao**. Express boats (2¼hr., 7:30am, 400฿) and **speedboats** (1¾hr., 7:30am, 400฿) leave from piers at **Hat Sai Ree,** 10km outside town. **Midnight boats** ("slow boats") leave at midnight from a different pier (6hr., 200฿). Tickets are readily available in Chumphon at tourist agencies and guesthouses. By far the best deal in town is through **New Chumphon Guest House** (p. 356). Express boat and speedboat tickets 350฿ with full refund if boat is a no-show (a benefit not granted

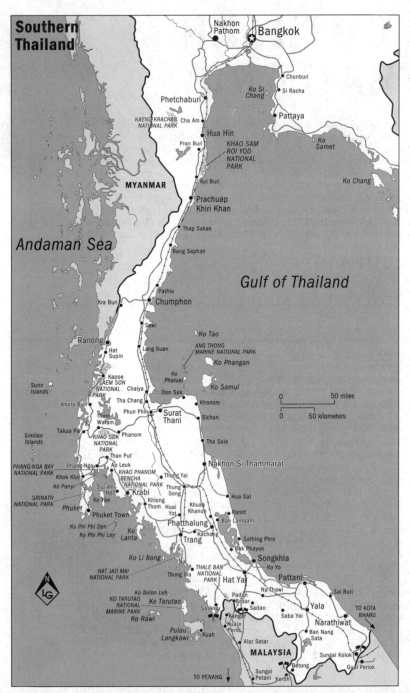

**Southern
Thailand**

Nakhon
Pathom

Bangkok

Chonburi

Ko Si
Chang   Si Racha

Phetchaburi

Pattaya

KAENG KRACHAN   Cha Am
NATIONAL PARK

Hua Hin

Pran Buri   *Ko*
KHAO SAM   *Samet*
ROI YOD
NATIONAL
PARK

MYANMAR   Kui Buri

Ko Chang

Prachuap
Khiri Khan

Andaman Sea   Thap Sakae

Bang Saphan

Gulf of Thailand

Pathiu
Kra Buri   **Chumphon**

Sawi

Ranong   Ko Tao

Hat   *ANG THONG*
Supin   Lang Suan   *MARINE NATIONAL PARK*

Surin   Kapoe   *Ko*   *Ko Phangan*
Islands   *LAEM SON*   *Phalui*
NATIONAL   Chaiya   *Ko Samui*
Khuru Buri   *PARK*   Don Sak
Tham   Tha Chang   Khanom
Similan   Waram
Islands   Phun Phin   **Surat**
Takua Pa   **Thani**   Sichon

KHAO SOK   Phanom
NATIONAL
PARK   Tha Sala

Than Put

PHANG-NGA BAY   Phang-Nga   Ao Leuk   **Nakhon Si Thammarat**
NATIONAL PARK
Khok Kloi   *KHAO PHANOM*
Ko Panyi   *BENCHA*   Thung Yai
NATIONAL PARK
Susam-   Thung   Hua Sai
SRINATH   Hoi   Song
NATIONAL PARK **Krabi**   Khlong
Ko Yao   Thom   Khuan   Ranot
Phuket   Huai   Khanun
Phuket Town   Yot   Ban Lampam

Ko Phi Phi Don   **Phatthalung**
Ko Phi Phi Ley   *Ko*   Kachong
Lanta   **Trang**   Sathing Phra

Ko Li Bong   *THALE BAN*   Rak Phayun
NATIONAL
HAT JAO MAI *PARK*   **Songkhla**
NATIONAL   Thung Wa   *Ko Yo*
PARK   **Hat Yai**
Ko Bulon Leh   **Pattani**
KO TARUTAO   Padan   Na Thawi
NATIONAL   Besar   Sai Buri
MARINE PARK *Ko Tarutao* Sadao
Satun   Kangar   Saba Yoi   **Yala**
Ko Rawi   Kuala   **TO KOTA**
Perlis   Alor Setar   **Narathiwat** **BHARU**
Pulau   Kuah   Ban Nang
Langkawi   Sata   Sungai Kolok

MALAYSIA   Betong   Gual Periok

TO PENANG   Sungai   Keroh
Petani

0 ___ 50 miles
0 ___ 50 kilometers

N
LG

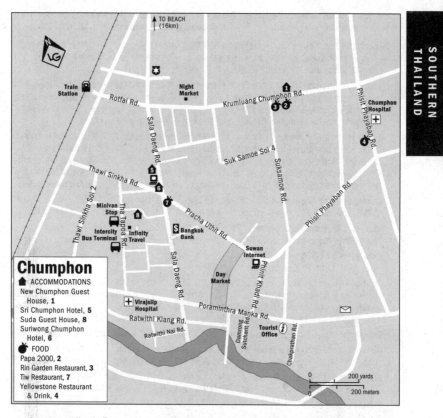

Chumphon

🏠 ACCOMMODATIONS
New Chumphon Guest
House, **1**
Sri Chumphon Hotel, **5**
Suda Guest House, **8**
Suriwong Chumphon
Hotel, **6**
🍎 FOOD
Papa 2000, **2**
Rin Garden Restaurant, **3**
Tiw Restaurant, **7**
Yellowstone Restaurant
& Drink, **4**

by most sellers). Free wake-up call and pick-up from anywhere in town and transportation by car to the pier. Most sellers in town provide free transportation for express and speedboat passengers but charge 50฿ for those taking the midnight boats. To visit **Ko Maphraw** (Coconut Island), contact a tourist office 15 days in advance.

Local Transportation: Motorcycle taxis can be found on almost every street in town. It should cost 10฿ to go anywhere in town. **Infinity Travel Service** (see **Tourist Office**, below) rents **motorbikes** (150฿ per day) and **cars** (1000฿ per day). **Suda Guest House** (p. 356) also rents motorbikes (150-200฿ per day). The **Chumphon Cabana Resort** (☎504 442) rents **diving equipment**. Open daily 9am-8pm.

✴ 🛈 ORIENTATION AND PRACTICAL INFORMATION

Chumphon lies 498km south of Bangkok. The town is deceptively compact, and its main streets roughly follow a grid system. **Krumluang Chumphon Road,** home of the town's impressive night market, runs east from the train station, forming the northern edge of town. **Poraminthra Manka Road** marks the southern limit; look here for the hospital, post office, and tourist office. The bus station and several travel agencies line **Tha Tapoa Road,** running north-south through the western part of the city. Parallel to Tha Tapoa Rd. and one block east is hotel- and eatery-studded **Sala Daeng Road.** "V"-shaped **Pracha Uthit Road** straddles the city center with the day market, *songthaew* to Ko Tao-bound ferries, and Hat Thung Wua Laen.

Tourist Office: Tourist Information (☎ 511 024, ext. 120), near the post office. Friendly and English-speaking, but most questions can be answered at the more convenient tourist agencies. Open daily 8:30am-4:30pm.

Tours: Commercial tourist agencies sell boat tickets and arrange tours on Tha Tapoa Rd., near the bus station. **Infinity Travel Services,** 68/2 Tha Tapoa Rd. (☎ 501 937), provides ferry tickets, advance booking for trains and buses, luggage storage, arrangements for scuba diving on Ko Tao, and showers. Open daily 7am-11pm.

Ecotourism and Adventure Travel: Most of the travel offices, including **Infinity Travel,** offer adventure travel tours into the lush wilderness nearby. The **Phato Rainforest Ecotourism Club** offers whitewater rafting adventures and ecotourism trips into the nearby Phato Rainforest. A 3-day package includes hands-on educational studies of the rainforest watershed system. 600-1500฿. Bookings can be made through **Suda Guest House.**

Currency Exchange: Bangkok Bank, 111/1-2 Sala Daeng Rd. (☎ 511 446). **24hr. ATM.** Open M-F 8:30am-3:30pm. Ko Tao has no ATMs, so pick up extra if you need it.

Markets: Day market, between Pracha Uthit and Poramintha Manka Rd. Open daily 5am-5pm. **Night market,** on Krumluang Chumphon Rd. Open daily 6-11pm.

Police: (☎ 511 505), on Sala Daeng Rd., about 50m north of the intersection with Krumluang Rd. Little English spoken. Open **24hr.**

Medical Services: Virajsilp Hospital (☎ 503 238), at the south end of Tha Tapoa Rd., a 5min. walk from the bus station. Great service. No credit cards. Open **24hr.** Also has a **pharmacy.** Convenient to town, **Chumphon Hospital** (☎ 503 672), on Phisit Phayaban Rd. where it curves up towards Krumluang Rd., also offers **24hr. emergency** care.

Telephones: Several guesthouses and tourist offices have **international phone** service.

Internet Access: Suwan Internet, on Pracha Uthit Rd. at Phinit Khadi Rd. near the market. 20฿ per hr. Open daily 9am-10pm. Also at **Infinity Travel.** 1฿ per min. 20฿ min.

Post Office: GPO, 192 Poramintha Manka Rd. (☎ 511 041), southeast of town, past the tourist office, on the left. *Poste Restante.* Open M-F 8:30am-4:30pm, Sa 9am-noon.

Postal Code: 86000.

ACCOMMODATIONS

Chumphon has a surprisingly good selection of budget accommodations. Most hotels and guesthouses cluster near the bus station, either on Tha Tapoa Rd., Sala Daeng Rd., or in the alleyways connecting the two.

Suda Guest House, 8 Soi Bangkok Bank Thatapao Rd. (☎ 504 366), just around the corner from Infinity Travel near the bus station. Immaculate facilities and homey atmosphere add to this place's considerable charm. Spotless bathrooms have hot showers. Singles 180-250฿; doubles 300-350฿. Add 80฿ for use of A/C in rooms. ❷

Sri Chumphon Hotel, 127/22-24 Sala Daeng Rd. (☎ 570 536). Impersonal but spacious rooms come with luxuries like TVs, private baths, and hot water. Tea and coffee downstairs. Singles and doubles with fan 250฿, with A/C 350฿. ❷

Suriwong Chumphon Hotel, 125/30 Sala Daeng Rd. (☎ 511 203), next to Sri Chumphon, has slightly nicer rooms for slightly higher prices. Rooms with fan 300฿, with A/C 380฿. ❸

New Chumphon Guest House (☎ 502 900), 600m from the railway station, off Krumluang Chumphon Rd., on a side street to the left. Nicely removed from the hubbub, but still close to the night market. Clean, basic rooms in Thai-style houses with shared baths. Patio and friendly service. Breakfast 60-80฿. Singles and doubles 120-160฿. ❷

🏠 FOOD

For Chumphon's finest victuals, head to the markets. The **day market ❶** offers *gluay lep meu* (fingernail bananas) and a variety of other fruits. The **night market ❶** on Krumluang Chumphon Rd. offers *pad thai* (20฿) and other Thai staples. (Open daily 5-11pm.) The **bakery** on the corner of Sala Daeng and Pracha Uthit Rd. sells great pastries. (Most pastries 4-15฿. Open daily 6am-5pm.) Restaurants line Krumluang Chumphon Rd., and several of them offer live entertainment.

▨ Papa 2000, 188 Krumluang Chumphon Rd., 2 blocks from the intersection with Sala Daeng Rd. The place to see and be seen for hip, wealthy Chumphonites, Papa is also quite tourist-friendly. Outdoor seating and live music most nights make this a fun, relaxed dining experience. Delicious Thai dishes 80-100฿. Open daily 10am-11pm. **❸**

Yellowstone Restaurant & Drink, 161 Phisit Phayaban Rd., across from the Chumphon Hospital. Well-maintained indoor restaurant. Typical Thai dishes, plus great seafood specialities (butterfish with Chinese plum 220฿). The adventurous (or vengeful) will try the "fried crispy pigeon" (80฿). Most dishes 80฿. Open daily 10am-10pm. **❸**

Rin Garden Restaurant, on Krumluang Chumphon Rd. at Suksamoe Rd. Very affordable dishes in a pleasant outdoor setting. Curried crab with vegetables 70฿. Most dishes 50-70฿. Open daily 10am-10pm. **❷**

Tiw Restaurant, on Sala Daeng Rd. across from Suriwong Chumphon Hotel, offers rice and curry dishes until early morning. Entrees 15-40฿. Open daily noon-6am. **❶**

🏃 DAYTRIP FROM CHUMPHON

For extended excursions to explore the caves and other sights in the vicinity, it's best to book a tour with one of the tourist agencies such as Infinity Travel (p. 356) or guesthouses such as Suda and New Chumphon. Two popular destinations are the **Rab Ro Caves** and the **Ka Po Waterfalls,** 30km from Chumphon. Prices vary depending on the number of people, but expect to pay at least 500฿.

HAT THUNG WUA LAEN

In Chumphon, bright yellow songthaew to Hat Thung Wua Laen (sometimes called Cabana Beach) leave from the market along Pracha-Uthit Rd. in front of 7-Eleven and stop at Chumphon Cabana Resort at the south end of the beach (25฿). You can also take Cabana Beach Resort's shuttle (1, 6pm; return 12:30, 5:30pm) from its office on

ISLAND LUXURIES

If paradise doesn't satisfy you, ambrosia will. It's tough to have a bad meal in southern Thailand—in fact, it's hard to have a bad day.

Southern Thai food, largely influenced by the Muslim population, is rich, spicy, hot, and heavy. Fresh tumeric, not the dried powder found in classic Thai food, is commonly used to flavor fish and other meats. Curries in the south are also different from those in the northern provinces. Muslim-style curries, particularly *massaman*, seem more Indian than Thai because they are made from roasted, not raw, herbs and roots.

Some southern dishes to try:

Roti: A dense, flaky pancake often stuffed with banana and covered in sweetened condensed milk—a southern specialty.

Khao moek gai: A chicken dish served with yellow rice, flavored with roasted spices and sweet-and-sour chili sauce.

Dtom kem gkati plaa doog: The name says it all. Catfish rounds simmered in tumeric and coconut sauce with lemongrass and red shallots.

Kluai buat chi: This dessert, made of bananas cooked in coconut milk and served either hot or cold, tastes like pudding.

Also look for sun-dried squid and soft shell crabs stir-fried with coconut milk and jasmine leaves. For a snack, buy big green pods at a market and munch on their *sadtaw* (seed). Or try them in *pad ped sadtaw,* an intensely spicy shrimp and red curry dish.

Tha Tapoa Rd. near the bus station directly to its resort on the beach. Free for Cabana's patrons. To return to Chumphon, walk 1km to the main road and catch a songthaew.

The area's premier beach, Hat Thung Wua Laen, is a 2km long beach that remains pristine, thanks to the lack of foreigners and rules forbidding further development. During the week, it is often completely deserted, save for fishing boats anchored several hundred meters out at bay.

Concrete bungalows and restaurants line Moo 8, the road running the length of the beach. Near the mini-mart in the center of town, the owner of the New Chumphon Guest House (p. 356) operates a number of **tourist bungalows** ❷ that are the most affordable accommodations at the beach. Her son will even drive you from Chumphon to the beach at no charge. (Contact New Chumphon for more info. ☎502 900. Bungalows 150-400฿.) At the northern end of the beach, **Seabeach Bungalows** ❸, 42 Moo 8, is covered in bougainvillea. (☎560 115. Doubles with bath 300฿; bungalows with bath and fan 400฿, with A/C 600฿; quads with bath and A/C 600฿.) **Clean Wave Resort** ❸, at the midpoint of the beach, has small, tidy, hotel-like rooms. (☎560 151. Rooms 200-300฿, with A/C 500-600฿, with hot water 700฿.) Their excellent **restaurant** ❷ serves Thai food for 40-100฿. **The View Restaurant** ❷, 13/2 Moo 8, has savory seafood plates (50-70฿), and well-maintained **bungalows** ❹ across the road, with amenities like TVs and phones. (☎560 214. Bungalows 400฿, with A/C 600-700฿, with A/C and hot water 800-900฿.)

Divers or those with a bit more time may want to visit two popular islands off the shores of Hat Thung Wua Laen, **Ko Ngam Yai** and **Ko Ngam Noi,** prized for their swallows' nests, coral reefs, and soaring cliffs. They are seldom visited but well worth the trip. Chartering a boat is expensive; it's best to book with an organized tour. Ask at the Chumphon Cabana Resort or at their office in town.

RANONG ☎077

Most foreign visitors stop in Ranong just long enough to get directions to the Burmese border for a "visa run" and then move on. While it serves this purpose well, Ranong also deserves an overnight stay to enjoy its small-town atmosphere, affordable Thai-Burmese cuisine, and the natural hot springs just 2km from the town's center. These attractions may not make it a destination in itself, but it is a good place to go to get away from the congestion of other cities in the south.

◪ **TRANSPORTATION. Ranong Airport** is about 20km south of town on Phetkasem Hwy. **Phuket Airlines** (www.phuketairlines.com) flies from Ranong to Bangkok (1¼hr.; 3:05pm; one-way 1895฿, round-trip 3790฿) and Phuket (1¼hr.; 4:15pm; one-way 900฿, round-trip 1700฿). The **bus station** is on Phetkasem Hwy. near the stadium, about 1km from the Spa Inn. **Buses** run to Bangkok (10hr., 5 per day 8am-8pm, 190-260฿), Chumphon (3hr., 6 per day 6am-8pm, 50-70฿), Krabi (6hr., 5 per day 8am-4pm, 100-130฿), and Phuket (5hr., 5 per day 8am-6pm, 100-140฿). Within town, **songthaew** run up and down Ruangrat Rd. about every 10 seconds. (5฿). **Motorcycle taxis** will take you anywhere within the market area for 10฿, from Ruangrat Rd. to the bus station for 15฿, and to the hot springs for 20฿.

◪ **PRACTICAL INFORMATION. Ruangrat Road,** which runs north-south, is the town's main street and the location of almost everything you'll need while you're here. **Phetkasem Highway** runs to the south of town, and is where you'll find the bus station and the road that leads to the hot springs.

Travel agencies lining Ruangrat Rd. specialize in visa runs (universally 300฿) and trips to nearby Ko Chang. **Pon's Place,** on Ruangrat Rd. just north of the Sin Tavee Hotel, operates visa runs and tours and arranges tickets and bookings. (☎823 344.

Tours of Ko Chang and other nearby areas 600-1000฿ per day. Open daily 8am-midnight.) Other services include: a few **banks** on Ruangrat Rd. at Tha Meuang Rd., on the part of the road closest to Phetkasem Hwy., including **Krung Thai Bank,** with a **24hr. ATM;** the **police station,** on Dupkadee Rd. just off Ruangrat Rd. on the opposite side of town (☎821 681; open **24hr.**); **Ranong Hospital,** on Kamlangsap Rd. a block from Phetkasem Hwy., with **24hr. emergency** care; a fully-stocked **pharmacy,** 87/1 Ruangrat Rd., in the middle of town (open daily 8am-midnight); and the **GPO,** about 1km down Dupkadee Rd. away from Ruangrat Rd., at the intersection with Chonraua Rd. (Open M-F 8:30am-4:30pm, Sat 9am-noon.) **Postal Code:** 85000.

🛏🍴 ACCOMMODATIONS AND FOOD. Most hotels in Ranong are run-down, overpriced, or both. In the center of town, **Sin Tavee Hotel ❷,** 81/1 Ruangrat Rd., offers a decent deal. Look for the large, yellow "Kodak Express" sign. Some rooms have hot water and balconies. (☎811 213. Singles 160฿; doubles 200฿, with A/C 280฿.) A bit further up Ruangrat Rd., away from the market, **Rattanasin Hotel ❷,** 226 Ruangrat Rd., is dirt-cheap, which comes as no surprise when you see the fan rooms and squat toilets that typify the place. (☎811 242. Rooms 100฿.) On Phetkasem Hwy. just a short walk from the hot springs, the **Spa-Inn Hotel ❸,** 1/15 Cholraeu Rd., pumps hot water from the springs into its baths. However, you pay a lot for the privilege and the rooms are drab. (☎832 692. A/C rooms 450฿.)

Good, cheap Thai-Burmese dishes can be found at the **day market ❶,** on Ruangrat Rd. in the center of town, and the **night market ❶,** on Kamlangsap Rd. near the hospital and a block from Phetkasem Hwy. Excellent and inexpensive restaurants line Ruangrat Rd. 🍴 **J&T Restaurant ❶,** on Ruangrat Rd. at Luvung Rd., a few blocks up from the market, offers meticulously prepared and presented Thai and Chinese dishes, and a delicious ice cream menu. (Dishes 20-45฿. Ice cream specialties 15-35฿. Open daily 10am-9pm.) A block farther from the market, **Boat ❶** is the classiest restaurant in town, and still quite inexpensive. It offers Thai-Chinese cuisine. (Entrees 25-60฿. Open 9:30am-9:30pm.) Three more blocks past Boat is **Sophon's Hideaway ❷,** an expansive outdoor restaurant with an enormous menu of breakfast, European and Thai entrees, and mouth-watering desserts. (Breakfast 30-70฿. Entrees 50-100฿. Desserts 35-45฿. Open daily 8am-10pm.) **Coffee House ❷,** 173 Ruangrat Rd., two blocks past Sin Tavee Hotel and before J&T, has the usual Thai fare plus an extensive sandwich list and delicious breakfast offerings. (Thai dishes 25-50฿. Sandwiches 30-55฿. Pineapple pancakes 25฿. Open daily 7am-8pm.)

📷 SIGHTS. The **Ranong Mineral Hot Springs,** 1km down Kamlangsap Rd. from Phetkasem Hwy., are good for a quick, relaxing, and, most importantly, 🔵 **free** dip. In the past, spa and bath privileges cost 100฿ at the nearby, über-pricey **Janson Thara Ranong Hotel,** 2/10 Phetkasem Hwy. (☎822 516), but the newly constructed addition to the public park at the springs includes fountains for bathing. The sulfuric springs themselves bubble up from underneath at a temperature of roughly 70°C, hot enough to burn skin. It's also hot enough to boil an egg, and opportunistic hawkers sell eggs and receptacles to boil them in (5฿ per egg). Coming from Phetkasem Hwy., three fountains on the left bank contain pure, steaming-hot water straight from the springs. They represent the three distinct springs that lie beneath the park and vary slightly in temperature and sulfuric content. You can stick your hand in and out of these fountains very quickly, but prolonged exposure will cause burns. In the newly constructed central island at the park, pumps mix purified river water with water from the springs to form natural jacuzzis of sorts. Go ahead and dip your feet in; the water's warm.

SOUTHERN THAILAND

PHANG-NGA TOWN ☎076

While most travelers explore the breathtaking natural beauty of Phang-Nga Bay National Park by speedboat from nearby Phuket, there are several advantages to coming instead to small Phang-Nga Town, the provincial capital of Phang-Nga (often pronounced "PUNG-aah"). Phang-Nga Town offers more bay tour options than Phuket, and at much more affordable prices. Perhaps even more importantly, coming to Phang-Nga Town allows you to explore the many other cultural and natural sights that lie nearby. From the now-famous Phang-Nga Bay to the ancient Buddhist temple caves at Suwan Kuha to the nearby rainforest, Phang-Nga remains a largely undiscovered gem, long concealed by Phuket's large shadow.

TRANSPORTATION. Phang-Nga's bus station is on **Phetkasem Highway** near the center of town. **Buses** run to Bangkok (13hr., 6 per day, 357-460฿); Hat Yai (6hr., every hr. 8am-2pm, 220฿); Ko Samui (6hr.; 9:30, 11:30am; 240฿ includes ferry); Krabi (1½hr., every 30min. 7:30am-8pm, 35-59฿); Phuket (1½hr., 14 per day, 50-65฿); Surat Thani (2½hr., 5 per day 9:30am-5pm, 60-130฿); and Trang (4½hr., every hr. 7:30am-8:30pm, 139฿). Blue **songthaew** run along the highway from the bus station to Wat Suwannakuha (20฿), the pier (20฿), and points around town (10-15฿). **Motorcycle taxis** cost about 20฿ around town.

PRACTICAL INFORMATION. Phang-Nga Town is easy to navigate but difficult to walk. It's easy to navigate because the entire town is on or within a half-block of **Phetkasem Highway,** but it's difficult to walk because the town's linear, spread-out nature makes it rather long. From the bus station, Phetkasem Hwy. runs north to Phang-Nga Guest House and a few blocks beyond. To the south, the town runs along the highway about 3km, and most of the government offices are 2km south of the bus station.

The **travel agencies** near the bus station provide most tourist services. These agencies (day tours 250-550฿; overnight tours to Phang-Nga Bay 750฿; park admission 200฿) are also about 200-400฿ cheaper than the agencies operating out of Phuket and Krabi. **Sayan Tour,** next to the bus terminal, is one of the more established tour operators. (☎430 348. Open daily 6am-9pm.) Another reputable tour company is **M.T. Tour,** which operates out of the Muang Tong Hotel. The owner, the inimitable Mr. Hassim, has a wealth of information on almost everything. (☎412 132. Open daily 8am-8pm.) Other services include: a **Thai Farmers Bank,** 126 Phetkasem Hwy., across the street from the bus station, with a **24hr. ATM** (open M-F 8:30am-3:30pm); the **police station** (☎430 390), on Soi Policestation, 1km from the bus station away from Phang Nga Guest House; **Phang-Nga General Hospital,** 436 Phetkasem Hwy., 2km from the bus station in the same direction as the police (☎412 034; open **24hr.;** English spoken; no credit cards); and a **post office** on Phetkasem Hwy. with *Poste Restante* and **international phone.** (☎412 171. Open M-F 8:30am-4:30pm, Sa-Su 9am-noon. Phone daily 8:30am-4:30pm.) **Postal Code:** 82000.

ACCOMMODATIONS AND FOOD. Without question, the best budget place in town is the ◙**Phang-Nga Guest House ❷,** on Phetkasem Hwy. near Krug Thai Bank, two blocks to your right as you exit the bus station. The owners are rightfully proud of their spotless rooms and "just-right" mattresses. (☎411 358. "American" breakfast 50฿. Singles with fan 200฿, with TV and A/C 300฿; doubles 250฿/400฿.) The best high-end place in town, the **Phang-Nga Inn ❸,** is owned by the same family. Located just off Phetkasem Hwy. on the opposite side of the bus station, most of these equally immaculate rooms have a hot shower and cable TV. (☎411 963. Rooms 450-1200฿.) A good budget option is the **Muang Tong Hotel ❷,** at 128 Phetkasem Hwy., between Phang-Nga Guest House and the bus station, on the opposite side of the street. Aging rooms have a bare minimum of amenities, but are cheap. (☎412 132. Singles with fan 150฿, with A/C 300฿; doubles 250฿/450฿.) A bit farther from town is the **Luk Muang Hotel ❷**, 1/2 Phetkasem Hwy. Walk about 10min. past Phang-Nga Guest House from the bus station, past the temple and the "Have a Good Trip" sign. The hotel offers large but somewhat stuffy rooms, some with TV and phone. (☎411 512. Singles 200฿; doubles 250- 300฿.)

Phang-Nga has several good dining options near the bus station. The best restaurant around, **Duang Restaurant ❷**, at 122 Phetkasem Hwy. next to Thai Farmers Bank and opposite the night market, serves hot-and-sour seafood soup. (Dishes 50-100฿. Open daily 9am-10:30pm.) **Bismilla ❸**, 247 Phetkasem Hwy., on the same side of the street as the bus station, is a Muslim restaurant with wonderful *roti*, curry, and soup—especially lemon. (Breakfast *roti* 30฿. Entrees 80-120฿. Open daily 7am-11pm.) The **restaurant ❶** on Phetkasem Hwy. at the bus station road serves good pork dishes. (Most items 30฿. Open daily 7am-midnight.) The **day market ❶**, off Phetkasem Hwy., two blocks to your left as you leave the bus station, sells fruit from 4am to 6pm. The **night market ❶** sets up near the post office on Phetkasem Hwy. and along Riverside Rim Kong Rd. (Open daily 4:30pm-midnight.)

◙ SIGHTS. Most of the interesting sights lie a bit outside of town, but the **Pung Chang Cave,** located off Phetkasem Hwy. past the post office on the far end of town from the Phang-Nga Guest House, is worth a visit. A stream runs through the cave, with entrances 1.3km apart on opposite ends of a towering tree-covered limestone mountain visible from anywhere in town. It is especially notable for its well-preserved ancient cave paintings. Sayan Tours operates **rafting** trips through the cave, although the most interesting paintings are accessible on foot from the far entrance. (Open daily 8am-6pm. Motorcycle taxis will take you there for 30฿.)

▣ DAYTRIPS FROM PHANG-NGA TOWN. These sites offer more than the usual tourist attractions, providing insight on both the natural and the cultural life of the region.

PHANG-NGA BAY NATIONAL PARK. The park stretches over 400km², 80 percent of which is water, and encompasses more than 120 postcard-perfect limestone islands. Although the bay's status as a national park has aided in its conservation, responsible ecotourism is critical to prevent damage to the islands. Most tourists make a beeline for the park's twin jewels: beautiful Ko Khao Ping Gan and its satellite, Ko Tapu, better known as "James Bond Island" (scenes from the Bond flick *The Man With The Golden Gun,* were filmed here). While the image of the thin limestone rock that is Ko Tapu (literally, "Nail Island") slicing into the bay is quite striking, be prepared to throw elbows at shell-vendors and tourists to stake a prime photo-taking spot. If it gets too crowded, head to Ko Khao Ping Gan, where a small pier juts into the bay for more spectacular panoramas. If you have time, be sure to paddle through the Tam Lod Grotto, a sea-level, open-ended cave dripping with stalactites. Ko Khien displays 300-year-old drawings of boats and animals on the mountain's edge. *Songthaew* (20฿) run from Phang-Nga bus station to the pier, where longtail boats are chartered (300-400฿ for a few hours; be prepared to bargain).

While larger boats visit from Krabi and Phuket, the most common tours from Phang-Nga are on **longtail boats,** which, while a bit shakier, are able to maneuver through the narrower caves and waterways that the larger speedboats can't even come close to. Most tours include swimming and lunch on the beach. **Sayan Tour** offers half-day (200฿), full-day (500฿), and overnight trips (extra 250฿), which include a memorable stay at Ko Panyi. The latter option, tacked on after a half-day or full-day tour, is highly recommended. Another way to tour the bay is by **kayak.** This pricey alternative (roughly 2000-3000฿ for a full day) allows you to fully explore the hidden lagoons without the deafening buzz of the longtail motor. Whichever way you decide to visit the bay, be sure to dress to get wet. The "land" excursions entail wading through knee-high streams, and rainstorms on the bay can completely drench you in a matter of minutes. *(Park admission 200฿.)*

KO PANYI AND THE MUSLIM FISHING VILLAGE. Though technically part of the Phang-Nga Bay National Park, Ko Panyi is certainly worth a visit by itself. About 250 years ago, Muslim fishermen from Indonesia settled on the island, constructing homes and businesses on stilts above the water. Almost three centuries later, the Muslim Fishing Village is alive and well, though nowadays it seems to cater more to tourists than to fish. Other than the prominent town **mosque,** there's not much to see in the village (besides a gorgeous sunset and sunrise); the real fascination is ambling down the rickety, suspended streets to watch the town inhabitants go about their daily chores in this most unusual setting. Overnight stays are recommended, as the village assumes a different character after daytrippers return to the mainland. It's possible to arrange a room with the locals or book an overnight stay through a travel agency for 250-350฿. The best accommodations in town are at the brand-new **bungalows** operated by Sayan Tour. The nine rooms are tidy and run by an extremely friendly staff; home-cooked dinner and breakfast are included with your stay. (Rooms with private bath 250฿, with full-day park tour 350฿.) For a more authentic, if somewhat less comfortable experience, M.T. Tour can arrange **homestays.** (150-250฿ per night. Long-term discounts available.) The company's owner, Mr. Hassim, is a native of Ko Panyi and knows just about everybody in town—walking the streets with him is a particular pleasure.

WAT THAM SUWANNAKUHA. A popular stop for most tourist groups, this pleasant Buddhist temple, known by locals as Wat Tham, consists of several caves, the largest of which is 40m long and houses an impressive 15m-long reclining Buddha. The temple (and its resident monkeys) is best visited late in the afternoon when the tourist buses have returned to Phuket, leaving the temple relatively undisturbed. *(8km outside Phang-Nga, off Phang-Nga Koke Kloy Rd. Take a blue songthaew from the town center for 20฿ and ask to be dropped off at Wat Tham. Free.)*

SA NANG MANORA FOREST PARK. This park, a small, secluded patch of dense rainforest bisected by a roaring brook, makes for an adventurous day of hiking. Well-marked trails criss-cross the brook and its accompanying waterfalls, often on rather precarious "bridges" that are actually just two logs nailed together. **Exercise extreme caution during and immediately after rainfall.** Points of interest along the main 2km path include limestone cliffs, Shell Cave (which serves as an impressive reminder of the area's oceanic past), giant trees, poisonous plants, and a grand finale known as Bat Cave. The payoff at the end isn't spectacular, but as usual, the best part is the journey itself. Sayan Tour offers 6hr. guided tours of the park for 250฿. *(7km from town, off a small, winding road that branches to the right from Hwy. 4 about 4km from town. Motorcycle taxis charge 50฿ from the town center. Free.)*

PHUKET ☎076

A tropical playground of international renown, Phuket begs comparison to Bali and other over-touristed tropical paradises. Thailand's biggest island in the Andaman Sea and its most wealthy province, Phuket draws tourists looking for anything but a cultural or solitary experience. Most visitors arrive by plane and are swiftly shepherded into A/C taxis, which deposit them at five-star luxury resorts. Here they frolic for a week or two, safely avoiding almost everything having to do with Thailand. As such, Phuket can be less than friendly for the budget traveler,

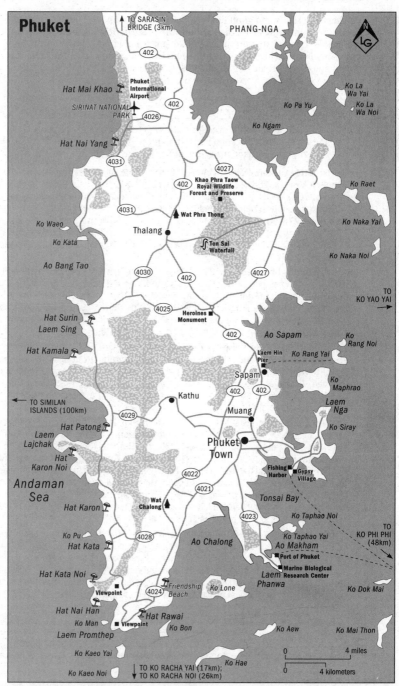

but there are still some good deals to be found, especially if you travel in the low season or if prime sleeping digs are not the most important thing in the world to you. Backpackers relax on beaches like Hat Kamala and Hat Karon by day and cruise the discos in legendary nightlife hub Hat Patong by night. The mantra is simple: give up your dreams of idyllic seclusion for a few nights, soak up a raucous good time with fellow *farang*, and make the most of the "Jewel of the South."

TRANSPORTATION

Because Phuket lacks public transportation, getting around is expensive. By far, the cheapest and most convenient way to explore the island is by motorbike. However, it is also the most dangerous, resulting in many casualties every month.

Flights: Phuket International Airport, 28km outside of Phuket Town on Rte. 4026. **Bangkok Airways**, 158/2-3 Yao Warat Rd. (☎225 033, open daily 8am-5pm) and **Thai Airways**, 78/1 Ranong Rd. (☎211 195, open daily 8am-5pm), across from the local bus station, run most domestic and international flights. To: **Bangkok** (1½hr., every hr. 8am-8pm, 2730฿); **Hat Yai** (45min., 12:50am, 1180฿); **Ko Samui** (40min.; daily 11:15am, 4:20pm; 1480฿; M, W, F, Su 11:10am; 1480฿); **Kuala Lumpur, Malaysia** (1½hr., daily, 3730฿); **Penang, Malaysia** (Tu, F, Su 12:30pm; 2230฿); and **Singapore** (4 per day, 6085฿).

Buses: Intercity bus station (☎211 480), off Phang-Nga Rd. in eastern Phuket Town, behind a shopping plaza. TAT office has a good, free bus schedule. A/C and non-A/C buses to: **Bangkok** (14hr., 21 per day 6am-7pm, 278-755฿); **Hat Yai** (7hr., 14 per day, 150-270฿); **Khao Sok National Park** via **Takua Pa** (7:30, 9am; 70-100฿); **Krabi** (4hr., 22 per day, 65-117฿); **Phang-Nga** (1½hr., 26 per day, 36฿); **Surat Thani** (5hr., 14 per day, 104-180฿); **Trang** (6hr., 20 per day 6am-6:30pm, 105-189฿).

Boats: Boats to **Ko Phi Phi** depart from Tonsai Bay (9am, 2:30pm; 250-450฿), the deep-sea port on the southeast coast. The cheapest way to buy tickets is through **Mark Travel Service** inside the On On Hotel. Transportation from in-town hotels to the pier is included. Tickets are cheaper in Phuket Town than elsewhere on the island. They are also less expensive in Ko Phi Phi, so unless you're getting a round-trip discount, it is best to buy your return ticket there.

Local Transportation: Local bus station on Ranong Rd. in Phuket Town, near the market. Labeled **songthaew** (every 30min. 7am-5pm) to: **Hat Kamala** (25฿); **Hat Karon** (20฿); **Hat Kata** (20฿); **Hat Patong** (15฿); **Hat Rawai** (20฿); **Hat Nai Yang** (30฿); **Hat Surin** (20฿). **Tuk-tuks** to: **Hat Kamala** (250฿); **Hat Kata** (150฿); **Hat Nai Yang** (300฿); **Hat Patong** (150฿); **Hat Rawai** (100฿); and **Hat Surin** (250฿). **Taxis** (from airport to Phuket Town 300฿) and **tuk-tuks** cruise between the beaches and airport. Blue-and-yellow **metered taxis** are almost impossible to find, but if you do grab one, they are very comfortable and not a bad deal at 30฿ for the first 2km and 4฿ for each additional km. Within Phuket Town, *tuk-tuks* charge 10-20฿; rates are negotiable to other points on the island and go up after 5pm.

Rentals: Motorbikes (150-300฿ per day) and **jeeps** (600-1000฿ per day) are available all over the island. Like most everything else, vehicle rentals are cheapest in Phuket Town and more expensive near the beaches. All vehicles are uninsured, and accident rates for *farang* are alarmingly high. Helmets are required for all drivers in Phuket, and the rule is strictly enforced in the most touristed areas. Cops sometimes run stings to ensure that all *farang* drivers possess a valid International Driver's Permit (p. 62).

ORIENTATION

Getting around Phuket is not particularly complicated, but given the island's size (570km²), traveling can take some time. Phuket is connected to the mainland by

Route 402, the island's main north-south artery, and the **Sarasin Bridge.** Bordered by the Andaman Sea, the west coast is lined with beaches. The northern beaches, especially **Hat Kamala, Hat Surin,** and **Laem Sing** are quieter and prettier, while south of Kamala, party central **Hat Patong** has a sensory overload of tacky bars, cabaret shows, and gimmicky tourist stalls. Farther south are the gentle duo **Hat Karon** and **Hat Kata,** while a few smaller, less attractive beaches fringe the island's southwestern tip. Phuket's bleak and muddy eastern coast is filled with mangroves, prawn farms, and bobbing boats. On the island's southeast corner, **Phuket Town,** the island's lifeline, offers financial, postal, and telecommunications services in addition to a bevy of authentic budget restaurants.

⚡ PRACTICAL INFORMATION

Tourist Office: TAT, 73-75 Phuket Rd. (☎212 213), in Phuket Town, northwest of the clock tower and hidden among furniture stores. Helpful English-speaking staff provides maps, bus schedules, and accommodations lists. Open daily 8:30am-4:30pm.

Tours: Tour operators are a dime a dozen in Hat Karon, Hat Kata, Hat Patong, and Phuket Town. Most can arrange tours to Phang-Nga Bay and nearby islands (450-650฿) and bus or ferry transportation to Krabi and Ko Phi Phi. **Mark Travel Service,** located in the **On On Hotel** (p. 367) is one of the cheapest.

Currency Exchange: In Phuket Town, a slew of banks are on Phang-Nga Rd. in front of the On On Hotel, and several more are 1 block down on Ratsada Rd. **Thai Farmers Bank,** 14 Phang-Nga Rd. (☎216 928), has a **24hr. ATM.** Currency exchange booths and ATMs abound on the larger beaches, especially Hat Karon, Hat Kata, and Hat Patong. Open daily 8:30am-5pm.

Supermarket: Tops, on Tilok Uthit Rd. 1 next to Paradise Cinemas and KFC, offers better prices and selection than neighborhood marts. Open **24hr.**

Local Tourist Police: 81-83 Satun Rd. (☎225 361), in the far northwest part of town. Open **24hr.** English spoken. Smaller booths are found on major beaches.

Medical Services: Bangkok Phuket Hospital, 21 Hong Yok-H-Thit Rd. (☎254 421), on the northwest side of Phuket Town. **Phuket International Hospital,** 44 Chalerm Prakiat Rd. (☎249 400), on the way to the airport. Credit cards accepted. English spoken. Both open **24hr.**

Telephones: Phuket Telecommunications Center, 112/2 Phang-Nga Rd. (☎216 861), in the building under the radio tower. **International phone**/fax and Internet. Generally cheaper than services provided by travel agencies. Open daily 8am-midnight.

Internet Access: Cybercafes line Montri Rd. and Tilok Uthit 1 Rd. and charge 25฿ per hr. **Hi-Tel,** on Ong Sim Phai Rd. at Tilok Uthit 1 Rd., has particularly fast connections. Open daily 8am-midnight. Also available in the On On Hotel (p. 367).

Post Offices: GPO, 12/16 Montri Rd. (☎211 020), on the corner with Thalang Rd. *Poste Restante.* Open M-F 8:30am-4:30pm, Sa-Su 9am-noon.

Postal Code: 83000.

PHUKET TOWN   ☎076

Lacking the glamour of its neighbors, Phuket Town is the place to stay for late-night or early-morning transit or to stock up on supplies before heading out to the beaches. For those interested in design, Phuket has wonderful examples of Sino-Portuguese architecture (an eclectic mix of Western with Chinese and Thai styles, characterized by the use of arches). Despite the scant entertainment options, Phuket Town's budget hotels and restaurants make it a popular springboard for exploring the rest of the island.

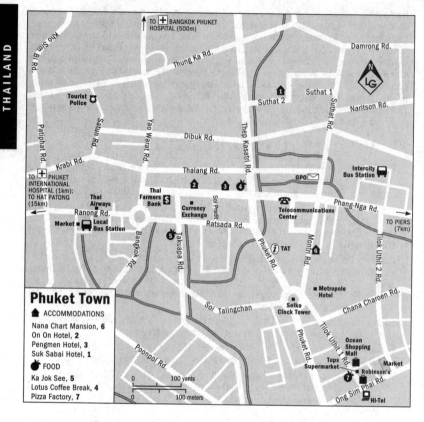

Phuket Town

🏠 ACCOMMODATIONS

Nana Chart Mansion, **6**
On On Hotel, **2**
Pengmen Hotel, **3**
Suk Sabai Hotel, **1**

🍴 FOOD

Ka Jok See, **5**
Lotus Coffee Break, **4**
Pizza Factory, **7**

ORIENTATION

Most of Phuket Town's tourist services and accommodations are concentrated within a small area. The island's **intercity bus terminal** is one block north of the main road, **Phang-Nga Road**, which runs west from the station to the On On Hotel and many banks. Past the Telecommunications Center (distinguished by its clock tower), Phang-Nga Rd. intersects **Phuket Road**, which runs south past TAT and **Navamindra Memorial Square** to the **Seiko Clock Tower**, a main landmark in the southern part of town (not to be confused with the Telecommunications Center clock tower) next to the towering and overpriced Metropole Hotel. The **local bus** and **songthaew station** is adjacent to the market on **Ranong Road**, on the west side of town. A newer part of town is near Tilok Uthit 1 Rd. (toward the bay from the Metropole Hotel), which contains a number of dining, shopping, and entertainment options, including landmarks, such as the Ocean Shopping Mall and Robinson's Department Store, that cater to *farang* and upper-class Thais.

ACCOMMODATIONS

Phuket Town has the widest selection of budget accommodations on the island. In the low season, you can sometimes find cheap accommodation on one of Phuket's beaches (as guesthouses are open to bargaining), but in general, Phuket Town is your best bet. ◪ **Talang Guest House** ❷, 37 Thalang Rd., is clean and well maintained, run by a friendly family. The third-floor rooms cost a bit more, but the fresh air and views are worth it. (☎211 154; www.talangguesthouse.com. Breakfast included. Rooms 260-300฿, with A/C 360-400฿.) **Pengmen Hotel** ❷, 69 Phang-Nga Rd. This Chinese hotel is most easily recognized by its always-crowded seafood restaurant on the ground floor. Rooms are old but fairly clean, and they're the cheapest beds this side of the Sarasin Bridge. (Singles and doubles with shared bath 120฿.) A few houses past the Pengmen Hotel away from the bus station, **On On Hotel** ❷, 19 Phang-Nga Rd., is architecturally significant and the oldest hotel in town. Prices draw a devoted backpacker crowd. (☎211 154. Internet 25฿ per hr. Rooms 150฿, with bath 250฿, with A/C 360.) Opposite the Pearl Hotel, the **Nana Chart Mansion** ❷, 41/34 Montri Rd., has modestly-sized rooms with crisp new sheets and ultra-clean Western toilets. (☎230 041. Singles and doubles 250฿, with TV 300฿, with TV, A/C, and hot shower 350-450฿.) To find **Suk Sabai Hotel** ❷, 82/9 Thep Kasatri Rd., from the bus station, travel west on Phang-Nga Rd., make a right onto Thep Kasatri Rd., and turn onto the small alley before the Ford dealership; the hotel is at the end. Suk Sabai's main advantage is its quiet location. (☎212 287. Singles 220฿; doubles 300฿.)

◖ FOOD

Phuket is famous for its culinary delights, including *tao sor* (Chinese crepes) and *kanom jin Phuket* (breakfast noodles in spicy curry). The day and night **markets** are at the junction of Tilok Uthit 2 and Ong Sim Phai Rd. ◪ **Baan Thalang** ❷, on Talang Rd. a few doors down from Talang Guest House toward Phang-Nga Rd., is a quiet Muslim restaurant that serves great Thai dishes (40-120฿), Indian-influenced curries (85฿), and absolutely fantastic *roti* (20฿) that taste like a piece of heaven when eaten with sugar and sweetened condensed milk. A good place to grab a Western breakfast or a sandwich is **Lotus Coffee Break** ❶, at the corner of Phang-Nga and Phuket Rd. (Tea 10฿. Thai dishes 35-65฿. Shakes 20-25฿. Open daily 7:30am-9:30pm.) The expensive but excellent **Ka Jok See** ❹, 26 Takuapa Rd., is several shops south of the Ratsada Rd. intersection, hidden by plants. The staff treats you like royalty. (Try the *tom yum* or *goong-sarong*, either 150฿. Chinese and Thai dishes 80-380฿. Open Tu-Su 6-11pm.) **Pizza Factory** ❸, on Tilok Uthit 1 Rd. across from the Paradise Cinemas near Ong Sim Phai Rd., is an Asian chain that offers slight twists on Italian pies. (Pizza 99-359฿. Open daily 10am-midnight.)

HAT PATONG

If you're looking for peace and relaxation, don't come to Hat Patong—quiet is one of the few things money can't buy you here. If, however, you're in the market for seedy drunken revelry and a crowded beach full of *farang*, then you've come to the right place. On Phuket's west coast, Patong is the island's nightlife and entertainment center. A tasteless mix of girlie bars, strip shows, Thai boxing, and gaudy souvenir stalls will disappoint—unless that's what you're looking for. Overpriced, overcrowded, and oversexed, Patong is worth visiting to see the spectacle. Then, for better prices and some peace, retreat to beach towns to the north and south.

■ **ORIENTATION.** Hat Patong is defined by two roads that run parallel to the 3km of beach. Closest to the water is **Thaweewong Road,** crowded with expensive seafood restaurants, outdoor bars, and souvenir stalls. One block east, **Song Roi Pee Road** (known as **Ratuthit Road** north of the **Bangla Road** intersection) is home to more restaurants and Hat Patong's few budget hotels. Phuket's raciest bars cluster in alleyways off Bangla Road, which connects Ratuthit and Thaweewong Rd.

◨◪ ACCOMMODATIONS AND FOOD. Accommodations in Hat Patong are among Phuket's most expensive, although they can be bargained down during the low season. Those who come here to party but don't have a place to stay will have to fork over 200-300฿ for a taxi back to Phuket Town. The cheapest places to stay are on Ratuthit Rd. on the north side of the beach. **Touch Villa ❺**, 151/4 Ratuthit Rd., offers the best combination of location and affordability. Located on a small road heading east from Ratuthit Rd. just north of Bangla Rd. (look for the signs), Touch has smallish rooms that are close to the action, but removed enough to be spared some of the noise. (☎344 011; touch-villa@hotmail.com. Rooms 350฿, with hot water, A/C, and fridge 550฿; low-season 250฿/350฿.) For clean A/C rooms, try **Shamrock Park Inn ❹**, 31 Ratuthit Rd. (☎340 991. Singles 600฿, low-season 500฿; doubles 700฿/550฿.) Popular with backpackers is the **PS2 Bungalow ❹**, 21 Ratuthit Rd., a 15min. walk north from the Bangla Rd. intersection. Large, squeaky-clean bungalows surround a pool and boast hot water and micro-fridges. (☎342 207; www.ps2bungalow.com. Rooms 600-900฿, with A/C and TV 1500฿; low-season 350-500฿/600฿.) **Orchid Guesthouse ❹**, 169/24, 28-29 Soi Saensabai, located just a block down Bangla Rd., is a well-situated hotel with a friendly staff. All rooms have cable TV, A/C, refrigerators, and hot water. (☎345 168; www.phuketorchid.com. Rooms 700-1200฿; low-season 500-800฿.)

Like everything else in Hat Patong, food is generally expensive. The **market ❶** on Ratuthit Rd., two blocks south of the Bangla Rd. intersection, provides the cheapest meals. **▨ Restaurant Number 6 ❷**, on Ratuthit Rd. just north of Bangla Rd., is a rare exception to the rule of overpriced, undercooked faux-Western dishes. This coastal eatery serves delicious and affordable Thai dishes in a very casual setting. (Dishes 40-100฿. Open daily 8am-11pm.) **The Pizzeria Hut ❸**, on Song Roi Pee Rd., one block south of the Bangla Rd. intersection, serves brick-oven pizza (100-200฿) on a shaded outdoor patio. (Open daily 11am-11pm.)

◧◪ ENTERTAINMENT AND NIGHTLIFE. Night after night, hot-blooded Western lads come to Hat Patong by the thousands, eager to chat up the pretty, young, Thai "waitresses" who smile seductively from the bars on every corner. Bangla Rd. is the epicenter of the girlie bar scene, and no guidebook is needed to find what you're looking for there. For some plain ol' boozing, head to **Molly Malone's Irish Pub**, 68 Thaweewong Rd., toward the south side of the beach, underneath KFC. Guinness and Kilkenny beer on tap, live Irish music, and "traditional pub grub" round out this slick but expensive bar. (Open daily 11am-2am.) Once you're ready to pick up (or be picked up), head to the center of the action on the streets off Bangla and Sawatdirak Rd. Dozens of gay venues with names like "Hot Boys" and "Connect Bar" cluster on Ratuthit Rd., while the renowned **Simon Cabaret**, 8 Sirirat Rd., just south of town, has a hilarious transvestite extravaganza. (☎342 011. Shows nightly 7:30 and 9:30pm. 500-600฿.) A popular club, **The Banana Disco** on Thaweewong Rd., two blocks south of the Bangla Rd. intersection, features two levels: a ground-floor lounge/restaurant and a disco upstairs. (Cover 200฿. Lounge open daily 7pm-2am. Disco open daily 9pm-2am.) **Tai Pan**, on Ratuthit Rd. at Bangla Rd., plays Western music and features live music on weekends. (Open daily 8:30pm-2am.)

HAT KARON AND HAT KATA

Popular with backpackers and package tourists alike, the adjacent beaches of Hat Karon and Hat Kata have the best balance of lively nightlife, plentiful dining options, and beautiful sand. Perhaps most importantly, they are blissfully free of the go-go bars that dominate Hat Patong. Though new resorts seem to spring up every day, Hat Karon and Hat Kata remain pleasant getaways, at least for now.

▉ ORIENTATION. Hat Karon and Hat Kata are actually three separate beaches. To the north, luxury resorts dot the 3km of Hat Karon. To the south, a hilly, rocky cape separates Hat Karon from Hat Kata. Here, budget restaurants and hotels cluster around **Taina Road,** which winds inland from the beachside **Patak Road.** Hat Kata itself is split into the beaches of **Hat Kata** and **Hat Kata Noi.** While Hat Kata is monopolized by the gargantuan **Club Med,** Hat Kata Noi to the south, smaller and a bit rocky, is the most solitary beach of the three. The tiny tree-covered island of **Ko Pu** lies a few hundred meters out from shore between Hat Kata and Hat Karon; the distance is manageable for experienced swimmers when the green flags are flying.

▉▉ ACCOMMODATIONS AND FOOD. Budget accommodations branch off the beach along Taina Rd. on the cape separating Hat Karon from Hat Kata. One of the best budget hotels is the Scandinavian-themed ▉ **Little Mermaid Guest House ❹,** on Taina Rd. at the far end of the block of beach hotels and restaurants. The four-story multicolored building has rooms with hot water, phones, and optional fridges and TVs (50฿ extra each). Two restaurants, three bars, a pool table, a swimming pool, and Internet access (1฿ per min.) are provided for general use. Try to get a room in the back to avoid late-night noise from the road and the bars across the street. (☎ 330 730; www.littlemermaidphuket.net. Rooms with fan 365฿, with A/C 500฿; bungalows with A/C 590฿; low-season 265฿/365฿/850฿. Discounts for long-term stays.) A great escape is the **Kata On Sea ❸.** On Taina Road, turn up the steep driveway next to the 7-Eleven, and walk up to the top of the hill. Accommodations are in large, basic bungalows with fans, or in recently renovated rooms with A/C, cable TV, and hot water. The friendly staff is quick to help with area info. (☎ 330 594. Motorbikes 300฿ per day. Reservations recommended in high season. Basic bungalows 400฿; deluxe rooms with A/C 600฿. Low-season 300฿/450฿.)

Karon lacks the superb budget options of Kata, but there are a number of mid-level selections. The **Melon Karon Beach Hotel,** 516 Patak Rd., offers 27 A/C rooms with hot water and a great corner location near a number of good restaurants.

Both Hat Karon and Hat Kata have a good selection of inexpensive restaurants, as well as some nicer, pricier ones. In Kata, the restaurants line up along Taina Rd. closest to the beach. **The Kwong Seafood Shop ❷,** on Taina Rd., is a no-frills place to get a fast bite to eat. (Chicken and beef dishes 50-80฿. Seafood dishes 80-200฿. Open daily 9am-midnight.) **Thai Kitchen ❷,** on Taina Rd., offers good, cheap Thai dishes. Locals eat here—always a good sign. (Entrees 40-80฿. Open Su-F 9am-11pm.) **La Banana ❷,** also on Taina Rd., offers great Italian dishes in a setting that is best described as "Venetian jungle." (Dishes 80-380฿. Open daily 9am-midnight.)

In Karon, the restaurants are on Patak Rd. just inland from the roundabout. The best of the bunch is **Papaya Restaurant ❷,** which serves Thai dishes in an open-air setting. Papaya also has an extensive vegetarian menu and selection of cocktails. Coming from the beach, turn left on the side street at the Crystal Beach Hotel and walk 2min. (Dishes 60-210฿. Drinks 100-140฿. Open daily 9am-midnight.)

▉▉ ACTIVITIES AND ENTERTAINMENT. For those with the cash, Hat Karon and Hat Kata are perfect for exploring some of the world's best **snorkeling** and **diving** around the Similan and Racha Islands. Head to PADI-certified **Siam Dive n' Sail,** 68/14 Patak Rd., Moo 2, behind Club Med near the Jiva Resort. They specialize in live-aboard diving trips—all the rage in Phuket now. Four-day trips to Similan and Surin start at 14,500฿ per person, seven-day trips to Myanmar start at 57,000฿, and daytrips start at 2000-3100฿. Gear rental costs 700฿ per day. All trips include transportation from your hotel, tanks, weights, and most meals and drinks. (☎ 330 967; www.siamdivers.com. Open M-Sa 11am-8pm. MC/V.) Hat Kata center's **night scene** offers loud music at nondescript bars lining the street. **Dino Park Mini-Golf** provides more innocent fun. (Open daily 10am-midnight. 240฿, children 180฿.)

HAT SURIN, AO BANG TAO, AND HAT NAI YANG

Once known to harbor the most beautiful and undeveloped beaches on Phuket, the island's northwestern shore has exploded with luxury resorts over the past decade. **Hat Surin** is no exception, though there are some cheaper guesthouses closer to the highway. Unfortunately, swimming is not recommended here due to strong winds and heavy surf. **Surin Sweet Hotel ❺**, 107/8 Moo 3, on the beach road, has large rooms with sea views and top-notch amenities. The higher the floor, the less the street noise and the better the view. (☎270 863; fax 270 865; surinhotel@hotmail.com. Rooms 1700฿; low-season 400฿.) Outdoor restaurants crowd the beach area with Western and Thai offerings at similar prices (dishes 80-180฿). On the southern end of Surin Beach, **Diver's Place ❷** is a beachfront pub with a friendly expat crowd (beers 60฿). Diver is a good person to ask about the surf.

If you bring your own food, a towel, and a book, attractive **Ao Bang Tao** makes a decent daytrip, especially between May and July, before the heavy rains hit but after the crowds have skedaddled. Ao Bang Tao is dominated by two resorts that monopolize access to the water. Squeezed between the two beaches on the road from Surin to Ao Bang Tao, **Bangtao Lagoon Bungalows ❺**, 72/3 Moo 3 T. Cherngtalay, has compact, comfortable huts with a blue patina and marble floors. The bungalows range from standard to deluxe. Ask the bus driver from Phuket Town to drop you off here or you may never find it. (☎324 260; http://phuket-bangtaolagoon.com. Bungalows 680-1780฿; low-season 400-1000฿. Extra bed 200฿.)

Sirinat National Park, further north at **Hat Nai Yang,** is a park spanning hundreds of kilometers of coconut trees and coral reefs. In the rainy season, Hat Nai Yang has Phuket's most dangerous riptides. The **Visitors Office** is near the entrance. (☎327 407. Open daily 8:30am-4:30pm.) It's possible to rent **tents ❷** (2-to-3-person tent 200฿; camping 20฿). **Park bungalows ❹** on the beach are popular among Thai vacationers (600-1200฿).

HAT KAMALA

Escape to quiet **Hat Kamala** on the way to Hat Surin from Phuket Town (*songthaew* 20฿). There are no luxury hotels and the beaches are decent. Rooms at **Benjaim Resort ❺**, 83 Moo 3, have ocean views, A/C, TV, and hot water. While regular rates are beyond the reach of most budget travelers, low-season discounts make this place a steal. (☎385 145; www.phuketdir.com/benjaminresort. Rooms 1200-1500฿; low-season 350-500฿.) To get to the spotless **Malinee House ❺**, 74/7 Moo 3, follow the beach road from the south end of the beach until it curves inland; the restaurant and guesthouse are on the right. An Internet cafe is below. (☎324 094. A/C singles and doubles 1000฿; low-season 500฿.) The excellent **Gourmet Restaurant ❸**, at the corner where Moo 3 turns inland, serves delicious Thai and Western dishes and great beach views. (Dishes 80-210฿. Open daily 8am-11pm.)

HAT RAWAI AND AO CHALONG

Squashed into the southeastern tip of Phuket, **Hat Rawai** caters mostly to locals. The beach's narrow strip of sand and muddy water render it unappealing; try its more attractive neighbor **Hat Nai Han**. Hat Nai Han slows down considerably during rainy season, and Rawai shuts down altogether. At Hat Rawai, **Pornmae Bungalows ❸**, 58/1 Wiset Rd., inside the hair salon opposite the central part of the beach, has simple rooms with fridges. (☎/fax 381 300. Singles and doubles 300-400฿.)

Pleasant **Ao Chalong,** north of Hat Rawai on the island's southeastern side, is the largest bay on Phuket. Because of its size and shallow, muddy waters, the bay is primarily used for docking. Though the bay makes for mediocre swimming, it's a good place to stay if you want to learn more about the active Andaman Sea yachting culture. A good place to meet other sailors is **Friendship Beach ❺**, 27/1 Soi Mittrapap, about 2km north of Hat Rawai toward Phuket Town on the southern side of the bay, across from the Phuket Shell Museum. Friendly and relaxed, it has bungalows, a **restaurant ❸**, Sunday jam sessions, a pool table, cable TV, and Internet for 1฿ per min. (☎381 281; fax 381 424. Bungalows 800฿; low-season 400฿.)

SIMILAN ISLANDS ☎076

While the southern Thailand backpacker superhighway swallows up other islands, Ko Similan, a national park consisting of nine small islands, remains the untouched virgin beauty of the Andaman Sea. Relative inaccessibility and higher expenses have helped preserve Ko Similan both below and above water. Due to its outstanding 30m underwater visibility and magnificent coral gardens, the Similan Archipelago is considered one of the best deep-water dive sites in the world. Though primarily known for diving and snorkeling, Ko Similan has spectacularly fine beaches, majestic rock formations, and fascinating wildlife. If time and budget are not an issue, Ko Similan is worth the trip (only open Nov.-Apr.).

TRANSPORTATION. There are three reasonable ways to access the Similan Islands by boat, either from **Ban Thap Lamu** pier (3hr., 8am, 2100฿) closest to Phang-Nga Town, from **Amphoe Khuru Buri** pier (3hr.) farther north, or from Phuket (1½hr., 8am, 700฿). **Met Sine Tours** (☎443 276), at Ban Thap Lamu is the most reliable booking agent. In Phuket, contact **Songserm Travel Center** (☎076 222 570). Keep in mind that rough seas might result in cancellation or a nauseating journey.

PRACTICAL INFORMATION. The nine islands 60km off the west coast of Phang-Nga are numbered from north to south. The second-largest island, **Ko Miang**, is where boats dock and is the only island that allows overnighters. It's also the site of the **Visitors Center, Park Headquarters,** and the only drinking water. Irregular boat trips between the islands cost 250฿ per person. It's best to contact the **Similan National Park Office** (☎411 913) at Thap Lamu pier for questions regarding transportation and practicalities. There's a 40฿ admission fee to the park, collected at Ko Miang upon arrival. Services on the Similan Islands are more than limited—they're non-existent.

ACCOMMODATIONS AND FOOD. Ko Miang has the only accommodations, a **campground** offering both **tents ❷** (150฿) and **bungalows ❺** (4 beds 600฿). There's a small fee for those who bring their own tent. Elsewhere in the Similan Islands, camping and campfires are prohibited. If you're not camping, it's necessary to book in advance through the Park Headquarters. Ko Miang also has the only restaurant, a rather over-priced affair, so bring your own food.

ACTIVITIES. From November through February, sea turtles lay eggs on the beach at **Ko Hu Yong. Khao Lak,** on the mainland, is the launching point for tours exploring the underwater landscape. A typical dive leaves from Phuket, lasts four days/three nights, and includes 10 dives (10,000-20,000฿). If you're not interested in diving, there's superb snorkeling and hiking (with fantastic views) and, well, whatever else one fancies to do in a timeless paradise.

KO PHI PHI DON ☎075

The secret is out. Beautiful Ko Phi Phi Don (generally known as Ko Phi Phi)—once an untouristed island dotted with swaying palms and isolated spits of sand surrounded by shimmering turquoise waters—is now second only to Phuket as a destination for *farang* in southern Thailand. Packed with backpackers, bikinis, bars, and booze, Ko Phi Phi is no longer the place to come to get away from it all—tourists seem to out-

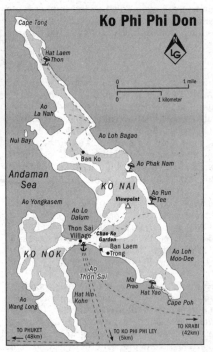

number locals about five to one. Visitors will now find street after street filled with restaurants, travel agencies, and guesthouses. However, the commercialization of the island still has not entirely destroyed its natural beauty—you just have to look through more people and construction to see it. The beaches are still clean and well maintained, and the ban on cars and motorbikes means teenagers on bicycles are the main road hazard. Nearby, the island preserve of Ko Phi Phi Ley, accessible by boat from Ko Phi Phi Don, provides a somewhat more serene atmosphere, although it too has suffered, especially since its role as the title character in the 2000 Leonardo DiCaprio film *The Beach*. Ko Phi Phi may no longer be a secluded island paradise, but it still promises a relaxing, enjoyable visit.

◨ TRANSPORTATION

To get to Ko Phi Phi, leave from Ko Lanta, Krabi, or Phuket; **ferries** depart regularly to and from Ko Phi Phi and these destinations. Some ferries may not operate May to September due to rough seas. From Ko Phi Phi's **Thon Sai Pier,** boats head to Ko Lanta (2hr.; 11:30am, 2pm; 200฿); Krabi (1½hr.; 9am, 1:30, 2:30pm; low season no 2:30pm boat; 200฿); and Phuket (1½hr.; 9am, 1:30, 2:30pm; low season no 1:30pm boat; 250฿). Tickets can be purchased at any of the travel agencies located in Thon Sai Village. **Boats** to uninhabited Ko Phi Phi Ley depart from the pier. It is best to hire **longtail** boats for more remote beaches (prices vary, generally 150฿ per hr.).

◪ ⁊ ORIENTATION AND PRACTICAL INFORMATION

Shaped like a lopsided dumbbell, Ko Phi Phi is small and devoid of roads. It's easy to walk the entire island, save the high cliffs. The main port of call is pretty but polluted **Ao Thon Sai,** nestled in the narrow part of the island, where travelers come to eat, check email, and party. Only a decade ago this area was relatively undeveloped, but now a slapdash network of businesses have turned Ao Thon Sai into a busy, tourist-oriented village. This narrow isthmus connects the two main chunks of island, Ko Nok to the west (left as you exit the pier) and the much larger Ko Nai to the east. On the other side of the village, beautiful **Ao Lo Dalam** has several pricey bungalows. Smaller, less-developed beaches ring the island's outer peninsulas, the most popular of which is **Hat Yao** (Long Beach), east of Ao Thon Sai on Ko Nai. The more rugged interior affords stellar views of the bays and surrounding islands.

Tourist Office: TAT in Krabi serves Ko Phi Phi.

Tours: Ao Thon Sai agencies arrange trips to Ko Phi Phi Ley and boat/train/bus combos to Bangkok and Malaysia. **Maya Tour & Travel** (☎ 612 403), in Tonsai Bay, offers tours, including a good snorkeling excursion. From the pier, take a right; it's 20m on the right.

Currency Exchange: The **Siam Commercial Bank** in Ao Thon Sai exchanges cash and gives credit card advances. Open daily 9:30am-7:30pm. Scattered **ATMs** in the village.

Local Tourist Police: (☎622 369), off the pier in Ao Thon Sai. English spoken. Open daily 8:30am-7:30pm. **24hr. police booth** past the Chao Khao Lodge in Ao Thon Sai.

Medical Services: Phi Phi Islands Hospital (☎622 151), in Ao Thon Sai, to the left of the pier. Offers basic medical services and relief from swimming injuries. English spoken. Open **24hr.** The closest full-service hospitals are in Krabi and Phuket.

Telephones: Private travel agencies in Ao Thon Sai offer expensive connections. Unless it's an emergency, wait until you get back onto the mainland.

Internet Access: It's hard to throw a coconut and *not* hit a computer with Internet in Thon Sai. Their abundance doesn't make them cheap—the going rate is 2฿ per min.

ACCOMMODATIONS

Ko Phi Phi's bungalows are plentiful, but vary widely in price and quality; guesthouses follow suit. Generally, the island is more expensive than its neighbors, but rooms are cheaper on the edges of the village and on the more isolated beaches. It pays to explore the outer rims of the island, where fewer mainstream backpackers venture. Don't trust the touts who meet your boat at the pier and tell you there are no accommodations below 300-400฿ on the island—if you go with one of them, you're probably paying too much. Low-season discounts up to 50% are available, but be ready to haggle for them. Accommodations are listed by beach.

AO LO DALAM AND AO THON SAI. For budget travelers, there is a row of cheap accommodations on the east side of the village. From the pier, turn right, walk about 100m, and then turn left at the bronze statue of the big fish. Follow the path past the V Shop, a **24hr.** minimart. On your left you'll find a number of restaurants and tattoo parlors that double as **guesthouses** offering spartan rooms with private baths for 250-400฿ per night. On your right you'll approach **The Rock Backpacker ❷**, with the cheapest beds in town. Rooms are bare and hardly large enough to hold the bed. All baths are shared and have cold water. (☎612 402. Singles 150฿; doubles 300฿.) If you keep walking down the path, you'll reach a blue sign on the right denoting **Rim Na Villa ❸**, a moderately priced set of bungalows with private baths. (☎618 086. Basic bungalows with fan 400฿, with A/C 700฿.) If you turn left at the Rim Na Villa sign instead of right, you'll cross a small wooden bridge and, 20m later, reach the unmarked, unlabeled set of guest rooms called **Ammarin House ❸**. The fan rooms are spotless, reasonably priced, and come with private bath. (Rooms 400-600฿, low-season 200-250฿.) Popular on the island, the slightly upscale **Charlie Beach Resort ❺** is located on the quieter and cleaner Ao Lo Dalam, across the isthmus from the pier. It has bungalows with great sea views, as well as a lively **restaurant ❷**. Bungalows in the back are a bit noisier. (☎620 615; www.ppcharlie.com. Bungalows with fan 750฿, with A/C 1200-1400฿.)

HAT HIN KOHN AND LAEM HIM. Just southeast of Ao Thon Sai, a path by a rocky hill leads to flat Hat Hin Kohn, a long stretch of sand generously sprinkled with bungalows. The beach is decent, but far from the island's best. **Andaman Guest House ❹** has new rooms that are plain but fairly clean. (Singles and doubles 500-600฿.) The similarly named but more professional **Andaman Resort ❹**, at the end of the beach, has clean, white bungalows that occupy a quiet spot by the island's sole primary school. (Bungalows 500-800฿, with A/C 1000-2900฿.) Heading right from the pier next to the coast takes you along a paved walkway and around a small promontory known as Laem Him. Past Laem Him is a stretch of quieter beach, which is completely overrun with longtail boats. **Gypsy 1 ❸**, inland from the path after the mosque and about 100m from the shore, has clean and basic bungalows with baths at rock-bottom prices by Phi Phi standards, as does **Gypsy 2 ❸**, 50m farther on. (☎01 229 1674. Bungalows 350-600฿.)

⬛ MA PRAO AND HAT YAO (LONG BEACH). The best option in the area is just before Long Beach on a lush promontory called Ma Prao. ⬛**Ma Prao Resort ❸** has charming wood and bamboo huts gathered against the hill only a stone's throw from the water—like staying in a jungle tree house with a tropical pool only meters away. The restaurant has excellent food, drink, and music. (☎622 485. Basic bungalows 300-800฿.) Just over the hill, past Ma Prao, is Hat Yao, commonly known as Long Beach. It has Ko Phi Phi's best sand and swimming, although the utter lack of nightlife keeps partiers away. Hat Yao's good mix of accommodations complements its pleasant beach. It's possible to walk here from Ao Thon Sai by continuing past Hat Kin Kohn through some rocky jungle, but the 1hr. walk is tedious. Longtail boats (100฿) from Ao Thon Sai's pier are more convenient. The most wallet-friendly accommodation is the cheerful, expat-run **Long Beach Resort ❷**, offering little more than four walls and a bed, but with a smile. (☎612 217. Singles and doubles 150-350฿.) Farther up the beach, away from Ma Prao, is the pricey but pleasant **Phi-Phi Natural Resort ❺**. Spacious, well-equipped bungalows offer water views. (☎07 622 3636; www.phiphinatural.com. Bungalows with A/C 1400-3800฿.)

📷 🎵 FOOD AND ENTERTAINMENT

Ko Phi Phi offers an outstanding range of international cuisine as a result of its expat population, many of whom have started businesses on the island. Homesick tourists munch on faux Italian, Mexican, and Swedish fare in restaurants all over the island. The cream of the crop is ⬛**Cosmo Resto ❸**, an Italian restaurant with exceptional handmade pasta. Run by an Italian expat, the restaurant is only open for dinner and closes on random days of the week for preparation. When it's open, the tiny, unassuming place is one of Thailand's best restaurants. (Dishes 120-380฿. Open roughly 5 days per week.) The **Lemongrass Restaurant ❷**, off the main drag in Ao Thon on Sat., is one of the only places to get good Thai food. (Rice dishes 60-80฿. Curries 70-120฿. Open daily 9am-11pm.) **Pee Pee Bakery ❷**, offers delicious donuts and cakes, plus cheap Western and Thai dishes. The film showings are a huge favorite. (One location on the pier road, and another on the path to The Rock Backpacker at the east end of the village. Pastries 5-20฿. Dishes 40-120฿. Italian wine 40฿ per glass. Open daily 7am-10pm.) **Garlic 1992 Restaurant ❷**, proud of its relative old age (as compared to other Phi Phi restaurants), sure loves its garlic. Everything, Thai and Western, is spicy and delicious. (Located just past V Shop in the village. Watch the board at the entrance for pizza-plus-beer specials. Dishes 40-90฿.) On the other side of the island, Ma Prao Bungalows has a charming **restaurant ❷**, which serves quality Thai food. Plenty of pancake stalls on the streets in Thon Sai Village serve up a modified version of *roti* (20฿) for tourist consumption.

By night, Ao Thon Sai becomes an impressive hotbed of nightlife activity. Backpackers wander about, mingling more as alcohol makes the world friendlier. **Jordan's Irish Bar** relinquishes anything Irish in favor of music that will make *farang* wave their hands in the air. The **Rolling Stoned Bar** blasts chill music, much of it live, until sunrise. The **Reggae Bar** has a large dance floor and a boxing ring featuring nightly matches (around 10pm). **Carlito's Bar,** on the walkway toward Long Beach, has live entertainment. Look for drink specials at all of the above bars.

🏊 WATER SPORTS

Ko Phi Phi's waters are so clear you almost don't need to bother with a mask to check out the marine life. **Bamboo Island** and **Mosquito Island** are famous dive sites and there are many dive shops and tour agents extremely eager to serve you. PADI certification courses generally cost 10,000฿ (far more than Ko Tao). **Visa Diving Center** is one of the best. **Hippo Divers**, an expat-run outfit located a quick left from the pier, offers a range of area dives for 800-3200฿. (☎618 200; www.hippodivers.com. Open daily 10am-9:30pm.) In addition to diving, snorkeling is also popular and far cheaper (usually 500฿ for a daytrip including lunch and gear). Longtail boats provide for a more intimate, enjoyable experience than the larger motor boats. **Maya Tour & Travel** (p. 372) runs quality half-day and full-day tours.

🏝 DAYTRIP FROM KO PHI PHI DON: KO PHI PHI LEY

Getting to Ko Phi Phi Ley from Ko Phi Phi Don usually involves some sort of organized tour. Plenty of Ao Thon Sai agencies arrange daytrips to the island, but individual longtail boat tours (600฿) around the island cost less.

Five years ago, "The Beach" was filmed on Ko Phi Phi Ley. The real reason to visit the island is for the beauty that made it such a spectacular location in the first place.

While the limestone cliffs practically enclosing white-sand **Ao Maya** make the island stunning, the row of longtails and wandering tourists mean that it hardly ever lives up to expectations from the film. Both Ao Maya and Ko Phi Phi Ley are really just another stop on any snorkeling or day tour from Ko Phi Phi Don and are nothing to get too excited about. Tours generally include a look at the prehistoric paintings in the **Viking Cave** at the northeast point on the island as well.

KRABI ☎075

The last bastion of serene beach beauty in southern Thailand is being invaded by droves of backpackers, and the town of Krabi is the staging ground for their assault. Tourists come here because the beaches of Ao Nang, Rai Ley, and Ko Lanta are within a short commute. The town of Krabi itself is little more than a necessary transit point, but it has a mellow vibe all of its own, and the emergence of excellent budget accommodations more than justifies an overnight stay.

🚌 TRANSPORTATION

Buses: The **bus station** (☎611 804) is 5km north of town along Utarakit Rd. Buses to: **Bangkok** (12hr., 8 per day 8am-5:30pm, 378-710฿); **Hat Yai** (5hr., every hr. 9am-3:20pm, 173฿); **Phuket** (5hr., every hr. 9am-5pm, 117฿); **Satun** (5hr.; 11am, 1pm; 175฿); **Surat Thani** (4½hr., every hr. 9:30am-1:30pm, 80฿; A/C: 3½hr., 5 per day 7am-1pm, 120฿); **Trang** (2½hr., every 2hr. 9am-5pm, 90฿).

Minivans: Private travel agencies operate A/C minibus service to various towns in Thailand and Malaysia. They are the primary mode of transit to **Ko Lanta** when ferries aren't running. They usually run every hr. 7am-7pm, but during the low season service drops to 4 times per day (2hr., 100฿). Minivans pick up at most hotels in the Chao Fah area; inquire at your hotel or a nearby travel agency.

Ferries: Longtail boats leave from **Chao Fah Pier** on Kongka Rd. for **Hat Rai Lay** (30min., 8am-5pm, 70฿) and **Ko Lanta** (2½hr.; 10:30am, 1:30pm; 200฿). From the shiny new **Passenger Marine Port** 5km south of town, **express boats** go to **Ko Phi Phi** (1½hr.; 10:30am, 2:30pm; 200฿). In low season, service decreases and Ko Lanta ferry service shuts down altogether. Tourist offices and travel agencies have up-to-date boat schedules and information.

Local Transportation: Songthaew run up and down Utarakit Rd. and go to: the **bus station** (20฿ from the center of town); **Ao Nang** (after 6pm 50฿); the **Shell Cemetery** (16-20฿); **Wat Tham Sua** (20฿); other places near Krabi. **Tuk-tuks** go to the center of town from: the new passenger pier (30฿); the bus terminal (50฿); the airport (100฿).

Rentals: Travel agencies and guesthouses on Utarakit Rd. rent **motorbikes** for 150-200฿ per day. Some also rent **jeeps** (1200-1500฿ per day).

✴ 🛈 ORIENTATION AND PRACTICAL INFORMATION

Central Krabi is compact and easily navigable by foot. **Utarakit Road,** the city's main street, runs parallel to the **Krabi River** and is home to most services. Parallel to Utarakit Rd. and one block over, **Maharat Road** has shops and eateries. Boats to Hat Rai Lay and Ko Lanta leave from **Chao Fah Pier** on **Kongka Road,** which branches off Utarakit Rd. and runs along the river. **Chaofa Road,** running from the pier past Utarakit Rd. is home to several *farang*-oriented hotels and restaurants.

Tourist Offices: TAT (☎612 740), on Utarakit Rd. near Chaofa Rd. Good maps. English spoken. Open daily 8:30am-4:30pm.

Tours: For boat tickets, go to **PP Family** on Chao Fah Pier (☎612 463). The company operates most ferry services from Krabi. Open daily 7:30am-9pm.

Currency Exchange: Several banks line Utarakit Rd., including **Bangkok Bank,** 147 Utarakit. Open M-F 8:30am-3:30pm.

Markets: A market sets up on Sukhon Rd. across from City Hotel. Open daily 8am-11pm.

Police: (☎637 208), 500m past the post office. Little English spoken.

Medical Services: Krabi Hospital (☎611 227), on Utarakit Rd., 2km north of town. Some English spoken. No credit cards. Open **24hr.**

Internet Access: All along Utarakit Rd. in cafes and guesthouses. The going rate is 1฿ per min. or 40฿ per hr., with a 10฿ min.

Post Office: 190 Utarakit Rd. (☎611 497), on top of the hill on the left. *Poste Restante.* Open M-F 8:30am-4:30pm, Sa 9am-noon.

Postal Code: 81000.

🏠 ACCOMMODATIONS

Krabi has a good selection of budget choices, most of which lie near the pier along **Utarakit Road.** Room prices are generally 100-200฿ cheaper in the low season.

▨ K Guest House, on Chaofa Rd., 1 block down from the intersection with Utarakit Rd. A very clean, comfortable guesthouse. Wood-paneled upstairs rooms conjure up images of a tropical log cabin. Singles and doubles 200-250฿, with private bath 300฿. ❷

Ban Chaofa, 20/1 Chaofa Rd. (☎630 359; banchaofa@hotmail.com), just past K Guest House and across the street. This small, elegant hotel is worth visiting just for the bathrooms, which offer full-pressure faucets and hotter-than-hot showers. Add, the hotel manager, will keep you entertained. Big-screen TV downstairs. Rooms with A/C 500-800฿; low-season rooms with fan 300฿, rooms with A/C 400-500฿. ❹

Chan-Cha-Lay Guest House, 55 Utarakit Rd. (☎620 952), on the slope uphill. This recently opened guesthouse is already one of the hippest digs in town, with ultra-clean, bright rooms sporting showers. Popular restaurant and super-friendly staff to boot. The airy blue interior brings the ocean to you. Shared baths. Laundry. **Internet.** Reservations recommended. Prices may rise upon completion of renovations. Singles and doubles 200฿; doubles with twin beds 250฿. ❸

Grand Tower Hotel, 9 Chaofa Rd. (☎621 456), at the intersection with Utarakit Rd. Multi-storied, it's not your typical guesthouse, but it and its bar are popular with those waiting for the next ferry. Plain, somewhat stuffy rooms with double mattresses. International phones, **Internet,** and fax service. Singles and doubles 150฿, with bath 300฿, with A/C 500฿; doubles with twin beds and bath 400฿, with A/C 700฿. ❷

City Hotel, 15/2-3 Sukhon Rd. (☎621 280), between Utarakit and Maharat Rd. in the heart of downtown, a block from Utarakit Rd. Spacious, well-furnished rooms, all with cable TV and phone. Singles and doubles with fan 400฿, with A/C 550-650฿; newer rooms with hot water 700-900฿. ❸

Siboya Guest House, 69 Utarakit Rd. (☎623 561). Modestly sized, cheap rooms are cozy, with funky, fresh decor. Singles and doubles 120-150฿; low-season 100-120฿. ❷

⬛ FOOD

There are two **night markets** ❶, one opposite the City Hotel (open until 9pm) and one by the pier. Several *farang*-friendly restaurants and cheap food stalls with everything from Thai food to grilled cheese cluster on **Kongka Road,** just north of the pier. For an interesting dining experience, try **Ruenmai Thai** ❷ on Maharat Rd., 2km from town past the hospital (motorcycle taxi 30฿). This huge outdoor restaurant has tables surrounded by jungle-like vegetation. For 60฿, try the blissful coconut-cream prawn soup with *pak mieng* or edible ferns with fish. (Open daily 10am-10pm.) The **restaurant** ❷ in the Ban Chaofa hotel, which specializes in pizza and pasta dishes, also serves a delicious vegetarian *pad thai.* (Thai dishes 40-70฿. Italian dishes 130-170฿. Open daily 7am-10pm.) **Corner Restaurant** ❷, between Ban Chaofa and K Guest House on Chaofa Rd., has great daily curry specials for 70฿. (Thai dishes 40-100฿. Western dishes 80-180฿. Open daily 9am-11pm.) **Kwan Restaurant** ❷, 30 Kongkha Rd., serves reliable and affordable Thai and Western meals and shakes. (Entrees 40-100฿. Open daily 7:30am-9pm; low season 7:30am-5pm.)

⬛ SIGHTS

Krabi's most impressive sight is **Wat Tham Sua,** 8km north of town along Utarakit Rd. An operating monastery comprised of monks, nuns, and tourists, the *wat* is best known for its **Tiger Cave.** Legend has it that a large tiger once lived here, and its footsteps adorn the *wat's* entrance (donation requested). Apart from a fairly large Buddha statue, the cave itself isn't much to see. Outside, stairs by the rear of the monastery lead up the mountain (30-45min.) to a pair of **Buddha's footprints.** Enlightenment isn't easy; be prepared for a grueling climb. A peripheral benefit to the hike is a fantastic view of Krabi and the surrounding area from the top. A second set of steps in the rear leads you to a promontory overlooking a valley within a preserved national forest, a good picnic site. Utarakit Rd. *songthaew* (15min., 10฿) drop you off at an access road 2km from the *wat.* Otherwise, walk or take a motorcycle taxi (5min., 10฿) to the entrance.

⬛ DAYTRIP FROM KRABI

The world-renowned beaches near Krabi are some of Thailand's most popular, so if you're planning on staying at Ao Nang or Hat Rai Lay, it's best to bypass Krabi and head straight for the sand. Locals heartily embrace *farang* arrivals, mostly for the sake of their wallets. A regional festival in November even celebrates the coming of a prosperous tourist season. Still, a supreme mellowness prevails.

KHLONG THOM

To get to the trail, take a motorbike from Krabi or a songthaew to Khlong Thom. Mr. Koyou at the Krabi Bird Club, 24 Phetkasem Rd., will haul tourists around in his pickup truck (300฿). Contact him by calling the park's tourist office (☎622 124); TAT can also track him down. If hiring a motorcycle taxi from Khlong Thom (100฿), be sure to arrange return transportation.

The **Khao Nawe Choochee Lowland Forest** is one of the last remaining forests of its kind in Thailand. Among the 290-plus bird species that nest in the forest is *Pitta gurneyi*, a brightly colored, ground-dwelling bird of which only 150 remain. The **Thung Tieo Nature Trail** (2.7km) traverses some of Thailand's most lush and undisturbed slices of nature. Hop into the natural pool or hot spring for relaxation.

HAT RAI LAY AND HAT PHRA NANG ☎075

With spectacular limestone cliffs dropping onto sand beaches and luminous, turquoise waters, Hat Rai Lay has become a haven for both climbers and beach lovers. For those who prefer that their feet stay on the ground, Hat Rai Lay also offers hiking trails, a mellow nightlife, and peaceful beaches, while Hat Phra Nang's caves provide hours of exploring potential.

■ **ORIENTATION.** Hat Rai Lay is actually two beaches, **Hat Rai Lay East** and **Hat Rai Lay West,** which occupy opposite sides of a peninsula that juts out into the sea. Rai Lay East is little more than a littered mangrove forest, but Rai Lay West's beach is a good deal nicer. The best way to get to Hat Rai Lay is by **longtail boat** docking at Hat Rai Lay East from Ao Nang (20min.; shared 50฿, chartered 200฿) or Krabi (30min., 70฿/300฿). In low season, Ao Nang becomes inaccessible by longtail boat; they instead go to Ao Nam Mao (15min., 40฿/200฿), a short *songthaew* ride from Ao Nang (15min., 10฿). The east side of the peninsula has a few budget accommodations, climbing schools, mangrove trees, and the gorgeous and largely undisturbed **Hat Phra Nang.** To get to Hat Phra Nang from Hat Rai Lay East, with your back to the boats, turn left and walk to the end of the beach; a dirt path to your right snakes to Hat Phra Nang. Hat Rai Lay West can be reached easily by cutting through Sand Sea Bungalows or Rai Lay Bay Bungalows.

■ **ACCOMMODATIONS AND FOOD.** Finding good deals on Hat Rai Lay between October and May can be more difficult than scaling its toughest climb. During the low season, however, prices plummet by 50 percent or more—if you're looking for a little quiet and a good deal to boot, this is the time to come. De facto segregation keeps backpackers on Hat Rai Lay East. **Ya-Ya Bungalow ❸**, the most popular among budget travelers, has the best off-beach location and a lively restaurant. (☎622 593. Closed in low season.) On the northern end of Hat Rai Lay East, **Viewpoint Bungalow ❸** has clean, modern bungalows with enormous windows that put the "view" in Viewpoint. (☎622 588. The only **Internet** access on the beach. Bungalows with fan 400฿, with A/C 1200-2000฿; low-season 200฿/400-700฿.) **Diamond Bungalow ❸** has some of the cheapest accommodations on the island. (Singles and doubles 400฿, with bath 500฿, with A/C 900-1200฿; low-season 200฿, with A/C 400-600฿.) Just before Viewpoint Bungalow, coming from the dock, **CoCo Hotel ❸** has cheap, rustic bungalows with fans. (400฿, low-season 100฿.) Inland from the beach, **Railay Highland Resort ❸** has peaceful bungalows away from the hubbub of the beach. (☎621 730. Bungalows with fan 750฿, low-season 200฿.)

Hat Rai Lay West has more upscale accommodations. **Rai Lay Village Resort ❺** charges twice as much as Hat Rai Lay East digs for posh bungalows with nicer

baths and landscaping. (☎ 622 578. Bungalows 1500-3000฿, low-season 500-1200฿.)
The unbelievably expensive **Dusit Rayavadee Resort ❺** dominates Hat Phra Nang,
though there never seems to be anyone staying there. It's much more practical to
find cheaper accommodations on Hat Rai Lay East and daytrip to Hat Phra Nang.

The hotels all have their own restaurants, and most of them serve similar, reasonably priced Thai and Western dishes and beach views. After a hard day of
climbing, many travelers flock to **CoCo Restaurant ❷** on the northern part of Hat
Rai Lay East for tasty Thai dishes. (Chicken wrapped in steamed leaves 60฿. Open
daily 8am-10:30pm.) **Cholay Pancakes ❶,** in a booth outside Ya-Ya Bungalow, serves
delicious *roti* for 15-30฿. (Open daily 9am-midnight.)

◙ ▣ SIGHTS AND ENTERTAINMENT. The Rai Lay beaches and environs have
become the **rock-climbing** capital of Southeast Asia, especially for beginners, and
several rock-climbing schools have popped up to meet the increasing demand.
Prices are the same everywhere. **Krabi Rock Climbing,** on Hat Rai Lay East, is well
known for its friendly staff. (☎ 01 676 0642. Half-day course 800฿, 1-day 1800฿, 3-
day 5000฿. Equipment rental also available.) **Hot Rock Climbing** (☎ 01 677 3727),
next to CoCo Restaurant on Hat Rai Lay East, is also popular. Don't let inexperi-
ence scare you—tons of others are first-timers too.

Adventures closer to sea level await you on Hat Phra Nang. Extending past the
water, dagger-like stalagmites protect **Princess Cave,** which can be explored by
land or sea with a flashlight. About halfway down the dirt path to Hat Phra Nang
from Hat Rai Lay East, another dirt path leads to a few mountain viewpoints and a
lagoon best visited at high tide. Bring sturdy footwear, expendable clothing, and
company for the challenging climb to the top. Closer to Hat Rai Lay East beach, a
hidden path leads to the popular **Diamond Cave,** whose walls sparkle with the precious stone. On the road to Railay Highland Resort behind Rai Lay East Village, a
protected, artificially lit cave called **Tham Pranangnai** is 100m long and impressively
high. (Open daily during daylight hours. Admission 20฿.)

Nights on Hat Rai Lay bring together opposite tourist factions: beach bums and
hard-core climbing/hiking/diving types. Everyone achieves equal party status
under the moon, relaxing at **Yaya's Bar, Last Bar,** or the **beachfront,** where fire dancers sometimes light up the beach to pulsing music.

AO NANG ☎ 075

Ao Nang's accessibility by car gives it a completely different atmosphere from
either secluded Rai Lay or Phang-Nga. With brightly colored shops, beachfront
hotels, and a pleasant boardwalk perfect for a sunset stroll, Ao Nang has a pleasant holiday feel. The bustle dies out past the Phra Nang Inn. From there, you can
walk down a dirt road into forested seclusion. Alternatively, rent a bike and zoom
through rice paddies, villages, and the ubiquitous waving kids.

Sea Canoe Krabi (☎ 612 740), near Gift's Bungalows, offers half-day (500-800฿)
and full-day (800-1200฿) self-paddled trips along the coast as well as equipment
rental. A guided trip, including meals, fruit, and water, costs 1200-1600฿. Rent
mountain bikes (30฿ per hr.) at **Ao Nang Adventure Travel and Tour** on the corner
before the main shops, coming from Krabi. Ask for a map. Full-day snorkeling
tours of the nearby islands by speedboat cost 1000-1200฿, but only 300฿ by slower
and noisier longtail boat. Low-season speedboat discounts (500-600฿) are available from **J. Mansion** (see below). **Nosy Parker's Elephant Trekking and River Camp**
(☎ 637 464) offers elephant treks (700฿) and half-day tours (1600฿).

On the road that runs past the beach, there are **moneychangers, ATMs,** a **minimar-
ket,** restaurants, and **tour offices.** There is a **police** substation on the town's main
road across from PK Mansion, just before it hits the beach. (☎ 695 163. Open daily

8am-midnight.) White Krabi-bound **songthaew** crawl down the beach road every 5min. during daylight hours (30฿ before 6pm, 50฿ thereafter).

Accommodations in Ao Nang vary, and many lodgings offer services besides room rental. **Blue Bayou ❸**, in the quiet outskirts of town, has kayak rentals (200฿ per 2hr.) and a volleyball court. The **restaurant ❸** serves Thai and Western cuisine. (☎637 148. Single and double bungalows with fan 350-500฿, with A/C 750฿; low-season 200-400฿/500฿.) If you happen to hit Ao Nang in the low season, you'll find some fabulous rates. The twin steals of **J. Mansion** and **J. Hotel ❹**, 302 Moo 2, are located about a 2min. walk from the beach. Rooms are big, clean, and come with hot shower, minifridge, and satellite TV. Try to get a fourth-floor room at J. Hotel for sea views. (☎695 128; www.krabidir.com/j_mansion. Fan rooms 600฿, with A/C 800฿; low-season 300฿/400฿.) **PK Mansion ❹**, located on the same *soi*, has similar rooms at similar prices. Another great low-season deal is **For You House ❺**, 245/11-12 Moo 2, which has hotel-style rooms with A/C, minibar, satellite TV, and hot showers. Get off the *songthaew* at Henry's Collection, and walk behind it. (☎637 805. 600฿, low-season 300฿.) Other cheap places are on the same *soi* as For You.

The best Thai food from the beachfront restaurants is available at **Ao Nang Cuisine ❷**, in the middle of the strip. (Thai entrees 45-75฿. Western dishes 80-200฿. Open daily 9am-11pm.) **Last Cafe ❷**, at the end of Ao Nang Beach, after the road becomes a dirt trail, is only open in the high season. (Muesli with fruit and yogurt 30฿. Omelettes 40฿. Thai noodle soup 30฿. Open daily 6:30am-midnight.) The ideally situated **Poda Restaurant ❷**, in Felix Phra Nang Inn in the circular building, is an alternative to bungalow basics. The green curry soup with shrimp is exceptional. (Most dishes 70-90฿. Open daily 7am-10pm.) Italian restaurants line the beach road. Among these, **Azzurra Ristorante-Pizzeria ❷** stands out for its homemade pasta, fresh bread, and focaccia with cheese, tomatoes, and lettuce (80฿). Mouth-watering homemade tiramisu (50฿) is a must-have. (Open daily 7am-11pm.)

KO LANTA YAI   ☎075

Ko Lanta Yai is an up-and-coming island on the *ko*-hopping backpacker trail. Because the island's industry has yet to be completely shelved in favor of tourism, there's a local flavor here that is lacking on tourist hotspots like Ko Samui. While the northern part of the island is fairly developed at this point, quieter, more serene parts can be found to the south, especially in the area surrounding the national marine park. During the high season, **boats** arrive regularly from Krabi at Ko Lanta Yai's Ban Sala Dan Pier (2½hr.; 10:30am, 1:30pm, return 8am; 200฿) at the northern tip of the island. Boats also leave from Ko Phi Phi for Ko Lanta (1½hr.; 10am, 1pm; 200฿). Otherwise, minivans depart year-round from Krabi and connect via ferry with Ko Lanta (2hr.; 11am, 1, 4pm; 200฿). **Ban Sala Dan** is the island's largest town, with tour operators, a police booth, a post office, **Internet** cafes, banks, a health center, and other conveniences. Much of the town closes down during the low season, however; during this time you are generally relegated to your resort due to meager transportation, dining, and entertainment options.

Outside of Ban Sala Dan, the island is extremely spread out. Most resorts offer free pickup from minivan and ferry drop-off points, as well as a free return, as long as you purchase your ticket through them. Because the resort trucks are the best mode of transportation, reservations are recommended one to two weeks in advance during the high season. This is often the only transportation option available, so visitors can be confined to the area immediately surrounding their resort. The roads on the island are extremely poor and very dangerous even for experienced drivers in many places, but for those who insist on going it alone, most tour agencies rent motorbikes for 200-250฿ per day.

Around the corner from Ban Sala Dan is Ko Lanta Yai's main sandy drag, **Hat Klong Dao,** a 2km beach sprinkled with quality resorts. Klong Dao has decent coral at its north end and the beach faces directly west, making for stellar sunsets. **Golden Bay Cottages ❺** offers spacious accommodations with huge price swings linked to the season. (Bungalows with fan 800฿, with A/C 1500฿; low-season 100฿/300-600฿.) Toward the more rugged south, overlooking the scenic Kanthiang Bay, the **Marine Park View Resort ❷** offers an excellent range of accommodations, from television-equipped A/C bungalows to more rustic rooms, all with private baths. The three-tiered **restaurant ❷** overlooks the peaceful bay. Most entrees are between 60-180฿. (☎01 397 0793; www.krabidir.com/lantampv. Rooms 150฿; bungalows with fan 400-900฿, with A/C 1500฿. Low-season 150฿/200฿/400฿.) Off the same drive as Marine Park View, **Top View Koh Lanta ❸** has new wooden and concrete bungalows with fans. The resort's **restaurant ❷**, precariously perched atop a west-facing cliff, has small portions but absolutely jaw-dropping sunset views. Most dishes are between 50 and 120฿; the view is free. (☎07 283 0135; lanta-top_view2002@yahoo.com. Wooden bungalows 300฿, concrete bungalows 500฿; low-season 100฿/200฿.) There are eight other beaches on the island, including the beautiful **Nin** and **Kanthiang** beaches, known for their scenery, and **Hin** beach, renowned for its snorkeling. There is also excellent diving and snorkeling at the offshore islands. There are a few outstanding daytrips to the interior, most notably to the **Tham Mai Ka** caves. You can also see **waterfalls** and go on **elephant treks.**

TRANG ☎075

Over the past 30 years, Trang has been rapidly developing. Although the provincial capital offers no special attractions, its relatively *farang*-free atmosphere provides relief from the southern Thailand tourist circuit. What's more, the province contains 119km of national-park beaches and a formidable collection of small islands, mostly undisturbed by the brazen bandits of large-scale development.

▐ TRANSPORTATION

Flights: Trang Airport (☎210 804), on Trang-Palian Rd., 7km south of the city. Take Trang Travel's airport vans (30฿) or a *tuk-tuk* (50฿) into town. **Thai Airways,** 199/2 Visetkul Rd. (☎218 066). Turn right at the clock tower onto Visetkul Rd.; it's several blocks down on the left, just past Soi 5. Open daily 8am-noon and 1-4:30pm. Daily flights to **Bangkok** (9:15pm, 2855฿).

Trains: Railway station (☎218 012), at the west end of Phraram 6 Rd. Trang is not on the main Southern Line, so train service is quite limited; buses and minivans are a better bet. Fares listed are 2nd-class express. Trains to: **Bangkok** (16hr. sleeper; 2:30, 5:20pm; 970฿) via **Chumphon** (7hr., 571฿) and **Surat Thani** (5hr., 201฿).

Buses: Bus station (☎215 718), on Huay Yod Rd., north of downtown. Check with TAT for buses that leave from other parts of city. Buses to: **Bangkok** (10hr., 4:30pm, 565฿); **Hat Yai** (4hr., every hr. 7am-7pm, 60-100฿); **Krabi** (2hr., every hr. 6am-8pm, 50-80฿); **Phuket** (5hr., every hr. 6am-6pm, 100-189฿).

Minivans: Leave from various parts of town. **Beach** minivans leave from Taklang Rd. near the railroad tracks (1½hr., every hr. 8am-5pm, 50฿). Service is less frequent during the low season. **Kantang Pier** minivans leave from Kantang Rd. in the opposite direction from Phraram 6 Rd. Minivans to **Surat Thani** (3hr., every hr. 9:30am-5pm, 125฿) leave from the train station. Check with hotel or any travel agency in town for departure location of minivans to: **Hat Yai** (every 30min. 6am-6pm, 70-99฿); **Krabi** (2hr., every hr. 7am-6pm, 90฿); **Nakhon Si Thammarat** (2½hr., every 2hr. 9am-5pm, 80฿); **Phang-**

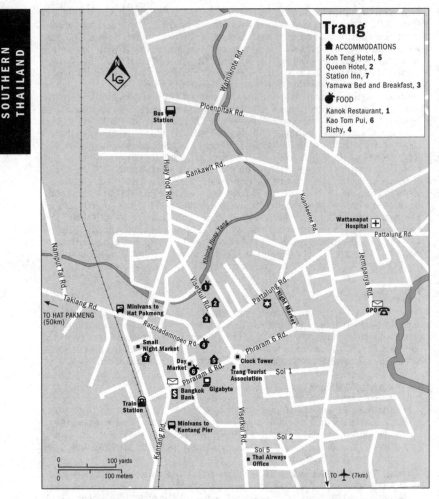

Trang

ACCOMMODATIONS
Koh Teng Hotel, **5**
Queen Hotel, **2**
Station Inn, **7**
Yamawa Bed and Breakfast, **3**

FOOD
Kanok Restaurant, **1**
Kao Tom Pui, **6**
Richy, **4**

Nga (4hr., every hr. 7am-6pm, 139฿); **Phuket** (5hr., every hr. 7am-6pm, 189฿); **Satun** (3hr.; 1:30, 3:30pm; 101฿).

Local Transportation: Pastel green **tuk-tuks** within the city run at a fixed 15฿ per person. They're a little difficult to find, but definitely the way to go since they cost the same as **motorcycle taxis,** which line every street corner. **Taxis** (15฿) and **minivans** (10฿) leave when full from different parts of town (every 20min. 5am-7pm).

ORIENTATION AND PRACTICAL INFORMATION

Buses arrive at the **bus station** near the intersection of **Ploenpitak Road** and **Huay Yod Road,** a 20min. walk north of town or 5min. by motorcycle taxi or *tuk-tuk* (both 20฿). The **railway station** sits at the west end of **Phraram 6 Road,** a large hotel-lined avenue with a landmark **clock tower** and most other tourist services. North of

Phraram 6 Rd., **Ratchadamnoen Road** (which becomes **Pattalung Road**) winds roughly parallel to the main day market and connects to Phraram 6 Rd. by **Kantang Road** to the west and **Visetkul Road** to the east by the clock tower.

Tourist Office: The **TAT** office in Nakhon Si Thammarat handles Trang queries. In town, try the **Trang Tourist Association** (☎/fax 215 580), next to the Trang Hotel on Phraram 6 Rd. Very helpful staff and free maps. Open daily 8am-5:30pm.

Tours: Travel agencies offering organized tours and transportation line Phraram 6 Rd.

Currency Exchange: Bangkok Bank, 2 Phraram 6 Rd. (☎218 203), 1 block from the train station on the right. **24hr. ATM.** Open M-F 8:30am-3:30pm.

Markets: The **day market** sells mostly produce and is near the train station. One **night market** is outside the Diamond Department Store near the train station; another, bigger one between Pattalung and Phraram 6 Rd., near the police station.

Police: 6 Pattalung Rd. (☎211 311). Some English spoken. Open **24hr.** There are no local tourist police.

Medical Services: Wattanapat Hospital, 247 Pattalung Rd. (☎218 585), at the intersection with Ploenpitak Rd., northeast of the clock tower. English spoken. Open **24hr.**

Internet Access: Gigabyte, 126 Phraram 6 Rd. 30฿ per hr. Open daily 9am-10pm.

Post Offices: GPO (☎218 521), at the bend on Jermpanya Rd., which branches north from Phraram 6 Rd., a 20min. walk from train station. *Poste Restante.* **International phones.** Open M-F 8:30am-3:30pm. **Branch office** on Phraram 6 Rd., 1 block from train station. Open M-F 8:30am-4:30pm, Sa-Su 9am-noon.

Postal Code: 92000.

ACCOMMODATIONS

Trang's budget accommodation situation is beginning to brighten as word spreads about the offshore islands and trekking opportunities near the town.

Koh Teng Hotel, 77-79 Phraram 6 Rd. (☎218 148), 5 blocks from the train station on the left. Located 1 block before the clock tower, Koh Teng pitches itself as the best place in town for backpackers, and it's hard to argue. Large rooms are clean, comfortable, and a great value. Try to get a room facing outside, for more fresh air. Singles and doubles 180฿, with satellite TV 220฿, with A/C 280฿. ❷

Yamawa Bed and Breakfast, 94 Visetkul Rd. (☎07 521 6617; www.trang-yamawa.com), Excellent guesthouse is carefully decorated. TVs, reading rooms, a terrace, **Internet,** and massage parlor. Rooftop bar under construction. Staff is very helpful. Breakfast 50฿. Closes periodically in low season. 200฿ per person. ❷

Queen Hotel, 85-89 Visetkul Rd. (☎218 229; fax 210 415), diagonally across from Yamawa. A nondescript, reasonably clean business hotel, although there's not much reason to stay unless Koh Teng and Yamawa are full. Singles 250฿, with A/C 350฿. ❷

Station Inn (☎223 393), 100m left of the train station and the closest option to the station. Not really good for more than a quick overnight; otherwise, walk 10min. to one of the other places. Large doubles are old and passably clean. Rooms with fan 320฿. ❸

FOOD

Trang's cuisine has a distinct Chinese flavor. Crispy roasted, honey-dipped pork, Chinese doughnuts *(paa tong ko)*, and *dim sum* make delicious breakfasts. The town is also famous for its fresh-brewed coffee, available at shops and restaurants everywhere. Trang has two **night markets** ❶, both open daily 6-10pm. There's also an expansive **day market** ❷ by the train station with fresh produce. English menus can be a bit hard to come by in town, but most places have one buried away somewhere. **Kanok Restaurant ❷,** 31/1 Visetkul Rd., just down the street from the Queen Hotel, has good standard Thai fare in a set-back, garden-party atmosphere. (Dishes 40-80฿. Open daily 9am-9pm.) **Koh Teng Restaurant ❶,** below the hotel of the same name, has tasty Chinese and Thai dishes for lunch or an early-bird special. (Dishes 30-90฿. Open daily 7am-5pm.) **Kao Tom Pui ❸,** 111 Tarad Rd., halfway up Phraram 6 Rd. from the train station on the left, is an open restaurant with excellent Thai fare, perfect for a late-night bite. (Open daily 5pm-3am.) **Richy ❷,** 126 Ratchadamnoen Rd., is a popular and clean place with breakfast, lunch, and dinner, though the portions are a bit small. (☎211 126. Most dishes 60-90฿.)

🎵 ENTERTAINMENT

The nightlife certainly doesn't rival that of Phuket or Ko Phi Phi, but Trang offers a different kind of entertainment. Early in the day traders sell colorful **fighting fish** on Phraram 6 Rd. Makeshift **cock fighting** arenas set up below stilt houses, and **bullfights** are staged once or twice per year. (Direct *tuk-tuk* drivers to Sanam Wuah Chon (10฿) near the bullfight field. Tickets from 100฿.) The Trang Chamber of Commerce organizes commercial events, like the **Cake Festival** (August) and **Barbecue Festival** (September), which celebrate Trang's famed dessert and pork.

🔆 DAYTRIPS FROM TRANG

The area surrounding Trang offers a bevy of attractions, from caves to natural oceanside Edens, most of them overlooked by travelers making a beeline from Surat Thani to Ko Phi Phi, Phuket, or Malaysia. Expect few travelers even in relatively populated places like **Ko Mook** and **Pakmeng** and only a smattering of locals on isolated **Hat Yong Ling.** Most towns are accessible from Trang by **minivans** that depart from various points around town. **Boats** to islands near Pakmeng, such as **Ko Hai** and Ko Mook, leave from **Pakmeng Pier** (100-600฿). Boats to **Ko Sukorn** leave from the pier at Tasae Cape in southern Trang Province.

🏝 HAT YONG LING

Minibuses (50฿) to Hat Yong Ling leave every hr. or when full from the station by the beach. During the low season, it may be necessary to hire a taxi or minivan from Trang or Pakmeng (400฿).

Hat Yong Ling National Park has two coves sheltered by wild-orchid-covered rocky mountains. Trek through forest and a bat cave to reach one of the best sand-and-sea combos around. Spelunkers should bring flashlights. Along the mountain base, the waves have carved out coves where locals camp and grill seafood. Hat Yong Ling's **National Park Headquarters,** actually located on the southern end of **Hat Chang Lang** (see below), also serves its distant neighbor **Hat Chao Mai.** (☎213 260. Open M-F 9am-5pm.) There is a **ranger station** in the center of Ban Yong Ling.

HAT PAKMENG

Minivans (45min.; every hr., low season every 2hr.; 50฿) from Trang will take you to the center of the beach or to the popular Pakmeng Resort. To return to Trang, flag down a white van from the main road.

Busy Hat Pakmeng is the only mainland beach with a significant commercial presence, as evidenced by the numerous seafood stalls and restaurants serving customers in their beach chairs. This beach is long but shallow, so not good for swimming, although several picturesque limestone formations dotting the horizon make it pleasant. The popular **Pakmeng Resort ❹,** farther south, offers tidy bungalows and private baths. (☎210 321. Singles and doubles 400฿, with A/C 750-800฿.)

HAT CHANG LANG

Located due south of Hat Pakmeng, Hat Chang Lang is a remarkably peaceful and long (5km) strip of sand. Walk all the way to the southern end of the beach at low tide to see the astonishing number of seashells the tide brings in. There are only two resorts in the area—a branch of the high-end **Amari Resort** chain on the northern end, and the more reasonable **Changlang Resort,** 131/1 Moo 5, closer to the middle of the beach. Changlang Resort offers clean, comfortable bungalows, some with A/C and satellite TV, at reasonable prices. (☎213 369; fax 291 008. Bungalows 500-1600฿, low-season 300-800฿.) **The National Park Headquarters,** with large bungalows and campsites, is located at the southern end of the beach. (☎213 260. 2- to 3-person tent 200฿; 3- to 4-person 300฿; 6-person bungalows 600฿.)

KO MOOK

Take a minivan to Pakmeng Pier (1hr., 50฿) and hop on a boat to the island (1hr.; 11am; 400฿, alone 600฿).

Easily accessible from Pakmeng Pier, Ko Mook is the most popular choice among European budgeters, and with four resorts, it's the most developed of the Trang Province islands. **Emerald Cave,** so named for its tinted waters, is a spectacular sight. To reach the cliff-surrounded lagoon at the center, visitors must swim. The lovelier and cheaper western side of the island boasts a great white-sand beach. Of the island's four resorts, **Had Farung Bungalows ❷** is the least expensive (bungalows 200฿, with bath 300฿), and **Sawatdee Resort ❷** has a highly recommended restaurant. (Bungalows 300฿.) On the west side, similarly-priced **Muk Resort ❷** (☎214 441; bungalows 300฿) and **Muk Garden Resort ❷** (☎211 372; bungalows 300฿) can arrange transportation to the island from their offices in Trang.

KO HAI (KO NGAI)

The ferry to Ko Hai leaves from Pakmeng Pier at 11:30am and returns at 8am the following day (150฿). Otherwise, charter a longtail boat for the 1hr. ride (600฿ each way).

With white-sand beaches and three pricey resorts, teardrop-shaped Ko Hai (sometimes spelled "Ko Ngai") is a true tropical paradise and an excellent dive and snorkeling spot. **Koh Ngai Villa ❹** has the cheapest rooms and arranges trips to and from the island. (☎210 496. Bungalows with fan 500-800฿; low-season 300-500฿.) More upscale **Koh Ngai Resort ❺** has a diving center. (☎210 317. Bungalows 600-780฿.)

KO KRADAN

Beautifully pristine, Ko Kradan, under the protection of the **Hat Jao Mai National Park,** contains only one high-end resort. Since **Ko Kradan Paradise Beach ❻** knows you're a hostage, the food is as expensive as the rooms; bring your own from the mainland. (☎211 391. Bungalows 600-2500฿, low-season 400-1000฿.)

> The info for Hat Yai, Satun, Ko Tarutao, Ko Bulon Leh, Sungai Kolok, and Songkhla was gathered during 2002; recent unrest in the area has prevented us from updating it and kept travelers away. For more detailed info see. p. 21.

HAT YAI   ☎074

Crowded and noisy Hat Yai is southern Thailand's transportation and commerce center. As there is not much to see or do, travelers should bypass the town, although there are quality lodgings if a stay is essential.

▐▀ **TRANSPORTATION. Thai Airways** flies out of Hat Yai's **airport,** heading to: Bangkok (1½hr., 6 per day, 2885฿); Kuala Lumpur (2hr.; F and Su 2:25pm; 9890฿);

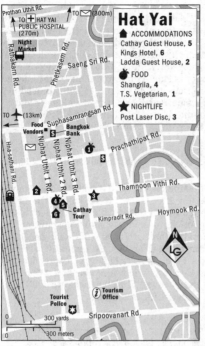

Hat Yai

🏠 ACCOMMODATIONS
Cathay Guest House, **5**
Kings Hotel, **6**
Ladda Guest House, **2**

🍴 FOOD
Shangrila, **4**
T.S. Vegetarian, **1**

⭐ NIGHTLIFE
Post Laser Disc, **3**

Phuket (45min., 11:15am, 1180฿); and Singapore (2½hr., 1:10pm, 5760฿). The **train station** at the west end of Thamnoon Vithi Rd. has **trains** to: Bangkok (16hr., 5 per day 2:45-6:10pm, 275-1200฿); Butterworth, Malaysia (5½hr., 7:40am, 233฿); Sungai Kolok (3-4hr., 4 per day 6:30am-12:15pm, 60-159฿); and Surat Thani (4-5hr., 5 per day, 215฿). In the southeast corner of town, the **bus station** on Ranchanawanit Rd. has **buses** to: Bangkok (14hr., 9 per day 7am-7pm, 535-830฿); Krabi (5hr., 11am, 173฿); Phuket (7hr., 13 per day 5:30am-9:30pm, 150-420฿); Sungai Kolok (4hr., 1:30pm, 148฿); and Surat Thani (5½hr., 10 per day 5:20am-3pm, 103-160฿). Locally, **tuk-tuks** (10฿ inside town, 20฿ outside) and **motorcycle taxis** (20฿) are the most popular modes of transportation.

🔏 PRACTICAL INFORMATION. Most travelers arrive at the train station on the west side of town at the intersection of **Rathakarn Road** and **Thamnoon Vithi Road,** one of the main commercial thoroughfares. Cheap guesthouses and tourist services cluster near the train station. Buses enter the city on **Phetkasem Road** and drop passengers off in the rather confusing market area north of downtown. Central Hat Yai is organized by a grid system, marked by **Suphasarnrangsan, Prachathipat,** and Thamnoon Vithi Rd., running eastward from the train station; **Niphat Uthit 1, 2,** and **3 Road** intersect them from north to south.

Services include: **TAT,** 1/1 Soi 2, Niphat Uthit 3 Rd. (☎243 747), with free timetables and maps; **Cathay Tour,** 93/1 Niphat Uthit 2 Rd. (☎234 535); the **immigration office** on Phetkasem Rd., west of the train tracks (☎233 760; open M-F 8:30am-4:30pm); **Bangkok Bank,** 39 Niphat Uthit 2 Rd. near Suphasarnrangsan Rd. (☎235 330; open daily 8:30am-3:30pm); a **morning market** on Niphat Uthit 3 Rd. by the clock tower; **day** and **night markets** between Montri 1 and 2 Rd. north of the bus station; **tourist police** on Sripoovanart Rd. (☎246 733; open **24hr.**); **Hat Yai Public Hospital** on Rathakarn Rd. (☎230 8001; open **24hr.**); and the **GPO** at the corner of Niphatsongkraw 1 Rd. and Soi 4 with **international phone** upstairs. (☎243 013. *Poste Restante.* Open M-F 8:30am-4:30pm, Sa-Su 9am-noon.) **Postal Code:** 90110.

🏠🍴 ACCOMMODATIONS AND FOOD. Many of the cheapest hotels in Hat Yai have poor reputations; opt for one of the slightly more expensive but reputable guesthouses suggested by TAT or stick to the tried-and-trusted train station area. A few blocks from the train station, **Cathay Guest House ❷,** 93/1 Niphat Uthit 2 Rd., at the corner with Thamnoon Vithi Rd., is reminiscent of a university hostel. The friendly staff offers good tourist services. (☎243 815. 4-bed dorms 90฿; singles 160฿; doubles 200฿; triples 250฿.) A little more expensive, **Kings Hotel ❸,** 126/134 Niphat Uthit 1 Rd., has over 75 rooms. Very well-kept, all rooms have standard amenities such as TV, A/C, and shower. (☎261 700. Singles 390฿; twins and doubles 490฿; triples 590฿.) Five minutes from the train station is **Ladda Guest House** ❷, 13-15 Thamnoon Vithi Rd. with clean baths and a friendly staff. (☎ 220 233. Singles with fan 200฿, with A/C 360฿; twins with fan 240฿.)

Muslim and Chinese influences are apparent in Hat Yai's *dim sum* restaurants and *roti* shops. Near Cathay Guest House on Thamnoon Vithi Rd. is **Shangrila** ❸, respected for its *dim sum*. (Open daily 6am-3pm.) **Food vendors** ❶ set up day and night in the Niphat Uthit Rd. area and near the plaza market and cinema on Phetkasem Rd. For local flavor, try *kanom bueng* (crepes with shredded coconut). **T.S. Vegetarian** ❶, 16 Prachathipat Rd., across from Central Department Store, lets you pick three cooked veggies with your rice. (Dishes 20฿. Open daily 7am-8pm.)

◸ ◰ SIGHTS AND ENTERTAINMENT. A 35x15m reclining Buddha rests in **Wat Hat Yai Nai**, 7km west of Hat Yai. (*Tuk-tuk* to *wat* 10฿ min. Open daily 8am-5pm.) Your trusty credit card may collapse from exhaustion on **Phetkasem Road.** For cheaper entertainment, check out **Post Laser Disc,** 82-83 Thamnoon Vithi Rd., about two blocks past Niphat Uthit 3 Rd., opposite Indra Hotel, where travelers gather upstairs to watch American movies. There's live music nightly and a daily happy hour 4-9pm. (☎ 232 027. 30฿ cover charge for a table upstairs. Open daily 9am-2am.) **Thai Boxing Stadium** hosts matches one or two weekends per month. (Approximately 180฿. *Tuk-tuk* to stadium 20-30฿.) **Bullfights** are staged on most weekend days. TAT has schedules and prices.

SATUN   ☎ 074

Satun is best known to travelers entering Thailand from Malaysia or passing through Ko Tarutao, the national park off the coast. Since Ko Tarutao is only open from October to May, Satun has few tourists during the other half of the year.

Orange buses leave from the school on Satunthanee Rd. for Hat Yai (2hr., every hr., 50฿) and from Sulakanukul, Burivanich, or Satunthanee Rd. for Trang (3hr., every 30min. 6:30am-5pm, 70฿). For A/C comfort to Hat Yai, take a **minivan** from the 7-Eleven on Satunthanee Rd. Mivivans also stop across the street from the Wangmai Hotel, in front of the open-air market (2hr., every 30min. or when full 6am-5pm, 150฿). A daily **ferry** service runs from Tamalang Pier to Pulau Langkawi (45min.; 9:30am, 1:30, 4pm; 180฿). In the high season, **boats** run from Pak Bara Pier, north of Satun, to Ko Lipe (departs 10:30am, returns 3pm; round-trip 440฿) and Ko Tarutao (departs 10am, returns 3pm; round-trip 300฿).

At its south end, **Satunthanee Road** forms a "T" intersection with **Samanthapradit Road.** South on Satunthanee Rd. just before the mosque, **Burivanich Road** splits to the right toward the **immigration office.** (☎ 711 080. Open M-F 8:30am-4:30pm.) Other services include: **Satun Travel and Ferry Service,** 45/8-9 Satunthanee Rd., which sells tickets and arranges tours (☎ 711 453; open daily 8am-5pm); the **Thai Military Bank** and **Bangkok Bank,** across the street, with **24hr. ATMs** (AmEx/Cirrus/MC/V); the **police** on the corner of Yarttrasawaddee and Satunthanee Rd. (☎ 711 025; open **24hr.**); **Pon Phasaj pharmacy,** 62 Burivanich Rd., near the police box (open M-Sa 7am-9pm); **Satun Hospital,** 55/1 Hatthakumsuksa Rd., on the corner of Yarttrasawaddee Rd. (☎ 732 460; English spoken; open **24hr.**); the **Telecom Office,** 7 Satun Thanee Rd., at the base of the red tower (open M-F 8:30am-4:30pm); and the **post office,** just east of the Satunthanee and Samanthapradit Rd. intersection. (*Poste Restante.* Open M-F 8:30am-4:30pm.) **Postal Code:** 91000.

The **Satultanee Hotel** ❷, 90 Satunthanee Rd., has spacious, bright rooms with private baths. (Singles with fan 210฿, with A/C 370฿.) Satun's budget choice is the **Rain Tong Hotel** ❷, 4 Samanthapradit Rd. From the Satunthanee Rd. intersection, walk toward the river; it's on the left. The old rooms are plain and clean, with squat toilets. (☎ 711 036. Singles and doubles 140฿.)

Satun's Muslim majority sets the tone for the local cuisine. Several breakfast *roti* places serve patrons throughout the day. Both the extensive **day market ❶** on Satunthanee Rd. and the **night market ❶** on Tammango Uthit Rd. whip up cheap meals. (Duck noodle soup 20฿. Both open daily 5pm-midnight.) For a spicy nirvana, ask locals to point you to **Sri Trang ❷**, 127 Satunthanee Rd., which has served curry and rice dishes for as long as anyone can remember. (Open daily 4-9pm.)

KO TARUTAO NATIONAL MARINE PARK

Once a pirate outpost and then an island prison, Ko Tarutao National Marine Park is an archipelago of 51 spectacular islands in the Andaman Sea. Home to a variety of wildlife, including deer, macaques, and four types of sea turtles, the park is an amazing and delicate ecosystem of coral and tropical jungle that is certain to become a popular tourist destination.

Ko Tarutao's beaches lie on its coral-filled west coast, while waterfalls, mountains, caves, and wildlife draw adventurous travelers inland. From October to January, **sea turtles** deposit eggs on **Ko Khai** (Egg Island), 15km southwest of Ko Tarutao. A popular way to explore is the 2hr. **hiking trail** from Ao Phante Melaka to Ao Talo Wao; the trail continues south to Ao Talo U-Dang (another 3hr.). For more information on Ko Tarutao, contact **Adang Sea Tour** (☎781 268) in Pak Bara.

To get to Ko Tarutao from Satun, take a **songthaew** to La-Ngu, 60km from Satun (30฿). Here, *songthaew* and **taxis** go to Pak Bara pier (12฿), from which **boats** leave daily for Ko Tarutao (10:30am, 3pm, return 9:30am; round-trip 300฿). Otherwise, charter a **longtail boat** from the Tarutao pier (from 500฿). From Hat Yai, board a **bus** to La-Ngu or go straight to Pak Bara by **minivan.**

Ko Tarutao is open from November to May. The park's main island is **Ko Tarutao** (Turtle Island), 56km from Langkawi Island. The largest of the park islands, covering 151km², Ko Tarutao was a labor camp for political prisoners during the 1940s. The **park offices** (☎729 002) at the northern tip of Tarutao on Ao Phante Melaka near the pier and at the pier in Pak Bara (☎07 478 3485) provide tourist information only during high season. The beaches along the west coast provide the best **campsites ❶** (about 10฿ per night). Bring your own tent. Otherwise, Tarutao provides **park housing ❷** (4-bed rooms 280฿; bungalows with two bedrooms and two baths 400฿; larger cottages with two bedrooms and one bath 600฿). Make reservations in advance with the National Park Division of the **Royal Forest Department** in Bangkok (☎02 579 0529) or in Pak Bara (☎781 285).

KO BULON LEH

While islands like Ko Tao and Ko Phangan contain pockets of seclusion, tiny Ko Bulon Leh exists free of any modern distraction. For those hoping to seriously unwind, Bulon Leh is a great choice.

If the handful of other beach-goers on the main beach is crowding your style, head to **Mango Bay,** a peaceful, rocky bay inhabited by *Chao Lay* fishing families—"sea gypsies" who have lived off the sea and in caves on the shore for centuries (p. 22). Or check out the activity at **Panka Yai Bay** or **Noi Bay,** where fishing boats go about their business.

Boats leave from Pak Bara pier (2hr.; 2pm, return 9am; round-trip 300฿). Service between islands is possible at a price (1000฿ for a longtail, more without a group). When the ferries approach Bulon Leh, they moor offshore, forcing you to pay a **longtail** for the last 5min. of the journey to shore (10-20฿ per person).

The island can be easily traversed on foot. **Pansand** and **Bulone resorts** are at either ends of the main beach where you are dropped off and **Ban Sulaida** is slightly inland from Bulone Resort. One path begins at Bulone Resort and cuts through the middle of the island—a 10min. walk takes you to the other side of the island where you'll find **Panka Yai** and **Panka Noi,** two bays side-by-side. Take the left along this path for **Mango Bay** and the smaller, rockier coves on other sides of the island.

The island offers almost no services besides those provided by resorts. Bring enough money to last and forget about checking your email. Bulone Resort has a **book exchange;** the island policeman regularly plays cards there as well. **Jeb's,** before Bulone Resort, slightly inland, can take care of basic needs.

There are now seven bungalow outfits on the island. The best of the bunch is **Bulone Resort ❸,** with basic bungalows along the waterfront and grounds. It also has the island's best **restaurant ❷.** (☎01 897 9084. Entrees 70-90฿. Bungalows 250-600฿.) Set on the nicest part of the beach, **Pansand Resort ❺** has gone upscale. One of the first operators here, it lacks the Bulone charm, though it has the most comfortable rooms. (☎01 397 0802. Modern bungalows 800-1500฿.) A newcomer, **Ban Sulaida Resort ❷,** right before Bulone Resort by Jeb's, offers four attractive, basic A-frame bungalows. (Bungalows 350฿, low-season 150฿.)

SUNGAI KOLOK   ☎073

Sungai Kolok is a raucous border town; most travelers go straight to the train station without staying at the hotels. Ban Taba, a small town 5km south of Tak Bai, is the preferred border-crossing point. Ferries from Ban Taba to Malaysia cost 15฿.

Thai Airways, 53 Soi 1, Charoenkhet Rd. (☎612 132), arranges transport to **Narathiwat Airport** (8am, 140฿), with daily flights to Bangkok (3hr., 10:40am, 2950฿) via Phuket (1hr., 1155฿). From the **railway station** (☎614 060) on Asia 18 Rd. on the right, trains leave for: Bangkok (21hr., 2:05pm; 28hr., 11:55am; 220-1493฿) via Chumphon (8-12hr., 150-334฿); Hat Yai (3½hr., 82-176฿); Surat Thani (8-9hr., 126-279฿). The **bus office,** 95 Vorakamin Rd. (☎612 045), is six blocks from the intersection with Charoenkhet Rd. **Buses** run to: Bangkok (19hr.; 8, 11:30am, 12:30pm; 546-1090฿) via Surat Thani (9-10hr., 277฿); Phuket (11hr.; 6, 8am, 5:30pm; 432฿) via Trang (7hr., 261฿); and Krabi (9hr., 335฿). **Minivans** (☎614 350) leave opposite the railway station on Asia 18 Rd., one block west from the intersection with Charoenkhet Rd., for Hat Yai (4hr., every hr. 6am-5pm, 150฿). **Motorcycle taxis** (20฿) wait just past TAT; **bicycle rickshaws** (40-60฿) may cost less on busier streets.

BORDER CROSSING: SUNGAI KOLOK/KOTA BHARU. The Thailand/Malaysia border, on Asia 18 Rd. near the Sungai Kolok River, is open daily 5am-9pm Thai time (1hr. behind Malaysian time). Thai buses do not cross through to Malaysia, nor do trains on the east coast. Those crossing over into Malaysia can take a share-taxi (RM5 per person; price doubles after dark) or bus #29 (every hr. until 6:15pm, RM2.70) from Rantau Panjang to Kota Bharu. Transportation on both sides of the border is most abundant in the morning. Before you cross, go to Thai Farmers Bank to exchange any leftover *baht* for Malaysian *ringgit.* Most banks in Kota Bharu are closed on Fridays.

The **border crossing** is at the end of **Asia 18 Road,** a broad avenue running parallel to the train tracks. Opposite the train station, **Charoenkhet Road** runs perpendicular to Asia 18 Rd., into the heart of Sungai Kolok. Other services include: the **Tourist Information Center** (☎612 126), on the right after passport control, with free maps and the **tourist police** (☎612 008; open **24hr.**); the **police station** (☎611 070), opposite the **Narathiwat Immigration Office,** 70 Charoenkhet Rd. (☎611 231; open M-F 8:30am-4:30pm); **Thai Farmer's Bank,** 1/6 Vorakamin Rd. (☎611 578; **24hr. ATM;** open M-F 8:30am-3:30pm); **doctors** on Saitong 6 Rd.; **medical** services (☎615 161); **CS Internet,** 2-4-6-8 Charoenkhet Rd. (☎615 444; 30฿ per hr.); and the **post office** on Prachawiwat Rd. (☎611 141. *Poste Restante.* Open M-F 8:30am-4:30pm, Sa-Su 9am-noon.) **Postal Code:** 96120.

There is no reason to spend a night in Sungai Kolok unless forced to. **Savoy Hotel ❷,** 34 Charoenkhet Rd., has a Chinese **restaurant ❷.** Its rooms have fans and bearable baths. Get a room off the street to avoid traffic noise. (☎611 093. Reception and restaurant open daily 6am-midnight. Singles with bath 150฿; doubles 170฿.)

Sungai Kolok's daily **market ❶** spreads out behind Asia 18 Rd. before the sun gets out of bed. At night, **food vendors ❶** along Shern Maroar Rd. sell local specialties. Those who want to sit while they eat can try the vendors along Vorakamin Rd., starting near the Thai Farmers Bank (fried vegetables on rice 20-25฿). **Siam Restaurant ❸,** 2-4 Shern Maroar Rd., cooks up several extravagantly garnished seafood dishes for 50-150฿. (☎611 360. Open daily 10am-3pm and 5-9pm.)

SONGKHLA   ☎074

Songkhla has a pleasant mix of museums, restaurants, and guesthouses. As a result of multinational oil companies and academic institutes, it's also conspicuously wealthier and more refined than the average Thai town. Its manicured, wide streets create a suburban appearance. If it's a beach you desire, Songkhla's got one, and nearby Ko Yo contains one of the country's most worthwhile museums.

Buses leave from the main **bus terminal** (☎354 333) on Ramwithi Rd. to Hat Yai (30min., every 15min., 15฿). In front of Wat Jaeng, **A/C minivans** also depart for Hat Yai (30min., 20฿). Services include: **TAT** in Hat Yai (p. 385); the **hospital** (☎447 446); **Internet** access at Dot Com, adjacent to the Abritus Guest House (2฿ per min; open daily 9am-10pm); and the **post office** on Nakhon Nai Rd. (☎311 145. Open M-F 8:30am-3:30pm, Sa 9am-noon.)

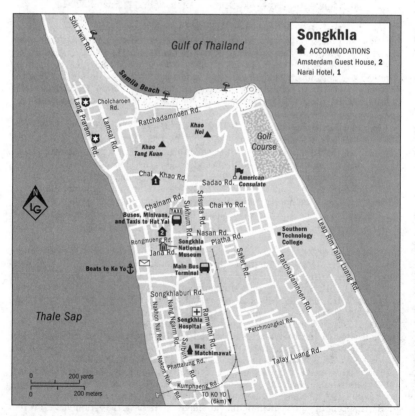

SOUTHERN THAILAND

Songkhla has a good range of guesthouses. ▨**Amsterdam Guest House ❷**, 15/3 Rongmueng Rd., across from the museum, is a civilized European oasis. (☎314 890. Rooms 180-2000฿.) One of the cheapest options in town is **Narai Hotel ❸**, 14 Chai Khao Rd., by the bottom of Khao Tang Kuan. (☎311 078. Singles 100฿; doubles 150฿.) A local favorite, **The Hot Bread Shop ❶**, 33/4 Srisuda Rd., has baked goods. (☎09 879 4424. Open M-Sa 10am-10pm.)

Songkhla National Museum, on Ronmueng Rd. across from Amsterdam Guest House, is an impressive structure, built in 1878. Originally the mansion of the governor, it now houses a mix of passably interesting artifacts dating to the prehistoric era, including pottery, Buddha images, and Chinese panels. (Open W-Su 9am-noon and 1-4pm.) At sunset, Songkhla residents gather at **Samila Beach** on Ratchamdanorn Rd. It's not suitable for swimming, but it's pleasant, with a stunning sky. The **golden mermaid** is one of Songkhla's most important landmarks.

Connected to Songkhla by Thailand's longest bridge, **Ko Yo** is 20min. from Songkhla. What may be Thailand's best museum, the ▨**Southern Folklore Museum,** can be reached via *songthaew* (10฿) from Jana Rd. The vast museum presents fascinating aspects of southern culture, from the process of bead-making to a display of coconut-scrapers. Spread over many rooms on a hillside (the exhibit halls themselves are reproductions of traditional Thai architecture), the museum also offers astounding views of the fishing activity—mainly hatcheries for shrimp, crabs, and sea bass—on Songkhla Lake and includes a shop and cafe. (☎331 184. Open daily 8:30am-5pm. 50฿.) Ko Yo is also famous for its cotton-weaving industry. The Ko Yo **cloth market** is 2km before the museum heading back to Songkhla.

NAKHON SI THAMMARAT ☎075

Located off the backpacker circuit, Nakhon Si Thammarat is a bustling city whose long and deep cultural history is evident in the town's markets and *wats*, which include the largest temple in all of southern Thailand. Buddhists come to here from all over the world to visit the massive Wat Phramahathat and stay for the several other *wats* and religious points of interest in the area. Known also for its fine jewelry and basketry, Nakhon Si Thammarat is a perfect choice for those looking for some cultural immersion and the chance to stock up on souvenirs.

▌ TRANSPORTATION

Flights: Airport (☎346 976), 20km north of town. **Thai Airways,** 1612 Ratchadamnoen Rd. (☎312 500), flies daily to Bangkok (1hr., 8:15am, 2525฿). Open daily 8am-7:30pm. Thai's "competitor," **PB Air** is located in the same office, reached via the same phone number, and does the Bangkok flight daily at 1:35pm for the same price.

Trains: Railway station, on Yommarat Rd. at Pagnagon Rd., 1 block from downtown. Nakhon Si Thammarat is on a spur off the Southern line, so service is somewhat limited. Fares given are 2nd class. Trains to: **Bangkok** (15-16hr.; 1, 2pm; 488-728฿); **Sungai Kolok** (9hr., 6:10am, 372฿); **Phatthalung** (2½hr.; 6:10, 10:20am, 3pm; 213฿).

Buses: The **bus terminal** (☎341 125) is off Phaniant Rd. past the mosque and across the railroad tracks. Buses go to: **Bangkok** (12hr.; 7am, 4-7pm; 350-454฿); **Hat Yai** (3hr., every hr. 4:30am-4:30pm, 73-102฿); **Ko Samui** (5hr.; 11:30am; 135฿, includes ferry fare); **Phatthalung** (3hr., 7 per day 6am-3:30pm, 43฿); **Phuket** (8hr., 7 per day 5:20-11am, 125-175฿); **Ranong** (6hr., 7:30am, 252฿); **Surat Thani** (2½hr., frequent 5am-5pm, 55-60฿); **Trang** (2hr.; 6, 9:10am, 2:50pm; 65฿).

Minivans: Leave from stands and travel agencies all over town, most within 1 block of Ratchadamnoen Rd. near downtown. Inquire at TAT or your hotel.

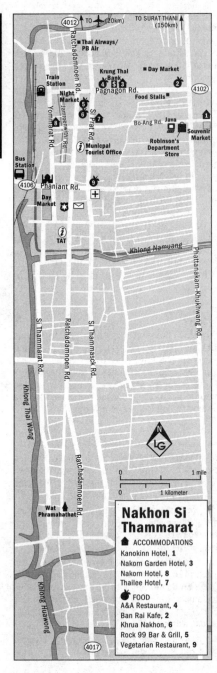

Nakhon Si Thammarat

🏠 ACCOMMODATIONS
Kanokinn Hotel, 1
Nakorn Garden Hotel, 3
Nakorn Hotel, 8
Thailee Hotel, 7

🍴 FOOD
A&A Restaurant, 4
Ban Rai Kafe, 2
Khrua Nakhon, 6
Rock 99 Bar & Grill, 5
Vegetarian Restaurant, 9

Local Transportation: An impressive and efficient **songthaew** fleet has rendered *tuk-tuks* obsolete in Nakhon Si. Blue *songthaew* ply linear routes on virtually every major street in town (every 2min. 6am-8pm, 6฿). **Motorcycle taxis** will do the same job for more *baht* and more adventure (20-40฿).

✴ 🛈 ORIENTATION AND PRACTICAL INFORMATION

Nakhon Si Thammarat is a large, 5km-long, linear town. Most of the city's sights and services are on or within a block of **Ratchadamnoen Road,** the main street. In the town's commercial center in the northern part of town, running parallel to Ratchadamnoen Rd., are **Yommarat Road** to the west and **Si Prat Road** to the east. Yommarat Rd. holds the **train station,** while Si Prat Rd. is the site of more **banks, hotels, restaurants,** and **shops.** Also between Ratchadamnoen Rd. and Yommarat Rd. is **Jamroenwithi Road,** a narrow street that is the location of the town's **night market.** **Pagnagon Road** is the city's largest east-west street, and runs from the train station past Ratchadamnoen Rd. in the heart of downtown to some good eateries, **hotels,** and a **day market.** A new portion of town lies east of center near **Phattha-nakarn-Khukhwang Road,** and contains a number of Western-style shopping centers.

Tourist Office: There are 2 official tourist offices in town. By far the more useful is **TAT** (☎ 346 515; tat-nksri@tat.or.th), near Sanam Na Meuang Park, a few blocks south of downtown, past the police station along Ratchadamnoen Rd. Helpful English-speaking staff dispenses a full range of information about the city. Ask for Bom, the office manager. Open daily 8:30am-4:30pm. In addition, the

Municipal Tourist Office—inside the City Hall complex on Ratchadamnoen Rd., just south of downtown—specializes in maps and directions, but not English skills. Open daily 8:30am-4:30pm.

Currency Exchange: Banks line Ratchadamnoen Rd. in the downtown area. Off the main road, try **Krung Thai Bank** on Pagnagon Rd., 1 block from Ratchadamnoen Rd. heading away from the train station. Open M-F 8:30am-4:30pm.

Markets: The whole town seems like one big market. There are 2 produce-oriented **day markets,** one on Yommarat Rd. just south of the train station and one on Pagnagon Rd. past the Nakorn Garden Hotel, a few blocks east of Ratchadamnoen Rd., heading away from the train station. The **night market** is on Jamroenwithi Rd., near its intersection with Pagnagon Rd.—which itself is also full of food and fruit stalls late into the night—between Ratchadamnoen Rd. and Phatthanakarn-Khukhwang Rd. to the east. There are good **souvenir markets** selling local jewelry, basketry, and pottery at good prices across Phatthanakarn-Khukhwang Rd. from Robinson's department store east of downtown, and near TAT on Si Thammarat Rd. south of downtown.

Police: (☎356 500). On Ratchadamnoen Rd. a few blocks south of downtown. Very little English spoken. Open **24hr.**

Hospital: Christian Hospital (☎356 214), at Si Prat and Phaniant Rd., is the best bet in terms of location and English skills. Open **24hr.**

Internet Access: Several places offer 20฿ per hr. Try **Java,** near Robinson's department store off Phatthanakarn-Khukhwang Rd. east of downtown. Open daily 8am-10pm.

Post Offices: GPO, on Ratchadamnoen Rd. across the street from the police station south of downtown. *Poste Restante.* Open M-F 8:30am-4:30pm, Sa-Su 9am-noon. Also convenient to downtown, there is a branch office on Pagnagon Rd. 3 blocks from Ratchadamnoen Rd., just past the Nakorn Garden Hotel on the right.

Postal Code: 80000.

ACCOMMODATIONS

Without the hordes of *farang* found in the rest of Thailand, Nakhon Si Thammarat does not have the usual range of accommodations. There are two types of places: nice middle-class A/C hotels and dirt-cheap digs.

Thailee Hotel, 1128-30 Ratchadamnoen Rd. (☎356 948), at the corner with Boh-Ang Rd. 1 block before City Hall coming from the train station. Clean rooms and professional service make this by far the best of the cheap places in town. You'll have to endure squat toilets, but the rooms are quite comfortable. Singles and doubles 120฿. ❷

Nakorn Garden Hotel, 1/4 Pagnagon Rd. (☎313 333; fax 342 926), just past Krung Thai Bank, 1 block from Ratchadamnoen Rd., heading away from the train station. This resort-style hotel set back from the road has greenery and fountains that almost let you forget you're in the middle of a bustling city. All rooms come with A/C, hot shower, minifridge, and satellite TV. Excellent attached restaurant. Singles and doubles 445฿. ❸

Kanokinn Hotel, 30/307-8 Ratchapruk Rd. (☎318 555; fax 346 271), east of Robinson's department store past Phatthanakarn-Khukhwang Rd. Away from downtown and the major sights, but convenient to the newest and nicest part of town, Kanokinn offers clean, comfortable A/C rooms with TV and hot showers. Some of the rooms are above a pool hall, but noise isn't much of a problem. Singles and doubles 280฿. ❷

Nakorn Hotel, 1477/5 Yommarat Rd. (☎356 318), 1 block to the right as you leave the train station. Nakorn's proximity to the bus and train stations is its biggest selling point. Very similar to Thailee, but you get a little less here for a little more. Very basic singles and doubles with fan and squat toilet 140฿. ❷

▐ FOOD

Curbside is the way to eat in Nakhon Si. The **night market** offers curries, rice, boiled corn, fried whole chickens, and other delicacies. The **food stall** ❶ on Jamroenwithi Rd. at the corner with Pagnagon Rd. is a particularly good place to grab a *roti* and pot of green tea. (Banana *roti* and tea 15฿. Open daily 6pm-midnight.) The **food stall** ❶ nearest to Phatthanakarn-Khukhwang Rd. on Pagnagon Rd. is known around town as the best place for curried rice dishes. (Most everything 15฿. Open daily 10am-midnight.) There is a small **vegetarian restaurant** ❷ on Si Prat Rd. near Phaniant Rd. that serves flour- and soy-based versions of Thai favorites. Get there early—it closes after lunch. (Most dishes 30-50฿. Open daily 8am-2pm.)

▨ **Khrua Nakhon,** inside Bavorn Bazaar just off Ratchadamnoen Rd. in the heart of downtown; turn into the small alley at the 7-Eleven. Come here around lunchtime for a real taste of Nakhon Si—Khrua serves delicious authentic regional cuisine. Fish curries served with coconut rice 40฿. Open daily 6am-3pm. ❷

A&A Restaurant, on Pagnagon Rd. just past Si Prat Rd. heading away from the town center. A large, pleasant Western-style cafe that serves delicious ice cream (7฿) and Thai dishes (40-90฿). Smoking ban allows weary travelers to breathe easy. Fresh-brewed coffee 20฿. Open daily 7am-midnight. ❷

Ban Rai Kafe, on Pagnagon Rd. at Phatthanakarn-Khukhwang Rd. Signs are in Thai, but look for the large, open-air bamboo-hut-style restaurant opposite the food stalls. Offering usual Thai fare, this place is best known for its freshly-brewed coffee and nightly music video sing-alongs. Dishes 50-120฿. Coffee 20฿. Open daily 8am-midnight. ❷

Rock 99 Bar & Grill, in Bavorn Bazaar next to Khrua Nakhon. The best place in town for grilled food; the pizzas (100-200฿) are especially good. Open daily 11am-midnight. ❸

◉ SIGHTS

WAT PHRAMAHATHAT WORAMAHA WIHAAN. The largest temple in southern Thailand, Wat Phramahathat covers an area of 40,800m². While the *wat* predates historical records of the region, it is said to be over 1000 years old. The temple is particularly important as the home of the Lanka Wong sect of Buddhism in Thailand. In AD 1157, King Chantharaphanu sent monks to study Buddhist teachings in Sri Lanka. In 1227 they returned to Thailand and set up shop at Wat Phramahathat. The province has been the home of the Lanka Wong sect in Thailand ever since.

A number of important artifacts and historical sights are housed within the *wat*'s compound. The most significant is the Phra Borom That Chedi, a pagoda that resembles a massive inverted concrete bell. It is estimated to have been built around AD 757, during the Si Wichai period. The pagoda has a base diameter of 23m and is 53m high, making it the second-tallest pagoda in all of Thailand. *(Located 2km south of downtown on Ratchadamnoen Rd. Take any songthaew heading south on Ratchadamnoen Rd. from the center of town (10min., 6฿). Open daily 7am-4pm.)*

NATIONAL MUSEUM. The museum contains a number of interesting and historically significant artifacts. Perhaps most impressive (not to mention a great source of local pride) is the throne of King Rama V. While the throne's exact origin is unknown, its intricate carvings exemplify the craftwork that is the signature of Nakhon Si Thammarat artisans. The museum also contains several Hindu and Sri Lankan Buddhist images and artifacts in addition to local artwork. *(3km south of town on Ratchadamnoen Rd. Southbound Ratchadamnoen Rd. songthaew (6฿) go past the museum entrance. Open W-Su 8:30am-4pm. 30฿.)*

SHADOW PLAYHOUSE. One of Nakhon Si Thammarat's most famous residents is the world-renowned puppet maker, Suchart Sabsin. From his small shop on the southern end of town, Sabsin and his apprentices work tirelessly on enormous buffalo-hide puppets. Sabsin is considered the premier maker of this particular Thai variety, used in performances in Bangkok and at privately sponsored (and undoubtedly exhausting) 9hr., overnight marathon events. A visit gives you the chance to watch the master at work. When enough visitors gather, he will even give a free live demonstration of his puppets at play; he does this at least twice per day. Also on the premises is the International Puppet Museum, featuring puppets from around the world and some of their history. *(On Thammasok Soi 3, 2km south of the city center. Take a blue songthaew (6฿) south from the city, or walk over 2 blocks from Wat Phramahathat. Open daily 8:30am-4:30pm. Free.)*

OTHER SIGHTS. The original **city walls** were built over 1000 years ago. The current ones occupy roughly the same location as the original ones and date back to the 18th century. They run 2238.8m north-south and 466m east-west. *(The northern gate is on Ratchadamnoen Rd. at the Khlong Namuang River just south of the city park.)*

There are a number of other historically interesting sights along Ratchadamnoen Rd., in the old part of town near Wat Phramahathat. The **Phra Phutthasihing** is a Buddha statue that is considered one of the most ancient and sacred in all of Thailand. There are now three statues that look exactly alike—one in Chiang Mai, one in the National Museum in Bangkok, and the one in Nakhon Si Thammarat. All three have advocates who claim theirs as the original. In Nakhon Si Thammarat, it is believed that the king of Sri Lanka commissioned the statue in AD 157 and, when the Thai king asked for the statue as a gift, it was sent to Nakhon Si Thammarat. However, most historians believe that the statue was moved to Chiang Mai in the 16th century. *(Off Si Thammarat Rd., behind the provincial office from Ratchadamnoen Rd. 1.5km south of downtown before Wat Phramahathat.)*

Buddhism isn't the only religion in Nakhon Si Thammarat. The town **mosque**, with its large green cupolas, is considered one of the most ornate in southern Thailand and is worth a quick look, even if it's just from a *songthaew* on the way to the bus station. *(On Phaniant Rd. 2 blocks toward the bus terminal from Ratchadamnoen Rd.)*

Nakhon Si Thammarat was also the original settling point for Hindus journeying east from the Indian subcontinent, and their former existence here is marked by the remnants of two temples that face each other across Ratchadamnoen Rd. On the west side (the same side as Wat Phramahathat), farther down the road, is **Phra Isuan,** the site of a Brahmin temple dedicated to Shiva, the Hindu god of war. While the original chapel, constructed during the Ayutthaya period, has long since eroded away, a reconstructed replica lies on its former site. Across the street is **Phra Narai,** a Hindu temple from a similar time period, dedicated to the god Narai. *(Both are on Ratchadamnoen Rd. 1.5km south of downtown, just past the city walls.)*

SURAT THANI   ☎077

Few people linger in Surat Thani, and the city's tourist industry is only built to cater to those waiting around for the next boat to Ko Samui or the next bus heading west or south. The increasing prevalence of joint bus, train, and boat tickets means that only a few stay here long enough for more than a quick stroll down the river promenade or a snack at the day market. While overnight visitors are able to indulge in the vibrant local night market, there is not much more to see or do in Surat Thani than check your watch and re-examine your ticket out.

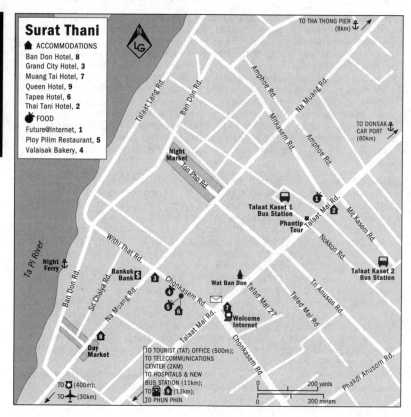

Surat Thani

ACCOMMODATIONS
Ban Don Hotel, 8
Grand City Hotel, 3
Muang Tai Hotel, 7
Queen Hotel, 9
Tapee Hotel, 6
Thai Tani Hotel, 2

FOOD
Future@Internet, 1
Ploy Pilim Restaurant, 5
Valaisak Bakery, 4

TRANSPORTATION

Flights: Airport (☎253 500), 30km outside of town. **Thai Airways,** 3/27-8 Karoonrat Rd. (☎441 137), flies daily to **Bangkok** (1hr.; 12:40, 7:15pm; 242฿). The Thai office, 2km inland from the pier, is quite remote; **Phantip Tour** (p. 397) handles bookings from the city center. More destinations are accessible from Ko Samui's more expensive airport, but with an 800฿ departure tax, this airport is the most expensive in Thailand. Vans leave from the Thai office and Phantip Travel for the airport 2-2½hr. prior to departure and make the trip back to town 30-60min. after flight arrivals (70฿).

Trains: Railway station (☎311 213), in Phun Phin, 13km from Surat Thani. Orange buses run constantly between the local bus terminal (Talaat Kaset 1) in town and the station; catch them anywhere on Talaat Mai Rd. (25min., every 5min., 10฿). Fares given are 2nd class. Trains to: **Bangkok** (12hr., 11 per day 11:25am-11pm, 47-508฿) via **Chumphon** (3hr., 138฿); **Butterworth, Malaysia** (11hr., 1:34am, 880฿); **Hat Yai** (6hr., 7 per day 9:20am-1:20am, 186-306฿); **Sungai Kolok** (10hr.; 1:20, 3, 4am; 231฿); **Trang** (5hr.; 6, 8am; 115฿).

Buses: Bus travel in and out of Surat Thani is somewhat complicated. There are 3 bus stations, and tour and travel agencies will try to lure you to **private buses,** which often cost 50-100฿ more than public buses but take significantly less time.

Talaat Kaset 1: On Talaat Mai Rd. behind Phantip Travel at Nokkon Rd. Offers local and provincial travel. To: **Chumphon** (3hr., every 30min. 7am-6pm, 80฿) and **Surat Thani Province,** with frequent buses to the railway station.

Talaat Kaset 2: (☎272 341), behind Thai Tani Hotel next to the market, has regular and A/C buses departing for: **Hat Yai** (4-5hr., 120-380฿); **Krabi** (4hr., 80฿); **Phang-Nga** (3½hr., 60-130฿); **Phuket** (5hr., 100-160฿), as well as other southern destinations (roughly every 30min. 6am-5pm).

New station: Just outside of town toward the train station, with **Bangkok** buses (9-11hr., every 30min. 7am-11pm, 211-380฿).

Minivans: Run from Talaat Kaset 2 to **Nakhon Si Thammarat** (2hr., every hr. 7am-5pm, 95฿) and **Penang, Malaysia** (6hr., every hr. 6am-5pm, 450฿), among others. Shop around; many of the pushier Surat Thani travel agencies charge a rather large *farang* mark-up for popular tourist routes.

Boats: Ferries depart from several points in and outside of town. **Songserm Travel Center** operates a **daily express boat** that leaves from the **Tha Thong Pier** 8km outside of town to **Ko Phangan** (4hr., 7:30am, 250฿) and **Ko Samui** (3hr.; 7:30, 8am, 2pm; 150฿); ticket includes transportation to the pier. The same company operates a **night ferry** that sets off from the Surat Thani pier (known as Ban Don) at 11pm for **Ko Phangan** (6hr., 200฿) and **Ko Samui** (6hr., 100฿). **Samui Tours** offers buses (1hr., 7 per day 6:15am-4:30pm, 45-65฿) to the **Donsak Car Port,** about 60km from Surat Thani, where **Raja Car Ferry** goes to **Ko Phangan** (2½hr., 120฿) and **Ko Samui** (1½hr., every 2hr. 6am-6pm, 45฿). **Seatran** operates car and passenger ferries that leave from Donsak for **Ko Samui** (ferry 2hr.; 7am, 12:30pm; 250฿), with bus service included. The 7am boat continues to **Ko Phangan.** An agent will add a 50-100฿ surcharge.

Local Transportation: Few tourists stray from the bus-train-ferry station triangle, which is well served by the orange railway station bus. However, **tuk-tuks** (10-40฿), **motorcycle taxis** (10-20฿), and **songthaew** (10฿) roam the streets.

◢◪ ❼ ORIENTATION AND PRACTICAL INFORMATION

Trains arrive at **Phun Phin Railway Station,** 13km from Surat Thani. Phun Phin and Surat Thani are connected by the busy and noisy **Talaat Mai Road,** which enters Surat Thani from the southwest and passes the **tourist, police,** and **post offices.** Local buses leave from two separate **markets,** each just a block off Talaat Mai Rd., near the center of town. Ferries depart from the municipal pier on **Ban Don Road** (which runs along the banks of the **Ta Pi River**) and from piers outside town. Most budget **accommodations, travel agencies,** and conveniences are in the Ban Don area also, within easy walking distance of the pier and bus station.

Tourist Office: TAT, 5 Talaat Mai Rd. (☎288 817). A 20min. walk on Talaat Mai Rd. from the town center; it's best to jump on an orange local bus heading to the train station. Friendly staff, good info, and maps. English spoken. Open daily 8:30am-4:30pm.

Tours: Agencies abound near the pier and on Talaat Mai Rd. between the two markets. A number of fraudulent agencies have sprung up in Surat Thani in recent years, so ask questions and choose wisely. A well-respected, full-service travel agency is **Phantip Tour** (☎272 230; fax 281 223), located between the 2 bus terminals on Talaat Mai Rd. Hotel, train, plane, bus, and boat bookings can all be made here. Endorsed by TAT, Phantip also offers a great deal of local information.

Currency Exchange: Surat Thani's exchange rates are better than those on the islands. Banks with **24hr. ATMs** line Na Muang Rd. Most are open M-F 8:30am-3:30pm, although a few operate extended hours. **Bangkok Bank,** 195-7 Na Muang Rd. (☎281 298), has a booth in front. Open daily 8:30am-5pm.

Markets: A **day market** is on Na Muang Rd., near the Ban Don Hotel. The popular **night market** sprawls on a single street (Ton Pho Rd.) between Na Muang Rd. and Ban Don Rd. From the bus stations, head toward the river.

YES, WE HAVE NO BANANAS

When traveling in Thailand, there's no better way to get a taste of local flavor than by sampling the street stalls at local markets. There are few sights in Surat Thani, but there is what *Let's Go* calls a "vibrant" night market, so, come evening, I head over to check out the action.

The market is a lot of fun; there's a wide variety of inexpensive fruits (generally 15฿ per kilo) and a delicious Muslim dish called *roti* 15฿ each). This is not your—or, more accurately, my—mother's *roti*; this is a fried pancake stuffed with banana and topped with sweetened condensed milk or honey, and it's absolutely fantastic.

Around 11:30pm, I head back to my hotel room. I haven't walked more than 100m when I see a table full of bright yellow baby bananas on my right. A perfect nightcap!

There is a girl behind the table, smiling, pretty, probably somewhere between 16 and 19 years old. I point to the tiny bananas and ask "How much?" She points to an older man, maybe in his 50s, behind a desk inside a storefront off to her right. I look back to him and, still pointing in the general direction of the bananas on the table, ask, "How much?"

He tips his head down and looks at me frowningly from above his reading glasses in the way librarians do when they are...

[Cont'd on next page...]

Police: 188 Na Muang Rd. (☎272 095). Little English spoken. Open **24hr.**

Hospitals: Surat Thani Provincial Hospital (☎284 700), 1km past TAT on Talaat Mai Rd., on the way to privately-run **Phun Phin Taksin Hospital** (☎273 239). Staff at Taksin speak somewhat better English. Credit cards accepted. Open **24hr.**

Telephones: Surat Thani Telecommunications Center (☎283 050), on Donnok Rd., 2km from most hotels. Walk down Talaat Mai Rd. toward TAT from the intersection with Chonkasem Rd. and turn left onto Donnok Rd.; it's 20min. down on the left under the radio tower. Open daily 8am-10pm.

Internet Access: Next to the Muang Tai Hotel, **Welcome Internet** charges 20฿ per hr. Open daily 9am-midnight. Other places are on Chonkasem Rd. and Talaat Mai Rd. Expensive Internet access (2฿ per min.) is available at travel agencies around the pier.

Post Offices: GPO (☎272 013), near the corner of Talaat Mai Rd. and Chonkasem Rd. *Poste Restante.* Open M-F 8:30am-4:30pm, Sa-Su 9am-noon.

Postal Code: 84000.

ACCOMMODATIONS

Surat Thani has several good hotels with relatively low prices, although it lacks a quality backpacker option. Most establishments can be found within a few blocks' radius of the pier or around the markets.

Ban Don Hotel, 268/2 Na Muang Rd. (☎272 167), hidden between the 7-Eleven and the day market, a block from where the river meets the road. Extremely clean, well-maintained rooms make this the best place to stay in Surat Thani. Cheap Thai-Chinese restaurant downstairs open daily until 5pm (*pad thai* 25฿). Singles and doubles officially 250฿, with A/C and TV 450฿, but 50-100฿ can be bargained off the nightly rates. ❷

Muang Tai Hotel, 390-2 Talaat Mai Rd. (☎273 586), at the intersection with Chonkasem Rd. A solid, reliable option, but some rooms capture a lot of street noise from the busy intersection. Rooms are large and come with creature comforts such as TV, tables, cushy chairs, and private bath. Cheerful staff. Singles with fan 220฿, with A/C 360฿; doubles 260฿, with A/C 390฿, with A/C and hot water 440฿. ❷

Thai Tani Hotel, 442/306-308 Talaat Kaset 2 (☎272 977), off Talaat Mai Rd. between the 2 markets, right in the thick of things. Reception on 3rd fl. A fairly clean and popular establishment—a good option for quick overnights and early morning bus departures. Rooms include private bath. Singles 240฿, with A/C 320฿; doubles with twin beds 260-380฿. ❷

Tapee Hotel, 100 Chonkasem Rd. (☎272 575), mid-block between Na Muang and Talaat Mai Rds. Large, clean rooms with a very professional staff. Ban Don Hotel offers similar, better-maintained rooms at better prices, but Tapee is bigger and a quick walk from all inter-city transit options. Singles and doubles with fan 300฿, with A/C 450฿. ❸

Grand City Hotel, 428/6-10 Na Muang Rd. (☎272 560), at the corner of Chonkasem Rd. Clean rooms with standard amenities in a prime location, although some of the rooms garner more than their share of street noise. Singles and doubles 200฿, with hot water and A/C 350฿; twin beds with fan 250฿, with A/C 500฿. ❷

Queen Hotel (☎311 831), on the street directly opposite the railway station in Phun Phin. Cross the street from the station, turn left, and then turn right at the fork in the road; the hotel is about 50m down. Convenient for early or late trains. Small rooms are clean. Tourist services available downstairs. Internet 2฿ per min. Singles 200฿; doubles 250-400฿. ❷

🍴 FOOD

The **night market** ❶ is almost reason enough to spend the night in Surat Thani and is perhaps its most memorable aspect. With a variety of vendors offering a tremendous range of snacks, sweets, and meals, the market seems to draw everyone in town. From crunchy bugs and duck eggs to enormous oysters and oil-drenched crepes, this is the place to sample Thai cuisine (try *khao niaw mamuang,* sliced mango with sticky rice). **Talaat Kaset 1** and **Talaat Kaset 2** both have stalls and buffets displaying curries, meats, and vegetables ladled over rice. For a variety of Thai dishes and seafood in a lovely indoor air-conditioned English tea garden, try the 🔳**Ploy Pilim Restaurant ❷,** 100 Chonkasem Rd., in front of the Tapee Hotel, which has, in addition to the usual Thai chicken and seafood favorites, an impressive 25 vegetarian options—about 24 more than anywhere else in town. (Standard dishes 40-70฿. Specialties 60฿ and way up. Open daily 7:30am-11pm.) **Future@Internet ❶,** across from the Thai Tani Hotel, has a menu of mostly 30฿ items. Good for a quick bite between buses. The *tom yum* (35฿) is particularly good. (Open daily 8am-9:30pm.) Next door to Ploy Pilim is **Valaisak Bakery ❶,** which has donuts (9฿) that are mouth-watering when fresh. (Open daily 8am-8pm.)

informing you that the copy o
*Sports Illustrated's World's 50C
Most Babe-alicious Swimsui
Models* that you checked out a
year and a half ago will have to be
replaced at your expense. He and
the girl exchange a few words ir
Thai. Then he looks at me again
"One thousand *baht*," he tells me

There must be some misun
derstanding. That's 25 dollars
Does he think I want to buy the
whole table of bananas? I onl
want one kilo.

I mask my shock at the price—
it's bad form to do anything bu
smile during negotiations here, o
else both parties lose face—anc
losing face is bad. I stick my righ
pointer finger in the air and say
"Just one?"

He looks back at the girl and
with a single finger in the air, say
something more to her. She
replies sharply and a bit crossly
prompting a rebuke from him
When the chatter has died down
he looks back up at me, and says
"For you, she give one hour only
600 *baht*."

I look down at the table o
bananas and the girl, once again
smiling at me behind them, and i
finally occurs to me that the man
is not interested in selling me
bananas. And as the girl, looking
up at me, unpeels a banana anc
pops it into her mouth whole,
quickly mutter my thanks-but-no
thanks and go on my way.

Taste of local flavor indeed.
— *Nitin Shah*

🔁 DAYTRIPS FROM SURAT THANI

CHAIYA

The most direct way to get to Chaiya is to take a Chumphon-bound bus from Surat Thani's Talaat Kaset 1 bus station, get off at Suan Mokkha, and catch a north-bound songthaew to Wat Phra That. (1½hr.) Alternatively, you can catch a songthaew from Surat Thani all the way to Chaiya town (1½hr., 25-30฿) and walk the 15min. to the wats from there.

40km north of Surat Thani, the town of Chaiya, once a powerful and important city-state in the southern gulf coast, may not possess all the splendor of its northern cousins, but it does boast several *wats*, museums, and ruins, including one of the most revered Buddhist sights in the south, **Wat Phra Borommathat**. Known as Wat Phra That, this 1200-year-old pagoda is surrounded by 174 Buddha images. Unlike most Thai *wats*, it is consecrated to Mahayana Buddhism, the religion of the ancient Sumatran Srivijaya Empire. The elaborate stone *chedi* is considered a masterful example of Srivijaya art, and the *wat* is considered the best-preserved of the Srivijaya style in Thailand. Its three tiers are decorated with small *stupas*.

Next door, the small but interesting **National Museum** houses artifacts dating from Chaiya's heyday. (☎431 090. Open W-Su 9am-4pm. 30฿.) Situated in a forest along Hwy. 41, **Wat Suan Mokkha Phalaram** (Suan Mok) is more a working monastery than a tourist attraction. Established in 1932 by Phuttathat Phikhu, one of Thailand's most famous monks, the area contains few modern buildings, since it was designed to return Buddhist practice and teaching to a more traditional and serene setting (i.e., the woods), while incorporating modern influences. A daytrip may not bestow enlightenment but will certainly offer a glimpse of beautiful paths and a bizarre collection of modern Buddhist art. As if to combat the indulgent lifestyles of the nearby islands, Suan Mok urges restraint in all its attendees, discouraging vices such as smoking and mosquito-slapping. Anyone can attend **meditation retreats** held by monks. Retreats start on the last day of each month and run to the 11th day of the following month. It's not possible or necessary to reserve a spot; you need only show up a few days before the end of the month. (☎431 552. 1200฿ covers food, accommodations, and expenses for the 12-day retreat.)

KHAO SOK NATIONAL PARK

To get to Khao Sok, find a bus doing the Phuket-Surat Thani route (2hr., every hr. 6am-5pm, 50-70฿) and confirm that it will go to Khao Sok—some buses take routes that bypass the park. The buses drop you off at the start of the Khao Sok road, which goes to the park entrance (3km). The road is full of bungalows: you're sure to find a room by walking along it. Surat Thani travel agencies also offer a number of minivan departures (180฿), but they're overpriced, and they will try to make you stay at their affiliated accommodation in Khao Sok.

Nestled in the mountain ridge separating the eastern and western coasts of peninsular Thailand, splendid Khao Sok National Park is one of the more worthwhile interior destinations in southern Thailand. With travelers heading to the park from both coasts, it is also one of the most popular. A relic of the country's topological past, the 160-million-year-old rain forest (some date it as far back as 380 million years) covers roughly 650km², and is mostly comprised of jungle-covered foothills and protruding limestone formations. Its unique geography and generous rainfall allow it to sustain a remarkable ecosystem—it is home to hundreds of wildlife species, including gibbons, bears, elephants, guars, and languars. Supposedly, tigers and panthers also live here, but they are rarely spotted. However, the park's jewel is undoubtedly the native flora, which include dozens of species of orchids and ferns. Most spectacular is the *Bua Phut*, a lotus flower that can grow to 80cm.

SOUTHERN THAILAND

The **park headquarters** near the entrance dispenses trail maps and arranges guided hikes to some of the waterfalls and caves in the park. The two major trails depart from behind the **Visitors Center.** A fairly easy 7km trek to **Ton Gloy Waterfall** leads through several picturesque falls and gorges. A somewhat steeper and trickier 4km hike to **Sip-et-Chan,** a majestic, 11-tiered waterfall, takes you through extremely dense rainforest and has six river crossings. Watch out for **leeches.** Both trails are well maintained but have bridge crossings that can be tricky when wet.

The headquarters offers a **camping area ❶** (pitch your own tent) and **bungalows ❺** (sleeps 4; 1000฿). Also just inside the park at the Visitors Center is **Tree Tops River Huts ❷,** a set of tree houses and bamboo bungalows right on the river that puts you just a stone's throw from the trailheads. (☎395 129. Free bus station pickup available. Reservations recommended. Tree houses and bungalows 200-1800฿. All have private baths, some have A/C and hot showers.) For a more remote, romantic experience, come to **Lost Horizons Jungle House ❸,** located off a dirt road 1km before the park entrance. A small stream flows by the bungalows, which have a bare minimum of foot traffic. While the regular bungalows aren't a tremendous value, the large two-level tree houses are a great deal. (Make reservations through **Lost Horizons Asia** ☎ 02 860 3936; www.losthorizonsasia.com. Bungalows 400฿; tree houses 500-600฿.) Park admission is 200฿ for three days. For more information on the park's facilities call (☎ 299 150).

KO SAMUI ☎ 077

Thailand's third-largest island has come a long way since its "discovery" by backpackers in the 1970s. Ko Samui ("Coconut Island") is a major exporter of coconuts, the main source of income for its 40,000 occupants—over two million are shipped off the island every month. Thousands of travelers and package tourists rush to Ko Samui's beaches, which run the gamut from loud, shop-crammed Hat Chaweng and Hat Lamai to the quiet, tropical enclaves of Hat Bo Phut and Hat Choeng Mon. Those looking for a range of entertainment and sunbathing options will not be disappointed; but those looking for a deserted coconut island will be.

▚ TRANSPORTATION

Some travelers arrive on Ko Samui by **plane,** but most come by **boat** via the transportation hub of **Surat Thani** or from neighboring islands.

> **Flights: Samui Airport** is between Hat Chaweng and Hat Bangrak (Big Buddha Beach). **Bangkok Airways,** in Chaweng (☎422 234, at the airport 245 601), flies daily to: **Bangkok** (1-1½hr., every hr. 6am-9:20pm, 4200฿); **Krabi** (50min., 4 per week 1:30pm, 3200฿); **Phuket** (50min.; 9:20am, 3:20, 7:20pm; 2600฿); **Singapore** (1½hr., 3:50pm, 5500฿).

Ko Samui, Ko Phangan, and Ko Tao

KO TAO
TO KO NANG YUAN
TO CHUMPHON 2-5hr.
Mae Hat
Gulf of Thailand
1-3hr.
TO ANG THONG NATIONAL MARINE PARK
40min.
KO PHANGAN
Thong Sala
Hat Rin
30min.-1hr.
1hr.
2¼-7hr.
Hat Bo Phut
Na Thon
Hat Bangrak (Big Buddha)
TO SURAT THANI
TO DONSAK
2-5hr.
KO SAMUI
0   10 miles
0   10 kilometers
(Ferry times vary by boat)

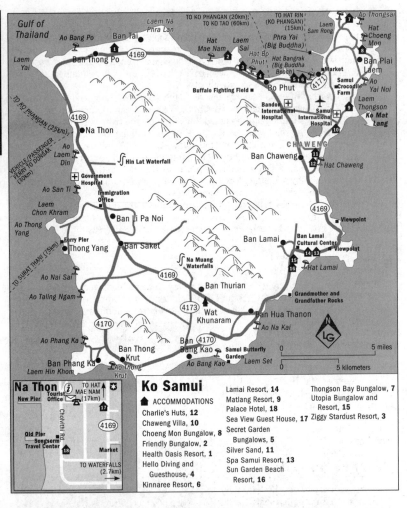

Book tickets at Bangkok Airways or any travel agency on the island. There is an exorbitant 800฿ departure tax at the Bangkok Airways-owned airport. **Thai Airways** offers cheaper flights to Bangkok through Surat Thani, and many travel agencies offer boat/plane packages through Surat Thani.

Trains and buses: Most travel agents can book joint boat/train or boat/bus tickets to the mainland. Prices vary slightly from agent to agent. Packages to **Bangkok** (16hr.; ferry and A/C bus 480฿, ferry and sleeper train 800฿) and **Kuala Lumpur, Malaysia** (22hr., ferry and A/C bus 1000฿).

Boats: There are 3 piers in Ko Samui. The main pier in **Na Thon** is dominated by **Songserm Travel Center,** which runs boats to: **Chumphon** (6½hr., 11am, 745฿); **Ko Tao** (2½hr.; 9, 11am; 345฿); **Krabi** (7hr., 2pm, 250฿); **Surat Thani** (3hr.; 12:30, 3:30pm;

150฿. Night boat 7hr., 9pm, 150฿); Ko Phangan's **Thong Sala** (45min.; 9, 11am, 5pm; 115฿). **Seatran** also sends express boats from Na Thon to **Donsak Pier,** 60km away from **Surat Thani** (1hr., plus 1hr. by bus; 8am, 3pm; 250฿ including bus to Surat Thani). A slower but cheaper **car ferry** also runs between Na Thon and **Donsak Pier** (5hr., 120฿). The **Raja Car Ferry** runs between a pier 10km south of Na Thon and Surat Thani (3hr., every hr. 5am-6pm, 200฿). The pier at **Hat Bangrak** has direct service to **Hat Rin** on **Ko Phangan** (1hr.; 10:30am, 1, 4pm; 100฿)

Local Transportation: Don't be fooled by the presence of yellow cars with "Taxi-Meter" signs; these are surplus cabs from the Bangkok taxi fleet, and the meters are rusted over from disuse. These A/C cabs, while the most comfortable means of getting around, will charge anywhere from 200 to 800฿ around the island. If you'll be traveling a considerable amount from beach to beach, the most convenient way to explore the island is to rent a **motorbike.** Clearly labeled **songthaew** congregate near the piers and circle the island frequently 5am-6pm. From Na Thon to: **Hat Bangrak** (30฿); **Hat Bo Phut** (20฿); **Hat Chaweng** (40฿); **Hat Lamai** (40฿); **Hat Mae Nam** (20฿). While these are official rates, in practice drivers will charge you more (especially if the truck is relatively empty), but it should never cost more than 50฿ per person from anywhere to anywhere else on the island by *songthaew.* Speedy **motorcycle taxis** also circle the island, providing a faster but more dangerous and expensive alternative to *songthaew.* From Na Thon to: **Hat Bo Phut** (150฿); **Hat Chaweng** (200฿); **Hat Mae Nam** (100฿). Many resorts on the island provide minivan transportation to and from the piers and the airport, sometimes for a 50-150฿ fee.

Rentals: Motorbikes 150฿ per day (200฿ for 150cc automatic bikes); **jeeps** 800฿ per day, with insurance 1000-2000฿. Rental places are everywhere, but choose a reputable vendor. Your hotel is usually a good choice.

✳❼ ORIENTATION AND PRACTICAL INFORMATION

The roughly oval-shaped Ko Samui is encircled by one road **(Route 4169),** making getting around fairly easy but somewhat time-consuming, due to the island's deceptive size. The main transportation hub and service center, **Na Thon,** lies on the west coast. From here, Rte. 4169 runs to **Ao Bang Po** and **Hat Mae Nam** on the northern coast and cuts down the east coast to **Hat Chaweng,** the island's most celebrated beach, and **Hat Lamai,** Hat Chaweng's smaller and more budget-oriented sibling. **Route 4171,** enveloping the island's northeastern peninsula, branches off Rte. 4169 just past Hat Mae Nam and reconnects with it in Chaweng. It passes through **Hat Bo**

THE BIG SPLURGE

TAMARIND SPRINGS

If you've prepared yourself to spend your hard-earned cash or 3-5hr. of bliss, Tamarind Springs is the place to do it. Located nea Hat Lamai on Ko Samui's south eastern coast, Tamarind Springs offers a unique blend of trad tional Thai massage with acupres sure and deep tissue techniques to remove all traces of physica and psychological wear.

Set in an expansive compound away from the beach, Tamarinc Springs offers friendly service anc an engulfing ambience of peace and relaxation. Steam saunas soothe the skin, while the coo dipping pool offers instan refreshment. Special massage packages include hot-stone mas sages and the herbal *prakop* mas sage treatment that uses warm fragrant oils.

When you are done for the day, retreat to one of Tamarinc Springs's villas, each individually designed to blend into its natura surroundings. The villas offe every possible luxury amenity, the staff is nothing short of doting and in-room massages are also available. The bar and restauran offer delicious Thai and Western dishes, plus drinks and cleansing juices. Once you're through, you'l be ready to return to the worlc outside, feeling just a little bi rejuvenated for the experience.

205/7 Thong Takian. (☎424 436; www.tamarindretreat.com. 3hr. packages begin at US$250 Villas US$300 per night. Spa open daily 11am-8pm.)

Phut (Fisherman's Village), **Hat Bangrak** (Big Buddha Beach), and the smaller beaches of **Ao Thongsai, Ao Yai Noi,** and **Hat Choeng Mon.** *Songthaew* circulate around Rte. 4169 and 4171, Hat Chaweng, and Hat Lamai; elsewhere you will have to take a taxi or ride a motorbike. In general, Na Thon, Hat Chaweng, and Hat Lamai are the liveliest areas and offer the most services, while Hat Mae Nam, Hat Bo Phut, and Hat Choeng Mon are quiet and more relaxed.

Tourist Office: TAT (☎/fax 420 504; tatsamui@samart.co.th), on Na Thon Rd. in Na Thon. With your back to the pier, turn left and follow the signs to a cluster of new buildings behind the post office. Helpful, English-speaking staff provides a wide range of maps and brochures on the island and environs. Open daily 8:30am-4:30pm.

Tours: Hundreds of establishments all over Na Thon, Hat Chaweng, and Hat Lamai sell identical boat/bus/train ticket combinations and arrange Ang Thon Marine Park tours (from 550฿), fishing trips, and elephant treks. In Na Thon, agencies line Na Thon Rd. near the pier. **Songserm Travel Center** (☎420 157), directly opposite the pier in Na Thon, operates most of the ferries (daily 5am-5pm).

Immigration Office: (☎421 069), 2km south of Na Thon at the intersection of Rte. 4169 and Rte. 4172. Visa extensions 555฿. Open M-F 8:30am-4:30pm.

Currency Exchange: Dozens of banks offering good rates for currency exchange, credit card advances, and **ATMs** line the main roads of Na Thon, Hat Chaweng, and Hat Lamai. Official **bank exchange booths** are also found along the main roads in Ban Plai Laem, Hat Bo Phut, Hat Mae Nam, Ban Thong Po, Ban Thong Krut, Ban Bang Kao, and Ban Hua Thanon. The exchange booths are generally open daily 9am-9:30pm. **Siam Commercial Bank** also operates perfectly legitimate **roving exchange vans** that wander the highways spreading *baht* and good cheer throughout the land.

Markets: The market on **Thaweerat Pakdee Road** in Na Thon has fresh produce. A small day and night market also sets up along the highway between the Big Buddha and the beach that takes its name, but it's mostly fresh fish.

Local Tourist Police: (☎421 281 or 1155), on Na Thon Rd. in Na Thon, 400m south of the pier. Fluent English spoken. Open **24hr.**

Medical Services: The island has 3 main hospitals: **Bandon International Hospital** (☎425 382), in Hat Bo Phut; **Government Hospital** (☎421 230), in Na Thon; and your best bet, the private **Samui International Hospital** (☎422 272), in Hat Chaweng. Smaller **nursing stations** can be found in Na Thon, Hat Chaweng, and Hat Lamai. English-speaking staff. Open **24hr.** Credit cards accepted.

Internet Access and Telephones: GPO, 2nd fl. Has **international calls,** fax, and cheap **Internet** (30฿ per hr.). Open daily 7am-10pm. Travel agencies around the island offer pricier international phone service and Internet access (1฿ per min.).

Post Offices: GPO (☎421 130), on Na Thon Rd., 50m left of the pier parking lot in Na Thon. *Poste Restante.* Open M-F 8:30am-4:30pm, Sa-Su 9am-noon. Licensed, private **branches** all along Rte. 4169 charge extra and offer limited services.

Postal Code: 84140.

■ ● ACCOMMODATIONS AND FOOD

Although Ko Samui caters to well-off tourists rather than backpackers, cheap beds can be found at just about all of the island's beaches at rates as low as 150฿ for a simple bungalow with shared bath. Several websites have good information on accommodation, dining, and entertainment options; www.samuidirect.com and www.sawadee.com are particularly thorough. Reserve ahead during the high season. Rates are 30-50% lower during other months; ask about discounts.

◪ **NA THON.** Na Thon is Ko Samui's waiting room for visitors killing time until the next ferry. Unless you have an early ferry to catch or the last *songthaew* has skipped town, there's little reason to spend the night. **Palace Hotel ❸**, 152 Cholvithi Rd., 100m on the right as you exit the pier, has small but comfortable rooms with sea views and a professional staff. (☎421 079. Singles and doubles 400-450฿, with A/C and TV 550-650฿; triples with A/C 800฿.) **Sea View Guest House ❷**, 67/15 Thaweerat Pakdee Rd., opposite the Shell gas station, has modestly sized rooms with showers. (☎420 052. Doubles with shower 200-400฿, with bath 300฿, with A/C 400฿.) On the waterfront, food carts sell fruit, noodles, sandwiches, and meat on sticks. Popular **Ruangthong Bakery ❶**, opposite the pier, serves breads, pastries, and Thai dishes for 20-100฿. It's a great place to grab a quick meal, cup of coffee, or snack before the ferry ride. (Open daily 6am-8pm.)

◪ **HAT MAE NAM AND AO BANG PO.** With its narrow strip of wet sand, the Mae Nam beach, stretching 4km along the northern coast of Ko Samui, is probably the island's least spectacular beach. Thanks to its seclusion (there is no road running along the beach and the way to access it is via dirt paths off Rte. 4169), Mae Nam draws long-term visitors and those looking for tranquility and respite from the bustle of the island's more popular beaches. On the way to Hat Bo Phut, the popular **Friendly Bungalow ❸** has standard beachside huts with baths and mosquito nets. (☎425 484. Small huts 300฿, large huts 400฿. 3-night min. during busy months.) On the other side of Hat Mae Nam at Ao Bang Po, the **Health Oasis Resort ❺** has clean, modern bungalows, although the high-end ones aren't a great value. The spa is known for its fasting and organ-cleansing programs. The popular colon-cleansing program, which requires a three- to nine-day commitment, will cleanse your wallet, too; it starts at 12,000฿. (☎420 124; www.healingchild.com. Rooms with fan 600฿, with A/C 1000-3000฿.)

◪ **HAT BO PHUT.** The charming Bo Phut, or Fisherman's Village, offers a pleasant combination of white sand and quiet atmosphere, as well as a selection of seafood restaurants and trendy shops. The beach is smaller and steeper than most others, but many overlook this imperfection because of the friendly locals and traditional architecture, which create an ambience that reminds you that you are, indeed, still in Thailand. Bo Phut is spread around one road that branches off Rte. 4169 (Samui's main road) and runs along the coast before reconnecting with the main road farther west. The area now has its own hostel, **Hello Diving and Guesthouse ❷**, a few meters from the pier, which boasts cheap dorm beds in a smartly restored wooden house. It doubles as a dive shop offering excursions to Ko Tao's dive sites. Those enrolled in diving classes stay free. (☎09 872 7056; www.hello-diving.com. Dorms with fan 100฿, with A/C 150฿.) The old-time favorite **Ziggy Stardust Resort ❹**, farther down the road, has beautiful, spacious rooms with old carved wooden furniture and clean full baths. The beachfront bar and restaurant features fabulous homemade yogurt. (☎425 173. Bar and restaurant open daily 7:30am-10pm. Small doubles with fan 400฿; larger rooms with A/C 1000฿.) For great and affordable Thai food, head to **No-name Restaurant ❷**, at the end of the road, right as it hooks back to Rte. 4169. (Dishes 35-70฿. Open daily 3-11pm.) Of all the restaurants serving up excellent seafood, try the **Summer Night Restaurant ❸**, in the heart of Bo Phut village on the beach. (Breakfast 80-110฿. Seafood 50฿ per 100g. Thai dishes 60-140฿. Open daily 7:30am-11:30pm.) Summer Night also runs a few clean **bungalows** across from the restaurant (400฿, with A/C 800฿).

◪ **HAT BANGRAK (BIG BUDDHA BEACH).** Big Buddha Beach lies north of Samui's northeastern peninsula, along Rte. 4171. Bungalows abound in this lively area, but the rocky, boat-filled beach is not conducive to swimming. **Kinnaree Resort ❸**, close to the Big Buddha pier and across from the primary school, is a villa among flower gardens, cooing doves, and beach views. (☎245 111. Motorbike rental. Singles and doubles 400฿, with hot shower and A/C 800฿.) **Secret Garden Bungalows ❹**, 200m to the right as you leave the pier, has very nice concrete bungalows with hot showers and other modern amenities. (☎425 419; www.secretgarden.co.th. Rooms with fan 500฿, with A/C 1500฿.) For food, try **Picnic Basket ❸**, 150m to the left as you exit the pier. Quiet and friendly Scottish owner Jimmy offers tasty breakfasts and build-your-own *à la carte* picnic offerings. (2 eggs cooked to order 30฿. Fresh fruit, vegetables, meats, cheese, and fresh baked bread each 30-120฿. Open daily 6am-7pm.) 100m farther down the road towards the airport turn-off, the open-air **One Dollar Cafe ❷** delivers as advertised—three-course breakfasts and Thai and Western entrees all cost 40฿. (Open daily 7am-10pm.)

◪ NORTHEASTERN PENINSULA: LAEM THONGSON, AO THONGSAI, HAT CHOENG MON, AO YAI NOI.

The northeastern cape wraps around some of the island's best views and most delightfully secluded coves. Beaches are down dirt roads off the mountain highway connecting northern Hat Chaweng to Rte. 4171 and are most easily accessible by motorbike. Solitude seekers should follow the signs 2km down to **Thongson Bay Bungalow ❸**, on the tip of the promontory. The beach here is rocky and scenic, but not suitable for swimming. (☎01 891 4640. Rustic bungalows with bath 250-500฿, on the beach 1000฿.)

North of Ao Yai Noi, bordering Ao Thongsai, and 4km north of Hat Chaweng, Hat Choeng Mon's serene beaches make it worth visiting, especially if crowds annoy you. **Choeng Mon Bungalow ❸** has modern, concrete bungalows with baths. (☎425 372. Singles 300฿, with A/C and hot water 600฿; doubles 450฿/1200฿.)

◪ HAT CHAWENG.

The biggest and brashest of Ko Samui's beaches, Hat Chaweng roars 5km over the eastern coast. As the sunbathing and party capital of the island, the beach is a loud, happy nation of superb sand, clean waters, cheap booze, and loud music. Even if you don't want to swim, people-watching provides hours of entertainment. Although the Chaweng area teems with luxury hotels, upscale tourist shops, and go-go bars, the quality beach makes it well worth a visit. Hat Chaweng's main road, **Chaweng Road,** is parallel to the beach and connected to Rte. 4169 via three access roads; most services are available along it.

Affordable accommodations in Hat Chaweng are scarce and fill up quickly. By far the best option for those on a budget is **Charlie's Huts ❸**, in the middle of the beach near the turn-off for the lagoon, which caters almost exclusively to backpackers and their ilk. Movies play every evening at 6pm in the attached restaurant. The spartan wooden bungalows set in a pleasant garden have thatched roofs, bamboo walls, and mosquito nets. A/C digs here are nicer, but you pay for them. (☎422 383. Doubles 300฿, with bath and closer to the beach 500฿, with A/C 700฿.) Next door, **Silver Sand ❷** has a few budget bungalows close to the water. The large ones have private baths, but are not in particularly good shape. (☎231 202. Bungalows 200-400฿, with A/C 800฿.) Old-timer **Matlang Resort ❸**, 1541 Chaweng Rd., in North Chaweng by the end of the cape, is a quiet hideaway from the main drag. The beach here gets a little too shallow for quality swimming at low tide but is more picturesque than anywhere else on Chaweng. (☎/fax 422 172. Singles and doubles with bath and fan 300-370฿, with A/C 1200฿.) If you're looking to spend a little more, one of the best higher-end options is **Chaweng Villa ❺**, right on the beach toward the northern end of Hat Chaweng. Very well-maintained modern bungalows are near the water and have a big pool and nice bars and restaurants. (☎231 123; www.chawengvilla.com. Bungalows with A/C 1700-2600฿.)

Budget accommodations on Chaweng may be scarce, but budget food is not. Inexpensive food stalls cramming the road by the Green Mango serve pizza, sandwiches, and Thai favorites to drunken night revelers. **Los Gringos Cantina ❹**, on an alley across from Pizza Hut towards the northern end of Hat Chaweng, does Tex-Mex very well, from the strawberry frozen margaritas (120฿) to the bottles of Tabasco on every table. Delicious tostadas, enchiladas, and burritos are each 160-

200฿. (Open daily 2-11pm.) **The Deck Restaurant ❺,** before the Green Mango as you approach from Na Thon, has great food (including vegan and vegetarian options), music, and three levels of cushions from which to enjoy it all. (☎230 898. 3-course breakfast 99฿. 5-course dinner 175฿. Thai dishes 60-80฿. Open daily 8am-2am.) Italian-owned **La Taverna ❹,** on the way to the Green Mango, cooks the best Italian food on the beach. (Pizza 160-250฿. Pasta 180-220฿. Open daily 10am-10pm.)

◪ **HAT LAMAI.** Hat Lamai is second to Hat Chaweng in terms of nightlife and beauty, but has a more family-friendly environment, good body surfing, and fewer crowds. Most tourist services can be found in South Lamai on the road running parallel to the beach, while the best budget accommodations are in North Lamai, some distance from the thick of things. **Spa Samui Resort ❷,** on Rte. 4169 before the Hat Lamai turn-off, has very simple bungalows with fan, and fancier ones with A/C. Many come here for the cheap rooms and stay for the excellent health spa, which features *tai chi* and yoga programs starting at 3000฿. (☎230 855. Bungalows with fan 250-600฿, with A/C 600-1800฿.) **Lamai Resort ❸,** in North Lamai, has sturdy, reasonably priced bungalows. (☎424 215. Bungalows with bath 200-650฿.)

Most establishments in south Lamai, the busier part of the beach, are solidly mid-range or above. The centrally located **Utopia Bungalow & Resort ❹** has nice bungalows, a more upscale clientele, and beautifully groomed gardens. The clean bungalows and rooms have private baths. (☎233 113. Bungalows 500฿, with A/C and hot water 1000฿.) The friendly owners of the **Sun Garden Beach Resort ❹,** next door, keep their rooms in good shape. All bungalows have baths. (☎418 021. Bungalows with fan 400-500฿, with A/C 900-1000฿.)

Most bungalows serve standard meals until 10pm and let more expensive restaurants and pubs along the main drag pick up the slack late at night. Street food abounds. **Il Tempio ❸,** in central Lamai just down the road from the Sun Garden Beach Resort, has very good Italian food in a casual setting. (Pizzas and pastas 130-230฿. Open daily 9am-2am.) The **Will Wait Bakery ❷,** in the center of Lamai Beach Rd., serves a standard menu of Thai and Western favorites. (Most dishes 50-150฿. Open daily 7:30am-10:30pm.) The **day market ❶** at Ban Hua Thanon sells munchies.

◉ SIGHTS

Ko Samui has a few sights to keep you entertained if you get too sunburned. Most are located off Rte. 4169 and are easily accessible by *songthaew*, foot, or motorbike. Travel agencies also offer one-day tours of the island for around 1000฿.

▨WAT KHUNARAM. Rather sensational as far as *wats* go, this temple, off Rte. 4169 in the island's southeast corner, is known for a mummified monk who died in 1973, but supposedly evaded decomposition via complex pre-death meditation.

THE BIG BUDDHA IMAGE (PHRA YAI). Ko Samui's most prominent landmark, the golden "Big Buddha" is located on a small island connected by causeway to Rte. 4171 on the island's northeast corner. Overlooking Samui Island from its location near Hat Bangrak (Big Buddha Beach), the 15m-tall statue was built in 1972 as a place for both islanders and *farang* to worship.

SAMUI CROCODILE FARM. The most fear-inspiring of the novelty animal sideshows on Samui, the Crocodile Farm, located near the airport, features 84 crocs in several holding pens, dozens of poisonous snakes, and several friendly monkeys who will perform acrobatic stunts in exchange for a rambutan and a back rub—if only the massage parlors and spas on the island would agree to a similar deal. If you come, the daily shows at 2:30 and 5pm, featuring fearless trainers who taunt the crocs, are a can't-miss. (*Off the airport road between Big Buddha Beach and Hat Chaweng.* ☎*01 894 4228. Open daily 9am-6pm. 270฿ admission includes shows.*)

SAMUI BUTTERFLY GARDEN. One of Samui's most popular non-beach attractions, the Butterfly Garden maintains over 24 species of southern Thai butterflies in addition to less spectacular (and less popular) species of insects. *(Off Rte. 4170, opposite central Samui Village. ☎424 020. Open daily 8:30am-5:30pm. 120฿, children 60฿.)*

WATERFALLS. Ko Samui boasts several waterfalls scattered around the interior of the island. Two-tiered **Hin Lat Waterfall,** 3km south of Na Thon, is the most accessible, though not the most beautiful. The two **Na Muang Waterfalls,** 11km south of Na Thon, are more impressive, but require a hike through the mountainous heart of the island. *(Difficult to reach without a motorbike. Taxis from Na Thon can drop you off at the foot of the waterfalls, and many travel agencies offer waterfall and trekking trips.)*

GRANDMOTHER AND GRANDFATHER ROCKS (HIN TA AND HIN YAI). According to an old Samui legend, an elderly couple was en route to the mainland to procure a wife for their son when a fierce storm pummeled the ship and killed the two seafarers. Their bodies washed ashore, and their respective genitals somehow petrified in the shapes of "Grandfather Rock" and "Grandmother Rock," a set of unusual, and slightly distasteful, natural formations. *(South of Hat Lamai.)*

THE SAMUI AQUARIUM AND TIGER ZOO. Thailand's only privately owned aquarium features fish native to the Gulf of Thailand, as well as sharks and turtles. The adjacent tiger farm houses several homesick-looking Bengal tigers. *(Off Rte. 4170, south of Hat Lamai near Ban Han. ☎424 017. Open daily 9am-6pm. 350฿.)*

BAN LAMAI CULTURAL CENTER. Located where Rte. 4169 takes a sharp right turn at Km 20, Lamai Cultural Hall's museum holds a small but interesting collection of photographs, pottery, and weaponry. *(Open daily 6am-6pm. Free.)*

🎵🍸 ENTERTAINMENT AND NIGHTLIFE

With dozens of pubs and go-go bars, Hat Chaweng is Samui's nightlife capital. Most places are open until at least 2am. The mega-pub **Green Mango** is a massive complex of six bars that draws a raging young drink-and-dance crowd. The mood picks up at around 11pm and doesn't fade until 4am. (Beer 80-100฿. Cocktails 120-150฿. Red Bull and vodka 130฿. Champagnes 800-2000฿. Open daily from 8pm.) The area around the Green Mango overflows with girlie bars and strip clubs, as well as a few good bars. One is the popular **Reggae Pub,** which attracts an older, more mellow crowd. Resembling an entertainment center rather than a pub, it comes complete with a tacky souvenir shop. Sunday nights attract party lovers to the weekly drinking contest. To get there, follow the signs to the boxing stadium across the lagoon. **Drop-In Bar,** a few blocks north of Green Mango, has a nice, laid-back atmosphere and good drink specials. (Beer 60-120฿.)

Hat Lamai has fewer nighttime options than Hat Chaweng, but bars and strip joints are popping up by the dozen. **Bauhaus Pub, Bistro and Disco,** south of the go-go area, is *the* hot spot for Lamai's young and restless. The foam party takes over on Friday nights, while the Saturday night Gin and Vodka party offers half-price cocktails. (Drinks 30-100฿. M-Tu and Th buy-1-get-1-free. Open daily 6pm-2am.)

Thai boxing demonstrations are put on at least a few times per week at the Chaweng stadium; watch for posters and flyers near the beach. (Matches usually Tu and F 9pm at Chaweng, W and Sa at Lamai Stadium. Admission 150-300฿.) For those interested in non-human bouts, **buffalo fighting** is a favorite local pastime. Matches are held throughout the island several times per week. The humaneness of the spectacle is an issue worthy of consideration, although the matches are readily compared to Spanish bullfighting, and unlike the latter, the buffalo here rarely suffer serious injury. (Admission 150-200฿.)

⚡ DAYTRIP FROM KO SAMUI: ANG THONG MARINE PARK

The only way to visit the marine park is on a tour through one of Ko Samui's travel agencies. Songserm (p. 404) sends daily boats at 8:30am from Na Thon's pier (return around 5pm, 550฿ includes lunch). If you have the money, a more worthwhile kayaking option (1800฿) allows you to explore the craggy island inlets.

The infamous setting for Alex Garland's *The Beach*, Ang Thong Marine National Park is a breathtaking collection of over 40 limestone islands 60km north of Ko Samui. Among the islands are **Ko Mae Ko** (Mother Island), popular for saltwater lake **Thalay Nai** (Lake Crater); **Ko Sam Sao** (Tripod Island), famous for its huge rock arch and fantastic snorkeling; and **Ko Wua Talap** (Sleeping Cow Island), home to the **park office**. Ko Lak and similar limestone formations tower 400m above the water. Dolphins dance in the water around the longtail boats that motor near **Ko Thai Plao**. The water at **Hat Chan Charat** (Moonlight Beach) is as good for diving as Ko Tao's. Visit the park on your own by arranging transportation with the tour ferry operator. If you end up staying on the island, the park office (☎ 286 025) rents several modest **bungalows ❸** for 1000฿; **camping ❶** is free.

KO PHANGAN   ☎ 077

Ko Phangan is a backpacker's heaven and hell. Sandwiched between Ko Tao to the north and Ko Samui to the south, the island's beaches range from unspoiled, laid-back beauties like Bottle Beach to the insanely overdeveloped, self-contained backpacker universes like Hat Rin Nok. With pirated films playing daily in restaurants and unbeatable drink specials at beachside bars, don't come to Ko Phangan to get away—come here to be in the middle of it all.

⬛ TRANSPORTATION

Boats: Ferries run between Ko Phangan and **Ko Tao, Ko Samui,** and **Surat Thani.** From Ko Tao, ferries leave from Mae Hat's southern pier (5 per day 9:30am-2:30pm, 180-350฿). From Ko Samui, boats leave from Big Buddha Pier for **Hat Rin** (1hr., 4 per day 9:30am-5pm, 100฿) and from Na Thon Pier for **Thong Sala** (9, 11am, 5:30pm; 95฿). Boats from Surat Thani leave from the Tha Thong Pier for Thong Sala. You can also head to Ko Phangan directly from Surat Thani via the **Donsak Car Port** (2½hr.; leaves Donsak 7, 10am, 2, 5:30pm; returns 6, 10am, 1, 7pm; 300฿) or the **town pier** (7:30am, 205฿; 11pm, 400฿). Ferries leaving Ko Phangan depart from Hat Rin Nai and Thong Sala. From the pier at Hat Rin Nai, boats go to: Ko Samui's **Hat Bangrak** (Big Buddha Beach; 1hr., 4 per day 10am-4pm, 100฿); **Hat Tian** (12:40pm, 50฿); **Than Sadet** (12:40pm, 80฿); **Thong Nai Paan** (12:40pm, 100฿). From the main pier at Thong Sala, boats go to: **Chumphon** (12:30pm, 650฿); **Hat Bangrak** (1hr., noon, 115฿); **Ko Samui's Na Thon** (30-60min., 7 per day 7:30am-4:30pm, 115-250฿); **Ko Tao** (2hr.; 10, 11:30am, 12:30pm; 180-350฿); **Surat Thani** (night boat 7hr., 10pm, 400฿; express boat via Ko Samui 4hr.; 7, 11am, 12:30, 1pm; 205฿).

Local Transportation: Getting around the island can be a bit costly. **Songthaew** (and their eager drivers) meet ferries at the pier in Thong Sala and run to the island's major beaches. To: **Ban Kai** (20-30฿); **Ban Tai** (20฿); **Chalok Lam** (50฿); **Hat Rin** (50฿); **Hat Yao** (50฿); **Thong Nai Paan** (100฿). In Hat Rin Nai, *songthaew* wait across from the police booth and go to **Thong Sala** (min. 3 passengers, 50฿). In addition, **longtail boats** make trips between the major beaches.

Rentals: Motorbikes are available for rent around the pier and on the main street of Thong Sala as well as from several guesthouses in Hat Rin Nai (150฿ per day with pass-

SOUTHERN THAILAND

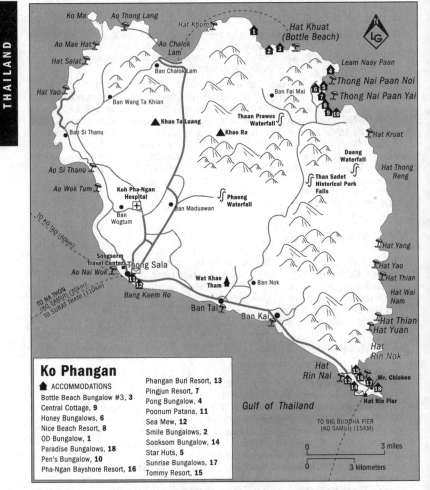

Ko Phangan

▲ ACCOMMODATIONS

Bottle Beach Bungalow #3, **3**
Central Cottage, **9**
Honey Bungalows, **6**
Nice Beach Resort, **8**
OD Bungalow, **1**
Paradise Bungalows, **18**
Pen's Bungalow, **10**
Pha-Ngan Bayshore Resort, **16**

Phangan Buri Resort, **13**
Pingjun Resort, **7**
Pong Bungalow, **4**
Poonum Patana, **11**
Sea Mew, **12**
Smile Bungalows, **2**
Sooksom Bungalow, **14**
Star Huts, **5**
Sunrise Bungalows, **17**
Tommy Resort, **15**

port deposit). Though paved, the last 5km of the road to Hat Rin is tremendously hilly, with enough traffic to result in **serious accidents** each year. Before heading to any remote destination, inquire about the road conditions.

✦ ⁊ ORIENTATION AND PRACTICAL INFORMATION

Ko Phangan is 100km northeast of Surat Thani and 12km north of Samui. While a few boats depart and dock at the Hat Rin pier, most arrive at the island's unsightly main city and port of call, **Thong Sala,** where many conveniences are located, including ATMs and travel agencies. From the Thong Sala pier, three paved roads cover most of the island; one runs 10km southeast along the coast to the party beach of **Hat Rin,** which is split into **Hat Rin Nai** to the west and **Hat Rin Nok** to the east. Midway along this paved road, a bumpy dirt road (only for experienced motorbikers) heads to the northeastern beaches of **Thong Nai Paan Yai** and **Thong Nai Paan Noi,** and other dirt trails stretch to more remote coves. A second paved road from Thong Sala (safe for most motorbikes) cuts 10km northward through the heart of the island to **Ao Chalok Lam,** a departure point for boats heading to lovely **Hat Khuat.** The third road (alternately paved and dirt) runs a scenic course west along the coast to the less-developed bays of **Ao Mae Hat**. More so than other islands, Ko Phangan rewards those who explore its far corners.

Tours: The helpful **Mr. Kim** (☎377 274), usually hanging around a few meters from the Thong Sala pier on the right, has encyclopedic knowledge of the island and books tickets. **Songserm Travel Center** (☎377 096), on the left side of the main road in Thong Sala. Boat and A/C bus packages to: **Bangkok** (450฿); **Krabi** (350฿); **Phuket** (350฿). Open daily 8:30am-5pm.

Currency Exchange: Several exchange booths line the street leading from the main pier in Thong Sala. **Siam Commercial Bank,** 30m from the Thong Sala pier on the left, has a **24hr. ATM.** Open M-F 8:30am-3:30pm. In Hat Rin, there are several bank exchange booths and ATMs on the road that leads from Hat Rin Nok to Hat Rin Nai.

Books: Carabou, next to the Siam Commercial Bank, has a selection of beach reads and refreshing A/C. Open daily 8:30am-8:30pm.

Police: Main office (☎377 114), 2km north of Thong Sala on the road to Ao Chalak Lam. English spoken. A small **police booth** operates at Hat Rin off Haadrin Rd., opposite the school. Some English spoken. Both open **24hr.**

Medical Services: Koh Pha-Ngan Hospital (☎377 034), 3km north of Thong Sala. English spoken. No credit cards. Open **24hr.** In Hat Rin, private **nursing stations** provide basic medical services. For serious medical attention, take a boat to Ko Samui.

Internet Access: The cheapest Internet providers (1฿ per min.) are on the road stemming from Thong Sala's main pier. More expensive places in Hat Rin charge 2฿ per min.

Post Office: GPO (☎377 118), in Thong Sala. From the end of the pier, walk down the main road, take the 1st right, and follow the road until it ends and turn left; the post office is on the right. *Poste Restante.* In Hat Rin, a private, licensed **branch** (☎375 204), on the southern road connecting Hat Rin Nok and Hat Rin Nai, offers expensive limited postal and courier services. Open daily 9am-midnight.

Postal Code: 84280.

ACCOMMODATIONS AND FOOD

Most travelers to Ko Phangan head immediately to the southern coast and the beaches of Hat Rin. Those looking for more attractive and secluded beaches should head north to lovely Hat Khuat (Bottle Beach) or mellow Thong Nai Paan Noi. Because transportation is costly and lengthy, chances are your accommodations will define your stay; consider splitting time between Hat Rin and one of the more relaxed bays. Accommodation prices and availability rise and fall with lunar tides. The island fills to maximum capacity in the days surrounding the full moon and its notorious party (see **Sex, Drugs, and Lunar Cycles,** p. 412). If you plan to be there for the party, arrive a few days early or be prepared to sleep on the beach. Better yet, make reservations in advance. Lunar fluctuations aside, prices jump about 100-200฿ during the high season, especially on the Hat Rin beaches.

THONG SALA. A concrete frying pan, Thong Sala is a lifeline for the island, boasting the cheapest Internet, most tourist services, and an aggressive barrage of *songthaew* drivers waiting at the pier. Staying here usually denotes an early ferry departure, an inability to find accommodation elsewhere, or a serious inertia problem, but some comfortable rooms do lie close to the pier. Near the waterfront, **Sea Mew ❷**, to the right heading from the pier, has a great staff. Enjoy the quirky restaurant and the cable TV. Mattresses may be back-straightening, but rooms are clean. (Singles with fan 200฿.) Across from the post office, as a last resort, the drab, multi-storied **Poonum Patana ❷** has large, passably clean rooms and tiled private baths. (☎377 089. Singles and doubles 250฿, with A/C 400฿.) The **Corner Kitchen ❷**, on the corner opposite Poonum Patana, serves extensive Thai, European, and Chinese cuisine (35-60฿). The **Swiss Bakery ❷**, just off the main road, is a good place for a pancake breakfast. (Dishes 30-200฿. Open M-Sa 6pm-5am.) Thong Sala's main drag has several decent Western eateries, though all are rather pricey.

> **SEX, DRUGS, AND LUNAR CYCLES.** For many, the fun of the Full Moon Party comes at a price, in more ways than one. Some ways to prepare for the night (and morning) ahead:
>
> **Reserve ahead.** Accommodations on Hat Rin Nok and Nai fill up as many as 4 days in advance of the big party. If you don't have a week to burn on Ko Phangan, reservations are strongly recommended. Otherwise, you may be stuck commuting from Ko Samui or paying 4000฿ for a room you're not even going to spend any time in.
>
> **Protect your stuff.** Full moon night is a huge night for theft. Avoid keeping valuable possessions in your bungalow or in obvious hiding places, such as under your pillow or mattress. Leave the expensive footwear behind: shoe theft on the beach is a major problem, much to the delight of nearby sandal vendors.
>
> **Protect your health.** Drug use is rampant on full moon night, with the most popular offenders being ecstasy, opium, and the local methamphetamine, *ya ba* (see **Crazy Medicine**, p. 414). Hundreds of people are forced to check into hospitals in Thong Sala, Ko Samui, and Surat Thani due to overdoses of impure substances that often weren't what the victims thought they were. What's more, an increasing number of travelers reportedly have been drugged or tranquilized and then robbed on full moon night.

 HAT RIN NOK (EAST). Introducing "Backpacker Land," where your every need can be fulfilled, the average age is 21, and the average personal savings are approaching zero. Hat Rin Nok is about as loud, obnoxious, and in-your-face as it gets. With all that's going on in the village at every turn, the sandy, boat-covered beach seems like almost an afterthought—until the night of the Full Moon Party, that is, when the waterfront takes center stage.

Songthaew from Thong Sala drop passengers off on the main road, just above Hat Rin Nai. From here, it's a 5min. walk to the beach or a 10min. walk to Hat Rin Nok's quieter twin, Hat Rin Nai. The two beaches are connected by several dusty roads, all of which intersect **Haadrin Road**, the area's main artery, running parallel to the beach. In this area, you can find most basic services.

Accommodations-wise, Hat Rin Nok brims with overpriced, flimsy bungalows along its beachfront road. It's worthwhile to shop around, if rooms are available. The winter months attract a crowd of 20-something, vacationing Europeans, while college coeds flock here during the summer. During the busy months (Dec.-Jan. and July-Aug.), accommodations on Hat Rin Nok fill up several days ahead of the full moon festivities. Book ahead, or your most convenient accommodations option may be on a different island. On Hat Rin Nok, your best bet is **Pha-Ngan Bayshore Resort ❸**, at the northern end of the road, a well-maintained set of bungalows reaching from the beach to the *songthaew* drop-off. At night, it's quieter than other resorts. (☎375 227. Basic bungalows with fan 400฿, with private bath 600฿, with A/C 1000-1800฿.) Toward the center of the beach, things get louder and more crowded, especially at night. **Sunrise Bungalows ❸**, in the middle of the beach, has breezy bamboo cottages with large beds. (☎375 145. Bungalows 250฿, with bath 350฿, with A/C 1000-1200฿.) At the opposite end of the beach from Pha-Ngan Bayshore is **Paradise Bungalows ❸**, the proud host of the first Full Moon Party in 1989. Bungalows are basic, but have balconies and are a bit removed from all the action. (☎375 244. Bungalows 200-250฿.) At the beach's northern end (just beyond Pha-Ngan Bayshore), **Tommy Resort ❷** is an old favorite with some of the cheapest beds on the island, but it shows signs of age. At night, brace yourself for pulsing techno from the beachside bar. (☎375 253. Bungalows 80-150฿, with bath 250-600฿.)

Restaurants representing at least half a dozen nationalities line Haadrin Rd. (which connects the southern ends of both Hat Rin beaches) and the small dirt alleys stemming from it. **Mr. Chicken ❷** is something of a landmark and local meeting place. It has chicken sandwiches (40฿) that will make you forget about *pad thai* for a while. Around the corner is **Niras Beach Kitchen and Bakery ❷**, which caters both to health-spa types and those with a sweet tooth. (Excellent chocolate croissant 50฿. Hummus sandwich on homemade bread 50฿. Kitchen open daily 8am-10pm. Bakery open **24hr.**) Across the street is **Sao's Kitchen ❷**, which dishes out decent tofu-based vegetarian food to customers reclining under low lights. (☎375 166. Vegetable curries 40฿. Pumpkin soup with coconut milk 40฿. Open daily 8:30am-10:30pm.) **BT Restaurant ❷**, on the main path to Hat Rin Nai, is a popular backpacker hangout with regular new movies. (Most dishes 40-120฿). **The Shell ❸**, toward the interior of the island near the small lake, is known throughout the province for its excellent Italian food, including fresh pastas and homemade gelato. (Dishes 90-220฿. Open daily 11am-11:30pm.)

All of Hat Rin Nok's nightlife essentially takes place right on the beach itself, with open-air bars where you can lounge or dance facing the ocean. During the day, flyers announce super-cheap drink specials. **Drop-In Bar** plays consistent Top-40 dance music. The most popular spot these days is the **Cactus Club,** which creates an outdoor ambience with its fleet of oil lamps, and hip, bottle-spinning bartenders. The **Outback Bar,** on the road between Hat Rin Nok and Nai, offers a laid-back yet sophisticated atmosphere and large crowds on most nights. Both offer nightly drink deals or happy hours worth checking out. The Full Moon Party is the stuff of legend. Each month under the full moon, thousands gather on this strip of sand. Bodies gyrate to the latest imported mixes and minds dance to the beat of illicit substances. Even when the moon isn't full, don't come here for a quiet beach. Hat Rin Nok is loud, brash, and proud of it.

◪ **HAT RIN NAI (WEST).** Though only a mere 100m west of Hat Rin Nok, Hat Rin Nai might as well be 1000km away from its party-loving neighbor. The strip of muddy sand at Hat Nai is hardly attractive, but the beach does have its perks—a good selection of bungalows, pretty sunsets, and a location that's close enough to take advantage of Hat Rin Nok's nightlife but far enough to retreat from it.

A number of basic accommodations, restaurants, and ticket agencies run along the ragged main drag heading toward the Hat Rin Pier. Budget beachside bungalows lie at the northern end of the beach, a 15min. walk from the pier and past a rocky outcropping. **Sooksom Bungalow ❷**, just past the outcropping, has simple, wooden huts and a vegetarian-friendly restaurant. (☎375 230. Bungalows 150-250฿, with bath 300-350฿.) Next door, **Phangan Buri Resort ❸** has more expensive, cleaner concrete bungalows with tiled patios. (☎375 330. Bungalows 300-800฿.)

◪ **HAT KHUAT (BOTTLE BEACH).** Set against lush green hills, this gorgeous and quiet ▨beach lures those who intend to stay for a few days into spending weeks or months instead. To get there, take a *songthaew* from Thong Sala to **Ao**

IN RECENT NEWS

CRAZY MEDICINE

Recently, Thailand has discovered that curbing the demand for one drug does not mean curbing drug demand.

In the mid-90s, opium use declined dramatically in Thailand because social and economic programs reduced both supply and demand. The big push worked—but only for opium. Just at the moment heroin became the world's hip drug, it was abundant, too—produced right in the Golden Triangle.

But heroin was only a passing fancy compared to the meteoric rise in the use of methamphetamines. Locally known as "ya ba" (crazy medicine), speed is Thailand's latest drug scourge. Ya ba became the intoxicant of choice among laborers during the boom years, but its use skyrocketed among disillusioned youth after the Asian Financial Crisis.

Ya ba is the perfect narcotic to attract new young drug users. Heroin prices are generally out of reach for new customers (price fluctuations influence the buying behavior of new users much more than addicts). Ya ba also fits the pop cultural trend: it's a club drug and cheap substitute for ecstasy, producing temporary hyperactivity, euphoria, confidence, alertness, and tremors. Users' heart rate, temperature, breathing, and blood pressure increase.

Violent behavior is common among drug users, as are anxiety, panic, paranoia, drowsiness, and...

[Cont'd on next page...]

Chalok Lam (10km, 20min., 100฿). The bay is the departure point for boats to **Hat Khuat** (9:30am, 3, 6pm; return 8am, 1, 5pm; 50฿.) It's also possible to walk the 4km from Ao Chalok Lam to Bottle Beach.

Once on Bottle Beach, your options are limited to four inexpensive bungalow operations, three of which are owned by the same family. **Bottle Beach 1 ❶**, in the middle of the beach, is the cheapest, with bathless bungalows starting at 100฿. **Bottle Beach 3 ❸** and **Smile Bungalows ❸**, at the far end of the beach, have bungalows with private baths and hammocks between 250฿ and 400฿. Bottle's bungalows sit on the beach but fill up quickly, while the ones at Smile are farther from the beach. All have similar facilities, including restaurants. **OD Bungalow ❶**, removed from the beach on a cliff, has great views. (Rooms with shared bath 100฿.)

◪ **THONG NAI PAAN NOI AND THONG NAI PAAN YAI.** With sparkling water and a relaxed atmosphere, these twin beaches offer ample reward for those who endure the hour-long *songthaew* ride from Thong Sala or the boat ride from Hat Rin. *Songthaew* stop first at Thong Nai Paan Noi, the more populated of the two and favored by backpackers. This bay is known for its long stretch of cheap and rustic bungalows. Near the *songthaew* drop-off, the popular **Star Huts ❷** is the largest operator on the beach and teems with long-term guests. (☎ 299 005. Bungalows 200฿, with bath 300-400฿.) Younger backpackers frequent **Honey Bungalows ❷**, behind Star Huts and away from the beach. The thatched-roof huts propped on concrete blocks aren't as nice as the ones at Star Huts, but the atmosphere is social. (Bungalows 250-350฿.) At the very northern end of the beach, a 15min. walk from the *songthaew* drop-off, **Pong Bungalow ❷** is well known for its popular bar. (Bungalows 150-180฿, with bath 250-300฿.) Most travelers take their meals at bungalow restaurants, though many recommend **Banglangon Vegetarian Restaurant ❷**, halfway up the beach and famous for its 150฿ pizzas.

To the south, Thong Nai Paan Yai is longer, less populated, and more suitable for swimming and snorkeling than Thong Nai Paan Noi. Ask the *songthaew* driver to let you off here, or make the pleasant 20min. walk across the small promontory from Thong Nai Paan's easternmost point. At the end of the road to Thong Nai Paan's easternmost point, **Nice Beach Resort ❷** has bright, whitewashed rooms with mosquito nets, high ceilings, and private baths. (☎ 238 542. Bungalows 200-600฿, with A/C 1000-1600฿.) Three bungalow operations cluster toward the middle of the beach: **Central Cottage ❸** provides simple but comfortable thatched bungalows and a restaurant (☎ 299 059; bungalows 350-400฿); **Pen's Bungalow ❸** has clean, white, wooden bungalows with peaceful porches and hammocks (☎229 004; bungalows 300-900฿); **Pingjun Resort ❷** contains charming bungalows on nicely cultivated grounds. (☎299 004. Bungalows 250-400฿.)

👁 SIGHTS

After full moons, beaches, and backpackers, **waterfalls** are Ko Phangan's major attraction. The most famous stretches of river run through **Than Sadet Historical Park,** a good daytrip from the beach. Kings Rama V, VII, and IX all walked along its bathtub-sized waterfalls and cascades, leaving their initials as seals of inspection. Longtail boats from Hat Rin (50฿) drop passengers off at the mouth of the river. From here, travel north on the road parallel to the river for 2.5km.

The Sanctuary is a backpacker's spa that comes highly recommended by Ko Phangan's long-term vacationers. It is noted for its seclusion, clean facilities, attentive staff, and free evening meditations. Many are happy to pay 60฿ for a dorm bed and splurge on yoga classes (150฿), oil massages (400฿), and 10-day fasts. Only accessible by **longtail boat,** 50฿ from Hat Rin. (☎01 271 3614; www.thesanctuary-kpg.com. Singles and doubles with bath 300-1000฿.)

KO TAO   ☎077

As one of Southeast Asia's most renowned dive sites, tiny Ko Tao lures an international crowd of underwater enthusiasts, ranging from scuba neophytes drawn to cheap certification courses to veterans who relish its clear gulf waters and outstanding reefs. For non-divers, the island offers superb sun-baked coves, many of which are so secluded they can only be reached by boat or a long hike. With no airport, few luxury hotels and roads, and a utilities crunch that causes power outages for at least half the day in most of the island, Ko Tao is certainly underdeveloped when compared with its island siblings. Despite its popularity, it remains a laid-back destination for scuba fans and backpackers alike.

📷 TRANSPORTATION

Boats: Ferries leave Ko Tao's **Mae Hat** for **Chumphon** (slow boat: 5hr., 10am, 200฿; faster boat: 2-3hr.; 10:30, 11am, 3pm; 300-400฿); **Ko Phangan** (3hr., 9:30am, 180฿; 1-2hr.; 9:30, 10:30am, 2, 3:30pm; 250-350฿); **Ko Samui** (4hr., 9:30am, 280฿; 2-3hr.; 9:30, 10:30am, 2, 3pm; 350-550฿); **Surat Thani** (6½hr., 10:30am, 500฿; 8hr., 9pm, 400฿). For **Bangkok,** there are ferry/bus combos (9½hr., 11am,

depression. Effects on the mind may include moodiness and lack of interest in friends, sex, and food. Continued use can cause personality changes, chronic paranoia, increased blood pressure, and brain damage.

The Thai Health Ministry estimates that 2.4 million of Thailand's 62 million people use the drug. Most users are ages 15-24, but addicts as young as 5 and as old as 68 have been documented. A *ya ba* tab, which can be smoked, injected, or swallowed, can cost as little as a dollar. Tabs have even become a form of currency—Bangkok taxi drivers short on *baht* have been known to return *ya ba* instead.

Ya ba is a supplier's dream, as it is cheaply made from available ingredients. With no fickle crop to deal with, labs can be quickly and easily dismantled. Runners can carry as many as 200,000 tabs in a backpack across the border from Myanmar. An estimated 700 million tablets—more than 10 per person in Thailand—entered Thailand in 2001, mostly crossing the 1300-mile border with Myanmar.

Officials believe *ya ba* use is plateauing. The Thai government is in the midst of a Southeast Asia-wide crackdown on the drug.

Derek Glanz is a freelance journalist and has written and edited extensively for Let's Go.

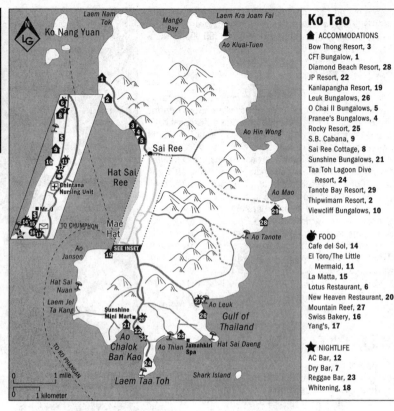

Ko Tao

🏠 ACCOMMODATIONS
Bow Thong Resort, **3**
CFT Bungalow, **1**
Diamond Beach Resort, **28**
JP Resort, **22**
Kanlapangha Resort, **19**
Leuk Bungalows, **26**
O Chai II Bungalows, **5**
Pranee's Bungalows, **4**
Rocky Resort, **25**
S.B. Cabana, **9**
Sai Ree Cottage, **8**
Sunshine Bungalows, **21**
Taa Toh Lagoon Dive
   Resort, **24**
Tanote Bay Resort, **29**
Thipwimarn Resort, **2**
Viewcliff Bungalows, **10**

🍎 FOOD
Cafe del Sol, **14**
El Toro/The Little
   Mermaid, **11**
La Matta, **15**
Lotus Restaurant, **6**
New Heaven Restaurant, **20**
Mountain Reef, **27**
Swiss Bakery, **16**
Yang's, **17**

⭐ NIGHTLIFE
AC Bar, **12**
Dry Bar, **7**
Reggae Bar, **23**
Whitening, **18**

550฿; 15hr., 3pm, 800฿). Boat service thins out somewhat in the low season.

Local Transportation: If you plan to explore the far reaches of Ko Tao's roads, the best way to do it is to rent a **motorbike**, available everywhere (150฿ for 24hr., passport deposit required). Otherwise, **pickup-truck taxis** go from Mae Hat to anywhere that's accessible by the island's few paved roads (30-60฿). **Taxis** between Mae Hat and Hat Sai Ree cost 30฿ per person, but you'll have to pay for 2 people if there's nobody else on board. Pricey **longtail boats** may be hired to reach otherwise-inaccessible bays. They go to **Nang Yuan** (100฿) and **Chalok Ban Kao** (150฿).

⚡ 🛈 ORIENTATION AND PRACTICAL INFORMATION

Boats arrive at **Mae Hat** (Mother Beach), where most services are. Facing the island from the pier, a paved road heads left over a hill to **Hat Sai Ree,** Ko Tao's most popular beach and the heart of the backpacking and scuba scene (3min. by taxi or 20min. on foot). The paved road uphill from the pier eventually bends right, leading to **Ao Chalok Ban Kao,** the main southern beach, and, 500m farther, **Ao Thian.**

Dirt roads branch off the island's only paved road to more beaches, including **Ao Leuk, Ao Tanote** (a fantastic snorkeling destination), **Ao Hin Wong** (on the east coast), and **Hat Sai Daeng** (in the island's southeastern corner). These sandy roads can be treacherous for inexperienced motorbike drivers. The island is difficult but manageable to explore by foot during the day; however, it's nearly impossible at night. Some exploration possibilities include the 20min. walk from Mae Hat to Hat Sai Ree and the 30min. walk from Mae Hat to Ao Chalok Ban Kao. Taxis go most places but can be hard to flag down in corners of the island. The free *Ko Tao Info* brochure is an excellent guide to the island. Jamahkiri Spa and Cafe del Sol also produce and distribute an excellent free fold-out map.

Tours: Tourist info and tickets are provided by private agencies lining the pier in Mae Hat and on the main road in Hat Sai Ree. All offer similar services and prices. **Mr. J** (☎ 456 066) claims to provide any type of service, from scoring visa extensions to arranging emergency loans. Find him at any of his 3 offices and shops on the hill just north of the pier, a 5min. walk down the dirt path right off the pier in Mae Hat, before the Buddha View Dive Center in Hat Sai Ree. All open daily 8am-10pm.

Currency Exchange: Exchange booths and **ATMs** abound. **Krung Thai Bank Booth,** left of the pier in Mae Hat, has mainland exchange rates. Open daily 9am-6pm.

Police: (☎ 456 260), a 10min. walk north of the pier on the hill heading toward Hat Sai Ree opposite the school. Some English spoken. Open **24hr.**

Medical Services: There is **no hospital** on the island. **Nursing stations** offering basic services are abundant around Ao Chalok, Hat Sai Ree, and Mae Hat. Dive shops recommend the **Chintana Nursing Unit** at the top of the hill to the left, on the road to Hat Sai Ree. Open daily 8am-8pm.

Telephones: Nearly all travel agencies and bungalows offer **international phone** service. About 80฿ per min.

Internet Access: Internet facilities in Mae Hat or Hat Sai Ree charge 1 or 2฿ per min. for good connections. A couple places in Sai Ree Village offer 1฿ per 2min. access, but they are only able to trim the price because they use prehistoric dial-up connections—another Ice Age might pass before your email screen loads.

Post Office: There is 1 privately licensed post office (☎ 456 122) on Ko Tao, on the main road in Mae Hat. *Poste Restante* (quite reliable). Open daily 8:30am-midnight.

Postal Code: 84280.

ACCOMMODATIONS AND FOOD

Dive agencies have bungalows that are rented almost exclusively to their clients, but there are plenty of budget places to stay in if you're not here to scuba dive. The cheapest rooms, usually with fan, overnight electricity, and attached bath, run 200-300฿. The closer you are to the beach, the more you'll pay. Prices listed reflect high-season rates; in the low season, you may be able to knock off 100-150฿.

MAE HAT. Mae Hat is the food, fuel, and ferry center of Ko Tao. The beach here is covered with boats, so it is unsuitable for swimming and there's little reason to linger upon arrival; you'll find better beaches and better vibes elsewhere on the island. Should an early-morning ferry departure keep you on Mae Hat, budget accommodations cluster south of the pier. Just before the Sensi Resort, the dive-oriented **Kanlapangha Resort ❷** has friendly management and cheerful bungalows, complete with hammocks. (☎ 456 058. Bungalows 250฿, with private bath 300-1000฿.) More bungalows hide north of the pier on the hill between Mae Hat and Hat Sai Ree, a 15min. walk from the pier. Though hardly beautiful, the area is closer to the beaches and dive shops of Hat Sai Ree. Jack-of-all-trades Mr. J owns several clean, well-maintained **bungalows ❸** just behind one of his stores across from the school. (Rooms with private bath and new fixtures 300-400฿.)

Even though Mae Hat may not be the best place to stay, it's one of the better places to eat. The best place to get Western-style bread, baguettes, pastries, and sandwiches is the **Swiss Bakery ❷,** just a few steps up from the pier on the right. Try the delicious tuna sandwich for 60฿. (Open daily 6am-6:30pm.) Across the street, **La Matta ❷** not only has authentic Italian pizza and pasta (100-160฿), but authentic Italians making it, too. They also serve up fresh salads (40-80฿) and tasty wine for 100฿ per glass. (Open daily noon-10pm.) **Cafe del Sol ❷,** on the way to La Matta from the pier, has good, fresh European and Mexican offerings in a pleasant, well-lit setting. (Dishes 60-220฿. Open daily 8am-11pm.) **Yang's ❶,** next to the Swiss Bakery, has fried noodles with chicken (40฿) and breakfast omelettes (30฿), among other cheap Thai eats. (Open daily 6am-10pm.) At night, **Whitening,** on the southern end of Mae Hat along the beach road, is the new place to be seen. Tasty Thai-Indian fusion dishes (80-220฿) are served in a setting that is, if nothing else, very white. Parties every Friday offer an excuse to drink. (Open daily 5pm-1am.)

◪ **HAT SAI REE.** Backpackers and divers congregate in the bungalows along this 2km beach, which is Ko Tao's busiest bit of sand. Despite its popularity, the beach is laid back; candlelit dinners fade into easy-going nightlife. However, for better-quality swimming, and snorkeling, head elsewhere. To get to the relatively inexpensive **Pranee's Bungalows ❸,** head to the northern end of Hat Sai Ree, a 20min. walk on sand from the start of the beach. With plywood walls and private baths, the accommodations are fairly standard, but the service is friendly and the clientele relaxed. (☎456 080. Bungalows 300-700฿.) A deservedly popular choice is the **Sai Ree Cottage ❷,** just past Scuba Junction. Their charming wooden bunga-lows get points for cleanliness, as does their social beachside restaurant, which boasts a menu of inexpensive Thai dishes, milkshakes, and cocktails. (☎456 374. Bungalows 250-600฿.) Two others to try are the **S. B. Cabana Bungalows ❷,** before Sai Ree Cottage, which has standard rooms (☎456 005; 250-400฿), and, closer to Mae Hat, **Viewcliff Bungalows ❸.** (Singles 350฿; doubles 600฿.) Near the far end of Hat Sai Ree, **O Chai II Bungalows ❷** is the cheapest place to stay on the beach (200-500฿). Just beyond O Chai, **Bow Thong Bungalows ❸** has bungalows ranging from spartan fan rooms to somewhat less spartan fan rooms for 300-1000฿.

For culinary offerings, Hat Sai Ree is second-best to Mae Hat. Most bungalows along the beach have good restaurants, ideal for quick between-dive meals and for evening pre-party drinks. The **Lotus Restaurant ❷,** past Sai Ree Cottage at the northern end of the beach, is one of the island's few non-bungalow restaurants, specializing in Thai cuisine. (Dishes 60-100฿.) The restaurant is romantic, quiet and also serves up affordable grilled food. (Open daily 6:30am-midnight.) **El Toro/ The Little Mermaid ❸,** despite its apparent identity crisis, has inauthentic but none-theless tasty Mexican and Swedish dishes. (Dishes 60-200฿. Open daily 5-11pm.) In the evening, divers put away their gear, and sunbathers slather on aloe vera in preparation for nights passed drinking by the beach and watching pirated movies in nearby restaurants. **AC Bar,** at the south end of the beach, draws partiers from all over the island with its theme nights. Smack in the center of the beach, stretch out with your feet in the sand, sipping a cocktail, at the **Dry Bar.** (Vodka and Red Bull 100฿. Happy hour until 10pm. Open nightly until late.)

◪ **LAEM NAM TOK.** The paved road continues through Hat Sai Ree town to the northwestern tip of the island, the relatively developed Laem Nam Tok. There are sev-eral bungalows along this road, the most scenic of which is the ▨**CFT Bungalow ❷,** at the end of the road. The walk is deceptively long; if you don't have a motorbike, it's best to take a taxi from Mae Hat (40฿) or inquire about boat transport. Its very simplis-tic huts are set among the large boulders that form the Nam Tok cape and offer spec-tacular views of Ko Nang Yuan and the sunset. Traditional massage (550฿ for 2hr.), yoga (12-day courses available), and Ayurvedic treatments at the attached **Here & Now** are an added bonus. Though there is no beach, it's worth making the trip out here in the late evening to sleep, but electricity is only available 6-10:30pm. (Bungalows with outdoor showers 100-600฿.) Along the way to CFT is the one of the only bona fide luxury resorts on the island, **Thipwimarn Resort ❺**, a quiet collection of bungalows built into a hill overlooking the water. The attached restaurant is quite reasonably priced. (☎456 409; www.thipwimarnresort.com. Bungalows 1650-4250฿. 30% low-season discount.)

◪ **AO LEUK AND AO TANOTE.** The two major bays on the eastern side of Ko Tao are ideal for solitude seekers and offer fantastic **snorkeling**. They can be accessed by a paved road branching off Ko Tao's main road just south of Mae Hat, which turns into a dirt road and is only recommended for experienced motorbikers because of its steep hills and sandy ditches. **Taxis** to both bays cost 50฿ from Mae Hat. Tiny Ao Leuk has a rocky, less-than-spectacular beach, but is much more peaceful than the ever-packed Hat Sai Ree. The best choice for lodgings on the bay is **Leuk Bungalows ❷**, which has airy, wooden bungalows with porches scattered about sprawling grounds. (Restaurant open daily 7am-10pm. Rooms 200-400฿.)

About 2km farther north from Ao Leuk along a winding dirt road is **Ao Tanote,** which is more populated and has a better beach than its smaller neighbor. For food, long-term vacationers recommend **Mountain Reef ❷**, a popular spot in the middle of the bay. (Thai and Western entrees 50-160฿.) On the north end of the beach, there's the slightly upscale **Tanote Bay Resort ❹**, with bungalows dotting the hill overlooking the bay. Bungalow No. 29 on the very top of the headland has incredible views of the sea. (☎01 970 4703. Basic bungalows 400฿, with shower and fan 500฿, on the beach 600-1000฿, with A/C 2500฿.) **Diamond Beach Resort ❸**, nearby, has reasonably priced rooms. (☎01 958 3983. Bungalows 400-600฿.)

◪ **AO CHALOK BAN KAO.** Chalok Ban Kao Bay is carved out of the island's south end, 3km from Mae Hat (45min. by foot, 50฿ taxi ride). A dense concentration of bungalows, dive shops, Internet cafes, and restaurants overwhelm the beach, meaning the bay is more convenient than scenic. Solution: head to gorgeous Ao Thian, a 10min. walk away. Most bungalows are affiliated with dive shops, but non-divers seek happy refuge in the new **▧JP Resort ❸**, smack in the center of the beach. Its cliffside bungalows are squeaky clean with private baths. Second-floor rooms have nice sea views, and a relaxed restaurant rounds out this relative newcomer. (☎456 099. **Internet** 2฿ per min. Rooms with fan 300-400฿, with A/C 1000฿.) **Sunshine Bungalows ❸** is also conveniently located but features less glamorous plywood bungalows with private baths (250฿). Behind the bungalows toward the island's main road is the **Sunshine Mini Mart,** a well-stocked shop selling everything from mosquito repellent and beach reads to liquor and clothes. (Open daily 8am-11pm.) The mellow, beachside **Reggae Bar,** at the left end of the beach when facing the water, serves drinks for 120-150฿. (Open daily 6:30pm-2am.)

◪ **AO THIAN.** An uphill walk south from Ao Chalok leads to a fork in the dirt road. The left path leads downhill to the small but stunning Thian Bay, also known as Rocky Bay or Shark Bay. The bay has an outstanding white-sand beach (perhaps the island's best), ideal for both swimming and snorkeling (equipment rental including fins 100฿, available on the beach). In addition, small bushes create sanctuaries of shade during the afternoon heat. The only accommodation is **Rocky Resort ❸**, on the bay's east end, with simple, tired-looking bungalows, some of which include balconies right over the water. Rocky also doubles as the beach's only restaurant, with decent, relatively inexpensive fare. (Bungalows 300-500฿.)

◪ **LAEM TAA TOH.** This lovely cape juts into the gulf, separating Ao Chalok from Ao Thian. To get here, follow the dirt road from Ao Chalok, taking the right path leading uphill at the fork. Besides spectacular views, the cape is home to the **Taa Toh Lagoon Dive Resort ❸**, on Taa Toh Beach halfway around the cape, which has simple bungalows. Many guests are divers-in-training at the resort's **scuba school.** (☎377 792; www.taatohdivers.com. Bungalows 300-100฿.) On the way up, stop at the romantic and atmospheric ◪**New Heaven Restaurant ❸**, which has a delicious menu and near-celestial views of Ao Thian. (Excellent Thai dishes 60-120฿. Seafood 200฿. Drinks 100-120฿. Open daily 11am-11pm.)

🔭 ACTIVITIES

Scuba diving is popular year-round in Ko Tao, although late September through December often brings heavy rains and choppy waters. The island also has a unique tide; September to May is high-tide season and better for snorkeling, while May to September is low-tide season and better for basking on the beach. Ko Tao has over 20 dive sites. **Chumphon Pinnacle,** where a granite tower rises 14m above the surface, is a favorite for deep dives. **Southwest Pinnacle** and **Shark Island** are known for gorgeous coral and leopard sharks. **Green Rock** and **Sail Rock** on the way to Ko Phangan are famous for rock "swim-throughs." Closer to Ko Tao, **Hin Wong Pinnacle** and **Ko Nang Yuan** (see below) have coral in waters suitable for snorkeling.

Scuba prices are standardized, so friendliness and professionalism are the key elements of a good dive shop. Four types of classes are available. Beginners can choose from the four-day open-water certification course (8500฿) or the supervised one-day "discover scuba" dives (2000฿, additional dives 800฿ each). Certified divers can hone their skills with the two-day advanced open-water course (6600฿) or tag along with any dive class on a one-day "fun dive" (1 dive 1000฿, 2-5 dives 900฿ each, 6-9 dives 800฿ each, 10 or more dives 700฿ each). Bring your own equipment for a 15% discount. Prices include accommodations in affiliated bungalows for the duration of the course. If you choose to stay in a non-affiliated lodging, however, prices only drop by 150฿, which means you'll almost certainly lose money, at least during the high season. Snorkelers can also take advantage of the dive scene by tagging along on shallower dives for around 50฿.

There are plenty of dive shops from which to choose, all with PADI certification. The following is an abbreviated list of dive shop operations. The Internet can be a good way to familiarize yourself with the various options, but be sure to talk to the staff and patrons about teaching and equipment before committing. The larger shops have representative offices on Mae Hat.

Ban's Diving Resort & Sunshine Divers (☎456 061; www.amazingkohtao.com).

Big Blue Diving Center (☎377 750; www.bigbluediving.com).

Buddha View Dive Resort (☎456 074; www.buddhaview-diving.com).

Scuba Junction (☎456 164; www.scuba-junction.com).

Taa Toh Lagoon Dive Resort (☎456 192; www.taatohdivers.com).

🎴 DAYTRIP FROM KO TAO: KO NANG YUAN

Ferries depart daily from the Mae Hat catamaran pier (right next to the boat and ferry pier) at 10am, 3, 5pm and return at 8:30am, 1, 4pm (round-trip 40฿).

About 2km off Ko Tao's northwest coast, lovely Ko Nang Yuan is actually three separate islets connected by a three-pronged stretch of white sand. The beach not only makes a good photo background, but its **snorkeling** is among Ko Tao's best. The steep climb up one of the islets to the **viewpoint** is well worth it. The island is best visited as a daytrip from Ko Tao, although there is one accommodation option, **Koh Nangyuan Dive Resort ❹**. Reservations are essential. (☎01 299 5212. Rooms with fan 700-1500฿, with A/C 2000฿.) The resort's **restaurant ❹**, aware of its monopoly over edibles on the island, also has steep prices. (Dishes 150-200฿.)

APPENDIX

COUNTRY CODES

Australia	61	Myanmar	95
Cambodia	855	New Zealand	64
Canada	1	Philippines	63
Hong Kong	852	Singapore	65
Indonesia	62	South Africa	27
Ireland	353	Thailand	66
Laos	856	UK	44
Malaysia	60	US	1

MEASUREMENTS

1 millimeter (mm) = 0.04 in.	1 inch (in.) = 25mm.
1 meter (m) = 3.28 ft.	1 foot (ft.) = 0.305m
1 kilometer (km) = 0.625 mi.	1 mile (mi.) = 1.6km
1 hectare (ha) = 2.7 ac.	1 acre (ac) = 0.37ha
1 gram (g) = 0.04 oz.	1 ounce (oz.) = 28.5g
1 kilogram (kg) = 2.2 lb.	1 pound (lb.) = 0.45kg
1 liter (L) = 1.057 US qt.	1 US quart (qt.) = 0.94L
1 wa = 2 m	1 meter (m) = 0.5 wa

LUNAR CALENDAR

Use the chart below to help you figure out the dates of local festivals, which are often based solely on the lunar calendar. Also, if you plan to attend a full moon party, we've listed the optimum arrival date to ensure you get accommodations..

NEW MOON	OPTIMUM ARRIVAL DATE	FULL MOON
January 10, 2005	January 20, 2005	January 25, 2005
February 8, 2005	February 19, 2005	February 24, 2005
March 10, 2005	March 20, 2005	March 25, 2005
April 8, 2005	April 19, 2005	April 24, 2005
May 8, 2005	May 18, 2005	May 23, 2005
June 6, 2005	June 17, 2005	June 22, 2005
July 6, 2005	July 16, 2005	July 21, 2005
August 5, 2005	August 14, 2005	August 19, 2005
September 3, 2005	September 13, 2005	September 18, 2005
October 3, 2005	October 12, 2005	October 17, 2005
November 2, 2005	November 11, 2005	November 16, 2005
December 1, 2005	December 10, 2005	December 15, 2005
December 31, 2005	January 9, 2006	January 14, 2006

CLIMATE

High and low tourist seasons roughly correspond with rainy and dry seasons in Southeast Asia. There is no uniform seasonal pattern for Thailand, except that it is generally very hot. Keep in mind that the monsoon is rarely an impediment for travel in the region. Generally, rainfall peaks from May to September, and from December to March. For a rough conversion of Celsius to Fahrenheit, double the Celsius and add 30. To convert more accurately from °C to °F, multiply by 1.8 and add 32. To convert from °F to °C, subtract 32 and multiply by 0.55.

TEMPERATURE CONVERSION

°CELSIUS	-5	0	5	10	15	20	25	30	35	40
°FAHRENHEIT	23	32	41	50	59	68	77	86	95	104

AVERAGE TEMPERATURE

City	JANUARY			APRIL			JULY			OCTOBER		
	High (F/C)	Low (F/C)	Rain (in)	High (F/C)	Low (F/C)	Rain (in)	High (F/C)	Low (F/C)	Rain (in)	High (F/C)	Low (F/C)	Rain (in)
Bangkok	91/33	71/22	0.4	96/36	80/27	2.4	92/33	78/26	5.7	91/33	78/25	7.2
Phuket	90/32	73/23	1.8	93/34	77/25	6.1	88/31	78/25	10.2	88/31	76/24	14.3

LANGUAGE

The Thai language is extremely different than English; few people pick up more than the basic rudiments during a short trip. Since it is so difficult to learn and since few travelers make the effort, however, even the most basic Thai words are greeted with excitement when used by a *farang*. This section will help you prepare for your trip and give you a few key phrases to practice.

PRONUNCIATION KEY

TONES: Thai (like Lao, Burmese, and Vietnamese) is a tonal language; word meanings are partially determined by intonation and pitch. The five tones in Thai are neutral, low, high, falling, and rising. Neutral tones (unmarked) are spoken in a level voice in the middle of a speaker's vocal range. Low (à) and high (á) tones are spoken in level pitch, and come from the bottom and top of a speaker's range respectively. Falling tones (â) begin high and end low, as in the English pronunciation of "Hey!" Rising tones (ä) begin low and end high, as in the English interrogative "What?"

VOWELS: Vowels are very roughly pronounced as in English, except for the "eu" sound in Thai, which corresponds to the vowel sound in the French "bleu."

CONSONANTS: Consonants are very roughly pronounced as in English. Some notable exceptions are "th," pronounced "*t*"; "ph," pronounced "*p*"; and "kh," pronounced "*k*". Sometimes the "*l*" sound is substituted for "r" so that a word like *aroy* ("delicious") is pronounced *aloy*. Occasionally, when there are two consonants next to each other in a word, Thai native speakers will drop the second consonant so that a word like *glai* ("far") is pronounced *gai*.

APPENDIX

POLITENESS: In order to be polite, men should add *krap* to the end of their sentences, and women should add *ka* to the end of theirs. These words have no specific meaning, but are used in place of words like *please* and other pleasantries.

PHRASEBOOK
The section below offers a few key phrases to help you travel through Thailand, as well as a some very basic grammar rules. Of course, the information provided should only serve as a basic conversation guide.

TOP SIX PHRASES		
mai pet	may-pet	not spicy
mai bpen rai	may-pen-ray	no problem
sawat di	sawat-dee	general greeting
khap khun	kap-koon	thank you
thao rai	tao-ray	how much
...yoo tee nai	you-tee-nay	where is...?

PRONOUNS. Aside from the five tones, Thai is complicated for many other reasons, including its large number of pronouns. Some of these are gender specific, while others vary according to the relationship between the people conversing. The pronouns below are commonly used, and appropriate for informal use.

I	pom/chan (male/female)	We	rao
You	khun		
He/She/It	khao	They	puak khao

GRAMMAR. Grammatically, Thai is very simple. There are no indefinite or definite articles and verbs are not conjugated to express tense. Questions are formed by adding *mai* to the end of any verb; for example, to inquire if someone is hungry (*hew*), you would ask *hew mai* ("Are you hungry?"). Answering a question is equally simple: to answer affirmatively just repeat the verb. From the example above reply with, *hew* ("I am hungry"). To answer negatively, place *mai* in front of the verb—from the example above, *mai hew* ("I am not hungry").

USEFUL PHRASES.

Meetings/Greetings		Eating	
Hello.	sawat di	I only eat vegetarian.	pom/chan kin jeh
How are you?	sabai di mai	Are you hungry?	khun hew mai
I am fine.	sabai di	Yes, I am hungry.	hew
What is your name?	khun cheu arai	No, I am not hungry.	mai hew
My name is Steve.	pom/chan cheu Steve	Is it spicy?	pet mai
Yes/No.	chai/mai chai	Not spicy!	mai pet
Thank you.	khap khun	**Getting Around**	
Excuse me.	khaw toht	Please repeat.	pood iik khrang dai mai
I can't speak Thai.	phut pasa tai mai pen	Where is...?	...yoo tee nai
I don't understand.	mai khao jai	to the left	sai meu
Shopping		to the right	khwa meu
How much?	thao rai	Straight ahead	dtrong bpai
I don't want it.	mai ao	Do you have a room?	mee hawng waang mai
It is too expensive.	paeng bai	Do you speak English?	phut pasa ungrit pen mai
Do you have...?	mee...mai	Where is the bathroom?	hong naam yoo tee nai
I want...	ao...	Help!	chuay duay

APPENDIX

VOCABULARY

1	neung	glasses	wairn dta
2	sawng	guesthouse	bahn pak
3	sahm	help!	chuay duay
4	see	have	mee
5	hah	hospital	rohng pa ya ban
6	hok	hungry	hew
7	jet	ice	naam khaeng
8	bpet	immediately	tun tee
9	khao	insect repellant	yah gun mai lairng
10	siep	island	ko
11	siep-et	late	chah
20	yi-siep	massage	noo ot
100	neung roy	market	dta laht
1000	pun	mosquito	yoong
Monday	wun jun	motorbike	rot mo dter sai
Tuesday	wung ung khan	passenger	poo doy-ee sahn
Wednesday	wun poot	pharmacy	raan khai yaa
Thursday	wun pa reu hut	plane	kreuang bin
Friday	wun sook	pineapple	sap pa rot
Saturday	wun sao	police	dtam ruat
Sunday	wun ah tit	pomelo	som oh
accident	u bahti het	pork	moo
airport	sa nahm bin	post office	prai sa nee
arrive	mah teung	rambutan	ngaw
bank	ta na khan	rain	fon
battery	bair dta ree	restaurant	rahn ah-han
bay	ao	rice	khao
beach	hat	school	rohng ree un
beautiful	suay	silk	mai
beef	nua	sore throat	jep kor
bicycle	juk gra yahn	station	satanee
bus	rot meh	stomach ache	bpoo ut torng
car	rot yon	sunblock	yah tan guh dairt
cheap	took	tailor	rahn dtut seu-a
chicken	gai	taxi	rot taek-see
coffee	gah fair	telephone	toh ra sup
doctor	morw	thirsty	hew naam
durian	too ree uhn	ticket	too-ah
early	ray oh	today	wan nee
emergency	chook chern	toilet	hong naam
ferry	reu-a kahm fahk	tomorrow	prung nee
fever	kai	toothbrush	bpairn see fun
fish	plaa	toothpaste	yah see fun
fire	fai mai	train	rot fai
food	ahaan	want	ao
fruit	pon la mai	water	naam

INDEX

INDEX

INDEX

ABOUT LET'S GO

GUIDES FOR THE INDEPENDENT TRAVELER

At Let's Go, we see every trip as the chance of a lifetime. If your dream is to grab a machete and forge through the jungles of Brazil, we can take you there. If you'd rather bask in the Riviera sun at a beachside cafe, we'll set you a table. We write for readers who know that there's more to travel than sharing double deckers with tourists and who believe that travel can change both themselves and the world—whether they plan to spend six days in London or six months in Latin America. We'll show you just how far your money can go, and prove that the greatest limitation on your adventures is not your wallet, but your imagination. After all, traveling close to the ground lets you interact more directly with the places and people you've gone to see, making for the most authentic experience.

BEYOND THE TOURIST EXPERIENCE

To help you gain a deeper connection with the places you travel, our researchers give you the heads-up on both world-renowned and off-the-beaten-track attractions, sights, and destinations. They engage with the local culture, writing features on regional cuisine, local festivals, and hot political issues. We've also opened our pages to respected writers and scholars to hear their takes on the countries and regions we cover, and asked travelers who have worked, studied, or volunteered abroad to contribute first-person accounts of their experiences. We've also increased our coverage of responsible travel and expanded each guide's Alternatives to Tourism chapter to share more ideas about how to give back to local communities and learn about the places you travel.

FORTY-FIVE YEARS OF WISDOM

Let's Go got its start in 1960, when a group of creative and well-traveled students compiled their experience and advice into a 20-page mimeographed pamphlet, which they gave to travelers on charter flights to Europe. Four and a half decades later, we've expanded to cover six continents and all kinds of travel—while retaining our founders' adventurous attitude toward the world. Our guides are still researched and written entirely by students on shoestring budgets, experienced travelers who know that train strikes, stolen luggage, food poisoning, and marriage proposals are all part of a day's work. This year, we're expanding our coverage of South America and Southeast Asia, with brand-new *Let's Go: Ecuador, Let's Go: Peru,* and *Let's Go: Vietnam.* Our adventure guide series is growing, too, with the addition of *Let's Go: Pacific Northwest Adventure* and *Let's Go: New Zealand Adventure.* And we're immensely excited about our new *Let's Go: Roadtripping USA*—two years, eight routes, and sixteen researchers and editors have put together a travel guide like none other.

THE LET'S GO COMMUNITY

More than just a travel guide company, Let's Go is a community. Our small staff comes together because of our shared passion for travel and our desire to help other travelers see the world. We love it when our readers become part of the Let's Go community as well—when you travel, drop us a postcard (67 Mt. Auburn St., Cambridge, MA 02138, USA) or send us an e-mail (feedback@letsgo.com) to tell us about your adventures and discoveries.

For more information, visit us online: www.letsgo.com.

go the distance with

HOSTELLING INTERNATIONAL

An HI membership card gives you access to friendly and affordable accommodations at over 4,000 hostels in 60 countries, including all across Asia.

HI Members also recieve:
FREE Travel Insurance
FREE stay vouchers*
Global reward points*
Long distance calling card bonus

Join millions of members worldwide who save money and have more fun every time they travel.

Get your card online today!
HIUSA.ORG

*at participating hostels

CATCH YOUNG MONEY!

YOUNG MONEY is the premier lifestyle and money magazine for young adults. Each issue is packed with cutting-edge
articles written by the nation's top college journalists.

Whether your goal is to save money, make more cash or get
ahead in your career path, YOUNG MONEY will help you
make smarter financial decisions. So subscribe now. It's one
decision you will never regret.

Subscribe Online TODAY and Receive Your **FREE ISSUE**
www.youngmoney.com

your life. *right now.*

LONG ON WEEKEND. SHORT ON CASH.

The fastest way to the best fare.

AND GO!™

©2004 Orbitz, LLC.

MAP INDEX

MAP LEGEND

✚ Hospital	℞ Pharmacy	♠ Wat	▲ Mountain
Police	✈ Airport	🏛 Museum	◠ Cave
✉ Post Office	🚕 Taxi Stand	Hotel/Hostel	Pedestrian Zone
ⓘ Tourist Office	🚐 Minibus Taxi	Food & Drink	Park
$ Bank	🚌 Bus Station	Shopping	
Embassy/Consulate	🚃 Train Station	★ Nightlife	Beach
■ Site or Point of Interest	M METRO STATION	Internet Café	Water
☎ Telephone Office	⚓ Ferry Landing	Hotsprings	
Theater	Church	Pass	The Let's Go compass always points NORTH.
Library	Mosque	Border Crossing	